EDUCATING EMOTIONALLY DISTURBED CHILDREN AND YOUTH:
Theories and Practices for Teachers

SECOND EDITION

JAMES L. PAUL
University of South Florida

BETTY COOPER EPANCHIN
University of South Florida

Merrill, an imprint of
Macmillan Publishing Company
New York

Collier Macmillan Canada, Inc.
Toronto

Maxwell Macmillan International Publishing Group
New York   Oxford   Singapore   Sydney

Cover art: Mike Strickler
Editor: Ann Castel
Production Editor: Victoria M. Althoff
Art Coordinator: Vincent A. Smith
Photo Editor: Gail Meese
Text Designer: Debra A. Fargo
Cover Designer: Russ Maselli
Production Buyer: Pamela D. Bennett

This book was set in Souvenir.

Photo credits: p. 9 by Susan Hartley; p. 39 by Andy Brunk/Macmillan; p. 47 by Mike
Penney; pp. 107, 166 by David Napravnik/Macmillan; pp. 127, 437 by Marjorie
McEachron/Cuyahoga County Board of Mental Retardation; p. 130 by Strix Pix;
p. 195 by Ulrike Welsch; p. 231 by Harvey Phillips; p. 254 by Jean-Claude LeJeune;
p. 360 by Michael Siluk; p. 379 by Constance Brown/Macmillan.

Macmillan Publishing Company
866 Third Avenue, New York, NY 10022

Collier Macmillan Canada, Inc.

Library of Congress Cataloging-in-Publication Data
Educating emotionally disturbed children and youth : theories and
  practices for teachers / [edited by] James L. Paul, Betty Cooper
  Epanchin. —2nd ed.
      p.   cm.
    Rev. ed. of: Emotional disturbance in children.
    Includes bibliographical references and index.
    ISBN 0–675–21211–1
    1. Mentally ill children—Education. I. Paul, James L.
  II. Epanchin, Betty Cooper. III. Emotional disturbance in children.
  LC4165.E46 1991
  371.94—dc20   90–60622
                                                                            CIP

Printing: 1 2 3 4 5 6 7 8 9   Year: 1 2 3 4

Preface

Since 1982, when the first edition of this textbook was published, the field of educating emotionally disturbed children has undergone important changes. This second edition reflects what the authors believe are the significant changes in philosophy, theories, and practices in this field.

The 1980s were rich in the development of knowledge about emotionally disturbed children and, more specifically, the development of strategies and technologies for use in the classroom. The philosophy of educating these children has been aggressively debated, especially on the issue of integration. Presently, there is an appreciation in the field for the needs of some of these children to be served in pull-out services or, in some cases, in special settings. However, the overarching philosophical orientation is one of teaching the child in the regular classroom. Research has increased our understanding of the nature of emotional disturbance, and the field is now guided by an integrated base of knowledge about practice.

While there was more emphasis on a single perspective, especially a behavioral perspective in engineering changes in the behavior of emotionally disturbed children in the late 1970s and early 1980s, there is now an appreciation for the contributions of different perspectives and bases of knowledge. While the development of behavioral technologies in the 1980s was very strong and enhanced the professional area of educating emotionally disturbed children, there were concurrent developments in other fields, especially in child psychiatry, developmental neurology, and psychopharmacology, which have substantially increased our knowledge about the neurological bases of behavior and the potential for chemical interventions in a broad interdisciplinary program for these children.

In the early 1980s there certainly was an appreciation for the interaction of the developmental vulnerabilities of these children and the social environments in which they develop and in which they become identified as emotionally disturbed. In the 1990s the reality and power of that interaction will be recognized and emphasized even more. There is now more understanding of the contribution of developmental and neurological factors to the interaction with social factors. Attention is now focused on more interdisciplinary programming and more effective interagency coalitions in communities.

Another important development in the field of educating emotionally disturbed children has been an increase in the attention given to the needs of children and youth who have been underserved or inappropriately served; that is, the seriously emotionally disturbed and the aggressively acting-out child. Considerable advances have been made in these areas.

In the early 1980s there was very limited information about programs and limited programmatic research related to educating emotionally disturbed children. Now there is a developing literature on programs and significant attention being paid to the need for programmatic research.

In the 1960s the education of emotionally disturbed children was significantly advanced by ideological changes and attention to the rights and interests of children as part of the larger civil-rights reform. The inclusion of all children in an appropriate educational program, including those children with emotional and behavioral problems, became a part of the national social agenda. In the 1990s the ideological context affecting the development of educational programs for emotionally disturbed children includes more than a children's rights initiative. It includes significant professional reform and a rapidly shifting undercurrent of change in the philosophy of science and an understanding of how to teach these children.

The boundaries of different disciplines, such as clinical child psychology, developmental psychology, behavioral psychology, child psychiatry, and pediatrics, no longer have the clarity they once did. Even the traditional distinction between scientific knowledge and the humanities does not have the ring of truth and endorsement of scientists and scholars it once did. The researcher is viewed as a constructor, rather than a benign discoverer, of knowledge. Knowledge of the values, beliefs, race, and gender of those who study emotional disturbance, therefore, becomes important in understanding the "findings." Objective data are now more suspect, and the subjective nature and meaning of data in social criticism and social histories, for example, are being appreciated across disciplines in the sciences and humanities.

The sociology of knowledge is changing, and there is a "blurring of genres" which is making it more reasonable to look at questions from perspectives with different value premises. Furthermore, the methods of inquiry are changing to reflect this more wholistic and inclusive view of reality. This is opening up possibilities for addressing new questions because of the rules of inquiry imposed by a single epistemological perspective. This change has the strong potential for completely changing the approaches to understanding and teaching emotionally disturbed children. During the 1970s and 1980s, the field focused on different theoretical perspectives and the relative merits of one or more theories. Debates centered on the depth of a single perspective versus eclectic views. There are now serious questions about the epistemological tradition of the social sciences that many believe has resulted in a limited view of knowledge and knowing. Many familiar distinctions in the theoretical and clinical literature are now considered problematic, including the presumption that there are two realities indicated in distinctions, such as between cause and effect, problem and symptom, education and treatment, child and family, biology and social context, affect and cognition, theory and practice, and others.

More fundamentally, our "theories" approach to structuring knowledge, so basic in psychology and education, must now be questioned. The distinction between theory and practice has troubled every clinical discipline. The debates take on political dimensions as theorists argue the practicality of "good theory" and the practioners question the clinical value and utility of theory. The emergence of a new scientific paradigm is forming an important new intellectual context within which to understand and develop research on emotionally disturbed children and approaches to education and healing. This paradigm focuses on a systems perspective and an integration of knowledge and questioning the assumptions of objectivity, reductionism, and linearity in traditional science.

The field of educating emotionally disturbed children is in transition. There continues to be a strong development of theories within the traditional scientific paradigm while the emerging paradigm formulates an alternative for research and practice. This edition includes both the continuing development and the new developments in the field. It is both an update on research about emotionally disturbed children and special education programs for these children, and a discussion of the changes that may well alter our most basic understanding and practices in special education.

The book is divided into three parts. Part One discusses the historical, professional, and social contexts for the field. It examines the history and philosophy of educating emotionally disturbed children, the definition and demographics of emotional disturbance in children, and the mental health and educational service delivery systems. A significant addition to this edition is a chapter on families of these children. Part Two presents the major theoretical perspectives of the field. Two new chapters have been added, one on cognitive development and one addressing the new paradigm. Part Three deals primarily with the applied areas of assessment, behavior management, instruction, and teaching social behavior. Several chapters that were in the first edition have been deleted, and all of the chapters retained were completely revised to reflect the philosophical changes and the development of knowledge in the 1990s. The structure of the book and the perspective of each chapter seek to present an integrated view of theory and practice and to provide the beginning student with the basic information needed to understand the field and to begin professional studies in the education of emotionally disturbed children.

The extensive revision of the text was accomplished with the cooperation of all chapter authors and the assistance of several individuals who made important contributions to the final editing. We wish to especially express our appreciation to Dr. Mary Sue Rennells and Ms. Margaret Darrow, without whom we would still be trying to finish this project. We also want to thank Mr. Thom Buddish, whose drawings make an important addition to this edition of the book. We gladly acknowledge the contributions of the following reviewers: Dr. Carl R. Smith, Buena Vista College, Storm Lake, Iowa; Dr. Jerome J. Schultz, Leslie College, Cambridge, Mass.; and Ms. Kathryn B. Brady, Fitchburg State College, Princeton, Mass. They substantially improved the book by their careful reading and excellent critiques. Finally, we are deeply grateful to the wonderful staff at Merrill, an imprint of Macmillan Publishing, especially Vicki Knight who started us in this revision with enthusiasm and Ann Castel who patiently helped us finish it.

Contents

EDUCATING EMOTIONALLY DISTURBED CHILDREN AND YOUTH

PART ONE

Teachers of emotionally disturbed children wear many professional hats—those of teacher, friend, parent, counselor, judge, and nurse.

Educating Emotionally Disturbed Children and Youth

The field of educating emotionally disturbed children began, as a serious commitment in public education, in the mid-1960s. It developed because of civil and social reforms that changed public policies, professional practices, education, and mental health. Although Public Law 94–142 was not passed until 1975, attention to the rights of all children to an appropriate education and treatment forced attention on the systems in which services had been traditionally provided, the practices of professionals providing those services, and the understanding of the problem of emotional disturbance in children. Since the mid-1960s an extensive knowledge base and a broad array of educational programs have been developed. Attitudes about emotional disturbance in children, understanding the nature and causes of emotional disturbance, and the roles of special educators and other professionals in treating and teaching these children have changed dramatically since the 1960s.

The field continues to develop in an environment of changes in social values, legislative priorities, public policy, and knowledge about emotional disturbance in children. Part One describes the current context of the field. Chapter 1 focuses on education reform in the 1980s and the changing paradigm of special education. These factors have significant implications for the education of emotionally disturbed children. Chapter 2 examines the educational and mental health systems that provide services for these children. Emphasis is placed on collaboration among and between disciplines and service delivery systems that provide integrated services for these children and their families. Chapter 3 focuses on the families of emotionally disturbed children. Historically, parents often were blamed for the problems of their children. This chapter emphasizes a systems view of families in which causes are usually not easily discerned but the effects on a family can be substantial. Collaborative approaches between professionals and families are emphasized.

1
Emotional and Behavior Disorders in Children*

MAIN POINTS

1. Our understanding of emotionally disturbed children has increased substantially as a result of the integration of knowledge about child development and child psychopathology.

2. We have improved the education of emotionally disturbed children by integrating our knowledge about instruction with our knowledge about the needs and learning characteristics of these children.

3. The future of educational services for emotionally disturbed children depends on the outcome of the educational reform movement and the changing philosophy of education.

4. Professionals disagree about how to define emotional disturbance. No single definition is entirely satisfactory from an educational perspective.

5. We can view emotional disturbance as a psychological disorder or a form of social deviance, but the educational consequences are of primary concern to the teacher.

6. Teachers and clinicians from mental health fields have different roles, interests, types of investment, and views of the problems of emotionally disturbed children.

---

*This chapter was written by James L. Paul, University of South Florida.

> Our visions are undergoing a radical change toward the multiple,
> the temporal, and the complex.
>
> *Prigogine & Stengers, 1984, p. xxvii*

The quality of education for emotionally disturbed children in the 1990s rests both on the integration of knowledge about child development and child psychopathology, and on improving the art and science of teaching. Policies governing educational services for these children will depend, in part, on the outcomes of the education reforms of the 1980s, which sought to change the educational system.

During the 1970s and 1980s our knowledge about cognitive development, the role of the family and other components of the child's social ecology, and the contribution of psychoneurological factors to behavioral pathology greatly increased (see Chapters 2, 3, and 4). The development of social and behavioral technologies and the use of drugs to control behavior and/or to facilitate learning have occurred at a rapid rate. Exciting developments in the social and neurosciences that increase our ability to control behavior also increase our need for concern about who sets the goals of behavior change and by what criteria interventions should be evaluated. In the future, it will be necessary to balance the development of technical competence for teachers with attention to making responsible ethical choices in the classroom.

Research on teaching, which has examined the relationship between specific instructional strategies and classroom performance of students, has added substantially to our knowledge about effective teaching (Berliner, 1984; Bickel & Bickel, 1986; Bennet, 1986; Hunter, 1984). There is, therefore, a much better understanding of what ought to occur in the classroom and a more definitive set of standards for evaluating teaching than in previous years. Many of the standard teaching practices are effective with emotionally disturbed children. However, some of these children do not respond to educational strategies that work with other children.

The development of a body of knowledge on effective teaching has important implications for educating emotionally disturbed children. Many of these children fail or are at risk for failure in the classroom under the best instructional conditions. This tends to amplify the negative effects of ineffective teaching strategies. Specific instructional strategies especially designed for children with learning problems have been developed and used effectively with emotionally disturbed children. These strategies integrate learning theories and instruction (Bos & Vaughn, 1988; Deshler & Schumaker, 1986). The improvement of instruction, therefore, should reduce the incidence of educational and psychological casualties associated with poor teaching.

In addition to the advances in our understanding of children with emotional and behavioral disorders and the development of knowledge about instruction, another change that has had an important impact on the education of emotionally disturbed children is the reform of schools. Since 1980, many important studies of the public education system in the United States have been undertaken (Boyer, 1983; Carnegie Forum, 1985; Goodlad, 1984; National Commission on Excellence in Education, 1983; Sizer, 1984). Attention to problems in public schools was generated because of a concern about school dropout rates and declining math and science scores that were lower than those in several other countries. There was an overarching concern with the country's position in international competition and a recognition that the educational system has a major responsibility in our future as a knowledge-based society. In an attempt to improve education and restore confidence in the public education system, many changes in educational policies and practices have been instituted. The reform of education that occurred in the late 1980s emphasized more learning time, more attention to curriculum content, increased graduation requirements, increased testing, stronger certification requirements for teachers, more extensive teacher evaluation systems, better educated teachers, higher salaries to attract and retain good teachers, and efforts to professionalize the teacher's role.

These ongoing changes have important impacts on schooling. The vulnerable child is affected by the increased emphasis on science, math, and humanities, and by the acceleration of competition among students. Some emotionally disturbed children have a low frustration tolerance, low impulse control, specific learning problems, and/or low self-esteem. Therefore, they are less likely to do well in competitive environments, and their needs will require special attention as the context and culture of schooling change.

An important policy initiative relevant to the education of emotionally disturbed children that is embedded in the education reform movement of the late 1980s is the **regular education initiative** (REI). Advocates of this initiative call for an integration of special and regular education services, citing problems of lack of coordination between special and regular education, overidentification of some handicapped children, lack of evidence of differences in instruction in regular and special education, and the inherently unequal and discriminatory nature of special education (Reynolds, Wang, & Welberg, 1987; Stainback & Stainback, 1984; Will, 1986). Strong opponents of this initiative argue that children with behavior disorders are underserved and the special educational environments, technologies, and teachers they need are different from what is available in the regular education programs (Braaten, Kauffman, Braaten, Polsgrove, & Nelson, 1988; Hallahan, Keller, McKinney, Lloyd, & Bryan, 1988; Kauffman, Gerber, & Semmel, 1988). Opponents of the REI believe it jeopardizes the limited services available to these students and probably results in many students failing or dropping out of education altogether. The executive committee of the Council for Children with Behavior Disorders (CCBD) takes the position that "the REI . . . threatens to undo much of the yet unfinished advocacy for appropriate education of behaviorally disordered students. . . ." CCBD shares many concerns of REI advocates such as those focused on procedures used to identify behavior disorder students, the need for preventive services for at-risk students, improving the training of regular classroom teachers, and generally improving the relationship between regular and special education. However, the council questions the assumption that most students served in special education should not be considered handicapped. The council points out that research on the effectiveness of special education in separate settings is mixed. Additional research is needed to guide education policies and practices in this area.

The REI debate addresses issues that are fundamental in the provision of public education for these children. These issues are partially empirical, having to do with the behavioral and achievement outcomes of alternative educational programs; partially political, having to do with the relative costs of the different options; and partially value-based, having to do with what society, especially educators, parents, and legislators, considers to be priority interests. The relationship between the special education program for all handicapped children, including those with behavioral and emotional disorders, and the regular education program will continue to be very important in the future.

THE CHANGING UNDERSTANDING
OF EMOTIONAL DISTURBANCE

As the philosophy and practice of education change, so do the educational system's perceptions of students. Students' needs are understood in relation to the values and beliefs of school administrators, teachers, pupil personnel specialists, and parents. The culture of schools—the goals of education, language, curriculum; approaches to teaching; and expected/accepted behavior of students—reflects the values of the society. The culture constructs its own realities about educational practice and crafts its own images of students with special needs.

Eisner (1988) pointed out that the way we understand something is influenced by the conceptual tools and the linguistic system we use. He stated that language "functions not only as a means for conveying our ideas to others, but also as an agency that shapes what we see" (p. 15). Theories, whether in physics, psychology, or education, "provide their portraits" and "harbor their own assumptions." Eisner observed the following:

> When the term "stimulus" entered the lexicon of psychological discourse, we began to think about humans as responding to what the stimulus evoked. Our major aim was to discover the connections between stimulus and response. Mind did not mediate. It was not, except in physiological terms, a part of the picture. When consciousness re-emerged in the language of psychology, when information processing became a salient paradigm, when the mind was likened to a computer, a sponge, an iceberg, and a growing organism, our thinking about thinking altered and our way of seeing the world changed. What we experienced was shaped by the theoretical language through which we became professionally socialized. To this day, theories of nature and of culture provide powerful agents for guiding our perceptions. (p. 15)

A paradigm is a way of understanding something that determines the way we "see" it (Rappaport, 1977); when the paradigm changes, we see it differently. The paradigms that have guided special education practices for emotionally disturbed children reflect an interaction of the beliefs and values of the culture and advances in the social, behavioral, and neurosciences. As our beliefs, values, and knowledge have changed, so have our paradigms; that is, our way of "seeing" emotional disturbance. For example, in the prescientific period of our history, the behavior of emotionally disturbed children was thought to be the work of the devil or a vengeful God punishing someone, frequently a parent, for his or her sin. Society viewed the behavior of these children as demonic or morally depraved. When we started to think about behavioral variance as a mental illness or sickness (Freud, 1923/1963; Freud & Charcot, 1986), we started seeing symptoms rather than evil spirits. When we started to understand the functions of the brain, we started to see behavior as being brain-based and behavioral anomalies as evidence of organic brain pathology (Goldstein, 1939). When we learned about socialization and the role of culture in behavior, we started seeing deprivation, values, and lack of opportunity as being involved in producing retarded social development and maladaptive behavior (Parsons, 1949); Kirk, 1952). When we understood the paradigms of learning, we started seeing behavior as responses to stimuli. What we look for and what we "see" when considering the behavior and the needs of emotionally disturbed children depend on our beliefs, our values, and our assumptions of the theories we employ.

Paradigms change as a function of social values, the political climate, and the advances of scientific knowledge. Paradigm changes have fashioned new images of emotional disturbance and have helped us understand children and their needs in different ways.

Paradigm Changes in the Social Context of the 1960s

While paradigms of learning, social development, and brain-based behavioral dysfunction developed over a long period of time, it was not until the 1960s that alternative paradigms became significant as competing views of the etiology and treatment of emotional disturbance in children. Prior to that time, the mental health system was the primary service provided for these children, and the psychodynamic perspective, described in Chapter 5, was the primary view of emotional disturbance. Virtually no community-based services for these children existed and, except in rare instances, public schools made no special provisions for them. Therefore, children with emotional and behavior disorders who could not function in the regular classroom in the public school dropped out of school, were expelled because of behavior problems or truancy, got into difficulty with the law and became involved in the juvenile correction system, or, if they were totally unable to cope in any other setting, were treated in a psychiatric hospital. Emotionally disturbed children were seen as having needs that could not be met in educational programs.

This situation changed in the 1960s as a result of several social and political factors. First, the 1960s was a time of fundamental social change. The rights of individuals, including the right to be different, were established. The multicultural nature of our society was affirmed through social reform, a commitment towards valuing individual differences began. At the same time, distrust of social institutions deepened; policies and rules were challenged that had denied access to and otherwise oppressed minorities, women, children, persons with disabilities, and persons of poverty. The strong advocacy movements and the broad social reforms of the 1960s and early 1970s resulted in the legal establishment of many basic rights for children, including the rights to treatment and due process. These reforms produced many changes in education and human services policies, and raised important philosophical and technical issues. Our understanding of the social and educational implications of emotional disturbance changed, and there was a redistribution of public responsibility for the care and treatment of these children.

The traditional view of the mental health system prior to the 1960s was that emotional disturbance was an illness requiring treatment with the aim of curing the condition. This view presented several problems. First, the opinion that any child diagnosed as being emotional disturbed should be the responsibility of the mental health system, even though that system lacked sufficient resources to provide the necessary treatment, resulted in many children not being served. Second, since schools are not hospitals and teachers are not doctors, there was no central role for education. Third, the fact that these children were not the responsibility of the public schools meant that the presence of a diagnosed emotional disorder was regarded as an explanation of the child's failure in school and was, therefore, used as the basis for the school reducing its efforts and not being expected to provide relevant primary intervention.

This situation changed in the late 1950s and early 1960s. First, the "medical model," which viewed emotional disturbance as a sickness needing treatment by medical specialists with the aim of cure, was questioned (Szasz, 1961). Previously, psychoanalytic theory was employed to explain and treat an emotional disorder as a sickness. The psychotherapeutic practices associated with this theory were questioned on the basis of outcome research (Eysenck, 1952). Second, an important manpower study by the Southern Regional Education Board found that the medical model of understanding and treating emotionally disturbed children and their families was not workable (Albee, 1956). This study found that, at that time, there were not enough mental health specialists (psychiatrists, psychologists, and social workers) in the entire southeastern part of the United States to meet the mental health needs of children in the least populated state. Further, it was not likely that increasing the productivity of training programs could keep up with the increasing morbidity of children. It seemed reasonable, therefore, to consider an alternative view of the problem.

When the public schools began to assume responsibility for teaching these children in the 1960s, an alternative view became especially important. Although important concepts of psychopathology relevant to education in the broad psychoanalytic view of personality development existed (Rezmierski & Kotre, 1972), there were difficulties involved in translating these views into educational practices in the classroom. The difficulties included an imprecise definition of the problem, the need for considerable time to learn psychotherapeutic practices, and the belief that causes rather than symptoms should be the focus of interventions. The conditions of public school classrooms did not lend themselves to many of the intervention concepts. Consequently, the public schools relied upon mental health professionals as consultants who were sympathetic to the educational context of schools. These consultants were often not available and, if they were, resources to support consultation were limited. Because of these and other difficulties with the traditional psychodynamic understanding of the problem and the urgency felt in the 1960s to provide appropriate educational as well as mental health services for these children, there was a commitment to find alternative approaches.

While other models of behavior and of intervention were available, they had not been systematically applied to the treatment of emotional disturbance in children. Since the 1970s, these models have become important in our understanding and education of emotionally disturbed children. Ecological psychology, for example, was a major source of ideas. This view, discussed in Chapter 9, understood emotional disturbance as a problem of the fit between children and their environments rather than as a problem of children with personality or conduct disorders. This view emphasized understanding behavior in the context

Emotional disturbance is an invisible handicap. To the casual observer emotionally disturbed children look no different from children who are socially and academically successful.

of social systems and the importance of liaison between systems. Experimental psychology, another important source of knowledge, cast the problem of emotional disturbance in the context of learning. This view, discussed in Chapter 6, perceived the problem as learned behavior that is causing difficulty for the child and/or others. Specific principles guide interventions to change the problematic behavior. Neuropsychology was another important perspective and source of knowledge about the child's behavior. This view, described in Chapter 4, emphasized the role of the central nervous system in behavior and the use of drugs to control behavior and to facilitate learning. Communication between teachers and physicians was, therefore, essential.

Another source of knowledge about the problems of children labeled emotionally disturbed was developmental psychology. The developmental perspective, which has become increasingly important, is reflected in Chapter 5 on psychodynamic theory, and Chapter 7 on cognitive development. The psychodynamic view emphasizes the development of the child's sense of self and autonomy, the acquisition of a sense of trust in self and others, and the ability to learn from and successfully interact with others. The cognitive developmental perspective views behavioral and emotional reactions as mediated, in part, by how children perceive their environment and how they think about responding to their perceived tasks and problems. The family system perspective, presented in Chapter 3, reflects the contributions of developmental and ecological theories and general systems theory. This perspective provides a framework for understanding the processes whereby the family influences the child, the child influences the family, and both are influenced by the broader community or cultural context. This perspective complements the theories of psychopathology presented in other chapters.

A COMPLEX SOCIAL AND PSYCHOLOGICAL PROBLEM

Emotional disturbance is one of the most complex problems that can occur in childhood. It does not take the form of a single, simple condition. Rather, it involves the total physical, psychological, and social being of the child. Emotional disturbance may be manifested by inappropriate behavior, faulty thinking, excessive variations in mood, depressed intellectual functioning, symptoms of physical illness, developmental lag in social and emotional maturity, and/or underachievement. The ways in which emotionally disturbed children are noticeably different from their peers may be social, behavioral, psycho-organic, or educational. The label, *emotional disturbance,* is applied to many different characteristics.

Professionals who label a child as emotionally disturbed may be guided by different paradigms and, therefore, disagree on what constitutes disturbance. The characteristics vary with different children, and the assessment of those characteristics varies with different professionals who identify, diagnose, and label these children. Different professionals have different approaches, philosophies, methods, and languages for evaluating the child and drawing the conclusion that the child is emotionally disturbed.

The problem of emotional disturbance may be manifested in different ways in different settings. For example, a child's pattern of difficulty in the school may be such that he is identified and labeled emotionally disturbed, but the same child may not be singled out as noticeably different from his peers in his home or neighborhood. The child may have more difficulty in his role as a student than as a son, brother, or friend. The more seriously disturbed child is more likely to be noticeably different ("disturbed") in all of his roles in his environments.

Emotional disturbance affects the child, his family, his teachers, his school, and his community. Whether the child attacks the world around him or psychologically leaves that world and creates his own internal world, his interactions with others are difficult—not only for the child but for those around him. Emotional disturbance is acted out as a series of negative transactions and failures. Sorting out the roles of the different actors in each scene—the child himself, his teachers, parents, siblings, friends, and neighbors—is difficult. The interactions change over time as the developmental needs and skills of the child and the expectations of others change. These changes alter the nature of the problems that must be addressed.

Our knowledge of the causes and treatment of serious emotional disturbance in children is limited. While substantial gains have been made in understanding the problems of emotional disturbance in children, there are still many things we do not understand about the various types of problems grouped under the label **emotional disturbance.**

As we look deeper into the problem of emotional disturbance, keep in mind the following:

1. The complexity is real, and no individual or group of individuals has all of the answers needed. The problems defy a single solution.
2. No single paradigm of emotional disturbance is adequate to guide educational practice.
3. Teachers must understand the needs of emotionally disturbed children in a way that helps them provide an appropriate educational program in an appropriate setting.
4. Other professionals have points of view, knowledge, and skills that can be helpful to teachers.
5. The teacher needs to understand the perspectives of other professionals, value the contributions other professionals and parents can make, and be able to use their help.

DEFINITIONS OF EMOTIONAL DISTURBANCE

Many definitions of emotional disturbance and behavior disorders in children have been proposed. No single definition, however, is adequate for the purposes of everyone who works with children identified as emotionally disturbed or behavior disordered. (Hence, a variety of terms are used to describe this condition.) Psychiatric definitions, for example, which historically were applied to seriously disturbed children found in hospital and clinical settings, are of limited value in defining emotional disturbance in educational settings. There are several reasons for this. First, children treated in special clinical settings are likely to represent a more restricted range of disturbances and to be more severely disturbed than most children needing special educational services in the public schools. Second, the theoretical framework of psychiatric definitions is likely to be unfamiliar to teachers. Third, psychiatric definitions do not lead to specific educational interventions. However, psychiatric approaches, as well as other approaches that define, describe, and explain emotional disturbance, can be useful to teachers in planning educational programs if they understand the theoretical perspective upon which the definition is based. Furthermore, the creative integration of several perspectives in defining emotional disturbance results in a richer professional foundation for understanding the complex social and emotional problems presented by these children and the educational consequences of those problems. Kauffman accurately observes that "the definition of behavior disorder or emotional disturbance is unavoidably a subjective matter" (1981, p. 14). He notes that those who disagree at a conceptual or theoretical level are not likely to agree upon a practical definition. The definition must serve the "purpose of the social agents who use them" (Kauffman, 1981, p. 15). Cullinan and Epstein (1979) point out that a definition can be useful in guiding the delivery of services through administrative channels, reflecting a particular theoretical position or describing a population for research purposes.

The various definitions of emotional disturbance in this text will be discussed in light of their educational relevance. Definitions are presented in the context of each perspective and the educational merits are examined. For an excellent discussion of definition, see Wood and Lakin (1979).

The purpose of defining emotional disturbance in children in educational settings is to identify those children who have certain problems that interfere with their educational success. The definition should conversely assist decision makers in identifying children who are not emotionally disturbed. While no single definition of emotional disturbance is entirely adequate for identifying emotionally disturbed children for educational purposes in the public school, it is possible to describe criteria for a satisfactory definition.

1. The definition should relate to some theoretical formulation of the problem of emotional disturbance. This does not mean the definition has to relate exclusively to one theory; the definition can, in fact, have an eclectic orientation. The definition, however, should reflect a theoretical orientation and that orientation should be clear.
2. Assumptions regarding the setting in which the emotionally disturbed child is to be identified and educated should be specified.
3. A definition should apply to the child as a student, particularly the academic and social aspects of that role.
4. A definition of severe emotional disturbance should be interdisciplinary in nature.

5. A definition should exclude cultural difference as a criterion for disturbance; it should incorporate the concept of cultural pluralism, distinguishing cultural difference from psychopathology.
6. A definition should avoid indicting children, parents, or social institutions as responsible for the disturbance. Broad generalizations regarding the etiology of emotional disturbance have not been well supported in the research literature. The problems of emotional disturbance are sufficiently complex that multiple correlates rather than single or specific causes are identified. Even in instances in which the etiology is known, that knowledge may be of little specific value to the teacher in developing an appropriate educational program for the child. It is important to recognize the interactive nature of the problems of emotional disturbance. The teacher needs to understand the variables that are involved in the child's difficulties in school and, as much as possible, the relationship between these variables.
7. The definition should specify the relationship between emotional disturbance and other disabilities, such as mental retardation and learning disabilities. In particular, the concept of severity must be incorporated in a definition. Algozzine, Schmid, and Conners (1978) differentiate two types of emotional disturbance in children. Type One is the milder form of emotional disturbance that may appear in school but not at home. Curriculum modifications may be sufficient in successfully educating these children. The more severe type of disturbance, Type Two, involves children who are disturbed and disturbing in different settings. Type Two disturbance is more pervasive and self-limiting in the lives of these children, and they are more likely to require a comprehensive clinical program. A definition should take the qualitative differences of these populations into account.
8. The definition must contain concepts that can be put into effect to facilitate measurement.
9. The definition should facilitate the process of identifying the child.

Walker described the difficulty posed for the field of behavior disorders:

> Because of competing models of human behavior, psychological assessment and therapy, and a reliance upon medically-based clinically-oriented definition and classification systems that often have limited applicability to the school setting, the field (behavioral disorders) has exhibited a kind of paralysis and ambivalence regarding its legitimate domains of activity. (1982, p. 52)

Part of the reason that there is not an agreed upon definition of emotional disturbance or behavior disorders is that there are different paradigms of disturbance in use at the present time. Recognizing this difficulty, Wyne and O'Connor (1979, p. 31a) suggest three types of definition that illustrate the relationship between theoretical approach and definition of emotional disturbance:

1. Psychodynamic: Impairment of emotional growth during one or more of the stages of ego development resulting in feelings of inadequacy, distrust of others, and hostility or withdrawal in reaction to anxiety.

2. Behavioral: Inadequate, inappropriate, or undesirable behaviors that are learned and that can be changed or eliminated by the use of applied behavioral analysis.
3. Developmental/Ecological: All forms and degrees of behavioral deviance, irrespective of etiology, which result in behavior and environmental maladaptation and personal-social alienation.

While no single definition satisfies all of the criteria and interests of different professionals working with emotionally disturbed children and takes into account the different theories applied to the understanding, treatment, and education of emotionally disturbed children, the definition by Bowers (1969) has been most widely accepted by educators. This definition is included in the 1975 Amendments to the Equal Educational Opportunity Act and P.L. 94-142, and is accepted by the U.S. Department of Education and many state departments of education. This definition states that a serious emotional handicap in children is behavior that is developmentally inappropriate or inadequate in educational settings and is indicated by one or more of the following characteristics:

- An inability to learn that cannot be explained by intellectual, sensory, or health factors.
- An inability to build or maintain satisfactory interpersonal relationships with peers or teachers.
- Inappropriate types of behavior or feelings under normal circumstances.
- A general or pervasive mood of unhappiness or depression.
- A tendency to develop physical symptoms or fears associated with personal or school problems. (*Federal Register,* 1977, p. 42478)

The behavior must be of sufficient duration, frequency, and intensity to call attention to the need for intervention on the child's behalf to insure educational success. The term *emotionally disturbed* does not include children who are socially maladjusted, unless it is determined that they are seriously emotionally handicapped. (P.L. 94-142 does include schizophrenia and autism in the definition.)

The concepts of duration, rate, and intensity are particularly important. All children at some time engage in behaviors that are inappropriate or unexpected for their chronological age, since normative behavior is a statistical concept and some variance or deviation is expected and accepted. Also, all children at some time act in ways that are inappropriate and unacceptable in specific social settings like the classroom. Emotionally disturbed children, however, violate age-appropriate and setting-specific norms at a rate that is significantly greater than the deviations of normal children, over a longer period of time, and with greater intensity.

In a position paper, the executive committee of the Council for Children with Behavior Disorders described the major difficulties with the federal definition and made recommendations for developing "a functional educational definition of this handicapping condition" (1987, p. 16). The council argued that a revised federal definition should eliminate the arbitrary exclusion of groups of children such as the socially maladjusted, focus on sources of data collection, emphasize alternative models of service delivery, and increase the federal priority for meeting the needs of emotionally disturbed children.

Historically, the professional literature has tended to associate the terms *emotional disturbance* and **social maladjustment** (Rhodes & Paul, 1978). It is not necessarily the case that emotionally disturbed children are socially maladjusted, or that socially maladjusted children are emotionally disturbed. Delinquent behavior and predelinquent behavior, for example, are considered to be forms of social maladjustment. Such behavior, however, may be primarily the result of the social or economic circumstances of the child's life rather than of a psychological disorder.

Grosenick and Huntze (1980), who collected information in a national needs analysis of behavior disorders, recommended deleting the exclusion of social maladjustment from the definition of emotional disturbance. They concluded that "there is no clear-cut evidence or thought in the field which delineates the distinctions" between emotional disturbance and social maladjustment (p. 23). While professionals disagree about this issue (Algozzine, Schmid, & Connors, 1980), the executive committee of the Council for Behavior Disorders argued for a revision of the federal definition, including eliminating the arbitrary exclusion of children who are socially maladjusted.

Grosenick and Huntze (1980) suggested substituting the term **behavior disorder** for *emotional disturbance*. They argued that the term *behavior disorder* could include the concept of social maladjustment and avoid some of the stigmatizing and conceptual difficulties associated with the definitions of *emotional disturbance*. Grosenick and Huntze and other researchers (Epstein, Cullinan, & Sabatino, 1977) pointed out, however, that most states label these children as emotionally disturbed and apply a wide range of definitions. Wood and Lakin (1979) noted the variability of definitions used in research studies that has contributed to the confusion about the nature of behavior disorders and emotional disturbance.

CLASSIFICATION SYSTEMS

Just as there are several theories and definitions of emotional disturbance and behavior disorders, there are also several systems for classifying behavior. The assumptions and values of a theoretical perspective are reflected in the codification of behavior. That is, each perspective has its own labels or vocabulary, concepts, and definitions. The labels are applied to different behaviors or groups of behavior manifested by different children. Some perspectives incorporate the concept of etiology in the classification scheme, while others recognize only manifested behavior. Each classification system has its own merits relative to its uses. That is, different professionals use perspectives and classification schemes that are appropriate to their particular professional responsibilities. Many common classification systems, such as DEM III and GAP (see Chapter 11), were developed for use in clinical settings. Quay (1972, 1975) and others tried to develop more educationally relevant classifications. However, just as there is not a single definition or theoretical perspective that is entirely adequate for teachers, there is not complete agreement on a single classification system to be used by teachers.

There are also many generic problems in labeling children that cut across different classification systems (Mercer, 1973). These are problems in the organization and administration of special education, especially the placement of children. Hobbs (1979) suggested that the difficulties involved in classifying children with behavior disorders were so great that only interventions should be classified. This is a serious and promising proposal but not yet a reality. It is important to understand the uses and limitations of different systems. Changing or even doing away with labels and categories does not reduce the need for a clear diagnostic understanding of the child. Morse (1967) long ago cautioned against throwing out the diagnosis with the label. Classification will be discussed further in Part 2 of this book. Chapter 4 discusses screening, identification, and diagnosis of emotional disturbance.

At the present time, it is important for teachers to understand that there are different systems for classifying children. Each has its own utility, but a single system has not been accepted by all special educators.

PREVALENCE OF EMOTIONAL DISTURBANCE IN CHILDREN

Citing current research (Gilmore, Chang, & Coron, 1984; Gould, Wunsch-Hitzig, & Dohrenwend, 1980), it was noted that there is general agreement that "over 11% of children (approximately 6 to 8 million) have a mental health problem in need of treatment" (Saxe, Cross, & Silverman, 1988, p. 800). There continues to be a wide range of prevalence estimates. Morse (1975) reviewed survey reports and found that 0.1% to 30% of the school-age population was considered behavior disordered. This wide variation in prevalence estimates is largely the result of differences in definition and criteria for behavior disorders. Wood and Zabel (1978) suggested that much of the variability in prevalence estimates is also due to differences in the ways in which data are collected.

The U.S. Office of Education uses a 2% estimate of prevalence for behavior disorders. Kelly, Bullock, and Dykes (1977) reported that teachers identified about 20% of their students as suffering from some kind of emotional disturbance. Morse and Coopchick (1979) pointed out that there is much evidence indicating that emotionally disturbed children are among the least adequately served in schools. The behavior of many of these children is not severe enough to fit state definitions. These children are largely unidentified and unserved (Kauffman, 1980). He noted that "statistics show that about 0.5% of school-age children are receiving special educational services as seriously emotionally disturbed, only about ¼ of a very conservative estimate of prevalence" (1981, p. 58).

Morse and Coopchick (1979) suggested that at least 3% of the total student population are very seriously disturbed and need intensive help. Of the 2% to 3% of the school-age population considered to be seriously emotionally disturbed, 6% have a primary diagnosis of mental retardation and 7% have physical disabilities. They suggest that the remaining 87% of the 2% to 3% of the student population considered seriously emotionally disturbed are the "true socio-emotionally disturbed" (p. 60).

EMOTIONAL DISTURBANCE AS AN EDUCATIONAL HANDICAP

In providing an appropriate education for an emotionally disturbed child, the teacher's concern is with the child's mental health and psychological well-being, his achievement and general success as a student, and the welfare of the classroom, including the integrity of the environment and the maintenance of normative procedures and activities. Since emotional disturbance is generally viewed as a psychological disorder or a form of social deviance, an understanding of both psychological and social principles will help teachers meet the educational needs of emotionally disturbed children.

Psychodynamic, psychoneurological, and behavioral theories (see Chapters 4–6) have made important contributions to the broad area of social education for emotionally disturbed and behavior-disordered children. During the past 15 years, however, special educators have become increasingly aware of the value of social theories in understanding the nature of emotional disturbance. Ecological, social, and cultural theories (see Chapters 8 and 9) have viewed emotional disturbance as a form of social deviance or a product of a mismatch between a person and the environment. Social theories have not been as prominent as psychological theories, because the mental health system, historically the primary service delivery system for emotionally disturbed children, conceptualized emotional disturbance as a *psychological* problem. The task of educators is different from that of clinicians in mental health treatment settings. Therefore, as educators assumed responsibility for teaching emotionally disturbed children, it was necessary to expand the framework within which emotional disturbance is understood. Social and ecological theories have contributed to the growing conceptual and knowledge base of special education for emotionally disturbed children. These interactional views of disturbance have contributed to an educationally relevant understanding of disturbance; this fact is indicated by the growing professional and research literature in this area during the 1980s.

Neither social nor psychological theories alone can guide educational programming for emotionally disturbed children. Teachers are specifically and uniquely concerned about emotional disturbance as an educational handicap. The psychological and social aspects of the problem are important in helping the teacher understand the child and plan an appropriate educational program. The teacher, however, must view emotional disturbance in the context of the classroom in which specific problems exist, and she must understand it in ways that lead to appropriate interventions.

A classroom is a social setting in which certain prescribed activities occur. The teacher is in charge of activities in the classroom, and students are expected to participate in prescribed ways and achieve at certain levels. The expectations for students are to be appropriate to the age and developmental status of students in that classroom. While all of the students in the classroom may be approximately the same chronological age, they may not all be able to achieve at equal rates or to respond with equal proficiency.

Many children have difficulty succeeding as students because of emotional problems. The relationship between the psychological status of a child and his performance of the social roles of a student, including achieving academically, is very complex. A few brief examples will illustrate the problem of emotional disturbance as an educational handicap.

In order for a child to be a successful student, he must be able to participate as a member of his class. For some children, successful group participation is almost impossible because they experience a high level of anxiety as group members. Speaking in the group, taking one's turn, reading out loud, asking or responding to a question, or making a presentation to the class is a nightmare for some children. A child who is afraid of groups, or of speaking to a group, may try to disrupt the class in order to relieve his anxiety and ultimately be placed somewhere else. If the child is asked to leave the room, his anxiety is reduced and the disruptive behavior is rewarded. The next time the child is asked to perform verbally for the class, the teacher might well expect this disruptive behavior to occur again. In asking the child to leave the classroom, the teacher may not have punished the behavior or reduced the likelihood that the behavior will occur again. Quite the contrary, the teacher may have rewarded the behavior and increased the likelihood that, under similar circumstances in the future, the behavior will recur.

Students are constantly being evaluated. The child must develop the skill of taking tests if he is to succeed as a student. Being evaluated, however, has psychological implications for the child. If a child feels reasonably good about himself, is relatively secure, and is fairly successful as a student, a test of his comprehension and retention of certain material presented in class may well be reliable. If, on the other hand, the child is extremely fearful, has a low self-esteem, and is failing most of time as a student, taking a test may increase his fear, causing him to be angry and resentful. A child who experiences evaluation in this way is not going to apply his normal intellectual resources for analyzing, recalling, and reporting appropriate responses to questions.

Being a good student requires the ability to attend. Attending has psychological and motor implications. For example, in order to attend to the teacher talking to the class, the child must be able to sit quietly at his seat. This means that motor impulses to fidget or to pester a neighbor must be inhibited. In order to listen to and understand the teacher effectively, the child must also be able to focus his attention on what the teacher is saying. This means that the child must inhibit other psychological activities such as daydreaming.

The emotionally disturbed child may not be able to control his attending behavior. Hallucinations, for example, of which the teacher may or may not be aware, make the child's successful participation in a group learning experience almost impossible. Some children, who may or may not be emotionally disturbed, experience intrusive interference when trying to attend because of seizures. The teacher may or may not be aware of petit mal seizures, which may effectively negate all of her teaching during the seizure episodes. The teacher may question, "Weren't you paying attention to what I just said?" or "Didn't you understand what I just said?" Such questioning is understandable but not very helpful. The child may not have been attending because of a psychological process over which he had no control, such as hallucination or distractibility.

The child may also express a need to gain the teacher's individual attention. Attention-getting behavior may be symptomatic of emotional disturbance. But saying that behavior has occurred simply to get attention explains nothing. Knowing why the child wanted individual attention and why he sought it in an inappropriate way, too often, or at an inappropriate time may help the teacher find a way to help the child meet this need in more appropriate ways.

The ability to attend is learned; it is acquired through practice over time. Norms related to attending change over time. As the child grows older, his attention span increases, his ability to inhibit inappropriate psychological or motor responses improves, and he can maintain an appropriate focus on relevant visual or auditory stimuli. The child's normative development in this area, however, relies on an intact central nervous system and emotional and intellectual resources in a relatively normal range.

In order for the child to be successful in the student role, he also must exhibit certain attitudes toward authority. The teacher is an authority figure and is in charge of the classroom. A child must be able to listen to, or in some instances read, understand, and obey the teacher. The teacher provides a structure for the classroom. It is a complex social, psychological, and instructional structure. The teacher makes decisions about the physical space, the curriculum, the materials, the schedule and activities for the day, rules governing appropriate behavior, and consequences for inappropriate behavior. The teacher determines the emotional climate as well as the nature and quality of social activity in the classroom. This arrangement generally works because both students and significant others outside the classroom understand that the teacher has authority and is in charge in the classroom.

While this arrangement works for most children, some have serious problems with authority. Some children, for example, have resisted the authority structure of their own homes by defying their parents. Many emotionally disturbed children have long-standing patterns of defiant and disruptive behavior. These children are particularly upsetting to teachers because they challenge the teacher's role and threaten the order and composure of the classroom. Some of these children exhibit the feelings needed to get what they want (i.e., to manipulate others), but they don't experience the feelings. These children often are able to identify weaknesses in the teacher and exploit them.

Children who over time defy the authority structure of the classroom, whether from neurotic needs, unreasonable emotional demands, anger, or a defect of character, may be at high risk for delinquency later in life. Robbins (1966), in a 30-year follow-up study, found that the sociopathic child grows up to be an unproductive and asocial adult. Children who refuse or fail to learn to live within the authority structure of the classroom may have difficulty with the authority structure of society. These are the children who are serious discipline problems in school and develop a reputation that follows them through school. These children reinforce and are reinforced by their reputations. Within this group, the children who are defiant and manipulative and seem to have little sense of right and wrong or guilt have, as a group, been least responsive to psychological treatment and educational remediation.

Impulse control is another important characteristic of a successful student. The child who is constantly out of his seat, who is always picking on his neighbor, who repeatedly gets into fights, who has temper tantrums, or who exhibits some other disruptive behavior pattern probably has low impulse control. That is, he acts spontaneously, without analyzing the appropriateness of the response, alternative responses, or the consequences of his response. Such children are **stimulus bound;** that is, they behave predictably in the presence of certain stimuli. They are very vulnerable in their peer group to being set up, teased, and exploited as the group scapegoat or clown. A child who cannot inhibit impulses in the presence of certain stimuli is easily manipulated. Stimulus-bound behavior can be extinguished easily. The teacher who understands the child's behavior—that is, the prompts for and consequences of his behavior—will be able to systematically extinguish that behavior.

THE EMOTIONALLY DISTURBED CHILD IN THE CLASSROOM

Teachers recognize emotionally disturbed children either through their own observations in the classroom (this is usually the case) or when parents make the teachers aware of some special difficulty the child is having. In the past, a child was more likely to be identified as emotionally disturbed if he created a disturbance in the classroom. Defiance, inability to get along with other children, insensitivity to the needs of other children, lack of respect for classroom rules, hyperactivity, destruction of property, and other social and behavioral offenses were likely to be noted by the teacher and ultimately resulted in the child's being labeled emotionally disturbed. Now, however, as a result of improved teacher education, increased public awareness of the needs of handicapped persons, and the implementation of P.L. 94-142, teachers are much more likely to be sensitive to the wide range of emotional needs of children. For example, the teacher is more likely to be aware of the special needs of an excessively shy and fearful child, who may not in any way disrupt the normal operation of the classroom or make the teacher uncomfortable. Teachers are now more likely to be concerned about the child who has a self-defeating relationship with his peers and therefore becomes the class clown or scapegoat. In general, today's teachers are likely to understand the sociology of their classroom and the psychology of their instructional strategies. They probably understand the way the classroom setting influences their own behavior, the curriculum, and the growth and development of children.

The increased awareness of teachers to the wide range of issues involved in emotional disturbance in children is evident in teachers' remarks about their students. In teacher's lounges, in teacher conferences, in parent-teacher conferences, in the cafeteria, and outside the classroom, one hears comments like the following:

- I don't seem to be getting anywhere with Billy. I have tried everything I know, but he seems terrified every time I go near him. And when I talk with him, I have a feeling he doesn't hear or understand a thing I am saying.
- I spend most of my time controlling Jerry. He won't keep his hands to himself. I can't get him to stay in his seat; he is interrupting my lessons; and quiet work at his seat is simply out of the question.
- Mark is a real problem. He does all right in the classroom, but anytime we have an unstructured activity he picks a fight with the other kids. He has created trouble on the playground and in the lunchroom almost every day for the last 2 weeks.
- I'm really concerned about Mary. She just sits and stares out the window. She doesn't give me any problems in class, she does what I ask her to, and she is doing her work at a passing level, but she is performing far below her ability.
- Michael is a charmer and very smart, but he seems to enjoy misrepresenting the truth. He worries me; he's so manipulative and convincing. He doesn't seem to care about others at all.

Obviously, a single occurrence of disturbed behavior does not make an emotionally disturbed child. The behavioral themes running through these teacher comments are, of course, very familiar in the school. They indicate that something is going on with the child that is concerning or perhaps even upsetting the teacher.

Not all children identified by teachers as having or causing some kind of problem in the classroom become identified as emotionally disturbed. In some instances, the problem is acute and transient. While alarming at the time it occurs, the difficulty subsides in a reasonable period of time. "Reasonable" is defined by the teacher who has two norms in mind—the child and the class. The difficulty may pass without teacher intervention. An example of a transient disturbance that often passes without special teacher intervention is the otherwise well-adjusted child who becomes belligerent or very withdrawn because of anxiety over a serious conflict between his parents. The death of a family member may cause anxiety or depression, triggering a transient behavior problem in the classroom. When the disturbance in the family subsides or the child finds ways to cope psychologically with his feelings, the child's normal and acceptable behavior returns. In the normal course of things, teachers support and encourage children through these difficult periods, and the trauma passes without receiving formal, institutional attention.

In other instances, an acute behavior problem is brief in duration because of the skillful intervention of a teacher. For example, a child who is regularly creating a group disturbance at approximately 9:30 every morning will prompt the skillful teacher to question what is happening in the curriculum and class-room activities at that time each day. If the class started oral reading 2 weeks ago and about that time Billy started creating difficulties in the class, the teacher should investigate possible difficulties in Billy's oral reading ability, or his anxiety about reading out loud in class. The teacher obviously has some leads to inves-tigate and, depending on her findings, she may use instructional or other inter-vention techniques to help Billy reduce his anxiety and succeed. The classroom disruption subsides and a potentially chronic behavior problem is prevented.

The special educational needs of emotionally disturbed children come to the attention of teachers primarily when some unacceptable behavior is dem-onstrated. As noted earlier, the behavior may be unacceptable because it violates classroom norms or the norm for that particular child. Unacceptable behavior is not necessarily bad or offensive behavior. Offensive behavior interferes with the normal routine activities of the classroom. Some behavior, such as excessive daydreaming or an unusual amount of sadness, may not interfere with the normal classroom activities but may arouse the teacher's concern about the child's psychological welfare which, of course, ultimately will affect the child's educational achievement.

Two aspects of behavior determine its acceptability in the classroom. The first aspect is the quantity of a particular behavior. The amount of a certain kind of behavior that is acceptable depends on the setting in which the behavior occurs, the teacher, and the nature of the activity in progress. For example, the amount of talking that is acceptable is greater in a reading group where the meaning of a short story is being discussed than it is when the teacher is making a presentation of a basic arithmetic fact to the entire class.

Quality is the second important aspect of behavior. That is, the timing and amount of a behavior may be appropriate, but the intensity and quality may be unacceptable. For example, as the students are preparing to go outside on a cold day, the teacher reminds Phyllis to button up her coat. Phyllis screams at the teacher, "Go to hell." Or consider Larry, who cries when the teacher asks the class to clear all of the books off their desks, and get out clean sheets of paper and well-sharpened pencils to prepare for a test.

Unlike the student who exhibits excessive or otherwise inappropriate be-havior, such as frequently being out of his seat, fidgeting, or picking at his neighbor, the child whose behavior is qualitatively unacceptable violates the norms of a setting. These include, but are not limited to, norms of authority, rules for conduct, and the intensity in teacher-student relationships that is tolerated. The qualitatively variant behaviors are provocative and suggest to the teacher that something is wrong with the child.

The specific types of behavior that have been described either interfere with the normal operation of the classroom, with the child's success as a student, or both. The child's behavioral, attitudinal, or affective deviation may offend social or psychological norms. The identification and diagnosis of a child as emotionally disturbed, however, depends upon the nature, intensity, and dura-tion of the offense. A child may be considered emotionally disturbed when, in the absence of a primary diagnosis of mental retardation, neurological, sensory or other physical impairment, he cannot derive reasonable benefit from the normal curriculum in the regular classroom without making excessive demands on the teacher's time and energy. The problem of emotional disturbance in the classroom is characterized by its intractability, its resistance to modification by normal teacher intervention, and its persistence over time in the presence of reasonable variations in classroom curriculum, structure, and routine.

DIFFERENT ROLES—DIFFERENT VIEWS

Just as different theoretical orientations give rise to different views of behavior and strategies for intervention, the type of involvement—personal, educational, or professional—one has with an emotionally disturbed child affects one's perception of the issues. Parents, teachers, and clinicians each may have a different perspective. The teacher's concerns are specific to the task of educating the child, usually in the context of a group of children and in the administrative, legal, and social context of a school. Parents and clinicians, however, often have different concerns, interests, and responsibilities with respect to the child. The teacher is in a unique position because she can draw upon the technical perspective of clinical specialists and the personal perspective provided by parents.

Often different views of the child exist. They may all be correct but not all equally useful to the teacher. The teacher needs to recognize and accept these differences and can often be very helpful in harmonizing different interests. The views of clinicians and parents should be recognized, understood, respected, and incorporated when possible in planning for emotionally disturbed children. The orchestration of effective interventions for the child is best accomplished when there is mutual respect among teachers, parents, and special clinical professionals working with or on behalf of the child. Since Chapter 3 is devoted to a discussion of parents, attention here will focus primarily on the views and roles of teachers and clinicians.

Teachers

The teacher is concerned with the child as a student in her class. If there is a behavioral issue, the question is, How can the behavior be controlled so that the educational business of the classroom can proceed? However, the teacher is interested in more than simply controlling behavior; she also is interested in teaching the child. If the child is not motivated to learn, how can she motivate him? If the child is failing in reading, how can she teach him to read? If the child is in the sixth grade and is reading at a second grade level, where can the teacher find materials for the child to read that are appropriate to his level of interest? If the child is excessively shy or withdrawn, how can the teacher help the child become comfortable participating?

A child who has low impulse control, who seems to be angry at the world, who has no skills or interest in developing skills as a student, or who shows some other behavior disorder or emotional disturbance is a challenge. Some behaviors are very threatening to teachers. Behavior that seriously interferes with the teacher's control of the class is particularly threatening. Also, a teacher does not like to find herself unable to teach a child because her professional self-image directly is affected by her ability to teach.

The teacher is concerned about the disturbed child in relation to the rest of the children for whom she has educational responsibility. Sometimes the teacher has difficulty making decisions about dividing her time and attention. Some emotionally disturbed children seem to have an almost limitless need for attention. A teacher, who may understand some things she could do to assist the child beyond what she is doing, may feel resentful that one child is occupying more of her time than she feels can be justified in a classroom with 26 other children.

The teacher sees the emotionally disturbed child as a student. She is concerned with that student's individual welfare, but she also is concerned with the collective welfare of her class. She is likely to approach the problem from the perspective of understanding and controlling the child's behavior in the classroom at a level where instruction is possible. Beyond this she is likely to focus on academic needs and curriculum decisions that will facilitate the child's academic achievement. In the following section, the teacher's view will be further described in relation to the views of clinicians.

Clinicians

The mental health professionals involved directly in the psychological or psychiatric treatment of emotionally disturbed children are primarily psychiatrists, psychologists, and social workers. While the teacher is concerned about the consequences of a child's emotional conflict and wants to help the child achieve, the clinician is more likely to be concerned about the source of the child's emotional conflict, and the nature and basis for the child's motivation, or lack of it. Because of his theoretical orientation and professional task, the clinician, therefore, is more likely to engage the child in a process to "work through" or resolve these difficulties. The process will vary with the particular theoretical orientation of the teacher or of the clinician. The clinician will have a specific theoretical framework in which to analyze and understand the child's behavior.

The clinician is concerned with the specific nature of the emotional disturbance—its causes and treatment. The clinician is concerned with the psychopathology of the child and with effective treatment to reduce or otherwise alter the child's behavior.

The perspectives of clinicians and teachers differ in several important ways. One difference is that teachers usually have a normative orientation to child growth, development, and behavior. Most of the children with whom the regular classroom teacher works function within normal social, psychological, and academic limits. The clinician, on the other hand, has more direct experience with emotionally disturbed children. The clinician spends most of his professional time working with children who are characterized by some negative deviation from norms for mentally healthy adjustment and functioning.

The teacher's task is to help the child learn and use information and skills. The teacher, therefore, is primarily involved in the constructive intellectual and behavioral development of the child. The clinician, on the other hand, has professional responsibility for working with the problems that exist, helping repair emotional damage, and correcting the child's defective thought processes and conclusions about himself or the world. The clinician, therefore, has treatment goals whereas the teacher has teaching and educational goals.

Teachers work with students; clinicians work with patients. If all goes well, students learn, achieve, and are promoted; patients improve and get well. The generic label for the role a child occupies is different in each case, and the child is treated differently. The expectations of the child and of the professional—teacher or therapist—are different. The clinician's standard is the child. Progress is measured in terms of the child's own level of functioning and the nature of the particular problem involved. The teacher's standard is the class and the universe of children of similar age. Children are expected to perform at certain grade levels, depending on their age.

The settings in which clinicians and teachers work are different. Clinicians work in one-to-one or small-group situations. Teachers usually work with large groups. Even when teachers work on a one-to-one basis with a child, it is typically in the context of the larger class. Clinicians work with children on the basis of appointments. Teachers have responsibility for children for most of the day, 5 days a week. The behavior setting in which the teacher works is the classroom. The behavior setting in which the clinician works is more likely to be an office, a room in the clinic, or a room in the hospital.

The child's motivation to change his behavior in the classroom may be different from that in the clinical setting. The approaches of teachers and clinicians, therefore, are likely to be different.

Teachers and clinicians have different orientations to behavior. The teacher is likely to be primarily interested in manifested behavior and the "fit" of that behavior with expectations for social and academic performance in the classroom. Teachers view behavior as intentional, primarily an act of the child's will that is expressed in a context of intellectual capacity on the one hand and teacher expectations and task requirements on the other hand. The teacher may view behavior that does not fit the normative requirements and expectations in the classroom as good or bad, since it is a function of a child's will; or she may view it from the perspective of competence, as success or failure, since the child's capacity is involved. The teacher is more concerned with the consequences of behavior than with the psychological nature, origin, and quality of the behavior.

The clinician, on the other hand, is more interested in how and why the behavior occurs as it does. The clinician is likely to be working with reports about the behavior rather than with the behavior itself. The teacher deals directly with the behavior in the classroom. The clinician frequently deals with abstractions, memories of what occurred, reports of what occurred, and interpretations of patterns of behavior. The clinician is interested in a psychological assessment of the behavior: What motivates the behavior? What feelings and thoughts produce the behavior? What are the internal psychological consequences and effects of the behavior? A teacher is interested in the child's succeeding as a student at a level that corresponds generally with his ability. The clinician is interested in a psychologically healthy child whose intellectual and emotional resources can be expressed in a well-integrated, socially adjusted personality.

The interests of clinicians and teachers are distinguished here in terms of primary interests. Both the clinician and the teacher are interested in psychologically healthy and happy children, and the child's success as a student is both primary evidence of, and a major source of nourishment for, his psychological health. The clinician and teacher approach a mutual goal from different perspectives.

The teacher has a very important role in planning and implementing appropriate educational services for these children. Considering the complexity of the needs and the interdisciplinary challenge of educational programming for emotionally disturbed children, the teacher must be able to give and receive information to facilitate appropriate programming. The teacher's relationship with other professionals, especially clinicians, and parents is often an important factor in developing and implementing appropriate services. The teacher must be aware of the different needs, perspectives, and potential contribution of each of the individuals involved in planning and programming. Reconciling the different perspectives in the interest of a common understanding and a consistent approach to the child is an important part of helping emotionally disturbed children.

THE NATURE AND ROLE OF THEORY

Theory is important to the development of special education for emotionally disturbed and behaviorally disordered children. Theory provides an intellectual framework for reality. A theory must, however, meet certain technical requirements. It must be at least potentially subject to verification, and it must have a technical language in which terms are clearly and operationally defined. In addition to its technical requirements, a good theory has two additional features. First, it recognizes and builds upon existing knowledge. Second, it leads us to some understanding of the practical working of some part of the world. In other words, good theory is practical (Lewin, 1951).

Different types of theories serve different purposes. Rapport (1970) suggests three types of theories: (1) **deductive theory,** the logical system of mathematics that deals only with the conceptual level of reality and proof of propositions, is determined by the validity of logical deductions rather than by correspondence with observable reality; (2) **predictive theory,** comprised of empirically based models of the real world, is subject to observable data-based proof and has as a primary purpose the discovery of the laws that operate in and control the real world; and (3) **heuristic theory,** which helps make sense out of something and, to that extent, explains it, does not predict anything and, therefore does not enable one to control any aspect of reality.

Our progress in developing knowledge about emotionally disturbed children and how to work effectively with them relies in part on our development of theory. Many theories about human functioning are heuristic although some psychological theories purport to be predictive. Theories of intelligence, for example, are predictive. It is in the area of predictive theory that psychological science is developing.

Many psychological and social theories have been applied to the understanding and education of emotionally disturbed children. Unfortunately, these theories have not always met the criteria of good theory. Many theories have not, for example, always taken account of existing knowledge or alternative theories. Second, the theories applied have not always specified variables and relationships between variables that are quantifiable and ultimately verifiable. Finally, theories applied to the education of emotionally disturbed children have not always had predictive appeal; that is, they have been heuristic in nature. Consequently, "theory" as a whole has suffered a great deal of criticism. Practitioners in particular have found theory irrelevant to the practical realities of education.

The role of theory in making educational decisions is important. The teacher is interested in the child's positive and constructive participation in class and in his educational achievement. If the teacher is confronted with behavior that interferes with or negates the child's positive psychological and social participation as a student in the class, she must make decisions about the meaning and significance of the behavior to the child and to the class. Based on her understanding of the behavior, the teacher must make a decision about intervening. If she intervenes, she must decide what the nature and objective of the intervention will be. If, for example, in response to the teacher's direct request that he clean off his desk in preparation for the test, Jerry says, "Go to hell, you bastard," how should the teacher respond? If Mary, who is a second grader, is a new student in the school and the teacher notices that Mary is masturbating during class, what should the teacher do?

As any teacher will tell you, you must "know the child," meaning that, in addition to knowing the child's age and academic ability, you must know something about the child's pattern of behavior, his history and, in some instances, what is going on in the child's personal life. How does the teacher decide what she needs to know about a child? How does the teacher know if she knows enough? How does the teacher organize what she knows in some way that helps her make sense out of the behavior that is problematic in the classroom and make decisions about what, if anything, should be done about the behavior?

Teachers are guided in their day-to-day activities by theories of behavior and instruction. In fact, according to a concept of theories developed by Argyris (1970), we all use different theories to guide our behavior. We operate from some set of assumptions or theoretical framework in making decisions about our activities. The theories teachers use may or may not be conscious and well thought out. The theories may or may not be well founded in terms of existing research about human behavior and instructional strategies in the classroom. Some teachers are more informed than others, and some teachers are more effective than others, but all teachers make thousands of decisions about the meaning of the behavior of children and about their own behavior as a teacher in response to the child's behavior. These decisions are based on the teacher's theory. For example, a teacher sees Behavior A and decides that she simply wants to get rid of Behavior A or replace it with Behavior B. Based on the teacher's understanding of behavior change, she selects Strategy X. She selects Strategy X for the intervention because it is a part of, or can be made a part of, her behavior repertoire and she predicts that the objective will be accomplished by it. If the objective was accomplished, then the theory was a good one. This is not to say that the theory was more effective or efficient than another theory might have been, but the teacher will use it again because she was reinforced by the fact that it worked.

Numerous theories of behavior and deviance have been applied to understanding, treating, and educating emotionally disturbed children. Some of these theories are more useful than others, and some are more efficient than others. Some are based on a more solid foundation of research knowledge than others.

This book reviews some of the most important theories that are useful in understanding and educating emotionally disturbed children. The theories have been selected because of and are reviewed primarily in terms of their practical merit and appeal to teachers. While we have made no attempt to expand existing theory or to develop new theory, we have attempted to place educational practice with emotionally disturbed children in a broad theoretical context. We emphasize the applications of theory and the theoretical foundations of good practices.

AN ECLECTIC APPROACH

Throughout this book the terms **theories, views, perspectives, frames of reference,** and **models** are used interchangeably. Although these terms do not have the same technical meaning, they are used interchangeably in the special education literature. For example, the technical distinctions between a model and a theory and the technical problems associated with terminology have been discussed by Rhodes and Paul (1978). For the purpose of this book, the distinctions are not meaningful.

The basic issue is this: Human behavior is complex and there are several different definitive scientific and quasi-scientific ways to understand it. It is a mistake to argue that one perspective is correct and the others are incorrect, or that one is necessarily more correct than others. The various theories or perspectives are not mutually exclusive and, as the reader will discover in the chapters that follow, each perspective is useful to teachers in understanding emotional disturbance and in providing an educational program for emotionally disturbed children.

For the teacher, the perspectives are part of the intellectual framework within which she works. The teacher's ability to understand the child's needs and plan and carry out interventions that respond to those needs is, in part, directly related to her ability to analyze the problem of disturbance from different perspectives. Maslow (1966) suggested that if one only has a hammer, one tends to treat everything like a nail. If a teacher has only been exposed to a psychodynamic perspective, she will tend to view the disturbance more in terms of the child's inner life, primary transactions, and social history. On the other hand, if the teacher has only been exposed to a behavioral perspective, she will tend to view the problem more in terms of actions and their consequences. A focus on a single perspective obviously limits the teacher's ability to understand and to help the emotionally disturbed child.

The different perspectives presented in the chapters that follow facilitate analysis and discussion of different ways of thinking about the problems of emotional disturbance. They are not presented to encourage the reader to think about emotional disturbance simply in terms of philosophical categories. Rather, a teacher should be both flexible and critical in analyzing emotional disturbance. This is especially important when interventions are not working or when the teacher finds herself saying, "I just don't know what to do with Gregory; I have run out of ideas." Moreover, teachers need the assistance of other professionals in understanding the needs and developing educational services for disturbed children. An appreciation for the various perspectives and approaches to understanding emotional disturbance will help the teacher be a better "consumer" of related professional services in her work with these children.

The integration of the different perspectives begins as an intellectual task. The teacher must think about emotional disturbance as a problem or a set of problems that can be seen through different lenses (Montgomery, 1979), each having some value in suggesting how to plan and implement an educational program for the child. The curriculum, the approach to managing behavior, and the educational methods used to help the child with a particular problem, such as reading, must reflect integration. Indeed, all of the educational decisions the teacher must make and the educational program that must be described in the child's individual education program (IEP) should reflect an integrated framework or "critical eclecticism" (Hewett & Taylor, 1980).

THE TEACHER AS DECISION MAKER

Some children are psychologically unable to interact with others or to compete with their classmates academically. Other children present behavior problems for the teacher because they are defiant. Still other children present problems for other students in the class because they are disruptive. Many different combinations of problems for the child, the class, and the teacher exist in the academic life of the emotionally disturbed or behavior disordered student. No single perspective is sufficient to effectively and efficiently guide the teacher's understanding of all problems.

The teacher is a decision maker and a problem solver who must decide about the most appropriate educational methods, curriculum, and approaches to behavior management in the classroom. Figure 1.1 outlines some of the relevant factors involved in the decisions teachers make. The teacher must decide if there is a problem, the nature of the problem, and what to do about it. The teacher's decisions are influenced and guided by personal values, personality, and the professional context in which she is working well as her under-

Decisions Teachers Make	Background of the Teacher	Conceptual Models for Viewing the Emotionally Disturbed Learner
1. Is there a problem?	1. Values and philosophy of life and education	1. Psychodynamic
2. What is the problem?		2. Organic
3. What interventions are available?	2. Personality needs and style	3. Behavioral
4. Which interventions best meet the child's particular needs?	3. Norms of the teaching setting	4. Ecological
		5. Sociological
5. Did the selected approach work?		6. Cultural

FIGURE 1.1
The Decisions to Be Made in Teaching Emotionally Disturbed Children Are Complex.

standing of alternative conceptual models that she can use in understanding the child and how to work with him.

Since the teacher decides when a problem exists, she must have some idea of what constitutes a problem before a specific problem occurs. Teachers have individual definitions of a problem, which differ in their concrete details and their theoretical sophistication. The teacher's definition of a problem is related to her view of classroom rules, her behavioral expectations, her values and philosophy, both personal and educational, as well as her scientific knowledge of child behavior, learning, and teaching.

Emotional disturbance involves many factors that are expressed differently in each child and in each classroom. The teacher must make the most informed educational decision she can in each instance. There are no patent answers. She is guided by an understanding of several theoretical perspectives, each of which may be useful in helping her respond to a particular child. The teacher must also consider the norms of the teaching setting in which she is working. The primary conceptualization of the problems associated with a child is likely to be different from the way the problems are viewed in an educational program in an inpatient psychiatric treatment facility.

The teacher's own values and philosophy of education also affect her view of the child and the approach she chooses. The teacher is most likely to understand the child's needs and be guided in her interventions by perspectives that fits with her view of life and can be comfortably incorporated into her teaching style.

One or several perspectives may be useful when the teacher plans for a specific child. All perspectives will be helpful when the teacher works with other helping professionals in planning for a child. These professionals may sometimes hold views that differ from those of the teacher. A basic understanding of alternative perspectives, however, will improve communication with other professionals in planning appropriate services for these children.

SUMMARIES

Emotional disturbance is a label associated with many problems that affect a child's life. Professionals are not in agreement on a single definition, a label, the causes, or the most appropriate way to conceptualize the problem. Emotionally disturbed children do not comprise a homogeneous group from an educational perspective. Estimates of the prevalence of the problem vary widely.

Parents, teachers, and clinicians have different types of concerns about emotional disturbance because they have different roles and responsibilities in relation to the child. These differences must be recognized and the efforts of parents and professionals orchestrated if the child's best interests are to be served.

Several different conceptual views on theories of emotional disturbance are useful to the teacher in understanding the educational needs of these children. These views assist the teacher in making appropriate decisions about educational programming.

DISCUSSION QUESTIONS

1. What barriers have prevented the development of an appropriate definition of emotional disturbance?
2. What is an educationally appropriate definition of emotional disturbances?
3. Give some examples of classroom problems associated with emotional disturbance in children.
4. What are some of the strategies for effectively harmonizing parent, clinical, and educational perspectives?

REFERENCES

Albee, G. W. (1956). *Mental health manpower trends.* New York: Basic Books.

Algozzine, R., Schmid, R., & Conners, R. (1978). Toward an acceptable definition of emotional disturbance. *Behavior Disorder, 4* (1), 48–52.

Argyris, C. (1970). *Intervention theory and method: A behavioral science view.* Reading, MA: Addison-Wesley.

Bell, R. G. (1977). Socialization findings re-examined. In R. O. Bell & L. V. Harper (Eds.), *Child effects on adults* (pp. 121–159). New York: John Wiley & Sons.

Bennett, W. J. (1986). *What works: Research about teaching and learning.* Washington, DC: U.S. Department of Education.

Berliner, D. C. (1984). The half-full glass: A review of research on teaching. In P. O. Hosford (Ed.), *Using what we know about teaching* (pp. 51–77). Alexandria, VA: Association for Supervision and Curriculum Development.

Bickel, W. E., & Bickel, D. D. (1986). Effective schools, classrooms, and instruction: Implications for special education. *Exceptional Children, 52,* 489–500.

Bos, C., & Vaughn, S. (1988). *Strategies for teaching students with learning and behavior problems.* Boston: Allyn & Bacon.

Bowers, C. A. (1984). *The promise of theory: Education and the politics of cultural change.* New York: Longman.

Bowers, E. M. (1969). *Early identification of emotionally handicapped children in school.* Springfield, IL: Charles C. Thomas.

Boyer, E. L. (1983). *High school: A report on secondary education in America.* New York: Harper & Row.

Braaten, S., Kauffman, J.M., Braaten, B., Polsgrove, E., & Nelson, C. M. (1988). The regular education initiative: Patent medicine for behavioral disorders. *Exceptional Children, 55,* 21–29.

Breuer, J., & Freud, S. (1950). *Studies in hysteria.* Boston: Beacon Press.

The Carnegie Forum. (1986). *A nation prepared: Teachers for the 21st century.* New York: Carnegie Corporation.

Cullinan, D., & Epstein, M. H. (1979, February). *Administrative definitions of behavior disorders: Status and directions.* Paper presented at the Advanced Institute for Trainers of Teachers of Seriously Emotionally Disturbed Children and Youth, Charlottesville, VA.

Deshler, D., & Schumaker, J. (1986). Learning strategies: An instructional alternative for low-achieving adolescents. *Exceptional Children, 52,* 583–590.

Eisner, E. W. (1988, June/July). The primary 'pf' experience and the politics of method. *Educational Researcher, 17,* 15–20.

Epstein, M. H., Cullinan, D., & Sabatino, D. A. (1977). State definitions of behavior disorders. *Journal of Special Education, 11,* 417–425.

The executive committee of the Council for Children with Behavior Disorders. (1987). Position paper on definition and identification of students with behavioral disorders. *Behavioral Disorders, 13,* 9–20.

Eysenck, J. J. (1952). The effects of psychotherapy: An evaluation. *Journal of Consulting Psychology, 16,* 319–324.

Federal Register (1977, August). Washington, D.C.: U.S. Government Printing Office.

Freud, S. (1963). Studies in hysteria. In J. Strachey (Ed.), *The standard edition of the complete psychological works of Sigmund Freud, Vol. 2.* London: Hogarth Press. (Original work published 1923)

Geertz, C. (1988). *Local knowledge.* New York: Basic Books.

Gilmore, L. M., Chang, C., & Coron, D. (1984). Defining and counting mentally ill children and adolescents. In *A technical assistance package for the Child and Adolescent Service System Program, Vol. 2.* Rockville, MD: National Institute of Mental Health.

Goldstein, K. (1939). *The organism.* New York: American Book.

Goodlad, J. I. (1984). *A place called school.* New York: McGraw-Hill.

Gould, M. S., Wunsch-Hitzig, R., & Dohrenwend, B. (1981). Estimating the prevalence of childhood psychopathology: A critical review. *Journal of the American Academy of Child Psychiatry, 20,* 462–476.

Grosenick, J. K., & Huntze, S. L. (1980). *National needs analysis in behavior disorders: Severe behavior disorders.* Columbia: Department of Special Education, University of Missouri.

Grosenick, J. K., & Huntze, S. L. (1983). More questions than answers: Review analysis of programs for behaviorally disordered children and youth. *National Needs Analysis in Behavior Disorders.* Columbia: University of Missouri.

Hallahan, D. P., Keller, C. E., McKinney, J. D., Lloyd, J. W., & Bryan, T. (1988). Examining the research base of the regular education initiative: Efficacy studies and the ALEM. *Journal of Learning Disabilities, 21,* 29–35.

Heshusius, L. (1988). The arts, science, and the study of exceptionality. *Exceptional Children, 55,* 60–66.

Hewett, F. M., & Taylor, F. D. (1980). *The emotionally disturbed child in the classroom* (2nd ed.). Boston, MA: Allyn & Bacon.

Hobbs, N. (1979). *Helping disturbed children: Psychological and ecological strategies, II; Project Re-ed, twenty years later.* Nashville, TN: Center for the Study of Families and Children, Vanderbilt Institute for Public Policy Studies, Vanderbilt University.

Hunter, M. (1984). Knowing, teaching, and supervision. In P. L. Hosford (Ed.), *Using what we know about teaching* (pp. 169–192). Alexandria, VA: Association for Supervision and Curriculum Development.

Kauffmann , J. M. (1981). Where special education for disturbed children is going: A personal view. *Exceptional Children , 46* (7), 522–527.

Kauffman, J. M., Gerber, M. M., & Semmel, M. I. (1988). Arguable assumptions underlying the regular education initiative. *Journal of Learning Disabilities, 21,* 6–11.

Kelly, T. J., Bullock, L. M., & Dykes, M. K. (1977). Behavioral disorders: Teacher's perceptions. *Exceptional Children, 43,* 316–318.

Kirk, S. A. (1952). Experiments in the early training of the mentally retarded. *American Journal of Mental Deficiency, 56,* 692–700.

Lewin, K. (1951). *Field theory in social science: Selected theoretical papers* (D. Cartwright, Ed.). New York : Harper & Row.

Maslow, A. H. (1966). *The psychology of science.* New York: Harper & Row.

Mercer, J. (1973). *Labeling the mentally retarded.* Riverside, CA: University of California Press.

Montogomery, M. D. (1979, September). Personal communication.

Morse, W. C. (1967, November). *Some approaches to meeting the needs of emotionally disturbed children in a public school setting.* Speech delivered at 19th Annual Conference of Exceptional Children, Charlotte, NC.

Morse, W. C. (1975). The education of socially maladjusted and emotionally disturbed children. In W. M. Cruickshank & G. O. Johnson (Eds.), *Education of Exceptional Children and Youth* (3rd ed.). Englewood Cliffs, NJ: Prentice-Hall.

Morse, W. C., & Coopchik, H. (1979). Socioemotional impairment. In W. C. Morse (Ed.), *Humanistic teaching for exceptional children: An introduction to special education.* Syracuse, NY: Syracuse University Press.

National Commission on Excellence in Education. (1983). *A nation at risk: The imperative for educational reform.* Washington, DC: Author.

Paluezny, M. J. (1979). *Autism.* Syracuse, NY: Syracuse University Press.

Parsons, T. (1949). *Essays in sociological theory, pure and applied.* Glencoe, IL: Free Press.

Paul, J. L., & Beckman-Bell, P. (1981). Parent perspectives. In J. L. Paul (Ed.), *Understanding and working with parents of children with special needs.* New York: Holt, Rinehart & Winston.

Prigogine, I., & Stengers, I. (1984). Order out of chaos: Man's new dialogue with nature. New York: Bantam Books.

Quay, H. C. (1972). Patterns of aggression, withdrawal and immaturity. In W. C. Quay & J. S. Werry (Eds.), *Psychopathological disorders of childhood.* New York: John Wiley & Sons.

Quay, H. C. (1975). Classification in the treatment of delinquency and antisocial behavior. In N. Hobbs (Ed.), *Issues in the classification of children* (Vol. 1). San Francisco, CA: Jossey-Bass.

Rapport, A. (1970, February). *Modern systems theory: An outlook for coping with change.* Paper presented at the John Umstead Lectures, North Carolina Department of Mental Health, Raleigh.

Rapport, J. (1977). *Community psychology: Values, research and action.* New York: Holt, Rinehart & Winston.

Reynolds, M. C., Wang, M. C., & Walberg, H. J. (1987). The necessary restructuring of special and regular education. *Exceptional Children, 53,* 391–398.

Rezmierski, V., & Kotre, J. (1972). *The psychodynamic model.* A study of child variance. Ann Arbor: University of Michigan Press.

Rhodes, W. C., & Paul, J. L. (1978). *Emotionally disturbed and deviant children: New views and approaches.* Englewood Cliffs, NJ: Prentice-Hall.

Robbins, L. (1966). *Deviant children grown up.* Baltimore, MD: Williams & Wilkins.

Saxe, L., Cross, T., & Silverman, N. (1988). Children's mental health: The gap between what we know and what we do. *American Psychologist, 43,* 800–808.

Schopler, E., & Reichler, R. J. (Eds.). (1976). *Psychopathology and child development: Research and treatment.* New York: Plenum.

Sizer, T. R. (1984). *Horace's compromise: The dilemma of the American high school.* Boston: Houghton Mifflin.

Stainback, W., & Stainback, S. (1984). A rationale for the merger of special and regular education. *Exceptional Children, 55,* 102–111.

Szasz, T. S. (1961). *The myth of mental illness.* New York: Harper & Row.

Walker, H. M. (1982). Assessment of behavior disorders in the school setting: Issues, problems. and strategies. In M. M. Noel & N. G. Haring (Eds.), *Progress or change: Issues in educating the emotionally disturbed,* Vol. 1: Identification and program planning (pp. 11–42). Seattle: University of Washington.

Will, M. C. (1986). Educating children with learning problems: A shared responsibility. *Exceptional Children, 52,* 411–415.

Wood, F. H., & Lakin, K. C. (Eds.). (1979). Disturbing, disordered or disturbed? *Perspectives on the definition of problem behavior in educational settings* (pp. 1–17). Minneapolis: Advanced Institute for Trainers of Teachers of Seriously Emotionally Disturbed Children and Youth. Department of Education Studies, University of Minnesota.

Wood, F. H., & Lakin, K. C. (1979, February). *Defining emotionally disturbed/behavior disordered populations for research purposes.* Paper presented at an Advanced Institute for Trainers of Teachers of Seriously Emotionally Disturbed Children and Youth, Charlottesville, VA.

Wood, F. H., & Zabel, R. H. (1978). *Making sense of reports on the incidence of behavior disorders/emotional disturbance in school populations.* Minneapolis: University of Minnesota.

Wyne, M. D., & O'Connor, P. D. (1979). *Exceptional children: A Developmental view.* Lexington, MA: D.C. Heath.

2
Meeting the Needs of Emotionally Disturbed Children*

MAIN POINTS

1. Emotionally disturbed children are served in a variety of settings, ranging from regular education settings to psychiatric hospitals. However, the professional literature contains few comprehensive descriptions of these programs and limited data about program effectiveness.

2. Research and clinical observations indicate that education is a beneficial process for emotionally disturbed children, but little is known about why this is so.

3. Since P.L. 94-142 mandated that exceptional children be served in the least restrictive alternative, there has been an increase of models for serving children in mainstream settings. A number of prereferral, teacher assistance, and consultation models have been described and evaluated in the literature.

4. Because emotionally disturbed children are disruptive and destructive, programs frequently are challenged to find ways of setting limits on unacceptable behaviors while also maintaining children in the program.

5. Mental health agencies have developed some creative, multidisciplinary programs for multiproblem children and their families. These programs emphasize relevance, connectedness, and competence.

6. Teachers are at the heart of programs for emotionally disturbed children. To do their job well, they must be able to think through many problematic situations and to develop positive, working relationships with students.

---

*This chapter was written by Betty C. Epanchin and James L. Paul, both from the University of South Florida, Tampa.

A teacher of emotionally disturbed children must wear many hats. To do this successfully, he must also be "a decent adult; educated, well trained; able to give and receive affection, to live relaxed, and to be firm; a person with private resources for the nourishment and refreshment of his own life; not an itinerant worker but a professional through and through; a person of hope, quiet confidence, and joy; one who has committed himself to children and to the proposition that children who are disturbed can be helped by the process of reeducation."

(Hobbs, 1966)

In a landmark study conducted for the Council of Exceptional Children and the National Institute of Mental Health in 1963, existing public school programs for emotionally disturbed children were described, and the effects of these programs on the children they served were explored (Morse, Cutler, & Fink, 1964). Using data gathered from the U.S. Office of Education and the state departments of education, a total of 117 programs were identified. It was estimated that these programs represented 75% of all public school programs for emotionally handicapped children. All of these programs were surveyed by mail and 54 were visited; thus, the study provided valuable information about the approaches used in public schools roughly 10 years before the passage of P.L. 94-142.

The authors of the study acknowledged the importance of social institutions such as the school and the family in preventing and treating emotional problems. They also posed several important questions that needed to be investigated. As they observed, "While it is apparent that the schools should be playing a central role in preventive and early remedial efforts, it is by no means so clear just what this role should be. Mental health is but one of many competing goals. Even if mental health were the schools' primary function, there is little agreement on how the mental health goal is to be served. Procedures and boundaries are vague and varied" (Morse et al., 1964, pp. 1–2).

Today virtually every school in the United States has services or access to services for emotionally disturbed children. As Grosenick, George, and George (1987) reported, 99.4% of all public school classes for emotionally disturbed children developed after the passage of P.L. 94-142. However, while the numbers of available classes, identified children, and types of services have increased dramatically, some problems still persist.

The National Needs Analysis Study examined many facets of the service system and service needs of emotionally disturbed children (Huntze & Grosenick, 1980). The authors of the study concluded, "It is apparent as one examines the major and related issues surrounding servicing behavior disordered children and youth, that this is an area in dire need of attention. One is also impressed (if not overwhelmed) with the complexity and enormity of the problems involved in trying to overcome the reality and obstacles confronting service to this population" (p. 116).

As part of the National Needs Analysis in Behavior Disorders, Grosenick, George, and George (1988) examined the availability of program descriptions in the field of serious emotional disturbance. They found that only 3.5% of the 145 districts surveyed had comprehensive written descriptions of their programs.

If the lack of program descriptors reflects a lack of comprehensive program development, then these findings may indicate that most programs are compilations of programming methods and strategies unique to individual teachers rather than coherent, structured educational interventions. The significance of these findings rests on the assumption that quality provision of services is based upon "program competence," rather than individual teacher competence (Morse, 1976). Program competence is defined by the existence of certain program components and by the efficient and effective functioning of these components. As Morse noted, too often it is a limited program rather than the limited teacher that negatively affects the quality of services.

After reviewing their data on programs for emotionally disturbed children, Grosenick et al. (1987) concluded: "Clearly the field is in need of direction in the area of evaluating progress and programs. It is time to move beyond examination of numerical increases and to confront the issues of quality, effectiveness, and program standards" (p. 168).

In his statements to the Senate Subcommittee on the Handicapped regarding the reauthorization of the Education of the Handicapped Act, Forness (1989) addressed a number of needs that he felt impeded the provision of quality services to emotionally disturbed children. He identified the absence of a continuum of services for emotionally handicapped children and the absence of federal guidance and support in developing such programs. When services are not available, communities must resort to residential treatment services. Forness also noted that individual educational plans (IEPs) often fit the child to available services rather than designing appropriate, *individualized* plans and that they often focus on educational goals with little attention given to psychosocial needs.

Clearly, a number of authorities agree that we need to focus on improving both the quality of programming for emotionally handicapped children and youth and the coordination of services. However, there is less agreement about what constitutes an effective program. Service providers in education and mental health continue to struggle with several significant questions: What can and should schools do to meet the mental health needs of emotionally disturbed children within an educational context? How are services best provided? What is the role of mental health? Who should provide these services? What type of training should these persons have? These questions are the focus of this chapter.

WHAT CAN SCHOOLS DO TO MEET THE MENTAL HEALTH NEEDS OF CHILDREN?

Clinicians and progressive educators have addressed this question for years. As Ekstein and Motto (1969) noted in their volume *From Learning for Love to Love of Learning,* until the late 1930s progressive teachers trained with psychoanalysts, and both groups of professionals worked to undo the overly strict,

Collaboration among teachers and other child-caring professionals improves the quality of care that children receive.

traumatic effects of the Victorian culture. Many saw education as harmful to children as demonstrated by this quotation:

> Leave your children alone. . . . It might be better if the teachers were to write a thousand times in their copy book, "I should leave the children alone!" instead of having the children write, "During school sessions one is forbidden to speak!" One speaks of the century of the child. But this will begin only when the adults will understand that the children have to learn less from them than they have to learn from the children." (Wittels, 1926, p. 6)

Four years later Anna Freud (1931) discussed the danger of "the lack of all restraint."

Gradually clinicians began to realize that education can be "a force which releases growth potentials and fosters development and maturation in a positive way" (Ekstein & Motto, 1969, p. 3). While these authors viewed education as therapeutic, they also saw it as having a different purpose and function from therapy. They stated:

> Between teaching and healing, between education and psychotherapy, there is a boundary line not in terms of understanding the child, but rather in terms of differentiation of function, of purpose and purpose-geared technique. . . . It is the task of the therapist, through psychotherapeutic intervention, to restore lost function. It is the task of the teacher and the educator not to restore function, but to develop functions by helping the child to acquire skills, knowledge and correct attitudes." (p. 158)

They explained that psychotherapists "remove the inner obstacles which have been created in the child and which prevent him from making use of what life has to offer . . . to restore inner controls which have broken down" (p. 158). The teacher helps the child "acquire various kinds of learning. One might say that the educator brings controls from outside, from without, to help the child to learn techniques to live" (Ekstein & Motto, 1969, p. 158).

For children who live with chaos, whether imposed from within or without, school can provide a sense of order, stability, and predictability. Speaking to this point, Fenichel (1976) described the early days of the League School, an excellent program for emotionally disturbed children. The assumption was made that teachers should be permissive and "therapeutic," but Fenichel stated, "Our children taught us otherwise. We learned that disorganized children need someone to organize their world for them. . . . Disturbed children fear their own loss of control, and need protection against their own impulses. . . . [They have] the need for a highly organized program of education and training that could bring order, stability, and direction to minds that are disorganized, unstable, and unpredictable" (Fenichel, 1976, p. 225).

Not understanding a concept or not knowing how to perform a skill forces a child to feel helpless and inadequate. Mastery represents not only an increase in knowledge or skills but also a victory over such feelings. This process alone can be beneficial, especially among children who present a facade of indifference and boredom. The actual process of trying to learn, of feeling inadequate but persisting, and finally of triumphing over one's inadequacies is beneficial. As Fenichel states, "The differentiation often made between education and therapy becomes largely a semantic one. A teacher who fosters self-discipline, emotional growth, and more effective functioning is doing something therapeutic. Any educational process that helps to correct or reduce a child's distorted perceptions, disturbed behavior, and disordered thinking, and that results in greater mastery of self and one's surroundings is certainly a therapeutic process" (1976, p. 229).

The student-teacher relationship is another aspect of the educational process that potentially has therapeutic value. Many emotionally disturbed children presume that authority figures are critical, demanding, distant, and punitive. For such children, the experience of learning to like an authority figure and perceiving that person as positive, supportive, interested, and empathic as well as firm and secure is therapeutic. Such an experience reeducates the child. It provides the child with a different, more benevolent perception of authority and helps to neutralize the child's feelings about authority figures.

Empirical support also exists for the tenet that education is a therapeutic process. Whalen, Mendez de Saman, and Fortmeyer (1988) conducted a study to address the question, Does achievement precede adjustment or vice versa? Based upon their literature review, they hypothesized that academic success contributes to students' feelings of self-worth and that teachers can manipulate variables so that children are able to be academically successful and therefore feel better about themselves. They collected data about children's feelings prior to and after tutoring sessions for 15 consecutive days and concluded that "achievement precedes adjustment. It should be discerned that teachers—acknowledged experts in instruction—can influence a pupil's internal feelings, often referred to as self-concept or self-worth. That influence, of course, is a function of assisting a pupil to perform successfully in school-related tasks" (p. 316).

Another study with a different design and question found similar results. Coie and Krehbiel (1984) studied the effects of social skills training on groups of rejected, low-achieving fourth-grade children. They found that social skill training resulted only in significant reading comprehension progress, while academic skill training produced significant improvement not only in math and reading but also in their peers' feelings toward the children. Furthermore, the reading and social preference gains were maintained at the fifth-grade followup. The groups receiving academic skills training also were observed to become less off-task and less disruptive. They also received more positive teacher attention.

HOW SHOULD PUBLIC SCHOOLS SERVE EMOTIONALLY DISTURBED CHILDREN?

Schools have developed a multitude of creative approaches to working with emotionally disturbed children, and no set pattern of service delivery appears to be preferred (Danielson & Bellamy, 1989) or more effective. Federal guidelines, however, have mandated several principles that are reflected in all service models.

The first principle is the one set forth in P.L. 94-142 that mandates services for children in the **least restrictive alternative.** This means that all handicapped children should be served, as much as is possible, in mainstream settings. Related to the principle of the least restrictive alternative is the expectation that school systems develop within their district a **continuum or array of services** that range from consultative, indirect services in mainstream settings to restrictive, residential, hospital settings. Figure 2.1 identifies and defines the six different educational placements about which all states report data annually to the Office of Special Education Programs (OSEP) in the U.S. Department of Education. Another principle that guides decision making is the right to an **individualized education program.** Clearly, these principles interrelate. When an array of services are in place and when programs on a continuum are cooperatively working together to provide appropriate services for children, options exist to aid in planning individualized educational programs for children in the least restrictive setting.

These principles have been difficult to put into operation, however. Recent data suggest that many children with negative school labels are being segregated into separate classrooms or separate facilities (Blackman, 1989). Funding and accountability regulations, rather than individual child needs, have been cited as forces that have shaped the way in which children are served.

When discussing the current patterns of service delivery, Blackman (1989) observed that every state reimbursement program is significantly underfunded

Regular Class includes children who receive a majority of their education in the regular class and receive special education and related services for 21% or less of the school day. It includes children placed in regular class but receiving special education within regular class, as well as children placed in a regular class and receiving special education outside the regular class.

Resource Room includes children who receive special education and related services for 60% or less of the school day and at least 21% of the school day. This may include resource rooms with part-time instruction in the regular class.

Separate Class includes students who receive special education and related services for more than 60% of the time and are placed in self-contained special classrooms with part-time instruction in regular class or placed in self-contained class full-time on a regular school campus.

Separate School Facility includes students who receive special education and related services in separate day schools for the handicapped for greater than 50% of the school day.

Residential Facility includes students who receive education in public residential facilities for greater than 50% of the school day.

Homebound/Hospital Environment includes children placed in and receiving education in hospital or homebound programs.

FIGURE 2.1
Placement Categories Used by the Office of Special Education Programs (OSEP)

and this has encouraged school systems to seek the cheapest, not necessarily the best, pattern of providing services. He stated, "we will make little progress until our funding programs are driven by our values" (p. 461).

Algozzine, Christenson, and Ysseldyke (1982) and Sevick and Ysseldyke (1986) supported Blackman's position. These authors found that 92% of all children referred for testing actually go through the formal testing process and 75% of all children tested are placed. Children are referred because someone in the system, often the classroom teacher, perceives the child as having difficulty; however, in many systems services have not been available to children until the children were identified. Given the subjective nature of the identification process, it is possible to qualify a child for identification and thereby to provide services.

Pugach and Johnson (1989) observed that the referral process requires that the referring teacher defend his reason for referring the child and this defense automatically becomes part of the information shared with the school-based committee. "No mechanism exists for a reinterpretation of the teacher's initial perception of the situation, although such early perceptions may not represent an accurate reflection of the actual problem. The problem as it is initially conceptualized by the referring teacher may be concretized prematurely" (p. 218).

The section that follows describes the array of services that need to be available for emotionally disturbed children if they are to be served appropriately. The least restrictive services such as mainstream consultation and resource rooms are school based, whereas the more restrictive settings such as self-contained classrooms are often district based. The most restrictive settings such as day treatment programs and residential programs are often designed to serve several school districts.

PREREFERRAL PROGRAMS

Programs set up to serve nonidentified children in mainstream classrooms, called prereferral programs, are required in many states in an effort to help children with relatively minor problems remain in mainstream settings, to improve services to children in mainstream settings, and to provide on-the-job training for mainstream teachers. These services require a shift in focus from assessing and placing children in special settings to developing alternatives in regular classrooms. There are a variety of preintervention models, but all provide systematic, documented interventions to children having mild problems in mainstream settings (Carter & Sugai, 1989; Chalfant, Pysh, & Moultrie, 1979; Friend, 1984; Graden, 1989; Hayek, 1987; Maher & Zins, 1987; Ritter, 1978). When such programs are implemented, they often result in a reduction of the number of referrals, but this typically is not a primary goal of such programs.

Prereferral programs typically have several phases of intervening (Curtis, Zins & Graden, 1987). Action is initiated when a teacher or a parent requests assistance. This request for assistance is *not* a referral nor is the child suspected of being handicapped; rather, a classroom problem that needs attention exists. Parents and teachers work together to plan an intervention.

Once assistance is requested, the problem is identified and analyzed. This involves specifying in objective terms the nature of the problem and identifying classroom-environmental variables that affect student performance. Other professionals may conduct classroom observations in an effort to identify the variables that are impacting upon the child's behavior. For example, observations may reveal that a child has more attentional problems when she is transitioning from one activity to another or that the child does not possess the classroom survival skills necessary to meet the demands of the situation.

When agreement is reached about the nature of the problem, an intervention is planned. Clearly, this intervention is based upon how the problem is conceptualized. When the intervention plans are complete, the plan is implemented and evaluated. Interventions that are frequently implemented include social skills training, peer tutoring, change in seating or schedules (environmental manipulation), contracts/reward programs, and learning strategies. Formative evaluation data are gathered and used to modify and revise the intervention.

Prereferral programs have several advantages, in addition to decreasing special education enrollments, enabling handicapped children to compete in mainstream settings, and providing on-the-job training for teachers. Heufner (1988) maintains that prereferral programs may reduce the special education costs, reduce the stigma of pull-out programs, increase understanding across disciplines, reduce mislabeling of nonhandicapped children, benefit regular students through "spill-over" effects, and help in the creation of a role for "master" teachers.

MODELS FOR MAINTAINING IDENTIFIED CHILDREN IN MAINSTREAM CLASSROOMS

Once children are referred and identified by the schools, the least restrictive setting is a mainstream classroom. Identified children are served within the regular setting in a variety of ways. Emotionally disturbed children may be maintained in regular classrooms with administrative modifications, with support from a special education consultant, with access to a crisis teacher when needed, or with special instructional modifications by the regular classroom teacher. Each model is characterized by flexibility and individualization.

Administrative Modifications

Administrators can make a number of modifications in the regular program that can help handicapped children be maintained in mainstream settings. For example, administrators can assign fewer students to a teacher in exchange for having one or more emotionally handicapped children in the classroom. The rationale for this model lies in the recognition that most emotionally handicapped children require more teacher attention but also benefit from having good role models with whom to interact.

Consultation

Consultation models are used to provide services to the regular classroom teacher (Polsgrove & McNeil, 1989; Reisberg & Wolf, 1986; Tindal, Shinn, Walz, & Germann, 1987). These approaches may be classified as indirect or direct. The indirect model of consultation focuses on work with the classroom teacher. The consultant rarely, if ever, has contact with the child. The other model, often called a resource-consulting model, involves alternating between direct and indirect services. In this approach, the consulting teacher works with the classroom teacher (indirect) as well as with the child (direct).

Collaborative consultation has been carefully described in the literature (Idol, Paolucci-Whitcomb, & Nevin, 1986; West & Cannon, 1988; West & Idol, 1987). This is a problem-solving model that involves regular and special education teachers as collaborators who *equally share* responsibility for intervention. It has been defined as "a process that enables people with diverse expertise to generate creative solutions to mutually defined problems. The outcome is enhanced, altered, and produces solutions that are different from those that the individual team members would produce independently. The major outcome of collaborative consultation is to provide comprehensive and *effective* programs for students with special needs within the most appropriate context, thereby enabling them to achieve maximum constructive interaction with their non-handicapped peers (Idol et al., 1986, p. 1). Table 2.1 compares schools that use the consultation model with traditional schools that do not.

TABLE 2.1
Characteristics of Instruction for Handicapped Children

	Consultation Schools	Nonconsultation Schools
Referral	1. Classroom teacher assumes primary role in referral	1. Special educator or guidance counselor assumes primary role in referral
	2. Classroom teacher assumes primary responsibility for IEP (individual education plan) development	2. Special educator assumes primary responsibility for IEP development
	3. Staffing process allows regular education personnel opportunity to provide referral input	3. Staffing process allows special education personnel to obtain approval of referral
Assessment	1. Basic staffing team shares responsibility for test selection and interpretation	1. Special educator assumes primary responsibility for test selection and interpretation
	2. Criterion-referenced tests used	2. Norm-referenced tests used
	3. Basic staffing team assumes responsibility for diagnosis	3. Special educator assumes responsibility for diagnosis
Curriculum	1. Staffing process allows regular education personnel opportunity to share in development of skill sequences	1. Staffing process allows special education personnel to obtain approval of selected skill sequences
	2. Locally developed skill sequences used	2. Commercially developed skill sequences used
	3. Curriculum referenced to school specific standards	3. Curriculum referenced to classroom specific standards
Teaching & Learning	1. Classroom teacher assumes primary responsibility for instruction	1. Special educator assumes primary responsibility for instruction
	2. No student spends more than 10% of time outside of regular classroom	2. Some students spend more than 10% of time outside of regular classroom
	3. Staffing process allows regular education personnel opportunity to provide instruction input	3. Staffing process allows special education personnel to obtain approval of instruction
Evaluation	1. Classroom teacher assumes primary responsibility for measures	1. Special educator assumes primary responsibility for measures
	2. Measures usually same as measures used for most children in classroom	2. Measures usually different than measures used for most children in classroom
	3. Staffing process allows regular education personnel opportunity to evaluate student progress	3. Staffing process allows special education personnel to obtain confirmation of evaluation

From "A 4-Year Evaluation of Consulting Teacher Service" by Knight Meyers, Paolucci-Whitcomb, Hasazi, and Nevin, 1981, *Behavioral Disorders, 6(2),* pp. 95–96. Reprinted by permission.

Team Teaching

One variant of the consulting teacher model that involves direct service to children is the team-teaching model. In this approach the regular classroom teacher and the special education teacher coteach some activities or classes. Typically the special education teacher combines his students with those of the regular teacher, and the two teachers alternate teaching responsibilities. One day the regular classroom teacher may have all but two or three children in her class while the special education teacher tutors the few who are having trouble. One day the special education teacher may teach most of the class while the regular classroom teacher works with a small group of children. The grouping changes often avoiding the stigmatization associated with static grouping. The regular classroom teacher is able to learn techniques used by the special education teacher, and the special education teacher is able to learn which techniques work in mainstream settings.

Crisis Teacher

The crisis teacher model involves assigning one teacher the responsibility of working with children who are having temporary difficulty (Morse, 1985). For volatile children, this can be especially helpful. The regular classroom teacher sends the child to the crisis teacher when she appears to be upset, when a situation arises that may cause trouble, and when the child indicates that she needs respite from the pressures of the regular classroom. For example, a student may be sent to the crisis teacher to take a test or to get focused and settled after a stressful event. Such programs are available to children on an as-needed basis.

Curricular Programs

A variety of programs have been developed to teach children how to improve their social skills, study skills, and self-monitoring strategies. A number of these programs are discussed in Chapter 14. While these programs are particularly beneficial to the identified child, they are usually of value to all students in the class.

RESOURCE ROOMS

The resource room is the most widely used educational service for mildly handicapped children (Friend & McNutt, 1984). Although there is a great deal of variation in how a resource room is implemented, it involves scheduling handicapped children in a special education setting for set periods of time but maintaining the regular classroom as the primary instructional setting (Wiederholt, Hammill, & Brown, 1983). There are noncategorical, cross-categorical or mul-

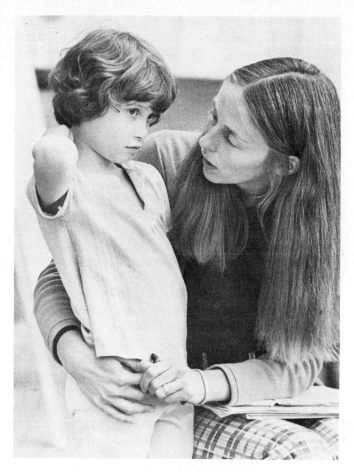

The relationship between teacher and student can be a positive, therapeutic experience for emotionally disturbed children who view school and authority figures as punitive.

ticategorical, categorical, and itinerant resource room programs. Noncategorical programs are those in which mildly handicapped children are placed in classrooms with other mildly handicapped children, and none of them are categorically labeled. Cross-categorical or multicategorical programs label children categorically, but place mild to moderately handicapped children of different labels in the same classroom. Categorical classrooms label and place by category. Itinerant classrooms involve a special education teacher traveling to several different schools to serve a few identified children in each school.

These models represent different belief systems about educating handicapped children as well as different financial and administrative realities. Proponents of noncategorical programs maintain that children labeled mildly handicapped, learning disabled, mentally retarded, and sensory impaired cannot be separated precisely and that mildly/moderately handicapped children have similar functional or instructional needs (Vallecorsa, 1983). Categorical programs, in contrast, are based on the assumption that students with similar labels have similar characteristics and instructional needs. Cross-categorical programs acknowledge the differences among handicapped groups, but these differences are not seen as significant with respect to instructional needs.

The persistence of different resource room models also is supported by economic and administrative convenience. In small, rural communities where there are not enough students in a given category to justify a school-based classroom for each handicapping condition, administrators tend to prefer cross-categorical or itinerant classes (Morsink, Thomas, & Smith-Davis, 1987). Cross-categorical or itinerant programs enable administrators to provide services to a number of different types of handicapped children in one classroom.

Research supports the position that differences do exist between students by category and that these differences become more obvious the more handicapped the child is (Morsink et al., 1987). Research, however, does not consistently support the position that instructional methods need to be different for the different groups. In fact, it appears that the majority of professionals advocate matching instructional methods with student characteristics rather than with category.

Problems arise with cross-categorical resource rooms, however, when large numbers of children with significantly different needs are placed together. After studying this model, Sage and Fenson (1985) reported that too many pupils were assigned, both at one time and overall, for effective instruction to occur. Furthermore, they found that many students stayed in such classes most of the day, which mixes models inappropriately. Finally, they reported that many classrooms had "unreasonable" age ranges in the same class. Hocutt and Schulte (1987) concluded that such conditions lead to teacher burnout and lack of individualized attention.

A number of studies have investigated the effectiveness of the resource room model, but available data are somewhat mixed. Given the lack of agreement regarding the efficacy of different models, researchers have examined classroom and instructional variables that affect outcome. For example, Haynes and Jenkins (1986) compared reading instruction in 28 resource rooms with reading instruction in regular education classrooms. They found that "resource rooms showed substantial variability in time scheduled for instruction. . . . Student characteristics such as achievement level were weakly linked to scheduling and to the amount of reading instruction received, challenging the view that special education programs are congruent with individual student needs. Instructional process variables seemed more a function of program and school context variables, such as district philosophy of curricula selection, than of student characteristics" (p. 188). Although significant variability was found among classrooms in general, students in regular classrooms received more reading instruction and had more teacher-led reading instruction than students in the resource rooms. Furthermore, no differences were found in the nature of reading instruction when the two settings were compared. Given these results, the authors questioned whether resource rooms would be able to close the gap between handicapped and nonhandicapped students.

How the resource room model is implemented clearly affects outcome. After an extensive review of the literature, Leinhardt and Pallay (1982) concluded that the variables most necessary for successful student outcomes can occur in a variety of settings; therefore, educators need to be less concerned about where instruction occurs and more concerned about effective teaching practices. The variables associated with student growth that Leinhardt and Pallay identified included small class size, high content overlap between teaching and learning activities and the outcome criteria, mastery learning systems, increased time spent on cognitive activities, reasonably rapid pacing, a formal management system, positive teacher affect, increased teacher instructional time, and positive self-concept.

SELF-CONTAINED CLASSROOMS

The self-contained classroom is the most common model for providing services for severely disturbed children, according to data gathered as part of the National Needs Analysis Project (Grosenick et al., 1987). The public schools serve two to four times as many severely disturbed children as do other agencies. The classrooms in these schools are usually designed for approximately 8 to 12 severely disturbed children who receive all of their instruction in one classroom from one teacher and one teacher aide. As with resource rooms, there is much variation in how this model is implemented.

Based upon the limited descriptive studies of these classes, it seems likely that most classrooms are highly structured, as a means of helping children maintain behavioral control. The classes are remedial in focus, in an effort to help the children become academically competent. How teachers program for children's emotional and social needs, however, apparently varies considerably.

Jennings, Mendelsohn, May, and Brown (1988) studied 147 elementary school students who were enrolled in self-contained classes in a large, urban, northeastern city. They found that black males were very much overrepresented (65% of the males were black whereas 55% of the males in the school population were black). Seventy percent of the sample were diagnosed as having one of the acting-out disorders: conduct disorder, oppositional disorder, or attention-deficit disorder with the most frequent diagnosis being oppositional disorder (33%). The children earned slightly lower than average scores on IQ tests (mean = 91.5) and on achievement tests (87 to 89 on tests where the mean was 100). On both measures, the range was large; approximately 80 points differentiated the high from the low scores.

ALTERNATIVES TO PUBLIC SCHOOL CLASSROOMS

Honig v. Doe was the first case considered by the Supreme Court that dealt with the discipline of special education students. The two students cited in the case had emotional disabilities and aggressive tendencies.

One of the students (John Doe) was a 17-year-old with a history of impulsivity and aggression that was documented in his IEP (individual education plan). He was enrolled in a developmental center for disabled students. One day, in response to taunts from a peer, he choked the child with enough force to leave abrasions on the student's neck. He was escorted to the principal's office and en route he kicked out a window. He was suspended for 5 days and the principal recommended that he be expelled. Suit was brought on his behalf and the federal district court directed the school to return John Doe to his school placement.

The second student was Jack Smith, an emotionally disturbed sixth grader who had a history of physical and emotional abuse. Jack had been enrolled in several alternative school settings, starting in the second grade. By sixth grade he was placed in a special education setting that was housed in a middle school. In this setting, he experienced a number of problems that included stealing, extorting money from classmates, and making sexual comments to his classmates. Because of his difficulties, his school day was reduced to half-days, but he continued to make lewd comments to female students which caused him to be suspended for 5 days and recommended for expulsion. His grandparents brought suit on his behalf.

The cases of John Doe and Jack Smith were joined together, and the district court ruled in favor of the students. The school district and the state appealed to the court of appeals. Generally the court ruled in favor of the students. Bill Honig, California Superintendent of Public Instruction, appealed to the Supreme Court, and the Court agreed to consider two issues: (1) whether schools may unilaterally expel special education students for dangerous or disruptive behavior that stems from their disability when their parents have filed an appeal, and (2) whether the state must provide educational services to a student when the local school district refuses or neglects to do so.

The justices voted 6 to 2 in favor of the ruling that handicapped students could not be expelled while waiting for administrative review. The justices were split 4 to 4 on the matter of requiring the state to provide direct services to students. Thus, the Ninth Circuit ruling was allowed to stand that the state must provide services when the local district fails to do so.

The significance of this case rests in the responsibility it places on educational professionals to find satisfactory placements and interventions for handicapped students who are dangerous to themselves and/or others. "If a program formerly deemed to be appropriate for such a child is not working satisfactorily, as demonstrated by severe inappropriate behavior, school administrators cannot any longer exercise the easy alternative of expulsion. Instead, the staffing team will have to be creative in making adjustments to the existing program, find an appropriate alternative placement, or gather evidence to take before a judge to seek a longer removal from school. Even then, . . . removal for longer than 10 days is appropriate only as a temporary reprieve for the educators seeking an appropriate alternative placement. At some time, the student will likely be ordered back to school or to an appropriate alternative placement" (Bartlett, 1989, p. 358).

As reflected in the Supreme Court case, *Honig v. Doe* (1988), public school programs are struggling with how to deal with disruptive, handicapped students. Grosenick (1981) pointed out that severely disturbed children constitute the group that is most likely to be removed from the public schools. She stated that "removed from the system" are key words used when describing public school services for severely disturbed students. She observed that "because this handicap often manifests itself in defiant rule-breaking behavior, severely disordered students, more than any others, find themselves at odds with school rules and discipline policy. Most personnel felt that by imposing sanctions on severely behavior disordered students for school rule breaking, such students are effectively barred from an appropriate education" (p. 186). She also described a number of ways in which students exhibiting serious behavior problems are excluded from schools. Some of these demotion procedures include the following:

- *In-school suspension*—The student is suspended from a class and assigned to the in-school suspension teacher, where students work on their assignments until their suspensions end.
- *Continuous suspension*—The student is suspended for 3 days, returns to school briefly, and then is suspended again. This practice has been discouraged because the student's handicapping condition is commonly the cause of the suspension. This is viewed to be an illegal practice.
- *Shortened school day*—The student is scheduled for less time in school.
- *Homebound instruction*—The student is taught at home.
- *Alternative school placement*—The student is placed in an alternative school where she may work on her degree requirements.
- *Ignored truancy*—The school system fails to seek truant warrants for children with behavior disorders.

While most of the school demission procedures can be very appropriate means of providing relief to stressed students or providing natural consequences for inappropriate behaviors, they can also be abused by persons wishing to expel a student from a school setting. After discussing the implications of *Honig v. Doe* (1988), Bartlett (1989) concluded that "school officials would be well advised not to consider expulsion a viable solution to a student's problem" (p. 365). As an alternative in cases of severe misconduct, he recommended the IEP change of placement procedures be used for making appropriate changes in educational placement.

More restrictive settings are often recommended for students who cannot be maintained successfully in the public schools. Most of the successful, more restrictive programs reflect cooperative, collaborative arrangements between public education, mental health, and other related agencies such as public welfare and the courts.

MENTAL HEALTH SERVICES

Historically, mental health agencies have been responsible for the provision of services to emotionally disturbed students, and they continue to be major providers. Agencies in urban areas offer services ranging from outpatient therapy for mildly handicapped children who may not receive any special services in the public school to intensive, all-day or 24-hour specialized care. In rural areas services are likely to be less available and spread out over large geographic areas. Unlike education that is mandated for all children, most mental health services are optional and depend upon the willingness of the client to seek treatment.

Unfortunately, this very basic difference in mandate, combined with differing philosophies and training of professionals providing treatment, often results in conflict and discord between education and mental health. Too often service providers do not communicate with each other about their work, or the communication is characterized by distrust and misunderstandings. This lack of collaboration has been identified as a major problem and efforts are underway to alter this. For example, a survey of the State Mental Health Representatives for Children and Youth found that interagency collaboration was of greatest concern to respondents (Florida Mental Health Institute, 1988–89). Creative programs that enable blended funding among agencies to optimize the quality of services are also being developed.

Most of these collaborative programs reflect a commitment to the following principles set forth by Stroul and Friedman (1986): a "system of care should be child-centered, with the needs of child and family dictating the types and mix of services provided" and "the system of care should be community-based, with the locus of services as well as the management and decision-making responsibility resting at the community level" (p. 17). They elaborate on these core values in the guiding principles for a system of care as depicted in Figure 2.2.

The primary therapeutic interventions identified in individual treatment plans for emotionally disturbed children are outpatient psychotherapy for an individual child and her family, in-home counseling and support (often called family preservation), specialized foster care, day treatment, and residential treatment. Case managers coordinate services for children receiving help from multiple agencies and professionals. They also work with all involved to adjust these "wrap-around" services as the needs of the child and family change.

Psychotherapy With Children and Youth

For decades the effectiveness of psychotherapy with children has been debated in the professional literature. Casey and Berman (1985) reviewed 75 studies that evaluated the effectiveness of psychotherapy with children (mean age = 8.9). They found that the average outcome of children receiving treatment was more than two-thirds of a standard deviation better than that of the untreated control groups. They also examined the types of problems that appeared to be most amenable to treatment and found that children who were hyperactive, impulsive, phobic, and had somatic complaints were more successfully treated than children with social adjustment problems. Interestingly, these authors also found that peers and teachers reported significantly less improvement than did parents and therapists. The authors attributed these findings to the intractable nature of peer and teacher impressions.

1. Emotionally disturbed children should have access to a comprehensive array of services that address the child's physical, emotional, social, and educational needs.

2. Emotionally disturbed children should receive individualized services in accordance with the unique needs and potentials of each child. These services should be guided by an individualized service plan.

3. Emotionally disturbed children should receive services within the least restrictive, most normative environment that is clinically appropriate.

4. The families and surrogate families of emotionally disturbed children should be full participants in all aspects of the planning and delivery of services.

5. Emotionally disturbed children should receive services that are integrated with linkages between child-caring agencies and programs and mechanisms for planning, developing, and coordinating services.

6. Emotionally disturbed children should be provided with case management or similar mechanisms to ensure that multiple services are delivered in a coordinated and therapeutic manner, and that they can move through the system of services in accordance with their changing needs.

7. Early identification and intervention for children with emotional problems should be promoted by the system of care in order to enhance the likelihood of positive outcomes.

8. Emotionally disturbed children should be ensured smooth transitions to the adult service system as they reach maturity.

9. The rights of emotionally disturbed children should be protected, and effective advocacy efforts for emotionally disturbed children and youth should be promoted.

10. Emotionally disturbed children should receive services without regard to race, religion, national origin, sex, physical disability, or other characteristics, and services should be sensitive and responsive to cultural differences and special needs. (Stroul and Friedman, 1986, p. 17)

FIGURE 2.2
Guiding Principles for the Care System of Emotionally Disturbed Children

Family Preservation Services

These services are based upon the assumptions that (1) preservation of the family is beneficial to family members and that (2) intensive interventions that focus on helping the family become more functional can prevent the psychological and social crisis evoked by the removal of an emotionally disturbed child from her family. This reflects a radical shift in thinking from earlier approaches in which the child was removed from the home and placed in what was presumed to be a more therapeutic setting. Follow-up studies of children treated out of the home have consistently indicated that children's treatment gains are not maintained if changes in the ecology do not also occur (Lewis, 1988).

Family preservation programs have developed all over the United States (Knitzer & Yelton, 1989). Homebuilders, a model started in the state of Washington, has provided a model for similar programs. The purpose of Homebuilders is to keep youngsters with their families while also providing the most effective type of intervention and controlling costs (Haapala, 1984; Knitzer, 1982). Staff are trained to help families learn how to be more skillful in relating to each other, to manage feelings better (particularly anger), and to stop self-defeating patterns of behavior. They accomplish these goals by entering the homes and providing 24-hour help, if needed. The types of services provided include the following: support, crisis counseling, advocacy, case management, and education in life skills. Families admitted to the program are on the verge of disintegrating because of multiple problems that include alcohol and drug abuse, spouse and child abuse, intense family conflicts, the child's commitment of a status offense, or failure to meet the child's serious emotional, behavioral, or developmental needs.

Specialized Foster Care

An example of the specialized foster care model is the Pressley Ridge Youth Development Extension (PRYDE) (Hawkins, Meadowcroft, Trout, & Luster, 1985). The mission of this program is to "provide troubled and troubling children and adolescents with a noninstitutional treatment alternative in the private homes of treatment parents and to return these youths to their communities or families better adjusted: that is, more skilled, more effective, more confident, more adequately equipped to deal with their natural ecology in the present and future" (Hawkins et al., 1985, p. 221). The program utilizes an in-home treatment model that utilizes as the "agent of treatment" the "professional parent." The foster parents have been trained to manage behavior, negotiate and solve problems with children, advocate for their children, deal with minor medical emergencies, and keep good records of progress. Outcome data are promising, and the program is clearly cost-effective.

Day Treatment

Day treatment is an intermediate step between residential care and self-contained classes in the public school. In this model, educational and mental health services are provided to both children and their families. The provision of vocational and other remedial services helps students develop social, psychological, educational, vocational, and economic skills. One of the major advantages of these programs is the in-house coordination of services. Professionals working with the children and their families share similar goals and cooperatively work with each other to achieve the goals.

City Lights is a day treatment program that has been in operation since 1981, and since that time it has reported positive outcomes for a number of very difficult children (Tolmach, 1985). City Lights was designed to create "an environment that guarantees the novelty of success to experts at failure" (p. 214). Critical elements of the program are remedial and vocational education, group and individual therapy for the students, and family therapy. The multidisciplinary team works together to help students develop skills and find positive and productive ways of getting involved in their community and their families.

Residential Services

Prior to the early 1960s most professional services for seriously emotionally disturbed children were provided in residential settings. These services were on the psychodynamic model, and the primary treatment staff were psychiatrists, psychologists, social workers, and nurses, with support services being provided by teachers, speech therapists, and physical therapists, among others. There was no continuum of care, and services for those children who were not disturbed enough to require hospitalization and who were experiencing serious behavioral and learning problems in school were very limited.

The focus on residential services as the primary system of care for seriously emotionally disturbed children changed radically in the 1960s. This was due in part to the human rights movement, which supported the right of all people to live in their own community. The shift from residential treatment also was supported by data that questioned the efficacy of residential services and by developments in the behavioral sciences that created more knowledge about the nature and treatment of emotional disturbance. Since the 1960s, with the implementation of the policy requiring children to be educated and treated in the least restrictive environment and with the legislative requirement that all children be provided a free appropriate education, residential services have been used much less frequently.

In a review of follow-up studies of children treated in psychiatric hospitals, Blotcky, Dimperio, and Gossett (1984) reported that approximately 15,000 children were in over 300 residential treatment centers in the United States. In their review they found many problems with the quality of the available research, including poor designs, focus on single variables, poorly defined dependent variables, and generally poor descriptions of the treatment programs. Because of the significant problems with the data about children treated in psychiatric hospitals, general conclusions about the efficacy of such treatment were impossible. However, good prognosis was positively correlated with adequate intelligence, the absence of antisocial symptoms, nonpsychotic and nonorganic diagnoses, adequate length of stay, healthy family functioning, and involvement in aftercare. They emphasized the need for quality longitudinal studies of long-term treatment effects.

Curry (1986) conducted an extensive review of the psychiatric hospitalization and residential treatment outcome literature and concluded that 60% to 80% of the youngsters treated in such programs improve or are functioning adequately at follow-up. He identified a number of factors that appear to be related to successful status at follow-up. Some were related to client characteristics, such as academic ability and capacity for relationships, but many were related to the continuity of care during and after discharge.

Case Management and Wraparound Services

In an effort to maintain children in their communities and to provide coordinated services to the children and their families, a number of states have developed case management or wraparound service policies. These policies or service provisions are based on the practice of first determining what the individual child and her family need and then providing individualized services based on these needs, rather than providing services based upon available programs and services (see Figure 2.3).

Case managers are professionals who work with a team to develop a coordinated, individualized treatment plan for each client in their caseload. They also monitor the appropriateness of services and plans developed for their clients. Children assigned to case managers are typically severely disturbed children who will need services over a number of years and who need services from a variety of different agencies and professionals. Case managers regularly com-

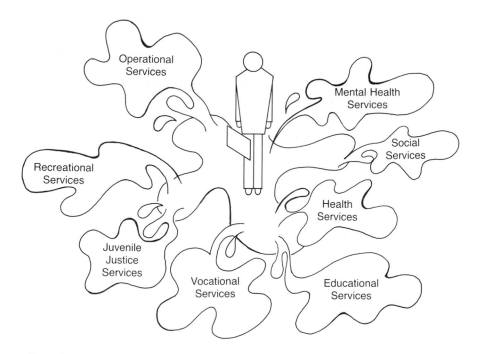

FIGURE 2.3
Case Management—The "Glue" That Holds the System Together (From "Update: Case Management," by FMHI Research Training Center, University of South Florida, *Update, 2(2).* Reprinted by permission.)

municate with the child and her family to be certain that treatment is progressing appropriately and that the needs of the child and family are being addressed.

Wraparound services are provided through policies and funding mechanisms that enable case managers to be more flexible in the provision of services. Essentially case managers are able to "wrap services around" the child and family so that individual treatment goals can be addressed. An example of such a practice is found in the Kaleidoscope Program in Chicago. When a child is referred to this program for services, a careful assessment is conducted, and treatment plans are generated on the basis of the assessment. Once an individualized treatment plan is developed, funds are requested to allow the plan to be implemented. This is in direct contrast to traditional approaches that require the children and their families to fit into existing services that are bound by the constraints of available funding.

THE TEACHER'S ROLE IN HELPING EMOTIONALLY DISTURBED CHILDREN

The majority of emotionally disturbed children receive most or all of their services from teachers, but what teachers should and can do to help children continues to be a topic of much debate. Research on teaching has revealed the complexity of the teacher's role (Berliner, 1986; Lortie, 1975). Two major factors have contributed to this complexity: (1) the changing paradigm of teaching and knowledge about instruction, and (2) the understanding of the social and cognitive behavior of children. These changes have important implications for understanding the role of the teacher of emotionally disturbed children.

The teacher's role is the education of students; however, the lack of agreement on the nature of the educational process makes the teacher's task unclear. In the past, there were two general views of the teacher's role. The first viewed the teacher's responsibility as the instruction and discipline of students with the aim of social and intellectual competence. The second viewed the teacher's responsibility as the facilitation of the social and intellectual development of children with the aim of emotional well-being as well as cognitive competence. The former focused primarily on the nature of knowledge and what was to be learned at each grade level. The latter focused more on the learner and how learning was to occur. This distinction is clearly present in the history of educating emotionally disturbed children. However, the distinction is more difficult to make in view of present theories of teaching and learning which more directly link knowledge about the learning task and the learning process.

The development of knowledge about educational practice is guided by theories of teaching and learning. Part of the complexity of the role of the teacher has been a result of confusion about an appropriate theoretical base for teaching. The teacher's role has been influenced by different perspectives on the nature of the learner. The humanistic perspective, for example, focused on the value and the intellectual and moral resources of the individual student and resulted in a curriculum that emphasized the freedom and experience of the student. On the other hand, the behavioral perspective focused more on observable and measurable teacher behavior, and emphasized known positive correlations with achievement.

Educational research both reflects and influences the prevailing theories of teaching. In the 1960s research on teaching focused on student-teacher interactions and on the personality of the teacher as a predictor variable in successful teaching. In the 1970s and 1980s there was specific interest in the discrete behavior of teachers that correlates with student achievement. This research reflects what Gage and Berliner (1988) characterized as the "process-product" view of teaching. This view emphasized academic learning time (Fisher & Berliner, 1985) and a structured approach to instruction (Good & Brophy, 1986). This view of the teacher's role has been supported by the school reform movement which has focused on the academic achievement of students (Carnegie Forum, 1986) and on the nature and structure of knowledge to be learned (Adler, 1984).

More recently, a perspective on the nature of teaching and the role of the teacher has emerged which has important implications for teaching emotionally disturbed children. This perspective, situated cognition, is described by Woolfolk (1989). Emphasizing the use of information to solve teaching problems, this view calls attention to two basic aspects of teaching. The first is the use of specialized knowledge structures by teachers to interpret situations, identify relevant resources, plan strategies, and implement those strategies. These knowledge structures enable teachers to recognize new situations and problems and to create novel solutions to those problems. The second is the particularistic and situational knowledge of teachers which enables them to apply what they know to a specific situation.

Unlike the process-product research, the situated cognition view of teaching focuses on "how teachers understand (the) observed conditions of effective teaching, how these conditions are established in classroom situations, (and) how effective teachers (acquire) their abilities" (Woolfolk, 1989, p. 56). The emphasis in the emerging framework, which is based on research in teacher cognition, is on the tasks teachers perform in the classroom and on the knowledge structures that enable them to perform those tasks. Tasks, which involve goals, circumstances or "problem space," and resources, are accomplished successfully by "interpreting the problem space accurately (e.g., discovering what the problem of achieving order is in a particular class) and organizing resources (activities, rules, physical space) in ways that 'fit' or account for the features of that problem space" (Woolfolk, 1989, p. 57). Within this view, actions are said to be "situated." Whether a particular teaching behavior, such as questioning or praising, is effective or appropriate depends upon the task being performed.

The situated cognition perspective on teaching is important to teachers of emotionally disturbed children because it broadens the process-product perspective by taking into account more directly the nature of tasks to be performed in the classroom. It also takes into account the knowledge structures on which the accomplishment of tasks is based and the processes for acquiring those knowledge structures.

There are several implications of this view for understanding the role of the teacher of emotionally disturbed children. He brings into the classroom a particular understanding of the nature of the problem of emotional disturbance, whereas other teachers of these children may have very different views. He also feels that certain educational tasks are important, and his views may be very different from those of other teachers of these children. Some teachers focus strongly on academic goals, others on social behavior, while still others focus on therapeutic goals. The teacher's own personal resources and understanding of himself as a teacher of these children is particularistic. That is, just as there is not an agreed upon theory of emotional disturbance, there is no common philosophy of education or a single curriculum for these children. Furthermore, the circumstances under which these children are taught vary greatly. Administrative support, an important issue for the teacher, varies from school to school, as does the educational policy regarding special versus integrated settings. When we view the teacher's role in the education of emotionally disturbed children, we must acknowledge the complexity and variability of the goals, the "problem space," the resources, and the teacher's teaching behavior.

Changes in paradigms of teaching have had profound implications upon the role of the teacher of emotionally disturbed children. Whether teaching is a humanistic task, influenced by the personal traits of the teacher, an engineering task, requiring a particular repertoire of teaching behaviors for managing instruction, an orchestration task, involving the facilitation of positive interaction between students and learning opportunities, or an intellectual task, which emphasizes the goals, circumstances, and resources for teaching, depends upon the paradigm of teaching.

Just as the paradigm of teaching has changed in important ways during the past 20 years, so has the understanding of the learner. The cognitive revolution of the 1980s, which sought to integrate the neurosciences, linguistics, anthropology, psychology, and the arts, emphasized both the complexity of the learner and the intellectual challenge of teaching (Gardner, 1985). The renewed emphasis on emotions (Sampson, 1988) produced by the cognitive revolution has minimized the distinctions among behavior, affect, and cognition and integrated the traditional clinical psychodynamic and cognitive perspectives. The focus was on the integrity of the learner as a whole person. There was a corresponding appreciation of the interactive nature of teaching. The social ecology of the classroom was recognized as influencing and being influenced by the values and personality of the teacher and of the students. There were, therefore, strong centripetal forces in the arts and sciences contributing to our understanding of teaching that emphasized the connections and relationships among students, the curriculum, and teachers. These changes affected our perceptions and understanding of the teacher's role.

Another philosophical change with important implications for the role of the teacher had to do with a concern for the quality of the teacher's relationship with students. Gilligan (1982), Noddings (1986), and others developed the concept of care in education. This view emphasized affective concerns and a valuing of subjective reality which balances the concern with objectivity in moral perspectives, for example. The focus was on the quality of connections among persons. Studies of the role of the teacher conveyed in literature and observational studies of the caring of teachers are developing the construct of care (Noblit & Kendricks, in press).

Changes in the perceptions of teachers of emotionally disturbed children reflect the shifts in educational philosophy and research. The role is, however, influenced by the knowledge of the characteristics of these children and the particular challenge of meeting their educational needs. Teachers of these children have been viewed as therapists, as having a special natural talent or endowment for working with these children (Hobbs, 1964), as behavioral engineers (Hewitt, 1967), and as "ego banks" (Rappaport, 1968). In addition to technical and clinical skills, different theorists have noted the importance of the personal and moral resources of the teacher, his authenticity (Moustakas, 1966), his tolerance for deviance (Trippe, 1963), and his own mental health.

Knowledge of instructional technologies is not sufficient. The teacher's values, self-esteem, self-confidence, anger, fear, and need for control are all ultimately a part of the encounter with children who are in conflict with themselves and others. A teacher of emotionally disturbed latency age children wrote in her diary about a large 10-year-old student in her class (Epanchin & Paul, 1982):

> It is hard to think straight. I'm mad at Jerry. I've never been hit and attacked like he hit me today. I was really frightened. He was out of control, and I could not get away from him. I don't know what set him off, but he went home hating me. I need to deal with my own anger before I see him tomorrow.

On another day, she was feeling frustrated by circumstances thwarting her efforts to teach these children:

> Today was mass confusion! I cannot keep my kids on task when workers are remodeling the classroom next door and banging on my wall all morning. Half the day was lost.
>
> I feel schizophrenic. It's bad enough moving from teaching beginning sounds to one student to finding common factors or exponents with the next student. Amidst this confusion comes collecting bus fare money, lunchroom staff saying the lunch count is incorrect, people arriving unannounced to observe.
>
> Taxi problems again. We had such a good day only to have it spoiled by Jerry spitting at passersby as the taxi drove away. We still have a long way to go.

At times this teacher also felt some success in teaching these children. The same teacher, on another day, wrote:

> Some positive things happened today. I was more relaxed and so were the kids. They worked together, and Mary actually participated in decorating Jerry's birthday cake. Today I feel like I did some things right.

A teacher in a private residential school who had had a good day wrote (Epanchin & Paul, 1982):

> Tremendous day! Billy did not have a single fight. No one tore up his homework. Everyone worked at his desk when the visitor came to observe.

Stress associated with teaching emotionally disturbed children can be reduced by meeting with other teachers of these children. One teacher wrote:

> It did me a lot of good to listen to the experiences of other teachers and to share mine. It was comforting to hear them talk about their frustrations, anger, and feeling inadequate. I am no different.

Having the necessary personal resources, the ability to repair one's self, and the required knowledge of child behavior and teaching are not enough. The teacher's role as a professional is also very important. The ethics and standards of professional practice are important for teachers of emotionally disturbed children who work with other teachers and other professionals. Teachers of emotionally disturbed children constantly deal with confidential information, daily face ethical issues involving decisions about fairness or behavior in the classroom, and interact with parents who may be dealing with difficult family issues.

The personal and professional complexity of the teacher's role with emotionally disturbed children can be expressed as follows:

> In the course of their development, their demands—for external controls, and psychological structure, for comfort and reassurance and for time and attention—exceed what is normally expected for their age. These demands are made independent of the convenience or emotional resources of the teacher. The healing of the child's relationships and his memories of past failure involves working on present relationships. The teacher is an important person in the child's present environment and, therefore, becomes a part of the disturbed or disturbing relationship which is a primary focus of the treatment and re-education. Teaching emotionally disturbed and behaviorally disordered children is, therefore, personally demanding—sometimes arousing feelings of anger, self-doubt, fear, and resentment, as well as feelings of satisfaction and joy. Teachers use themselves as well as the curriculum in the re-education of emotionally disturbed children. Sometimes this work is defeating, sometimes rewarding and, almost always, personally challenging. (Epanchin & Paul, 1982, p. 241)

SUMMARIES

Since the early 1960s when Morse, Cutler, and Fink (1960) surveyed educational services for emotionally disturbed children, things have changed dramatically. The public education system has assumed responsibilities for these children, and there is a commitment to providing a continuum of services. The social forces in schools that moved emotionally disturbed children into segregated services or out of schools altogether have been countered by a public policy and services that make support available to these children in regular education settings. The therapeutic role of education and the importance of the teacher as a therapeutic agent are now recognized. While the needs of many emotionally disturbed children are unmet, schools are increasingly able to provide for the needs of these children on a more systematic and professional basis than ever before.

1. Observe or think about various educational settings, and detail the nature of the expectations teachers have for students in those settings. Do the same for peer groups. Describe what children are expected to do to fit into various peer groups. Then think about an emotionally disturbed child you know. What types of skills and abilities does the child need to develop to fit into regular education setting?
2. It has been said that emotionally disturbed children are the most difficult population to mainstream. Why do you think this is so?
3. Why is the teacher of emotionally disturbed children likely to communicate with other professionals? What barriers to collaboration have you observed?
4. What should education's role be in working with children's emotional problems? What do you think is therapeutic about education?

REFERENCES

Adler, M. J. (1982). *The Paidcia Proposal: An educational manifesto.* New York: Macmillan.

Algozzine, B., Christenson, S., & Ysseldyke, J. (1982). Probabilities associated with the referral to placement process. *Teacher Education and Special Education, 5,* 19–23.

Bartlett, L. (1989). Disciplining handicapped students: Legal issues in light of *Honig v. Doe. Exceptional Children, 55,* 357–366.

Blackman, H. P. (1989). Special education placement: Is it what you know or where you live? *Exceptional Children, 55,* 459–462.

Blotcky, M. J., Dimperio, T. L., & Gossett, J. T. (1984). Follow-up of children treated in psychiatric hospitals: A review of studies. *The American Journal of Psychiatry, 141,* 1499–1507.

The Carnegie Forum. (1986). A nation prepared: Teachers for the 21st century. New York: Carnegie Corporation.

Carter, J., & Sugai, G. (1989). Survey on prereferral practices: Responses from State Departments of Education. *Exceptional Children, 55,* 298–302.

Casey, R. J., & Berman, J. S. (1985). The outcome of psychotherapy with children. *Psychological Bulletin, 98,* 388–400.

Chalfant, J. C., Pysh, M. V. D., & Moultrie, R. (1979). Teacher assistance teams: A model for within-building problem solving. *Learning Disability Quarterly, 2,* 85–96.

Coie, J. D., & Krehbiel, G. (1984). Effects of academic tutoring on the social status of low-achieving, socially rejected children. *Child Development, 55,* 1465–1478.

Curry, J. (1986). Outcome studies of psychiatric hospitalization and residential treatment of youth: Conceptual and research implications. Paper presented at Symposium on Out-of-Home Placement Division 37, American Psychological Association, 94th Convention, August 26, 1986.

Curtis, M. J., Zins, J. E., & Graden, J. L. (1987). Prereferral intervention programs: Enhancing student performance in regular education settings. In C. A. Maher & J. E. Zins (Eds.)., *Psychoeducational interventions in the schools.* New York: Pergamon Press.

Danielson, L. C., & Bellamy, G. T. (1989). State variation in placement of children with handicaps in segregated environments. *Exceptional Children, 55,* 448–455.

Ekstein, R., & Motto, R. L. (1969). Psychoanalysis and education—An historical account. In R. Ekstein and R. L. Motto (Eds.), *From learning for love to love of learning: Essays on psychoanalysis and education* (pp. 3–27). New York: Brunner/Mazel.

Epanchin, B. C. & Paul, J. L. (1982). *Casebook for educating the emotionally disturbed.* Columbus, OH: Merrill.

Fenichel, C. (1976). Psychoeducational approaches for seriously disturbed children in the classroom. In N. J. Long, W. C. Morse, & R. G. Newman (Eds.), *Conflict in the Classroom* (3rd ed.) (pp. 223–229). Belmont: CA.: Wadsworth Press.

Fisher, C. W., & Berliner, D. C. (1985). *Perspectives on instructional time.* New York: Longman.

Florida Mental Health Institute (1988–89). *Update, 4* (1). Tampa, FL: University of South Florida.

Forness, S. R. (1988). Planning for the needs of children with serious emotional disturbance: The national special education and mental health coalition. *Behavioral Disorders, 13,* 127–133.

Forness, S. R. (1989). *Statement of the National Mental Health and Special Education Coalition to Senate Subcommittee on the Handicapped Act.* Statement presented at Washington, D.C.

Freud, A. (1931). *Introduction to Psychoanalysis for Teachers.* London: Allen and Unwin.

Friend, M. (1984). Consultation skills for resource teachers. *Learning Disability Quarterly, 7,* 246–250.

Friend, M., & McNutt, G. (1984). Resource room programs: Where are we now? *Exceptional Children, 51,* 150–155.

Gage, N. C., & Berliner, D. C. (1988). *Educational Psychology* (4th ed.). Boston: Houghton Mifflin.

Gardner, H. (1985). *The mind's new science: A history of the cognitive revolution.* New York: Basic Books.

Gilligan, C. (1982). *In a different voice: Psychological theory and women's development.* Cambridge, MA: Harvard University Press.

Good, T. L., & Brophy, J. E. (1987). *Looking in classrooms* (4th ed.). New York: Harper & Row.

Graden, J. L. (1989). Redefining "prereferral" intervention as intervention assistance: Collaboration between general and special education. *Exceptional Children, 56,* 227–231.

Grosenick, J. K. (1981). Public school and mental health services to severely behavior disordered students. *Behavioral Disorders, 6,* 183–190.

Grosenick, J. K., George, M. P., & George, N. L. (1987). A profile of school programs for the behaviorally disordered: Twenty years after Morse, Cutler, and Fink. *Behavioral Disorders, 12,* 159–168.

Grosenick, J. K., George, N. L., & George, M. P. (1988). The availability of program descriptions among programs for seriously emotionally disturbed students. *Behavioral Disorders, 13,* 108–115.

Haapala, D. A. (1984). A discrimination of successful treatment outcomes for in-home family therapy: Homebuilders Model. Unpublished paper available from author at Behavioral Sciences Institute, 1717 South 341 Place, Suite B, Federal Way, WA 98003.

Hawkins, R. P., Meadowcroft, P., Trout, B. A., & Luster, W. C. (1985). Foster family-based treatment. *Journal of Clinical Child Psychology, 14,* 220–228.

Hayek, R. A. (1987). The teacher assistance team: A prereferral support system. *Focus on Exceptional Children, 20,* 1–8.

Haynes, M. C., & Jenkins, J. R. (1986). Reading instruction in special education resource rooms. *American Educational Research Journal, 23,* 161–190.

Heufner, D. S. (1988). The consulting teacher model: Risks and opportunities. *Exceptional Children, 54,* 403–414.

Hewett, F. (1968). *The emotionally disturbed child in the classroom: A developmental strategy for educating children with maladaptive behavior.* Boston: Allyn and Bacon.

Hobbs, N. (1966). Helping disturbed children: Psychological and ecological strategies. *American Psychologist, 2,* 1105–1115.

Hobbs, N. (1982). *The troubled and troubling child.* San Francisco: Jossey-Bass.

Hocutt, A. M., & Schulte, S. T. (1987). *A study of noncategorical special education: A literature review.* Research Triangle Institute Report #3727/01-01TP, Research Triangle Park, NC.

Honig v. Doe, 108 S.Ct.592 (1988).

Huntze, S., & Grosenick, J. K. (1980). *National needs analysis in behavior disorders.* Columbia: University of Missouri-Columbia, Department of Special Education.

Idol, L., Paolucci-Whitcomb, P., & Nevin, A. (1986). *Collaborative consultation.* Rockville, MD: Aspen.

Jennings, R. D., Mendelsohn, S. R., May, K., & Brown, G. M. (1988). Elementary students in classes for the emotionally disturbed: Characteristics and classroom behavior. *American Journal of Orthopsychiatry, 58,* 65–76.

Knitzer, J. (1982). *Unclaimed children: The failure of public responsibility to children and adolescents.* Washington, DC: Children's Defense Fund.

Knitzer, J., & Yelton, S. (1989). Interagency collaboration. *Update: Improving Services for Emotionally Disturbed Children, 5*(1), 12–14. Tampa, FL: Florida Mental Health Institute.

Leinhardt, G., & Pallay, A. (1982). Restrictive educational settings: Exile or haven? *Review of Educational Research, 52,* 557–578.

Lewis, W. W. (1988). The role of ecological variables in residential treatment. *Behavioral Disorders, 13,* 98–107.

Lortie, D. C. (1975). *School teacher: A sociological study.* Chicago: University of Chicago Press.

Maher, C. A., & Zins, J. E. (1987). *Psychoeducational interventions in the schools: Methods and procedures for enhancing student competence.* New York: Pergamon Press.

Morse, W. C. (1976). Competing in teaching socio-emotional impaired. *Behavioral Disorders, 1,* 83–88.

Morse, W. C. (1985). *The education and treatment of socio-emotionally impaired children and youth.* Syracuse, NY: Syracuse University Press.

Morse, W. C., Cutler, R. L., & Fink, A. H. (1964). *Public school classes for the emotionally handicapped: A research analysis.* Washington, DC: Council for Exceptional Children.

Morsink, C. V., Thomas, C. C., Smith-Davis, J. (1987). Noncategorical special education programs: Process and outcomes. In M. C. Wang, M. C. Reynolds, & H. J. Walberg (Eds.), *The handbook of special education: Research and practice* (Vol. 2). Oxford, England: Pergamon Press.

Moustakas, C. E. (1966). *The authentic teacher: Sensitivity and awareness in the classroom.* Cambridge, MA: H. H. Doyle Publishing Co.

Noblit, G., & Kendricks, D. (Eds.). (In press). *Contexts of Care.* Available from senior author: School of Education, University of North Carolina at Chapel Hill.

Noddings, N. (1984) *Coring a feminine approach to ethics and moral education.* Berkeley: University of California Press.

Polsgrove, L., & McNeil, M. (1989). The consultation process: Research and practice. *Remedial and Special Education, 10,* 6–13.

Pugach, M. C., & Johnson, L. J. (1989). Prereferral interventions: Progress, problems, and challenges. *Exceptional Children, 56,* 217–226.

Rappaport, J. (1977). *Community psychology: Values, research and action.* New York: Holt, Rinehart & Winston.

Reisberg, L., & Wolf, R. (1986). Developing a consulting program in special education: Implementation and interventions. *Focus on Exceptional Children, 19,* 1–13.

Ritter, D. A. (1978). The effects of a school consultation program upon referral patterns of teachers. *Psychology in the Schools, 15* (2), 239–243.

Sage, D., & Fenson, H. C. (1985). *Study of mixed category special education programs in Pennsylvania.* Final report to the Pennsylvania Department of Education, Bureau of Special Education.

Sampson, E. E. (1988). The debate on individualism: Indigenous psychologies of the individual and their role in personal and societal functioning. *American Psychologist, 43* (1), 15–22.

Sevick, B. M., & Ysseldyke, J. E. (1986). An analysis of teachers' prereferral interventions for students exhibiting behavioral problems. *Behavioral Disorders, 11,* 109–117.

Stroul, B. A., & Friedman, R. M. (1986). *A system of care for severely emotionally disturbed children and youth.* Available from CASSP Technical Assistance Center, Georgetown University Child Development Center, 3800 Reservoir Road, NW, Washington, DC, 20007.

Tindal, G., Shinn, M., Walz, L., & Germann, G. (1987). Mainstream consultation in secondary settings: The Pine County Model. *The Journal of Special Education, 21,* 94–106.

Tolmach, J. (1985). "There ain't nobody on my side": A new day treatment program for black urban youth. *Journal of Clinical Child Psychology, 14,* 214–219.

Trippe, M. (1963). Conceptual problems in research on educational provisions for disturbed children. *Exceptional Children, 29,* 400–406.

Vallecorsa, A. L. (1983). Cross-categorical resource programs: An emerging trend in special education. *Education, 104*(2), 131–136.

West, J. F., & Cannon, G. S. (1988). Essential collaborative consultation competencies for regular and special educators. *Journal of Learning Disabilities, 21,* 56–63.

West, J. F., & Idol, L. (1987). School consultation (Part I): An interdisciplinary perspective on theory, models, and research. *Journal of Learning Disabilities, 20,* 388–408.

Whalen, R. J., Mendez de Sammon, L., & Fortmeyer, D. (1988). The relationship between pupil affect and achievement. In E. L. Meyen, G. A. Vergason, & R. J. Whelan (Eds.), *Effective Instructional Strategies for Exceptional Children* (pp. 307–318). Denver: Love Publishing.

Wiederholt, J. L., Hammill, D. D., & Brown, V. (1983). *The resource teacher: A guide to effective practices* (2nd ed.). Austin, TX: Pro-Ed.

Wittels, F. (1969). Die befreiung des kindes [The liberation of the child]. In R. Ekstein & R. L. Motto (Eds.), *From learning for love to love of learning: Essays on psychoanalysis and education* (pp. 3–27). NY: Brunner/Mazel. (Original work published 1926).

3
Emotionally Disturbed Children and the Family*

MAIN POINTS

1. A family systems perspective offers the teacher an overall framework for identifying the processes whereby the family influences the child, the child influences the family, and both are affected by their broader environment.

2. Family systems theory does not compete with various theoretical models used to explain child emotional disturbance; rather, it allows a convergence or integration of several views.

3. An understanding of Sameroff and Chandler's (1975) transactional model is critical for understanding the relationships among the emotionally disturbed child, the family, and the school.

4. Family systems theory implies that a teacher cannot intervene with a child without intervening with the family, that the results of what the teacher does with the child have an effect on the family, and that the effects of what the teacher does with the child are mediated by the family.

5. The properties of a system, such as those described by Laslzo (1973), are useful for identifying the complex processes active among the emotionally disturbed child, family, and school.

6. Several concepts borrowed from family systems theory and family therapy are especially relevant to the education setting: bidirectionality, transactions, boundaries, subsystems, and triangulation.

7. Myths about parents can result in barriers to parent involvement with the school; a systems perspective can be helpful in more appropriately understanding parent behavior and identifying parent needs.

---

* This chapter was contributed by Karen J. O'Donnell, Duke University Medical Center, and Thomas A. Fiore, Research Triangle Institute.

Those Winter Sundays

Sundays too my father got up early
and put his clothes on in the blueblack cold
then with cracked hands that ached
from labor in the weekday weather made
banked fires blaze. No one ever thanked him.

I'd wake and hear the cold splintering, breaking.
When the rooms were warm, he'd call,
and slowly I would rise and dress,
fearing the chronic angers of that house,

Speaking indifferently to him,
who had driven out the cold
and polished my good shoes as well.
What did I know, what did I know
of love's austere and lonely offices?

(Hayden, 1975)

The love as well as the chronic angers of families form the context from which children negotiate relationships with all others. One of the most important aspects of teaching emotionally disturbed or behaviorally disordered children is to understand and maintain a relationship with the child's family. Just as the relationship between a child and his family affects the child's well-being outside the family, the nature of the relationship between teacher and family can determine the effectiveness of the educational experience. Unfortunately, teachers often receive little formal training in understanding and working with families.

The most obvious question a teacher encounters when preparing to work with a troubled child and his family is whether the family situation caused the child's problems. Myriad theories of developmental psychopathology suggest, directly or indirectly, that parents cause their child's emotional difficulties. Alternative perspectives indicate that the problem resides within the child's biological makeup. Recent theoretical models argue that child development is much more complex than either view; a child's emotional or behavioral problems may be affected by family functioning, but also the family is affected by the child. These more complex theories of child and family functioning present new challenges for teachers; they instruct about the inevitability of the teacher's involvement with families, and they identify processes active among children, families, and teachers.

In this chapter, we offer teachers a theoretical perspective for viewing child and family relationships that derives from family systems theory. This family systems view does not compete with the theories of child psychopathology presented in Part 2 of this text. In fact, it is congruent with the ecological theory described in Chapter 9. The family systems perspective offers the teacher an overall framework with which to identify the processes whereby the family influences the child, the child influences the family, and both are affected by their broader community or cultural context. However involved or uninvolved a family may be in the child's educational setting, the teacher is involved with the family and with the child's relationship to the family. Teacher and educational interventions are influenced by the family's functioning.

This chapter outlines child developmental processes as seen from a general systems perspective. Developmental psychology, predominately normal or average development, are discussed. In fact, much of the chapter describes normal developmental processes and applies them to understanding child and family issues in child emotional disturbance. The chapter also explores implications for abnormal child development from a family systems framework. Implications from systems theory for working with a child and family in a school setting are also discussed.

THE RELATIONSHIP BETWEEN THE CHILD AND THE FAMILY

The family systems perspective represents a way of thinking that does not compete with but rather allows a convergence of several theoretical views. For example, both the psychoanalytic and ecological views can be integrated into an overall theoretical framework with systems theory. The approach to child, family, and school is seen as an integrative one; it is both more simple and more abstract than other models; it can be used as a metatheory for those perspectives that follow.

ABOUT THEORIES

Various models for understanding the child and family relationship have emerged from practice and research in child development and developmental psychopathology. The teacher of emotionally disturbed and behavior disordered children is faced with the difficult task of translating theories and research findings into practice in the classroom and into encounters with the child's family. The literature is vast. Shifts from one acceptable theoretical perspective to another are relatively frequent and can be confusing for the practitioner. Theoretical models cannot be ignored, however; teachers need a model or a framework with which to understand child and/or parent behavior, to problem solve about interventions, and to test the effectiveness of interventions.

Teachers who try to respond to developments in the field frequently find themselves in a bind. They want to integrate existing models and research into their teaching, but the usefulness of various and competing constructs or strategies may not be obvious or direct. Jens and O'Donnell (1982) proposed an "as if" approach to models and theories to be helpful in this bind. That is, the family systems approach, like the ecological perspective (see Chapter 9) or the cognitive view of child behavior (see Chapter 7), as well as other models, should be approached by the practitioner "as if" it is true.

The "as if" approach suggests that the model represents currently accepted principles of child development, not universal laws. Use of a view "as if it is true" gives the practitioner a framework from which to work with a child and his family; then, educational interventions are not random but are driven by specific assumptions. While the structure and order of a theory is needed, the "as if" approach provides the freedom, flexibility, and humility to know that the theory merely represents a currently acceptable understanding and that more than one point of view often is needed to solve a practical question about an emotionally disturbed child.

THE CHILD-FAMILY RELATIONSHIP IN THE STUDY OF CHILD DEVELOPMENT

The relative contributions of nature and nurture, constitution and environment, and inheritance and experience for the child's development have been a matter of controversy for centuries. Our awareness of the complexity of the relationship between the child and his context in determining intellectual and emotional development has increased significantly, particularly over the last 20 years.

The first turf on which the modern nature versus nurture battle developed was in the area of intelligence (Gould, 1981); that is, the study of genetic and environmental variation and intellectual outcome. Was a person's intelligence inherited from the parent or from the race? Were differences between people in intelligence determined by variation among environments? When examining systematically the effects of different environments on intellectual development, scientists focused initially on parents' educational and socioeconomic levels. Eventually, studies of the effects of different care-giving environments (e.g., institutions and homes) led to the conclusion that differences in environmental stimulation accounted for some differences in intellectual development. In fact, this notion is consistent with our American folk philosophy: the assumption that man is what his environment makes him (Sears, 1975).

Freud (1949) and others introduced similar theoretical frameworks for understanding a child's emotional development. Freud emphasized both instinct and experience; his postulation of a psychobiological interaction and his assumption that there were forces, outside the purely physical, active in behavior and development contributed to a growing interest in identifying forces active in development and, therefore, methods for intervening in developmental processes.

Freud's observations were underlined by the severe intellectual and emotional delays documented in children who did not receive sufficient, individual, and consistent care in institutions (Spitz, 1945). Generally, these theories and findings contributed to the social, political, and scientific environment of the first half of the twentieth century, which focused on the effects of parents and families on child development. This period was characterized by more books on child rearing (Spock, 1946), arguments about specific child-rearing practices and their positive and negative effects (e.g., methods of toilet training), and a growing scientific literature on the effects parents have on their child's develpment.

Subsequently, efforts in the 1960s included programs, such as Head Start, that were designed to intervene in children's environments to improve their developmental, particularly intellectual, outcomes. Arguments for constitutional causes of less optimal development continued as well (Jensen, 1969). The views of heritability versus environmental deprivation as explaining developmental outcome can be seen as competing views that continued the nature versus nurture argument well into the second half of this century.

Research in child development in the late 1960s and 1970s still did not provide a simple answer to the nature-nurture argument. In fact, developmental processes came to be seen as not so straightforward or one-dimensional as nature versus nurture. Contemporary models indicate that the developmental context significantly influences the range of developmental possibilities for a particular child. Furthermore, aspects of the child's development and behavior are seen as affecting care givers. Dimensions of the broader cultural, community, and family context affect both child and family. Systems theory provides an overall framework for describing the nature of these complex and reciprocal influences.

One of the first theoretical discussions of reciprocal influences in the child-family relationship examinined the direction-of-effects issue in child development research (Bell, 1968). Bell reviewed several studies in animal and human research on mothers and their offspring. He suggested that the assumptive model of research to date—that the effect was parent to child—was too limited to accommodate the actual findings. He asked if aspects of child functioning are associated statistically with variation in parent functioning. Might the child be influencing the parent as well as the parent influencing the child? If, for example, juvenile delinquency is found to be associated with poor parenting skills, does poor parenting cause delinquency or could it be that out-of-control children cause parents to give up on behavior management? In other words, a significant statistical association proves neither explanation. Bidirectional effects are not only possible but likely.

The challenge to unidirectional causal models for child development was supported by the popular work on infant temperament in the New York Longitudinal Study (see also Chapter 9 for a discussion of child temperament) (Thomas, Chess, Birch, & Hertzig, 1960; Thomas, Chess, Birch, Hertzig, & Korn, 1963). In this extensive study of temperament, parents' descriptions of their children's characteristic behavior (e.g., predominant mood, persistence, adaptability) were collected every three months for the first 18 months, every 6 months until 5 years of age and yearly thereafter. Ratings of a child's behavior based on the interview data led to the creation of nine categories of infant and child temperament and of three broader categories: easy, difficult, and slow to warm up (Carey & McDevitt, 1978). There is significant controversy about the concept of and research in temperament; for example, in several studies the stability of child descriptions on these dimensions did not hold true for children over 2 years of age. Nonetheless, the proposition of constitutional differences from birth contributed to the growing awareness that children bring their own characteristics into care-giving relationships.

In Sameroff and Chandler's (1975) review of the literature on perinatal biological risk factors as they relate to developmental outcome, the mechanisms of the mutual influences of child and family were described. Prior to this review, models for viewing the outcome of asphyxiated, low-birth weight, or otherwise medically compromised newborns included the "continuum of reproductive wastage" (Lilienfeld & Parkhurst, 1951) and the "continuum of reproductive casualty" (Pasamanick & Knobloch, 1966). Both models indicated that a range of biological conditions was associated with a range of subsequent developmental outcomes. For example, a major medical insult during birth might result in cerebral palsy or mental retardation; and a less devastating insult might cause a learning disability. In other words, biological conditions or events were responsible for development that deviated from normal.

In fact, Sameroff and Chandler (1975) were not able to identify these simple developmental links. They found, instead, that socioeconomic and familial factors overshadowed biological ones in predicting developmental outcome. They concluded that the care-giving environment could minimize or maximize a child's developmental potential. They postulated that the range of outcomes found in high-risk infants could be attributed to better or worse care-giving environments; they identified the term **continuum of care-giving casualty** as an explanatory model. The shift in models from the purely biological to include environmental influences is analogous to thinking about a constitutional predisposition for or the inheritance of mental illness. Again, the general conclusion is that biology alone is too simple an explanation.

THE TRANSACTIONAL MODEL

Sameroff and Chandler (1975) identified three models that have been used to describe the process of child development. The first, a **single-factor model,** assumes that a single factor, whether environmental or constitutional, is sufficient to predict the status or condition of a child at a later date. Examples from the literature on child emotional disturbance include the "refrigerator mother" hypothesis used previously to explain childhood autism (Bettelheim, 1950) and the "double bind" hypothesis (Weakland, 1974) of schizophrenia; these represent single factors from the environment. Similarly, the notion that adults who were abused as children will abuse their own children because of an inherited factor also is a single factor model. In their review, Sameroff and Chandler (1975) indicated that there simply is no research evidence in support of a single factor model.

The second theoretical model is referred to as an **interactional model.** This model suggests that constitutional risk factors are combined with environmental ones in an additive manner. That is, the effects of biological risk can be reduced or augmented by better or worse environments. This is a static model in which neither the constitution nor the environment is seen as changing.

The interactional model provides an explanation for development that is still too simple. The notions that effects between child and family are bidirectional and that children bring their own behavioral characteristics into care-giving relationships suggest that neither children nor caregivers are constant over time. A child with a difficult temperament may affect his parents' feelings of frustration and helplessness so much that they, in fact, do provide less optimal nurturance as time goes on. Their withdrawal from the child could promote less behavioral organization and more irritability in this already difficult infant.

These types of mutual influences led Sameroff and Chandler (1975) to formulate a third, or transactional, model. An understanding of the **transactional model** is critical for thinking about the emotionally disturbed child and his family and about the educator's influences on family functioning. The transactional model stresses the importance of both child and family characteristics in predicting child status at any point in time. The major theme in this model is that development involves an ongoing relationship between the child and the context in which he develops.

Sameroff and Chandler (1975) concluded that a single factor or an interactional model does not provide a sufficient explanation for the ontogeny of a developmental disorder. Often, even the child with a genetic abnormality has a range of possible developmental outcomes. Neither the child nor his family is constant over time; at each moment, month, or year children and caregivers change as a function of their mutual influences.

In a later paper, Sameroff (1982) extended his explanation of the transactional model by clarifying aspects of the environment that exert important influences. In the 1975 paper, Sameroff and Chandler addressed transactions between the child and the immediate context or, specifically, the caregivers. In the 1982 paper, Sameroff specified three components of the transacting relationship: the child's status, the functioning of parents and the immediate family, and aspects of the broader cultural and social context. The last, the broader context (or ecosystem as described by Bronfenbrenner, 1977; see Chapter 9), includes the family's social and economic group, cultural norms, and other sources of stress and support in the life of the child and his family. The transactional model indicates that a child's development is related to the ongoing and reciprocal relationship between the child and family and between the family and the broader context.

For educators working with emotionally disturbed and behavior disordered children, the transactional model indicates that the relationship between child and family is regulated by complex and dynamic processes. The notion that the child develops in immediate and broader (cultural) environments is consistent with an ecological perspective (Hobbs, 1966; see Chapter 9). Behaviorists also believe that child and family influences are reciprocal (Bandura, 1978; see Chapter 6). General systems theory adds conceptually to these models in suggesting that child and family not only function by transactional processes; they function also as a system or a whole.

GENERAL SYSTEMS THEORY AND CHILD DEVELOPMENT

Theories about child and family relationships have moved to still another level of complexity with the application of general systems theory. Systems theory changes the unit of focus or study from the individual child or parent to the system itself (Power & Bartholomew, 1987). It is suggested that educational interventions that address the child and family as a system with understanding and planning for relationships among child, family, and school are the most effective ones.

General systems theory is not a true theory as traditionally defined by the ability to explain and predict. In that way, its application to families is different from behavioral or psychoanalytic theories or their explanations for child emotional disturbance. Rather, general systems theory is a paradigm in which the components of a system (in this discussion, child and family) are seen as interacting in an organismic, or whole, manner. General systems theorists take the interactionists' position that parts of a system cannot be understood in isolation from other parts. From that perspective, systems theorists describe the organization and properties of systems, whatever their specific domain or content may be.

The idea of a general systems theory often is attributed to von Bertalanffy (1968) who attempted to frame biological processes as an organized system. He insisted that to understand any science, one must understand not only the elements of the science but their interrelationships. To that end, he studied interdisciplinary isomorphisms or correspondences; in other words, he suggested that all areas of study have components that form a system and that the relationships among components and the system as a whole follow the same rules. An atom and a family each have component parts that form a system; rules for action and interaction are the same for parts of an atom or members of a family. General systems theorists describe such actions and interactions in terms of relationships, transactions, and teleology. Similarly, Boulding (1980) and Miller (1978) described general systems theory as a general field theory that provides theoretical constructs about components of concern, regardless of the content of the system.

How is general systems theory relevant to the teacher of the emotionally disturbed child? The perspective suggests that a family with an emotionally disturbed child interacts according to certain rules or processes. The family system is seen as and planned for as a whole. In addition, the family systems perspective implies that a teacher cannot intervene with a child without intervening with the family, that the results of what the teacher does with the child will have an effect on the family, and that the effects of what the teacher does with the child are mediated by the family. An understanding of these processes enables the teacher to be aware of the nature of the school's involvement with children and their families.

Several general systems theorists have identified specific properties of systems (see Laszlo, 1972). When these properties are applied to the developing child who is emotionally disturbed or behaviorally disordered, they describe the complex processes active between child and family. Laszlo described five properties of systems, and Sameroff (1984) applied them to child development. These properties are outlined briefly in the following sections because they are useful in understanding and intervening with families with emotionally disturbed children.

Wholeness and Order

Laszlo's first property of a system is wholeness and order. The system as a whole is greater that the sum of its parts because the whole adds the property of relationships between parts to the parts. For example, when a man kicks a dog, the reaction of the dog depends not only on the laws of physical science but also on the relationship between the man and the dog (Hoffman 1981). The dog can respond in several ways, depending on the history of that relationship as well as what the kick may mean to the dog. The kick is news about the relationship to the dog and may affect the dog's subsequent behavior toward the man; the dog's response is news to the man and may affect subsequent behavior toward the dog.

For teachers of emotionally disturbed children, the wholeness and order property indicates that any intervention with the child invariably affects the family. If a teacher teaches a child to express feelings instead of act them out, the parent's view of the child may be affected and they may become responsive to the child's expressed emotional needs. This educational intervention also may threaten a family system that focuses on the child's bad behavior instead of confronting dysfunction in the family. The child who is willing to say what he feels can become a threat to family stability. Even the teacher who never actually sees the child's parents is intervening in the family system.

The effects of educational and behavioral strategies with the child also are mediated by the family. In the previous example, the family may intentionally or unintentionally thwart the child's attempts to state his feelings—by interrupting, ignoring, or belittling. The child quickly learns that these efforts do not pay off; in fact, he may feel punished for expressing his feelings. The family may not actually be trying to keep the child dysfunctional. For example, if the child's acting out plays some familiar and needed role for the family as a whole, there may be attempts to maintain such behavior.

Educational strategies that help a very impulsive child pause and problem-solve before acting out may positively affect the child's overall organization at home. When the behavior is reinforced at home, it is strengthened. Needless to say, the child's improved organization and problem-solving skills may give the family an opportunity to appreciate some of the child's strengths. Various aspects of the family's functioning will influence its ability and willingness to support and follow through on intervention strategies provided by the teacher. The family's response to the change in the child will influence the extent and stability of change. Again, the teacher cannot choose to be uninvolved with the family system.

Adaptive Self-Stabilization

Laszlo's second property of a system's functioning is self-stabilization. If the system's environment presents change or threat, a system has the need and capacity to buffer the threat, maintain the status quo, and protect its identity. The system avoids input from the outside by coordinated efforts; stress on the system is reduced.

Families of emotionally disturbed children are capable of reducing their stress by using self-stabilizing strategies. These strategies are necessary to maintain the family's identity and to carry out day-to-day activities. An example of adaptive self-stabilization is defense mechanisms that parents sometimes use concerning their child's illness or behavior (O'Donnell, 1985). Every teacher has met parents who do not seem to realize that their child's behavior is not normal or adaptive. Every teacher has talked to parents who did not seem to hear what was being said to them. Many parents become instant experts on their child's condition and needs from a purely intellectual perspective.

The important and helpful notion in adaptive self-stabilization is that the parent's behavior may be necessary for the stability of the family system. Defenses, especially denial or intellectualization, can present one of the most difficult problems for the educator in attempts to support and communicate with parents. Defenses can deprive the teacher and the parent of a common basis from which to discuss the child. On the other hand, a parent may be defensive in order to manage the intense stress that reality brings with it. A temporary adjustment of reality may not be pathological for the parent. However, educators must understand and work with such adjustments.

The parents of an emotionally disturbed child are faced with guilt, blame, frustration, feelings of helplessness. Often they have no real explanation for the child's condition. Defenses can be self-buffering and prevent the emergence of tremendous stress. Defenses work because they sacrifice reality, in one way or another, until the threat is reduced or the parent is better able to cope with it. Parents who do not seem to hear information about the child's condition or who do not seem to grasp the gravity of the situation may be trying to maintain enough control and stability to go to work, to care for other children, or to get themselves to the school for a meeting.

Defenses, of course, can be maladaptive, particularly when they become a way of life, independent of an initial real threat. Defense mechanisms can interfere with the care and cooperation needed for the child's special needs. It is important to remember that defenses often are adaptive, allowing the family to do the best it can in an intensely threatening situation.

Adaptive Self-Organization

When faced with new forces or threats in the environment, such as information that a child is emotionally disturbed, and when self-stabilization strategies are not sufficient to maintain the system, a system can reorganize itself to meet new demands. A classic example used by general systems theorists is that of cold-blooded animals becoming warm-blooded animals. The animals could no longer survive in an environment of changing temperatures without the internal thermostat of the warm-blooded organism.

Families with emotionally disturbed children often are faced with reorganizing the sytem when the existing one is not adequate to meet the child's needs. A parent may become reeducated by learning about the child's psychological, medical, and educational condition and needs. Families readjust their position in and their use of community service delivery systems, calling upon support systems that they previously may not have known existed. They sometimes even reorganize the service delivery system to better meet the needs of their child. Parents often have to redefine their relationship to the child and their understanding of the meaning of the child's behavior. Adaptive self-organization is at the heart of family assessment and planning for helping the emotionally disturbed child within the family context by helping the family's reorganization.

Teachers should know that reorganization for any system is done with great difficulty and only after attempts at self-stabilization have failed. Families benefit greatly from support for system changes, but a teacher cannot just make it happen.

Systemic Hierarchies

The fourth property of a system argues that any system develops in the direction of increasing structure and complexity. As a system accommodates the needs of the whole, struggles to maintain identity and stability, and reorganizes as necessary to external demands, it increases the complexity of and fragility in its functioning. That is, the system's functioning becomes more specialized and requires greater coordination among components. Remember the cold-blooded animal? In many ways, life was simpler at this level. Warm-blooded animals survived, but the price for change was more structure and complexity, more working parts, and an increased need for the coordination of parts to make the whole system work.

Development and change for a family system of an emotionally disturbed child are complex. In some ways, the family's stability becomes fragile. The property of systemic hierarchies is apparent to the teacher when a family seems to adapt, reorganize, and achieve a new stability in meeting the needs of the system and of the emotionally disturbed family member. When an additional threat is posed, such as the onset of puberty, change of schools, or a birthday, the family's adjustment deteriorates. The parent may begin again to deny the child's condition or its severity; the parent may return to intellectualizing about the child's needs.

It is very helpful for the educator to view these events in terms of the hierarchy of development or change for the system. A family may be well organized around the child's special needs, but its stability may become more vulnerable. As noted, a threat can precipitate a return to a lower level of functioning. It is extremely helpful for the teacher to understand what has happened and not to give up on the family out of frustration.

The property of systemic hierarchies has implications for the ideals of **family adjustment, acceptance,** or **coping.** Often, these constructs are presented to teachers and other interventionists as goals of support services. In other words, the family must complete certain tasks to function with and support the child. From the family systems perspective, these are foolish and misleading objectives. Because family development is hierarchic, new adaptation is challenged and can fail periodically. Usually the system's return to a lower level of functioning is only temporary; the family resumes its previous level of adaptation more readily than before. These ideas underline the importance of teacher expectations about family functioning. The last thing a stressed family needs to deal with is a teacher's unrealistic expectations and disappointment.

Dialectic Movement

Any part or component of a system, through its functioning, changes the sytem, creating a new context, which requires further changes in the part or component, and so on. A dialectic refers to a constant mutual change among parts and the whole. The emotionally disturbed child affects his parents, siblings, and the family as a whole. The child alters the system, and the changed system affects the child's behavior and development. Implications of the dialectic are very similar to Piaget's (1952) descriptions of accommodation and assimilation in the development of cognitive structures (see Chapter 7).

Successful intervention with the parents likely will affect the child and, subsequently, the family as a whole. Changing a child's behavior, such as temper tantrums, will affect the parents' behavior toward the child, which may support more optimal child behavior in other areas. In other words, an educational/behavioral intervention that affects the child will affect the family, which then provides a changed context for the child.

CHILD PSYCHOPATHOLOGY AND THE FAMILY SYSTEM

In the preceding pages, we used models from normal child development to identify the important components of and processes active in the child and family relationship. A general systems perspective was adopted and applied to the child developing within a family system. It was suggested that an educator can use this family systems framework for understanding the relationship between the emotionally disturbed child and his family, and for developing educational plans for the child from that perspective.

The theoretical assumptions of a family systems approach offer the educator much in terms of comprehending child and family behavior. Family therapy as a specific treatment modality developed from earlier work in general systems theory (Hoffman, 1981). Several major assumptions about child psychopathology and the family derive from systems theory, family therapy, and related approaches and can be useful in an educational setting.

Bidirectionality and Transactions

Teachers very often find themselves allied with the children in their classrooms as they observe the apparent effects that a dysfunctional family can have on a child. In their interactions with emotionally disturbed children, teachers also gain some empathy with the parents who care for these sometimes difficult children. Whether a dysfunctional family or a dysfunctional child comes first may not be relevant to the classroom setting. We assert, however, that a professional's belief system about the child and family will influence interactions and the provision of services.

The concepts of bidirectionality and transactions give the teacher a way to view complex child and family interactions without judgment or blame. In addition, the educator is given a model with which to assist in positive adaptation for child and family. Helping a parent find respite care may have more positive effects on the family system and, subsequently, on the child than many other more child-oriented interventions. Teaching a child alternatives to temper tantrums might affect not only the child but overall family stability; the family may then be able to provide more appropriately for the child's other needs.

RELEVANCE OF THE FAMILY TO THE CLASSROOM

The family systems approach to serving emotionally disturbed children—particularly the property of wholeness and order—assumes that the child's behavior has meaning for the family and fits into the system in some way. For example, when a family therapist conducts an interview, he may find that an individual's behavior may seem quite bizarre. However, when the same person is observed in the family group, it sometimes becomes apparent that the behavior no longer looks so bizarre; rather, it somehow fits. Though certainly controversial, some family therapists even suggest that a thought disorder can be understood in terms of family communications, particularly in terms of the "double bind" or mixed messages in parents' communications (Weakland, 1974).

Aspects of social learning theory parallel these comments on the relevance of the family to the child's interactions outside the family. Patterson (1974, 1980) developed a behavioral model that also emphasizes the interactive nature of maladaptive child behavior. He began by referencing Bell's (1971) notion of bidirectional causality and the role of the infant in shaping his parents' behavior. Crying is the first aversive stimulus a child uses to control his environment. Crying is a negative reinforcer since it ends when the parents responds. In this way, the child trains the parent in proper care-giving skills. As the child ages, he adds to his repertoire of coercive behaviors. Patterson identified 14 "noxious" behaviors that the average 3-year-old child has learned.

The existence of these noxious behaviors does not indicate deviance, according to Patterson. What marks deviant patterns is a higher rate of occurrence of coercive or aversive behaviors and the lack of a decline in their use as the child ages. Patterson recognized that some children seem to have an innate propensity for higher levels of coercive behavior. The model is interactive in that a significant factor in the child's coercive behavior is the response he receives from parents and siblings. An erroneous application of reinforcement (both rewards and punishment) supports the continuation and even escalation of coercive behaviors. Of course, the child transfers this maladaptive pattern of behavior to relationships outside the family, including those with teachers and classmates. The teacher should view coercive behaviors in the classroom from the context of long-standing, initially adaptive, family patterns gone awry. Figure 3.1 is Patterson's (1974) representation of child-family interaction and the problem child.

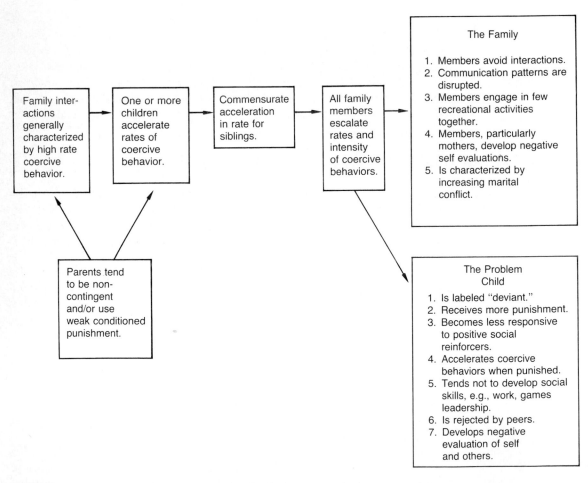

FIGURE 3.1
Child-Family Interactions (From "The Aggressive Child: Victim and Architect of a Coercive System" by G. R. Patterson. In *Behavior Modification and Families* (p. 287) by E. J. Marsh, L. A. Hamerlynch, and L. C. Handy (eds.), 1974, New York: Brunner/ Mazel.)

It is important for a teacher to consider the possible relevance of an emotionally disturbed child's behavior in the family or, indeed, in the classroom itself. Armed with the assumption that all behavior has meaning, the teacher may try to understand how a seemingly negative behavior works for the child, the family, and/or other children. Then the teacher can employ strategies for decreasing the behavior with a more sophisticated understanding of potential outcome.

Boundaries, Subsystems, and Triangulation

Another central concept in a family systems view is boundaries around the family and around subgroups in the family. If you believe that the child's behavior has meaning for the family system, it becomes difficult to think of teaching the child in isolation from the family. Minuchin's scheme (1974) is particularly helpful in assessing family boundaries.

He described a continuum of family boundaries that ranged from rigid to diffuse. Well-functioning families have clear boundaries and are represented by the middle of the continuum. Families with diffuse boundaries are enmeshed and have an increased sense of togetherness, which may require a loss of autonomy for individuals. In fact, growth and differentiation from the family is discouraged and, when possible, hindered. In contrast, families with rigid boundaries are disengaged and individuals may function independently. In these families, individuals may lack the capacity for interdependence and for requesting support when needed. Importantly, isolation characterizes families at either end of Minuchin's continuum (see Figure 3.2). School interventions, especially those that put families together with other families, can erode some of the isolation.

Some families readily join with a teacher and actively participate in the child's education. Other families resist involvement. Consistent with the notion of adaptive self-stabilization, an enmeshed family can protect itself by closing ranks against outsiders. Such a family may view a teacher trying to have a parent-teacher conference as an outsider and a threat. Wynne (1963) used the term **rubber fence** to describe what happens to an outsider who attempts to penetrate the defended family boundary—he bounces off. On the other hand, the disengaged family may need help and involvement but be unskilled or unfamiliar with obtaining information or support.

DISENGAGED	CLEAR BOUNDARIES	ENMESHED
(rigid boundaries)	(normal range)	(diffuse boundaries)

FIGURE 3.2
Minuchin's Continuum of Family Boundaries (Reprinted by permission of the publishers from *Families and Family Therapy*, p. 54, by Salvador Minuchin, Cambridge, Mass.: Harvard University Press, Copyright © 1974 by the President and Fellows of Harvard College)

Planning for an enmeshed family may entail very different strategies than those used for a disengaged family. If an enmeshed family seems reluctant to respond to the teacher's requests for communication, the teacher should determine the most powerful person in the system and elicit his help. This family needs to know that the teacher is going to challenge its beliefs or insist on change.

Minuchin (1974) also identifies the existence and importance of subsystems within the family. Around these subsystems are relatively diffuse, clear, or rigid boundaries. Subsystems are composed of various family members. The parents form a subgroup, the children form another, and the grandparents form still another. Subgroups overlap and interconnect. For example, a girl is part of the sibling subgroup; she is also part of the female subgroup in conjunction with her mother, grandmother, and any female siblings. Subgroups also can be based on particular relationships; a boy and his mother may form a subgroup with the father excluded, or a father and his own mother may form a significant subgroup in relation to the father's wife and children.

Identifying significant subgroups in a child's family may be very instructive for the teacher. The child may not be completing his homework because, in his family, the parenting subsystem consists of the father who works in the evenings. The son and his mother psychologically form the ''child'' subsystem and watch television instead of doing homework. Intervention with this dysfunctional subsystem arrangement may require family counseling, but the teacher's understanding of the situation likely will affect her interactions with the child and the parents.

Also related to boundaries is the concepts of triangulation. Many family systems theorists and clinicians underline the triangular patterns of interaction within a system (Haley, 1976, 1981). The idea here is that two stressed people may try to relieve the stress by pulling in another person. For example, a triangle can occur over homework. A conflict between the teacher and student over homework can be acted out by the student bringing his parent into the conflict. If the child presents his homework as overwhelming and unreasonable, the parent often will enter the conflict and support the child in not doing homework. The teacher and parent are now in conflict, and the child is off the hook for the time being. Stress between child and teacher is reduced temporarily.

APPLICATIONS FOR TEACHERS

A family systems perspective dictates that educators see the family as an inseparable part of the child's educational program. In addition, the teacher needs to recognize the system-wide impact of working with the child, even in entirely child-oriented interventions. Making the rather abstract ideas in family systems theory seem live in educational planning requires some thoughtfulness and honesty from a teacher. She must confront myths about parents, deal with barriers to working with them, and develop strategies that meet the child's and family's individual needs. Each of these needs is elaborated below.

School Myths

Parents are to blame for their child's problems. Our contemporary models for understanding child and family interactions indicate that blaming parents is a single-factor model with little research evidence to support it. Many resilient children grow up well in adverse environments; other children develop abnormally in apparently supportive and nurturing environments. The teacher's view that the parent affects the child and that the child also affects the parent better facilitates good relationships with families.

Parents are not at all responsible for their children's problems. This notion, which assumes the entire problem is within the child, may imply that change is not possible. The parent who turns over complete responsibility for the child's problems also may turn over complete responsibility for the child's education and care. It is important that the parent be helped to feel effective with the child, not guilty about the child.

Fathers do not want to be involved. Many fathers are waiting for the opportunity to be involved. While many families adhere to traditional values that place child care and school-related issues with the mother, fathers often feel that they do not have a role rather than feel that they do not want one.

From a systems perspective, consider what it might mean for the parenting subsystem to have all communications about the child be with one parent. At least two negative effects could occur. First, the informed parent becomes the messenger, the bearer of bad news at times, and consequently the potential recipient of the other parent's unhappiness and frustration. Second, the situation gives the informed parent unequal power, perhaps by association with the authority. The other parent may feel jealous, unimportant, and resentful. Only seeing parents together is a good policy for teachers to have, although every teacher will have to break it.

If parents do not come to conferences, it is because they do not care. Parents fail to come to conferences for a variety of reasons. Some are as simple as logistics: no babysitter, no transportation, no time off from work. Other reasons are more subtle and warrant consideration before the teacher concludes that the parent does not care about the child or about his education.

Barriers

Even if the teacher has a goal of parent involvement, there will be parents who do not comply. There may be many reasons for a parent's reluctance to work with educators. Several are listed below:

- A parent may have a personal history of school problems. Working with teachers may bring back fears and unpleasant memories of his own experiences.
- A parent may feel inferior to school personnel in terms of educational level or socioeconomic status. It is important to remember that, from the parent's perspective, the teacher has the power.

- A parent may blame himself for the child's problems or he may fear that school personnel will blame him.
- A parent may be relieved to have someone else take responsibility for her problem child and may wish to avoid continued repsonsibility herself. She may feel she needs or deserves a break.
- A parent might have a long history of failure in dealing with this child, in working with professionals, or both.
- Parents may disagree with one another regarding the causes and treatments for their child's problems.
- A parent may not share the teacher's opinion that the child requires special services.
- A parent may wish to hide other family problems (such as abuse or alcoholism) and be reluctant to involve outsiders.
- A parent may be overwhelmed with his own problems.

Similarly, it should be recognized that educators may resist working with families for reasons of their own:

- Most teachers and administrators are not trained to work with families and may feel inadequate about their interviewing skills and their ability to conduct meetings and conferences.
- Parents have strong feelings about their children. Many educators would prefer to avoid dealing with the intense anger, sadness, and anxiety that parents can bring to meetings.
- Teachers and parents sometimes see one another as adversaries. Teachers may be afraid that the parent will demand more than the teacher is prepared to provide.
- Teachers are overworked; often, parent meetings require staying after school.
- A teacher may feel partly responsible for the child's problems at school.
- A teacher may be intimidated or discouraged by a family's reputation for being difficult.

Strategies

Regardless of myths and barriers, the most important family intervention a teacher can make is to involve the family in the education of the emotionally handicapped child. This can take many forms. The most obvious plan for involvement is to follow the guidelines of the federal laws for educational services for handicapped children (P.L. 94-142 and P.L. 99-457), and to provide ample opportunity for parents to help develop plans for their child. Further involvement, at school or at home, can include opportunities for parents to participate in academic or social-emotional interventions.

Perhaps the most powerful parent intervention that is within the scope of the school is to bring parents together with other parents. This can take many forms, including parenting skills groups, parent support groups, parent advocacy groups, family social gatherings, or parent auxiliary acitivities. The primary agenda, again, is to reduce isolation and to provide support for the primary caregivers of the emotionally disturbed student. The family systems view indicates that this may be one of the most important interventions for the child's well-being.

Research in special education and mental health indicates that many successful interventions with parents create a collaboration between parents and professionals. Various models include parent training (O'Connell, 1975; Sandler, Coren, & Thurman, 1983; Trautman & Trail, 1983; Zelitch, 1980), partnerships between parents and professionals (Fox, 1985; Honig, 1978; Jones, 1973), and self-help groups (Cain, 1976; Hatfield, 1981).

All of these collaborative efforts are within the domain of special education. They differ significantly from psychotherapy as traditionally offered by the mental health system in that they are largely educational with teaching components or self-discovery activities more similar to educational processes than to insight-oriented psychotherapy.

SUMMARIES

The family systems theory offers educators an overall theoretical model for understanding the family's mutual influences and interactions with educational programs and strategies for emotionally disturbed children. The view is seen as not competing but integrative of other explanatory models for child emotional disturbance. Furthermore, an understanding of the family as a system has implications for the direct involvement of the teacher with the child's parents.

DISCUSSION QUESTIONS

1. The authors describe the family systems perspective as an integrative one. Outline your understanding of the tenets of this perspective, and explain why it is an integrative perspective.
2. Define and differentiate among the following three models for describing the process of child development: single-factor model, interactional model, and transactional model.
3. Explain the concept of bidirectionality in relation to family interactions.
4. Discuss Laszlo's five properties of a system: wholeness and order, the concept of adaptive self-stabilization, the concept of adaptive self-organization, systemic hierarchies, and dialectic movement. Define each of these concepts and explain their importance and usefulness in understanding parental behavior.
5. Describe the types of interactions one would expect to see in a "disengaged family" and in an "enmeshed family," using Minuchin's scheme for describing family boundaries. Explain the relevance of these concepts to teachers.
6. Discuss specific ways in which schools and individual teachers can involve families in the educational process. Survey local schools to determine what approaches to family involvement are being used.

REFERENCES

Bandura, A. (1978). The self system in reciprocal determinism. *American Psychologist, 33,* 344–358.

Bateson, G. (1970). *Mind and nature.* New York: E. P. Dutton.

Bateson, G. (1972). *Steps to an ecology of mind.* New York: Ballantine.

Bell, R. (1968). A reinterpretation of the direction of effects in studies of socialization. *Psychological Review, 75,* 81–95.

Bell, R. Q. (1971). Stimulus control or caretaker behavior by offsprings. *Developmental Psychology, 4,* 63–72.

Belsky, J. (1984). The determinants of parenting: A process model. *Child Development, 55*(1), 83–96.

Bettelheim, B. (1950). *Love is not enough.* Glencoe, IL: Free Press.

Boulding, K. E. (1980). Universal physiology, *Behavioral Science, 25,* 35–39.

Bronfenbrenner, U. (1977). Toward an experimental ecology of human development. *American Psychologist, 32,* 513–530.

Cain, L. F. (1976). Parent groups: Their role in a better way of life for the handicapped. *Exceptional Children, 42,* 432–437.

Carey, W. B., & McDevitt, S. C. (1978). Revision of the Infant Temperament Questionnaire, *Pediatrics, 61*(5), 735–738.

Fox, M. (1985). Maternal involvement in residential day treatment. *Social Casework, 66,* 350–357.

Freud, S. (1949). *An outline of psychoanalysis.* New York: Norton.

Gould, S. J. (1981). *The Mismeasure of Man.* New York: W. W. Norton.

Haley, J. (1976). *Problem-solving therapy.* New York: Harper & Row.

Haley, J. (1981). *Reflections on therapy, and other essays.* Chevy Chase, MD: Family Therapy Institute.

Hatfield, A. B. (1981). Self-help groups for families of the mentally ill. *Social Work, 66,* 350–357.

Hayden, R. (1975). *Angle of ascent.* New York: Liveright.

Hobbs, N. (1966). Helping disturbed children: Psychological and ecological perspectives, *American Psychologist, 21,* 1105–1115.

Hoffman, L. (1981). *Foundations of family therapy.* New York: Basic Books.

Honig, A. S. (1978). *Parent involvement and the development of children with special needs.* Paper presented at the Teachers College Institute on Parenting Education for Handicapped Children, Columbia University, New York, NY. (ERIC Document Reproduction Service No. ED 165904).

Hoppe, P. (1979). How to organize self-help groups in the schools. *Exceptional Parent, 9,* E22–E23.

Jens, K., & O'Donnell, K. (1982). Bridging the gap between research and intervention with handicapped infants. In D. Bricker (Ed.), *Interventions with at-risk and handicapped infants* (pp. 31–43). Baltimore: University Park Press.

Jensen, A. R. (1969). How much can we boost IQ and scholastic achievement? *Harvard Educational Review, 33,* 1–123.

Jones, E. F. (1973). *Parents as staff partners: A program for parent involvement in a short term preschool psychiatric center. Volume II, No.*

1. The staff training prototype series. Austin, TX: Texas University, Department of Special Education. (ERIC Document Reproduction Service No. ED 133 936).

Laszlo, E. (1973). *Introduction to systems philosophy: Toward a new paradigm of contemporary thought.* New York: Harper & Row.

Lilienfeld, A. M., & Parkhurst, E. (1951). A study of the association of factors of pregnancy and parturition with the development of cerebral palsy: A preliminary report. *American Journal of Hygiene, 53,* 262–282.

Miller, J. G. (1978). *Living systems.* New York: McGraw Hill.

Minuchin, S. (1974). *Families and family therapy.* Cambridge, MA: Harvard University Press.

O'Connell, C. (1975). The challenge of parent education. *Exceptional Children, 41,* 554–556.

O'Donnell, K. (1985). Defenses in the nursery. In I. Wilhelm (Ed.), *Advances in neonatal special care* (pp. 118–126). Chapel Hill: University of North Carolina.

Pasamanick, B., & Knobloch, H. (1966). Retrospective studies on the epidemiology of reproductive casualty: Old and new. *Merrill Palmer Quarterly, 12,* 7–26.

Patterson, G. R. (1974). The aggressive child: Victim and architect of a coercive system. In E. J. Mash, L. A. Hamerlynck, & L. C. Handy (Eds.), *Behavior modification and families.* New York: Brunner/Mazel.

Patterson, G. R. (1980). Mothers: The unacknowledged victims. Monograph of the Society for Research in Child Development, 45(5).

Power, T. J., & Bartholomew, K. L. (1987). Family-school relationship patterns: An ecological assessment. *School Psychology Review, 16*(4), 498–512.

Sameroff, A. (1982). The environmental context of developmental disabilities. In D. Bricker (Ed.), *Intervention with at-risk and handicapped infants.* Baltimore: University Park Press.

Sameroff, A. (1984). Developmental systems: Contexts and evolution. In Kessen, W. (Ed.), History, theories, and methods (Volume I) of Mussen, P. H. (Ed.), *Handbook of Child Psychology.* New York: Wiley.

Sameroff, A., & Chandler, M. (1975). Reproductive risk and the continuum of caretaking casualty. In F. D. Horowitz (Ed.), *Review of Child Development Research* (Vol. 4). Chicago: University of Chicago Press.

Sandler, A., Coren, A., & Thurman, S. (1983). A training program for parents of handicapped preschool children: Effects upon mother, father, and child. *Exceptional Children, 49,* 355–357.

Sears, R. R. (1975). *Your ancients revisited: A history of child development.* Chicago: The University of Chicago Press.

Spitz, R. A., & Wolff, K. (1946). Anaclitic depression. In A. Freud et al. (Eds.), *Psychoanalytic Study of the Child.* New York: International Universities Press.

Spock, B. (1946). *Baby and child care.* New York: Duell, Sloan, & Pearce.

Thomas, A., Chess, S., Birch, H. G., & Hertzig, M. (1960). A longitudinal study of primary reaction patterns in children. *Comprehensive Psychiatry, 1,* 103–112.

Thomas, A., Chess, S., Birch, H. G., Hertzig, M. & Korn, S. (1963). *Behavioral individuality in early childhood.* New York: New York University Press.

Trautman, R. C., & Trail, A. (1973). *Parent involvement in the treatment of disturbed preschoolers.* Paper presented at the Annual International Convention of the Council for Exceptional Children, Detroit, MI. (ERIC Document Reproduction Service No. ED 229 982).

von Bertalanffy, L. (1968). *General systems theory.* New York: Braziller.

Weakland, J. (1974). The double-bind theory by self-reflexive hindsight. *Family Process, 13,* 269–277.

Wynne, L. C. (1963). Pseudo-mutuality in the family relations of schizophrenics. *Archives of General Psychiatry, 9,* 161–206.

Zelitch, S. R. (1980). Helping the family cope: Workshops for the families of schizophrenics. *Health and Social Work, 5,* 47–52.

PART TWO

Professionals' views about the nature of emotional disturbance affect the way they see problems and the type of treatments they recommend.

Major Theoretical Perspectives

Since the early 1970s when William C. Rhodes codified the theoretical basis for the field, the education of emotionally disturbed children has had a "theories" approach. There is a behavioral theory of emotional disturbance, a psychodynamic theory of emotional disturbance, and so forth. Textbooks on educating emotionally disturbed children generally review and update the theories, with some variation in which theories are included. Some texts use a single theory of emotional disturbance, reviewing the alternative views in a general chapter on theory. This text, like several others, examines the major theoretical perspectives in individual chapters, advocating the view that each perspective offers useful information and ways of understanding the problem for teachers.

Part Two includes chapters on behavioral, psychoneurological, psychodynamic, and ecological theories. The current state of knowledge and formulation of the perspective as well as the general practices associated with the theories are presented. Three additional chapters on theory which reflect the changing intellectual horizons of the field also are presented. Chapter 7 examines the cognitive development of children and the nature of emotional disturbance in the context of developmental theory. Chapter 8 discusses the social and cultural construction of emotional disturbance, emphasizing the nature and role of the political and social organization of schools, and the process of constructing culture, order, and curriculum in schools. Chapter 10 presents the new scientific paradigm and considers implications for the field of educating emotionally disturbed children. This chapter, which challenges the traditional assumptions of science on which the formal theories of emotional disturbance are based, is coauthored by Rhodes, who directed the Child Variance Project that codified those theories.

4
Psychoneurological Theory and Practice*

1. The neurological bases for childhood learning problems can be summarized through congenital, developmental, or acquired theories.

2. The majority of children who are referred to physicians for possible pharmacologic management of school-related problems do not show clear signs of neurological dysfunction when given traditional physical exams.

3. Psychostimulant compounds are the most commonly prescribed medications to assist in the management of school-related problems.

4. Medications can suppress negative behaviors that interfere with classroom learning.

5. It is unlikely that any medication will correct and/or eliminate a core learning disability.

6. A childhood traumatic brain injury, mild or severe, can result in significant learning and/or behavior problems.

7. While medications can bring about significant positive changes in a child's ability to participate in the classroom, they should not be used until possible nonneurologic sources for the child's difficulty have been thoroughly examined and other nonmedication efforts have been used.

8. Effective medication management in the school setting requires the active participation of the educator and physician as partners in the decision to medicate and in the evaluation of the medication once implemented. Schools of education need to offer courses on commonly used medications and the medical aspects of the learning process.

---

*This chapter was written by Randall W. Evans, CAROLINA Community Re-Entry Program.

9. Severe neurological conditions (e.g., autism, mental retardation) cannot be cured with medications; rather, negative behaviors/symptoms often *associated* with these conditions can be reduced with some medications.

10. Some medications, particularly the major tranquilizers, can have significant negative side effects that can actually impair the learning process. Therefore, the teacher, with the assistance of the physician and possibly a psychologist, should evaluate and determine if a particular medication is negatively affecting the student's learning ability.

Weighing less than sixteen hundred grams (three pounds), the human brain in its natural state resembles nothing so much as a soft, wrinkled walnut. Yet despite this inauspicious appearance, the human brain can store more information than all the libraries in the world. It is also responsible for our most primitive urges, our loftiest ideals, the way we think, even the reason why, on occasion, we sometimes don't think, but act instead. The workings of an organ capable of creating Hamlet, the Bill of Rights, and Hiroshima remain deeply mysterious. How is it constructed? How did it develop? If we learn more about the brain, can we learn more about ourselves? Indeed, are we anything other than our brain?

(Restak, 1984, p. 1)

This chapter reviews contemporary thinking, with reference to theoretical and data driven literature, concerning the neurological bases of common emotional and behavioral disorders in children. Discussion is supported with analyses of treatment interventions attendant to these disorders and to some of the approaches which may be of value in a classroom setting.

It is not necessary for teachers to be well versed in behavioral neurology or pathophysiology. However, they do need to have an understanding of basic central nervous system function (and consequently, central nervous system dysfunction) as it relates to disordered emotional and behavioral functioning. The lack of this understanding may lead to misdiagnosis and improper educational treatment. This chapter reviews collaborative efforts between neurological and psychological approaches toward the understanding of severe emotional and behavioral dysfunction.

The interaction between "organic" functioning and "psychological" functioning as they relate to problems that compromise the child's ability to succeed in the classroom are discussed. Special attention is given to treatment techniques involving physiological manipulation (e.g., medications) to bring about signifi-cant behavioral and emotional changes.

This chapter will focus on congenital theory, developmental theory, and acquired theory. **Congenital theory** assumes that a basic defect of genetic struc-tures exists (e.g., trisomy 21 resulting in Down's Syndrome) or that damage to the developing central nervous system occurred during gestation (e.g., infec-tions, toxins, and anoxia can all cause certain neurological disorders). Congen-ital theory implies that the individual at birth possesses an irreversible neurolog-ical defect that may have mild to severe consequences upon learning and educational development. **Developmental theory** assumes that the individual's biological endowment at birth is essentially "normal" but that the interaction between the individual and the environment can result in developmental dys-function, or developmental "lag." Finally, **acquired theory** accentuates the ar-rest or regression of normal development as a consequence of a distinct, iden-tifiable event (e.g., traumatic brain injury).

It is important for the educator of the neurologically impaired child to have an appreciation for the theoretical basis of a particular disorder in the classroom. Such an understanding will affect educational planning and the eventual aca-demic outcome of the child.

CONGENITAL THEORY

Congenital theory assumes that factors influencing embryo and fetal develop-ment have an exceedingly powerful effect upon the individual's eventual phys-ical, emotional, and cognitive development. This is not a new or revolutionary position; rather, it emphasizes that certain prenatal events can have considerable impact upon a child's eventual classroom performance. This model also implies that learning difficulties caused by prenatal conditions are more resistant to modification through environmental manipulation (Schroeder & Schroeder, 1982). **Mental retardation, severe learning disorder,** and **autism** are promi-nent syndromes, each associated with behavioral problems, which may have strong congenital bases.

Mental Retardation

Strictly speaking, mental retardation is a common disorder, **statistically** repre-senting at least 5% of all school-aged children. Mental retardation denotes a level of behavioral (i.e., intellectual) performance without specific reference to etiol-ogy. It does not necessarily imply prognosis, particularly in mild cases. None-theless, certain prenatal and perinatal events such as genetic disorders or toxic exposures are strongly correlated with mental retardation. Therefore, it is ap-propriate to discuss mental retardation within a congenital framework. Addition-ally, the lower the intelligence quotient (a standard but partial method of deter-mining mental retardation), the greater the likelihood that other deficits exist, including physical malformations such as microcephaly or crippled limbs (Erickson, 1978), giving further evidence of prenatal dysfunctions.

It is beyond the scope of this chapter to review the enormous amount of literature relating genetic and nongenetic (e.g., prenatal, perinatal) factors to mental retardation. Baroff (1986) provides an excellent summary of this important literature. Although the etiology for the majority of mental retardation cases, particularly mild cases, remains unknown, two major mental retardation syndromes—Down's syndrome (LeJeune, Gautier, & Turpin, 1959) and Klinefelter's syndrome (Jacobs & Strong, 1959)—have genetic linkages.

Other forms of mental retardation are associated with various prenatal and perinatal hazards (Baroff, 1986). These hazards include the following:

- Infections (rubella, toxoplasmosis, syphilis)
- Drugs and alcohol (psychotropics, tobacco, cocaine)
- Chronic maternal health problems (diabetes, hypertension)
- Asphyxia (prolapse of umbilical cord)
- Environmental toxins (e.g., lead poisoning)
- Prematurity
- Maternal-fetal irradiation

Mental Retardation and the Right to Education.   Prior to P. L. 94–142, public schools created special education classrooms for the mentally retarded based on IQ scores which usually placed the children in either the educable mentally retarded (EMR) group or a trainable mentally retarded (TMR) group. Students in the EMR group had IQs between 55 and 69; those in the TMR group had IQs of less than 55. Professionals assumed that students in the EMR group could learn fundamental school subjects (i.e., reading, writing, arithmetic), as well as practical living skills and noncompetitive occupational training. On the other hand, the goal for TMR training involved basic self-care skills and social adjustment. It is generally now believed that individuals who once fell in the EMR group have a considerably more favorable prognosis than those in the TMR group for normalized living in society. Individuals formerly placed in TMR classrooms do in fact require considerable special education and are probably best served in an environment where highly trained professionals can carry out specialized programming.

Therapeutic Use of Medications in Mental Retardation.   The use of medications for **behavioral control** in the mentally retarded population was the original arena for investigating widespread drug use. Therefore, proper attention must be paid to this population in order to establish an appreciation for using psychoactive medications for behavioral control in other populations.

Psychotropic medications (i.e., drugs which have a known impact upon central nervous system functioning) are typically used in the mental retardation population for **symptomatic** control of certain associated negative behaviors. It is now common knowledge that drugs were initially used in excess in this population (Lipman, 1970) and that drug misuse continues to exist (Bates, Smeltzer, & Arnoczky, 1986). It is important to emphasize the use of these medications in

TABLE 4.1
Some Commonly Used Drugs for Controlling Behavior

Indication	Drugs	Drug Class
Behavior control	Thorazine, Mellaril Stelazine, Prolixin	Tranquilizer
Seizure control	Dilantin, Phenobarbital Carbamazepine	Anticonvulsants
Mood elevation/ antidepressants	Tofranil, Elavil, Aventyl	Stabilizer

this population since the same drugs are used in other populations for different purposes. Drugs are most commonly prescribed for behavior control (e.g., taming aggression, assault, self-injury), for seizure control, or for elevating mood. See Table 4.1 for a listing of commonly used drugs.

As in any situation where drug therapy is considered, it is critical that the prescribing physician and other professionals involved in the medication decision consider each case individually. Drug use in the mentally retarded population appears to be most appropriate "where the retarded individual experiences symptoms associated with an acute schizophrenic (psychotic) or affective (mood) disorder, in some hyperactive retarded children with major attention and concentration problems, and in persons with seizures" (Rivinus, 1980). Remember that some drugs (e.g., anticonvulsants or tranquilizers) can impair learning ability (Evans, Gualtieri, & Amara, 1986). Therefore, drug use in a population with known learning difficulties should be prudently investigated prior to implementation. This responsibility lies with the prescribing physician to understand the cognitive side effects of commonly used medications. Additionally, it is the teacher's responsibility to alert physicians of potential negative side effects on the child's learning skill while under the influences of the medication.

Little evidence suggests that prescribed drugs can effect a significant **positive** change upon learning or behavior beyond amelioration of a significant negative symptom in the mentally retarded population. That is, medications that have been shown to exert positive effects upon "normal" functioning (e.g., stimulant medications in improving memory abilities) cannot be expected to have similar effects in the retarded population. The use of medications in a classroom setting for the mentally retarded individual should be limited to only where other, less intrusive techniques have failed to remove or lessen a negative behavior.

Severe Learning Disorder—Dyslexia

Debate remains on whether a severe learning disability is a consequence of either a congenital anomaly or a developmental, dysmaturational lag (Galaburda, LeMay, Kemper, & Geschwind, 1978; Kinsbourne, 1973). It is not the intent of this discussion to solve this debate. However, from a neurological perspective, there is considerable evidence that certain learning disabilities exist within families and that there are critical periods of embryonic development for specific high-level cognitive abilities to develop (Kemper, 1984). It is in this context that a neurological theory behind severe dyslexia will be presented. **Dyslexia** is a measurable reduction or, in severe cases, an absence in the ability to read. This inability occurs in the face of normal intellect and normal sensory functioning, despite intensive efforts to otherwise remediate. Dyslexia exists on a continuum, and some individuals experience only mild to moderate difficulties with reading compared to other academic or cognitive tasks.

Lou, Henricksen, and Bruhn (1984) suggest that severe language disorders in children (including dyslexia) may result from morphological brain abnormalities. Their study, based upon regional cerebral blood flow measurements, did not address the potential confounding variables that these children also suffered from other disorders, including hyperkinesis and visuospatial problems. Therefore, these children were not a genuine dyslexic group; rather, they represented a group with heterogeneous deficits, of which dyslexia was a prominent feature. Nonetheless, Lou et al. hypothesized that each child's language disturbance was attributable to an early hypoxemic-ischemic lesion, perhaps secondary to prenatal injury.

Bishop (1987) discusses potential causes of specific developmental language disorders, and cites possible prenatal and/or perinatal factors. One popular notion regarding the etiology of dyslexia focuses upon the observation that since neurological disease in childhood is relatively rare (aside from trauma), then prenatal or perinatal factors must account for specific language disorders. This argument is basically one of diagnosis by exclusion, or alternatively by lack of reasonable evidence. Therefore, it is highly suspect. Bishop emphasizes that there are no satisfactory retrospective studies of the birth histories of language-disordered children. Related investigations (Fundudiss, Kolvin, & Garside, 1979; Pasamanick, Constantinou, & Lilienfeld, 1956) suggested a correlation between low birth weight, reduced gestational age, and eventual language disorders; however, their experimental group also included children who showed delays in other milestones as well.

Bishop (1987) concludes: "In general, studies of children with verifiable lesions do not support the idea that specific developmental language disorders are caused by early (prenatal, perinatal) localized brain damage" (p. 8). This statement is supported by studies showing that early, postnatal damage to the left cerebral hemisphere, which typically governs language functioning, does not necessarily produce selective language impairments (Woods, 1980).

Finally, it is almost impossible to examine the dyslexia literature without discovering that there appears to be an inevitable blend of neurogenic and developmental (i.e., assumed to be not neurologically driven) factors leading to dyslexia. The developmental model of dyslexia assumes that the dyslexic individual is merely delayed (e.g., 1, 2, or more years) in the acquisition of a specific skill (i.e., reading). This model implicitly assumes that the individual will eventually catch up and that her reading abilities will coincide with other cognitive skills. The fact remains, however, that many individuals do not catch up, and this is the population which is of special interest to geneticists and developmental psychologists.

Dyslexia and Medications.   When medications are considered for treating the dyslexic child, the medication trial is usually intended to correct a behavioral problem (i.e., hyperactivity, aggressiveness), a specific cognitive deficit (i.e., poor attention span), or a psychological symptom (i.e., depression, anxiety, phobia). Until very recently, there was little evidence to suggest that a medication could actually decrease or eliminate dyslexia.

In general, the efficacy of psychotropic drugs, particularly stimulant drugs, for the remediation of academic underachievement has been a topic of controversy for decades (Gadow, 1986). The ability of stimulant compounds to produce desired short-term benefits in attention and memory functioning is well established (Evans, Gualtieri, and Hicks, 1986), as is the efficacy of stimulant medications to bring about desired changes in the activity level of highly overactive children (Hensen, 1986). However, the few longitudinal studies targeted to look at the long-term academic achievements of children prescribed stimulants fail to support the notion that stimulant drugs can result in global improvements in academic performance (Gadow, 1983). Positive short-term effects upon academic achievement have recently been reported following stimulant treatment (Richardson et al., 1988), although this short-term effect was related to a significant reduction of behavior problems. Kavale (1982) is optimistic about the potential positive effects upon overall academic performance, and he advocates for more rigorous statistical analyses and better control of the experimental design of such studies.

In any event, it is highly unlikely that stimulant compounds will lead to any substantial, quantitative changes in a dyslexic child's basic ability to read. Perhaps a child's reading ability may increase following administration of a stimulant compound. However, available research indicates that this improvement is probably secondary to improvement in attention span, a cognitive component in reading ability, rather than to a neuropharmacologically induced alteration of the child's primary reading skill. After reviewing methodologically sound research in this area, Aman (1982) concluded that there "is no compelling evidence to date that drugs in **isolation** result in improved reading performance" (p. 46). This statement holds true today, although a recent national multicenter study renewed the potential for medications to improve reading ability (Wilsher, Bennett, & Chase, 1987).

Wilsher et al. (1987) suggested that the drug Piracetam (Nootropil) may influence language areas of the brain. This medication, as well as others purported to exert cognitive-enhancing effects warrant considerable investigation prior to providing the population at large with such compounds.

Clinical and research practices show that positive academic changes can result from proper pharmacotherapy. However, any positive effects are likely consequent to (1) a reduction of hyperactive and inattentive behavior and (2) a possible improvement of a child's memory functioning (i.e., acquisition and retrieval of carefully presented information). "Core" reading ability appears to be unaffected by medications. Medication side effects can occur. In the case of tranquilizers and anticonvulsants, sedation, lethargy, and cognitive blurring are the most common. In the use of stimulant medications, irritability, decreased appetite, headaches, and insomnia can occur. Fortunately, these side effects are usually completely reversible following withdrawal of the medications.

Autism

From a neurological perspective, autism is an impossible concept. That is, there is no known specific pathophysiologic defect that causes autism. It is a syndrome that embraces a wide range of individual deficits, and individuals who are autistic differ widely in clinical presentation, developmental level, etiology, associated disorders, and prognosis. Research has failed to uncover any single biologic mechanism which may explain the diversity of behaviors associated with autism. Therefore, the hope for a specific biological "treatment" is in vain.

Autism is characterized by lack of responsiveness to other people, gross impairment in communication skills, and bizarre responses to various aspects of the environment (American Psychiatric Association, 1987). There is often a pronounced failure to develop interpersonal relationships with an associated failure to develop normal attachment behaviors. The impairments in communication include both verbal and nonverbal skills. In severe cases, language may be totally absent. In the nonverbal realm, the autistic individual does not readily grasp facial expressions and gestures. Autism is considered a chronic disorder although some autistic individuals are able to live independently. However, the overwhelming majority of autistic individuals are unable to live independent lives and usually reside in group homes or some other type of institution.

From an educational standpoint, special education facilities are almost always necessary. It is usually impossible to place autistic children in a regular classroom due to their disruptive behavior and profound deficits in cognitive status. Schopler and Mesibov (1987) present a thorough description of the actual educational process for autistic people.

The Medical Treatment of Autistic People.   As mentioned, there is no formal medical treatment for autism. However, there are treatments for seizure disorders that can afflict autistic people, and there are also medical treatments that can mitigate many of the destructive behaviors that autistic individuals develop. When these treatments are properly used, they are probably no more toxic for autistic persons than for other individuals who are treated for seizures or behavior disorders (Gualtieri, Evans, & Patterson, 1987).

All medication treatments for autistic persons are symptomatic and are aimed at reducing seizures, undesirable behaviors, or their attributes. There is a relative lack of experienced psychopharmacologic care for autistic individuals.

Anticonvulsant and psychopharmacologic drugs and even vitamin combinations have been tried, although the long-term effects of these medications are unknown. Additionally, parental dismay over the marginal quality of traditional medical services and treatments has led to an understandable uncertainty about how to proceed. Brief descriptions of some commonly used medical approaches to autism will be offered. As mentioned, these approaches are intended to facilitate the special education needs of the autistic child. It is highly unlikely that such therapies will lead to the mainstreaming of autistic children into the classroom setting. Medications that have received the most attention for autistic individuals include neuroleptic or antipsychotic drugs, Fenfluramine, megavitamins, and anticonvulsant drugs.

Neuroleptic (antipsychotic) drugs are the most commonly prescribed psychotropic medications given to autistic children (Rimland, 1977). Neuroleptics (especially Haldol in low doses) have been shown to reduce symptoms of stereotypy, withdrawal, hyperactivity, and fidgetiness in young (i.e., age 2–8) autistic children. Clinical improvement in such areas would naturally be expected to render children more accessible in the classroom and presumably more amenable to a learning environment. There is tentative evidence to support this hypothesis (Campbell, Anderson, & Cohen, 1982). The precise manners in which these compounds work for epileptics and autistic children is unknown. The neuroleptics may exert a specific antipsychotic effect, a tranquilizing effect, or a combination of both. Whenever neuroleptics are given in any clinical situation, considerable attention must be given to potential side effects of these compounds. Neuroleptic medications are known to induce severe defects in motor abilities; the most severe being tardive dyskinesia (i.e., involuntary abnormal motor movements).

Fenfluramine, an atypical stimulant medication, has gained some attention in reducing the negative behaviors and improving the cognitive status in autistic children. The safety of Fenfluramine is open to question; this issue will not be resolved until the drug has been used for many years.

Megavitamins have been proposed as a possible adjunctive treatment for autism, although there is little scientific evidence to support these claims (Gualtieri, Evans, & Patterson, 1987). It is supposed that water-soluble vitamins have a prophylactic use for the negative symptoms of autism. Megavitamin treatment may be relatively safe, but is not completely free of untoward effects. Such treatment should be undertaken only under the supervision of a physician who is knowledgeable about autistic symptoms.

Because autistic children are vulnerable to seizure disorders (particularly complex-partial-type seizures), anticonvulsant medications are commonly prescribed. When seizure disorders occur in autistic children, the disorders often carry poor prognoses and therefore are likely to require long-term anticonvulsant treatment. It is important to reiterate and to emphasize that anticonvulsants carry potential cognitive and behavioral toxic reactions and, therefore, should generally be used in the smallest possible therapeutic dose ranges. The anticonvulsants of particular relevance are Dilantin, Phenobarbital, and Carbamazepine.

DEVELOPMENTAL THEORY

In some respects, developmental theories of aberrant behavior probably came about as a consequence of scientific inability to account for an observable physical disorder or syndrome. A primary component of the developmental perspective is that aberrant behavior may be the result of an environmental stimulus and a subtly disturbed central nervous system (CNS). Otherwise stated, no direct observations of damage or significant disturbance to the CNS are made; rather, the aberrant behavior leads to a possible conclusion of existing CNS pathology. Such a model assumes that specific types of treatment (including symptomatic uses of medications) can ameliorate the aberration. In its simplest form, this is a post hoc explanation; that is, no theory exists that accurately *predicts* which medications will be successful and which will not. Attention Deficit Disorder (ADD) and Conduct Disorder (CD) are the two most common syndromes considered within this developmental framework.

Attention Deficit Disorder

Childhood hyperactivity, attention deficit disorder, previously known as childhood hyperactivity (American Psychiatric Association, 1987) can have a profound, negative impact upon a child's academic performance. In the most severe form of ADD, a child cannot attend in any given situation for a period exceeding several seconds. In such circumstances, the child usually displays associated severe behavior problems. It is believed that a cognitive component—severely reduced attention span—is the underlying problem in hyperactive children. Consequently, correcting the attentional deficit will lead to more organized, goal-directed behavior.

No single known etiology for childhood ADD exists, although several factors have been labeled as potential agents. Because some evidence suggests that childhood ADD is characterized by an irregular neurotransmitter system, genetic theories abound. However, ADD symptoms can be evoked by severe psychological or environmental changes. Therefore, developmental theories exist as well. For purposes of clarity, we will consider ADD as a developmental syndrome. In the majority of cases, this syndrome develops during childhood and can diminish when adulthood is reached, with proper treatment.

In its purest form, ADD is a syndrome in and of itself. While overactivity is the most common characteristic of the disorder, cognitive factors also compose part of the diagnostic picture (American Psychiatric Association, 1987). Certainly, some of the other clinical populations discussed in this chapter suffer from both behavioral and cognitive difficulties. However, the American Psychiatric Association recently has developed strict criteria for ADD. These criteria are as follows:

The child displays, for her mental and chronological age, signs of developmentally inappropriate inattention, impulsivity, and hyperactivity. Adults in the child's environment, such as parents and teachers, must report these signs.

Because the symptoms are typically variable, they may not be observed directly by the clinician. When the reports of teachers and parents conflict, primary consideration should be given to the teacher reports because of greater familiarity with age-appropriate norms. Symptoms typically worsen in situations that require self-application (e.g., in the classroom). Signs of the disorder may be absent when the child is in a new or in a one-to-one situation.

Symptomatic display usually occurs between the ages of 8 and 10, the peak age range for referral. In younger children, more severe forms of the symptoms and a greater number of symptoms are usually present. The opposite is true of older children. The following outline lists characteristics of attention deficit disorders.

A. Inattention. Displays at least **three** of the following:
　1. Often fails to finish things she starts
　2. Often doesn't seem to listen
　3. Easily distracted
　4. Has difficulty concentrating on schoolwork or other tasks requiring sustained attention
　5. Has difficulty sticking to a play activity

B. Impulsivity. Displays at least **three** of the following:
　1. Often acts before thinking
　2. Shifts excessively from one activity to another
　3. Has difficulty organizing work (this not being due to cognitive impairment)
　4. Needs a lot of supervision
　5. Frequently calls out in class
　6. Has difficulty awaiting turn in games or group situations

C. Hyperactivity. Displays at least **two** of the following:
　1. Runs about or climbs on things excessively
　2. Has difficulty sitting still or fidgets excessively
　3. Has difficulty staying seated
　4. Moves about excessively during sleep
　5. Is always "on the go" or acts as if "driven by a motor"

D. Onset before the age of 7.

E. Duration of at least 6 months.

F. Not due to schizophrenia, affective disorder, or profound mental retardation.

Among the more popular developmental theories of ADD is that espoused by Kinsbourne (1973). Termed a "dysmaturational" disorder, Kinsbourne's model views ADD as a predictable component of the normal bell-curve distribution of human behavior. That is, if one assumes the theoretical perspective that all human behavior follows a normal bell-curve distribution, then a specific percentage of that behavior will fall at the extreme of the distribution at some point in development. This theory implies that the child does **not** display overt evidence of a biological disorder, although certain "soft signs" (i.e., asymmetrical reflexes, delayed learning, minor physical aberrations) may be present. This developmental perspective hypothesizes that these statistical deviations will eventually remit during the normal course of maturation. Finally, this model places considerable importance upon the influence of the environment. For example, an impoverished environment can have a measurable negative impact upon the child who is experiencing "dysmaturation."

Therapeutic Uses of Medication in Attention Deficit Disorder. Medical treatment for the ADD child should occur only following a thorough evaluation of the child's emotional, environmental, and biological states. A physician or psychologist trained in pediatric neuropsychiatry should evaluate whether the child meets DSM-III-R (*Diagnostic and Statistical Manual III-Revised*) criteria for ADD, and whether the ADD child and those around her can be greatly aided by the child being placed on medications.

It is estimated that between 750,000 to 1,000,000 American children receive medication treatment for ADD symptoms. The majority of these children receive stimulant medications, particularly Ritalin. The efficacy of stimulant medications for ADD symptoms is well established (Barkley, 1977; Evans, Gualtieri, & Hicks, 1986). Two other popular drugs for ADD are Dexedrine and Cylert. The pharmacokinetic profiles of Dexedrine, Ritalin, and Cylert are provided in Table 4.2.

Stimulant medications exert their therapeutic effect by normalizing an imbalanced neurotransmitter system, particularly one rich in monoamines (a specific class of neurotransmitters). Stimulant medications facilitate the transmission of monoamines which leads to behavioral and cognitive improvements in the ADD child. From a pharmacological point of view, stimulant drugs "stimulate"

TABLE 4.2
Pharmacokinetic Profiles

	Dextroamphetamine (Dexedrine)	Methylphenidate (Ritalin)	Pemoline (Cylert)
How supplied (mg)	5, 10	5,10, 20	18.75, 37.5, 75
Single dose range (mg/kg/dose)	.15–.5	.3–.7	.5–2.5
Daily dose range (mg/kg/day) (mg/day)	.3–1.25 5–40	.6–1.7 10–60	.5–3.0 37.5–112.5
Usual starting dose (mg)	2.5 daily or BID	5 daily or BID	18.75 daily
Onset of behavioral effect	1 hour	1 hour	Variable
Duration of behavioral effect (hours)	4	3–4	Not available

the child to become more attentive in thought and in action by increasing arousal in the child's central nervous system.

Several studies showed the efficacy of stimulants in controlling severe behavior and attention problems of ADD children in the classroom setting (Connors, 1971; Solanto, 1984). With regard to the most optimal therapeutic dose, it appears that higher doses (still within the therapeutic range) of medication are required in children placed in settings with less structure than in those placed in highly structured settings (e.g., one-to-one tutoring).

As mentioned earlier, few studies have examined the long-term effects of stimulant medications upon a child's overall academic performance. One could assume that increasing a student's attention span and memory performance would have notable effects upon her performance; however, this assumption has not been reliably investigated (Gadow, 1983). Gadow emphasizes that stimulant medications should be used properly to control activity level and to improve a child's cognitive skills in the short term. He states that long-term results are much more difficult to predict.

Conduct Disorder (CD)

According to DSM-III-R, the essential feature of conduct disorder is a "repetitive and persistent pattern of conduct in which either the basic rights of others or major age-appropriate societal norms or rules are violated. The conduct is more serious than the ordinary mischief and pranks of children and adolescents" (American Psychiatric Association, 1987, p. 45). Typical conduct disorder behaviors include impulsivity, poor organization, "calling out" in class, difficulty staying seated, poor turn-taking ability, and the like. Like ADD, conduct disorder is more prevalent among males, although no clear neurological cause for the disorder has been established. There are four types of conduct disorder: (1) undersocialized, aggressive; (2) undersocialized, nonaggressive; (3) socialized, aggressive; (4) socialized, nonaggressive. There is usually an obvious impairment in social and school functioning, in any of these types. Refer to DSM-III-R (American Psychiatric Association, 1987, pp. 47–50) for a more thorough diagnostic description of the four types.

Among all the childhood diagnoses/syndromes presented in this chapter, conduct disorder has probably the least amount of support in the literature as a neurological problem. Although excessive impulsivity, poor attention span, and acting-out behavior—characteristics that are common to CD—could be attributed to improper frontal lobe functioning (Cox & Evans, 1987), this is a tenuous proposition. Genetic studies have failed to produce a genetic "marker" for familial behavior disorders. Rather, most clinical and research evidence support the notion that CD may be a "learned" disorder. Only in extreme CD cases, in which CD coexists with ADD or another syndrome, are neurological hypotheses plausible.

In spite of the lack of knowledge regarding the etiology for conduct disorder, a small number of studies have documented potential positive effects from medication trials. These studies are briefly reviewed herein.

Recent reports show that conduct disorder and attention deficit disorder coexist (Werry, Reeves, & Elkind, 1987). Therefore, psychostimulant drugs, which are frequently employed in ADD, are used symptomatically in CD. It is clear, however, that stimulant compounds do not have the effectiveness in children with CD **and** ADD **or** CD that they have in children with only ADD. Therefore, other medication approaches have been advanced for the CD child.

DeLong and Aldershof (1987) investigated the possible utility of lithium in 33 CD children; they found that only five children (15 percent) responded favorably to lithium. Campbell, Perry, & Green (1984) report a more favorable potential of lithium in CD children. They found that lithium was clearly superior to Haloperidol (Haldol), a major tranquilizer, both clinically and in its side-effect profile. The mechanism of action for lithium effectiveness in CD children is unknown, although it has been speculated that lithium is more likely to be successful in CD children when affective, particularly depressive, symptoms are also present.

As mentioned previously, the utility of pharmacotherapy in children with conduct disorder is dubious at best. Since considerable evidence exists that many of the behaviors of CD can be modified through behavioral intervention, educators and physicians should first investigate the potential contributions of the child's environment to the behavior problem. It is not desirable to medicate the behaviorally disordered child before trying other treatment choices. Consultation with the school psychologist can often lead to a nonmedical solution for what most consider a nonmedical problem.

Anecdotal clinical experience and research findings consider most conduct disorders as environmentally produced and environmentally maintained. In cases where conduct disorder coexists with other diagnoses (e.g., ADD, dyslexia), the argument can be made that a biological factor, or predisposition, is likely.

ACQUIRED THEORY

Acquired theory is self-defining. In this model, an identifiable physical stressor exists that creates a transient or chronic deficit in one's behavior. Common acquired stressors are traumatic brain injury (TBI), metabolic disturbances, tumors, or strokes. TBI, usually secondary to automobile accidents, is by far the most common source of disability in young children and adolescents.

Acquired Brain Injury

Until the recent AIDS (acquired immune deficiency syndrome) epidemic, injury was cited by the National Academy of Sciences as the principal public health problem in America. In 1985, injury was predicted to affect one out of every three Americans. Injuries are, in fact, thought to be the most significant contribution to childhood disease, disability, and death. Over 25% of all emergency department or hospital clinical visits are for treatment of injuries. Furthermore, a Massachusetts study conducted in 1980–81 reports that of every 1,000 chil-

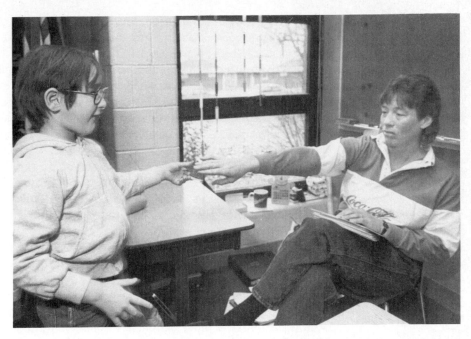

Research has identified a number of physical stressors that create transient or chronic behavior problems.

dren, a minimum of 200 emergency room injury-related visits occur each year (Gallagher, Finison, & Guyer, 1984).

Among childhood injuries, head trauma emerges as the major contributor. Although data are sparse in regard to epidemiological studies of this problem as it relates to specific age groups in the pediatric population, it has been suggested that "head trauma is a serious cause of morbidity and mortality and accounts for 43% of all deaths in children aged 5–9 years" (Klauber, Marshall, & Toole, 1985).

Etiology. Although researchers agree that most brain injuries in young children are not due to motor vehicle accidents, opinions differ regarding the causative factors. For example, falls have been reported to account for anywhere from 40 to 65% of brain injuries; motor vehicle accidents for 30 to 40%; "other" causative factors (e.g., abuse, sports-related injuries) for 10 to 30% (National Head Injury Foundation, 1986).

While head injuries in children less than 12 months of age pose a special problem and are overrepresented by inclusion of birth-related injuries, the contemporary view is that child abuse or nonaccidental brain injury is on the rise and is the major contributor to nonvehicle accidents (Matthews, 1988). In fact, child abuse is believed to be the most common diagnosis in children under 2 years old.

Minor head injury (i.e., trauma resulting in less that 1 hour of unconsciousness) is by far the most prevalent form of brain injury. Although moderate and severe injuries are less significant from an epidemiological standpoint, they do have substantial societal impact. It is estimated by a current practitioner that 6 or more children per 100,000 per year suffer severe brain injury and are in need of sophisticated rehabilitative treatment (Matthews, 1988).

Academic Treatment Intervention.   Once medical stability has occurred for children, integration into the community must be tied to the developmental aspects of both the short- and long-term effects of the brain injury. Taking into account a child's often rapid and more complete **physical** recovery, as well as her extended period of **psychological/cognitive** recovery, much of a child's progress after traumatic brain injury will occur contemporaneously while she is functioning as a member of her family, community, and school (Brink, Garrett, & Hale, 1970; Brink, Imbus, & Woo-Sam, 1980; Klonoff, Low, & Clark, 1977). A combination of factors, including early return to the community (or no separation at all), the interaction of development and recovery, and the prolonged nature of gains after injury, are common to most children after traumatic brain injury (Lehr, 1988). Physical recovery from brain injury is usually fast and easy to observe. On the other hand, cognitive, psychosocial, emotional, and behavioral issues are more difficult to observe and consequently are often denied and/or underestimated.

The immediate and long-term effects of injury are generally related to the neurodevelopmental processes that are dominant through each period (Shapiro, 1985). During infancy, injury affects cell migration and the organization of the brain. In toddlers, injury affects the rapid cortical myelinization of the primary and secondary association cortices. In preschool and primary-school-aged child, injury may interrupt and interfere with the rapid connection and myelinization of the tertiary association cortices. When children are in the middle-school-aged period, the effects of myelinization of the frontal/limbic structures are of critical importance.

Since delayed effects can appear long after the onset of injury and after immediate medical/rehabilitation management has ended, community-based personnel must be aware of the potential for emerging deficits, possibly many years after injury.

Moderate to severe head injuries in children can lead to cognitive and information-processing deficits. Recent studies document deficits in memory, attention, concept learning, adaptive problem solving, and sensory-perceptual and sensorimotor abilities (Levin, Eisenberg, & Wigg, 1982). The frequency and severity of these deficits are presumed to be directly related to evidence of the severity of the head injury, such as duration of the posttraumatic amnesia and coma, depth of coma, or global severity. As with the learning disabled child, head-injured children can exhibit significant and continuing impairment of their learning skills, while at the same time obtaining IQs that fall within normal range, particularly during the first year after trauma.

Accurate information regarding the learning capabilities of head-injured children is very important since most are returned rapidly to the school environment where they are expected to function effectively with their age and peer group. For those head-injured students placed in special education classrooms, baseline information is critical in determining appropriate program development.

P.L.94–142 mandates that an individualized, age-dependent educational developmental program be constructed for handicapped children. In order to develop a realistic program, a measure of the adaptive abilities that reflect impairment of the various dysfunctional systems within the brain must be obtained. The Reitan-Indiana Neuropsychological Test Battery (for children 5 to 8 years of age), and the Halstead-Reitan Neuropsychological Test Battery (for children 9 to 14 years of age), developed and standardized by Ralph Reitan, measure abilities demonstrably sensitive to dysfunction of brain-behavioral relationships in children (Reitan & Davison, 1974). Because of the need for evaluating academic performance, augmentation of the neuropsychological battery with measures of reading, spelling, writing, and arithmetic skills is essential. The specific tests in the Halstead-Reitan and Reitan-Indiana batteries are usually categorized according to the skills that they purportedly measure. Rourke, Young, Strang, and Russell (1986) have conducted extensive research regarding the existence of various "subtypes" of learning disabled children. These subtypes are defined through careful neuropsychological and academic performance analyses and have been shown to have relevance to academic remediation and even to adaptive behavior in adulthood (Rourke, Young, Strang, & Russell, 1986).

Educating the Traumatically Brain Injured Child.   Traditional educational goals may be inappropriate for head-injured students. For example, most curricula stress integrating basic processing abilities (i.e., visual and auditory skills, language comprehension and expression, and fine motor abilities) while teaching academic subjects such as reading and mathematics (Haarbauer-Krupa, Moser, & Smith, 1985). However, to complete academic subjects, students also must be able to attend, remember information, and organize thoughts and materials. In general, the educational system does not teach "attending" or "remembering." In fact, it is often assumed that these skills are automatic and intact. But when students cannot learn, it may be because of cognitive deficits, and teachers or neuropsychological consultants may have to develop students' cognitive skills before teaching academics (Cohen, 1986). The general issue of cognitive rehabilitation is reviewed by Light et al. (1987). The cognitive problems listed in Figure 4.1 affect how children perceive, interpret, and respond to life situations, including school tasks.

It is easy to misread behaviors and not recognize cognitive deficits. For instance, a student may be able to demonstrate how to complete a worksheet, but when she is given this assignment, she cannot get started. The problem? Initiation. Or a student may be able to give short answers to questions about a story, but cannot make any sense when asked to relate large parts of the story. The problem? Expressive organization. Therefore, success in an academic environment traditionally entails integrating and using many sophisticated and interrelated skills, such as listening, language comprehension, reading (i.e., visual perception, tracking, sequencing), remembering, writing and discussing (i.e., thought organization and expression). However, success in an academic environment for the head-injured child may be relegated simply to paying attention, to waiting to be called upon, to controlling the impulsive tendency to

Orientation	Rate of Performance
Attention and Concentration	Flexibility v perseveration
Memory and Retrieval	Staying on Task or on topic
Impulse Control	Initiation
Comprehension: concrete or abstract	Generalization
	Judgement
Organization (of thoughts, expression, tasks)	Problem solving
	Frustration tolerance
Overload: comprehension breakdown	Fatigue or stress
	Inconsistent performance
Rate of Processing	

FIGURE 4.1
Cognitive Problem Areas

speak out, to responding to questions without drifting away from the topic, or to completing certain stages of, rather than an entire, assignment.

Success must be measured in terms of a child's unique ability. Educational goals will vary accordingly, and should be continuously reevaluated and redefined in an effort to effect a nonstandardized, dynamic process rather than a static process. Flexibility is a critical component of this process and is necessary for maximizing the brain-injured student's success in the academic environment.

With this as a basis of understanding, it makes sense to have an interdisciplinary collaborative effort between the rehabilitation treatment team (specifically the psychiatrist, the neuropsychologist, the behavioral analyst) and the child's educators (counselors, special educators, teachers, and the school principal). The family must be included in the assessment, planning, and ongoing evaluation, as they, too, are a critical element in maximizing the child's potential.

Therapeutic Uses of Medications in Traumatic Brain Injury. At this time, the use of medications for children with traumatic brain injury is guided by clinical practices from other pediatric populations who have similar problems. This symptomatic approach is certainly not an endpoint for rational pharmacology in TBI; rather, the cognitive and behavioral problems experienced by children with severe TBI are worthy of immediate attention. Therefore, health professionals must borrow treatment techniques from other patient groups until the pathophysiologic mechanisms of TBI are better understood.

The medications used for treating cognitive and behavioral disorders in TBI are similar to those used with the previously discussed populations. For example, psychostimulant compounds alleviate or reduce cognitive deficits, particularly memory and attention problems (Evans, Gualtieri, & Shear, 1987); anticonvulsants have proven effective for the treatment of some seizure disorders as well as behavioral problems following TBI; and minor and major tranquilizers may possess short-term benefits for reducing anxiety and severe agitation.

When considering the use of medications in a classroom setting to assist in the control of negative behaviors, it is critical that the prescribing physicians have considerable experience in the use of psychoactive compounds. If they do not have this experience, they are advised to consult with an experienced physician. Traumatic brain injury is a very poorly understood condition from a therapeutic pharmacological perspective. Without proper deliberation prior to medication use, serious negative drug reactions and side effects can occur. For an up-to-date review of the state of this literature, refer to the *Journal of Head Trauma Rehabilitation,* Vol. 2.

PHYSICIAN/TEACHER PARTNERSHIP

How can the educator communicate with physicians to enlist their support for a medication trial? One possible solution to this issue is to follow these recommended steps to enlist the physician's support/advice. The "good" physician must elicit this information from teachers who might be intimidated by previous experiences with medical professionals. The educator should do the following:

1. Describe the behavior/symptom that is significantly interfering with the child's academic progress. These behaviors/symptoms include excessive activity, poor attention span, and acting-out behavior.
2. Describe the circumstances in which the behavior/symptom occurs (e.g., pervasive vs. situation specific).
3. Propose possible sources for the behavior/symptom. Is there a known stressor, such as family disruption or a recent move?
4. Determine if academic reasons can account for the behavior/symptom. For example, does a specific learning disability exist?
5. Determine if the child has been prescribed medication previously for similar difficulties. If so, what was the outcome of the medication trial?
6. Investigate possible medical problems, or past medical trauma, which could account for the behavior/symptom. For example, is there a history of neurological dysfunction/trauma?

Investigating the answers to these six questions can often reveal possible sources for the child's apparent difficulties in the classroom. Answers to these questions can also provide the physician with the starting point from which to consider the potential benefits to pharmacotherapy.

As emphasized earlier, medications are likely to be helpful in situations where a negative behavior (e.g., severe acting out, very poor attention span) can be reduced or eliminated. In such circumstances, taking the medication allows the child to participate more fully in her academic challenges. It does not make the child "smarter"; rather, the child is more likely to access the information presented to her (Richardson et al., 1988). Additionally, it should be emphasized that medications, particularly the stimulant compounds (see Table 4.1) are unlikely to significantly improve the child's overall academic skills (i.e., writing, reading, arithmetic) in the long term if the child does not possess the innate capacity to perform these skills. It is unlikely that any drug will make up for gross deficiencies in these areas.

SUMMARIES

The efficacy of medications in the aforementioned populations is both a reason for optimism and a caution for use. It is encouraging that neuroscientists are conducting sound research to better understand the pathophysiologic bases for aberrant cognition and behavior. It is important to emphasize that great caution is needed when employing drugs with serious negative side effects. The current trend toward reducing the uses of tranquilizing agents in the mentally retarded population is a good example of this movement.

Caution is also advised in circumstances where medications are used without deliberate attempts to monitor possible side effects. Additionally, it is the extremely rare case in which medications alone will lead to a total normalizing of behavior and cognition in the populations described in this chapter.

DISCUSSION QUESTIONS

1. What class of medications are most commonly used in the educational setting? What is the intended use of such medications?
2. Briefly explain congenital, developmental, and acquired theories.
3. Describe two indications for medications in traumatic brain injury.
4. Briefly describe how you would go about determining if a medication trial is indicated. How would you communicate this information to the physician?
5. What are the common features of attention deficit disorder?

REFERENCES

Aman, M. Stimulant drug effects in developmental disorders and hyperactivity: Toward a resolution of disparate findings. (1976). *Journal of Abnormal Child Psychology, 4* (4), 389–410.

American Psychiatric Association. (1980). *Diagnostic and statistical manual of mental disorders (3rd ed.).* Washington, DC: Author.

American Psychiatric Association (1987). *Diagnostic and statistical manual III—Revised.* Washington, DC: Author.

Barkley, R. A review of stimulant drug research on hyperactive children. (1977). *Journal of Child Psychology and Psychiatry, 18,* 137–165.

Baroff, G. S. (1986). *Mental retardation: Nature, cause and management.* Washington, DC: Hemisphere Publishing.

Bates, W. J., Smeltzer, D. J., & Arnoczky, S. M. (1986). Appropriate and inappropriate use of psychotherapeutic medications for institutionalized mentally retarded persons. *American Journal of Mental Deficiency, 90,* 363–370.

Bishop, D. V. M. The causes of specific developmental language disorders ("developmental dysphasia"). (1987). *Journal of Child Psychology and Psychiatry, 28* (1), 1–8.

Brink, J. D. Garrett, A. L., & Hale, W. R. (1970). Recovery of motor and intellectual function in children sustaining severe head injuries. *Developmental Medicine and Child Neurology, 12* (5), 565–571.

Brink, J. D., Imbus, C., & Woo-Sam, J. (1980). Physical recovery after severe closed head trauma in children and adolescents. *Journal of Pediatrics, 97* (5), 721–727.

Campbell, M., Anderson, C. T., & Cohen, I. C. (1982). Haloperidol in autistic children: Effects on learning, behavior, and abnormal involuntary movements. *Psychopharmacology Bulletin, 18,* 110–112.

Campbell, M., Perry, R., & Green, W. H. (1984). The use of lithium in children and adolescents. *Psychosomatics, 25,* 95–106.

Cohen, S. Educational reintegration and programming for children with head injuries. (1986). *Journal of Head Trauma Rehabilitation, 1,* 22–29.

Conners, C. K. (1971). Recent drug studies with hyperactive children. *Journal of Learning Disabilities, 4,* 476–483.

Cox, D. R., & Evans, R. W. Measures of frontal-lobe functioning in bright children. *Journal of Clinical and Experimental Neuropsychology, 9,* 28.

Delong, G. R., & Aldershof, A. L. (1987). Long term experience with lithium treatment in childhood: Correlation with clinical diagnosis. *Journal of American Academy of Child and Adolescent Psychiatry, 26,* 389–394.

Erickson, M. T. (1978). *Child psychopathology; Assessment, etiology, and treatment.* New Jersey: Prentice-Hall.

Evans, R. W., Gualtieri, C. T., & Amara, I. (1986). Methylphenidate and memory: Dissociated effects in hyperactive children. *Psychopharmacology, 90* (2), 211–216.

Evans, R. W., Gualtieri, C. T., & Hicks, R. E. (1986). A neuropathic substrate for stimulant drug effects in hyperactive children. *Clinical Neuropharmacology, 9,* 264–281.

Evans, R. W., Gualtieri, C. T., & Shear, P. K. (1987). Childhood hyperactivity. In B. C. Epanchin & J. L. Paul (Eds.), *Emotional problems of childhood and adolescence: A multidisciplinary perspective* (pp. 143–161). Columbus, OH: Merrill.

Fundudis, T., Kolvin, I., & Garside, R. F. (1979). *Speech retarded and deaf children: Their physiological development.* London: Academic Press.

Gadow, K. (1983). Effects of stimulant drugs on academic performance in hyperactive and learning disabled children. *Journal of Learning Disabilities, 16* (5), 290–299.

Gadow, K. (1986). *Children on medication* (Vols. 1 & 2). San Diego: College Hill Press.

Galaburda, A. M., Lemay, M., Kemper, T., & Geschwind, N. (1978). Right-left asymmetries in the human brain. *Science, 199,* 852–856.

Gallagher, S. S., Finison, K., Guyer, B., & Goodenough, S. (1984). The incidence of injuries among 82,000 Massachusetts children and adolescents: Results of the 1980–1981 Statewide Injury Prevention Program Surveillance System. *American Journal of Public Health, 74,* 1340–1347.

Gualtieri, C. T., Evans, R. W., & Patterson, D. R. (1987). The medical treatment of autistic people. In E. Schopler & G. B. Mesibov (Eds.), *Neurobiological issues on autism.* New York: Plenum Press.

Haarbauer-Krupa, J., Moser, L., & Smith, G. J. (1985). Cognitive rehabilitation therapy: Middle stages of recovery. In Yluisaker, M. (Ed.), *Head injury rehabilitation: Children and adolescents* (pp. 247–274). San Diego: College Hill Press, 1985.

Hensen, M. *Pharmacological and behavioral treatment: An integrative approach.* (1986). New York: John Wiley and Sons.

Jacobs, P. A., & Strong, J. A. (1959). A case of human intersexuality having a possible XXY sex determining mechanism. *Nature, 183,* 302–303.

Kavale, K. (1982). The efficacy of stimulant drug treatment for hyperactivity: A meta-analysis. *Journal of Learning Disabilities, 15,* 280–289.

Kemper, T. L. (1984). Asymmetrical lesions in dyslexia. In N. Geschurad & A. M. Galaburda (Eds.), *Cerebral dominance: The biological foundations* (pp. 75–89). Cambridge: Harvard University Press.

Kinsbourne, M. (1973). Minimal brain dysfunction as a neuro-developmental lag. *Annals of the New York Academy of Science, 205,* 263–273.

Klauber, M. R., Marshall, L. F., & Toole, B. M. (1985). Cause of decline in head injury mortality rate in San Diego County, California. *Journal of Neurosurgery, 62,* 528–531.

Klonoff, H., Low, M. D., & Clark, C. (1977). Head injuries in children: A prospective five year follow-up. *Journal of Neurology, Neurosurgery, and Psychiatry, 40,* 1211–1219.

Lehr, E. (1988). Personal communication.

LeJeune, J., Gautier, M., & Turpin, R. (1959). Etude des chromosomes somatique de neuf enfants mongoliens. *Comptes Rendus de l'Academic des Sciences, 248,* 1721–1822.

Levin, H. S., Eisenberg, H. N., & Wigg, M. D. (1982). Memory and intellectual ability after head injury in children and adolescents. *Neurosurgery, 11,* 668–673.

Light, R., Newman, E., Lewis, R., Morecki-Oberg, C., Asarnow, R., & Satz, P. (1987). An evaluation of a neuropsychologically based re-education project for the head injured child. *Journal of Head Trauma Rehabilitation, 2* (1), 11–25.

Lipman, R. S. The use of psychopharmacological agents in residential facilities for the retarded. In F. J. Menolascino (Ed.), *Psychiatric approaches to mental retardation.* New York: Basic Books.

Lou, H. C., Henrickson, L., & Bruhn, P. (1984). Focal cerebral hypoperfusion in children with dysphasia and/or attention deficit disorder. *Archives of Neurology, 41,* 825–829.

Matthews, D. (1988). Personal communication.

National Head Injury Foundation (1986). *Comparative incidence and prevalence of brain damage from trauma and other neurological disabilities.* Framingham, MA: Author.

Pasamanick, C. E., Constantinou, F., & Lilienfeld, A. M. (1956). Pregnancy experience and the development of childhood speech disorders: An epidemiologic study of the association with maternal and fetal factors. *American Journal of Diseases of Children, 91,* 113–118.

Reitan, R., & Davison, R. (1974). *Clinical neuropsychology: Current status and applications.* New York: Wiley.

Restak, R. (1984). *The brain.* Toronto: Bantam Books.

Richardson, E., Kupletz, S., Winsberg, B., Maitinsky, S., & Mendell, N. (1988). Effects of methylpnenidate dosage in hyperactive reading-disabled children: II. Reading achievement. *Journal of the American Academy of Child and Adolescent Psychiatry, 27* (1), 78–87.

Rimland, B. (1977). *Comparative effects of treatment of child's behavior (Vol. 34).* San Diego: Institute for Child Behavior Research.

Rivara, F., & Mueller, B. A. (1986). The epidemiology and prevention of pediatric head injury. *Journal of Head Trauma Rehabilitation, 4,* 7–15.

Rivinus, J. M. (1980). Psychopharmacology and the mentally retarded patient. In L. S. Szymanshi & P. E. Tanguay (Eds.), *Emotional disorders of mentally retarded persons.* Baltimore: University Park Press.

Rourke, B. P., Fisk, J. L., & Strang, J. D. (1986). *Neuropsychological assessment of children: A treatment oriented approach.* New York: Guilford Press.

Rourke, B. P., Young, G. C., Strang, J. D., & Russell, D. L. (1986). Adult outcomes of central processing deficits in childhood. In I. Grant & K. M. Adams (Eds.), *Neuropsychological assessment of neuropsychiatric disorders.* New York: Oxford Press.

Schopler, E., & Mesibov, G. (1987). *Neurobiological issues in autism.* New York: Plenum Press.

Schroeder, S., & Schroeder, C. (1982). Organic theories. In J. Paul & B. Epanchin (Eds.), *Emotional disturbance in children: Theories and methods for teachers* (pp. 153–183). Columbus, OH: Merrill.

Shapiro, K. Head injury in children. (1985). In D. P. Becker & J. T. Poulistroch (Eds.), *Central nervous system status report, 1985.* Bethesda, MD: National Institute of Neurological and Communicative Disorders and Stroke.

Solanto, M. V. (1984). Neuropharmacological basis of stimulant drug action in attention deficit disorder with hyperactivity: A review and synthesis. *Psychopharmacology Bulletin, 95* (3), 387–409.

Werry, J. S., Reeves, J. C., & Elkind, G. S. (1987). Attention deficit, conduct, oppositional, and anxiety disorders in children: II. Clinical characteristics. *Journal of American Academy of Child Adolescent Psychiatry, 26,* 144–155.

Wilsher, C. R., Bennett, D., & Chase, C. H. (1987). Piracetam and dyslexia: Effects on reading tests. *Journal of Psychopharmacology, 7* (4), 230–237.

Winogron, H. W., Knights, R. M., & Bawden, H. N. (1984). Neuropsychological deficits following head injury in children. *Journal of Clinical Neuropsychology, 6,* 269–286.

Woods, B. T. (1980). The restricted effects of right-hemisphere lesions after age one: Wechsler test data. *Neuropsychologia, 18,* 65–70.

5
Psychodynamic Theory and Practice*

MAIN POINTS

1. Psychodynamic theory views the development of the student's sense of self and autonomy as the central organizing principle of humanistic education.

2. Psychodynamic theory and education have influenced each other mutually and beneficially since the early 1900s.

3. A central theme of normal development, from the psychodynamic point of view, is the child's acquisition of a sense of trust of others, confidence in himself, and the ability to be curious and take initiative in order to learn about the self, significant others, and the inanimate world.

4. The child's confidence, initiative, and ability to learn and perform develop out of the caretaking environment and the child's innate potentials acting in combination.

5. Emotional disturbance occurs when a child experiences persistent developmental lags or excessive, prolonged subjective distress, such as anxiety or depression.

6. A student's developmental lags and subjective distress are usually associated with distorted perceptions of the self and others which are transferred to the classroom environment.

7. A careful diagnostic study of the student and his environment is crucial to discovering the primary locus of the emotional disturbance which in turn determines the appropriate treatment.

8. A wide range of psychodynamic consultation and treatment modalities are available to assist students and their caretakers and teachers. These modalities may occur in training settings, schools, clinics, and hospitals.

---

*This chapter was contributed by Charles Keith, M.D., Department of Psychiatry, Division of Child and Adolescent Psychology, Duke University Medical Center.

The recurrent confusion of contract, community, and domination fails . . . to explain the unlimited quality of people's fear of one another . . . . People fear one another, in a way that goes beyond the horror of subjection and depersonalization, because they require not simply an exchange of particular advantages and a recognition of their membership in well-defined communities but also a more radical acceptance of their own selves. They want a sign that there is a place for them in the world, a place where they can undertake certain limited experiments in self-knowledge and self reconstruction without risking material and moral disaster. (p. 97)

Roberto Mangabeira Unger, (1984)
Passion: An Essay on Personality. New York: The Free Press.

Psychodynamic theory is the study of the dynamics of the human psyche or mind. Most current psychodynamic schools of thought grew out of psychoanalytic theory, and all share certain basic principles. A central principle of psychodynamic theory as applied to education is that the child's psychic life is the nodal point of education. Thus, the ultimate usefulness of any educational practice depends on its ability to enhance the forward progression of the child's psychic life.

What is this psychic life of the child? It consists of the child's beliefs about himself in relation to others and to work tasks; the child's moral values, dreams, and fantasies; the child's sense of mastery and competency; and a collection of past feelings, experiences, and relationships that have crystallized into a character with unique coping styles. This psychic life is both conscious and unconscious; it is for the most part experienced as being inside oneself. But while it is felt to be private and inner, at the same time this psychic life is constantly being played out in the public realm including the classroom (Berlin & Szurek, 1965; Bower & Hollister, 1967; Brenner, 1973; Cameron, 1963; Ekstein & Motto, 1969; Jones, 1962; Kessler, 1966).

Psychodynamic theory and education have had a reciprocal impact on each other for over seven decades. Though the influence of psychodynamic theory has waxed and waned as other personality theories have moved across the stage of education, its place within educational psychology remains secure due to its emphasis on (1) the child's autonomy and positive sense of self; (2) the child's perception of the world and the tasks of learning; and (3) the child's developmental forces and symbolic mental processes that may enhance or interfere with learning and performance.

Psychodynamic theory began in the 1890s with the seminal discoveries of Sigmund Freud (Jones, 1953). Though Freud said he discovered nothing about children that nurses and mothers had not known for centuries, he presented to the startled scientific and educational world the news that the child's mind is not what most adults had wanted to believe. He described how the normal child has intense bodily needs and wishes, more passionate than those experienced in adult life. These needs are reinforced by the normal magical and egocentric thinking of childhood which makes the child experience his own needs as the center of his being and the pivot of his world. Most alarming, though certainly not new, was Freud's description of the child's sexual and aggressive needs and wishes (Freud, S., 1966a; Freud, S., 1966b). Freud's discoveries helped to usher in a new era of appreciation of the child's inner mental life. A new respect and understanding of the child were also reflected in the major social reforms of the era, such as child labor laws, school attendance laws, settlement house programs, the creation of the juvenile courts, and the inauguration of school social work (Levine & Levine, 1970). Dewey (Levitt, 1960), Montessori (1964), and others were breathing new life into educational philosophy and practice. Nearly every facet of the child's life in the Western world was affected by this revolution in the care and understanding of the child in the early decades of this century.

With the discovery of the child's unreasoning guilt and excessive repression of sexual and aggressive urges, early psychodynamic clinicians worked with educators to create repression- and guilt-free schools. (See Wiener [1967] for a description of Tolstoi's guilt-free school prior to Freud.) Some of these early experiments were doomed to failure unless directed by unusually gifted teachers. One reason many failed was that some guilt and repression were found to be necessary for a child's normal development and academic learning, a fact ruefully noted by Freud (1966c). These early, collaborative educational efforts, however, drew many gifted educators such as Anna Freud (1979), Aichhorn (1955), Fleischman (1967), Erikson (1959), and Redl (1966) into the psychodynamic movement. These pioneers retained their interest in education and built many bridges of understanding between psychodynamic theory and education through their prolific writings and work with educators (Ekstein, 1969).

In the 1930s and 1940s, psychodynamic clinicians became more aware of the role of the child's caretakers, usually the mother and later the teacher, in shaping the child's character, providing structure and "taming" the child's tumultuous drives (Cameron, 1963). Also, these were the years when child psychology came of age, particularly in the cognitive sphere. Psychodynamic theory and educational psychology recognized the importance of the child's naturally unfolding cognitive and intellectual abilities and how these shape and determine a child's perception of the world (Anderson, 1956; Flavell, 1963; Gelman & Baillargeon, 1983; Piaget, 1962; Watson, 1953).

NORMAL DEVELOPMENT: THE PSYCHODYNAMIC VIEW

Before examining the emotionally disturbed child's development from a psychodynamic perspective, we will look at the development of the normal child. According to psychodynamic theory, there are few qualitative differences between normal and emotionally disturbed children. Most of the differences are quantitative. For example, a disturbed child may have excessive, prolonged fears, perhaps lasting months or years, about monsters or robbers entering the bedroom at night, whereas in the normal child, these fears might exist for a few weeks and disappear with parental reassurance.

In presenting this scheme of normal development, several crucial assumptions will be made. First, it will be assumed the child described has an intact central nervous system and normal physical growth and development. Though children who are significantly damaged in their brains or bodies undergo the same psychological stages of development as normal children, a discussion of the complexities of the interaction between psyche and soma in these cases lies outside the scope of this chapter (Kessler, 1966; Kessler, Smith, & McKinnon, 1976; Koop, 1983; Work, 1979).

Another important assumption, for this discussion, is that the children described were born and raised in an "average expectable environment," which means that each child has a parent who has enough interest, sense of parental responsibility, and personal resources to give emotionally to the child. Thus, we will not be dealing in this chapter with children who have been severely brutalized, abandoned, starved, or disadvantaged by extreme poverty. Children who grow up under these cruel conditions go through a similar sequence of developmental stages as do children from more benign environments. Their problems, however, often call for special interventions which, again, would take us beyond the scope of this chapter (Graffagnino, Bucknam, Orgun, & Leve, 1970; Mattick & Murphy, 1973; Meers, 1970; Pavendstedt, 1967).

The narrower scope of this discussion is fitting since the majority of emotionally disturbed pupils in the average classroom are those who have an average expectable environment and who stray quantitatively from the normal scheme of development. On a nationwide basis, neurologically damaged and severely deprived children are statistically a small minority, though of course their problems loom large in education.

A guiding principle in the psychodynamic developmental scheme is the concept of **epigenesis** (Erikson, 1959), a term borrowed from embryology. The concept grew out of the finding that injury to a part of the embryo hampers or prevents the development of future body parts which include the damaged part in their developmental sequence. The earlier the damage to the embryo, the more future body parts are affected. As applied to human development, the epigenetic concept means that one developmental stage must reach a certain threshold of successful completion to allow the next developmental stage to unfold, and so on through the developmental sequence eventually leading to adulthood. The earlier and more massive the trauma or damage to the young child or infant, the more difficult it is for the subsequent developmental stages to unfold and be successfully completed. The fact that many individuals can surmount and master problems traceable to unfavorable earlier developmental periods through therapy, inner strengths, and changes in life circumstances points to the resilience and complexity of the human psyche but does not invalidate the epigenetic concept in human development. (For an alternate viewpoint, see Kagan, Kearsley, & Zelazo [1978].)

Stage 1: The Early Mother-Infant Matrix

The human infant is the most dependent and helpless of all young mammals. This fact underscores the crucial importance of the early caretaking environment which supplies all that the infant needs for survival, growth, and humanization. The early caretaking environment and the infant who develops within it make up the first extrauterine ecosystem, the two elements acting on each other reciprocally. To acknowledge the importance of environment, however, is not the same as saying that the infant is born a tabula rasa. Each infant enters the extrauterine world with his own unique set of coping styles. Some infants are passive, some active; some are quiet, some loud. These innate patterns have been called by various names such as basic temperament (Thomas, Birch, & Chess, 1968), activity patterns (Fries & Woolf, 1953), or autonomous ego structures (Hartmann, 1958).

In recent years it has been shown that infants also have a surprising repertoire of perceptual and communicative skills, though, again, sensitive mothers have always known this. An infant only a few days old can detect and show preference for complicated visual patterns and can distinguish his caretaker from strangers, as detected by changes in his heart and respiratory rates when the caretaker approaches for a feeding (Stern, 1984, 1985). A tiny infant moves in rhythm to the inflections in his mother's voice. Not surprisingly, infants are most responsive perceptually to the external world after a satisfying feeding and when not in a state of marked bodily tension. A tense, crying, unsatisfied infant has trouble scanning and taking in the world about him. Thus, adequate maternal† care increases the opportunity for the infant to contemplate, perceive, take in information, and exercise his inborn skills (Kagan, Kearsley, & Zelazo, 1978). The attachment that derives from these early learning experiences between the infant and mother in the first few hours or days of life has been called **bonding,** a concept roughly analogous to **imprinting** in certain animals. Failure to achieve satisfactory bonding has been shown to have detrimental effects throughout the child's early developmental stages (Klaus & Kennel, 1979), though many caution about overuse of the concept (Brody, 1981).

This very early learning about the world becomes connected in the infant's mind with a satisfied feeling state if the caretaker has performed well. Though it is always risky to impute feelings and states of mind to the infant, our empathic observations suggest that the normal, sufficiently contented infant develops a sense of confidence and trust in himself and the caretaking world which allows him to enjoy learning and performing (Erikson, 1959).

Piaget and his students have outlined in detail some of these early forms of intelligence that are subsumed under the rubric of sensorimotor stage of development. The following vignette illustrates a learning task at this stage:

> At five months, while he is trying to grasp a doll suspended from the crib, the child strikes it by chance. After his initial surprise at the result, he repeats the striking movement rather than trying to grasp the doll, and at the same time looks with interest at the doll; then he systematically practices "striking to make the doll swing again" (Wolff, 1960, p. 84).

The infant is practicing on the world and learning that he can make things happen. Of course, all of this depends on the mother being present physically

---

†In this chapter, the word **maternal** connotes the principal caretaker, be it biological mother, father, relative, day-care supervisor, or housekeeper. Increasingly in our society, the primary maternal figure is not the biological mother.

and emotionally to provide the props and a sufficiently good holding environ-ment. The infant "believes" he is really making things happen, though in truth, the mother is making it possible. The "good enough" mother realizes and accepts this, and enjoys the infant's egocentric activities (Winnicott, (1965). In these first few weeks and months of life are present all the necessary ingredients of successful learning, performing, and teaching in later school life.

Stage 2: The Autonomous Self

If learning in Stage 1 has been sufficiently successful, the infant is ready to move on to the next phase of development in which the central task is to define oneself as an individual separate from the primary caretaker. In Stage 1 the infant shows few signs of distinguishing himself from the caretaker, but Stage 2 marks a forward thrust into autonomy and selfhood. There are three developments that make this possible: (1) the onset of crawling and walking around 8–12 months of age; (2) the increase in cognitive skills such as the ability to conceive an object having a separate existence from oneself (Piaget, 1962); and (3) the vital ma-ternal support and care that encourage exploration away from the mother but not so far that the toddler cannot readily return, both physically and emotionally, when anxious and in need of refueling (Mahler, 1975). This heady plunge into the world is accompanied by the onset of language and several major, formi-dable learning tasks. As every parent knows, two central educational issues for the toddler are learning to respect the word *no* and learning to control bladder and bowels, which in our society usually occurs around 18–24 months. Thus, with the newfound freedom of movement and expressive language, the toddler paradoxically must learn for the first time to limit his natural impulses. In other words, for the infant to gain something through learning, he must also relinquish something, a basic pedagogical principle and stumbling block for many children.

Learning problems make their appearance during this stage if the child and the maternal caretaker-cum-educator develop too many conflicts within them-selves and in their relationship. There is no precise formula for the optimal learning environment for the young child, but generally it must include a proper balance of love and firmness. Too much guilt, anxiety, hostility, or indifference in the caretaker can keep her from being realistically firm, instructive, and nurturing to the toddler who is struggling to become socialized. Similarly, too much fear, hostility, and anxiety in the child, such as anxiety about the mother's absence, can inhibit the child's nascent sense of competence and skill growth.

Another development occurring at this stage can help to explain how later learning problems develop. During this early stage, the infant or toddler is taking in and laying down mental representations of the innumerable daily interactions with the maternal caretaker as a representative of the external world. The child takes in the world via the mother in a process called **internalization,** which provides the child with the necessary building blocks of his inner psychic life. All children have good and bad experiences. The more normal the child, the more predominant are the good mental representations laid down in his mind. Similarly, the more disturbed the child, the more one finds negatively tinged representations. These mental representations are the eyeglasses through which the growing child views the world. In order to live in the real world, the child must develop methods of integrating his inner world with the demands of the external world. He does so by developing his own unique combination of coping skills, habits, and defense mechanisms (Freud, A., 1936).

These marvelously complex coping skills and defenses can be adaptive or maladaptive. For instance, a 2-year-old child may overcome a fear of receiving injections from a doctor by lining up dolls or playmates and giving them play shots with great panache. Another child might try to cope with this fear of injections by becoming afraid of people who wear white uniforms and refusing to enter any building reminding him of a doctor's office. Clearly the former child's coping style would be considered more adaptive and could lead to further advances in other related social and play skills. The latter child has developed a less adaptive coping style which could in turn lead to further social isolation.

Many of these coping skills, such as the child's playing out fears in order to master them (Peller, 1954), are rather obvious and easily explainable from common sense. Other coping skills and defense mechanisms, however, are much harder to understand. Many coping devices or defenses disguise the true state of affairs within the child's mind so that what appears on the surface is really not what the child is experiencing inside. In this situation caretakers and teachers can become easily confused and misled. For example, a child who is fearful of being hurt or attacked by others will sometimes adapt to this fear by becoming like the attacker, a defense called **identification with the aggressor** (Freud, A., 1936). Such a child often becomes super-tough, combative, and pugnacious. An aggressive response to such a child may only increase the child's underlying fear and spur him on to more attacking behavior. What is needed instead is an understanding of his underlying terror. A strategy of verbalizing fears or reducing the sources of fear will lessen the child's attacking stance. Taking defenses at face value rather than understanding how they function to protect a child from inner and outer anxieties and fears is one of the most common reasons for the frustration and misunderstanding on the part of parents, educators, and therapists.

By age 2–3 the young child has clearly become separate in his own mind from his caretaker and has developed an inner psychic life with elaborate coping skills and defenses of his own making. The normal child of this age can take care of many of his bodily functions and can explore and learn about his immediate environment. Of course, he is still quite dependent on adults and will remain so for many years. Also, egocentrism and magical thinking, in which the thought equals the deed, still abound, leading the child to distort and misunderstand events in his life. For example, if a child's parent dies or disappears, the child will almost universally blame himself due to his egocentric and magical thinking. The child's reasoning goes something like this, ''My parent is gone because I am bad. It is my fault. If I were good and lovable, my parent would have stayed with me.'' This type of thinking, quite normal for a child of age 2–3, is the main reason why early parental loss creates such a high risk for future problems (Furman, 1974; Nagera, 1970; Wallerstein & Kelly, 1975; Ragan & McGlashan, 1986).

Stage 3: Sexual Identity and Conscience

Up to now, the child knows he or she is a boy or girl or, in other words, each has developed a **gender identity** and has assumed many of the cultural characteristics of a boy or a girl. The child's psychic life, however, has been taken up by such matters as autonomy, controlling oneself, and practicing language. As far as we know, a child prior to the age of 2 or 3 does not think much about himself or herself as a boy or a girl, but instead learns the cultural role through basic conditioning processes. Around age 3–4, however, a dramatic change takes place as both the girl and the boy develop wishes and fantasies about what it means to be a girl or a boy, particularly from the sexual-genital point of view. These wishes and beliefs become the foundation of one's sexual identity. As with other forms of development, growth in this stage does not occur in a vacuum but in relation to the father and mother. If a child does not have one or both parents, fantasy parents are created in his mind. These fantasy parents are usually inflated to superhuman proportions by the child's magical thinking which if left unchecked by reality experiences can create many problems for the child (Neubauer, 1960).

In this phase of learning about oneself as a sexual person, children become intensely aware of their genitals as pleasurable organs and are avidly curious about the genitals of the opposite sex. For instance, boys and girls may ask why girls do not have penises, and they may create stories of badness and punishment to account for the absence of a penis in girls. Children's avid interest in anatomy is matched by their curiosity about babies and how they are made, grow within the mother, and arrive on the scene, though the baby's actual arrival is often greeted with mixed feelings by the older child, who feels displaced. Within the normal child's tender love relationship for each parent, possessive sexual feelings toward the opposite-sex parent arise, along with rivalrous, hostile feelings toward the same-sex parent. Children's passions at this age are the most intense they will ever experience around these issues (Brenner, 1973). Understandably, children experience much psychic conflict because of these rivalrous, competitive feelings for the parent of the same sex and the sexual longings for the opposite-sex parent. This constellation of feelings and fears that all children have toward their parents has been called the **Oedipus complex,** a name derived from the play **Oedipus Rex** by Sophocles in which a man unknowingly slays his father and marries his mother. For example, frequently a boy in this stage will tell his mother that he wishes daddy would not come back from work or a trip so that the boy could marry and take care of mother. The normal parent accepts these wishes and knows that the boy also loves the father and that this stage will pass.

The normal child finally resolves these conflicts through the crystallization of conscience (superego), which reaches its peak around age 5–7 (Hoffman, 1970). The hostile, competitive feelings toward the parent of the same sex are turned against the self so that the child now experiences guilt, or the pangs of conscience, and believes that such hostile thoughts and wishes are bad. Likewise, the child's sexual possessiveness toward the opposite-sex parent is pushed into the unconscious mind by the defense mechanism of repression, which is reinforced by the pressures of conscience. Of course, only the unacceptable hostile and sexual wishes and thoughts toward the parents should be repressed, leaving the child free to express love and friendship toward both parents in everyday family life. This repression should not be so excessive and widespread that the child's intense sexual curiosity, possessiveness, and competitiveness also go underground into the unconscious and are not available to the child as he prepares to enter school. If this occurs, the child is in danger of becoming one of the many pupils who appear to be uninterested in learning and afraid to compete in the classroom, suffering from what Erikson calls a sense of inferiority (Erikson, 1959). The normal child retains an acceptable sense of initiative which allows him to feel safe in exhibiting his skills to explore the mysteries of school subjects and to create and produce in the classroom.

For an in-depth review of research concerning the development of moral values and the conscience, see the chapter "Moral Development" in Hoffman (1970). Hoffman masterfully discusses the theories of Piaget, Kohlberg, Freud, and others in this area.

Stage 4: Industriousness and the Social Self

Around age 6–7, with the development of conscience and the repression of the Oedipus complex, the boy and girl undergo dramatic changes. They become much less preoccupied with sexual matters and what their parents are doing, which allows them to turn their curiosity and mental energy toward school tasks. This crucial developmental fact explains why most children in our Western culture are ready for the structured classroom setting around age 6. It also explains, in part, why early attempts at formal academics usually fail. Of course, as any first grade teacher knows, sexual interests do not disappear entirely but become quiescent and relatively latent; hence the term **latency period** for the years between ages 6–11 (Erikson, 1959; Sarnoff, 1976).

The normal child's character structure and defense mechanisms become much more solidified and resistant to regressive pressures. Children in the developmental phase of latency become interested in rules, learn to enjoy habitual ways of doing things, and appreciate adult structure as long as it allows some freedom of thinking and does not reinforce their already strong sense of guilt. Their motor and cognitive skills have advanced so that they can manipulate tools and, as Erikson says, enjoy a sense of industry. Industriousness for the latency-age child is analogous to work in adult economic life. The child gains pleasure from making and producing in the classroom. The rewards come from the teacher and peers and from satisfying one's inner ego ideals, which can be defined as "what one wants to be." Child development observers have postulated a competency drive or an instinct to master which is also satisfied when the child works successfully (White, 1963).

As the child progresses through the latency years, his conscience becomes less rigid. Hence, he is less preoccupied with right and wrong and fears of blame.

The child moving into late latency (age 9–11) develops more give and take, learns to compromise and accepts responsibility for wrongdoing.

Throughout the latency years, boys and girls prefer their free play to be with their own sex. This helps to reduce sexual stimulation which the latency child experiences as a source of anxiety and an interference with work tasks.

The latency period also includes a major step forward in the child's conceptual skills which Piaget has described as the stage of concrete operations. To illustrate, a third grade teacher shows her pupils models of three tigers and two elephants. She asks, "Are there more animals or more tigers here?" Most of the class should answer, "More animals," since tigers are a subclass of animals. This seemingly simple cognitive task, however, is not mastered by most children until age 7–8. These emerging classification and conceptual skills can only be used for productive learning in the classroom if the child's general development is proceeding well.

EMOTIONAL DISTURBANCE AND LEARNING: THE PSYCHODYNAMIC VIEW

Using the normal developmental scheme as a reference point, we can define emotional disturbance as a disorder that arises when something goes wrong developmentally for too long. All children, of course, suffer from brief emotional disturbances in which they feel guilty, anxious, and inhibited in their work (MacFarlane, Allen, & Horzik, 1954). Hence, it is important to keep in mind the distinction between brief and "too long." This is not too difficult for the perceptive teacher who has the opportunity to work with the child over the weeks and months of the school year. More specifically, emotional disturbance can be conceptualized according to objective or subjective criteria.

Conceptualizing Disturbance in the Classroom

Objective Criteria.   Emotional disturbance may occur when the child strays too far from the normal developmental sequence for too long a time (Freud, A., 1966). Sometimes problems arise when development proceeds too rapidly (e.g., when a child undergoes pubescence at an unusually early age). Much more commonly, however, emotional problems ensue from lags in development. A child at age 8, for instance, is normally expected to show features of latency-age development as described in the normal developmental scheme. Some children age 8–9, however behave more like a younger oedipal child; they may be preoccupied with wooing the teacher and gaining her attention through seductiveness and age-inappropriate sexual behavior. Often this interferes with their ability to concentrate on the learning tasks within the classroom.

Subjective Criteria.   From a subjective point of view, a child may not experience a developmental lag but, instead, may experience too much internal suffering and distress that go on for too long. The depressed child and the obsessive child, for example, would both be regarded by this criterion as emotionally disturbed. Depression is common in childhood (Rie, 1966; Cytryn & McKnew, 1987). It can be manifested through a sad, forlorn look, preoccupation with death or injury, lackluster performance, or actual self-destructive behavior, which is more common in children than we often realize. The obsessive child often has above-average intelligence, but instead of applying his intelligence to schoolwork he may become obsessed in thinking about decisions. Children of this type may appear quite unsure when making up their minds on schoolwork and play activities, may erase their written work innumerable times trying to find just the right word, may appear rigid with themselves and others, and may have trouble showing the usual range of emotional expression (Freud, A., 1966).

With both the objective and subjective criteria, the child is the "experiencer," the carrier of the developmental imbalances and internal suffering. The psychodynamic clinician is cautious about using parent or teacher complaints to define emotional disturbance. For example, many psychodynamic clinicians have concerns about the frequent diagnosis of hyperactivity which is often based primarily on teacher rating scales. According to the psychodynamic perspective, the child's development and personal experiences are the final determiners in a decision about emotional disturbance (Rhodes & Paul, 1978). Observations and concerns of parents and teachers are invaluable indicators of the child's relationship with significant others, but can also lead the clinician astray since parents and teachers have their own modes of perceiving. A child can be mislabeled on the basis of parental, teacher, family, or school needs.

Childhood emotional disturbance in the classroom can be most clearly conceptualized if the child is in an "average expectable classroom," analogous to the "average expectable family" we hope the child was born into. The more atypical the classroom, the more the needs of a teacher or school system intrude on the pupil's normal developmental progression (Snow, 1969). For example, elementary counselors often note that particular teachers refer a large number of children for counseling. Too many referrals from a classroom may signal that the classroom teacher is in distress and needs assistance in handling her classroom or perhaps has an interfering personal problem. In such a situation, therapeutic efforts ideally should be directed to the teacher's problem, though, of course, the children could still have problems in their own right in such a classroom. Fortunately, most classrooms are "average expectable." This means that they are not ideal, nor will they ever be, but that they fall within a broad range of normal teaching and organizational styles which make up a typical public school.

Internalization and Transference

What happens when a child lags developmentally for too long or suffers too much anxiety, guilt, depression, or other internal stress? Remember that all children, especially the very young, experience developmental lags or excessive painful feelings from time to time. These ups and downs of life are experienced within the context of a relationship with someone important, usually the mother, father, siblings, caretakers, or extended family. These all-important people try to

The ups and downs of a child's life are experienced in the context of a relationship to an important caretaker.

help the child learn, become less anxious and move forward in development. At the same time, however, these important people may block the child's learning and increase his distress because of their own particular limitations or blind spots resulting from their past development and their own unique life experiences. In the hundreds of daily, caretaking interactions, the child lays down mental representations about himself and these caretaking people. For instance, one child may develop a belief that his mother is usually there to help him when he is frightened. Another child, however, may develop the belief that mother is not available and develop predominantly angry feelings around the mental representation of the mother. One child may think of fathers as generally safe and kind, and another child may believe that fathers are scary or angry.

With all children there is normally a mixture of good and bad mental representations. The more normal the child, the greater the preponderance of good representations. In the emotionally disturbed child a preponderance of negative, hostile, and fearful feelings develop in connection with these important mental representations, which are compounded by the child's own intense needs and magical thinking. These internalized beliefs in turn set up expectations within the child's mind about how others in the world will behave. A vicious spiral can result when a child's expectations lead the adult to fulfill these expectations, particularly when the adult is struggling with the same issues as the child is. Thus, a great danger in emotional disturbance is that these spirals become internalized in a semipermanent fashion. The emotionally disturbed child comes to believe that he is mean, bad, anxious, or is a poor performer, and lives out these patterns with others outside the family. This process has been described as **transference,** which means simply that the child transfers past beliefs and experiences onto new people and situations. Normal children also transfer, but they transfer generally positive expectations for themselves and others onto new situations and, hence, their transferences are usually not considered problems. Notice that in this description of the emotionally disturbed child, we have intentionally stayed away from diagnostic categories, important as they are, and have focused on emotional disturbance as a process.

What happens when an emotionally disturbed child enters the average, expectable classroom? The internalized beliefs about the self and others are transferred onto the significant people in the classroom, primarily the teacher but often fellow pupils and the learning tasks set forth for the child in the classroom (Baron, 1960). If the teacher and enough of the pupils have primarily positive outlooks or transferences, the emotionally disturbed child's transferences seem out of place and incongruent with the goals, tasks, and working relationships necessary for the functioning of a normal classroom (Pearson, 1952).

Consider the immature child who has insufficiently entered the latency period and is still struggling with the mother over control of the bodily functions, such as bowel training or speech. This child may set up the same struggles with the classroom teacher, the mother's representation in the classroom. Such a child will quickly seem out of place and out of step with his peers who for the most part will already have worked through these issues and be more interested in pleasing the teacher by doing good work and receiving realistic praise from the teacher.

Another child, experiencing more internalized suffering, might exhibit performance inhibition or depression. Many children with these behaviors have come to believe that performing and being competitive is hostile and destructive. They feel they deserve to be punished, either by others or by suffering the pangs of guilt from conscience. These children may become quite guilty and anxious when asked to perform or, if the problem is sufficiently severe, may act dumb. This particular problem is at the root of many elementary school failures, particularly in boys (Prentice & Sperry, 1965; Colarusso, 1980). The developmental lag these children suffer is not easily observable, namely the persistence of magical thinking by which they view their performance in the classroom as magically hurting someone else or themselves. The internal suffering arises out of the guilt and secondary depression from their poor performance which is viewed negatively by themselves and others.

Emotionally disturbed children who are prone to live or act out their transferences in the classroom often draw their teachers into pitfalls. Even a very good teacher may unwittingly become drawn into the transference and either act it out with the pupil or react defensively against it. Compliance with a child's transference occurs frequently in the very common situation of the class clown, who is most often a boy. This child is often intelligent and lovable in a distressing sort of way, and usually manages to be the focus of banter and laughter through his classroom antics. The teacher can sense the hostile provocativeness behind this clowning facade and often senses that she is being set up continually by the clowning pupil. Another teacher, however, may find herself unwittingly cooperating with the clowning, teasing the child in provocative ways such as saying, "Well, guess who's done it again." In other situations, a teacher may react defensively to a child's transference. When a child may view the teacher as a hostile, noncaring maternal figure, the teacher may find herself becoming irritated or angry with the child who doesn't seem to appreciate her good teaching qualities. If the teacher finds this response in herself unacceptable, she may become excessively loving and kind toward the pupil in order to demonstrate that she is not mean or uncaring but is actually very nice and loving. Needless to say, teachers who cooperate with a child's transference or react defensively to it will have trouble maintaining the proper teacher stance.

The goal of the teacher is to recognize the child's transference for what it is, to view it as a signal for help, to utilize it for classroom interventions with the pupil, and to keep the transference from pulling her off of the proper teaching stance. Recognizing a child's transference and not reacting to it blindly can by itself be a powerful intervention. Many children who show emotional disturbance in the classroom have experienced faulty, blind reactions from important figures in the past and present life. For a teacher to maintain her teaching perspective and not get caught up in the transference is often for these children a new experience which can lead to personality change and educational growth. In clinical parlance, it is called a **corrective emotional experience** when a child expects and wants, consciously or unconsciously, a particular response from an important person or situation, but instead gets another, often unexpected response. The experience has surprise value and can spur the child to productive learning and relating in the classroom.

An emotionally disturbed child may perform poorly in most classes or even for several years in a row, then suddenly hit it off with a particular teacher; his performance improves for that class or school year and sometimes thereafter. These teachers are thought of having an undefinable charisma for certain pupils (Pederson, Faucher, & Eaton, 1978). One partial explanation for their success is that they may have the intuitive ability to detect these transferences from emotionally disturbed pupils and are not pushed off base by them.

Referral and Teacher Intervention

The preceding discussion gives us some guidelines to the often-asked question, when is the best time to refer a pupil for outside help? Assuming an average expectable teacher and classroom environment, the best time to ask for outside help is, when utilizing her best teaching skills, the teacher has worked with the

Trust between the child and adult is a prerequisite for learning.

child for a sufficiently long period of time and has concluded that the progress has not been sufficient. Some teachers believe that a child should be referred as soon as a problem arises, but this early referral may prevent the teacher from understanding the transference and working with the child in the classroom. Referring a child can become a subtle form of extrusion even though the child usually remains in the classroom while receiving outside help. The danger here is that the teacher will ignore the emotional problems of the referred child. Of course, there are a number of children whose emotional distress is obvious and who need referral when the problem is first noted. But after a referral, it is important that the teacher remain interested in working with the child's problems and look upon the referral as an opportunity to develop new insights rather than a chance to have someone else take over or take away the problem.

Take the following case, for example. Masturbation by both boys and girls is a relatively common issue in elementary classrooms. Having approached a consultant, a second grade teacher stated that a girl was obviously masturbating to the point that it was distracting to the teacher and the girl's peers and was interfering with her concentration. The teacher felt certain that this was a problem requiring referral and was out of her domain. Hence, she was surprised when the consultant asked what she had tried so far to help the girl with the problem. There followed a discussion of whether it was possible or even proper for a teacher to address such a problem with a classroom pupil. When the two concluded that it is all right for the teacher to address any issue which is interfering with a child's learning in the classroom, the consultant suggested that the teacher go back and talk with the child about the masturbatory activity to make sure the child was consciously aware of what she was doing and to suggest that she might do this at home in privacy rather than in the classroom.

In addition to wondering to what extent they should get involved with a child's emotional problems, some teachers believe that there are specific solutions to those problems. They may want to be told specifically what to do with particular children in their classrooms. By focusing on the teachers' knowledge of their pupils, psychodynamic clinicians try to assist teachers to gain insight into their own techniques rather than offering a list of "how to's" which may have little relevance in the particular classroom environment. Such "how to" lists may foster a teacher's sense of inferiority and prevent her from using her own skills and classroom techniques. These techniques emerge and become usable when a teacher feels that she understands a situation, a child, or a problem more clearly (Berlin & Szurek, 1965). Average and better-than-average classroom teachers usually have a large repertoire of learned and intuitive techniques but are often hesitant to use them because of their own anxieties about a child with problems or a belief that it is not proper for them to be actively involved with an emotionally disturbed pupil. This is one of the greatest dangers of labeling a child as emotionally disturbed: not that the child will be physically extruded from the classroom (only a minority are) but that the teacher will not feel free to work with the child so labeled (Minuchin & Shapiro, 1983). Being told specifically what to do by a consultant is sometimes misread by the teacher as a subtle suggestion that she not act and be herself with the child. It may be that what she is told to do is not really suitable for her and her teaching style. Once a teacher feels free to say what is really on her mind about the pupil in question, she can come up with creative ideas to help the child and create a climate for change and growth in the classroom. If a teacher remains fixated on the level of "tell me how to do it," this may indicate that she is not developing professionally.

Teachers and all those who work with children must be constantly aware of the natural impulse to cure or rescue the child. This has been called the "rescue fantasy" by clinicians. The teacher's main goal in the regular classroom is to free up and protect the child's learning process. This focus on protecting and fostering learning helps keep the teacher from wandering into areas of the child's emotional life, such as relationships with parents, that are not clearly related to learning. Delving into a child's relationship with a parent can stir up tumultuous, anxious feelings and fantasies that the child may then attach to the teacher. In the child's mind, the teacher may then be viewed as a parent and some of the advantages of the relatively neutral, objective teaching role will be lost.

The following vignette illustrates how a teacher was able to help ensure that both she and the child focused on educational tasks, and not family problems, in the classroom. A third grade boy entered the classroom each morning distraught, unkempt, and lashed out at those about him. The teacher was aware that this pupil was bringing anxiety and distress from his home environment into the classroom. The parents had declined the recommendation that they seek professional help for their family problems. As with all children with emotional problems in the classroom, the teacher must continue to work with the child whether or not he or the parents are seeing counselors, mental health clinicians, or other outside professionals. Rather than becoming involved with the boy's family problems, the teacher worked out a plan that allowed the boy to leave his problems at the door. By talking with the boy for a minute or two after he got off the school bus, the teacher could appraise how the student was feeling, what kind of morning it was going to be in the classroom, and whether the child would be able to remain on top of his problems. Or, at the classroom door the teacher would chat with the boy a moment or two while the other children filed past. In this way the teacher was helping this boy build a psychic wall between his problems at home and the classroom where he needed to have his mind more at ease in order to concentrate on the learning tasks.

MISCONCEPTIONS ABOUT PSYCHODYNAMIC THEORY

With the preceding skeletal outline of the psychodynamic development of the normal child and that of the emotionally disturbed child freshly in mind, we can address several common misconceptions which educators often have and which appear in some educational texts. In reviewing these misconceptions, we will see how important the distinction is between theory and how some people put a theory into practice. All the following misconceptions have been stated and practiced by psychodynamic clinicians. Fortunately, theory does not stand or fall by how it is put into practice.

Misconception #1: Psychodynamic Theory Merely Seeks to Diagnose and Label.   Diagnoses and labels are not ends in themselves but are merely general summations of one's detailed understanding of a child's development and how the child is currently functioning internally and in relation to the external world. The use of labels implies that there are important differences between, for instance, a child diagnosed as **autistic** and another child diagnosed as **psychoneurotic.** By analogy it is important to know that a car is a Ford in order to fix it and order the right parts, but it does not tell you what to do. Knowing a child has a bad cough does not tell you whether he has tuberculosis or a cold. A diagnosis is the main heading of a more detailed outline. The various outlines are based on data and observations collected over time and organized to form a scientifically valid conceptual scheme.

Of course, diagnoses do not automatically tell us what to do to help a child since in treatment or in educating one must constantly move from a general conceptual scheme into the concrete world of motivation, individuality, and the thorny issue of what is realistic and what isn't. Thus, a label by itself is not enough, but it does convey important information. Even people who recognize the value of labels, however, may fear that people will be reduced to their labels, or stereotyped according to them. For example, a child's race might not be mentioned in a treatment conference for fear it might "label the child." But leaving out such a vital piece of information may end up doing the child a disservice. The same principle applies to outlawing the use of IQ tests. Some wish to discard diagnostic understanding entirely because of its past misuses and replace it with other schemes which are often related more to administrative experience than the child's needs. Such schemes appeal because of their simplicity but are unlikely to further our understanding of the child.

Misconception #2: Psychodynamic Theory Places Too Much Emphasis on the Intrapsychic Life of the Child.   In one textbook, psychodynamic theory was depicted by a picture of a child surrounded by arrows pointing out from his body to represent his interactions with the outside world; these arrows were cut off, so that the child appeared as if in a vacuum. This diagram was intended to show that psychodynamic theory focuses only on the inner workings of the child's mind and pays no attention to the child's external world. The developmental scheme outlined earlier should help to dispel this notion. There is no fetus without a surrounding mother; there is no infant without a holding, caretaking environment; there is no aggressive or sexual wish without someone or something in the real world who is or once was a target of the wish; there is no real learning without a teacher. Currently, educational theorists are scrutinizing the educational ecosystems of the child and their potential for good or harm (Mortimore, Ansten, Rutter, & Mangham, 1979). Likewise, in recent decades, psychodynamic theorists have focused on the child's interaction with the caretaking environment (Winnicott, 1965).

Misconception #3: Psychodynamic Theory Places the Burden of Change on the Child Rather Than the System.   As a blanket statement, this is incorrect. It would be unethical and unrealistic to prescribe treatment for a child because he is upset at having to spend 7 hours a day in a destructive classroom, or the rest of the day in a grossly destructive home, without taking steps to improve the child's environment. On the other hand, in the reality of everyday life some situations cannot be changed sufficiently, so emotionally disturbed children may have to be helped to adapt to a less-than-optimal situation. More commonly a child has problems with an adequate classroom or family setting because of his distorted perceptions of the external world. The child in this situation may be asked to change his perceptions through some type of therapy or educational intervention while the external world essentially holds steady. Clearly what is needed is a thorough diagnostic understanding of where the problem is and where the potential for change lies. The assumption that only one part of a system must always assume responsibility for change is a simplistic notion in a complicated world. This notion can actually depreciate the potential for change within the child. Often responsibility is equated with blame by the parties involved. To develop a sense of responsibility for oneself and one's actions is a worthy goal. To confuse it with being blamed or criticized may deprive a child or a parent of a crucial and necessary developmental step.

Misconception #4: Psychodynamic Theory Places Too Much Emphasis on the Past.   The developmental approach we have outlined illustrates how the past is only known and lived out in the present. Understanding how the past is being lived out in the present permits one to take steps to work with the child in the here and now in order to eventually alter the child's perception of his past life.

EDUCATIONAL AND THERAPEUTIC INTERVENTIONS

Many of the techniques and interventions described in this section are practiced by clinicians and educators from diverse schools of thought. Psychodynamic clinicians, however, carry out these interventions in a manner that reflects the psychodynamic point of view. Many of these interventions can be implemented in educational settings, and some are preferably performed there (Stickney, 1968).

Interventions in Educational Settings

Teacher training. Psychodynamically oriented teacher training programs stress the acquisition of self-knowledge and understanding the meaning of behavior. Through small-group seminars, tutorials, and case study approaches, all of which require a high teacher-student ratio, teacher trainees have the opportunity to understand more about themselves and discover what a powerful tool this approach can be in the classroom.

Techniques for interviewing parents and pupils are also emphasized in psychodynamic teacher training programs. At times, teachers and parents blame each other for a student's problem. This common, destructive spiral can often be interrupted by a teacher who feels confident and is nondefensive in talking with the parents (Lightfoot, 1978).

How to talk with pupils in a noncritical, open-ended fashion and yet maintain a focus on the immediate problem is a valuable technique which can be learned by teachers. This technique has been called the **life space interview,** a term first used by Redl (1959). The hub of the interview is helping the child articulate and conceptualize the issues going on in his immediate life space. The teacher helps the child to reach a preliminary closure to the problem and to verbalize the agreed upon course of action. Usually the interview is most effective when it is carried out in physical and temporal proximity to the problem. In other words, the teacher talks with the child whenever and wherever the trouble occurs.

Interventions in the regular classroom.   Because they function as caregivers, authorities, group leaders, and providers of information, teachers have the opportunity to foster a child's learning processes and to protect them from outside interference, which includes the emotionally troubled child's turbulent affects and distorted thinking. The classroom teacher has a wide range of techniques available, assuming she has both inner and outer permission to carry them out. Some of the techniques are reassurance, clarification, educative correction of distorted thinking, and teaching normal behavioral responses to peers and authority and to the pupil's learning tasks. These techniques comprise a powerful set of tools at the teacher's command (Bower & Hollister, 1967). Specific teaching strategies are described in more detail in Chapters 13 and 14, in Rhodes and Tracy (1974) and in Long, Morse, and Newman (1980).

Therapeutic tutoring and other specialized techniques. Therapeutic tutoring involves a teacher or special educator working with a child or small group of children over a period of time to help the child understand what is interfering with the academic learning process (Templeton, Sperry, & Prentice, 1967). For instance, if a child begins to daydream and look away or becomes stubborn each time a teacher presents an appropriate learning task, the teacher may talk to the child about his response and eventually the child can understand what fears are making him turn away from performing. This technique is often practiced intuitively by gifted teachers but for most it requires special training. Therapeutic tutoring is distinct from psychotherapy. Therapeutic tutoring maintains a constant focus on the learning and performing in the classroom and whatever interferes with it, whereas psychotherapy is more open-ended and delves into the child's perceptions of past relationships and his fears and fantasies about them.

Consultation. Psychodynamic consultation within a school setting has been going on for several decades (Berlin, 1979; Berlin & Szurek, 1965; Caplan, 1970; Newman, 1967). Consultants try to help teachers to understand themselves better in their work with students, parents, and colleagues; consultants avoid providing specific "how to" lists that may inadvertently foster continued dependence on others and reinforce a teacher's already sagging self-esteem. Psychodynamic consultation often requires a period of many weeks or months before a trusting, comfortable relationship is established between the consultant and the teacher. This trust can become a powerful force for change in the individual teacher, her peer group, and sometimes even the entire school environment. Because such consultation emphasizes the teacher's own enhanced sense of self and helps her feel more confident about her work, consultation sessions usually center on the teacher's own presentation of her work with pupils. This approach helps to keep the focus on the learning process in the classroom and prevents the sessions from wandering into the teacher's personal life.

Clinical psychotherapeutic work in school settings. Carrying out clinical or therapeutic work in the child's school setting has both pros and cons. Some professionals are concerned that the roles of the teacher and the mental health clinician will merge, with the mental health clinician becoming swallowed up in the school system. With agreed-upon safeguards, this need not be a problem. In rural school settings where there are large geographical distances between mental facilities and schools, mental health clinicians may travel to school settings on a regular basis to provide diagnostic and treatment services in the school setting. If the school system and the clinic are comfortable with each other and are not caught up in administrative or territorial issues, treatment programs for children can often be worked out in school settings.

Treatment Modalities in Clinical Settings

All recommendations for treatment should be based on diagnostic evaluation. The purpose of a diagnostic evaluation is not to place a label on a child or family. Diagnosis is actually short-term treatment in which the clinician, parents, and the child establish a working relationship, agree on what the problems are, and then set up a realistic treatment program. In a well-conducted diagnostic evaluation, the child and his family gain a new perspective on themselves and their situation. A diagnostic evaluation that does not go well often leaves the parents and the child feeling that they didn't learn anything and that the clinician was not in tune with them. A well-conducted diagnostic evaluation is a challenging, formidable task. It is carried out by a child psychiatrist, psychologist, social worker, or other clinic personnel through regular meetings with the child, the parents, or the family. Sometimes two or more clinicians work with the child and family; at other times one clinician performs the diagnostic evaluation alone. Sometimes psychological testing may be done to help elucidate personality patterns and conflicts in the child or parents; most clinicians try to do psychological testing selectively rather than routinely. The diagnostic evaluation concludes with the important interpretive phase in which the clinician pulls together his impressions and findings in lay language for the parents and the child and then makes recommendations for further treatment, or no treatment if none is indicated. The clinician hopes that the parents and the child have been gaining insight throughout the diagnostic evaluation so that his findings will not come as a bolt out of the blue. Many evaluations include telephone conversations or school visits with educators and talks with the child's pediatrician, social service caseworker, or other agency people involved with the family and child. In these multiple communications maintaining confidentiality appropriate to the case is important, yet at the same time clinicians must have the freedom to talk with school personnel, pediatricians or caseworkers in a frank manner, to ask questions, to share impressions and to obtain relevant information. Nowadays, complicated forms are signed by parents and clinicians to provide legal safeguards. The best safeguard of all is mutual trust among the parties involved.

For any treatment to be successful, both the parents and the child must believe it will work and that they have the emotional strength to utilize it. Often treatment recommendations are made in the face of parental or child anxieties, doubts, and resistances which may drive the parents to seek advice and consultation elsewhere. Deciding on a treatment program is a major decision for the child and parents since it usually involves a large commitment of their emotions, finances, and time. Parents often feel that accepting the treatment program is an admission that they have been bad parents or have a bad child and that they will now be liable to criticism from others and from their own consciences. Thus, an important task of the clinician is to help the parents and the child achieve a receptive frame of mind before making recommendations.

Once a child, parents, or family have completed a diagnostic evaluation and a specific treatment is recommended, then comes the problem of matching the treatment proposed with what is actually available in a particular community. Treatment is available through two primary sources. First, there are publicly funded mental health clinics and training institutions in which the treatment staff is paid by tax monies. Fees for services are usually charged in these facilities, but because salaries and operating expenses come from other sources, the patient's fees can be scaled to fit the family's income and living style. For low-income families, the fees can range down to very low amounts, such as $1 per session. One might wonder why such fees are even charged when the administrative expenses in collecting such a low fee are greater than the amount of the fee obtained. It is generally felt in our society that paying for services engenders the client's respect for the treatment modality. The other principal source of treatment for children and families is in the private sector in which the treating personnel receive much or all of their income from fees paid by the patient. These private facilities and practitioners tend to be used predominantly by middle- and upper-income socioeconomic groups or those who have adequate insurance programs.

In most settings, whether public or private, treatment is usually carried out by individuals from a variety of mental health disciplines. In other words, psychologists treat children and families in addition to performing psychological tests. Likewise, many social workers treat children as well as work with parents. In recent years, increasing numbers of graduate-level educators have been working in mental health clinics. What treatment modalities are available in a particular community depends not only on the sources of funds and personnel available but also on the particular background, training, and interests of the therapists. Some clinics and private facilities are predominantly psychodynamically oriented, others behaviorally, and many are combinations of several schools of thought.

A major problem within the mental health field today, as within education, is to maintain quality of care through the upgrading of staff and continued training of clinic personnel. Both public clinics and private facilities vary widely in the quality of care provided. Unfortunately, many communities and school systems are handicapped by not having well-trained child mental health facilities available to them.

Individual psychotherapy.   In this treatment modality, the child usually meets once or twice weekly with a therapist. In child analysis, a more intense form of psychotherapy, the child and the analyst meet four times weekly. In psychodynamic psychotherapy, the child usually initiates each session by talking or playing out whatever is on his mind. Since this talking or playing usually reveals the child's fears and defenses against these fears, the therapist is in a position to gently, and at the child's pace, put these wishes, fears, and maladaptive defenses into words. Through this working together the child develops his own observing capacity, and the therapist assists the child to gain insight into and better mastery over conflicts that are interfering with the child's development and performance in school. Since it is very important to move at the child's own speed to allow the child maximum autonomy in the therapeutic process, individual therapy usually requires long periods of time, often 1, 2, or more years. Specific problems can be worked through in short-term individual psychotherapy, lasting from a few weeks to a few months. More general character or personality problems, however, usually require longer periods of time since any significant change in a child requires time and repetitive working through of the problems. The length of time required by psychotherapy is sometimes puzzling and discouraging to schoolteachers who must continue to work with the child in the classroom while therapy is taking hold (Cooper & Wanerman, 1977; Glenn, 1978; Coppolillo, 1987).

Parent therapy.   Many types of parent therapy are conducted in clinics today. These include open-ended group work with parents and instructional sessions emphasizing parenting techniques. One important type of parent therapy involves the parents working with the child's therapist while the child is undergoing individual therapy (Sperling, 1979). The support of one or both parents is necessary for any type of child therapy to exist and be successful. In parent therapy, the parents are free to bring up their concerns about their child's therapy and any doubts or criticisms they may have of the therapist and the therapeutic process. The purpose is to help the parents put into words any resistances or anxieties they may be developing about the child's therapy. It is almost universal that, when any child undergoes individual therapy, conflicts usually involving the parents are brought into the open. Thus, the child's problems reverberate in child-parent and the parent-parent relationships; parents need an arena for verbalizing their feelings so that these feelings will not pile up to destructive proportions and threaten the child's therapy.

In some parent work, the therapist also provides instructions or suggestions to the parents concerning their techniques of child rearing. However, experience has shown that these specific suggestions are often unsuccessful until the parents have had the opportunity to work through some of their own resistances and fears in their relationship with their child. Almost all parents initially take recommendations for therapeutic work with their children as criticism of their parenting. School personnel are sometimes approached by parents who have concerns about what the clinician has told them about their child's problems and their relationship to their child's learning difficulties. When this happens, it is extremely important that the teacher hear out the parents' concerns and, assuming the teacher has confidence in the clinician or clinic working with the parents, that she gently guide the parents back to the therapist and encourage the parents to put into words their concerns about their child's therapy. Sometimes, parent therapy is recommended as the sole treatment modality, though more often it is recommended in conjunction with child psychotherapy. Parent therapy in conjunction with child psychotherapy usually continues throughout the course of the child's therapy, though in the later stages parents may be seen less often as a child assumes more and more responsibility for his own improvement.

Group therapy with children.   In group therapy a therapist, or sometimes two co-therapists, meets one to three sessions/week with a group of children. Six to eight children comprise a group since experience has shown that this is usually the maximum number of group participants that can effectively work together. The younger the children, the more the group focuses on activities that the children and therapist engage in together and discuss. The older the children, particularly as they enter adolescence, the more group therapies are focused on talking rather than playing and physical activity (Kraft, 1979). This principle applies to all types of child therapy. The younger the child, the more the therapist works with play and play metaphors; the older the child, particularly in adolescence, the more the therapist and patient can talk directly about problems.

Group therapy necessarily must focus on the group interactional processes and is particularly helpful when a child's problems center around relationships with peers. Since the group interactional processes are so important in group therapy, it is crucial that group therapists select a proper mix of children who can interact productively, maintain some group cohesiveness, and have problems which are sufficiently similar. Some groups have a specific focus and the group work is highly structured by the therapist; other groups are more open-ended and the children talk spontaneously and bring in their own activities.

Family therapy.   In the past two decades, family therapy has become an increasingly important treatment modality (Lewis, 1979; Whiteside, 1979). Family therapy focuses on the interactional relationships between the parents, target child, and siblings. Since many, if not most, learning and emotional problems arise in the context of conflictual family relationships, the child often becomes the carrier of the family problems. The general goal of family therapy is to help the family achieve insight into how it is handling family problems so that a particular child is not made a scapegoat for the family conflicts. Through family awareness, the child is freed to pursue his own interests while the other family members, usually the parents, work out their problems between themselves. If problems have become firmly internalized within an individual in the family under treatment, then individual psychotherapy must sometimes be taken up; at other times, the child's problems clear up through family therapy alone. Family therapy is a powerful treatment modality for children since in our culture the child is normally quite dependent upon the parents. Some observers, however, are concerned that at times family therapy can focus on the interpersonal problems of the parents, and the child can slip into the background. How to include the child as an active member of family therapy is an issue under discussion among family therapists today.

Educational Programs in Clinical Settings

Just as clinical treatment modalities and facilities can be located in regular educational settings, therapeutic educational programs can exist in clinical facilities. These programs include therapeutic tutoring, special classrooms usually involving a small number of children and therapeutically trained, clinically oriented teachers, educational activity groups, and consulting liaison teachers operating out of a clinical facility (Berkowitz & Rothman, 1960). One advantage of these therapeutic educational activities within clinical settings is that they are free from the usual pressures in public school systems. Thus, the teachers are often freer to do their own programming and are not bound by some of the restrictions found in public schools. At the same time, however, therapeutic educational activities in clinic settings take place in physical isolation from a normal school environment, and role conflicts between teachers and other professional disciplines can develop in a clinic setting. In the historical development of clinical settings in our country, teachers were often the last professionals to join the clinic staff and hence are sometimes viewed as junior members. In recent years, however, special educational and therapeutic educational teachers have become accepted in many clinical settings as peers of professionals in the traditional disciplines.

Day treatment programs.   Many children, parents, and families require more than can be supplied in the usual outpatient treatment modalities. At the same time, they may not require inpatient hospitalization 24 hours a day, seven days a week. Their needs, in many cases, have been met by day treatment programs (Rosie, 1987).

Within the past 25 years, concurrent with the community mental health center movement, intermediate programs have sprung up in many localities. In these programs, the child can participate in specialized school settings and group activities during the day and return to his home in the evening or on the weekends. Often these children are having considerable difficulty functioning within the regular school classroom but are not sufficiently disturbed to require separation from their neighborhood and families for long periods of time. Sometimes such programs have been difficult to establish because the usual model for hospitalization in our country has been round-the-clock, full-time hospital care. The skyrocketing cost of inpatient hospitalization, however, has forced many communities to look at intermediate day programs in a more favorable light.

Day programs may consist of only 2 or 3 hours a day of school or structured play activities with other children to full 8-hour days of complete schooling and after-school recreational activities. In many clinical settings where sufficient treatment staff are available, the children in day programs also participate in individual and group psychotherapy while the parents and families are often involved in parent therapy or family therapy. One advantage of day treatment programs is that the child may return to his home and neighborhood in the afternoons and evenings, thereby minimizing the harmful effects of extrusion. (See Chapter 2.)

Inpatient hospitalization.   The hospitalization of children has come under considerable criticism in the past decade due to some actual abuses (e.g., keeping children in poorly staffed, inadequate hospitals) and fears of civil libertarians that a child's rights may be deprived unfairly. Another criticism is that the harmful effects a child may suffer by the extrusion process may outweigh any benefits obtained by hospitalization. Though such criticisms are sometimes valid, the fact remains that the children's psychiatric hospital, if well run with adequately trained and supervised staff, has a valuable and necessary place in the spectrum of child mental health services. (Bettelheim & Sanders, 1979; Stone, 1979). Hospitalization may be indicated when removing the child for a period of time would allow all parties involved—the child, parents, and siblings—to work on their mutual problems without having to deal with the destructiveness of their usual daily interactions. A well run, adequately staffed children's psychiatric hospital has the full complement of teachers, housemothers, recreational workers, psychologists, social workers, and occupational therapists, who can, in effect, supply most of the emotional and physical needs of the child. A child may be hospitalized briefly for a diagnostic evaluation and return to his community for outpatient or day treatment. When it is felt that continued hospitalization is important for the child and the family, the child may remain for longer periods of time ranging from a few months to several years. In most hospital settings, the parents visit with their child regularly or take him home for weekends and holiday visits. Most children's psychiatric hospitals require that the parents be strong enough to support the treatment and to participate actively in parent therapy.

If the parents are not motivated, or perhaps not even available, hospital treatment facilities are often less likely to accept the child. Such children at times do better in group homes or orphanages in which they may live for long periods of time. In recent decades, some group homes and orphanages for children have been closed due to fears that the children would be harmed by prolonged institutionalization. Though some of these facilities did not benefit the children they housed, it is unfortunate that orphanages acquired a bad name since many children are best served in such institutions. Currently there is a trend in this country to clearly distinguish group homes and orphanages from psychiatric hospitals. Hospitalization implies active treatment which is time-limited, usually involving some family support for the child. Commitment to an orphanage, however, often implies that parents are not available or not fit to take care of their children. Thus, orphanages and group homes function **in loco parentis,** and children stay until they reach young adulthood. Children in group homes and orphanages are educated within the facility or, if capable, attend nearby public schools.

Drug therapy. In general, the use of drugs to treat childhood emotional problems is not as widespread or thought to be as effective as with adults. Tranquilizers such as Thorazine for psychotic episodes, antianxiety drugs such as Valium for anxiety attacks, and antidepressants for childhood depression are sometimes prescribed for brief periods of time to help children through acute crises. Occasionally, the drugs are administered over a lengthy time period. Dexedrine and Ritalin have been prescribed extensively for the symptom of hyperactivity. Psychodynamic clinicians have had misgivings about the use of drugs with children, maintaining that drugs are often prescribed in lieu of a careful understanding of a child's problems. Through proper understanding of a child's problems and supplying the necessary environmental support, education, and therapeutic treatment, most children respond without the necessity of drugs. Furthermore, some drugs have harmful side effects if taken over long periods of time. If properly used, however, within the context of a thoughtful therapeutic program, drugs can provide a valuable treatment adjunct (Gadow, 1980).

SUMMARIES

Psychodynamic theory emphasizes the importance of understanding the individual child, how the child's mental life progresses through developmental stages, and how emotional problems arising from developmental difficulties are manifested in the classroom. Through knowledge of these developmental processes and self-awareness, the teacher can bring a wide range of teaching strategies into the regular classroom to assist the emotionally disturbed student by walling off and freeing his learning from emotional problems.

The treatment modalities used by psychodynamically oriented child mental health clinicians complement classroom teaching. Though clinicians and teachers use different techniques and may have different short-term goals, both have the same ultimate goal for the emotionally disturbed child: namely, to assist the child to achieve inner freedom in order to learn and to resume normal development.

DISCUSSION QUESTIONS

1. Describe the principal viewpoints of the psychodynamic theory of development.
2. How are these viewpoints relevant to the classroom setting?
3. How are these viewpoints similar to and different from the tenets of the other personality theories described in this text?
4. Define emotional disturbance from the psychodynamic point of view.
5. Describe five ways that emotional disturbance can be manifested in the regular classroom setting. How might these emotional disturbances have arisen in the child's development?
6. What are some of the important roles and functions served by the mother and father in the development of the child? How are these different from the role and function of the teacher in the classroom? How are they the same?
7. Describe five ways that clinicians and teachers can work together to understand and help an emotionally disturbed child in the classroom.
8. List three classroom techniques that a teacher can use to assist an emotionally disturbed student and discuss each technique from the psychodynamic viewpoint.
9. What is **transference** and why is it important for the teacher to be aware of her reactions to it?
10. Describe three treatment modalities and what types of children and families might best use each modality.

REFERENCES

Aichhorn, A. (1955). *Wayward youth*. New York: Meridian Books.

Anderson, J. (1956). Child development: An historical perspective. *Child Development, 27*, 181–196.

Baron, S. (1960). Transference and countertransference in the classroom. *Psychoanalysis and the Psychoanalytic Review, 47*, 76–96.

Berkowitz, P. H., & Rothman, E. P. (1960). *The disturbed child*. New York: New York University Press.

Berlin, I. N. (1965). Some learning experiences as a psychiatric consultant. In I. N. Berlin & S. Z. Szurek (Eds.), *Learning and its disorders.* Palo Alto: Science and Behavior Books, 1965.

Berlin, I. N. (1979). Mental health consultation to child-serving agencies as therapeutic interventions. In S. I. Harrison (Vol. Ed.) & J. O. Noshpitz (Ed.-in-Chief), *Basic handbook of child psychiatry,* (Vol. 3). New York: Basic Books.

Berlin, I. N., & Szurek, S. Z. (1965). *Learning and its disorders.* Palo Alto: Science and Behavior Books.

Bettelheim, B., & Sanders, J. Milieu therapy: The orthogenic school model. In S. I. Harrison (Vol. Ed.) & J. O. Noshpitz (Ed.-in-Chief), *Basis handbook of child psychiatry* (Vol. 3). New York: Basic Books.

Bower, E., & Hollister, W. G. (Eds.). (1967). *Behavioral science frontiers in education.* New York: John Wiley & Sons.

Brenner, C. (1973). *An elementary textbook of psychoanalysis* (rev. ed.). New York: International Universities Press.

Brody, S. (1981). The concepts of attachment and bonding. *Journal American Psychiatric Association, 29,* 815–829.

Cameron, N. (1963). *Personality development and psychopathology.* Boston: Houghton Mifflin.

Caplan, G. (1970). *Theory and practice of mental health consultation.* New York: Basic Books.

Colarusso, C. A. (1980). Psychoanalysis of a severe neurotic learning disturbance in a gifted adolescent boy. *Bulletin Menninger Clinic, 44,* 585–602.

Cooper, S., & Wanerman, L. (1977). *Children in treatment.* New York: Brunner/Mazel.

Coppolillo, H. P. (1987). *Psychodynamic psychotherapy of children.* Madison, CT: International Universities Press.

Cytryn, L., & McKnew, D. H., Jr. (1987). Childhood depression: An update. In J. D. Noshpitz (Ed.-in-Chief), *Basic handbook of child psychiatry,* (Vol. 5). New York: Basic Books.

Ekstein, R. (1969). Psychoanalysis and education.: A historical account. In R. Ekstein & R. Motto (Eds.), *From learning for love to love of learning.* New York: Brunner/Mazel.

Ekstein, R., & Motto, R. (Eds.). (1969). *From learning for love to love of learning.* New York: Brunner/Mazel.

Erikson, E. (1959). Identity and the life cycle. *Psychological Issues* (vol. 1). New York: International Universities Press.

Flavell, J. H. (1963). *The developmental psychology of Jean Piaget.* Princeton, NJ: Litton Educational.

Fleischman, O. (1967). *Delinquency and child guidance: Selected papers of A. Aichhorn.* Menninger Foundation Monograph Series (Vol.1). New York: International Universities Press.

Freud, A. (1936). *The ego and the mechanisms of defense.* New York: International Universities Press.

Freud, A. (1966a). *Normality and pathology in childhood: Assessments of development.* New York: International Universities Press.

Freud, A. (1966b). Obsessional neurosis: A summary of psychoanalytic views as presented at the congress. *International Journal of Psychoanalysis, 47,* 116–122.

Freud, A. (1979). *Psychoanalysis for teachers and parents.* New York: W. W. Norton.

Freud, S. (1966a). *Analysis of a phobia in a five year old boy.* In J. Strachey (Ed.), *Standard edition of the complete psychological works of Sigmund Freud* (Vol. 10). London: Hogarth Press and Institute of Psychoanalysis. (Original work published 1909.)

Freud, S. (1966b) *Civilization and its discontents.* In J. Strachey (Ed.), *Standard edition of the complete psychological works of Sigmund Freud* (Vol. 21). London: Hogarth Press and Institute of Psychoanalysis. (Original work published 1930)

Freud, S. (1966c). *Three essays on the theory of sexuality.* In J. Strachey (Ed.), *Standard edition of the complete psychological works of Sigmund Freud* (Vol. 7). London: Hogarth Press and Institute of Psychoanalysis. (Original work published 1910)

Fries, M., & Woolf, P. (1953). Some hypotheses on the role of congenital activity type in personality development. *Psychoanalytic study of the child, 8,* 47–54.

Furham, E. (1974). *A child's parent dies: Studies in childhood bereavement.* New Haven, CT: Yale University Press.

Gadow, K. (1980). *Children on medication.* Reston, VA: Council for Exceptional Children.

Gelman, R., & Baillargeon, R. (1983). A review of some Piagetian concepts. In J. H. Flavell & E. M. Markman (Vol. Eds.) & P. H. Mussen (Ed.), *Handbook of child psychiatry* (Vol. 3, 4th ed.). New York: Wiley & Sons.

Glenn, J. (Ed.). (1978). *Child analysis and therapy.* New York: Jason Aronson.

Graffagnino, P. N., Bucknam, F. G., Orgun, I. N., & Leve, R. M. (1970). Psychotherapy for latency-age children in an inner-city therapeutic school. *American Journal of Psychiatry, 127,* 86–94.

Hartmann, H. (1958). *Ego psychology and the problem of adaptation.* New York: International Universities Press.

Hoffman, M. (1970). *Carmichael's manual of child psychology,* ed. P. Mussen. New York: John Wiley & Sons.

Jones, E. (1953). *The life and work of Sigmund Freud* (Vol. 3). New York: Basic Books.

Jones, R. (1962). The role of self-knowledge in the educative process. *Harvard Educational Review, 32,* 200–209.

Kagan, J., Kearsley, R., & Zelazo, P. (1978). *Infancy.* Cambridge, MA: Harvard University Press.

Kessler, J. (1966). *Psychopathology of childhood.* Englewood Cliffs, NJ: Prentice-Hall.

Kessler, J., Smith, E., & McKinnon, R. (1976). Psychotherapy with mentally retarded children. *Psychoanalytic Study of the Child, 31,* 493–514.

Klaus, M., & Kennel, J. (1979). Early mother-infant contact: Effects on the mother and infant. *Bulletin of the Menninger Clinic, 43,* 69–78.

Koop, C. B. Risk factors in development. (1983). In M. M. Haith & J. J. Campos, (Vol. Eds.) & P. H. Mussen (Ed.), *Infancy and Developmental Psychobiology* (Vol. 2), Chap. 13, pp. 1081–1188, *Handbook of child psychology.* New York: Wiley.

Kraft, I. (1979). Group therapy. In J. Noshpitz (Ed.), *Basic handbook of child psychiatry.* New York: Basic Books.

Levine, M., & Levine, A. (1970). *A social history of helping services.* New York: Meredith Corporation.

Levitt, M. (1960). *Freud and Dewey on the nature of man.* New York: Philosophical Library.

Lewis, M. (Ed.). (1979). Family therapy in child psychiatry. *Journal American Academy of Child Psychiatry, 18,* 1–102.

Lightfoot, S., (1978). *Worlds apart: Relationship between families and schools.* New York: Basic Books.

Long, N. J., Morse, W. C., & Newman, R. G. (Eds.). (1980). *Conflict in the classroom* (4th ed.). Belmont, CA: Wadsworth.

MacFarlane, J. W., Allen, L., & Horzik, M. P. (1954). *A developmental study of the behavior problems of normal children between 21 months and 14 years.* Berkeley: University of California Press.

Mahler, M. (1975). *The psychological birth of the human infant.* New York: Basic Books.

Mattick, I., & Murphy, L. (1973). Cognitive disturbances in young children. In S. Sapir & A. Nitzberg (Eds.), *Children with learning problems: Readings in a developmental-interaction approach.* New York: Brunner/Mazel.

Meers, D. R. Contributions of a ghetto culture to symptom formation. *Psychoanalytic Study of the Child, 25,* 209–230.

Minuchin, P. A., & Shapiro, E. K. (1983). The school as a context for social development. In P. H. Mussen (Ed.), Socialization, personality and social development (Vol. 4 pp. 197–274), *Handbook of child psychology* (4th ed.). New York: Wiley.

Montessori, M. (1964). *The Montessori method.* New York: Schocken Books.

Mortimore, P., Ansten, J., Rutter, M., & Mangham, B. (1979). *Fifteen thousand hours.* Cambridge, MA: Harvard University Press.

Nagera, H. (1970). Children's reactions to the death of important objects: A developmental approach. *Psychoanalytic Study of the Child, 25,* 360–400.

Neubauer, P. (1960). The one-parent child and his oedipal development. *Psychoanalytic Study of the Child, 15,* 286–309.

Newman, R. (1967). *Psychological consultation in the schools*. New York: Basic Books.

Pavendstedt, E. (1967). *The drifters: Children of disorganized lower-class families*. Boston: Little, Brown.

Pearson, G. (1952). A survey of learning difficulties in children. *Psychoanalytic Study of the Child, 7*, 322–385.

Pederson, E., Faucher, T. A., & Eaton, W. (1978). A new perspective on the effects of first grade teachers on children's subsequent adult status. *Harvard Educational Review, 48*, 1–31.

Peller, L. (1954). Libidinal phases, ego development and play. *Psychoanalytic Study of the Child, 9*, 178–198.

Piaget, J. (1962). The stages of intellectual development. *Bulletin of the Menninger Clinic, 26*, 120–128.

Prentice, N. M., & Sperry, B. M. (1965). Therapeutically oriented tutoring of children with primary neurotic learning inhibitions. *American Journal of Orthopsychiatry, 35*, 521–530.

Ragan, P. V., & McGlashan, T. H. (1986). Childhood parental death and adult psychopathology. *American Journal of Psychiatry, 143*, 153–157.

Redl, F. (1959). The life space interview: 1. Strategy and techniques of life space interview. *American Journal of Psychotherapy, 29*, 1–18.

Redl, F. (1966). *When we deal with children: Selected writings*. New York: Free Press.

Rhodes, W. C., & Paul, J. L. (1978). *Emotionally disturbed and deviant children*. Englewood Cliffs, NJ: Prentice-Hall.

Rhodes, W. C., & Tracy, M. (1974). *A study of child variance*. Ann Arbor: University of Michigan Press.

Rie, H. E. (1966). Depression in childhood: A survey of some pertinent contributions. *Journal American Academy of Child Psychiatry, 5*, 653–685.

Rosie, J. S. (1987). Partial hospitalization: A review of recent literature. *Hospital and Community Psychiatry, 38*, 1291–1299.

Sarnoff, C. (1976). *Latency*. New York: Jason Aronson.

Snow, R. Unfinished pygmalion. (1969). *Contemporary Psychology, 14*, 197–199.

Sperling, E. (1979). Parent counseling and therapy. In J. Noshpitz (Ed.), *Basic handbook of child psychiatry* (Vol. 3). New York: Basic Books.

Stern, D. N. (1984). Affect attunement. In J. D. Call, E. Galenson, & R. L. Tyson (Eds.). *Frontiers of infant psychiatry* (Vol. 2). New York: Basic Books.

Stern, D. N. (1985). *The interpersonal world of the infant: A view from psychoanalysis and developmental psychology*. New York: Basic Books.

Stickney, S. (1968). Schools are our community mental health centers. *American Journal of Psychiatry, 124*, 101–108.

Stone, L. A. (1979). Residential treatment. In S. I. Harrison (Vol. Ed.) & J. O. Noshpitz (Ed.-in-Chief), *Basic handbook of child psychiatry* (Vol. 3). New York: Basic Books.

Templeton, R. G., Sperry, B., & Prentice, N. (1967). Therapeutic tutoring of children with psychogenic learning problems. *Journal American Academy of Child Psychiatry, 6,* 464–477.

Thomas, A., Birch, H. G., & Chess, S. (1968). *Temperament and behavior disorders in children.* New York: New York University Press.

Wallerstein, J., & Kelly, J. (1975). The effects of parental divorce. *Journal American Academy of Child Psychiatry, 14,* 600–616.

Watson, R. (1953). A brief history of clinical psychology. *Psychological Bulletin, 50,* 321–346.

White, K. R., & Greenspan, S. I. (1987). An overview of the effectiveness of preventive early intervention programs. In J. D. Call, R. L. Cohen, S. I. Harrison, I. N. Berlin, & L. A. Stone (Vol. Eds.) & J. O. Noshpitz (Ed.-in-Chief), *Basic handbook of child psychiatry* (Vol. 5). New York: Basic Books.

White, R. W. (1963). *Ego and reality in psychoanalytic theory.* Psychological Issues (Vol. 131). New York: International Universities Press.

Whiteside, M. F. (1979). Family therapy. In S. Harrison (Vol. Ed.) & J. Noshpitz (Ed.-in-Chief), *Basic Handbook of Child Psychiatry* (Vol. 3). New York: Basic Books.

Wiener L. (1967). *Tolstoi on Education.* Chicago: University of Chicago Press.

Winnicott, D. W. (1965). *Maturational processes and the facilitating environment.* New York: International Universities Press.

Wolff, P. (1960). *The developmental psychologies of Jean Piaget and psychoanalysis.* Psychological Issues (Vol. 11). New York: New York University Press.

Work, Henry. (1979). Mental retardation. In J. Noshpitz (Ed.), *Basic Handbook of Child Psychiatry* (Vol. 2). New York: Basic Books.

6
Behavior Theory and Practice*

1. Behavior theory as applied to clinical and educational work is a general orientation that uses an experimental problem-solving approach to skill development and behavior problems.

2. The behavioral approach to treatment and education consists essentially of four steps: (a) defining desired and undesired behavior in objective terms, (b) assessing the behaviors in question using observational techniques, (c) using intervention methods based primarily on learning and the science of human behavior, and (d) evaluating the effectiveness of the treatment program using observational techniques.

3. Behaviorists view inappropriate or "abnormal" behavior as learned and maintained in the same way as appropriate or "normal" behavior. Behavior is the result of a person's interaction with her environment.

4. The principles of how behavior is learned are essential to understanding a behavioral approach to treatment. The three most basic types of learning are respondent conditioning, operant conditioning, and observational learning.

5. Assessment is an ongoing process in the behavioral approach. Assessment targets not only the observable behavior, but also the social context of the behavior and the developmental level of the child.

6. Behaviorists do not have a comprehensive classification system for psychological disorders. The limited state of knowledge about the significance of particular variables in the development, treatment, and prognosis of most behavior clusters limits the usefulness of any classification system.

*This chapter was written by Carolyn S. Schroeder, Ph.D., and David B. Riddle, Ph.D., Pediatric Psychology, University of North Carolina at Chapel Hill.

7. Respondent conditioning, sometimes called Pavlovian or classical conditioning, is a form of learning in which an unconditioned stimulus (e.g., food in mouth) which elicits an unconditioned response (e.g., chewing and swallowing), is paired with a neutral stimulus (e.g., a bell), which comes to serve as a conditioned stimulus that elicits a conditioned response (e.g., chewing without food) similar to the unconditioned response (chewing and swallowing with food). Examples of treatment techniques that rely heavily on respondent conditioning are systematic desensitization, cognitive behavior modification, and biofeedback.

8. The basic principle of operant conditioning is that behavior is a function of its consequences. The likelihood of a behavior increasing or decreasing under certain stimulus conditions is a function of the consequences of that behavior. Treatment procedures focus on the consequences of behavior as well as the influence of ecological variables.

9. Observational learning, also called modeling, imitation, or vicarious learning, plays a key role in socialization. Three important effects of observational learning are (a) the observer can learn new behaviors previously not in her repertoire, (b) the observer's behavior may be inhibited or **disinhibited** by watching a model, and (c) previously learned behavior can be facilitated by watching a model. **Self-control** (to bring behavior under internal, rather than external control) is the ultimate goal of most of the treatment techniques based on observational learning. Specific problems addressed by these techniques include impulsivity, disruptive behavior, social skills difficulties, and academic behavior.

10. Behavior theory's departure from traditional views of personality and treatment techniques has given rise to criticism and misconceptions. While no one approach to deviant behavior can provide all of the answers to questions of the etiology, treatment, and prognosis of deviant behavior, the behavioral approach has proven to be an appropriate and viable therapeutic method.

If we are to use the methods of science in the field of human affairs, we must assume that behavior is lawful and determined.

(Skinner, 1965, p. 6)

Behavior theory as applied to clinical and educational work is best defined as a general orientation that uses an experimental problem-solving approach to the areas of skill development and behavior problems. The principles and findings derived from learning and other research in the behavioral sciences are used to teach new behaviors, to increase appropriate behavior, to decrease inappropriate behavior and to alleviate psychological distress. A behavioral approach to treatment involves essentially four steps: (a) defining desired and undesired behavior in objective, observable terms, (b) assessing the behaviors in question using observational techniques, (c) using intervention methods based primarily on learning principles and research in behavioral science, and (d) evaluating the effectiveness of the treatment program using observational techniques. A behavioral approach is also concerned with effecting behavior change that is socially significant (Kazdin, 1980). Behavior therapists, and hopefully all therapists regardless of orientation, are interested in helping an individual function more effectively in her environment. The terms **behavior therapy** and **behavior modification** describe the practical application of a behavioral approach to change or create new behavior.

ELEMENTS OF BEHAVIOR THEORY

Personality Development

Behaviorists define personality as the sum total of an individual's behavior and describe it as the likelihood of an individual to behave in similar ways to a variety of situations that comprise her day-to-day living (Goldfried & Kent, 1972). The focus is on what the person **does** in various situations. No reference is made to global traits, such as "she's a strong-willed child," that "make" a person behave in a particular way. This point of view contrasts sharply with most traditional views of personality which assume a person's actions are expressions of underlying motives, needs, drives, attitudes, defenses, and traits. Behaviorists contend that a person learns to behave in a certain way through interaction with the environment. They recognize that the individual inherits certain physical traits and a unique biochemical makeup which could help or hinder her interaction with the environment, but it is this interaction that determines behavior (Bijou, 1970). Rutter (1975) uses the analogy of the development of a river to demonstrate the interaction between environment and biological endowment. The lake provides the river with its main source of water, but the river is changed and altered by minerals, pollution, and additional tributaries that it encounters throughout its course. Each interaction of the river with the environment is influenced by the last interaction.

Like Rutter's river, the child's use of her potential for various types of behavior will in the final analysis be determined by past social learning history, the current environmental situation, and the environmental consequences of behavior. Behavior patterns, such as stubbornness, bad temper, leadership, and friendliness, are not inherited; rather, they are the result of the child's interaction with her environment. She has learned to behave in a particular way. What a person **does** is the focus of the behaviorist rather than what she **is** or **has.** For example, the observation that a child races around whenever she comes into the classroom is more important to understanding the child than saying she **is** active or **has** hyperactivity.

Normal vs. Abnormal Behavior

According to the behavioral approach, most behaviors, with the exception of simple reflexes, are learned. When a functional relationship between a stimulus in the environment and a child's response occurs, learning has taken place. For example, shortly after birth, a baby learns that crying will bring relief to hunger or discomfort; likewise, the child who gets what she wants by throwing a tantrum has learned this behavior as a result of its effect on the environment. Thus, behavior labeled **abnormal** is learned and maintained in the same way as behavior labeled **normal.** The abnormality of the behavior is inferred from the degree to which the behavior deviates from the expected social norms in a particular context. Therefore, at any given time, a particular culture, society, social situation, or the subjective judgment of a particular person (i.e., parent, teacher, or even the child) can set the criteria for behavior judged as abnormal or normal.

The task of the behaviorist is to assess the conditions under which the desired or undesired behavior occurs or does not occur, and to determine what changes in the environment and/or the child's behavior can help the child learn the more socially adaptive responses. The abnormal or undesired behavior can most often be explained by past learning experiences or by the failure to receive or profit from various learning experiences.

Types of Learning

The behaviorists define learning as a relatively permanent change in behavior as a result of practice. By identifying practice as a key condition for learning, the effects of heredity, maturation, and so on are excluded. For children, however, one must keep in mind their developmental level in determining their readiness for learning particular skills. Theory and research in learning occupies a key role in psychology; but for our purposes, only the principles essential to understanding a behavioral approach to treatment of emotional/behavioral disturbance will be discussed. The three most basic types of learning are **respondent condition-**

ing (sometimes called Pavlovian or classical conditioning), **operant conditioning** (sometimes called instrumental conditioning), and **observational learning** (also called modelling).

Respondent Conditioning.   In the United States, interest in the use of conditioning with humans began with Pavlov's 1906 Huxley lecture published in *Science* under the title, "The Scientific Investigation of the Physical Faculties or Processes in Higher Animals." The initial discovery of the importance of respondent conditioning for "the mental hygiene of the school child," however, was made by a graduate student, Florence Mateer, who was taking a course from W. H. Burnham on this topic at Clark University in 1913. Her experiments constitute the pioneer study of conditioning in this country (Kimble, 1961). While trying to condition very young children, she accidentally discovered that placing a bandage over the child's eyes immediately before feeding elicited chewing and swallowing **before** food was presented. The words of her dissertation in 1918 testify in a contemporary fashion to what many teachers have observed repeatedly since then:

> The great significance of the method came to me all at once about the fourth or fifth day of my first experiments with Phil, in 1914. I learned that even acceptance of a test posture, or entrance into the experimental laboratory, was a conditioning factor and that these and other casual environmental factors had to be unconditioned through disuse before any arbitrary conditioning factor might be used as predetermined in a planned procedure. Even with babies who could not sit up, the bandage was a conditioning factor, as valuable as other stimuli in evoking response. Neither Bekhterev nor Krasnogorski prepared me for this, and, though I had read Pavlov, it took personal experience to show how significant the minutiae of an experimental setting must be. (as cited in Kimble, 1961)

Mateer's experiment is an excellent example of respondent conditioning. Food in the mouth was an **unconditioned stimulus** which reliably elicited the **unconditioned responses** of chewing and swallowing. By temporally pairing a bandage over the eyes with the presentation of the unconditioned stimulus (food in the mouth), the bandage came to serve as a **conditioned stimulus** which itself elicited a **conditioned response** (mouthing and chewing without food) which was very similar to the original **unconditioned response** (the actual mouthing and chewing of food). Mateer also noticed that Phil **generalized** the conditioned response, that is, he also swallowed and chewed in the presence of other stimuli, such as assuming the test posture and entering the laboratory. These generalized responses had to be unconditioned or **extinguished** through disuse. In other words, the experimenter had to make sure that these stimuli were never paired with food in the mouth before the conditioned stimulus (bandage) was **discriminated** by the subject so that only it elicited the conditioned response (chewing). There are many more important elements to respondent conditioning, but Mateer's experiment contains the essentials: (a) elicitation of a conditioned response by a conditioned stimulus when it has been repeatedly paired with an unconditioned stimulus which reliably has been eliciting an unconditioned response;

(b) discrimination learning by extinction of the conditioned response to generalized conditioned stimuli. These processes have lawful, or predictable, relationships to one another which are relevant to a wide variety of behaviors. There are several types of behavioral treatment today which rely heavily on respondent conditioning, such as **systematic desensitization** (Wolpe, 1969) which is primarily for treatment of anxiety reactions, **cognitive behavior modification** (Meichenbaum, 1977), **biofeedback training** (Budzynski & Stoyva, 1969), and **aversion therapies** (Rachman & Teasdale, 1969) which are used to decrease behaviors such as excessive eating, drinking, or deviant sexual behavior.

Operant Conditioning.   Early Pavlovians originally made no distinction between **classical** and **operant** conditioning. The latter term, which was originally known as **instrumental** conditioning, was derived from the work of Thorndike as early as 1898. The term emphasized that instrumental conditioning differs from classical Pavlovian procedures in that the subject's behavior is instrumental in producing reward or avoidance of punishment. But it was Skinner (1938) who made the most forceful case for distinctions between respondent and operant conditioning. Respondent conditioning, he pointed out, occurs basically by association, whereas operant conditioning is under the control of reinforcement or punishment. Also, respondent conditioning operates mainly on autonomic, or involuntary, responses such as heart rate or a startle reaction to a loud noise, whereas operant conditioning works with voluntary responses such as social behavior. Each type of conditioning is subject to a different set of laws. Another unique feature of operant conditioning is that behavioral law can be examined without reference to other organismic hypotheses such as temperament, and analyzed as single cases in free-responding situations. Skinner's approach was unorthodox when first introduced. It took 25 years before it began to have a strong impact on learning theory.

The basic principle of operant conditioning is that behavior is controlled by its consequences. In effect, a behavior can ''operate'' or have some influence on the environment and generate a consequence. Examples of operant behavior include talking, sitting quietly, attending to the teacher, having tantrums, or hitting. Procedurally, the sequence in operant conditioning or learning is as follows: (1) a child is presented with a stimulus that (2) may be followed by her response; (3) the response may have a consequence which itself acts as a stimulus to repeat the sequence at the next opportunity. This consequence then reinforces the connection between the original stimulus and the response, that is, increases the probability of the response recurring under the particular stimulus conditions. For example, a young child asks to use a toy and his friend gives it to her; in the future she repeatedly asks for toys and is given them. In this example, asking (the operant behavior) is followed by getting the desired object and thereby is reinforced. However, if her friend repeatedly says ''no'' and she stops asking, then the consequence, ''no,'' has acted as a punisher. The event following the behavior either increases (reinforces) or decreases (punishes) the probability of its recurrence. One knows if a particular stimulus is a reinforcer or a punisher only by observing its effect on behavior. Note no inference is made that a punisher has to be **aversive** or noxious. Behaviorists disagree on whether punishers need to be aversive. The problem seems to be a technical one, because some aversive events increase behavioral probabilities.

In operant conditioning, a discriminative stimulus has a higher probability of being followed by the conditioned response than do other stimuli. Likewise, when the discriminative stimulus is absent, the conditioned response is not likely to occur. For example, children may have been conditioned to be quiet when a particular teacher is in the room. When he is absent, they are no longer quiet. The teacher thus has become a discriminative stimulus for the children's quiet behavior. When this set of relationships prevails, the occurrence of the response is **contingent** upon the presence of the discriminative stimulus, and the behavior thus generated is called **operant behavior.** Operants, or behavior outcomes, themselves can be contingent stimuli for other operants so that, with the help of generalization, huge chains of behavior or habits can be formed. For instance, Skinner used the notion of **chaining** as his basic unit of analysis of language (1957).

The basic components of operant conditioning used in behavior therapy are

1. **Positive reinforcement.** Presenting a stimulus that increases the probability of a response.
2. **Punishment.** Presenting a strong stimulus that decreases the probability of a response.
3. **Negative reinforcement or avoidance conditioning.** Increasing the probability of a response that removes or avoids an aversive stimulus.
4. **Extinction.** Decreasing the probability of a response by noncontingent withdrawal of a previously reinforcing stimulus.
5. **Time-out.** Decreasing the probability of a response by contingent withdrawal of a previously reinforcing stimulus.
6. **Differential reinforcement of other behavior (DRO).** Decreasing the probability of a response by reinforcing the omission of it.
7. **Satiation.** Decreasing the probability of a response by reinforcing it excessively.

Sometimes a combination of the above procedures is more effective than any one alone. The treatment technique overcorrection (Foxx, 1978), for example, has two components: (1) gradual guidance, which stops the undesirable behavior and physically prompts desired behavior; and (2) restitution, which requires the individual to repair the disrupted environment to better than its original condition. For example, if a child throws her books on the floor she would have to pick up or be guided to pick up her books, and she would have to pick up any other objects on the floor, and perhaps sweep and mop the floor. This treatment approach probably involves punishment, avoidance, and time-out, as well as other components of operant conditioning. Thus, each basic component of operant conditioning represents a class of procedures with many variations that can be suited to a particular child's problem in a particular setting.

Until recently, operant conditioning forms of behavior therapy have focused almost exclusively on managing the consequences of behavior. Currently

the influence of ecological variables (see Chapter 9), which in operant terminology comprise the area of differential stimulus control, is receiving more attention.

Behavioral programs in applied settings such as the school are based
primarily on operant conditioning. Academics, social skills, aggressive behavior,
withdrawn behavior, and life skills are operant responses which can be increased,
decreased, maintained, or developed by altering the consequences which follow
the behavior. The environment sets the stimulus conditions for learning.

Observational learning.   Observational learning has been studied under a
variety of levels: modeling, imitation, vicarious learning, identification, copying,
social facilitation, contagion, and role playing. Observational learning occurs
when an individual observes a model's behavior, but makes no overt response
nor receives any direct consequences. New behavior is learned simply by observing or watching a model. The modeled response is assumed to be learned
through a cognitive or covert coding of the observed events (Bandura, 1977).
Three main effects of modeling can be distinguished: (1) The observer can learn
new behaviors previously not in her repertoire; (2) the observer's behavior may
be inhibited or disinhibited by watching a model; and (3) previously learned
behaviors can be facilitated by watching a model. The distinction between **learning** and **performance** is important, since the observer may learn a response but
may not perform it unless some consequence or incentive is associated with the
response. This type of learning thus includes both respondent conditioning by
learning through association and operant conditioning with performance being
affected by the consequences of the behavior.

Kazdin (1980) reported on an early study by Bandura (1965) that dem-
onstrates both learning and performance in three groups of children who observed a film where an adult modeled kicking and hitting a large doll. For one
group the model's aggressive responses were rewarded, for another the model's
aggressive responses were punished, and for a third group no consequences
followed the adult's behavior. When given the opportunity to perform the aggressive responses, those who observed the punished model gave fewer aggressive responses than those who observed the aggression rewarded or ignored.
When all three groups were offered an incentive for performing aggressive
responses, there were no differences in aggressive responses. They all **learned**
the aggressive behavior, but the consequences to the model determined whether
the aggressive responses would be performed.

Some of the factors which affect observational learning are differential
reinforcement and punishment of the model; similarity of the observer to the
model; status, prestige, power, or expertise of the model; and whether the
responses to be modeled are motor, cognitive, attitudinal, or emotional
(Bandura, 1977b). In general, imitation of a model is likely to be greater when
several models perform the same behavior, when the model is more prestigious,
has more status and expertise, and when the model is similar to the observer,
such as in age.

Observational learning has been used to desensitize fears, train social skills,
and teach new behavior (Hermecz & Melamed, 1984; Kendall & Braswell,

1985). Even in treatment procedures primarily based on operant or respondent conditioning, modeling plays an important role in helping the child understand the exact desired behaviors.

To summarize, the three types of conditioning are not fundamentally different; they are just different forms of the same basic process. What distinguishes one type of learning from the others is that the learning process responds differently to manipulation of some experimental variables. In a given learning situation, respondent, observational, and operant processes are likely to overlap. It is impossible, for example, to perform a purely operant conditioning sequence. When reinforcement occurs, there is always a chance for the reinforced responses to become classically conditioned to stimuli or cues present at the time. By the same token, isolating a pure example of classical conditioning is very difficult, since the conditioned response usually has some effect on the probability of recurrence of the unconditioned stimulus. In the complex interactions occurring in the classroom, all forms of learning may occur as part of a single teaching episode. For instance, a severe reprimand in class by the teacher might simultaneously punish a student's undesirable operant response (e.g., talking out), elicit a conditioned emotional fear response whenever the teacher is subsequently near the offending student, and serve as a model for a method of dealing with the same behavior of another child.

Human behavior is complex and even more so when dealing with behavioral and emotional problems of children who are constantly changing and developing. The research on human development, perception, cognition, affect, social interactions, and behavior genetics, as well as the learning protocols, are part of a behavioral approach to treatment (Ross, 1985). There have been a number of attempts to develop theories of behavior that integrate the different learning paradigms as well as environmental events and cognitive processes such as thoughts and beliefs. For example, Bandura's (1977) social learning theory provides a framework from which behavior in general can be explained by taking into account the multiple types of influences on behaviors that occur in the context of social development. To develop behavioral treatment programs, however, a knowledge of the different types of learning is important so that one can effectively explain how behavior is developed, maintained, and altered. Each learning paradigm offers something unique to the assessment and treatment process and, at the same time, most treatment procedures include aspects of all types of learning.

CLASSIFICATION OF PSYCHOLOGICAL DISORDERS

The purpose of a diagnostic label or classification system for psychological disorders is to group together children who have similar behaviors so that the study and understanding of the etiology, treatment, and prognosis of the behavior can be more effective. In effect, labels help to classify, sort, and put order into our worlds. With psychological or behavioral disorders, one looks for behaviors that "go together," that is, for the common denominators in the described behavior of a group of children. To have meaning, one category of behaviors has to be differentiated from another category in terms of sex distribution, age of onset, association with other problems, etiology, response to treatment, outcome, and so on (Rutter, 1975). For example, the labels **hyperactive, autistic, school phobic,** and **mildly retarded** should each describe the behavior of a group of children who have similar problems and are distinctly different from other groups of children. Unfortunately, the limited state of knowledge about the significance of particular variables in the development, treatment, and prognosis of most behavior clusters restricts the usefulness of any classification system (Quay, 1972).

While labels and classification systems are important in studying and communicating about particular problem behaviors, their true meaning and limitations often get lost in our daily use of them. Once a classification system is in use, we often fail to remember, or we simply ignore, the fact that there may be little experimental evidence to support a particular classification. Labels take on a life and meaning of their own. Soon they are used to *explain* why a child is behaving in a certain way rather than to *describe* the behavior. The child is said to run around the room *because* he is "hyperactive." A child does not do her schoolwork *because* she has "poor motivation." People use labels to assign reasons for the child's behavior and fail to look at environmental influences on the behavior. While there may indeed be a biological basis for the behavior, such as the self-biting or gnawing associated with Lesch-Nyhan syndrome (Nyhan, Johnson, Kaufman, & Jones, 1980), such occurrences are rare. Environmental influences must be manipulated to effect change even when physical correlates are found. Many responses previously considered involuntary (e.g., seizures, high blood pressure, and pain) have been altered by the environmental consequences which follow them. In short, labels do not give adequate information about the uniqueness of a child or her environment, and they do not always provide guidance in dealing with the behavior. In fact, assigning a label often takes the place of dealing with the behavior. Instead of helping a child change her behavior, we say, "Johnny can't go to school because he's aggressive," or "Mary cannot be in a regular class because she is hyperactive." Such statements imply that little can be done about behavior but accept it. The "accepting" environment then ensures the continuation of the behavior.

Behaviorists do not have a comprehensive classification system for psychological disorders. The difficulties in developing such a system are obvious, given the behavioral focus on an individual's unique interaction with the environment. Any classification system would have to take into account client and environment variables without setting universal criteria for what would be called abnormal behavior. A broad and flexible classification system is proposed by Goldfried and Davison (1976). They outline five general ways in which behaviors can be seen as deviant. Behavior problems can be the result of one or more of the following:

1. Poor stimulus control of the behavior
2. A deficient behavioral repertoire
3. A behavioral repertoire that others find aversive

4. A deficient incentive system
5. An aversive self-reinforcing system

Poor stimulus control of behavior means that the child responds inappropriately to social cues or has maladaptive emotional responses to some environmental stimuli. In the first instance, the child may have the appropriate behavioral repertoire, but she uses it at the wrong time or place. For example, when a teacher is talking with a visitor, the child might take this as a cue to talk, walk around the room, and stop working. Likewise, a child is often accidentally taught not to respond to appropriate stimuli. Many children do not respond to the first calmly stated request to be quiet, because neither positive nor negative consequences follow the children's response. When the teacher finally starts to count to 10, the children learn that they had better respond or negative consequences will follow! In the second type of poor stimulus control, intense aversive emotional reactions are elicited by objectively innocuous cues. The child starts screaming when she sees a dog, or a quiz sets the stage for a stomachache. These and other emotional reactions may be classically conditioned to stimuli either by direct or vicarious social learning experiences.

A child with a **deficient behavior repertoire** lacks the skills needed to deal with situational demands. For example, a child may have never learned to chat socially with other children, to give positive feedback to peers, to accept criticism, or to organize her time wisely. The skill deficit problem is often complicated by aversive consequences such as ridicule and rejection which result in negative subjective attitudes such as lack of confidence and anxiety (Goldfried & Davison, 1976).

A child with an **aversive behavioral repertoire** exhibits behaviors which are harmful or bothersome to others. She may know what to say or do but is excessive: for example, she talks very loudly or acts overly aggressive. She may exhibit behavior that is simply annoying to those around her; for example, she may wipe her nose with her hand or stand too close when talking to people.

Difficulties arising from a **deficient incentive system** result from the reinforcing consequences of the behavior. The individual's incentive system may be deficient or inappropriate, or the consequences available in the environment may be creating the problem. A child with a deficient incentive system does not respond to incentives such as approval which usually control other people's behavior. Conversely, the incentive system itself could be maladaptive in that the consequences sought (e.g., drugs or certain sexual practices) are harmful or disapproved of by society. The environment can also present conflicting incentive systems whereby a behavior is labeled inappropriate but inadvertently rewarded. For example, a mother may say her child should go to school yet indulge the child when she stays home. Incentive systems could also be lacking or unavailable to a person. For example, divorce often means the loss of a once available source of reinforcement for children.

A child with an **aversive self-reinforcing system** does not reinforce her own behavior. If a child views her behavior as continually inadequate or sets excessively high standards for herself, then she is unlikely to reward herself even when her performance is adequate.

By categorizing maladaptive behavior within a social learning context, Goldfried and Davison (1976) provide some guidelines for a behavioral analysis of deviant behavior. A person may have behaviors that fall in several categories, or a problem behavior may be complex enough to fall in more than one category. In either case, the system helps pinpoint those client and environmental variables that should be the targets of treatment.

VARIABLES TO BE ASSESSED

Two journals, *Journal of Behavior Assessment* and *Behavioral Assessment,* and several handbooks (Hersen & Bellack, 1976; Ciminero, Calhoun, & Adams, 1977) have focused exclusively on behavioral assessment. The assessment of specific childhood behavioral disturbances has been receiving growing attention (Mash & Terdal, 1981; Ollendick & Hersen, 1984). Refer to those works for an in-depth view of assessment techniques and procedures. In this section we will examine the relevant child and environmental variables that should be assessed when planning a behavioral program.

The ongoing process of assessment in a behavioral approach not only determines if there is a problem, but also generates hypotheses about what is maintaining the behavior and what treatment would be appropriate. Assessment can also evaluate the long-term effectiveness of a treatment program. The assessment process includes both a molecular (or specific) approach, as well as a contextual approach in determining the parameters of the behavioral disorder.

The first step in assessment is describing each problem behavior in objective, concrete, observable terms. The behavior should be defined in specific terms that allow it to be reliably observed and counted by independent observers. Descriptors such as "lazy" have to be translated into specific behaviors; for example, "the child does not get out of bed until 10:00," or "she refuses to take out the garbage, or to make her bed." Only when the **desired and undesired behaviors are described objectively** can one determine if the undesired behavior indeed is deviant. Once the behavior has been adequately described, observing antecedent and consequent events to the behavior can determine what environmental variables are controlling and maintaining the behavior. Often the antecedent and consequent events shape the type of intervention.

When a teacher or parent brings a behavior to the attention of a professional, it is often assumed that there is a problem and that the problem will warrant treatment. Children are particularly vulnerable to this assumption since they rarely have a choice in the referral process. Usually the parent, teacher, or some other adult raises a complaint or concern about a child's behavior. It is important, however, to determine if the adult's complaint or concern is a valid reflection of the child's behavior (Ross, 1980). Several studies using parent questionnaires, as well as home and clinic observations on both clinic and nonclinic populations, have found that factors other than the child's behavior contribute to parental labeling of a child as deviant (Bond & McMahon, 1984; Forehand, King, Peed & Yoder, 1975). Low parental tolerance, high expectations for child behavior, parental pathology, marital distress, and other family problems can play a major role in the parents' perceptions of their children's behavior. Assessment of these contextual variables is imperative before embarking on a program to change the child's behavior. Social context, as well as the specific aspects of the described behavior, should be considered.

Kanfer and Saslow's (1969) S-O-R-K-C model, an assessment paradigm, can guide the assessment process in integrating the specific and contextual factors which may be maintaining a child's behavior. This model allows for a thorough analysis of observable and unobservable behaviors. Unlike more rigid paradigms, it evaluates ecological, social, and cultural factors. The S in the paradigm represents the antecedent events to the behavior. These can be either internal or external stimulus events that are thought to be functionally related to the behavior. The O represents the biological or organismic variables influencing certain behaviors. In child assessment, this component also includes the developmental status of the child. R refers to the behavior of the individual. The behavior may be motoric, cognitive, verbal, or physiological/emotional. The fourth variable, K, stands for the contingency-related conditions. Factors such as the frequency and timing of responses are included under this heading. Finally, the C component refers to the events following the behavior, the consequences. The consequences may be either environmental or organismic events (Ollendick & Hersen, 1984).

In determining whether a behavior is deviant, Rutter (1975) employs nine criteria that take into account specific child and environmental variables: (1) age and sex appropriateness, (2) persistence, (3) life circumstances, (4) sociocultural setting, (5) extent of disturbance, (6) type of behavior, (7) severity and frequency of behavior, (8) change in behavior, and (9) situation specificity of the behavior. Behavior should also be assessed in terms of the social restrictions it places on the child, its interference with development, the suffering it is causing the child, and its effect on others in the environment. The addition of the physical state of the child rounds out the variables that should be given serious consideration in the assessment process. Methods that behaviorists use to assess these variables include parent interview; parent questionnaires; tests of parental skill; observation of the behavior in the clinic, home, school, or any other setting in which the behavior primarily occurs; observation of parent-child interactions or teacher-child interactions; and self-observations by the teacher parent or child. These assessment methods focus on the conditions under which the behavior occurs, the consequences of the behavior, and the frequency, duration, and intensity of the behavior. It is also important to gather information relative to the child, including physical, cognitive, social, emotional, and developmental level. Standardized tests that include normative data on children at different ages can be very helpful in this assessment. Observation of other children not having a problem can also help to define what behavior is appropriate in a given situation.

At the conclusion of a thorough assessment, some questions should be answered about the behavior. Is it a developmental problem? Are parental expectations, attitudes, or beliefs appropriate for the social situation, the age, and developmental level of the child? Are there environmental conditions contributing to the perception of the behavior or setting conditions for the behavior?

Should the child be referred for a medical evaluation? Are the consequences of the behavior creating a problem for the child, parents, or environment? Data gathered to answer these questions should provide information for defining the deviant behavior and for selecting treatment techniques. The continued assessment of the behavior and environment will determine the short- and long-term effectiveness of the program.

CLASSROOM INTERVENTION STRATEGIES

Strategies Based on Respondent Conditioning

Respondent conditioning is clearly recognized in behavioral interventions involving relaxation training, a technique originally pioneered by the physician Jacobson (1929). The basic notion is that anxiety can be inhibited by eliciting an incompatible state, namely, muscle relaxation. Identifying all of the essential ingredients to relaxation therapy is still the subject of research, but variations of this technique have been applied extensively with children. For example, it has been used to desensitize school phobia and other fears; to train aggressive delinquent girls in "stress inoculation"; to control psychosomatic asthma attacks; to control generalized anxiety attacks (i.e., fear of becoming overly anxious); to cope with stressful situations, such as fear of tests; and to control chronic headaches in adolescents.

Clinically it has been difficult to teach a "state" of relaxation to some children, since it requires them to attend to internal cues such as muscle tension. A study by Raymer and Poppen (1985) demonstrated with three hyperactive boys, ages 9 to 11, that simply teaching ten overt postures and behaviors such as slowing breathing, being quiet, and dropping the jaw, was effective in producing high levels of relaxed behaviors as measured by frontalis electromyograph (EMG) levels, self-report, and teacher ratings. The relaxed behaviors were taught through **behavioral relaxation training** which involved modeling, prompting, and feedback. This exemplifies how the three types of learning—respondent, operant, and observant—are all part of one treatment procedure. The objective nature of the relaxed behaviors made it relatively easy for the child to imitate and correct his performance, and for the experimenter to observe and consequate the child's performance. Thus, the children learned to engage in relaxed postures in school-related situations in which they were likely to display hyperactive behavior.

Chronic headaches among children and adolescents are frequent complaints, with 4.5% of preadolescents experiencing migraines and 13.3% having frequent nonmigraine headaches (Bille, 1962). The frequency of both types of headaches increases throughout adolescence, particularly in girls (Bille, 1981). Studies have shown the feasibility of relaxation training and biofeedback for chronic headaches with children as young as 8 years of age. A recent study with 16- to 18-year-olds demonstrated that a school nurse could assist students to learn to follow a taped relaxation program which could then be done at home with results equal to a therapist-assisted relaxation program done with groups of three or four students (Larson, Daleflod, Hakansson, & Melin, 1987). In a 5-month follow-up, not only were the treatment gains maintained but also the headaches had decreased even more. This work points to the feasibility of school personnel, with relatively little time, helping children with chronic headaches and thereby increasing their availability for learning.

Test anxiety, another potentially debilitating behavior, has been effectively treated in the school setting. Multifaceted programs using systematic desensitization, cue-controlled relaxation, self-monitoring, modeling, and study skills training have proven successful with 11- to 20-year-olds (Ploeg-Stapert & Ploeg, 1986). Unfortunately, it is difficult to determine what was the most significant component of the treatment package.

The study by Lazarus, Davison, and Polefka (1965) is a good example of desensitizing a 9-year-old school-phobic boy's fears through classical conditioning. First, a hierarchy of feared stimuli in the school situation was identified. Then the child was exposed to these school-related stimuli in gradually more difficult steps while incompatible anxiety-reducing stimuli, in this case the presence of the therapist, were present. Initially, the boy accompanied the therapist to the empty school on Sunday, then after school hours. Next the two stayed briefly to chat with the teacher. Within a week, the boy could stay in class a whole morning with the therapist outside the classroom door. During this period attending school was reinforced, while reinforcement (attention) for staying home was reduced. This basic procedure was replicated in another study with 50 children (Kennedy, 1965). Insistence on school attendance is an essential component in treatment of school phobia, since in phobia situations successful avoidance of the feared stimulus is itself reinforcing and may perpetuate the fear. In some cases, forced exposure promotes rapid extinction. It should, however, be used judiciously, since in some cases it could actually increase the fear.

Strategies Based on Operant Conditioning

Most classroom learning occurs in the operant conditioning paradigm. The individual educational plan (IEP) is a prime example where contingent relationships exist among students, teacher, parents, and supporting educational personnel. Low-frequency behaviors need to be increased, new skills need to be learned, and some inappropriate behaviors need to be supplanted with other more socially acceptable behaviors. These goals can be achieved through positive reinforcement, extinction, and punishment.

Positive Reinforcement Techniques.   A positive reinforcer refers to a stimulus which increases the probability of the recurrence of a response. When a new response is being shaped, immediate reinforcement usually produces a conditioned response more reliably than delayed reinforcement. In this example, continuous reinforcement is also more effective than intermittent or random reinforcement. Intermittent schedules, however, are usually more characteristic of natural reinforcement contingencies as they occur in the environment. It is thus desirable to build in tolerance for delay of reinforcement as soon as possible. The amount of reinforcement, quality or type of reinforcer, as well as the delay of reinforcement and the schedules of reinforcement, also play an important part in determining the effectiveness of a particular reinforcer for an individual child.

What types of reinforcers can be used in the classroom? **Food** and other **consumables** can be very potent reinforcers in the classroom. Some disadvantages of consumables, however, are that they are often not available in naturally occurring social settings; they run the risk of satiation; they are difficult to dispense immediately, especially to a group; and they disrupt the flow of a teaching episode while the child is distracted by consuming them. In most situations social reinforcers, such as hugs, pats, praise, smiles, attention, and nods of approval, may be less potent but more functional. The teacher must remember that social reinforcers are conditioned responses which are viewed differently by each child. Touches and eye contact may not be reinforcing for some withdrawn children or for hyperactive children whose problem is paying attention to the teacher. In some cases, information feedback may be sufficiently reinforcing, but with socially maladapted children it usually needs to be accompanied by social reinforcement, such as teacher approval. Teacher attention can be effective in modifying academic as well as adaptive behavior. Unfortunately, a teacher's attention is often given to inappropriate behavior ("be quiet", "sit down") versus appropriate behavior. A survey of public school teachers found that 77% of the teachers' interactions with their students were negative and only 23% of the interactions were positive (Madsen, Madsen, Saudargas, Hammond, & Egar, 1970). Thus, students could quickly learn that the only way to get teacher attention is to misbehave. It would be far more productive if teachers would provide positive attention and reinforcing activities when desired academic and social behaviors occur. It also would make the learning experience fun!

Tokens, or **symbolic reinforcers,** such as poker chips or points which can later be exchanged for a desired reward, are often effective with individuals or groups in the classroom. Tokens are economical, tangible, and not satiable; they also help train children to tolerate delay of reinforcement. Various academic subjects and social behaviors have served as target behaviors in token systems. Although the efficacy of token systems in classroom settings has been well demonstrated, the teacher should be aware that not all children respond to token reinforcement and that token systems are more difficult to implement than other reinforcers.

A recent study demonstrated that learning disabled youngsters with attentional deficits correctly and effectively self-administered points for sustained attention (Bowers, Clement, Fantuzzo, & Sorensen, 1985). In fact, the self-administered reinforcers were more effective than teacher-administered reinforcers. **Self-reinforcement** usually refers to determining for oneself the criteria for earning reinforcers and actually administering the reinforcers to oneself. Some studies have shown that there is a tendency for students over time to become lenient in the criteria necessary for reinforcement (Jones & Kazdin,

1981). Thus, teacher consequences may be needed to keep the students adhering to the contingencies. However, the advantages of self-reinforcement, such as involving the student directly in the contingencies of her behavior, cannot be overlooked.

Some additional methods for structuring occasions for reinforcement in student programs are priming, reinforcer sampling, group contingencies, and contingency contracting. **Priming** refers to procedures which initiate early steps in a chain of responses. Often when shaping a completely new response, the teacher may have to prompt the student to get her started. For example, if a child is learning to control her anger toward another youngster, the teacher might physically prompt her to move away from the other child by a light touch on the arm. Such priming may also facilitate learning later in the sequence. Of course, prompts need to be faded out after the criterion is met.

Reinforcer sampling may be necessary when students are likely to become satiated on reinforcers. Often the range of permissible reinforcers is restricted in the school setting. Occasionally, the teacher may have to reevaluate the value of reinforcers by recording the ones which children are still working for. This can be done by offering them a reinforcer menu and allowing them to choose preferred reinforcers (Ayllon & Azrin, 1968).

Group contingencies, or consequences dependent on the group's response, are also very effective in the classroom. Group contingencies can depend on one or several individuals within the group or on the entire group. Sometimes the classroom is divided into two competing teams, each of which can earn rewards and can earn an additional bonus for surpassing the other team or meeting a particular criterion first (Jones & Kazdin, 1980). Some advantages of this approach include the following: (1) less teacher effort since rewards are given on a group basis; (2) group contingencies can be enhanced by team competition; and (3) when peer contingencies compete with teacher contingencies, it allows this to occur in a positive way. For example, peers may reinforce each other's disruptive behavior; reinforcement contingent on group performance is not only likely to decrease the disruptive behavior but increase the appropriate behaviors targeted by the teacher. A recent study combined group-oriented contingencies with reciprocal peer management to increase math proficiency and improve classroom behavior in fifth and sixth grade students (Wolfe, Fantuzzo, & Wolfe, 1986). They converted the four distinct peer-administered operations (peer instruction, peer observation, peer evaluation, and peer reinforcement) into four separate roles: coach, scorekeeper, referee, and manager, each assigned to individual members of the treatment team. Not only did arithmetic competency and positive behavior increase, but sociometric data showed positive peer interaction trends both within the treatment group and also by their general classmates. While group contingencies have some real advantages, care must be taken that peer pressure does not get out of hand when group standards are set and reinforced.

Contingency contracting in the classroom (Homme, Csanyi, Gonzales, & Rechs, 1969) specifies, formally and in writing, the relationship between behavior and its consequences. The five key elements are detailed privileges and obligations, readily observable behaviors, sanctions for failure, bonus clauses for consistent compliance, and explicit methods for monitoring rate of reinforcers given and received. Contracts are very useful tools familiar to most teachers of the emotionally disturbed. They actively solicit the child's participation and agreement, and thus ensure that the program is fair and that the contingencies are acceptable to all parties participating in the program.

The **Premack principle** states that, of any pair of responses or activities in which a child freely engages, the more frequent one will reinforce the less frequent one. For example, if a child likes to play outside but does not like to finish her seat work, then the teacher could make playing outside contingent on completing seat work, thereby increasing seat work. Thus, a number of frequently performed behaviors such as being with friends, hobbies, or privileges can serve as reinforcers to other behaviors.

The **differential reinforcement of other behavior** (DRO) is one technique used to decrease undesirable behavior. By reinforcing all other behavior in the absence of the undesired behavior, its nonoccurrence is reinforced. One could also reinforce behavior that is directly incompatible with the unwanted behavior, thereby decreasing the frequency of the undesired behavior. For example, hyperactive behaviors such as being out of seat, running around the room, and speaking rapidly have been decreased by reinforcing with praise, tokens, and food, the desired behaviors of sitting in seat, on-task behavior, and speaking slowly (Kazdin, 1980). Suppression of behavior can also be accomplished by reinforcing behavior physically incompatible with the undesired behavior. The frequency of the behavior can be decreased by teaching more appropriate behavior that displaces the undesired behavior in the child's repertoire. For example, by reinforcing the number of arithmetic problems completed, disruptive behavior such as running around or talking to neighbors decreases as the number of completed problems increases.

Reinforcement of low response rates (DRL) provides reinforcement for reductions in the frequency of the undesirable behavior or for increasing periods of time when the behavior does not occur. The DRL (differential reinforcement of long interresponse times) schedule can completely eliminate a behavior by increasing the requirements for reinforcement. For example, a teacher could decrease thumbsucking by first reinforcing 1-minute intervals of no thumbsucking during a half-hour reading period and then gradually increasing the time interval as well as the activities across which nonsucking is reinforced. These techniques, DRO and DRL, point to the value of developing and reinforcing adaptive behaviors, even when a reinforcement program is initiated primarily to suppress undesirable behaviors.

For positive reinforcement to be effective in increasing behavior, one should deliver a highly preferred reinforcer immediately after the desired response on a continuous schedule. When the response is well established, substituting an intermittent schedule of reinforcement will enhance resistance to extinction.

The variety of reinforcers and reinforcement systems available in the classroom provides a great deal of flexibility in setting up reinforcement programs. A

Differential reinforcement of other behavior (DRO) is an effective technique for helping children develop alternatives to disruptive behavior.

program that incorporates a variety of reinforcers is likely to be more effective
than one in which few reinforcers are available. It is wise to use praise, activities,
and privileges before implementing a token economy, and praise should always
be paired with other reinforcers, since it ultimately increases the child's responsiveness to her social environment (Kazdin, 1980). Positive reinforcement is the
primary basis for behavioral techniques used in the school. Positive reinforcement programs not only increase behavior, but through differential reinforcement of other behaviors and differential reinforcement of low rates one can also
decrease or eliminate undesirable behaviors.

Extinction Techniques.   Extinction techniques consist of withholding reinforcement from a previously reinforced response. Nonreinforcement of the response
results in the eventual reduction or elimination of the behavior. Most often the
everyday use of extinction involves ignoring behavior that was previously reinforced by attention. For example, a child burps loudly in class and everyone
laughs. She continues to burp, but now the other students are instructed to
ignore the burping and may even be reinforced for ignoring. Sometimes desirable behavior is accidentally extinguished; for example, a child may never get
called on when she raises her hand. In school settings, extinction is used primarily for behaviors which have been positively reinforced. It can, however, be
used for behaviors that are maintained by negative reinforcement. These behaviors are performed to avoid anticipated aversive consequences, such as
studying for a test to avoid failure. Fear and anxiety are often conceptualized as
the basis of avoidance conditioning because people do not want to remain in the
fearful situation. Thus, it is very difficult to extinguish the fear. Derived from a

classical conditioning framework, systematic desensitization is an effective technique to gradually get the person to remain in the actual feared situation or imagine the feared situation. Kazdin (1980) points out that extinction of avoidance responses eliciting anxiety often decreases in therapy because the person talks about the fears in a safe nonpunitive environment.

On the surface it may appear that extinction of inappropriate behavior that has been positively reinforced is a simple procedure to implement, but this is far from the case in an uncontrolled setting like a classroom. First, all of the reinforcers maintaining the behavior must be correctly identified, and second, everyone in the child's environment must consistently and completely withdraw *all* reinforcement for the inappropriate behavior. Otherwise, the behavior will be intermittently reinforced, and spontaneous recovery will recur. Third, the responses may actually increase at the beginning of extinction. If the deviant behavior is inadvertently reinforced, it could actually increase. Fourth, the decrease in behavior is usually gradual, so if immediate intervention is needed, extinction may be too slow in decreasing dangerous or very disruptive behavior. Fifth, when reinforcement is no longer available, there may be side effects of anger, frustration, or aggression. To be effective, extinction is best used in combination with positive reinforcement for behaviors incompatible with the undesired behavior.

Negative Reinforcement.   Negative reinforcement refers to an increase in the frequency of a response by removing an aversive event immediately after the response is performed. Turning off an alarm to escape the loud noise or finishing work to get out of detention are examples of negative reinforcement. A behavior is performed to escape an ongoing aversive stimulus. Negative reinforcement can occur at a high rate in some classrooms; that is, the teacher may nag the children to turn in homework, make a child stay in until her work is done, or yell at a child to stop talking. However, this is not a widely used treatment technique because of undesirable side effects. For example, a child might try to avoid the person or situation that is providing the negative reinforcement. Consequently, the child could thus be missing opportunities to learn or avoid going to school.

Avoidance learning occurs when a person learns to avoid an aversive event. For example, a frown on a teacher's face stops children from running in the hall. The children stop to avoid punishment from the teacher. The behavior which reduces a threat is then negatively reinforced. Both classical and operant conditioning operate in avoidance learning. A good example of this technique involved teaching preschoolers to reduce the amount of time for morning clean-up from an average of 11.6 minutes to an average of 4.3 minutes by a "beat the buzzer" time limitation. While no consequences were provided for the children "beating the buzzer," the behavior was maintained over the school year and generalized to situations when the teacher was absent from the room.

Punishment.   Punishment refers to a decrease in response rate when the response is followed by an aversive consequence. Punishment can occur by the presentation of an aversive event (e.g., slap, reprimand, frown) or by the contingent withdrawal of a reinforcing event (e.g., time-out, response cost, fines). For example, a child is fined for every problem she misses or she is removed from the group every time she hits another child. Like reinforcement, punishment is defined by the effect it has on behavior, so an aversive stimulus for one child may not be aversive for another child.

While aversive events are part of our everyday life, one must be careful when using them in a treatment program. The effectiveness of punishment is affected by its intensity, manner of delivery (abrupt versus gradual), delay, schedule (continuous versus intermittent), source of reinforcement, timing and sequence in the response chain, and the presence of alternative reinforced responses. In general, punishment is most effective when it is intense and when it is applied abruptly, immediately, and on a continuous schedule to a response that currently is not being reinforced. It should also be introduced early in a response chain and in the presence of alternative responses that are being positively reinforced (Kazdin, 1980). Meeting all of these conditions in the classroom setting can be difficult.

Punishment has some potential negative side effects: conditioned anxiety responses, avoidance of or aggression toward the teacher by the child, and modeling of punishment by the child. Also, the child's behavior during punishment may be so aversive to the teacher that he avoids requiring certain behaviors from the child in order to avoid the child's negative response. These negative effects of punishment are not likely to occur if punishment is administered with careful planning and for well-specified behaviors. The primary criticism of punishment is that it only inhibits behaviors and does not necessarily promote desirable behaviors. It is rarely justified unless it is done in the context of appropriate positively reinforcing circumstances.

Response suppression by punishment is usually durable (i.e., it may be maintained for months). Spontaneous recovery often occurs; but when the punishment is reintroduced, suppression is more rapid. The punishment situation is usually highly discriminated by the student, and suppression may not generalize to other settings or persons unless it is specifically programmed.

Time-Out.   The removal of a positive reinforcement contingent upon some undesirable behavior is probably the most frequent form of punishment used by the teacher. Actually, different social situations define a variety of types of time-out.

1. **Contingent observation.** The child sits in the classroom where she can see others, but she cannot interact with them.
2. **Withdrawal time-out.** The adult leaves the child's environment contingent upon the child's undesirable behavior.
3. **Exclusion time-out.** The child is not allowed to participate in time-in activities.
4. **Seclusion time-out.** The child is removed to a restricted separate enclosure.

The most important feature of time-out is specifying a time period in which reinforcement is not available. In a review of the literature, Forehand and Baumeister (1976) found that time-out durations lasting between 5 and 30 minutes were most effective. The main effect of time-out may be disruption of an ongoing chain of inappropriate behavior. Effective time-out periods may be influenced by other variables, such as inhibiting responses during time-out, or how reinforcing the environment was from which the child was removed.

As noted previously, there are a number of ways to remove positive reinforcement or to "time-out" a child, and they do not all require the child's removal from the situation. Time-out also has the advantages of being brief and physically painless. To be most effective, there should be a variety of reinforcers available in the setting so that time-out from the setting is especially aversive.

Response Cost.   Response cost refers to a loss of a positive reinforcer or to a penalty involving some effort or work (Kazdin, 1980). In this procedure, there are no necessary time restrictions for available reinforcement as with other time-out procedures. In the classroom, response cost usually means a fine. For example, a child loses 5 minutes of free play for every time she talks without raising her hand. Response costs are often part of token economics, in which tokens are earned for some behaviors and lost for others. This is a useful technique because it can be part of a token system, it is easy to implement, and it is an effective yet practical way to decrease behavior. Research has shown that combining response cost with token reinforcement is most effective.

Strategies Based on Observational Learning

Vicarious **reinforcement, extinction,** and **punishment** all occur in the classroom. Children who hear praise given to other children improve their own behavior to increase the likelihood that they too will be reinforced. Children also respond to observed punishment and extinction. If they observe that no reinforcement or punishment follows certain behaviors, they are less likely to engage in those behaviors. The key to these examples is that the child observes the behavior and consequence connection, and learns the appropriate behavior without directly experiencing the reinforcer or punisher. This type of **observational learning** has served as the conceptual basis for the development of a variety of techniques used to modify behaviors. These techniques are characterized as cognitive-behavioral due to the dual emphasis on behavior and on cognitions, or thoughts. Cognitive-behavioral approaches are techniques that are "designed to alter cognitive processes in an attempt to modify clinically relevant child behaviors" (Meador & Ollendick, 1984, p. 25). Techniques which fall under the cognitive-behavioral heading include **self-monitoring, self-evaluation, self-reinforcement, self-punishment, modeling, cognitive restructuring,** and **overt or covert verbal self-instruction.** Treatment programs commonly use several different aspects of the cognitive-behavioral approach. Behavioral rehearsal or modeling has been useful in desensitization training, assertion training, and social skills training.

Self-control, which should be the ultimate goal of all conditioning techniques, is largely based on modeling and conditioned reinforcers. Self-control means that a person can reinforce herself for self-selected behaviors. Examples include leaving a room to avoid a fight, setting an alarm clock to wake up early, or jogging to stay healthy. In most cases, there is a considerable time lag between the positive consequences and the negative consequences of one's actions. In early life children's behavior is controlled largely by external standards, such as the rules of parents or teachers. The goal of self-control is to adhere to internal standards which are self-imposed and maintained by one's own rewards and punishments. This concept has alternately been referred to as **self-efficacy** (Bandura, 1977a) and **self-competence** (Routh & Mesibov, 1980).

Modeling is very important to the development of self-control because standards are largely adopted from observed models (Bandura & Kupers, 1964; Mischel & Liebert, 1966). According to Kazdin (1980), self-control patterns can be trained by five different techniques:

1. **Stimulus control.** Practicing specific responses to specific stimuli.
2. **Self-observation.** Monitoring one's own performance.
3. **Self-reinforcement and self-punishment.** Selecting one's own consequences for one's own actions, via vicarious reinforcement and rehearsal.
4. **Self-instruction.** Prompting oneself to develop and maintain the behaviors.
5. **Alternate response training.** Engaging in responses which interfere with or replace the response to be controlled or eliminated.

Role playing, a type of behavioral rehearsal, is especially advantageous for classroom settings: social interactions can be realistically simulated; each student's progress can serve a modeling function for other members of the group; and the social pressures in such settings encourage experimentation with one's newly learned behaviors. A main advantage of self-control training techniques is their range and ease of applicability. Typically, these techniques have been applied to problems of impulsiveness, deficient academics, disruptive school behaviors, and withdrawn or shy behavior.

A good example of using self-control training techniques with an impulsive hyperactive population is found in a study by Meichenbaum and Goodman (1971). These authors taught methodical work habits to hyperactive children who were in the habit of making impulsive errors. First, the experimenter modeled the tasks while continually instructing himself aloud with questions about the task, answering these questions, planning his actions, guiding his actions, and finally reinforcing himself. Then students imitated the model, first instructing themselves aloud, but later doing so without vocalizing or moving their lips. This type of self-instruction resulted in a reduction of impulsive errors compared to those of an untrained control group.

The components of the preceding study are more thoroughly outlined in a self-management training program developed by Kendall and Braswell (1985). The essential components of the program for impulsive children include self-instruction, self-rating of performance, response cost, modeling, and reward. In one of the original studies used to develop this program, Kendall and Wilcox (1980) focused on a group of 33 impulsive and hyperactive children who were 8 to 12 years old. Those children who had received self-instruction training, modeling, and response cost contingency techniques evidenced higher teacher ratings of self-control and decreased impulsivity compared to an attentional control group.

The population of children who exhibit academic deficiencies has also been the target of cognitive-behavioral strategies. Beck, Matson, and Kazdin (1983) describe an instructional package targeted to enhance the spelling performance of three emotionally disturbed children on an inpatient psychiatric ward. The program consisted of a six-page, self-instructional manual that depicted a cartoon character performing the required steps for the successful learning and recall of the spelling of word lists. The package contained numerous components, including self-assessment and self-reinforcement, and required minimal teacher involvement. Overall, the program enhanced the children's ability to spell accurately. Other studies have found improved reading comprehension and math achievement using similar self-instructional techniques, but with a model (Swanson & Scarpati, 1985).

Aggressive and disruptive student behavior has also been the focus of self-instructional efforts. A good example of such a technique for young children is the "turtle technique" (Robin, Schneider, & Dolnick, 1976). Children are taught to imagine they are turtles withdrawing into their shells, to practice muscle relaxation, and to use a problem-solving approach to generate alternative prosocial responses. A *Turtle Manual* explains the technique (Schneider & Robin, 1973).

In one of the largest self-management programs to date, Brigham, Hopper, Hill, De Armas, and Newsom (1985) demonstrated the effectiveness of a self-management program for 103 disruptive middle-school students. Components of the program included teacher and manual instruction on problem identification, self-assessment, self-monitoring, role playing, and modeling. Results of the 3-year program suggested that the self-management training procedures were effective in reducing the frequency of student detentions.

In addition to decreasing aggressive disruptive behaviors, self-management techniques have been used successfully with populations of children with social skills deficits (Plienis, Hansen, Ford, Smith, Stark, & Kelly, 1987), as well as with children who are socially withdrawn (Christoff, Scott, Kelley, Schlundt, Baer, & Kelly, 1985).

School children are not the only populations for which self-control procedures have proven successful. Recent studies have shown the effectiveness of using self-instructional techniques with school administrators and teachers. Maher and Illback (1985) investigated the effects of training four urban high school principals in problem solving with adolescents and their families. The training occurred over three sessions and involved didactic presentations, role playing, and feedback on performance. Assessment of training effects was accomplished through simulation and naturalistic settings, and revealed increases in problem-solving skills for the trainees.

Teachers experiencing job-related stress were the subjects of an intervention by Sharp and Forman (1985). Recognizing the relationship between high levels of stress and physiological, cognitive, and emotional problems, the authors developed stress inoculation training and classroom management training programs. They then investigated the effectiveness of the two programs in improving teacher affect and behavior. The stress inoculation component was modeled after Meichenbaum's (1977) model and consisted of three phases: education, skill acquisition, and application. Teachers were taught relaxation and rational restructuring, and were given the opportunity to rehearse the skills covertly and in role play. The classroom management component included the specification of problem behavior, the observation/recording of the behavior, and reinforcement and punishment techniques. Again, participants were given the opportunity to view live and videotaped modeling and to engage in role play. Results from the study suggest that both stress inoculation training and classroom management training are effective in helping teachers reduce school-related anxiety. There was no evidence for the superiority of either type of training.

The exact nature of self-control is not yet clearly understood. Several theories have tried to explain how it works, and theorists have debated the importance of external reinforcers and role models (Gross & Wojnilower, 1984; Stuart, 1972). Clearly, however, a child can be trained to manage a great deal of her own behavior without constant external controls. Conditioning programs that contain a high degree of external control should also include plans for fading the controls and moving toward self-control. This involves the technology of generalization and maintenance training (Stokes & Baer, 1977).

MISCONCEPTIONS ABOUT A BEHAVIORAL APPROACH TO TREATMENT

Behavior theory's departure from traditional views of personality and treatment techniques was a direct challenge to many long held beliefs about deviant behaviors. It is natural that questions about the behavioral approach to treatment should be asked and that misunderstandings should arise. At this time, no one approach to deviant behavior can provide all of the answers to the etiology, treatment, and prognosis of deviant behavior.

Some critics maintain that behavior therapy, or behavior modification, offers nothing different from other therapeutic approaches to changing behavior. While learning that involves the use of positive and negative reinforcement, extinction, and punishment is common in everyday life, the behavioral approach involves the systematic and consistent application of psychological principles to behavior problems. The response to be developed or changed is objectively defined and observed, and the intervention program is based on a systematic manipulation of environmental variables. The effects of the intervention are also carefully observed and evaluated. This is distinctly different from the random use of learning principles that occur in our everyday lives. Although the behaviorist approaches deviant behavior with a framework for ordering the complex data about the individual and environment, the knowledge of how to use basic psychological principles to bring about change is far from simple. A great deal of therapeutic experience and creativity is necessary to translate the principles of behavior to the clinical situation (Goldfried & Davison, 1976). The goals of

behavior therapy or behavior modification are not unlike Freud's goals of helping people love and work, but the methods of teaching those goals are distinctly
different.

A common misconception is that behavior therapists ignore the past. Behaviorists regard past learning experiences as very important in determining the
way a person responds to her environment, but rarely do the same conditions
under which the behavior was learned and maintained exist at the current time.
While behaviorists view the past as important and gather information on personal history, the treatment focuses on the variables affecting the current behavior and on providing the client with new learning experiences. Behaviorists
also have been accused of ignoring private events such as thoughts or feelings.
Behavior therapists themselves have disagreed about this issue; therefore, the
behaviorists' stand on this issue has not always been clear. Behaviorally oriented
professionals do not deny the existence of such private events as thoughts or
feelings, but they look for observable correlates of these behaviors (Ross, 1980).
The words people put to their thoughts and feelings often do not coincide with
their observable behavior. The behaviorist cautions that these subjective statements are not always reliable correlates of what a person *does*. Statements
regarding anger, joy, and frustration should not be accepted without some support from observable behavior.

Manipulation and **coercion** are words that often come up in connection
with behavior modification. The goal of the behavioral approach, however, and
hopefully of any type of therapeutic intervention, is to allow the client greater
self-control. Clients seek or, in the case of children, are brought to the attention
of a professional because they are not able to control certain aspects of their
lives. The fact that behavior therapists are effective in changing behavior does
not mean that the client is not actively involved in the change process. The
behaviorist's systematic approach to changing behavior clearly indicates that
there is no attempt to coerce people into doing things they don't want to do. It
is probably because behavior therapists take some of the mystery out of therapeutic intervention that some people see the approach as manipulative in a
coercive sense. The behaviorist teaches adaptive skills by primarily relying on the
systematic use of positive reinforcers rather than aversive consequences.

Another common misconception is that reinforcement is a form of bribery.
Some people see the use of reinforcement to increase a behavior as "buying"
the person in order to get her to perform a behavior. **Bribery,** however, refers to
the illicit use of rewards and gifts to influence someone to do something she
should not be doing. The behavioral therapist uses reinforcement to reward
socially desirable behavior. The desired behavior is usually nonexistent or at a
low level, and the systematic use of reinforcement is intended to strengthen the
behavior. The goal should always be to use naturally occurring reinforcers, such
as more time with other children for improved social skills or more time on the
playground for efficient and accurate completion of work. Extrinsic rewards or
rewards not usually available in a particular situation, such as food, tokens, or
activities, are often necessary to increase a particular child's behavior, but these
should always be faded back to the reinforcers that would naturally follow a

particular behavior. By now, the reader should understand that people don't do things because they "should"; rather, they learn under certain conditions to engage in certain behaviors because of the consequences.

Another concern with the behavioral approach is that children will refuse to do anything unless they are specifically rewarded. Actually, this rarely happens, but when it does it is usually because the parent or teacher has inadvertently reinforced the manipulative response. For example, if a child is told, "If you stop crying, you may have ice cream," she quickly learns that crying will set the stage for getting what she wants (Kazdin, 1980). Another possible reason for a child refusing to do things unless rewarded could be that she is getting only a very low level of reinforcement for other behaviors.

Teachers sometimes fear that reinforcing one child might increase the negative behavior of another child in order to get a reward. Teachers often voice this concern when a number of children in a class are on individual programs or only one child in a large class is receiving special rewards for increasing desired behavior. Such an increase in negative behavior has been reported in a classroom (O'Leary, Paulos, & Devine, 1972), but overall there has been little evidence to support this concern. Again, if the reinforcement level is generally high in the classroom, this problem is less likely to occur. On the other hand, reinforcing one child has been reported to have positive side effects on the behavior of other children. One way to avoid this potential problem is to have the target child's performance result in extra reinforcement for the entire group (Kazdin, 1980). In this way, all of the children are rewarded for a child's improved behavior, and they, in turn, are more likely to reinforce and encourage the child's behavior.

SUMMARIES

The behavioral approach is a general orientation to the clinical and educational work that uses an experimental problem-solving approach to the areas of skill development and behavior problems. Behavior, whether it is labeled normal or abnormal, is believed to be learned and maintained by the same principles. The strength of the behavioral approach lies in its insistence on defining problems in an objective manner so that they can be systematically observed and treated. The principles involved in three types of learning—classical conditioning, operant conditioning, and observational learning—were described and related to intervention strategies in the classroom setting. The specific strategies (e.g., a token system or the use of a time-out program) are less important than the scientific approach that is employed by the behaviorist which enables new methods to be tested and, consequently, new information to be generated. In essence, a behavior therapist employs an ever-changing and self-correcting approach to the treatment of deviant behavior.

1. Define behavior theory as applied to clinical and educational work.
2. Describe a behaviorist's view of personality and abnormal behavior and compare it with traditional views of personality and abnormal behavior. How do these views affect the approach to treatment taken by behaviorists and more traditional therapists?
3. Define **learning** and list the three basic types of learning discussed in this chapter. Give examples of each type of learning in the classroom.
4. Select four components of operant conditioning and, using hypothetical behavior problems, describe how each of the operant components could be used to develop new skills or change behavior in the classroom.
5. Describe the assessment process of the behavioral approach. Name at least four methods a behaviorist could use in assessing a problem behavior.
6. Give a behaviorist's response to the charge that (a) behavior therapists ignore the past, (b) behavior therapy is coercive, (c) rewarding behavior causes children to refuse to do anything unless a reward follows, and (d) if one child is reinforced, another child might increase her negative behavior to get a reward.

REFERENCES

Ayllon, T., & Azrin, N. H. (1968). *The token economy.* New York: Appleton-Century-Crofts.

Bandura, A. (1965). Influence of models' reinforcement contingencies on the acquisition of imitative responses. *Journal of Personality and Social Psychology, 1,* 589–595.

Bandura, A. (1977a). Self-efficacy: Toward a unifying theory of behavior change. *Psychological Review, 84,* 191–215.

Bandura, A. (1977b). *Social learning theory.* Englewood Cliffs, NJ: Prentice-Hall.

Bandura, A., & Kupers, C. J. (1964). Transmission of patterns of self-reinforcement through modeling. *Journal of Abnormal and Social Psychology, 69,* 1–9.

Beck, S., Matson, J. L., & Kazdin, A. E. (1983). An instructional package to enhance spelling performance in emotionally disturbed children. *Child & Family Behavior Therapy, 4,* 69–77.

Bijou, S. (1970). What psychology has to offer education—now. *Journal of Applied Behavior Analysis, 3,* 63–71.

Bille, B. (1962). Migraine in school children. *Acta Pediatrica, 136,* 1–151.

Bille, B. (1981). Migraine in children and its prognosis. *Cephalagia, 1,* 71–75.

Bond, C. R., & McMahon, R. J. (1984). Relationships between marital distress and child behavior problems, maternal personal adjustment, maternal personality, and maternal parenting behavior. *Journal of Abnormal Psychology, 93,* 348–351.

Bowers, D., Clement, P., Fantuzzo, J., & Sorensen, D. (1985). Effects of teacher-administered and self-administered reinforcers on learning disabled children. *Behavior Therapy, 16,* 357–369.

Brigham, T. A., Hopper, C., Hill, B., De Armas, A., & Newsom, P. (1985). A self-management program for disruptive adolescents in the school: A clinical replication analysis. *Behavior Therapy, 16,* 99–115.

Budzynski, T. H., & Stoyva, J. M. (1969). An instrument for producing deep muscle relaxation by means of analog information feedback. *Journal of Applied Behavior Analysis, 2,* 231–238.

Christoff, K. A., Scott, W. O. N., Kelley, M. L., Schlundt, D., Baer, G., & Kelly, J. A. (1985). Social skills and social problem-solving training for shy young adolescents. *Behavior Therapy, 16,* 468–477.

Ciminero, A. R., Calhoun, K. S., and Adams, H. E. (Eds.). (1977). *Handbook of Behavioral Assessment.* New York: John Wiley & Sons.

Eyberg, S. M., & Ross, A. W. (1978). Assessment of child behavior problems: The validation of a new inventory. *Journal of Clinical Child Psychology, 1,* 113–116.

Fantuzzo, J., Stovall, A., Schachtel, D., Goins, C., & Hall, R. (1987). The effects of peer social initiations on the social behavior of withdrawn maltreated preschool children. *Journal of Behavior Therapy and Experimental Psychiatry, 4,* 357–363.

Forehand, R., & Baumeister, A. A. (1976). Deceleration of aberrant behavior among retarded individuals. In M. Hersen, R. M., Eisler, & P. M. Miller (Eds.), *Progress in Behavior Modification* (Vol. 2). New York: Academic Press.

Forehand, R., King, H. E., Peed, S., & Yoder, P. (1975). Mother-child interactions: Comparisons of a non-compliant clinic group and non-clinic group. *Behavior, Research and Therapy, 13,* 79–84.

Foxx, R. M. (1978). An overview of overcorrection. *Journal of Pediatric Psychology, 3,* 97–101.

Goldfried, M. R., & Davison, G. C. (1976). *Clinical behavior therapy.* New York: Holt, Rinehart & Winston.

Goldfried, M. R., & Kent, R. N. (1972). Traditional versus behavioral personality assessment: A comparison of methodological and theoretical assumptions. *Psychological Bulletin, 77,* 409–420.

Gross, A. M., & Wojnilower, D. A. (1984). Self-directed behavior change in children: Is it self-directed? *Behavior Therapy, 15,* 501–514.

Hermecz, D. A., & Melamed, B. G. (1984). The assessment of emotional imagery training in fearful children. *Behavior Therapy, 15,* 156–172.

Hersen, M., & Bellack, A. S. (Eds.). (1976). *Behavioral assessment.* New York: Pergamon Press.

Homme, L., Csanyi, A., Gonzales, M., & Rechs, J. (1969). *How to use contingency contracting in the classroom.* Champaign, IL: Research Press.

Jacobson, E. (1929). *Progressive relaxation.* Chicago: University of Chicago Press.

Jones, R. T., & Kazdin, A. E. (1981). Childhood behavior problems in the school. In S. Turner, K. S. Calhoun, & H. E. Adams (Eds.), *Handbook of clinical behavior therapy.* New York: John Wiley & Sons.

Kanfer, F. H., & Saslow, G. (1969). Behavioral diagnosis. In C. M. Franks (Ed.), *Behavior therapy: Appraisal and status.* New York: McGraw-Hill.

Kazdin, A. (1980). *Behavior modification in applied settings* (revised edition). Homewood, IL: The Dorsey Press.

Kendall, P. C., & Braswell, L. (1985). *Cognitive-behavioral therapy for impulsive children.* New York: Guilford Press.

Kendall, P. C., & Wilcox, L. E. (1980). A cognitive-behavioral treatment for impulsivity: Concrete vs. conceptual training in non-self-controlled problem children. *Journal of Consulting and Clinical Psychology, 48,* 80–91.

Kennedy, W. A. (1965). School phobia: Rapid treatment of fifty cases. *Journal of Abnormal Psychology, 70,* 285–289.

Kimble, G. A. (1961). *Hilgard and Marquis conditioning and learning.* New York: Appleton-Century-Crofts.

Larson, B., Daleflod, B., Hakansson, L., & Melin, L. (1987). Therapist-assisted versus self-help relaxation treatment of chronic headaches in adolescents: A school-based intervention. *Journal of Child Psychology and Psychiatry, 1,* 127–136.

Lazarus, A. A., Davison, G. C., & Polefka, D. (1965). *Journal of Abnormal Psychology, 70,* 225–229.

Madsen, C. H., Madsen, C. K., Saudargas, R. A., Hammond, W. R., & Egar, D. E. (1970). *Classroom raid (rules, approval, ignore, disapproval): A cooperative approach for professionals and volunteers.* Unpublished manuscript, University of Florida, Tallahassee, Florida.

Maher, C. A., & Illback, R. J. (1985). Training urban high school principals in problem solving with adolescents and family members. *Child & Family Behavior Therapy, 6,* 13–21.

Mash, E. J., & Tardal, L. G. (Eds.). (1981). *Behavioral assessment of childhood disorders.* New York: Guilford Press.

Meador, A. E., & Ollendick, T. H. (1984). Cognitive behavior therapy with children: An evaluation of its efficacy and clinical utility. *Child and Family Behavior Therapy, 6,* 25–44.

Meichenbaum, D. H. (1977). *Cognitive-behavior modification: An integrative approach.* New York: Plenum.

Meichenbaum, D. H., & Goodman, J. (1971). Training impulsive children to talk to themselves: A means of developing self-control. *Journal of Abnormal Psychology, 77,* 115–126.

Mischel, W., & Liebert, R. M. (1966). Effects of discrepancies between observed and imposed reward criteria on their acquisition and transmission. *Journal of Personality and Social Psychology, 3,* 45–53.

Norton, G. R., Austen, S., Allen, G. E., & Hilton, J. (1983). Acceptability of time-out from reinforcement procedures for disruptive child behavior: A further analysis. *Child and Family Behavior Therapy, 2,* 31–41.

Nyhan, W., Johnson, H. G., Kaufman, I. A., & Jones, K. L. (1980). Serotonergic approaches to the modification of behavior in the Lesch-Nyhan syndrome. *Journal of Applied Research in Mental Retardation, 1,* 25–40.

O'Leary, K. D., Paulos, R. W., & Devine, O. T. (1972). Tangible reinforcers: Bonus or bribes? *Journal of Consulting and Clinical Psychology, 38,* 1–8.

Ollendick, T. H., & Hersen, M. (1984). An overview of child behavioral assessment. In T. H. Ollendick & M. Hersen (Eds.), *Child behavioral assessment: Principles and procedures* (pp. 3–19). New York: Pergamon Press.

Plienis, A. J., Hansen, D. J., Ford, F., Smith, S., Stark, L. J., & Kelly, J. A. (1987). Behavioral small group training to improve the social skills of emotionally disordered adolescents. *Behavior Therapy, 18,* 17–32.

Ploeg-Stapert, van der J., and Ploeg, van der H. (1986). Behavioral group treatment of test anxiety: An evaluation study. *Journal of Behavior Therapy and Experimental Psychiatry, 4,* 255–259.

Quay, H. C. (1972). Patterns of aggression, withdrawal, and immaturity. In H. Quay and J. S. Werry (Eds.), *Psychopathological disorders of childhood.* New York: Wiley.

Rachman, S., & Teasdale, J. (1969). *Aversion therapy and behaviour disorders.* Coral Gables, FL: University of Miami Press.

Raymer, R., & Poppen, R. (1985). Behavioral relaxation training with hyperactive children. *Journal of Behavior Therapy and Experimental Psychiatry, 4,* 309–316.

Robin, A., Schneider, M., & Dolnick, M. (1976). The turtle technique: An extended case study of self-control in the classroom. *Psychology in the Schools, 13,* 449–453.

Ross, A. O. (1980). *Psychological disorders of children.* New York: McGraw-Hill.

Ross, A. O. (1985). To form a more perfect union: It is time to stop standing still. *Behavior Therapy, 16,* 195–204.

Routh, D. K., & Mesibov, G. B. (1980). Psychological and environmental intervention: Toward social competence. In H. E. Rie & E. D. Rie (Eds.), *Handbook of minimal brain dysfunctions: A critical review.* New York: John Wiley.

Rutter, M. (1975). *Helping troubled children.* New York: Plenum Press.

Sackett, G. P. (1978). *Observing Behavior* (Vol. 2). Baltimore: University Park Press.

Schneider, M., & Robin, A. (1973). *Turtle manual.* Unpublished manuscript.

Sharp, J. J., & Formen, S. G. (1985). A comparison of two approaches to anxiety management for teachers. *Behavior Therapy, 16,* 370–383.

Skinner, B. F. (1938). *The behavior of organisms.* New York: Appleton-Century-Crofts.

Skinner, B. F. (1957). *Verbal behavior.* New York: Appleton-Century-Crofts.

Skinner, B. F. (1965). *Science and human behavior.* New York: The Free Press.

Stokes, T. F., & Baer, D. M. (1977). An implicit technology of generalization. *Journal of Applied Behavior Analysis, 10,* 349–367.

Stuart, R. B. (1972). Situational versus self-control. In R. D. Rubin, H. Fensterheim, J. D. Henderson, & L. P. Ullmann (Eds.), *Advances in behavior therapy.* New York: Academic Press.

Swanson, H. L., & Scarpati, S. (1985). Self-instruction training to increase academic performance of educationally handicapped children. *Child & Family Behavior Therapy, 6,* 23–39.

Wolfe, J., Fantuzzo, J., & Wolfe, P. (1986). The effects of reciprocal peer management and group contingencies on the arithmetic proficiency of underachieving students. *Behavior Therapy, 17,* 253–265.

Wolpe, J. (1969). *The practice of behavior therapy.* New York: Pergamon.

Wurtele, S. K., & Drabman, R. S. (1984). "Beat the buzzer" for classroom dawdling: A one year trial. *Behavior Therapy, 15,* 403–409.

7
Cognitive Development*

MAIN POINTS

1. Children's behavioral and emotional reactions are mediated, in part, by how children perceive their environment and how they think about responding to their perceived tasks and problems.

2. In adapting to their environment, children both assimilate and accommodate. For successful adaptation to occur, these two means of adaptation should be in equilibrium.

3. Cognitive shifts occur during certain age ranges (e.g., 5–7), resulting in qualitative changes in how children process information.

4. During development, changes occur in children's cognitive and social-cognitive processes, affecting their attention, memory, problem solving, and metacognitive self-guidance.

5. Unique patterns of deficits are apparent in these cognitive and social-cognitive processes in children with certain behavioral and emotional disorders.

6. Children with an attention deficit hyperactivity disorder have difficulty sustaining attention, have poor memory of complex information, have poor complex problem-solving skills, and have poor metacognitive regulation.

7. Aggressive children are overattentive to social and nonsocial cues in their environment, excessively interpret hostile intent as the cause of others' behavior, and think of too few verbal assertions and too many direct action solutions to social problems.

*This chapter was written by John E. Lochman, Duke University and Durham Community Guidance Clinic. The preparation and writing of this chapter were partially supported by a grant from the National Institute of Mental Health to the author (MH 39989).

8. Depressed children have negative expectations for, and perceptions of, their own performance on tasks, and they set overly stringent criteria for success.

9. In school and clinic settings, social problem-solving and self-instructional interventions can address these students' deficient cognitive processes, and thus reduce their behavioral and emotional difficulties.

Remember that foul words or blows in themselves are no outrage, but your judgements that they are so. So when anyone makes you angry, know that it is your own thought that has angered you. Wherefore make it your first endeavor not to let your impressions carry you away. For if once you gain time and delay, you will find it easier to control yourself.

(*The Manual, Epictetus*)

We can imagine a school situation in which a fourth grade child, Ronnie, jumps ahead of three other children in line to get to the cafeteria first. One of the three children, Chad, responds to this line-jumping by nervously shrinking back; a second child, Joanna, tells Ronnie firmly that he is not being fair and he should return to his place in line; and the third child, Bobby, steps forward, tells Ronnie that he is a scumbag just like Ronnie's mother, and then he hits Ronnie quickly in the face with his fist. These three children have responded to a particular stimulus, which was Ronnie's line-jumping, in three quite different ways. These differences in behavioral responses can be explained from different theoretical perspectives, including the points of view adopted by behavioral theory (see Chapter 6) and by psychodynamic theory (see Chapter 5). In this chapter, we will explore how these behavioral differences can be due to the characteristic ways in which various children cognitively process the stimulus situations around them and the responses they plan to make to these situations. Thus, Ronnie's line-jumping may have been perceived quite differently by the three other children, and their behavioral responses were due to their perceptions of the situation and to the available array of solutions that they have in mind to readily use in this kind of situation. Children's cognitive processing is related in important ways to their emotional and behavioral adjustment.

Children's perceptions of social situations govern their reactions.

Cognition refers to all the processes by which "sensory input is transformed, reduced, elaborated, stored, recovered and used" by the person (Neisser, 1967, p. 4). Cognitive theory hypothesizes that the use of cognition, as in the acquisition of knowledge, is an active, rather than passive, process. To really know something about objects, the young child must act on the objects such as beads, and transform them by connecting, combining, taking apart, and reassembling them (Piaget, 1983). For an older child, these transformations can be done internally through images and thoughts in the child's mind, rather than only through direct manipulation of physical objects. Thus, according to cognitive theories, the person actively incorporates information and decides what to do. In contrast, psychological learning theories depict a person as reacting to a stimulus by emitting a response that has been conditioned to that stimulus. Abstract learning is described in behavioral theory as the organism's ability to find commonalities or similarities among a range of similar stimuli, using discrimination and generalization among the stimuli. Once the stimulus is perceived, the response associated with that class of stimuli is passively evident, and the organism responds (Diamond, 1982). On the other hand, theories of cognitive development describe abstract learning as a process in which information is coded into abstract relational systems. The individual construes how an object (e.g., a red circular block) fits into logical hierarchies of categories (color, shape, size), and how responses themselves also come from meaningful related categories. Thus, as the child learns more about the properties of objects, he can eventually perceive that among a subset of red blocks, the blocks can be further categorized on dimensions of shape (circular, square) and size (large, small).

While the development of cognitive processing skills has a certain relationship to children's level of intelligence as operationalized in our commonly used intelligence tests, there also are major differences. Intelligence test scores provide a static, quantitative measure of how a particular child compares to the test's normative sample on the particular tasks used in that test. With only rare exceptions, intelligence tests were developed in a pragmatic fashion, and were not developed to assess theoretically interrelated cognitive processes. Thus, intelligence test scores are predictive of children's future academic achievement and are often used in school settings to assist in the evaluation of mental retardation and learning disabilities. However, intelligence tests do not comprehensively assess the sequence of cognitive processes involved in children's perceptions of stimuli and in their decision making, and they do not assess qualitative changes in children's thinking style as children become older. While intelligence test scores are often found to be positively correlated with cognitive and social-cognitive processes, these relationships are modest and intelligence tests are not effective means of assessing most of the cognitive processes discussed in this chapter.

In this chapter, we will examine cognitive developmental theories, and the manner in which the structure of children's cognitive processing changes at points in their development. We will examine several of the basic cognitive processes and social-cognitive processes that have become the center of research interest in recent years. We will then focus on how deficiencies and distortions in these cognitive and social-cognitive processes operate in children who have behavioral and emotional difficulties in the areas of conduct disorder and aggressive behavior, attentional deficits, and depression.

THEORY AND STAGES

Piaget's Theory

Clearly, the individual who has had the most influence on our understanding of cognitive development in children is Jean Piaget. Piaget was born in 1896, received his doctorate in biological sciences in 1918, and published his first research on developmental psychology in 1921. From his academic position at the University of Geneva, Piaget was enormously prolific in designing inventive studies and publishing ground-breaking results for five decades. Within the United States, initial interest in Piaget's work waned after the early 1930s, but since the early 1960s Piaget's theory has had seminal influences on a large portion of the child development research in this country (Baldwin, 1967).

Piaget's background in biology had a profound influence on his thinking about development. The biological concept of adaptation evident in Darwinian evolutionary theory describes how organisms adapt to the demands of their environment by restructuring their activities (Diamond, 1982). Following this model, Piaget's theory described how children actively adapt to their physical and social environment by making progressive changes in the organization and structure of their thought processes. Piaget described the structure of thought processes in logical and mathematical terms; the purpose of these structures was to organize thoughts and perceptions in a meaningful way, such that relationships between individual concepts, and the more abstract classification including these concepts, became increasingly delineated over time. Ideas, thoughts, and concepts are thus not just passively associated with each other, but, instead, the individual actively organizes his perceptions and thoughts. As early as 1 to 1½ years of age, babies have what Piaget (1983) called a "Copernican revolution" in which they actively reorganize their perceptions. Babies, because of their searching for and manipulation of objects, begin to transform their own understanding of themselves as objects in their environment. Rather than seeing himself as the motionless center of the universe, the infant perceives himself as "only one member of the set of the other mobile objects that compose his universe" (Piaget, 1983, p. 105). The child comes to recognize the permanence and independent movement of objects, such as a ball that rolls under the sofa and the mother who walks in and out of the bedroom doorway.

Piaget postulated that there are two types of adaptation that a child uses: assimilation and accommodation. With assimilation, the child seeks to understand the meaning of a new experience by determining how aspects of the new experience fit with prior structures. For example, students just beginning kindergarten will assimilate their experiences with their new teacher by determining if this teacher fits within their cognitive schemas or structures for other adults they know. To the degree that a child can readily assimilate a new experience into his set of prior experiences, then the child can readily and automatically respond to the stimulus with existing response strategies. However, if a child only used assimilation while perceiving new experiences, his cognitive structures and responses would never vary, and the child would be incapable of acquiring new knowledge. He would operate only in an extremely egocentric manner, without being able to change his perceptions of events or objects to meet objective differences between events, and he would be subject to major distortions in his perceptions.

However, when accommodation (i.e., the other adaptation process described by Piaget) occurs, the child changes his cognitive structures in response to new environmental events. Essentially, the child infers that the new events cannot be adequately interpreted within existing schemas, so change in the schemas takes place. Accommodation can lead ultimately to major, qualitative shifts in the child's cognitive structures, or ways of thinking, at certain stages of growth. These qualitative changes occur gradually, in a piecemeal fashion, over the course of time as the child progressively accommodates to environmental events. If the child used accommodation as his only adaptive mechanism, then his learning would be due exclusively to imitation, and the child's behavior and cognitive structures would have little stability or generality across different environmental events.

However, children learn and function best when assimilation and accommodation are in equilibrium, and this produces cognitive behavior that is both organized and creative. Optimal cognitive growth occurs when the child has experiences that are moderately different from those that he has already accurately perceived and comprehended (Cohen & Schleser, 1984); these new experiences cause the individual to both assimilate and accommodate. For example, on a spring evening recently, our 22-month-old son, Bryan, was being taken for a stroll around the neighborhood at dusk. As Bryan was being wheeled in his stroller, he looked over his right shoulder and enthusiastically said, "Moon, Moon," as he recognized one of his favorite objects in the sky (other favorite objects being airplanes and helicopters). Later, after turning a corner, he was asked where the moon was, and Bryan quickly turned to look over his right shoulder. He looked in that direction for several seconds, appearing puzzled to find the moon was no longer in that spot, and then be began haphazardly searching the sky until he again found the "Moon" behind him. A little later, after we proceeded down the curving street a littler further, Bryan was again asked to find the moon, but this time he only momentarily looked over his right shoulder, and then in a smoother, more systematic manner he scanned the sky until he again relocated the "Moon" in a different position behind him.

Bryan's behavior illustrates several of Piaget's key concepts. Bryan's understanding of object permanence, and in particular his understanding that an object continues its existence despite changes in the object's position in space and changes in the sensorimotor schemes required to locate that object, occurs because of Bryan's active interaction with, and adaptation to, his environment (Diamond, 1982). Adaptation occurred as Bryan assimilated his perception of the moon at different points in the sky into his already developed cognitive schema for the "Moon," and accommodation occurred as he developed in his ability to locate an object which has had a set of invisible displacements. By using both assimilation and accommodation, Bryan was nearing the completion of the sixth and final stage in Piaget's (1954) account of how children form the concept of permanent objects over the course of the first several years of life.

Developmental Shift at 5 to 7 Years of Age

In addition to the ongoing and progressive changes that children make in their cognitive structures due to accommodation, there are several periods of major, qualitative shifts in cognitive processing during childhood. The first and clearest of these shifts occurs between the ages of approximately 5 to 7 for most children. Children change from having their attention, problem solving, and reasoning being drawn to aspects of the stimuli, to a state where they begin to organize their experiences into more logical and specific categories. During this cognitive shift, their problem solving becomes more intentional and systematic (Paris & Lindauer, 1982).

One explanation for this shift involves the evident change in the younger child's predominant reliance on simple processing of visual and auditory stimuli (i.e., focusing on concrete similarities or differences on a perceptual dimension such as size) to the 7-or-8-year-old child's increasing reliance on language to mediate problem solving and to develop conceptual inferences (Flavell, 1977; Kendler & Kendler, 1962). The younger child also attends to isolated states, such as a peer's behavior at two different times, without accounting for processes that could induce changes between those states. A Soviet psychologist, Vygotsky (1962), has concluded that speech becomes internalized, or goes "underground," in children prior to the age of 7. Language, thus, becomes the symbolic tool that more effectively allows the child to classify his perceptions more effectively and to connect one perception with another perception in space or over time (Paris & Lindauer, 1982). During the shift, the child moves from an automatic, associative response to stimuli to a level of cognitive operations that is capable of functioning more slowly and deliberately. This shift from perceptual to semantic processing is also consistent with recent descriptions of how reading develops (Bakker, 1983). Prior to entering first grade, children rely primarily on right brain hemisphere functioning in reading, as they learn to discriminate the shapes of letters and simple words. Research has suggested that by the end of first grade, however, the most effective readers have shifted over to left-hemisphere dominance during reading tasks as they increasingly attend to the semantic, rather than merely the perceptual, qualities of what they read.

The most comprehensive conceptualization of this period of cognitive shift is evident in Piaget's description of the second and third of his major cognitive states: the preoperational period and the concrete operations period. During the **preoperational phase** which extends from about age 2 to 7, the child's developments include a large increase in language and vocabulary which permits the child to develop symbolic representations of his world. During this phase, an associated increase in fantasy and imagination occurs. However, the child remains egocentric and he is unable to adopt the perspectives of others. As the child attains the next level of cognitive development, the **concrete operations** period which extends from approximately 7 to 11 years of age, the child does not just add something significant to his cognitive skills; instead, he begins to experience a new reality because of the qualitative changes in cognition. In the concrete operations period the child develops systems of interrelated logical operations (Achenbach, 1982), with two of the major cognitive structural changes being conservation and classification.

Conservation refers to the child's ability to distinguish quantitative properties of objects (e.g., volume) from the various cues in the appearance of the object which do not affect these quantitative properties. Conservation becomes possible, in turn, because of the child's increasing development in being able to decenter and to perceive and anticipate the **reversibility** of actions (Diamond, 1982). In one of the classic experimental tasks used to assess a child's attainment of conservation, the child observes water being poured from a tall, thin cylindrical beaker into a short, wide cylindrical beaker. Then the child is asked if the amount of water in the second beaker is more, less, or the same as the amount of water in the first beaker. Children at the concrete operational level who have attained conservation will state that the amount of water is the same, and when their accommodation of this operation is complete, they can provide a logical explanation for why the water's amount is the same. In contrast, children at the preoperational level initially center on just one dimension of the beaker, such as the height, without taking into account other dimensions, such as the width, and they say that the water in the two beakers is not the same. The concrete operational child both decenters, by coordinating perceptions of multiple dimensions, and also cognitively reverses the water pouring, predicting accurately where the level of water will be in the first beaker if the water is poured back into the first beaker.

Another aspect of decentering involves the ability to perceive how an object would look if it was moved or if it was seen from a different vantage point. In another experiment, Piaget slid three colored beads (red, yellow, blue) which were strung on a wire to the right into a tube covering the middle of the wire (Baldwin, 1967). When the beads were hidden from the child's view inside the tube, the child was asked a series of questions about which color of bead would first come out of the right of the tube, which color of bead would come first back out of the left of the tube, and which color of bead would come out of the tube's ends if the entire apparatus was rotated one turn (180°), two turns (360°), as well as for additional turns. Children under 4 years of age did not predict consistently any of the responses, but children who were between 5 and 7 years of age, and in what Piaget called the **intuitive** stage, were often able to describe which bead would come out first even after one or two rotations. However, the child's intuitive understanding of the problem did not allow the 5-or-6-year-old to predict the bead sequence with more turns. These children responded as if they were rotating their remembered visual images of the beads, but this method of solving the problem became too difficult with multiple rotations. The concrete operational child, after about age 7, seemed to solve the problem in a different fashion, however. These older children understood the logic of the problem, in which one turn reversed the order of beads, the second turn restored the order of beads, and so on, and thus did not have to rely on rotating images of beads in their mind (Baldwin, 1967). Thus, decentering permits an individual to systematically perceive an object or event from other imagined viewpoints, and this cognitive operation has clear implications for social perception, as we will soon discuss.

The other major cognitive structural change involves **classification,** or concept formation. Classification is a cognitive operation in which the child determines how objects or experiences fit into various classes or logical groupings. Eventually, the child understands that certain classes are more general and abstract, and that they include subclasses of objects which can be more finely differentiated. As with decentering, Piaget believed that children proceeded through three stages before mastering true classification (Diamond, 1982). Children at the lowest level, below age 5, were unable to consistently group blocks that varied in shape and color into meaningful categories. The young child might begin by putting different colored rings together because they were rings, but then would also add a yellow square to the same group since one of the rings had been yellow. Children between 5 and 7, again in the intuitive period, can create meaningful classes from the colored blocks by separating them consistently by shape or color. On the surface these children appeared to have mastered classification, but Piaget noted that they had not yet understood **class inclusion,** or how subordinate parts of a classification system relate to the whole system. Only after age 7 when the children reached concrete operations were they able to successfully answer whether there were more rings or more blue rings (Diamond, 1982). Thus, by the time they achieve concrete operations, after a period of intuitive approximations and accommodations, children have made qualitative changes in their cognitive structure, and they have become capable of using such cognitive operations as decentering, reversibility, conservation, and classification.

Developmental Shift at 9 to 11 Years of Age

The second shift in cognitive reasoning has been less explored, and the range of changes in cognitive structure is less overtly dramatic than the cognitive changes evident by about age 7. However, Piagetian theory posits that by about age 11, children will begin to have a qualitative shift from the stage of concrete operations to the stage of formal operations, although this shift is not completed until later in adolescence. The central feature of logical operations is that adolescents seek to determine if the conclusions reached from a chain of reasoning are logically necessary. The adolescents' thought processes become less dependent on the direct experiences they have with objects in their environment, and they instead can imagine a range of possible solutions to a problem, and can anticipate the many possible future consequences associated with these solutions. In this way, the adolescent's thinking becomes analogous to the hypothetico-deductive reasoning that is evident in scientific endeavors (Neimark, 1982). The adolescent who has attained formal operations is more capable of considering what is possible, rather than merely what is real and immediately apparent, when solving problems (Cohen & Schlesser, 1984). One natural outgrowth of these changes in the ways in which adolescents think is that they become more idealistic and can be more abstract.

To assess children's transition into formal operations, Piaget and Inhelder developed a series of tasks to measure children's abilities to systematically understand the entire range of possibilities that can occur when events or objects are combined (Baldwin, 1967). In one of these tasks, children were presented with four large bottles and one small bottle containing different, unlabeled colorless liquids, and the children were asked to make a yellow-colored liquid by using any or all of these flasks. The correct solution to this problem was to combine liquids from the small bottle and from large bottles 1 and 3, thus producing a solution containing dilute sulfuric acid, oxygenated water, and potassium iodide. Children who had attained formal operations would solve this problem systematically by writing down all of the possible pairings of the bottles so that the entire set of possibilities could be examined. Children functioning at the concrete operations level lacked this deductive, systematic approach to considering all possible combinations, and instead tried haphazard sets of combinations in a trial-and-error manner, leading them to be successful only by chance.

BASIC COGNITIVE PROCESSES DURING DEVELOPMENT

In the prior section, we examined how children's cognitive development occurs in both continuous and discontinuous ways over time. We will now turn to some of the basic cognitive processes which have major implications for children's ability to adequately learn in school and to effectively modulate their emotional behavioral reactions. These basic cognitive elements of attention, memory, selection of strategies and solutions, and metacognition have been the focus of increasing research in recent years, leading to a clearer understanding of how children develop in their abilities to process the information they perceive in the environment around them.

Attention

A key developmental cognitive change that occurs during the preadolescent and early adolescent years involves children's increasing skill in focusing and sustaining attention on their tasks. The child selectively attends to only portions of the many sensations he experiences, and he thus screens out other elements. Attention can be conceived as a process that assists other cognitive activities, such as perception, memory, and learning (Cohen & Schlesser, 1984). Thus, the efficiency and accuracy of the attentional processes have major effects on the quality of the other cognitive processes.

As attentional skills develop, children learn not only to more adeptly focus on the central, relevant cues they wish to remember and to respond to, but they also should become better able to ignore and not attend to irrelevant, incidental stimuli. Thus, selective attention has an effect on both central and incidental recall. Hagen, using his Central-Incidental Recall Task, presents a series of seven cards to a child, instructs the child to pay attention only to the pictured animal, and then places the cards upside down in a row before the child (Hagen & Kail, 1973). The bottom of each card has a drawing of a different animal, while the top of each card has drawings of other objects (e.g., lamp, chair). For the Central Task, the child is then shown drawings of the various animals, and is asked to recall which of the turned-over cards has the same animal. For the Incidental Task, the child is given pictures of all seven animals and seven objects, and he is asked to identify which object had originally been on the cards with which animal. The Incidental Task assesses knowledge which should have been irrelevant, according to the initial instructions. Hence, children who do well on this part of the task have not screened out irrelevant stimulus information.

As children progress from first to seventh grades, they score progressively better on the Central Task, but their scores on the Incidental Task remain stable until approximately age 12, and then these Incidental scores begin to decline (Tarver, Hallahan, Kauffman & Ball, 1976). Therefore, children at the Piagetian level of concrete operations actively sort, label, and classify information, and they become increasingly proficient at this aspect of attention during the preadolescent years. However, older children know not only how to attend, but also when it is useful to attend. Formal operations children are less stimulus-bound; instead, they planfully direct their attention towards certain portions of a stimulus. They display more logical and strategic search behavior (Cohen & Schlesser, 1984; Paris & Lindauer, 1982).

The development of cognitive control over attention is also apparent in the more reflective, less impulsive cognitive style of children after ages 6 or 7. A reflective cognitive style is evident on tasks such as the Matching Familiar Figures Test when children take more time to compare drawn figures to see which are similar, and make more correct matches. Children who have achieved the Piagetian concrete operations stage scan stimulus details in a more systematic manner, and they are more reflective than preoperational children (Cohen, Schlesser, & Meyers, 1981). Developmental changes in the attentional capacities of children are evident in their reflective cognitive style, as well as their selective attention.

Memory

After information is attended to and perceived by the child, the information is ready to be stored in memory. Information is stored briefly in short-term memory, and the limited capacity of this short-term storage has some effect on how much information becomes stored in a permanent manner in long-term memory. Modest developmental changes are evident in short-term memory during childhood. Three-year-olds are able to remember about three items on a task involving the presentation of a series of numbers, 7-year-olds recall about five items, and 12-year-olds recall about seven items (Cohen & Schlesser, 1984). However, considerably more dramatic developmental changes during this age span are evident on tasks measuring long-term memory. Thus, short-term memory development has less effect on long-term memory than do the developmental changes that children display in their strategies for encoding and retrieving memory from storage. These memory, or mnemonic, strategies include (1) rehearsal and (2) awareness of the organization and meaning of the information. College students are likely to recognize the usefulness of these memorization strategies as they study for tests.

Interest in children's rehearsed strategies was stimulated in the 1970s by a frequently cited study by Flavell, Beach, and Chinsky (1966). A series of pictures were presented to 5-, 7-, and 10-year-old children, and then the children were asked to remember several of the pictures after a brief delay. During this interval, a visor was placed over the children's eyes, and their lip movements were recorded by a trained lip reader, as the children spontaneously labeled and rehearsed the content of the pictures. Rehearsal was evident on at least some trials in 10% of the 5-year-olds, and consistent rehearsal occurred with 25% of the 7-year-olds, and 65% of the 10-year-olds. Flavell concluded that rehearsal was not a common cognitive activity prior to 9 or 10 years of age, but after that time active rehearsal of information becomes a common means of enhancing memory.

Children's memory of information can also be enhanced by making the material more meaningful. Functionally, this means that information can be stored and retrieved more readily because there are more "tags" to the information and the information becomes more solidly embedded in existing hierarchical structures containing other memories. The developmental changes in how meaning is attached to perceptions and how memories are retrieved are exemplified in another of Piaget's creative experiments in which children's memory was found to actually improve over time. Piaget and Inhelder (1973) presented an ordinal set of 10 sticks to children who ranged in age from 3 to 8. The sticks were displayed in a serial order going from longest to shortest. When children were asked to draw the sticks from memory 1 week later, their Piagetian level predicted their responses. The youngest children (3 to 4 years old), who were preoperational and had no understanding of serial classification and ordering, drew lines of about equal length, and 6-to 8-year-old children, who were at the concrete operations level, had drawings that were generally accurate. The transitional, or intuitive, level children drew lines of various lengths, but the lines were not drawn in an organized order. When the children were asked to draw the set of sticks again 6 to 8 months later, 75% of their drawings had an improved portrayal of serial ordering. Ninety percent of the transitional, or intuitive, group demonstrated improvement. While replication studies have generally found more modest rates of improvement over time than Piaget's original study, the results still strongly support Piaget's hypothesis that developmental changes in cognitive structures will produce improvement in the memory of material that is processed by the changed cognitive structures. Children who have begun to understand the concept of ordering objects from biggest to smallest will have better memories of related information after the change than before.

Children may enhance memory by organizing, or "chunking," the material into relevant categorical associations. Children can better remember pictures of a shirt and of socks if they remember them as associated articles of clothing. When children below the age of 9 or 10 are presented with sets of pictures that can be grouped into categories such as animals, furniture, vehicles, and clothing, they do not cluster the picture to assist recall (Neimark, Slotnick, & Ulrich, 1971). However, 10-and 11-year-old children display substantial spontaneous categorization. Children's memory can also be enhanced when they add additional meaning to information, such as when they put pairs of words in sentences when they are asked to memorize the words (Paris & Lindauer, 1982). Thus, when concrete operational children begin to approach the transition to formal operations, they begin to use mnemonic strategies such as rehearsal and categorization to enhance their memory.

Selection of Strategies and Solutions

After a task has been perceived, the child can engage in deliberate selection of strategies to achieve task goals. Since the child cannot enact all of the possible strategies or actions that can be retrieved from memory, he selects certain strategies based on the personal significance of the goal, and the amount of effort required to use the strategy to attain the goal (Paris & Lindauer, 1982). According to Piaget, children become planful and reflective after attaining concrete operations; prior to that time the children's problem-solving efforts involve trial-and-error reasoning.

Younger children do not use feedback from the success of their prior actions to facilitate the planning of their behavior. When first-grade children forget items on a memory task, they do not select these items to study prior to another memory trial as often as third graders do (Masur, McIntyre, & Flavell, 1973). The preoperational children do not form a systematic plan for their study behavior to make the most of their efforts.

Metacognitive Regulation

Metacognition refers to an individual's awareness of, and active control over, his own cognitive processes. For children, this means that they are consciously aware of their planning, of their progress towards a goal, and of their capacity for changing and redirecting their own behavior, if necessary. Younger children do not keep track of their solution efforts on problem-solving tasks (Siegler & Liebert, 1975). In addition, preoperational-level children do not check or correct their own errors on tasks. By not attending to and responding to feedback about his own responses, the younger child persists in erroneous solution patterns or makes random changes. Neither strategy is likely to be competent on complex tasks.

Children begin to refine their metacognitive regulation as they internalize self-guiding speech. Vygotsky (1962) has described how children progress in their internalization of self-talk from audibly talking to themselves (Slow down! Slow Down! Careful!) to internalizing the talking. Luria (1961), who was Vygotsky's student, found that by age 6, children were able to inhibit behavior in reaction to their own self-directed instructions, and did not have to rely solely on adult direction.

SOCIAL-COGNITIVE PROCESSES DURING DEVELOPMENT

We can think of the basic cognitive processes which we have just reviewed (attention, memory, strategy selection, and metacognition) as essential "hardware'' processes that must develop during childhood so that children can function effectively on school tasks. To acquire information, the child has to be able

- To selectively attend to the stimuli in his textbook or worksheets
- To screen out other concurrent stimuli, such as an airplane flying over or another child talking disruptively in the seat behind him
- To remember the material that is read by using rehearsal and categorization strategies
- To planfully compare and select response options
- To guide himself through this process by reminding himself what his next step is in the learning process

In social interactions with other students and teachers, another level of cognitive processes is also important. Social-cognitive processing involves the child's cognitive perceptions and reactions to his social world, as well as the strategies he develops to cope with and influence his social encounters. Deficiencies can exist in children's social-cognitive processing either because of developmental delays in their ''hardware''processing, or because of children's inability to apply basically sound ''hardware'' processes to social situations. In the latter case, children who can function adequately on structured school tasks may be excessively impulsive and distracted when talking with peers, and may be too quick to take offense at slight frustrations with peers, leading potentially to intensely aggressive or emotional reactions. When these emotional and behavioral reactions are severe and chronic in children's social interactions, the accompanying arousal may cause deterioration in the academic functioning of even children with initially sound basic cognitive processing. In this section, we will briefly examine the development of social-cognitive processes during childhood to assist us in understanding the deficiencies in social-cognitive processing that some children experience.

Attention to and Memory of Social Cues

As children develop, their ability to pay attention to, perceive, and remember cues in social situations evolves. By the fourth or fifth grade, children pay attention to more aspects of a situation before deciding about the meaning of others' behavior; they are less subject to recency biases in recall; and they begin attending to different kinds of information from social situations. Dodge and Newman (1981) had children listen to stories about characters who were suspected of misdeeds, such as a child spilling somebody's bag of groceries. The children were then given the opportunity to listen to as many recorded testimony statements as they wished. In the testimony statements, various people reported their perceptions of the suspect. After this, the children decided whether the suspect was guilty or innocent. Ten-year-old children were found to listen to 50% more testimony statements than did 6-year-old children. Thus, the 10-year-olds paid attention to more details before interpreting the meaning of these social situations. This pattern is consistent with our prior discussion about developmental decreases in children's impulsive cognitive styles.

In addition to paying attention to fewer elements in social situations, younger children have a recency bias in their recall strategies (Austin, Ruble, & Trabasso, 1977; Surber, 1982). They remember best the last element that just occurred in an interaction. A younger child is more prone to become intensely activated by what a peer has just said or done to him, without the ability to adequately recall and take into account the enjoyable, cooperative play he may have had with the peer earlier in an interaction sequence.

As children become older, their attention and encoding patterns become more sophisticated. Their increasing ability to selectively attend extends into their perceptions of social situations. While younger children attend to concrete features of social situations (e.g., what happened, what people wore), older children attend to more general features of the situation which permit them to make guesses about other people's beliefs and traits (Livesley & Bromley, 1973). This refinement in their attention and immediate recall of situations assists children in their developing abilities to take other people's perspective and to interpret others' behavior.

Interpretation of Social Cues

The ability to accurately interpret the meaning of other people's behavior is a complex process which ultimately has considerable effect on children's ability to develop reciprocal, mutually satisfying relationships with peers and adults. Piaget regarded the social-cognitive process of being able to adopt the perspectives of others in social situations as being more difficult to acquire than the related basic cognitive process of imagining how physical objects, such as a vase with flowers, would look different from various points in a room (Achenbach, 1982). Piaget felt that children had a relatively uniform history of perspective-taking experiences with physical objects (i.e. seeing objects from different angles, seeing objects falling or rolling away), but their history of experiences with social objects was quite variable. An only child who had highly constricted, inhibited parents who rarely verbalized their feelings or ideas would likely have more difficulty developing social perspective-taking abilities than would a child who had expressive and articulate parents who often spoke about their own experiences and thoughts.

Social perspective-taking abilities have been a popular topic for developmental psychology research. To assess these abilities, children are often asked to tell a story about a central character in a picture or in a series of cartoons, and then they are asked to retell the story from the point of view of a bystander to the scene. Children who are relatively egocentric in their social perspective-taking will describe the bystander as knowing everything about the central character's private thoughts and feelings. Research findings indicate that as children become older, they become less egocentric (Feffer & Gourevitch, 1960; Kurdek, 1977).

Selman (1980) has extended Piaget's model of social perception, and has suggested that children move through four basic stages before fully achieving social perspective-taking (Selman & Byrne, 1974). First, the child is in a fully

As children develop, they acquire cognitive skills that enable more sophisticated social functioning.

egocentric state and is unable to differentiate the points of view of others. Second, the child can consider other people's ideas in a rudimentary way and realizes their thoughts can be different from his own. However, he has difficulty understanding exactly what the differences are. Third, although the child cannot consider others' and his own perspectives simultaneously, he can sequentially consider first his own perspective and then other's perspective. Finally, the child is able to think about both perspectives at the same time in an integrated manner, as well as having a "third person" perspective in which he can figuratively step back from the interaction and examine both sides' points of view (Kendall & Braswell, 1985). Selman, Jaquette, and Lavin (1977) have found in a longitudinal study that most children do advance in the expected direction up the perspective-taking stages, and mental age was found to correlate .77 with perspective-taking level. Thus, substantial evidence exists for developmental progression.

One aspect of perspective-taking that deserves particular attention involves affective perspective-taking and empathy. In a four-step sequence essentially consistent with Selman's model, Hoffman (1983) proposed that children progressively acquire not only a cognitive awareness of what others feel, but also actually experience feelings consistent with how they perceive others feel. These steps also start with an egocentric level, and then progress to a level where the child's and other person's feelings are often experienced in a mixed-up way. When a 2-year-old is with an adult who beings to cry, the child may respond by bringing the adult his teddy bear, thus attempting to comfort the adult in the way the child usually comforts himself. At higher levels of empathy, the child begins to recognize a wide range of emotions in others, and these recognized emotions produce similar, appropriate feelings in the child, especially as the child begins to be able to differentiate that the other's distress is chronic and not transitory. It is anticipated that children's abilities to empathically experience others' distress can stimulate prosocial behavior.

Finally, one last aspect of children's abilities to interpret social cues is evident not only in their inference of others' thoughts and feelings, but also in their attributions of others' intentions. When preoperational and early operational children have to determine who was at fault in a particular situation, such as when a child breaks one of the mother's favorite dishes, they base their decision about the child's "badness" on the consequences of the behavior, rather than on the child's apparent intentions. Thus, if something of value was broken, then the child is considered to be bad, but if the object was relatively trivial, then the child is judged less harshly. Children who are 9 or 10 years of age go beyond mere rule violations and consequences as the reason for assigning blame; instead, they seek to determine if the child's intentions were malevolent, or if the behavior may have been accidental (Costanzo & Fraenkel, 1987). Research supports Piaget's model, with kindergarten-age children being unable to differentiate between the positive and negative intentions of actors who produce negative consequences, while second and fourth grade children are progressively better in correctly inferring intentions (Costanzo, Coie, Grumet & Farnhill, 1973).

Selection of Social Strategies and Solutions

After children have perceived and interpreted the behavior of a peer or teacher with whom they are interacting, they then think about how they are going to respond to the interpersonal task they face. The task can entail trying to enter a new group of peers, talking to a teacher about difficulties on classwork, or trying to resolve a conflict with a peer or teacher. In deciding upon the social response they will make, children can operate cognitively in either an automatic processing mode or in a deliberate processing mode. In reality, most of the time both children and adults respond in an automatic manner, as they quickly select the most salient response from the "memory bin" that is associated with a particular class of social situation. However, in novel or complicated social situations, children will use deliberate processing, and will carefully consider a range of possible responses. After anticipating consequences that can follow from the alternative solutions to problems, then the strategy that leads to the most satisfaction and avoids the most aversive consequences is enacted. Spivack and Shure (1974) have developed a sequence of cognitive processes that occur in social problem-solving. Assessment is usually made of processes such as the number of alternative solutions generated for a social problem, the number of consequences children consider, and the ability of children to think about their responses as step-by-step, means-ends plans.

Developmental trends are noted in children's social problem-solving skills. Older children generate a larger number of varied and competent responses to hypothetical social problems than do younger children (Spivack, Platt & Shure, 1976). Different problem-solving skills have also been found to relate in different ways to adjustment at different ages. Spivack et al. (1976) reported that adjustment for preschool-age children is most related to the number of solutions generated and the number of consequences identified. By middle childhood means-ends thinking also becomes a correlate of adjustment, and by adolescence the ability to think of problem-solutions in a planful, means-ends manner was the most important problem-solving skill that mediated adjustment. This growing capacity to consider the logical, detailed way in which a given social response elicits certain expected reactions from others, and then leads to the next response is influenced by preadolescents' and adolescents' transitions to formal operations in their basic cognitive processing.

The developmental change in children's abilities to deliberately select solutions to social problems is reflected in their moral development as well. The cognitive approach to moral development originates in Piaget's theory and was related to children's development of social perspective-taking. Using Piaget's concepts, Kohlberg (1981) refined a cognitive theory of moral development that included six stages. At the earliest stages (Stages 1 and 2), children's moral judgments about responses to social dilemmas are based on a desire to avoid punishing responses from powerful others. Children choose how to respond due to their concern about immediate negative consequences. During Stages 3 and 4, which usually begin during preadolescence, the children become less impulsive and hedonistic, become more cooperative, and show mutual caring. They become more oriented towards acting in a just manner by conforming to conventional standards of behavior. Finally, in the latter stages of moral development, adolescents and young adults develop a sense of autonomous morality in which their conception of justice and fairness is that individuals rationally and cooperatively balance their competing claims and needs. Needless to say, not everyone attains the final stages of moral development in Kohlberg's model. There is less empirical support for the ordering of the latter stages of this sequence than for the early stages. However, the consensus of research findings is that as children become older, they generally move up the lower stages of moral development, or stay at the same level, with only about 7% of children moving down in the stage sequence over time (Carroll & Rest, 1982). Further support for the overall stage sequence is evident in correlational studies in which approximately 50% of the variance in moral judgment scores has been found to be due to the children's age. In a similar manner, Selman's theory of a stage sequence in children's use of interpersonal negotiation strategies, or problem solutions, hypothesizes that children progressively coordinate the perspectives of themselves and others when resolving interpersonal conflicts. Children can eventually become capable of negotiating mutually collaborative solutions, according to this theory (Brion-Meisels & Selman, 1984).

Children's enactment of the solutions they consider is part of a social interaction. As one child enacts a behavioral response in a peer interaction, the other child is busily perceiving the first child's response, inferring the meaning of the behavior, and selecting a counterresponse. Children's behaviors tend to evoke predictable behaviors from others (Meichenbaum, 1985). For example, if a child's behavior is aggressive, a reciprocal aggressive behavior is often elicited from others. On the other hand, if the child's behavior is submissive, a complementary dominance response is usually elicited. These predictable responses from others often reinforce the child's original interpretation of the other as hostile or controlling, even though the original interpretation may have been inaccurate. Because of the behavioral responses that an individual elicits, a child can become the architect of his own environment full of hostile or controlling people, which he then transposes onto one situation after another (Lochman & Allen, 1979).

The growing knowledge about the relationship between problem-solving skills and adjustment has had wide-ranging implications for the development of primary prevention programs in school settings (Allen, Chinsky, Larcen, Lochman & Selinger, 1976); Durlak, 1983; Kirschenbaum, 1983). Targeted at all the students in a classroom, not just the behaviorally and emotionally disturbed children, these innovative programs have used classroom tasks and role playing, often led by classroom teachers, to increase children's competence in using various problem-solving skills (e.g., generating alternative solutions, considering consequences). Research on the longer-term preventive effects of this kind of training is still being conducted, but initial results have been promising (Durlak, 1983).

Metacognition in Social Interactions

Children's metacognitive regulation of their thinking in social situations operates in a manner that is similar to that found in nonsocial situations. By the concrete operational stage, children are capable of using self-guiding verbalizations, or self-talk, to assist their other cognitive processes. Children can use internal self-statements to prepare for aversive events by focusing their attention onto other stimulus cues (e.g., "At least when I'm through with this dentist visit, I can go shopping and I won't have to come back here for 6 months"), as well as to guide their step-by-step problem-solving thinking ("What should I do next?").

One particular aspect of metacognitive development that has an effect on children's social functioning is their increasing ability to recognize and label their own states of arousal and their feelings. As children develop, they become aware of a finer differentiation in their moods and feelings, going from identifying only "glad" and "bad" to feelings such as "frustration" and "disappointment," and they become more accurate in their labeling (Larazus & Folkman, 1984). The way in which children label their arousal during social problem situations has a direct effect on their selection of solutions. In a threatening situation, a child can experience undifferentiated arousal as either fear or anger. If the child labels the feeling as fear, he is more likely to select an avoidant or nonconfrontation strategy than if he labeled the arousal as anger. Therefore, accurate labeling of feelings is an important developmental achievement.

CHILD PSYCHOPATHOLOGY

Deficits in Cognitive and Social Development

Now that we know what to expect over the course of development in children's cognitive and social-cognitive processes, we can turn our attention to deviations in the normal developmental patterns. If students with emotional and behavioral difficulties have particular patterns of distortions and deficits during their development of cognitive processes, then interventions can be designed to impact on these mediating cognitive processes. Cognitive and social-cognitive processes have been the focus of recent research in three areas of child psychopathology that are often apparent in special education and even mainstream classrooms. In this section, we will discuss attention deficits, conduct disorders, and depressive disorders, and we will briefly identify relevant intervention strategies.

Attention Deficit Hyperactivity Disorder

Children with an attention deficit hyperactivity disorder (ADHD) have central difficulties with inattention and with impulsivity, and they may also have associated difficulties with hyperactive behavior (Campbell & Werry, 1986). The core problem is the central attentional difficulty, rather than the surface behavioral manifestation of overactivity. ADHD children lag developmentally in the basic areas of cognitive processing of attention, memory, complex problem-solving, and metacognition. The social-cognitive deficiencies that do appear are less salient, and are generally reactive to the deficits in basic cognitive processing that we will examine next in this section.

Attention. A disorder labeled as attention deficit hyperactivity disorder would certainly be expected to have attentional deficits as major characteristics of the syndrome. Attentional difficulties are indeed apparent in research on ADHD children, although these deficits are less global than was originally believed. In comparison to children without attentional difficulties, ADHD students are less alert to incoming stimuli, and, most importantly, they are less able to sustain their attention on laboratory measures of reaction time and vigilant tasks. These children's difficulty with sustaining attention over time is in turn affected by their basic problem-solving style which deters their ability to organize and maintain their attention. The ADHD child can initially pay attention to task stimuli, but on more complex tasks which require extended periods of attention to the task, this child is unable to regulate his continuing attention and begins to scan his environment for other stimuli.

Is this child's inability to keep attending to the central task due to his inherent distractibility as he readily processes irrelevant as well as relevant information? Research indicates that the ADHD child is not merely more distractible. Using the Central-Incidental Recall Task discussed earlier, Peters (1977) found that ADHD children perform more poorly on Central Recall of relevant information, in comparison to control children, but the two groups of children were not different in their Incidental Recall of irrelevant information. In addition, the ADHD children's Central Memory scores were essentially the same in distraction and nondistraction conditions. While the ADHD children are not generally excessively distracted by irrelevant stimuli (e.g., flashing lights, noise), they do become more distracted than other children by highly salient stimuli when they are working on a boring, difficult task. Thus, an ADHD child tends to pay attention to irrelevant letters on a tedious worksheet only if the irrelevant letters are all made with his favorite color. In general, the conclusions emerging from research studies are that ADHD children have a central developmental deficiency in deploying and sustaining attention on tasks that require extended attention. While the cognitive problem for ADHD children is not simply "wandering attention," they can be prone to focus on irrelevant stimuli if the stimuli are of interest or value to them and if the task is sufficiently frustrating to them (Campbell & Werry, 1986; Douglas, 1983; Kendall & Braswell, 1985).

These findings have implications for certain assumptions that were made by educators in the 1960s and early 1970s. A movement grew at that time to try to teach attention disordered children in "stimulus reduced environments," so that all extraneous stimuli were removed from the students' work areas and from the classroom. These environmental changes were unsuccessful by themselves in improving children's academic performance (Douglas, 1983). This outcome is not surprising when the central problem for ADHD children is viewed as a developmental lag in focusing and refocusing attention on complex tasks, rather than as being easily distracted by any and all stimuli.

The ADHD children's attentional deficiencies are also implicated in their characteristic levels of physiological arousal. In the 1970s, it was hypothesized that children were hyperactive because their central nervous systems were overaroused. Stimulant drugs, such as Ritalin, were felt to have a "paradoxical" effect on the overaroused state. In the interim, studies examining skin conductance, heart rate, and evoked cortical potentials on the electroencephalograph have found that overactive, attentionally deficient children are no different from nonclinical controls in their resting levels of autonomic and central arousal. While they are neither over- nor underaroused at the resting level, the overactive children's physiological arousal was less reactive than control children to specific target stimuli that were introduced (Campbell & Werry, 1986). This lower level of arousal in response to central stimuli may then be associated with ADHD children's attentional difficulties, although it is still not clear if there is a simple causal link between arousal and attention.

Memory. In comparison to control children, ADHD children have been consistently found to be unimpaired in their basic memory recall and recognition in either short-term or long-term memory. These memory tasks have used both short strings of numbers or words to be remembered, as well as stimuli that can be classified together in logically meaningful ways (Douglas, 1983). However, memory weaknesses do become apparent for ADHD children when they have to recall longer sequences of stimuli. Therefore, they process stimuli at superficial and obvious levels, but they have less efficient recall strategies (Douglas, 1983), and they appear to be less effective than most concrete operational children in clustering information in logical ways. These results indicate that ADHD children's deficits on these memory tasks are due to the attentional and problem-solving deficiencies, rather than representing a pure memory deficiency (Campbell & Werry, 1986).

Selection of Strategies and Solutions. A principal characteristic of ADHD children is their inability to use effective inhibitory controls to guide their cognitive problem-solving efforts, thus leading to their cognitive impulsivity. On the Matching Familiar Figures Test (Kagan, Rosman, Day, Albert, & Phillips, 1964), the impulsive ADHD children responded more quickly and made more errors than matched controls. However, this kind of cognitive impulsivity is not specific to ADHD, since conduct disordered children display the pattern. The lack of inhibitory control in ADHD children is evident in their inability to withhold responding until target stimuli appear, their acting before they have understood a problem clearly, and their acting before they have given sufficient thought to possible solutions.

When they have adequate reinforcement and motivation, ADHD children actually demonstrate adequate problem-solving skills as simple concept-formation tasks where they choose between two options (Parry & Douglas, 1983). However, when tasks include large stimulus arrays, ADHD children perform more poorly as they attempt to determine the relevant dimensions in the stimulus array. Tant and Douglas (1982) presented ADHD and non-ADHD children with an array of 16 stimuli items that varied on four dimensions, such as type of letter (A or B), size of letter (large or small), position of letter (upright or sideways), and background shape (round or square). They then asked the children to find the "correct," preselected stimulus by asking as few questions as possible, in the form of the game "20 Questions." Efficient problem-solvers abstract out the dimensions on their own and ask their questions about these dimensions rather than about individual items. They then remove half of the remaining stimulus items with each question. ADHD children asked less efficient questions, identified fewer relevant dimensions, and made less efficient use of the dimensions they did identify. Instead, their problem solving often consisted of trial-and-error guesses about individual items.

The essential distinction between ADHD and non-ADHD children is that ADHD children rely on exploration of the stimulus situation rather than using search strategies which are directed by logical problem-solving abilities. ADHD children are developmentally delayed in their attention and problem-solving abilities. ADHD children function like younger children since their attention is controlled by highly salient, curiosity-producing features of the stimuli. Non-ADHD children function at a more advanced concrete operational level where these diffuse, exploratory behaviors have been replaced by the children's self-governed, goal-directed search strategies. These strategies allow the children to gather specific information from their environment which is required for solution of a task (Douglas, 1983). The ADHD child has a limited development of Piagetian cognitive structures which permit higher-order classification of concepts, and which would then enable more accurate perception and retrieval of information.

Metacognitive Regulation. ADHD children not only use less efficient problem-solving strategies, but they are less aware of the strategies they enact. ADHD children are less able to verbalize aloud to themselves, or to others, what their current strategy is (Douglas, 1983). As expected, they display less conscious and overt control over their own thinking.

Social-cognitive processing. While less research has been conducted on the social-cognitive processing of ADHD children, the available results indicate that the social-cognitive deficiencies are not as likely to be primary sources of children's difficulties as are the basic cognitive deficiencies. In certain social-cognitive processes, ADHD children, as a group, are not deficient. Thus, ADHD children have been found to think about the social perspectives of others as well as children in control groups (Ackerman, Elardo, & Dykman, 1979; Paulauskas & Campbell, 1979). However, ADHD children do have a low sense of self-esteem, they expect to fail on academic tasks, and they perceive themselves as relatively unpopular (Campbell & Werry, 1986). These latter self-perceptions are, in fact, accurate, since they do have poorer academic achievement, and their classmates actively reject them on sociometric, peer-nomination measures and indicate that their social skills often consist of aggressive, domineering behaviors (Cambell & Werry, 1986). Once these negative self-perceptions become firmly developed, the perceptions themselves can maintain the ADHD children's lack of sustained attention and organized problem-solving. The ADHD child who expects that he will not be successful on an academic or social task, will then process information in a cursory, defensive manner, will have a low frustration threshold, and will not persist in deliberate cognitive processing of how to respond to the task. Thus, while the self-perception may or may not have been central in the development of the child's attentional difficulties, the self-perception can certainly be a useful focus of intervention due to its potential for maintaining the difficulty.

Intervention Implications. Intervention in the school setting with the cognitive deficits of ADHD children includes medication, as well as behavioral and cognitive-behavioral approaches. Stimulant medications such as dextroamphetamine (Dexedrine) and methylphenidate (Ritalin) excite the central nervous system, and a large number of studies have indicated that these medications effectively enhance ADHD children's attention and reduce their motoric over-activity (Gittelman & Kanner, 1986). However, these gains in attention do not by themselves improve learning, and medication alone is not effective in increasing children's academic achievement. In fact, medication use can reinforce the external locus of control that already exists in ADHD children's expectancies. ADHD children on stimulant medication have been found to perceive both good and bad behavior as being out of their control; instead, they perceive these behaviors as being dependent on whether they have taken their medication (Whalen & Henker, 1980). Thus, careful clinical judgment is required in decisions about using medication with ADHD children, since both clear positive effects, as well as negative psychological and physical side effects, occur.

A variety of behavioral and cognitive-behavioral interventions have been used with ADHD children. Response-cost contingencies appear to have beneficial effects upon on-task classroom behavior, and response-cost procedures have produced stronger improvements than Ritalin on academic performance (Kendall, 1984). Cognitive-behavioral interventions are particularly well-suited for the basic cognitive deficiencies identified for ADHD, and these intervention packages can be adapted for use in school settings by teachers and counselors. Kendall has developed a 12-session Self-Instruction Training program for impulsive children (Kendall & Braswell, 1985). In this program, a child acquires a series of self-instructions that he will use to guide and reinforce his behavior on academic tasks, as well as in social situations (e.g., "What is the problem?" "What are my choices?" "I had better concentrate and focus in." "I think this is the right choice." "I really did a good job," or "I made a mistake. I'll go slower next time."). As suggested by Vygotsky and Meichenbaum, Kendall includes faded rehearsal in the intervention, which progresses from the therapist modeling the self-statements out loud while working on a task, to the child whispering the statements, and finally, to the child covertly saying the self-statements to himself. In comparison to control conditions, the Self-Instruction Training program has been effective in increasing impulsive children's self-control and decreasing their hyperactivity, according to teachers' ratings (Kendall & Wilcox, 1980; Kendall & Zupan, 1981). This type of cognitive-behavioral intervention has been more effective with concrete-operational, rather than preoperational, children (Cohen, Meyers, Schlesser, & Rodick, 1982), apparently due to the older children's greater capacity for developing metacognition and self-directed problem solving. Research has also suggested that, at least in certain areas, the combination of self-control training and of medication may be more effective than either intervention alone (Horn, Chatoor, & Connors, 1983).

Conduct Disorder

While children with attention deficit disorder appear to have central deficiencies in their basic cognitive processes along with relatively few identified deficiencies in the social-cognitive realm, the pattern of cognitive and social-cognitive deficiencies is reversed for conduct-disordered children. We will focus on conduct-disordered children who emit high levels of aggressive behaviors towards others. Aggressive children have a consistent pattern of social-cognitive deficiencies and distortions, and comprehensive information-processing models have been used more with aggression than with other disorders to effectively depict the interrelationship among this network of processes (Dodge, 1986; Lochman, 1984; Lochman, 1987, Lochman, Nelson & Sims, 1981). These social-cognitive deficiencies will now be examined.

Attention to and Memory of Social Cues.   Aggressive children perceive the cues in the environment around them in a different manner than nonaggressive children do. To examine how children attend to social cues, Dodge and his colleagues had children listen to a series of audiotaped interviews in which child actors say hostile, benevolent, and neutral things about their classmates. After listening to the interviews, the children were asked to remember as many statements as they could. Aggressive children remembered more of the last statements they heard, indicating that they had a developmental lag in this aspect of their processing, since recency effects in recall is more typical of younger children's memory (Milich & Dodge, 1984). In addition, when they had a choice about how long they would listen to taped statements about a fictional child before making decisions about that child's intentions, nonagressive boys listened to 40% more cues before making a decision than did aggressive boys. The aggressive boys' tendencies to not attend to very many multiple cues while trying to understand the meaning of others' behavior is similar to younger children's behavior, again representing a developmental lag (Dodge & Newman, 1981). However, in a recent study using these same audiotaped interviews, Lochman (1988) found that aggressive boys actually recalled significantly more of the taped statements they heard than did nonaggressive boys.

These findings indicate that aggressive children are hypervigilant in scanning their social environment, actually attending to more immediate cues than do nonaggressive children. However, the aggressive children tend to live for the moment, remembering briefly what has just happened around them, and then forgetting information that occurred earlier in the interaction. While they are hypervigilant in exploring their environment, aggressive children do not appear to be oriented towards using sustained search strategies which could planfully address more complex inferences about others' behavior, such as intentionality.

Interpretation of Social Cues.   In addition to perceiving social situations in their characteristic style, aggressive boys have been found to be 50% more likely than nonaggressive boys to infer that an antagonist in a hypothetical provocation had acted with hostile rather than benign intent (Dodge, 1980). This tendency for aggressive children to misinterpret others' intentions as being hostile has been replicated with both children and adolescents in a series of studies. A wide variety of experimental stimuli have been used in these studies, including written stories, videotaped vignettes, and observation of a hostile child knocking down the block-building project the target children had made (Milich & Dodge, 1984);

Nasby, Hayden & DePaulo, 1980; Steinberg & Dodge, 1983). Aggressive children and aggressive adolescents were less skilled in their social perspective-taking abilities (Jurkovic & Prentice, 1977). The hostile attributional bias has occurred more often when a child has attended to and recalled a higher proportion of hostile cues (Dodge & Frame, 1982). The attributional bias also appears to be significantly influenced by the aggressive child's prior expectations that the peer would be hostile towards him in the future (Dodge & Frame, 1982). Thus, the aggressive child's attributional bias is influenced by his perception of what just happened to him as well as by his expectations for what will happen in the future.

Recent research has found that, in actual competitive dyadic discussions with a nonaggressive peer, aggressive boys not only overperceive the aggressiveness of the peer, but they also substantially underestimate their own aggressiveness (Lochman, 1987). Due to their distorted perceptions of the peers and of themselves, aggressive boys do not appear to assume responsibility for the conflict that develops in these discussions, blaming the disagreements on the peer. This pattern of distortions would allow these boys to later feel quite justified in responding in an intensely aggressive manner.

Selection of Solutions to Social Problems. One feature that disrupts planful, goal-oriented problem-solving thinking by aggressive boys is their usual impulsive cognitive style (Camp, 1977). They rely on the quick, automatic mode of cognitive processing, and are less likely to deliberately, carefully process their choices of responses in a problem situation. By using automatic processing extensively, the effectiveness and competence of their social response is highly dependent on the content or type of the problem solution that is accessed at the top of the "memory bin" during automatic processing.

The content or type of solutions that aggressive children consider tend to be different than the solution choices of nonaggressive children. Using a set of hypothetical, open-middle stories, in which boys were asked to make up what could happen between the social conflict at the beginning of the story and the problem no longer existing at the end, aggressive boys considered more nonverbal, direct action solutions and fewer verbal assertion solutions (Lochman & Lampron, 1986). Neither group of boys frequently considered physical aggression solutions for these early stages of conflict, and the overall number of solutions considered were about the same for both groups. Thus, if the aggressive child sees that another boy is holding a basketball which he thinks belongs to him, the aggressive boy is likely to walk over and abruptly take the ball back. The nonaggressive boy is likely to go over and tell the other child to give him the ball back because it's his. By verbally labeling what they want, even in a simple, direct manner, the nonaggressive children's peers are better able to understand what the nonaggressive children's intentions are, rather than incorrectly assuming they may have been hostile.

The aggressive boys' reliance on direct action rather than verbal assertion is notably more pronounced when the antagonists in the stories have hostile rather than apparently nonhostile intentions. Thus, the hostile interpretations that a child makes about the intentions of others appear to narrow the aggressive child's thinking of solutions to less competent ones (Dodge, 1980; Lochman & Lampron, 1986). In a recent study, aggressive boys produced other, more competent solutions when they responded in the deliberate processing mode rather than the automatic mode (Lochman, Lampron, & Rabiner, 1987). When aggressive boys responded to a multiple-choice version of the Problem-Solving Measure for Conflict, rather than the usual open-middle format, they selected dramatically higher rates of verbal assertion and very few direct action solutions. Therefore, aggressive boys do appear to be potentially capable of accessing more competent solutions that are lower in their ''memory bin,'' and interventions can focus on making these existing, but unused, choices.

As children reason about which solution to enact, they can consider the consequences of their actions, and plan how the solution will be enacted. Aggressive children and adolescents have deficits in the latter planning, or means-ends thinking (Platt, Spivack, Altman, Altman & Peizer, 1974). Aggressive children are less able to specify and elaborate how their solutions would be enacted, and are less able to anticipate the potential obstacles that could frustrate their efforts to reach their goal. By considering the consequences and implications of their possible actions, children engage in moral judgment. Aggressive children and adolescent delinquents consistently have lower levels of moral reasoning (Edelman & Goldstein, 1981; Jurkovic & Prentice, 1977; Nucci & Herman, 1982). They reason at a preconventional level of moral development, primarily attempting to avoid the punishments of authority figures, rather than acting cooperatively to enhance the positive consequences for both themselves and others.

Basic Cognitive Processes. The problem-solving difficulties of aggressive children appear to be due primarily to deficits at the level of social-cognitive processing or reasoning about social situations, since these children display adequate basic concept-formation abilities when they work on nonsocial tasks (Lochman, 1988). However, the aggressive children's hypervigilant perceptual style with social stimuli is reflective of the perceptual style they use with nonsocial stimuli as well, indicating that this aspect of their processing may be ''hard-wired.'' Aggressive undersocialized delinquents have been found to be ''stimulation-seeking,'' since they excessively prefer novel and complex stimuli to more common stimuli (Skrzypek, 1969). In addition, aggressive children not only have better recall of audiotaped social statements, as discussed previously, but they also tend to recall more missing details in nonsocial drawings. They think that elements in the pictures have changed when they actually have not (Lochman, 1988). In general, aggressive children are extremely sensitive to cues in their immediate environment, regardless of whether the stimuli are social or not.

Intervention Implications. Focusing on these deficiencies and distortions in cognitive and social-cognitive processes, a variety of training programs have been developed for aggressive children (Camp, Blom, Herbert, & Van Doorninck, 1977; Forman, 1980; Kazdin, Esveldt-Dawson, French, & Unis, 1978; Kettlewell & Kausch, 1983) and aggressive adolescents (Feindler, Ecton, Kingsley, & Dubey, 1986). The Anger Coping Program (Lochman, Lampron, Gemmer, & Harris, 1987) is an 18-session intervention using cognitive-behavioral and social problem-solving training procedures that has been developed for use with aggressive children in school settings. Children meet weekly in a group at school, with four or five other children, and with two group leaders. The 18 sessions focus on (1) establishing group rules and reinforcement for group behavior, (2) using self-statements to inhibit impulsive behavior, (3) identifying the social perspectives of different children using pictured, role-played, and actual social problems, (4) generating alternative solutions (especially verbal assertion) and considering the consequences of alternative solutions to social problems, (5) viewing videotapes of children who are modeling physiological arousal when angry, using self-statements ("Stop! Think! What should I do?"), and using the complete set of problem-solving skills with social problems, (6) the children's planning and making of their own videotape of inhibitory self-statements and social problem-solving, and (8) implementing social problem-solving skills with children's current anger arousal problems through discussion and role playing. To enhance generalization to the classroom, the children in these groups set weekly classroom goals for themselves which are monitored daily by teachers.

Research has indicated that by the end of intervention, aggressive boys in the Anger Coping Program have reduced their disruptive-aggressive classroom behavior and their parent-rated aggressive behavior, in comparison to other aggressive boys in untreated or minimal treatment conditions (Lochman, Burch, Curry, & Lampron, 1984; Lochman & Curry, 1986). Children who were initially the poorest problem-solvers, and who potentially had the most to gain from this kind of intervention, made the greatest reductions in their disruptive and aggressive behavior (Lochman, Lampron, Burch, & Curry, 1985). In addition to being implemented by school teachers or counselors in small-group sessions, social problem-solving intervention strategies have also been effectively used on an ongoing basis in special education classrooms (Robin, Schneider, & Dolnick, 1976).

Depressive Disorders

In comparison to attention deficit hyperactivity disorder and to conduct disorder, less research has been directed at the cognitive correlates of depressive disorders. However, evidence indicates that deficiencies are selectively apparent in certain cognitive and social-cognitive processes for depressed children, and these processes have become an area of emerging interest in child psychopathology.

Memory and Problem Solving. Consistent with research findings on depressed adults, depressed children appear to have impaired functioning in their speed and accuracy of recall of nonsocial information, and in their complex problem-solving skills (Quay & LaGreca, 1986). In one study, happy, sad, or neutral states were induced in preschool children, whose performance on memory recall task was examined. Memories of the stimulus items were recalled more slowly by children in the sad affective state than by happy children (Barden, Garber, Duncan, & Masters, 1981). Similar patterns of slow memory retrieval and related attention disruptions have been suggested with seriously depressed children. Depressed fifth and sixth grade children have longer response latencies, as well as more errors, on the Matching Familiar Figures Test, in comparison to nondepressed children (Schwartz, Friedman, Lindsay, & Narrol, 1983).

Depressed children's problem-solving efforts on nonsocial concept-formation tasks were also deficient. Fifth and sixth grade children who had a high number of depressive symptoms on the Children's Depression Inventory performed poorly on two problem-solving tasks involving an anagram task and the Block Design subtest of the Wechsler Intelligence Scale for Children-Revised (Kaslow, Tanenbaum, Abramson, Peterson, & Seligman, 1983). Even though the depressed and nondepressed children in this study had similar vocabulary skills, the depressed children were less able on the anagram task to make new words from existing words (e.g., teacher, father) within a time limit. Another study replicated this pattern of results (Mullins, Siegel, & Hodges, 1985), and also found that the depressed children's problem-solving deficiencies did not extend over to the number of step-by-step solutions they could generate on an untimed, social problem-solving measure. Therefore, depressed children are slower in recalling information presented to them, apparently because of internal disruptions in their focusing of attention on the task. This slowness of cognitive processing, along with a reduced ability to sustain problem-solving strategies, leads to reductions in their performances on complex concept-formation tasks despite having the vocabulary skills to perform adequately on these tasks. This cognitive processing deficit occurs at the basic processing level, rather than merely surfacing with social stimuli

Attributions and Meaning of Social Cues. Depressed children tend to develop distinct and self-defeating ways of perceiving their own and others' behaviors. Depressed children have lower expectations for their performance on laboratory tasks, rate their performance on tasks in a more negative manner, and set overly stringent standards for success, in comparison to nondepressed children (Kaslow, Rehm, & Siegel, 1984). These distorted expectations and perceptions of themselves may then contribute to the depressed children's delayed and inefficient thinking on tasks. In a recent study of depressed children who were receiving services in an outpatient clinic, depressed children lacked a "self-serving attributional bias." According to the self-serving attributional bias, which has been consistently noted in social-psychological research, people normally claim credit for their successes and blame their failures and bad outcomes on external causes. Depressed children, in contrast, did not differ in their attributions of causes for good and bad events happening to them (Kaslow, Rehm, Pollack, & Siegel, 1988), and thus took more global self-blame for negative outcomes than did other children. This attributional style (internal, stable, global) is quite similar to the self-perceptions of socially withdrawn and anxious children

(Quay & LaGreca, 1986), who also were found to be self-deprecating and to have excessively strict internal standards. This suggests that there is a commonality in this aspect of cognitive processing for children with various kinds of internalizing disorders.

Intervention Implications. Little formal research has been conducted on interventions with these cognitive and social-cognitive processes. In the school setting, teachers and counselors can most effectively address the children's distorted attributions and expectations, and their potentially deficient social skills. Stress inoculation training (Meichenbaum, 1985) is one form of cognitive behavioral intervention with individuals with internalizing disorders. Within this framework, depressed children are asked to describe in detail what they think prior to, during, and immediately after stressful situations that include academic tasks and social encounters in everyday school life. Children may be asked to keep an ongoing diary of their reactions to these situations. Based on the children's typical negative self-thoughts, the counselor or teacher can work with the children to develop a set of coping self-statements to think about when they next encounter the stressful situation. The coping self-statements (Meichenbaum, 1985) include those to prepare for the stressor ("This could be rough, but I can work out a plan to handle it"), confront the stressful situation ("One step at a time; I can do it"), cope with feelings of being overwhelmed ("Time to take a deep breath and problem solve"), and evaluate the coping efforts ("I did pretty well," "It didn't work that time. That's OK"). In addition to reversing the child's negative expectations, social-skill training may be useful with depressed children who are also socially withdrawn. Coaching and role playing can be used to help children develop verbal and nonverbal skills to initiate interactions with others, respond to the initiation of peers, and keep the interactions going (Oden & Asher, 1977).

IMPLICATIONS FOR THE NEXT STAGE

If we adopt a developmental metacognitive perspective to examine our own current understanding of children's cognitive processing in general, and of cognitive processing in behaviorally and emotionally disturbed children in particular, we are left with a major conclusion found at the end of this chapter. Available evidence indicates that we are now ready for the next stage in the development of our understanding of these processes. Several critical questions will assist us with this cognitive shift, and these questions are likely to be the focus of energetic research in coming years.

First, what roles do the family and the peer group play in the child's development of unique means of perceiving and responding to his environment? It is likely that much of a child's deficient cognitive processing is due to the parents', peers', and teachers' ways of perceiving and responding to the child, but the means of transmission are not clear. Better understanding of the ways in which certain parental behaviors can lead to deficiencies and distortions in a child's cognitive processing, which in turn can lead to the child's maladaptive behavior in his immediate environment, will assist educational and mental health professionals in planning more effective preventive interventions for these disorders.

How are a child's feelings related to his cognitive processes? The study of children's cognitive processes has focused too heavily on these rational (or irrational) aspects of a child's development. We need to understand more clearly how intense feelings, such as anger or depression, can lead to certain cognitive styles, as well as how certain cognitive structures may result from the child's current emotional state, as well as initiating and maintaining the emotional states. In a similar vein, we need to know more clearly how certain cognitions (e.g., coping processes) lead to behavior change, as well as how behavior leads to cognitive changes.

Finally, can school-based cognitively oriented interventions have long-term effects on students' later adjustment? This is perhaps the most critical of these questions, and one that educators and psychologists can pursue actively during this next stage of inquiry. In many ways, cognitive theory fosters this spirit of inquiry by providing a framework to direct the researcher and the teacher in the classroom to creatively understand and accommodate to their children's ongoing and developing behaviors.

SUMMARIES

Children's ways of thinking about both social and nonsocial stimuli and tasks systematically develop during childhood and adolescence. Qualitative shifts in children's cognitive processing skills are typically observed at several points during this development. Children who have difficulties with focusing and sustaining attention on tasks, with their aggressive behavior, or with their depressive feelings can have clear deficiencies and distortions in their cognitive and social-cognitive processing. In many ways, these disturbed children seem to have developmental lags in their cognitive processing, so that they think about handling problems and tasks as younger children would. Thus, how children perceive and understand the events in their lives and how they decide to respond to those events have important implications for their behavioral adjustment.

The kinds of cognitive and social-cognitive processes discussed in this chapter are processes that teachers and school counselors can recognize in their students. Teachers and counselors have an excellent vantage point from which they can observe and try to understand their students' thinking processes. Educational professionals have the opportunity to assist their students in developing more workable and competent coping and problem-solving skills through their direct daily work with their students.

DISCUSSION QUESTIONS

1. A teacher notices that a 6-year-old student is upset that he received a wide, shallow can of clay. He says that he didn't get as much clay as the other children in the class who received tall, skinny cans, even though the teacher said before she passed out the clay that all the cans had the same amount of clay. Why might the child have perceived that he had received less clay?

2. A fifth grade teacher saw Sam claim that Jim had taken Sam's new backpack. Actually, Jim had just received a backpack that looked similar to Sam's. Sam grabbed the backpack out of Jim's hands, and Jim then told Sam to give it back. Sam refused, and a loud argument and pushing match ensued. Why did Sam, who has chronic problems with aggressive behavior, perceive and handle the situation in this way? What could a teacher or school counselor do with Sam?

3. When a psychologist observed Shirley in her second grade classroom, he found that Shirley frequently stared out the window, got up every 5 minutes to sharpen her pencils, and never completed her worksheets. Shirley has average intelligence, and she usually starts classroom tasks adequately at the beginning, but then soon has difficulty keeping her attention on the task. What cognitive processing deficiencies potentially contribute to Shirley's classroom difficulties? What can the teacher, counselor, or psychologist do to assist with the problem?

4. Frank is a seventh grader who has become increasingly dejected and morose during the course of the school year. He rarely seems to be happy. The teacher has noticed that Frank has become less able to complete school tasks, even though he had been regarded as a good student several years before. Frank often criticizes his work performance, and he says that he can't keep up with his classwork. What kinds of attribution and expectation biases is Frank likely to experience? What could be done to help him?

REFERENCES

Achenbach, T. W. (1982). *Developmental psychopathology* (2nd ed.). New York: Wiley.

Ackerman, P. T., Elardo, P. T., & Dykman, R. A. (1979). A psychosocial study of hyperactive and learning disabled boys. *Journal of Abnormal Child Psychology, 7,* 91–100.

Allen, G., Chinsky, J., Larcen, S., Lochman, J. E., & Selinger, H. (1976). *Community psychology and the schools: A behaviorally oriented multi-level preventive approach.* New York: Wiley.

Austin, V. D., Ruble, D., & Trasbasso, T. (1977). Recall and order effects as factors in children's moral judgments. *Child Development, 48,* 470–474.

Bakker, D. J. (1983). Hemispheric specialization and specific reading retardation. In M. Rutter (Ed.), *Developmental neuropsychiatry* (pp. 498–506). New York: Guilford.

Baldwin, A. L. (1967). *Theories of child development.* New York: Wiley.

Barden, R. C., Garber, J., Duncan, S. W., & Masters, J. C. (1981). Cumulative effects of induced affective states in children: Accentuation, inoculation, and remediation. *Journal of Personality and Social Psychology, 40,* 750–760.

Brion-Meisels, S., & Selman, R. L. (1984). Early adolescent development of new interpersonal strategies: Understanding and intervention. *Psychological Review, 13,* 278–291.

Camp, B. W. (1977). Verbal mediation in young aggressive boys. *Journal of Abnormal Psychology, 86,* 145–153.

Camp, B. W., Blom,G. E., Herbert, F., & VanDoornick, W. J. (1977). "Think Aloud": A program for developing self-control in young aggressive boys. *Journal of Abnormal Child Psychology, 5,* 157–169.

Campbell, S. W., & Werry, J. S. (1986). Attention deficit disorder (Hyperactivity). In H. C. Quay & J. S. Werry (Eds.), *Psychopathological disorders of childhood* (3rd ed.) (pp. 111–155). New York: Wiley.

Carroll, J. L., & Rest, J. R. (1982). Moral development. In B. Wolman & G. Stricker (Eds.), *Handbook of developmental psychology* (pp. 434–451). Englewood Cliffs, NJ: Prentice-Hall.

Cohen, R., Meyers, A., Schlesser, R., & Rodick, J. D. (1982). *Generalization of self-instructions: Effects of cognitive level and training procedures.* Unpublished manuscript, Memphis State University.

Cohen, R., & Schlesser, R. (1984). Cognitive development and clinical implications. In A. W. Meyers & W. E. Craighead (Eds.), *Cognitive behavior therapy with children* (pp. 45–68). New York: Plenum.

Cohen, R., Schlesser, R., & Meyers, A. (1981). Self instructions: Effects of cognitive level and active rehearsal. *Journal of Experimental Child Psychology, 32,* 65–76.

Costanzo, P. R., Coie, J. D., Grumet, J., & Farnhill, D. (1973). A re-examination of the effects of intent and consequence on children's moral judgments. *Child Development, 45,* 799–802.

Costanzo, P. R., & Fraenkel, P. (1987). Social influence, socialization, and the development of social cognition. The heart of the matter. In N. Eisenberg (Ed.), *Contemporary topics in developmental psychology* (pp. 190–215). New York: Wiley.

Diamond, N. (1982). Cognitive theory. In B. Wolman & G. Stricker (Eds.), *Handbook of developmental psychology* (pp. 3–22). Englewood Cliffs, NJ: Prentice-Hall.

Dodge, K. A. (1980). Social cognition and children's aggressive behavior. *Child Development, 51,* 162–170.

Dodge, K. A. (1986). A social information processing model of social competence in children. In M. Perlmutter (Ed.), *Cognitive perspectives on children's social and behavioral development* (pp. 77–125). Hillsdale, NJ: Erlbaum.

Dodge, K. A., & Frame, C. L. (1982). Social cognitive biases and deficits in aggressive boys. *Child Development, 53,* 620–635.

Dodge, K. A., & Newman, J. P. (1981). Biased decision-making processes in aggressive boys. *Journal of Abnormal Psychology, 90,* 375–329.

Douglas, V. I. (1983). Attentional and cognitive problems. In M. Rutter (Ed.), *Developmental neuropsychiatry* (pp. 280–329). New York: Guilford.

Durlak, J. A. (1983). Providing mental health services to elementary school children. In C. E. Walker & M. C. Roberts (Eds.), *Handbook of clinical child psychology* (pp. 660–679). New York: Wiley.

Edelman, E. M., & Goldstein, A. P. (1981). Moral education. In A. P. Goldstein, E. G. Carr, W. S. Davidson III, & P. Wehr (Eds.), *In response to aggression: Methods of control and prosocial alternatives* (pp. 253–315). New York: Pergamon.

Feffer, M., & Gourevitch, V. (1960). Cognitive aspects of role-taking in children. *Journal of Personality, 28,* 383–396.

Feindler, E. L., Ecton, R. B., Kingsley, D., & Dubey, D. R. (1986). Group anger-control training for institutionalized psychiatric male adolescents. *Behavior Therapy, 17,* 109–123.

Flavell, J. H. (1977). *Cognitive development.* Englewood Cliffs, NJ: Prentice-Hall.

Flavell, J. H., Beach, D. R., & Chinsky, J. M. (1966). Spontaneous verbal rehearsal in a memory task as a function of age. *Child Development, 37,* 283–299.

Forman, S. G. (1980). A comparison of cognitive training and response cost procedures in modifying aggressive behavior of elementary school children. *Behavior Therapy, 11,* 594–600.

Gittelman, R., & Kanner, A. (1986). Psychopharmacotherapy. In H. C. Quay & J. S. Werry (Eds.), *Psychopathological disorders of childhood* (3rd ed.) (pp. 455–494). New York: Wiley.

Hagen, J. W., & Kail, R. V. (1973). Facilitation and distraction in short term memory. *Child Development, 44,* 831–836.

Hoffman, M. L. (1983). Empathy, guilt, and social cognition. In W. F. Overton (Ed.), *The relationship between social and cognitive development* (pp. 1-51). Hillsdale, NJ: Erlbaum.

Horn, W. F., Chatoor, I., & Connors, C. K. (1983). Additive effects of Dexedrine and self-control training: A multiple assessment. *Behavior Modification, 7,* 383–402.

Jurkovic, G. J., & Prentice, N. M. (1977). Relation of moral and cognitive development to dimensions of juvenile delinquency. *Journal of Abnormal Psychology, 86,* 414–420.

Kagan, J., Roman, B., Day, D., Albert, J., & Phillips, W. (1964). Information processing in the child: Significance of analytic and reflective attitudes. *Psychological Monographs, 78,* (1, Whole No. 578).

Kaslow, N. J., Rehm, L. P., Pollack, S. L., & Siegel, A. W. (1988). Attributional style and self-control behavior in depressed and non-depressed children and their parents. *Journal of Abnormal Child Psychology, 16,* 163–177.

Kaslow, N. J., Rehm, L. P., & Siegel, H. W. (1984). Social-cognitive and cognitive correlates of depression in children. *Journal of Abnormal Psychology, 12,* 605–620.

Kaslow, N. J., Tanenbaum, R. L., Abramson, L. Y., Peterson, C., & Seligman, M. E. P. (1983). Problem-solving deficits and depressive symptoms among children. *Journal of Abnormal Child Psychology, 11,* 497–502.

Kazdin, A. E., Esveldt-Dawson, K., French, N. H., & Unis, A. S. (1987). Problem-solving skills training and relationship therapy in the treatment of antisocial child behavior. *Journal of Consulting and Clinical Psychology, 55,* 76–85.

Kendall, P. C. (1984). Cognitive processes and procedures in behavior therapy. In C. M. Franks, G. T. Wilson, P. C. Kendall, & K. D. Brownell (Eds.), *Annual review of behavior therapy: Theory and practice* (Vol. 10.) (pp. 123–163). New York: Guilford.

Kendall, P. C., & Braswell, L. (1985). *Cognitive-behavioral therapy for impuslive children.* New York: Guilford.

Kendall, P. C., & Wilcox, L. E. (1980). A cognitive-behavioral treatment for impulsivity: Concrete versus conceptual training in non-self-controlled problem children. *Journal of Consulting and Clinical Psychology, 48,* 80–91.

Kendall, P. C., & Zupan, B. A. (1981). Individual versus group application of cognitive-behavioral strategies for developing self-control in children. *Behavior Therapy, 12,* 344–359.

Kendler, H. H., & Kendler, T. S. (1962). Vertical and horizontal processes in problem-solving. *Psychological Review, 69,* 1–16.

Kettlewell, P. W., & Kausch, D. F. (1983). The generalization of the effects of a cognitive-behavioral treatment program for aggressive children. *Journal of Abnormal Child Psychology, 11,* 101–114.

Kirschenbaum, D. S. (1983). Toward more behavioral early intervention programs: A rationale. *Professional Psychology: Research and Practice, 47,* 778–780.

Kohlberg, L. (1981). *The philosophy of moral development: Moral stages and the idea of justice.* San Francisco: Harper & Row.

Kurdek, L. A. (1977). Structural components and intellectual correlates of cognitive perspective taking in first through fourth grade children. *Child Development, 48,* 1503–1511.

Lazarus, R. S., & Folkman, S. (1984). *Stress, appraisal, and coping.* New York: Springer.

Livesley, W. J., & Bromley, D. B. (1973). *Person perception in childhood and adolescence.* New York: Wiley.

Lochman, J. E. (1984). Psychological charcteristics and assessment of aggressive adolescents. In C. Keith (Ed.), *The aggressive adolescent: A clinical perspective* (pp. 17-62). New York: The Free Press.

Lochman, J. E. (1987). Self and peer perceptions and attributional biases of aggressive and nonaggressive boys in dyadic interactions. *Journal of Consulting and Clincal Psychology, 55,* 404–410.

Lochman, J. E. (1988). *Hardware versus software: The level of deficiency in cognitive and social-cognitive processing of aggressive boys.* Unpublished manuscript, Duke University Medical Center.

Lochman, J. E., & Allen, G. J. (1979). Elicited effects of approval and disapproval: An examination of parameters having implications for counseling couples in conflict. *Journal of Consulting and Clinical Psychology, 47,* 634–636.

Lochman, J. E., Burch, P. R., Curry, J. F., & Lampron, L. B. (1984). Treatment and generalization effects of cognitive behavioral and goal setting interventions with aggressive boys. *Journal of Consulting and Clinical Psychology, 52,* 915–916.

Lochman, J. E., & Curry, J. F. (1986). Effects of social problem-solving training and of self-instruction training with aggressive boys. *Journal of Clinical Child Psychology, 15,* 159–164.

Lochman, J. E., & Lampron, L. B. (1986). Situational social problem-solving skills and self-esteem of aggressive and nonaggressive boys. *Journal of Abnormal Child Psychology, 14,* 605–617.

Lochman, J. E., Lampron, L. B., Burch, P. R., & Curry, J. F. (1985) Client characteristics associated with behavior change for treated and untreated aggressive boys. *Journal of Abnormal Child Psychology, 13,* 527–538.

Lochman, J. E., Lampron, L. G., Gemmer, T., & Harris, S. (1987). Anger coping interventions for aggressive children: Guide to implementation in school settings. In P. A. Keller & S. R. Heyman (Eds.), *Innovations in clinical practice: A source book* (Vol. 6) (pp. 339–356). Sarasota, FL: Professional Resources Exchange.

Lochman, J. E., Lampron, L. B., & Rabiner, D. L. (August, 1987). *Salience effects in the social problem-solving of aggressive boys.* Paper presented at the American Psychological Association annual convention, New York.

Lochman, J. E., Nelson, W. M., III, & Sims, J. P. (1981). A cognitive behavioral program for use with aggressive children. *Journal of Clinical Child Psychology, 10,* 146–148.

Luria, A. (1961). *The role of speech in the regulation of normal and abnormal behaviors.* New York: Liverwright.

Masur, E. F., McIntyre, C. W., & Flavell, J. H. (1973). Developmental changes in apportionment of study time among items in a multi-trial free recall task. *Journal of Experimental Child Psychology, 15,* 237–246.

Meichenbaum, D. (1985). *Stress inoculation training.* New York: Pergamon.

Milich, R., & Dodge, K. A. (1984). Social information processing in child psychiatric populations. *Journal of Abnormal Child Psychology, 12,* 471–490.

Mullins, L. L., Siegel, L. J., & Hodges, K. (1985). Cognitive problem-solving and life event correlates of depressive symptoms in children. *Journal of Abnormal Child Psychology, 13,* 305–314.

Nasby, W., Hayden, B., & DePaulo, B. M. (1980). Attributional bias among aggressive boys to interpret unambiguous social stimuli as displays of hostility. *Journal of Abnormal Psychology, 89,* 459–468.

Neimark, E. D. (1982). Adolescent thought: Transition to formal operations. In B. B. Wolman & G. Stricker (Eds.), *Handbook of developmental psychology* (pp. 486-502). Englewood Cliffs, NJ: Prentice-Hall.

Neimark, E. D., Slotnick, N. S., & Ulrich, T. (1971). Development of memorization strategies. *Developmental Psychology, 5,* 427–432.

Neisser, U. (1967). *Cognitive psychology.* Englewood Cliffs, NJ: Prentice-Hall.

Nucci, L. P., & Herman, S. (1982). Behavioral disordered children's conceptions of moral, conventional, and personal issues. *Journal of Abnormal Child Psychology, 10,* 411–426.

Oden, S., & Asher, S. R. (1977). Coaching children in social skills for friendship making. *Child Development, 48,* 495–506.

Paris, S. G., & Lindauer, B. K. (1982). The development of cognitive skills during childhood. In B. B. Wolman & G. Stricker (Eds.), *Handbook of developmental psychology* (pp. 333–349). Englewood Cliffs, NJ: Prentice-Hall.

Parry, P., & Douglas, V. I. (1983). Effects of reinforcement on concept identification in hyperactive children. *Journal of Abnormal Child Psychology, 11,* 327–340.

Paulauskas, S. L., & Campbell, S. B. (1979). Social perspective-taking and teacher ratings of peer interaction in hyperactive boys. *Journal of Abnormal Child Psychology, 7,* 483–494.

Peters, K. W. (1977). *Selective attention and distractibility in hyperactive and normal children.* Unpublished doctoral disseration. McGill University.

Piaget, J. (1954). *The construction of reality in the child.* New York: Basic Books.

Piaget, J. (1983). Piaget's theory. In P. H. Mussen (Ed.), *Handbook of child psychology: History, Theory and Methods* (4th ed.) (pp. 103–128). New York: Wiley.

Piaget, J., & Inhelder, B. (1973) *Memory and intelligence.* New York: Basic Books.

Platt, J. J., Spivack, G., Altman, N., Altman, D., & Peizer, S. B. (1974). Adolescent problem-solving thinking. *Journal of Consulting and Clinical Psychology, 42,* 787–793.

Quay, H., & LaGreca, A. M. (1986). Disorders of anxiety, withdrawal, and dysphoria. In H. C. Quay & J. S. Werry (Eds.), *Psychopathological disorders of childhood* (3rd ed.) (pp. 73–110). New York: Wiley.

Robin, A. L., Schneider, M., & Dolnick, M. (1976). The turtle technique: An extended case study of self-control in the classroom. *Psychology in the Schools, 73,* 449–453.

Schwartz, M., Friedman, R., Lindsay, R., & Narrol, H.(1983). The relationship between conceptual tempo and depression in children. *Journal of Consulting and Clinical Psychology, 50,* 488–490.

Selman, R. L. (1980). *The growth of interpersonal understanding: Developmental and clinical analyses.* New York: Academic Press.

Selman, R. L., & Byrne, D. F. (1974). A structural-developmental analysis of levels of role-taking in middle childhood. *Child Development, 45,* 803–806.

Selman, R. L., Jaquette, D., & Lavin, D. R. (1977). Interpersonal awareness in children: Toward an integration of developmental and clinical child psychology. *American Journal of Orthopsychiatry, 47,* 264–274.

Siegler, R. S., & Liebert, R. M. (1975). Acquisition of formal scientific reasoning by 10- and 13-year-olds: Designing a factorial experiment. *Development Psychology, 10,* 401–402.

Skrzypek, G. J. (1969). Effect of perceptual isolation and arousal on anxiety, complexity preference, and novelty preference in psychopathic and neurotic delinquents. *Journal of Abnormal Psychology, 74,* 321–329.

Spivack, G., Platt, J. J., & Shure, M. B. (1976). *The problem-solving approach to adjustment: A guide to research and intervention.* San Francisco: Jossey-Bass.

Spivack, G., & Shure, M. B. (1974). *Social adjustment of young children: A cognitive approach to solving real-life problems.* San Francisco: Jossey-Bass.

Steinberg, M. D., & Dodge, K. A. (1983). Attributional bias in aggressive adolescent boys and girls. *Journal of Social and Clinical Psychology, 1,* 312–321.

Surber, C. F. (1982). Separate effects of motive, consequences, and presentation order on children's moral judgments. *Developmental Psychology, 18,* 257–266.

Tant, J. L., & Douglas, V. I. (1982). Problem-solving in hyperactive, normal, and reading-disabled boys. *Journal of Abnormal Child Psychology, 10,* 285-306.

Tarver, S. G., Hallahan, D. P., Kauffman, J. M., & Ball, D. (1976). Verbal rehearsal and selective attention in children with learning disabilities: A developmental lag. *Journal of Experimental Child Psychology, 22,* 375–378.

Vygotsky, L. (1962). *Thought and language.* New York: Wiley.

Whalen, C. K., & Henker, B. (1980). *Hyperactive children: The social ecology of identification and treatment.* New York: Academic Press.

8
The Social and Cultural Construction
of Emotional Disturbance*

MAIN POINTS

1. From the exceptionalistic perspective, special education should be for special children. Special services are added to existing regular programs. From a universalistic perspective, all students are seen as different and no sharp distinction is made between "normal" and "special."

2. From the exceptionalistic perspective, special children are defined as deviant, labeled, and assigned a negative cultural image.

3. Official labels, such as **emotionally disturbed,** help establish expectations and organize formal (organizational) and informal (interpersonal) ways of responding to the child.

4. The three phases of the labeling process include **confrontation, judgment,** and **placement.**

5. There are two major social and cultural theories of educational organizations: **loosely coupled,** and **organized anarchy.**

6. The stability of schools comes from teachers and the environment, and is essentially established by the political activities of bargaining and coalition making. In each school, a dominant coalition of people has a major effect on the cultural beliefs and social organization that is socially constructed.

7. Individuals actively construct their cultural beliefs through interaction and communication. Teaching involves the "communicative competence" to construct culture, knowledge, organization, and political networks.

---

* This chapter was written by George W. Noblit, University of North Carolina; James L. Paul, University of South Florida; and Phillip Schlechty, President, Center for Leadership in School Reform, Louisville, Kentucky.

8. Gilligan (1982) argues that in our culture two fundamental ethics are used in dealing with children: (1) the ethic of justice and (2) the ethic of caring. Special education involves both.

9. Culture is embedded in the structure of schools as social organizations.

10. Teachers of emotionally disturbed children can help construct the order of schools by focusing on their classrooms, their ongoing relationships with teachers from a range of networks, and their relationships with the administration. Regular involvement in a range of formal and informal networks is probably the best way to promote the values of special education, the special needs of students, and an overall effective school.

11. Establishing a cooperative learning technology in a classroom is a good way to establish an effective and orderly classroom.

12. Communicative competence (i.e., the ability to use the skills and knowledge learned in school to participate in society) is essential for teachers and for students. In order to actively participate in constructing wider social and cultural values, students must learn not only the knowledge we teach, but also that this knowledge itself is but one way of thinking and can be considered in its own right and, if desired, changed.

13. Political strategies which recognize the power configuration within a school are important in constructing culture.

> Let us never cease from thinking—what is this "civilization" in which we find ourselves? What are these ceremonies and why should we take part in them? What are these professions and why should we make money out of them? Where in short is it leading us, the procession of the sons of educated men?
>
> (*Woolf, 1936, p. 62*)

This chapter focuses on emotional disturbance from a sociological point of view. We will examine emotional disturbance (1) as a subfield of sociology, and (2) as one of the contributors to what we will talk about as the "new sociology of education." The ideological history of the field of educating emotionally disturbed children, discussed in Chapter 1, is briefly reviewed. This review provides a basis for formulating the alternative case, the nonpsychological case, for viewing the phenomenon of emotional disturbance in schools.

OVERVIEW OF IDEOLOGICAL HISTORY

Since its early development in the 1960s, the special education of emotionally disturbed and behaviorally disordered children has had a clinical focus. Understanding the problem of disturbance has mostly focused on the characteristics of children and the interventions needed to reduce the disturbing quality of those characteristics. Early views and practices were based on this orientation, which came directly out of psychiatry and clinical child psychology.

During this early period of development, special education for these children focused primarily upon the inner feelings of children and, later, upon the disturbing quality and/or inappropriateness of their behavior. The assumption was that if the troubling characteristics of these children could be changed, then their educational needs could be met in the regular classroom like those of other children. It was considerably later that the specific instructional needs of these children were addressed.

The early concern with the inner states of children and the subsequent shift to a more specific concern with observable behavior involved changes in assumptions about the nature of emotional disturbance and the nature of the educational task. The psychodynamic perspective, the predominant perspective until the late 1960s, viewed emotional disturbance primarily in terms of a developmental lag. This perspective focused on the child's experience of severe psychic pain and a poor self-concept. Emotional disturbance was viewed as an illness. This view guided thought about the nature of interventions and who should intervene. The language and concepts of treatment and cure are foreign to the work of teachers. Teachers teach. Their business is education, not treatment. They were seen, therefore, as paramedical or ancillary staff in treatment settings like psychiatric hospitals and child treatment centers.

In the 1960s, as a result of major changes, the perception of the social role of education changed and the role of teachers expanded. Special education teachers became more directly involved in addressing the self-concept, social behavior, and age-appropriate performance of children.

The changing view of the role of teachers in working with emotionally disturbed children was coupled with a changing paradigm of disturbance. There was a shift to explanations and descriptions of disturbed behavior grounded in ecological psychology and in experimental psychology. Ecological psychology viewed the problem of disturbance as an interaction of children and their social environment. The "trouble" was not exclusively in the child or in social systems such as the classroom or home. Rather, it was located in the child-system social matrix; thus, interventions were aimed at changing the nature and quality of those interactions. This interactional view challenged the inner-life view that had been associated with the psychodynamic view. The educational task became one of altering the curriculum materials and the behavior and instructional strategies of teachers, in addition to the attitudes and behavior of "disturbing" children.

Experimental psychology viewed all behavior as learned, including inappropriate or "disturbed" behavior. The label **emotional disturbance** was applied to children whose behavioral excesses or deficits were problematic or disturbing and needed to be changed. The specific problematic behavior of the student was identified, and behavioral objectives were established to eliminate that behavior and to teach prosocial or more adaptive behavior. The educational task, then, was to change the behavior to make the child amenable to instruction. The instructional environment was altered as needed, according to a specific plan designed to change the contingencies of behavior that needed to be extinguished, to model and reinforce different behavior, or to systematically change the child's response to stimuli.

These behavior theories and explanations of emotional disturbance have persisted during the past 20 years, and most educational programs are planned and explained more or less according to one or more of these perspectives. Sociology offers a different basis for understanding and intervening to change emotional disturbance in children. In the language of sociology, emotional disturbance is a social construction in which various groups of people participate. It is less a characteristic of the children so labeled than of conceptions and actions of psychologists, teachers, parents, and students negotiating the label. Emotional disturbance is more a classification than a diagnosis (Mehan, Hertweek, & Meihls, 1986).

The social construction notion that is at the basis of the "new" sociology of education has dramatic implications for how we think about emotional disturbance and how we might act in a "communicatively competent" way to educate those seen as emotionally disturbed (Bowers, 1984). To effectively participate in the social construction of emotional disturbance, one must understand how culture and social action are linked, how everyday reality is socially constructed, and what constitutes the social meaning of labels, as well as the social and political organization of schools. The communicatively competent social construction of emotional disturbance involves creating culture, social organization, and politics.

CULTURE AND SOCIAL ACTION

Culture is everything we think, believe, do, create, perceive, and so on. In our culture, one of the central beliefs is that "facts" are distinguishable from "values." Facts, in our culture, are believed to be objective and immutable things that exist independently of people's perspectives. On the other hand, values are matters of personal opinion or proclivity (MacIntyre, 1984) and are believed to be less stable and valuable than facts. Anthropologists and sociologists do not see this distinction as true or false, but as a central element of Western cultural beliefs. Certainly, the fact-value distinction is real if people believe and act on it. Moreover, a classic theorem in sociology attributed to W. I. Thomas says that "situations that men define as real are real in their consequences" (Brown, 1977, p. 146). Our beliefs give form and substance to what we believe, and if we believe in and assume a distinction, such as the fact-value distinction, we will not understand that a fact is really a value given to some phenomenon. For Westerners the fact-value distinction is a taken-for-granted cultural belief, and is involved in much of what we do. Reading a book such as this yields some factual information as well as a discussion of values. The point is that cultures both shape what we see and guide how we act.

Culture is all around us and in us. It is our conceptual schema and our language, and how we use both. Geertz (1973) argues that culture is best understood as the "webs of significance" people weave in their lives. Geertz, a prominent anthropologist, focuses on how people create the meaning or interpretation of social scenes. Seeing culture as webs of significance gives us two insights into culture. First, it is weblike. How people interpret their lives is based on the taken-for-granted assumptions their culture gives them and on how different people's taken-for-granted assumptions interact. In social interaction, people come together and weave an interaction, which each person then uses to weave further interactions based on his interpretations of prior interactions. The web is dense and pervasive. Second, significance is what is to be woven. Meaning and interpretations are not just opinions. They have substance. In conceiving that children could be handicapped, and in trying to deal with that classification, we dramatically alter the relationships between the child and society. Thus, meanings have dramatic significance for people and for social life.

Exceptionality is a human concept and therefore is a matter of culture and perception. Programs designed to deal with children with special needs reflect a particular perspective on the nature of exceptionality (Rhodes & Paul, 1978; Rhodes & Tracy, 1975). Ryan (1971) speaks of two major perspectives on special education: the exceptionalistic and the universalistic. From the **exceptionalistic perspective,** special education should be for special children. Those who act differently and learn differently, it is believed, **are** different from regular students. Special services should be added to existing regular programs. From the **universalistic perspective,** special education should add a new dimension to all programs. All students are seen as varying on numerous dimensions, with no sharp delineation between "normal" and "special." The goal of special education is to deal with "exceptional school situations," to modify regular programs, making them more appropriate for a wider range of students (Lillie, 1975, p. 48).

In schools, the exceptionalistic set of beliefs is well established. The message has been that "special" education for "special" children should involve "special" methods and materials, which can only be learned from "special" courses that lead to "special" certification and degrees. The universalistic perspective, on the other hand, has produced the mainstreaming movement and legislation, with an emphasis on change in the regular classroom for the benefit of children with special needs. One potential barrier to mainstreaming is the exceptionalistic perspective of classroom teachers, administrators, and parents. According to Sarason, "Segregation of problem children is the prepotent response to the professional and personal dilemmas that teachers face" (Sarason, 1971, p. 156). Teachers are likely to feel that they are unprepared to handle "special" children and parents. Teachers still believe in the exceptionalistic perspective. Most textbooks do not deal substantially with the cultural realities of schools that threaten well-intentioned innovation.

SOCIAL CONSTRUCTION OF REALITY

Culture is implicated in everything we do, but we are not passive carriers of culture. Indeed, we recreate our culture in every action, changing it as we conduct our everyday social affairs (Berger & Luckmann, 1967). Bowers (1984, pp. 35–42) has developed five propositions about how our culture is communicated, negotiated, and internalized:

1. Social reality is shared, sustained, and continuously negotiated through communication.
2. Through socialization, the individual's intersubjective self is built up in a biographically unique way, and this self serves as the set of interpretational rules for making sense of everyday life.
3. Much of the social world of everyday life is learned and experienced by the individual as the natural, even inevitable, order of reality. This natural attitude toward the everyday world is taken for granted.
4. The individual's self-concept is constituted through interaction with significant others. The individual acquires not only the socially shared knowledge but also an understanding of who she is in relation to it.
5. Human consciousness is characterized by intentionality; it is the intentionality of consciousness that insures that socialization is not deterministic.

Individuals actively construct their cultural beliefs through interaction and communication. These beliefs are taken for granted, and the will of humans changes the culture. The patterns that people create in this process become social rules, expectations about how social processes should unfold. Belief in the exceptionalistic perspective has meant that, in everyday interaction, children with special needs are defined as deviant. In the language of the social sciences, such children have been labeled, or assigned a negative cultural image.

THE SOCIAL MEANING OF LABELS

Not all social labels are negative. Some students are labeled "talented" or "gifted," while others are labeled "emotionally disturbed" or "behaviorally disordered." Labels are symbols of cultural assumptions and are real in their effects. Negative labels tend to create "careers" of deviance (Becker, 1963). Deviant careers begin with committing a nonconforming act. Lemert (1975) terms this **primary deviance.** When deviant acts are witnessed, they can have social consequences: stereotyping, retrospective interpretation, and negotiation (Schur, 1971). In stereotyping, people who witness a deviant act infer that the act itself is an indication of the kind of person the actor is, according to cultural archetypes. Retrospective interpretation involves a reevaluation of a person's history based on the new stereotype. Prior history is given a new meaning in line with the stereotype. Finally, labels are negotiated between the parties in social interaction. This is the point where the labeled person has some involvement in the meaning assigned to her behavior. Yet, to enter into a negotiation about the label and its consequences is to also accept the label as real. The labeled person's interaction becomes centered on dealings involving the label. **Secondary deviation** is the actions and interactions that result from the application of the label (Lemert, 1975). Indeed, juvenile delinquency research reveals that if you can stop the label from being applied, the juvenile is less likely to commit additional offenses than if the label is applied and the juvenile's life comes to revolve around addressing it (Gibbons, 1976). In Becker's (1976) language, a career of deviance is created when a person's life begins to revolve around the label and its consequences.

Labeling theory reveals the significance of cultural categories and their consequences. The emotionally disturbed student, in qualifying for needed special services, begins a deviant career. The student and others begin organizing classes, curricula, and social interactions with a stereotype in mind. The student's history is reinterpreted. The label creates a context in which the student negotiates the meaning of her behavior with those who have more power.

In the broadest sense, labels are neither good nor bad. Rather, they are symbols that have the effect of fostering shared definitions of a particular situation or behavioral episode. Some labels (e.g., mentally ill, criminal, and delinquent) have negative consequences for the person who is labeled. These kinds of labels encourage others to view any rule-violating behavior that the labeled person undertakes in terms of the label. For example, the child who has been labeled a behavior problem in school is more likely to be perceived as being rebellious when she does not turn in an assignment in class than is the child who has been labeled an honor student. When the honor student fails to turn in an assignment, others are prone to look for extenuating circumstances, quickly accept apologies, and see the behavior as forgivable. For the child labeled as a behavior problem, however, rule breaking is expected and is instantly labeled deviant.

Labels and the expectations they engender have considerable staying power. A child develops a reputation as a "trouble maker," a "very shy child," and so forth. When the expectations have been made public and institutional-

The labeling of a child as a "trouble maker" fosters expectations of rule-violating behavior.

ized, the officially labeled child may well be launched into a deviant career characterized by a specified role and relationship with the educational system. Mercer (1973) has described how children with mental retardation are labeled and therefore characterized.

While some labels set up circumscribing rules for behavior, other labels permit persons to violate rules that usually would bring formal sanctions. For example, a person viewed as a genius is expected to behave, or is more readily forgiven if she behaves, in erratic ways.

Thus, labels serve important social functions. Labels permit others to give meaning to behavior that violates norms or that occurs at the fringes of the range of behavior that is expected and required. Labels permit social life to proceed with some sort of order, even when individuals behave in what seem to be disorganized ways. Indeed, it could even be argued that groups and organizations establish their limits or boundaries through the labeling of certain behaviors or persons. In effect, organizations indicate that those who behave in deviant ways are at the edge of the group, if not outside it. Thus, the labeled person serves as an object lesson to those inside, or those who want to be inside the group. Labels and the broader sociolinguistic context contribute substantially to the process by which children with behavior problems are understood and controlled. Official labels, such as emotionally disturbed, help establish expectations and organize formal (organizational) and informal (interpersonal) ways of responding to the child.

THE LABELING PROCESS

In school, as in other organizations, children who exercise self-control, who know how to confess and how to be contrite, are less likely to be labeled than other children. Of interest, however, is the fact that children's groups often develop negative labels for children who are overcompliant, are quick to please, or are too able. Gifted children often learn, sometimes in cruel ways, that one should hide one's talents, especially when a test is given that is graded ''on the curve.'' Similarly, children who respond well and quickly to informal control mechanisms are not likely to be nominated for some negative label for their rule-breaking behavior.

There is evidence that the actual differences in amount of rule breaking are negligible when comparing adolescents who were caught and those who were not caught. The fact that there are rules creates violations. Of course, not all rule breakers become candidates for labeling, and the breaking of just any rule does not automatically make one a candidate. At some point, however, the conduct of a rule-breaking individual comes to the attention of social control agents, such as teachers and administrators. At that time, the individual's conduct is viewed as something that must be acted upon. When the behavior is publicly taken into account by those in power, the official control structure is activated and the labeling process begins.

According to Erikson (1964), the labeling process involves three phases: confrontation, judgment, and placement. Each of these phases is relevant to understanding the process by which emotionally disturbed children are labeled.

Confrontation

Confrontation includes those processes and activities associated with bringing the candidate for deviant labeling to the attention of the official representatives (e.g., psychologists) of the community in a way that suggests that here is a person about whom ''something must be done.'' Such confrontations sometimes involve a single episode, such as a child masturbating in the classroom. More frequently, however, these confrontations involve a series of mini-episodes, where the teacher, playing the role of informal control agent, finds the student unable or unwilling to respond to corrective feedback. Eventually, the teacher takes the role of official control agent and sets in motion actions that make the student a candidate for further attention in the system.

Two aspects of the confrontation phase are critical. First, the social control agent (e.g., the teacher) has considerable influence on the conditions under which confrontation will occur and the behaviors over which confrontation is likely to occur. In schools, adults establish most of the rules (i.e., they are seldom negotiated with children), and adults decide when and under what conditions they will be enforced. Second, certain rules make confrontations with some groups or categories of individuals more likely than with other groups or categories. For example, rules regarding personal hygiene are more likely to be violated by children from impoverished families than by children from families of the upper-middle class. Requiring children to do seat work in the late afternoon means that children who are hyperactive, or who have short attention spans, are more likely to break rules than are more docile youngsters. To understand how and why children are labeled as they are, it is necessary to understand those who do the labeling as well as those who are labeled, since labeling is a reciprocal-interactive process.

Judgment

The judgment phase of the labeling process concerns those activities associated with developing a verdict or diagnosis. In some fashion, social control agents (e.g., teachers) must develop an official meaning for the behavior violation and announce that meaning in a way that makes it stick. Since the enactment of P.L. 94-142, the judgment process used by schools has come under careful scrutiny, and a variety of efforts have been made to rationalize this set of activities. Perhaps even more important is the fact that in the judgment phase, the decision is made to give the offender either a label of forgiveness or a label of damnation.

Labels of forgiveness imply that rule violations by the person so labeled ought to be tolerated, accepted, or excepted. In effect, labels of forgiveness ask others to uphold specialty norms or to make exceptions for the person being labeled. Labels of forgiveness include **learning disabled** and **mentally retarded.** To say a person is disabled means that person would do what she should do if she could. To say that a person is mentally retarded means that person's deviant behavior can be attributed to inability rather than to unwillingness or some untoward motive.

Labels of damnation include **delinquent** and **character disordered.** These labels suggest that there is something wrong with the will or moral nature of the offender. The offender offends because she somehow wills it, not because she cannot do otherwise.

It is not accidental that mental illness, emotional disturbance and demonic possession often are confused by the general population. Before behavior variance was explained as mental illness and treated by medical doctors (i.e., up until the nineteenth century), it was explained as demon possession and witch doctors were primary care agents for those afflicted (Seeley, 1953). Also, while reform in the 1960s placed mental illness in a context broader than medicine and characterized the problem as one of social adaptation and coping (Szasz, 1961), the educational system continued to view the problem as belonging to the child and placed the burden of responsibility for change upon her. Unlike programs for the mentally retarded, in which prosthetic technology (i.e., the use of devices such as hearing aids, glasses, and artificial limbs) helped circumvent the disability to make it possible for the child to use the regular curriculum, emotionally disturbed children were expected to change. Prior to the mainstreaming movement which emphasized the need for some curricular modifications for handicapped children in the regular classroom, the special class for the emotionally disturbed had as its goal the reentry of the child into an unmodified regular curriculum (Trippe, 1963). Not surprisingly, many special educators in the 1970s substituted the label emotionally handicapped for emotionally disturbed, since handicapped suggests the possibility of understandable exception to the universal rule. The perception is that handicapped people would comply if they could. The labeling of children as emotionally handicapped in California in the 1950s was viewed as a reform in special education for emotionally disturbed children (Trippe, 1963).

Placement

Placement is the third phase of the labeling process. Placement refers to those activities associated with redefining the role of the person who is labeled in the social system. Among other things, it involves teaching others to behave toward the labeled person in a different way and teaching the labeled person to accept and internalize her new position. A variety of social mechanisms may be set in motion that cause the condition that has been judged to be the case; that is, the self-fulfilling prophecy (Merton, 1968) may cause deviant career development to take over. For example, the handicapped child may come to understand that because she is handicapped, less is expected, so she does less. The emotionally disturbed child may learn that she is expected to have temper tantrums in class, so she continues this behavior. In fact, on those days when the labeled child behaves normally, her behavior may be considered abnormal. The emotionally disturbed child who disturbs no one for a full school day is said to have had a good day, but the normal child is not said to have had a good day under similar circumstances.

The sociological perspective suggests that the simple paradigm of "seek, find, identify (label), and treat" is misleading when applied to the problem of emotional disturbance. The identification and labeling process is related to the rules of the setting in which the problem is "found" and to the values and power of the finder and the labeler. Emotional disturbance is not like a malignant tumor on which a biopsy can be performed. With a tumor, tissue pathology can be analyzed, a diagnosis of disease can be made, and a particular treatment can be recommended on the basis of the diagnosis. The clinical determination that a child is emotionally disturbed, however, does not imply the presence of an entity and the absence of other entities. It is, rather, a professional judgment that a child's failure to perform in customary ways in normal social settings is a result of her emotional weaknesses or inabilities. The expectations, values, and rules operating in the social setting of the classroom, therefore, become important in defining emotional disturbance.

From a sociological perspective, the incidence of emotional disturbance in schools could be reduced by altering the structure of relationships that occur in schools. For example, the reason some children cannot "keep their place" in school may be that their place is too confining. Actually, the most psychologically healthy persons in some organizations may be those who cannot, or refuse to, keep their place. Places, as well as people, can be insane (Goffman, 1971). Where is it written that emotional health is defined by one's willingness to do meaningless work, or passionately embrace boring tasks? Is it always the case that resistance to authority is a sign of emotional disturbance? Is one emotionally disturbed because one withdraws from a race one cannot win? Who are the rules for, anyway? What view of human nature and human ability do the rules imply?

A sociological view of emotional disturbance in schools brings into question the values and behavior of rule makers and rule enforcers. These rules might have as much to do with the incidence and effects of emotional disturbance in schools as does the behavior of children who eventually come to be labeled as emotionally disturbed. Teachers may view the rule-breaking behavior of girls or middle-class children differently than they view the behavior of boys or lower-class children. Because of teacher values, perhaps more poor children become labeled as emotionally disturbed than do children of the affluent (Hollingshead & Redlich, 1958). Or, it may be that lower-class children break rules that teachers value more. For example, lower-class children may be more likely to break rules that have moral content (e.g., one ought to be obedient to the demands of adults). The breaking of moral rules, in turn, is more likely to lead to a confrontation with the system than is the violation of aesthetic or technical norms.

Exceptionalistic cultural beliefs and labels in schools and society have dramatic consequences for students with special needs. The meanings of the student's life are vastly altered as the label is applied. However, labels are based in more than just stereotypic cultural beliefs. Labels are applied to students by those with power and authority, such as administrators, teachers, and parents.

THE SOCIAL ORGANIZATION OF SCHOOLS

The ability to shape and change social action and cultural beliefs is not equally distributed. Some members of society are more powerful than others. Power is based in many things. French and Raven (1960) identified five types of power. Legitimate power is power justified by law and/or custom. Some power is based in the ability to reward others for their actions and commitments, whereas some power is based in the ability to punish others. Referent power depends upon connections and the ability to involve support and/or protection from those connections with others. Finally, there is the power of expertise in socially valued endeavors. Types of power can overlap and be multiple. One of the enduring power struggles is the struggle to gain legitimacy, to have others believe your actions and values are justified, and thus be able to determine the cultural beliefs to be observed. However, legitimacy must be constantly negotiated to be maintained.

Schools and their officials are governed by many sources, including local and state legislation. This legislation by state departments of education, local school boards, and local governments has created a bureaucratic formal structure for schools. The formal structure includes official policy, the hierarchy of authority and decision making, and the division of labor. In the United States, official policies and the hierarchy of authority vary. Some states exercise considerable control, while in other states local school boards are largely independent. Goals and policies vary for the same reason. What does not vary much is the division of labor and everyday classroom experiences (Goodlad, 1984). In American schools, administrators maintain the legitimacy of the schools, while teachers instruct the children (Meyer & Rowan, 1978). Schools are "street-level bureaucracies" (Lipsky, 1980) that are in continual contact with the public, on the one hand serving the public and on the other hand serving the state and local government. In this situation, legitimacy is constantly at risk. Every act of disciplining a child both enforces the school's legitimacy by punishing a rule violation and threatens the school's legitimacy by alienating the children and their families from the school. The school principal and administrative staff balance these kinds of issues constantly. Decisions on such issues have dramatic impacts on how effective the school is thought to be (Katz & Kahn, 1978).

Teachers, on the other hand, are concerned about instruction. Even when principals and central school district specialists and supervisors try to affect instruction, they do it in such a way as to avoid disrupting the teacher's classroom. Staff development, planning, and faculty meetings typically are arranged to minimize disruption of classrooms, while at the same time attempting to change classroom practices. Evaluations of instruction are often ritualized, occurring only a few times a year and having some known evaluative format. Teachers complain about them precisely because they are largely rituals and do not examine the fullness of their classrooms. In any case, the division of labor is clear. Teachers are about the instruction of children. The administration is about the legitimacy of the school. Logically, this could cause conflict in school, but it usually does not. The traditional theories about organization fail to explain power in schools, the division of labor, and the basic lack of conflict (Noblit, 1986).

Educational organizations have been such an anomaly that they have shifted to more social and cultural theories (Noblit, 1986; Scott, 1978). Two main schools of thought are the **loosely coupled** theory (Weick, 1976) and the **organized anarchy** theory (Cohen & March, 1974). Both theories assume that since the formal structure does not determine the behavior of teachers, there must be some other basis for the striking similarity of classrooms across the United States (Meyer & Rowan, 1978). With reference to the "loosely coupled" theory, Weick (1976) argues that instead of the superordinate's determining the behavior of the subordinate, the two actually have only episodic relationships. Principals and teachers work in the same building, in the same organization, and on related affairs. They are coupled. However, the principals do not directly supervise the daily work of the teachers, nor do the teachers see the principals' daily work as directly affecting their teaching. The coupling of school is quite "loose," at least compared to that in other organizations.

The "organized anarchy" (Cohen & March, 1974) concept of educational organizations emphasizes the notion that people are not cooperating on similar tasks. Cohen and March see this largely as being due to four fundamental ambiguities that schools face: the ambiguities of purpose, of power, of experience, and of success. Schools have multiple and sometimes conflicting goals,

Social order in the school depends on the compliance of participants who are not fully socialized.

such as seeking both equality and excellence (Metz, 1978; 1986). As such, statements of purpose in schools are largely rhetorical. Power is ambiguous and, as we noted before, legitimacy must be maintained. Power and responsibility are constantly being negotiated throughout the organization, and their meanings are tenuous and variable. Experience, according to Cohen and March, can lead to considerable "false legitimacy" (p. 19). In many senses, what experience can teach us lags behind the "complexity of the phenomena and the rate of change in the phenomena" (p. 20). Success is usually recognized by either promotion or by operational measures of success (Cohen & March, 1974). Schools are relatively "flat" organizations (Bidwell, 1964), and promotion is not a usual result of a career in teaching. Teachers are likely to continue to be teachers throughout their careers. The promotion opportunities are few. Each school has only one principal and limited assistants. Recent proposals to "professionalize" teaching have tried to alter this by creating positions of **lead** teachers and **master** teachers. Even with the staff, program, and curriculum development responsibilities for these positions, it is clear that teachers will not normally have promotion as a way to measure success. Moreover, despite recent attempts to standardize instructional practice, student achievement is clearly not an adequate measure of teaching effectiveness. Variations in student ability and effort make such measures inappropriate. Because of such fundamental ambiguities, legitimacy is always at issue, social rules are negotiable, and efforts to establish stability and control are promoted whenever possible.

Administrative control of noninstitutional activity is understandable as a way for schools to maintain the loose coupling between instruction and outcomes. Schools are fragile organizations that are not adaptable to the industrial model of structure or management (McNeil, 1986). In some ways, effective schooling requires a variety of constituents (i.e., children, parents, and community leaders) who agree that what is occurring is appropriate and who believe that it will yield desirable effects. When a variety of constituents are involved in defining the meaning of what is occurring, however, the potential for conflict is likely to escalate. Thus, the ability of any school to satisfy the potentially conflicting demands of various constituents is certainly limited. Meyer and Rowan (1978) argue that this creates problems of legitimacy regarding schools and their practices. To counter this threat, administrators maintain tight control over "ritual classifications" and resort to a "logic of confidence" that assumes that instruction is being properly accomplished. By resorting to ritual classifications (e.g., teacher certification, student classifications, grade levels, topic classifications, and school accreditations), schools are able to maintain a loose, normative consensus among the various constituencies.

Meyer and Rowan (1978) also reveal the subtle dynamics of change in schools. Schools are effectively organized to insulate the organization from fundamental challenges. Problems are quickly isolated to particular curricula or teachers; any legitimacy challenges are transformed into technical and isolated problems. This means that schools have patterns of organization that are unlikely to be changed by immediate environmental forces. In other words, they are less likely to change substantially in response to environmental forces than are tightly coupled organizations. Loose coupling also means schools are fundamentally stable, not because of bureaucracy, but because of its absence.

The central conflict that promotes this organizational form is between the goals of educating students and controlling students; "thus the school is organized to be in conflict itself" (McNeil, 1986, p. 1). McNeil argues that bureaucratic controls "can easily trivialize the course content and thus undermine the educative goals of the institution," in turn contributing to student apathy and resistance (McNeil, 1986, p. 1). The loose coupling of the formal organization with instructional activity seems to offer some degree of protection for the educative goal.

Given all this, where does the stability and constancy in schools come from? Meyer and Rowan (1978) find the sources to be essentially environmental. While classrooms are buffered from fundamental challenge by isolating each challenge in an individual teacher's classroom, the structure and content of schooling is a well-ingrained set of cultural beliefs held by most U.S. citizens. The majority have experienced public education and are nostalgic about the experience. Teachers also have had this same educational experience. The teachers were students, and their models of teachers are largely drawn from those who taught them (LeCompte & Ginzburg, 1987). Stability in schools is not the result of the formal structure; rather, it is the result of widely shared experiences and values about what schooling should be. As we see, however, there is considerable order that can be generated within schools.

The structure of schools is such that the teacher enacts expectations in the classroom and in instruction. The power of teachers is significant in the lives of students and in their learning. This responsibility needs to be taken seriously. The stability and order of schools come from teachers and the environment, and is essentially established by the political activities of bargaining and coalition making.

POLITICAL ORGANIZATION OF SCHOOLS

For schools to be stable, the societal expectations of teachers and parents must be embodied in everyday social relationships. In many ways, beliefs are as durable as the people promoting them. Social anthropologists (Schmidt, Scott, Lande, & Guasti, 1977) have found two primary forms of political arrangements between people. The horizontal network is a coalition of people of relatively equal status who volunteer to reciprocate one another. The reciprocity is based on an overresponse to a favor so that it incurs a social obligation. The horizontal network (i.e. friends) is established when someone overresponds to the overresponse. The network is bound by reciprocal favors and obligations.

The second major form of political organization involves the relationship of a "patron" to a "client" (Schmidt et al., 1977). This form of relationship is quite common. The patron has sufficient power and resources to protect and sponsor some people. The client volunteers to enter into these relationships in order to get protection and a sponsor, usually in exchange for deference and loyalty to the patron. In schools, the principal may be a powerful patron and may also have official authority. Some teachers may be patrons in their own right or subpatrons under a patron principal. Additionally, the principal is also a member of various networks and probably a client to other patrons.

Schools are collections of networks that teachers, students, parents, staff, administrators, communities, and school boards construct together. They are linked via numerous social networks and political arrangements. These networks embody belief systems, values, and conflicts of interest (Kriesberg, 1982; Spring, 1988). The members of these networks bargain for power and status and, in many ways, involve the authentic interests and values of teachers independent of the rhetoric, the rituals, the classifications, and the logic of confidence described by Meyer and Rowan (1978). It is in the political organization of schools that values are promoted and/or lost.

One of the myths of education in the United States is that it is apolitical. The historical battle about politics and the schools in the United States was over the influence of political parties and bosses on the schools. The establishment of politically independent, nonpartisan boards of education was meant to make schools apolitical. However, social life is political in the sense of networks, patrons, and clients. This is how things get done in a loosely coupled or organized anarchy organization. Understanding and using the political organization are necessary for promoting everything from least restrictive environments to parent advocacy, from working with a classroom full of networks of students to working with a faculty, and from promoting values to sanctioning behaviors. In each school, a dominant coalition of people has a major effect on the cultural beliefs and social organization that is socially constructed (Benson, 1975).

THE POWER OF THE TEACHER

In recent years, there has been a call for teacher empowerment. Such empowerment is envisioned largely in formal decision making. Yet, it is clear that the formal structure of schools does little to give social organization to schools. Rather, schools are a social construction of various constituents holding various cultural beliefs transmitted via political networks. Schools are not a consensus, but an ongoing negotiation. Teachers—especially teachers of special students— should have a larger role in formal decision making, but teacher empowerment needs to be based on the actual organizational character of schools. Teacher empowerment involves the "communicative competence" to construct culture, knowledge, organization, and political networks (Bowers, 1984).

CONSTRUCTING CULTURE

In our culture, there are two fundamental ethics used in dealing with children: the ethic of justice and the ethic of caring (Gilligan, 1982). Justice refers to fair and equitable treatment. Much of the work of a teacher of emotionally disturbed children involves negotiating justice for his students in the wider school and determining appropriate and equitable treatment of students in the classroom. Caring refers to a different set of values. Values about connection, belonging, attachment, responsibility, respect, and love are part of an ethic of caring. Schools have a range of other values: mass education, identification of elites, and promotion of excellence and nationalism, to name a few.

The values of special education are relatively clear. Special education involves the ethics of justice and caring, diverse and appropriate services, least restrictive environments, and the integration of the handicapped into everyday society (i.e., mainstreaming). The values of special education often conflict with elitist beliefs and with efforts to provide mass education by teaching students similar content via just one format, often a didactic lecture.

It is difficult to change the culture of a school (Sarason, 1971). Since culture is the collection of the multiple perspectives of the participants, efforts to change it have many and complex results. Promoting change is itself a culture belief that conflicts with those whose interests are well served by current arrangements.

Changing culture is also tricky (Pettigrew, 1979). When change is sought, there is a range of possibilities. The school or classroom can respond to the notion of change rather than to the substance or value of the desired change.

Moreover, values are carried by people. People modify and adapt values and the social practices justified by values in the course of their everyday action. Given these conditions, it is probably best that one consider changes in culture and values more as the act of creating and sharing values. Culture is constructed through our rituals, our ceremonies, and our beliefs. Culture can be altered, but the teacher of the emotionally disturbed is not in the authoritative position to mandate change. Nonetheless, a teacher of emotionally disturbed children can have a dramatic effect on the culture of the school simply by paying close attention to the values of school and of special education and by participating within the "management of academic culture" in the school (Dill, 1982, p. 303).

As discussed previously, the values of special education include both the ethic of justice (i.e., fair, appropriate and least restrictive treatment of emotionally disturbed students) and that of caring (i.e., respect for the students, advocacy for their needs, and a personal connection with students). Developing these values in the classroom and the school involves painstaking attention to how culture is constructed and managed in schools. Dill (1982) provides us with a five-fold framework for this position. First, he argues that it is important to **nurture myths** about the classroom and school. Stories need to be told about the history, the key events, and issues, so that the meanings attached to behaviors become shared. Second, **unifying symbols** need to be identified. Often these are highly abstract, even rhetorical, sacred values that many can agree on. These symbols are the bases upon which the teacher of emotionally disturbed children can build. Therefore, it is important to look widely for values about cooperation, fairness, caring for children, and serving the community. Third, these unifying symbols must be **ritually observed.** Assemblies, banquets, and even the opening and closing routines of classrooms should reflect and celebrate the unifying symbols. Fourth, Dill argues, there needs to be **"canonization of exemplars"** (p. 35). Awards and status should be given to those who exemplify the various unifying symbols. Finally, he calls for the **"formation of guilds"** (p. 36), by the people who have been identified as exemplars of the unifying symbols, giving the values a new embodiment. If, for example, the teacher award for caring is granted by a group of teachers who have previously received the award after a process of nominations, applications, reviews and assessments, and who also have a celebration for the incoming member explaining the obligations of guild membership, the award gives school values considerable impetus. However, until a group of exemplars can be established, a panel of impartial judges may be necessary.

Constructing and managing culture takes some time and considerable effort. Indeed, existing values in a school are powerful impediments to change because they define what is significant and important to people. Changing the culture will jeopardize the meaning of people's lives and work, and people may be reluctant to see that happen. However, focusing on unifying symbols, ritually observing them, celebrating exemplars, and organizing guilds of exemplars will allow people to participate in the change, to find new meanings acceptable to them, and to promote the values of special education.

CONSTRUCTING ORDER IN SCHOOLS

Culture is also embedded in the structure of schools as social organizations. However, there is a dramatic difference between administrative structure and organizational structure. School administrators are taught to establish a division of labor and a hierarchy of authority. As we have shown, this has little to do with the instructional work of schools and classrooms. In loosely coupled organizations like schools, instructional work is based on a rather different notion. Educational organizations are constructed by the participants in interaction with each other and in interaction with their environments. In educational organizations, order emerges from the various participants more than from administrative structure.

Altering schools for the benefit of emotionally disturbed students requires a sophisticated understanding of educational organizations. Weick (1976, p. 109) summarizes the needed understanding in six themes:

1. There is less to rationality than meets the eye.
2. Organizations are segmented rather than monolithic.
3. Stable segments in organizations are quite small.
4. Connections among segments have variable strength.
5. Connections of variable strength produce ambiguity.
6. Connections of constant strength reduce ambiguity.

Weick is saying that in schools, effectiveness is due more to the collective actions of the participants than to the administrative structure, the formal program, or the procedures. The everyday work of schools is not that of a single organization, but of a network of independent organizations—the classrooms. The essential order of the school is generated in individual classrooms by teachers, groups of teachers, and departments. In many ways, these "small segments" of classrooms and formal and informal networks of teachers are related to each other in a complex pattern of ways and with varying intensity. Some networks of teachers rarely interact with each other. Ambiguity is created when networks do not have a regular pattern of interaction. On the other hand, ambiguity is reduced when students, teachers, administrators, and environmental constituencies (i.e., parents, community, and psychological services staff) have ongoing stable relationships.

The teacher of emotionally disturbed children can help construct the order of schools by focusing on their classrooms, and on ongoing relationships with teachers from a range of networks, as well as relationships with the administration and other constituencies. These ongoing relationships help stabilize the school.

Decisions made by teachers in small groups are the ones likely to affect classroom practices. Regular involvement in a range of formal and informal networks is probably the most effective way to promote the values of special education, the special needs of students, and an overall effective school. This involves a commitment of time to develop and manage the ongoing relationships. Both are worth the return.

CONSTRUCTING CURRICULA AND INSTRUCTION

Teachers should remember that a classroom's culture and order are created in small groups of students (Weick, 1976). Small, heterogeneously grouped instruction is a highly effective way to facilitate achievement and positive social relations as well as reduce prejudice. Establishing a "cooperative learning" technology in a classroom is a good way to establish an effective and orderly classroom (Slavin, 1980).

Moreover, even within the constraints of mandated curriculum and textbooks, it is apparent that teachers can develop "communicative competence" in their students, as well as for themselves (Bowers, 1984). Communicative competence is the ability to use the skills and knowledge learned in school to participate in the discourse about what values society should embody. This requires a level of thought rarely taught in school, with the result being to leave students to develop communicative competence through their own resources. Bowers (1984) sees communicative competence as an approach to curriculum development that is based on three principles: (1) using students' phenomenological culture; (2) using historical perspectives to deobjectify knowledge; and (3) incorporating a cross-culture perspective. To actively participate in construction of wider social and cultural values, students must learn not only the knowledge we teach, but also that this knowledge is only one way of thinking and can be considered in its own right and, if desired, changed.

Such "active citizenship" (Spring, 1980) is based in having students engage in "metaphorical thinking" (Bowers, 1984, p. 87) and in tracking language use in different contexts for the different metaphors employed. This is especially important to students who are at risk in some environments. Instead of teaching knowledge as a set of facts, we should frame knowledge in its historical context, giving students some perspective on the conditions in which the knowledge arose and its essential human authorship. Knowledge, students learn, is something to develop, to work on, rather than simply to recite. Finally, comparing key concepts and ideas with those of other cultures allows the students to "defamiliarize" (Marcus & Fischer, 1986) their own culture and conceive of alternatives in values and actions.

Teaching students to be communicatively competent is not easy. The teacher himself first needs to be communicatively competent; understand the assumptions, histories, and bases of values; and be able to think metaphorically. Second, the teacher must elaborate the curriculum, teaching the alternative conceptualizations of phenomena and their social, historical, and cultural bases. Third, students must participate in the discovery of these alternatives and perceive the implications for their everyday life and for the future of their society. In one sense, this type of instruction is what integrates the learning of skills and allows students to use these skills in understanding the philosophical bases of science, the cultural bases of literature, the historical bases of social science, and so on. This type of curriculum will take a while to develop and modify. Communicative competence does not develop overnight, nor will the curriculum and instructional processes which can enable it.

POLITICAL STRATEGY

Constructing culture, order, curriculum, and instruction is achieved through social networks. Schools have differing political arrangements. In some schools, a few teachers are powerful patrons. In others, the principal may be the primary patron. Some schools have horizontal networks of equal-status members. Schools with patron systems can more easily alter teacher behaviors if the patrons promote the change. A coercive patron system, however, promotes alienation of clients (Etzioni, 1961). Schools with horizontal networks may be slow to change, but when they do, they bring the added benefit of moral involvement. People make the change not because they must, but because they believe they ought to do so.

A political map of any school or organization can be constructed if one observes who interacts with whom with any regularity, who exchanges favors with whom, who are seen as friends and enemies, and who helps whom. From this, a map of the social networks can be constructed. Once this map is created, one can discern who is isolated from the networks, who belongs to more than one network (and serves or can serve as a broker between networks), which networks are of friends (horizontal networks), which networks are patron-client networks (vertical networks), who are the patrons, which networks are strong and which are weak, and which networks hold strong beliefs.

After discerning the networks in a school, a strategy can be made to align with powerful patrons, to become a patron in one's own right, or to join networks with persons of equal status. The goal is to participate in the dominant coalition in the school, in order to politically represent the values of special education and the needs of special students. If becoming a member of the dominant coalition is not reasonable, becoming a broker between networks is another valuable role. By belonging to multiple networks, the teacher of emotionally disturbed children can broker relationships and values across networks and, in the process, have considerable influence on the values and power relations in the school.

Classrooms are separate organizations in themselves in many ways, with the teacher having legal authority and position power. The teacher can use such power and authority in many different ways. Etzioni (1961) has categorized power as coercive (threats or punishments), remunerative (paying or exchanging for compliance), and normative (the belief one ought to do it). In general, the exercise of each type of power has predictable results. If a teacher uses coercive power, threatening students with punishment and punishing for misbehavior, the students will be alienated. They will comply but will not invest in the work. If the teacher uses remunerative power to set up a basis of exchange where students earn favors for work done or good behavior, the students will comply but will be calculating in their involvement. The teacher's power is relative to the value of the favors to the students. If the teacher uses normative power, (i.e., develops a positive set of values for learning, a belief on the part of students that they can learn, and sets of routines that accomplish this), students will comply with moral involvement. They will invest in the classroom activity and respect the teacher's authority.

The classroom will have networks of students, and potentially a set of patrons. The teacher is a powerful patron, but the students are also focused on each other. Some students will have more power to define social status than others. Classrooms often have a teacher as the strongest patron, with a set of subpatrons ("teacher's pets," helpful children, etc.), and competition among some students for power is keen. Handling this competition is often a true test of the teacher's power. The teacher, of course, has the legal authority to discipline children. Yet, as previously discussed, coercive power begets alienation. The teacher may end up exchanging one problem for another. Politically, it makes more sense to try to alter the networks in the classroom. This is what teachers are doing when they separate students by reassigning seats. Paying attention to students who may in the future be identified as disturbed is another way teachers break up networks. By focusing on school work in these encounters, teachers reinforce their power and the goal of learning. Cooperative learning systems have the advantages of using the students' interest in peers as part of the mechanism of learning and of reducing intergroup tensions. By considering part of the job of teaching to be the construction of political networks with and among students, teachers can reduce discipline problems and help establish positive routines for learning.

SUMMARIES

Viewing emotional disturbance as a cultural construction gives insight into how the teacher of emotionally disturbed children may best promote the values of special education and contribute to cultural change and social order in schools. While this approach requires a sophisticated understanding of the structure of schools, culture, politics, and social interaction, it allows relatively straightforward use of the teacher's power to create culture, knowledge, and social networks. Teachers of children with special needs are well situated to do both. If they become communicatively competent in the social construction of school life, they can have dramatic effects on school culture and organization, and on the meaning the school applies to emotional disturbance.

DISCUSSION QUESTIONS

1. How is reality socially constructed in schools?
2. Why is the social organization of schools problematic in bringing about changes?
3. How does the labeling process work in schools?
4. What are effective strategies for constructing order in schools?
5. How can teachers of emotionally disturbed children develop communicative competence in their students?

REFERENCES

Becker, H. (1963). *Outsiders: Studies on the sociology of Deviance*. New York: The Free Press.

Benson, J. K. (1975). The interorganizational network as a political economy. *Administrative Science Quarterly, 20,* 229–248.

Berger, P., & Luckmann, T. (1967). *The social construction of reality*. Garden City, NY: Doubleday.

Bidwell, C. (1964). The school as a formal organization. In J. G. March (Ed.), *Handbook of organization.* Chicago: Rand McNally.

Bowers, C. A. (1984). *The promise of theory.* New York: Longman.

Brown, R. (1977). *A poetic for sociology.* New York: Cambridge University Press.

The Carnegie Forum. (1986). *A nation prepared: Teachers for the 21st century.* New York: Carnegie Corporation.

Cohen, M., & March, J. (1974). *Leadership and ambiguity.* New York: McGraw-Hill.

Dill, D. (1982). The management of academic culture. *Higher Education II,* 303–320.

Erikson, Erik H. (1964). *Insight and responsibility.* New York: Norton Press.

Etzioni, A. (1961). *A comparative analysis of complex organizations.* New York: Macmillan.

French, J. R., & Raven, B. H. (1960). The basis of power. In D. Cartwright & A. Lander (Eds.), *Group dynamics* (2nd ed., pp. 607–623). New York: Row, Peterson.

Geertz, C. (1973). *The interpretation of cultures.* New York: Basic Books.

Geertz, C. (1983). *Local knowledge.* New York: Basic Books.

Gibbons, D. C. (1976). *Delinquent behavior.* Englewood Cliffs, NJ: Prentice-Hall.

Gilligan, C. (1982). *In a different voice.* Cambridge, MA: Harvard University Press.

Goffman, E. (1961). *Asylums.* New York: Doubleday.

Goldstein, K. (1970). Paul Broca, 1824–1880. In W. Haymaker & F. Sciller (Eds.), *The founders of neurology.* Springfield, MA: Charles C. Thomas.

Goodlad, J. I. (1984). *A place called school.* New York: McGraw-Hill.

Katz, D., & Kahn, R. L. (1978). *The social psychology of organizations.* New York: John Wiley & Sons.

Kirk, S. A., & Gallagher, J. J. (1989). *Educating exceptional children.* Boston: Houghton Mifflin.

Kriesberg, L. (1982). *Social conflicts.* Englewood Cliffs, NJ: Prentice-Hall.

LeCompte, M., & Ginzburg, M. (1977). How students learn to become teachers. In G. Noblit & W. Pink, *Schooling in social context.* Norwood, NJ: Ablex.

Lemert, E. M. (1975). Primary and secondary deviation. In S. H. Traub & C. B. Little (Eds.), *Theories of deviance.* Itasca, IL: F. E. Peacock Publishers.

Lillie, D. (1975). *Early childhood education.* Chicago: Science Research.

Lipsky, M. (1980). *Street-level bureaucracy: Dilemmas of the individual in public services.* New York: Russell Sage Foundation.

MacIntyre, A. (1984). *After virtue.* Notre Dame, IN: University of Notre Dame Press.

Marcus, G., & Fischer, M. (1986). *Anthropology as cultural critique.* Chicago: The University of Chicago Press.

McNeil, L. (1986). *Contradictions of control.* New York: Routledge and Kegan Paul.

Mehan, H., Hertweek, A., & Meihls, J. L. (1986). *Handicapping the handicapped: Decision-making in students' educational careers.* Stanford, CA: Stanford University Press.

Mercer, J. R. *Labeling the mentally retarded: Clinical and social systems perspectives and mental retardation.* Berkeley: University of California Press.

Metz, M. H. (1978). *Classrooms and corridors: The crisis of authority in desegregated secondary schools.* Berkeley: University of California Press.

Metz, M. H. (1986). *Different by design: The context and character of three magnet schools.* New York: Routledge and Kegan Paul.

Meyer, J., & Rowan, B. (1978). The structure of educational organization. In M. Meyer et al. (Eds.), *Environments and organizations* (pp. 78–109). San Francisco: Jossey Bass.

Noblit, G. W. (1986). What's missing from the national agenda for school reform? Teacher professionalism and local initiative. *The Urban Review, 18* (1), 40–51.

Parsons, T. (1949). *Essays in sociological theory, pure and applied.* Glencoe, IL: Free Press.

Pettigrew, A. (1979). On studying organizational cultures. *Administrative Science Quarterly, 24,* 570–581.

Rhodes, W., & Paul, J. (1978). *Emotionally disturbed and deviant children: New views and approaches.* Englewood Cliffs, NJ: Prentice-Hall.

Rhodes, W., & Tracy, M. L. (1972). *A study of child variance.* Ann Arbor, MI: University of Michigan Press.

Ryan, W. (1971). *Blaming the victim.* New York: Pantheon.

Sarason, S. B. (1971). *The culture of the school and the problem of change.* Boston: Allyn and Bacon.

Schmidt, S., Scott, J., Lande, C., & Guasti, L. (Eds.) (1977). *Friends, followers and factions.* Berkeley: University of California Press.

Schur, E. M. (1971). *Labeling deviant behavior: Its sociological implications.* New York: Harper & Row.

Scott, M. (1978). Theoretical perspectives. In M. Meyer et al. (Eds.), *Environments and organizations* (pp. 21–28). San Francisco: Jossey Bass.

Seeley, J. R. (1953). Social values, the mental health movement and mental health. *Annals of the American Academy of Political and Social Science, 286,* 15–24.

Slavin, R. E. (1980). Cooperative learning in teams: State of the art. *Educational Psychologist, 15* (2), 93–111.

Spring, J. (1980). *Educating the worker-citizen.* New York: Longman.

Spring, J. (1988). *Conflicts of Interests.* White Plains, NY: Longman.

Szasz, T. S. (1961). *The myth of mental illness.* New York: Harper & Row.

Temkin, O. (1947). Gaul and the phrenological movement. *Bulletin of the History of Medicine, 27,* 275–321.

Trippe, M. (1963). Conceptual problems in research on educational provisions for disturbed children. *Exceptional Children, 29,* 400–406.

Weick, K. (1976). Educational organizations as loosely-coupled systems. *Administrative Science Quarterly, 21,* 1–19.

Wiederhold, J. L., Hammil, D. D., & Brown, V. (1978). *The resource teacher: A guide to effective practices.* Boston: Allyn & Bacon.

Woolf, V. (1936). *Three guineas.* New York: Harcourt, Brace & World.

9
Ecological Theory and Practice*

MAIN POINTS

1. The ecological model as it applies to disturbing children is an evolving perspective. The perspective initially was defined in the 1960s and offered a new way of viewing and treating emotional disturbance.

2. According to the ecological model, a child is not disturbed. Disturbance is a result of discordance in the reciprocal interactions between a child and components of his social system.

3. A child's social system is generally very complex, with interactions occurring within and between several settings.

4. In this model, no one "owns" the disturbance and no one is "blamed" for it. The child or adolescent and key participants of the environment are contributing and receiving members of transactions, and both have responsibility for altering disturbing interaction patterns.

5. The goal of intervention is to make the system work, and to make it work, ultimately, without intervention.

6. Interventions may be based on any theoretical model or practical strategy. An important constraint is that interventions should not be designed to change only the child, leaving other components unchanged.

7. An important current issue in special education is the overrepresentation of minorities in classes for the retarded or disturbed and the equating of difference with disability.

8. Each effective ecological assessment approach contains two elements: (a) a process or sequence of steps to follow and (b) a particular selection of variables for evaluating the interaction of child and setting.

---

*This chapter was written by Susan McAllister Swap, Wheelock College, Boston, Massachusetts.

> We assume that the child is an inseparable part of a small social system, of an
> ecological unit made up of the child, his family, his school, his neighborhood
> and community.
>
> *(Hobbs, 1966, p. 1109)*

The ecological model was introduced to the field of special education during the 1960s. It provided a revolutionary approach to understanding and treating emotional problems in children and youth.

The most important concepts of the model are quite simple. First, context affects behavior. Environmental and interpersonal factors affect whether, when, and how children exhibit disturbing behaviors. In fact, the child is not even considered to be the source of the disturbance. Rather, the disturbance is located in the reciprocal interactions between the child and critical aspects of the environment. Second, the decision that a behavior (or a child) is disturbing is culturally relative. Whether or not a behavior is seen as disturbing depends on the values and expectations of key persons in the setting.

The easiest way to understand these concepts is to relate them to our own experience. Consider what helps or hinders your learning. Most of us have been in situations where we learn easily and well, and consequently feel confident and productive. We can usually identify those variables in the interpersonal and physical environment that help us to feel optimally challenged. Most of us also have been in situations where we feel unhappy and unproductive, sometimes to the point where we act out, stop trying to produce, or develop physical symptoms. These reactions may or may not be identified as disturbing by other participants in the setting.

Consider the following:

> A setting in which I felt unhappy, stupid, and unproductive was a required geography class that I took in seventh grade. I found the teacher's voice so monotonous, the omnipresent maps so confusing, and the lists we were to memorize so boring that one day I started to giggle—and could not (would not?) stop. Other students found the giggling infectious, and soon most of the class were laughing, too. The teacher, quite annoyed, sent me out of the room to get a drink of water and wait in the hall until I could get control of myself. My "giggling fits" recurred periodically during the rest of the semester in that class.

Several aspects of this short tale illustrate concepts important to the ecological perspective. For example, not all students found this class as intolerable as I did. Some liked it! My disturbing behavior was a product of the unique interaction between me and aspects of the setting; that is, between my particular learning style, temperament, and developmental phase and the particular characteristics of this academic setting, the teacher, and the peer group. For my giggling to be seen as a disturbing behavior justifying dismissal from class, the teacher had to identify it as such. My particular behavior (refusing to obey the teacher's directions to be quiet) was quite radical for a seventh grade female in a highly structured classroom in a suburban community in the 1950s. In other settings in that school (e.g., the playground or the lunchroom) or in a classroom in a different community, the giggling might have gone unnoticed or been ignored by adults in positions of authority.

Now let's consider another case:

> Gary, a sensitive, thoughtful 11-year-old moved into the district and joined a class of about 40 students who were team-taught by two teachers whom many considered to be the most creative and effective in the school. The peer group included about 11 children who responded slowly, if at all, to teacher direction. The teachers, exasperated at their inability to teach this group in their usual manner, would make frequent statements such as, "You kids just don't care about learning. You just don't want to learn." Although Gary had been a good student in his other school, he took these comments to heart, stopped doing his homework, complained frequently of stomachaches, and finally told his mother quite seriously, "I just want to die."

According to the ecological perspective, Gary was not a "disturbed child" and the teachers were not "bad" teachers. Rather, there was a lack of fit or match between the skills and expectations of the teachers and the skills and needs of several of the students.

Now let's look at another case:

> Joe was having a bad semester. In a self-contained class for disturbed children in grades K–2, Joe had a very difficult time focusing his attention. He was often out of his seat and both responded to and created distractions that interfered with his completion of assignments. The teacher was troubled by Joe's aggressive behavior: hitting and biting other children, and occasionally kicking and striking out at her. Most confusing to the teacher was Joe's inconsistency. On some days, he was calm, reasonably focused, and friendly to her and the other children. The teacher could not identify any compelling reasons for his behavioral inconsistency within the classroom.
>
> The teacher made several telephone calls to Joe's mother and went on a home visit. She learned that Joe's mother, a single parent, was an alcoholic whose boyfriend was occasionally abusive to her and Joe. Although the mother cared deeply about her son, it was difficult for her to provide a consistent and nurturing environment for him. In addition to her adult struggles, Joe's high activity level, difficulty in paying attention, and aggressive outbursts at home intensified the mother's feelings of parental incompetence.

This example illustrates an important clarification of the ecological perspective. Children's behaviors may be influenced by their interactions in many settings, even settings in which they do not directly participate. A child's environment is a very complex system, with interactions occurring within and between several settings. Ecological interventions are not designed to "fix" the child, but rather to "fix," or alter, the interactions within or between settings that are creating the disturbance. These basic concepts and case illustrations serve as an introduction to the ecological perspective as it relates to emotional problems in children. In the remainder of the chapter, the origins of this perspective in special education will be outlined; the assumptions of the model will be reviewed; and current issues, research insights, intervention strategies, and assessment practices that are helpful to the practitioner will be identified.

ORIGINS OF THE ECOLOGICAL MODEL

The ecological model as it applies to emotionally disturbed children is an evolving perspective. It was initially defined in the 1960s by Nicholas Hobbs (1966) and William Rhodes (1967). The "alternative model" they advocated was revolutionary in the field of special education because it rejected prevailing beliefs and practices in mental health, and offered a new way to view and treat emotional disturbance.

First Applications to the Education of Disturbed Children

Hobbs established a new kind of treatment program for disturbed youngsters. Inspired by visits to treatment programs in France and Scotland, Hobbs initiated Project ReEducation (ReEd) in Nashville, Tennessee, and Durham, North Carolina (Hobbs, 1966).

Re-Ed programs were (and continue to be) designed as short-term treatment sites, where connections are maintained between Re-Ed staff, the family, and the school. The focus is on teaching the child how to act appropriately in a range of situations, while at the same time helping teachers and parents to understand their reactions to the child and respond more adaptively. Unlike treatment programs based on the psychodynamic model where therapy and the role of the psychologist are emphasized, Project Re-ED emphasized education and the role of the liaison teacher-counselor.

According to Hobbs (1982), William Rhodes led the way in developing the model. He asked Rhodes to help him reconstruct the debates that occurred when they were working together in the early days of Re-Ed. In Rhodes' words:

> As I recall it from this distance, we were very concerned with the environmental relativity of the condition called emotional disturbance. We felt that environmental contributions had been totally ignored in traditional psychiatric treatment of children. We felt that "disturbance" was a relative term, that different settings saw different kinds of behavior as "disturbed" depending on the cultural values and expectations of that setting, as well as the particular predilections of the child's own parents and teachers.
>
> Also, we were aware of the problem of institutionalization and its contribution to the states and behaviors observed in child hospital units. We felt that, to avoid the negative influence of institutions, treatment had to be in a setting as nearly like the child's natural habitat as possible. Therefore, the residential treatment had to be radically modified to overcome the pathology created by the residential setting itself.
>
> We particularly felt that the then current practice of removing the child from school, "curing" him or her in isolation, and then returning the child to a

peer group which had been moving on in development and learning was non-sense. It was this idea, incidentally, which caused our first NIMH (National Institute of Mental Health) review committee to suggest a liaison person who would keep the child abreast of his or her own school and peer group.

Since there was then no current term for this environmental inclusion, we borrowed "ecology." . . . As part of "ecological treatment," we felt we had to go into the child's environment and alter it in just noticeable ways, so that, matched with the just noticeable changes in his or her behavior which we focused on in the child's brief stay in residence, we could bring about greater tolerance in the environment which was being disturbed by particular aspects of the child's behavior and performance. This, also, we saw as the role of the liaison teacher-counselor. (Hobbs, 1982, pp. 184–185)

Rhodes' retelling of the history of Project Re-ED and the reconceptualization of approaches to treating disturbed children does not quite capture the passion that led to his advocacy of this model. In Rhodes' own articles during this period (1967, 1971), he expressed a concern about the "culture-bearers" whose standards of behavior were impossible for increasing numbers of children to meet. He was concerned about "blaming the victim," focusing treatment only on the "flawed" child, and narrowing our tolerance of differences. He wrote:

The nucleus of the problem lies in the content of the behavioral prohibitions and sanctions in the culture. . . . The problem is multiplied by the fact that behavioral prohibitions and sanctions have accumulated over many centuries. It is very difficult to eliminate any of them from the culture even though they may be pure legends with no real basis. . . . With such an accumulation hanging over us, there are limitless forms of behavior which can disturb us. The range of children's behaviors to which we respond with upset is extensive. In our tendency to refer such upset within ourselves to the child who stimulates the upset, we blanket a large proportion of children under the category of disturbance. (Rhodes, 1970, p. 451)

As further elaborated by Rhodes and Paul:

School systems, business and industry, clubs and associations all seem to be combining to demand a narrower and narrower definition of prescribed behavioral types for their purposes. Further, there seems to be increasing convergence of agreement among these institutions with respect to the prescribed type. This draws a very tight band around acceptable or useful behaviors and relegates to extrasystemic and extrasocial a greater and greater array of individual differences both within the population and the individual. (1978, p. 213)

The late 1960s and early 1970s was a confusing, intense topsy-turvy period in our country's history. The assassinations of John F. Kennedy, Martin Luther King, and Robert F. Kennedy left the leadership of the civil-rights movement and other progressive causes in disarray. President Lyndon Johnson resigned because of the country's division over the Vietnam war. The Watergate scandal revealed a long list of immoral and unethical behaviors undertaken by the leaders of our country's executive branch. Individual experimentation with drugs, sexual practices, lifestyles, and philosophies was very common. Confusion and distress about what was right and wrong and who was moral or immoral prevailed. In this climate, Rhodes' questions about who or what was disturbed were widely shared.

Rhodes was instrumental in disseminating the concepts of the ecological model in special education. Through the Conceptual Project in Emotional Disturbance that he directed at the University of Michigan, Rhodes and others published several books and videos that highlighted the theories and interventions of each of the competing models of emotional disturbance, including the ecological model (Rhodes & Tracy, 1972). Several generations of graduate students in psychology, education, and special education in many different parts of the country were trained either with these materials or texts based on them. Their use supported an eclectic approach to working with disturbed children and a less exclusive reliance on the behavioral and psychodynamic approaches.

Development of the Ecological Perspective in Other Fields

Interest in the ecological perspective was not confined to special education. Ecology is an area of study within many fields, such as anthropology, biology, sociology, social psychology, and community psychology. Within each of these disciplines, investigators using an ecological perspective share a commitment to studying organisms or individuals in their natural habitat, discovering more about the reciprocal interactions between organisms and environments, and developing new methodologies for exploring these relationships.

Rhodes borrowed extensively from other disciplines in shaping his own conceptual framework (see Feagans, 1972, and Rhodes & Paul, 1978, for detailed reviews). Because the scope of the relevant literature is so large, I have chosen to highlight the origins of only two other strands of research and model building that continue to be important in special education today. These strands began with the work of Roger Barker and with Alexander Thomas, Stella Chess, and Herbert Birch.

Roger Barker and Associates at the Midwest Psychological Field Station. For over 40 years, Roger Barker and his associates developed the discipline known as **ecological psychology** (typified by Barker, 1968, or Gump, 1975). The goal of their studies was to develop an understanding of person-environment relations using a methodology that did not disturb the habitat or the interactions within them. Barker became interested in this type of research of his frustration with his graduate training in psychology. According to Barker (1987), he was taught to do experiments with children in which he created situations which almost never occurred in real life and had no significance to the adults working with children. Eventually, he opened a "field station" in a small town in Kansas where he and his colleagues learned to study and document the naturally occurring behavior of a wide range of inhabitants in a variety of settings in this community over time.

Gump (1977) summarized two important contributions from the Midwest Field Station research. First, these psychologists invented methodologies that would allow them to study natural environments. For example, several investigators developed methodologies for studying meaningful episodes of behavior as they occurred in the natural stream of events. Gump (1975) developed a way to assess environmental units, creating the concept of "behavior setting" that encompassed a physical milieu, a program of activities, inhabitants, and a location in time and space.

Second, the researchers learned to measure the effects of environments on human behavior. Barker was struck by the power to elicit behavior that settings had. He explained:

> We could not avoid asking what happens in Third Grade Music Class and Third Grade Recess Period to produce such narrow variation in the children's behavior within each setting despite the wide variation in the children's abilities and motives. We could predict a child's behavior better from place of occurrence than from personality. And how could it be that the "same" Third Grade Music Class occurred in 1948 and 1949 even though there was a complete turnover of inhabitants—both pupils and teacher?"(1987, p. 11)

Barker and his associates learned a great deal about how school settings affected children's behavior. For example, Willems (1967) found that the size of high schools was an important determinant of students' satisfaction with themselves, their sense of being valued, and their sense of obligation to the school. Students in the smaller high schools responded more positively, apparently because they were more needed to occupy central roles. Gump (1975) discovered that children spent more time on task in open than in traditional classrooms. Kounin (1970) learned that certain dimensions of teaching competence such as an ability to monitor several activities simultaneously and to manage transitions led to low deviancy rates among both disturbed and nondisturbed children.

Although the Midwest Field Station is now disbanded, psychologists continue to gather data that help them to understand how different variables in school settings affect children's behavior. Later the work of Moos, Trickett, and others who have raised several new questions about the effects of school settings on children's behaviors will be reviewed. Another line of research that has been influenced by Barker and associates is that of the ecobehavioral analysts (e.g., Rogers-Warren, 1984), who have applied ecological concepts and methodologies to the behavioral model.

Alexander Thomas, Stella Chess, and Herbert Birch.   Thomas and Chess, child psychiatrists, and Herbert Birch undertook a longitudinal study to evaluate the origins and evolution of behavior disorders in children and youth (Thomas, Chess, & Birch, 1968). Their initial sample, selected in 1956, was composed of 133 children in 84 families.

They developed a scale to measure children's temperamental differences. This scale evaluated a child's activity level, rhythmicity, approach/withdrawal, adaptability, threshold of responsiveness, intensity of reaction, quality of mood, distractibility, and attention span/persistence. Thomas, Chess, and Birch examined the interaction of temperament, other individual characteristics (e.g., intelligence, age, developmental differences), and situational factors over time.

In 1968, after 12 years of studying this population, Thomas, Chess, and Birch concluded that behavior disorders emerged as the result of the interactions between individual and situational characteristics. Although some temperamental constellations seemed to put children at a higher risk for developing emotional or behavior problems (e.g., the "difficult child" pattern), compensating individual characteristics and sensitive parental handling could avert the development of symptoms. As they worked with parents over time, the researchers recognized that parents were neither good nor bad, but behaved in an optimal or suboptimal way with a given child. The emphasis placed on parental education, preventive counseling, situational assessment, and naturalistic methodology was an important departure from traditional mental health practice and very influential for others in the field.

Assumptions of the Ecological Model

As applied to special education, there are three assumptions that summarize the ecological approach to emotional disturbance in children. These assumptions are based on the works of Apter and Conoley (1984), Swap (1978), Swap (1984), and Swap, Prieto, and Harth (1982).

Assumption 1: Each child is an inseparable part of a complex social system. As Hobbs explains:

> What is powerful in the concept of ecology is the idea that the child or adolescent cannot be juxtaposed with the environment, that she is an inextricable part of an ecological system. The only way we know how to talk about it precisely requires a circumlocution: our concern is with the ecological system of which, for our purposes, the child or adolescent is the defining member. The child, family, school, agency, neighborhood, work place, and community, with their dynamic interrelationships, make up a nonfractionable whole. (1982, p. 94)

Defining what is meant by an ecological system turns out to be quite complex. According to Swap (1978), it is useful to picture the ecological network in which a child participates as consisting of three nested systems or levels. The most basic unit is called a **behavior setting** and consists of a physical milieu, a program of activities and inhabitants, and a location in time and space (Gump, 1975).

The second level may be called **patterns of behavior across settings** and encompasses the child's interactions in different settings and the feedback among them. Examples include a child's contrasting behaviors in a biology class and on the football field, or at circle time in kindergarten and at dinnertime at home. The third level is defined as **patterns of behavior settings in the community and culture.** It is at this level that group norms, expectations, and values for behavior are defined. This level includes not only subcultural norms, but also national, state, and community policies and patterns of service delivery that influence those who are seen as disturbed and how they are treated.

Bronfenbrenner (1979) also developed a model for understanding social systems based on the notion of a nested arrangement of structures. This model, which has been very influential in the field, includes four components. As summarized in Apter (1984), these include the following:

- **The microsystem,** or pattern of activities, roles, and interpersonal relations experienced by the developing person in a given setting
- **The mesosystem,** which encompasses the interrelations among two or more settings in which the developing person actively participates
- **The exosystem,** which includes one or more settings that do not actively involve the developing person but affect systems in which the developing person does participate (e.g., the decision to strike by school bus drivers may affect a child's experiences on the first day of school)
- **The macrosystem,** which encompasses the overarching institutional patterns of the culture or subculture, including values and beliefs, that provide the basis for consistency in form and content of lower-order systems

Assumption 2: The child is not disturbed. Disturbance is a result of discordance in the reciprocal interactions of a child and components of the child's social system. The disturbing behavior of a child is the product of interactions among the child's characteristics, the characteristics of the environment, and the interactions among them.

In this formulation, no one is blamed for the disturbance. Rather, the problem reflects "poorness of fit" between an individual's characteristics and the demands and expectations of the environment. This approach recognizes that "negative reciprocal interaction patterns can create, maintain, and increase the frequency of disturbing interactions, whereas positive reciprocal interactions can lessen or eliminate disturbance" (Swap, 1984, p. 108). Further, according to Hobbs (1982), both the child or adolescent and also the key participants in the environment are contributing and receiving members of transactions, and both are responsible for altering disturbing interaction patterns.

In this model, a child does not "own" the disturbance, carrying "it" with him unchanged from setting to setting. Disturbance is created by **interaction** and by the expectations and values that define whether those interactions are seen as disturbing or within the normal range. Thus, a child's behavior may be seen as disturbing by the head teacher in a classroom but not by the assistant teacher, depending on their interactions with the child and their expectations about how children should behave. Furthermore, a child may be involved in disturbing interactions with teachers at school but not with parents at home, because the settings and players elicit different interactions and/or because the expectations and values of the key players are different. Finally, different communities and cultures may develop different values and expectations about "normal" behavior, so a child's behavior may be seen as normal in one community and bizarre in another.

From the perspective of this model, one can worry about the rate of referral as much as about the children who are referred. For example, Rubin and Balow (1978) collected data about behaviors that teachers in Minnesota considered disturbing. In their sample of 1,586 children, 65% of the boys and 48% of the girls were identified by at least one teacher as having a behavior problem in the course of a 3-year period. They concluded that behavior that at least one teacher is willing to classify as a problem is the norm rather than the exception for elementary school children.

Daniels, Wilkinson, and O'Connor (1984) found that "the reality . . . is that we cannot distinguish between positive and effective personal functioning and ordinary middle-class conformity." Klassen's treatment outcome data, for example, suggests that individuals who were considered as most improved by the treatment facility were often those who changed least but were most typically middle class in patterns of behavior and demographic characteristics on treatment entry (1977, p. 332). The implication is that professionals in positions to identify children as disturbed must be alert to narrowness in their tolerance of differences and sensitive to important variations in cultural expectations that may influence a child's behavior.

There may be great variation in the relative contributions of individual characteristics or environmental factors to the production of discordance. At one extreme is the child or adolescent who creates disturbing interactions in most behavior settings in which he participates. However, environmental influences may still play a part in exacerbating or mitigating the disturbing interaction. For example, Lichstein and Wahler (1976) found that an autistic child exhibited a diversity of behavior over time in a given setting and across settings. They found that he looked healthiest at school during the afternoon unstructured playtime, as opposed to structured group activities in the morning, or self-directed play at home in the late afternoon.

On the other hand, there are some environments that are so stressful that they create disturbing responses in most of the inhabitants. Consider the children whose countries are at war and who immigrate to the United States. As Valero-Figueira summarizes:

> They have survived experiences that are beyond our comprehension. They have experienced violence at its peak, seen their families killed or mutilated, and lived in fear for their own lives. Those who have lost their parents have realized a child's greatest fear, the fear of being abandoned by both parents. . . . These children are at risk for "post-traumatic stress disorder." (1988, p. 48)

Even with these children, experiences can be exacerbated or mitigated by their resilience, their capacity to identify and use sources of support, and the particular pattern of defenses they mobilize.

Assumption 3: The goal of intervention is to make the system work, and to make it work, ultimately, without intervention. As Hobbs asserts, "The goal of ReEd is not to 'cure' the child but to enable an ecological system, of which the child is the defining member, to work reasonably well" (1982, pp. xiii–xiv). He later elaborates:

> We are not concerned with the general adequacy of a family, or with the goodness of a school for all the children it serves, or with the community in general, but with goodness of fit of family, school, and community with the needs of a particular child. And we are quite as much concerned with the ability of the

child or adolescent to meet the requirements of her family, her school, her neighborhood, her workplace, her community. We are not concerned with her adequacy to meet the demands of all possible roles—of all tasks that a school might produce, of all the possible expectations of a family, or of the competences for all job settings—but simply with unmet expectations that keep a particular system from working reasonably well. (p. 195)

The possible interventions may be based on any theoretical model or practical strategy. For example, parent education may support the parent's development of listening skills; an in-service program for teachers on multicultural education may enhance their understanding of some sources of a child's differences; teachers and students from a fifth grade class may go on a camping trip to increase their ability to work collaboratively; a child may have a behavioral contract to help him focus his attention on academic work for longer intervals; a "big sister" may be sought as an extension of a child's support system. Interventions designed according to the ecological model are uniquely defined for each system where discordance is present. An important constraint is that interventions should not be designed to change only the child, leaving the other components of the system untouched.

An opportunity provided by this model is to "think big" and borrow widely. Interagency coordination may be useful. An intervention program might combine a behavioral program at school and family therapy. Persons functioning in liaison roles could create bridges between home, school, and the community. A 13-year-old who is acting out in school might be best helped by facilitating the father's access to homemaker services and a job-training program. (See Apter & Conoley, 1984, for additional ideas about "systems" intervention.)

CURRENT ISSUES

Who is Disturbed and Why? Problems in Identification

As we have seen, the ecological perspective suggests that the identification of disturbing behaviors is subjective and culturally relative. As Kauffman (1984) points out, "Many of the children with whom we are concerned—probably **most** of them, in fact, are **arguably** emotionally disturbed. Their designation as emotionally disturbed or not disturbed is a matter of subjective judgment of the costs and benefits involved. And that judgment carries with it a considerable burden of responsibility, because the consequences of designation or nondesignation may be extreme. Identification is no trivial matter" (1984, p. 63).

Kauffman identifies several contexts that affect such decisions, including the political, legal, research, technological, and professional climate. He asserts that the political context of identification has changed, from the great liberal surge in the beginning of the 1960s to what he characterizes as today's "flaming hot conservative revival." He suggests that a by-product of the current conservative political climate is the serious underidentification of emotionally disturbed children.

When the physical structure of the classroom is rigid, deviant behavior may be more noticeable and hence more disturbing.

Another issue in identification is that some children are significantly over-represented in certain special education classes, such as those for the educable mentally retarded (EMR), trainable mentally retarded (TMR), and severely emo-tionally disturbed (SED). These overrepresented children are members of par-ticular cultural, racial, and ethnic minorities. This trend has concerned educators for the last two decades. A 1987 analysis of four surveys of elementary and secondary school populations by the Office of Civil Rights reveals that the problem persists.

The overrepresentation of blacks in EMR, TMR, and SED categories of excep-tionality remains at twice the level which would be expected from the percentage of blacks in the school population. The nationwide data show a decrease from 1978 to 1982 in the number of Hispanics referred for special classes of educable mentally retarded students. In 1984, however, the prevalence moved upward. (Chinn and Hughes, 1987, p. 45)

Chinn and Hughes also point out the overrepresentation of American Indians in classes for the retarded in several of the surveys. The comparative underrepresentation of white children and Asian and Pacific islanders is also noteworthy. Although it is not clear why these imbalances are occurring, one question that must be asked is whether particular kinds of cultural and ethnic differences between teachers and learners are interfering with the learning process. As explained by Ramirez:

> Both the literature and practical experience continually remind us of the importance of understanding the cultural, linguistic, and socioeconomic backgrounds of students. Inaccurate perceptions, stereotypes, and lack of familiarity with ethnic groups, their culture and history, and contemporary experiences can lead to low expectations and unwarranted generalizations about their educational potential. (1988, p. 45).

As an illustration of this kind of negative process, consider the research of Shirley Brice Heath (1983). She conducted an ethnographic study of two very small working-class communities in the Carolina Piedmonts. The inhabitants of Trackton were black and the inhabitants of Roadville were white. The inhabitants in these communities differed in their literature and oral traditions, in methods of teaching children to talk, and in a wide array of cultural values and expectations. When children from these communities went to school in the nearby city, it was clear that their teachers represented a third culture, and that children from both groups inadvertently violated many of the norms of behavior and language expected by their teachers.

For example, the teachers' expectations that children in preschool would be able to enjoy particular activities within a specified time frame (e.g., juice time, free playtime, clean-up time) caused frustration for Trackton youngsters. According to Heath's study, Trackton children were raised in an environment in which time flowed easily and the amount of time spent on an activity was based on interest, the availability of supplies, and the accessibility of adults. When told to interrupt an activity, the children felt very frustrated, some protesting shrilly. Many other differences separated the cultures of the Trackton children and the teachers, including expectations about storytelling, learning through questioning, and demonstrating respect for generalized "others."

Teachers made judgments very early about the students' potential for learning, given these "uncooperative" behaviors. One of the highlights of the study occurred when a teacher, Ms. Gardner, was assigned a class of 19 black first grade students who had been designated as potential failures based on their reading readiness scores. All these children were from Trackton or Trackton-like communities.

Ms. Gardner had been working with Heath and a group of other teachers to try to understand differences in the ways language was used in Trackton and Roadville and to discover ways to alter teaching methods and materials to accommodate these different styles of learning. Ms. Gardner used several methods to support the children's learning, including visiting the parents, cutting up old tires to represent letters of the alphabet and scattering them on the grass outside the classroom, asking children to identify letter shapes as they appeared in their own neighborhoods, using hardback primers, teaching small function words by studying their configurations as they were projected on a large screen in the auditorium, and enlisting the children's eager help in predicting story endings. She used these and other methods that took advantage of the way these children learned best. "At the end of the year, all but one of the children . . . were reading on at least grade level; eight were at third grade level, six at second grade level, and the rest were at grade level" (p. 287).

The pressure is increasing on teachers and special educators to learn how to work effectively with children from diverse cultures. More minority students are entering our schools. It is projected that by the year 2000, 40% of public school students will be from ethnic minorities as opposed to the current 30%. In many large city school systems, the proportions already exceed 80% (Ramirez, 1988, p. 45). Many new Americans, including refugees from Asia and Central America, are contributing to the rising minority population.

It is important that we recognize the importance of these changing demographics and seize the opportunity to enhance our appreciation of cultural differences and their effects on the learning process. What is required is much more complex than identifying and sharing the artifacts of a particular culture, such as holidays, foods, and special dress (Banks, 1987: Montero-Sieburth, 1988). The hope is to learn, through respectful study, the differences in children's approaches to such things as talking, writing, figuring, discussing, competing, the teacher, their family, and space/time boundaries. Those variables frame how children learn and develop best. Such an approach might well lessen the equating of difference and disability and the overidentification of children from some minorities as retarded or emotionally disturbed.

National Policies Affecting Special Education

Public Law 94-142 is a national policy that affects the way any child in a public school system is referred and placed in a special education program. Two developments are occurring now in education that have the same kind of potential as P.L. 94-142 for altering the education received by emotionally disturbed children throughout the country. These developments within the macrosystem are (1) the efforts to improve our schools that are taking place at the federal, state, and local levels and (2) the agitation to reunite regular and special education.

Recommendations designed to improve today's schools have appeared in many studies, such as the Carnegie Foundation's *A Nation Prepared* (1986), the Holmes' report *Tomorrow's Teachers* (1986), Bennett's *First Lessons: A Report on Elementary Education* (1986), Goodlad's *A Place Called School: Prospects for the Future* (1984), and the report by the Education Commission of the States (1986). Some recommendations emerge repeatedly, such as the importance of greater teacher involvement in curriculum planning and decision making, and the usefulness of career ladders and higher salaries in the teaching profession. The Carnegie Foundation's and Holmes' reports recommended that teacher training be improved by greater exposure of students to the liberal arts and interdisciplinary study, the requiring of masters' degrees, and the collaboration of college professors and mentor teachers in the preparation of new teachers. Goodlad (1984) advocated more local control of the schools, with problem-solving and long-range planning undertaken by committees consisting of the principal, teachers, parents, and community representatives. State governments are invited to take leadership roles in requiring teachers to pass minimum standards of writing and mathematical proficiency, in upgrading certification standards, and in fostering excellent schools and teaching through incentive programs.

This focusing of interest in education by such diverse groups already has led to some important changes in schools. In Massachusetts, for example, there are several different kinds of incentive grants available for teachers; new minimum salary levels; new certification regulations that require masters' degrees of new teachers and their joint preparation by mentors and college teachers; a state-supported teacher center that offers conferences, resources, and regular newsletters to teachers throughout the state; and school improvement grants offered to each school in the system. Applications for admission to teacher training institutions are increasing. Many schools are seeking funds to become professional development schools or Carnegie schools; there is new energy and excitement around teacher empowerment, teacher-directed staff development, and leadership training for administrators.

The implications for children with special needs are not yet clear. On the one hand, if school environments become healthier places for the educators, children are likely to benefit also. The effects of systematic curriculum review, career ladders for teachers, less tracking, more local control of school programs, and better prepared teachers are likely to be of some support to children who have not functioned well within the existing system. On the other hand, many special educators are concerned that little or no mention is made of special education in the national calls for educational reform. Their concern is that the emphasis on certain reforms, such as requiring more English, math, and science courses for high school graduation, will penalize children with special educational needs.

Another macrosystem issue is the potential merger of regular and special education (Lieberman, 1985; Reynolds, Wang, & Wahlberg, 1987; Wood, 1988). Hotly debated, proponents of the merger insist that long-term special education placements are not in the best interests of children; opponents argue that a range of options is needed to suit individual needs, and that many children with special needs are likely to get inadequate attention in the mainstream. The format for service delivery does have profound implications for emotionally disturbed children. Neither format has thus far worked as well as it might to lessen the production of disturbing behaviors in classes or to alter the ecology of disturbing systems once negative cycles have started.

RESEARCH INSIGHTS

Creating a Good Fit Between Children and Settings

Proponents of the ecological model are interested in finding studies which help them understand how to improve the fit between children and their environments. One fruitful direction of recent research has been to assess children's learning styles and the effects of curriculum modification on the children's academic progress. Carbo and Hodges (1988), for example, have differentiated students according to whether their reading style is global or analytic. Analytic students process information logically and sequentially, like to follow step-by-step directions, can understand a rule without examples, can decode words out of context, and like to do reading skill exercises. On the other hand, global students concentrate and learn best when information is presented as a gestalt or whole; tend to like fantasy and humor; process information subjectively and in patterns; are unconcerned about dates, names, or specifics; and recall information easily when it is presented in the form of an anecdote.

Matching reading materials with the student's preferred style has resulted in sharp decreases in stress and significant gains in reading comprehension. Carbo and Hodges (1988) cited a 1-year research study with learning disabled children, which resulted in a 17-month gain in reading comprehension for students whose learning styles and instruction were matched as compared to a 4-month gain for students not so matched.

In addition to their work with specific reading styles, the authors also learned in working with at-risk students that "the majority of these youngsters learn best in an informal, highly structured environment that contains soft light and has headsets available for those who learn best with quiet or music—such environments that seldom are provided in our schools" (Carbo & Hodges, 1988, p. 55). Since most instruction offered in schools is based on the analytic approach, Carbo and Hodges offer many suggestions that would support global learners, such as beginning lessons globally that demonstrate the importance and context of a skill, and replacing much of the typical skills work with "listening to and reading good literature, acting in plays, creating models, drawing pictures and writing about them, and using puppets for storytelling" (p. 57). Moreover, sharing information with students about their learning styles tends to make them feel valued and empowered and results in sharply decreased discipline problems.

The research of Thomas, Chess, and Birch (1968), mentioned earlier, has been expanded. Chess and Thomas (1984) continued to gather data on the initial population of 133 subjects, extended their work with a Puerto Rican sample, and stimulated related research by other investigators.

Chess and Thomas (1984) commented about the relationship of temperamental characteristics to the goodness of fit between children and their settings in school. For example, they indicate that high-activity children suffer if required to sit for long periods of time, and distractible children may have trouble learning if they are expected to concentrate at length. "Slow-to-warm-up" children may perform below par in the initial weeks of the school year, and incorrect and undesirable judgments with unfavorable consequences may be made by teachers'' (p. 286). The authors cite Barbara Keogh's work at the University of California at Los Angeles (UCLA) on temperament and teachability. She points out that variations in children's temperament affect teachers' expectations of the children's teachability, ability, and performance.

Chess and Thomas elaborate on the goodness of fit concept, finding it ''a most useful conceptual framework within which to trace the vicissitudes of individual psychological development from infancy to early adult life'' (1984, p. 288). They explain that the goodness of fit concept does not specify that any one pattern of individual-environment interaction is required for favorable psychological development to occur. To illustrate, they describe differential outcomes for children with the ''difficult'' temperament who live in different cultures. (Children with ''difficult'' temperaments are irregular in body function, negative in response to new stimuli, slow to adapt to change, and intense, often negative in mood.) Children with these characteristics in a middle-class New York sample were at risk for behavior disorders. It was the authors' belief that ''difficult'' children did not fit easily with their parents, who had high expectations for predictable infant schedules and quick adaptation to new situations. For their Puerto Rican sample, conformity to a predictable schedule was not a necessity for the children, and there was no correlation between the ''difficult'' temperament pattern and behavior problems. For a sample of children from the Masai tribe in Kenya whose region was experiencing drought, of the seven ''easy'' babies, five died, while all six of the ''difficult'' babies survived! The authors have used information about children's temperament, together with data about the child's other characteristics and the setting demands, to help parents anticipate appropriate placements, to counsel parents and school personnel about how to support particular styles, and to help older students gain insight into their own profiles and options for themselves.

Schalock and Jensen (1986) presented an assessment procedure they used to determine the goodness of fit between the behavioral capabilities of retarded citizens and the expectations for performance in six different types of community living arrangements (e.g., group homes, supported apartments). They found that the quality of life index was highest if there were matches between required behavioral capabilities and the performance requirements identified by caretakers in the setting.

Effects of Environments on Groups of Children

The research initiated by Barker (1963, 1968) explored the effects of particular settings on groups of children. A significant body of research has followed this tradition, and a few of these studies are highlighted here.

Smith, Adelman, Nelson, Taylor, and Phares (1987) studied the relationship between students' perceptions of control at school and their attitudes toward schooling. Compared to controls in regular education classes, the children in special education classes perceived themselves as having less control at school and reported themselves to be less happy. On the other hand, an alternative program for children with special needs that was designed to enhance students' perceptions of control resulted in more positive attitudes toward school than either of the other samples. The authors suggested that these findings should make us wary of school programs that emphasize greater use of external control and management of problem behavior, since their use may intensify the psychological reaction and negative behaviors they are designed to eliminate. Instead, the researchers advocate programs that stress intrinsic motivation and interventions that emphasize enhancement of perceptions of control and self-determination.

Nielsen and Moos (1978) studied the relationship between high school students' preferences for exploration (i.e., willingness to take part in activities and to be a change agent in the environment) and the opportunity for exploration in various high school settings. They discovered that students with a strong interest in exploration were significantly more satisfied with schooling when placed in an environment that permitted high levels of exploration.

Other investigators were curious about the characteristics of special education classrooms in secondary schools. Polsgrove, Okolo, Bahr, and Eckert (1987) were surprised to find that the special education classrooms were characterized by teachers providing much of the instruction, depending on individual seat-work activities, and giving little monitoring or feedback to students. The researchers were concerned that teachers did not use those procedures ordinarily associated with high student achievement, such as small-group instruction, direct instruction, and corrective feedback.

Forness, Guthrie, and MacMillan (1982) used the Classroom Environment Scale (Moos & Trickett, 1974) to assess a range of classes for the retarded on the dimensions of classroom structure, support, and psychological climate. They compared the classroom characteristics with mentally retarded children's observable classroom behavior. They discovered that the classes were generally characterized by higher than average levels of involvement, clarity, flexibility, friendliness, and support, and that differences in the amount of these characteristics led to changes in the students' observable behaviors. For example, they discovered that in the classrooms they described as "problematic," with low scores on student involvement, teacher control, order and organization, the students were inattentive and tended to be disruptive.

Lentz and Shapiro (1986) explored the relationship between classroom variables and academic performance or achievement. They identified three factors that affected achievement: allocated instructional time, on-task behavior, and opportunities to respond. Also related directly to students' progress and performance were teacher behaviors such as goal setting and progress monitoring; direct questioning about academic work; and praising, prompting, and contacting students during individual seatwork. The authors coined the term **academic ecology** to encompass the network of relationships among student and classroom variables affecting student engagement and achievement in academic tasks.

Effects of Family on School Performance

Because a child is part of a nonfractionable social system, it is often important to gather data about aspects of the child's life in settings other than school. Two studies are presented offering somewhat similar views of family characteristics that might place a child at risk for low academic achievement or troublesome behaviors. In both cases, the compelling data were not the family structure variables such as single-parent or two-parent status, but the complex network of behaviors and attitudes that supported or did not support children's positive involvement in school.

Ramsey and Walker (1986) examined the family management practices of parents of antisocial boys. Subjects were recruited from the three major school districts in Eugene, Oregon, and compared with a control group. Using home observations, the investigators discovered that parents of antisocial boys were significantly less competent than control-group parents on each of five family management constructs which included discipline, monitoring, positive reinforcement, involvement, and problem solving.

Status variables which did not differentiate the two groups included family structure, number of siblings, birth order, and parental income. However, more of the antisocial group had parents who were not married (26% vs. 4%) and fathers who had ben arrested (29% vs. 7%). The authors agreed with literature reviews suggesting that family correlates of antisocial behavior patterns present "a characteristic profile of family management practices and patterns of interaction . . . that converge on the side of negativism, harsh discipline practices, inconsistency, lack of structure, and lower levels of competence in parenting skills" (Ramsey & Walker, p. 198).

A more optimistic picture is presented by Clark (1983), who investigated the relationships between family life and school achievement for black children. Based on intensive interviews with 10 families, Clark argued that structural characteristics such as poverty, single-parent status, limited parental education, or working-mother status were not predictive of academic achievement in black families. Rather, Clark hypothesized an assortment of activities, attitudes, and relationships that supported school success. The school survival skills possessed by high achievers and their parents included frequent school contact initiated by the parent, some stimulating supportive teachers, calm interactions between child and parents, expectations for lots of parent and child involvement in schooling, and infrequent family conflicts. Parents' expectations for their child's postsecondary training were important, as was their involvement in achievement-training activities. Offering clear role boundaries, actively monitoring the student's compliance with rules, and providing nurturance and support were additional recipes for success.

Both of the preceding studies suggest the importance of reaching out from the school to families to offer resources, opportunities for parent support, and information on how parents can enhance children's achievement.

CURRENT PRACTICES

An Intervention That Works: Project Re-ED Revisited

Project Re-ED is no longer a project, but it is an approach to treatment of children and adolescents that is being used in 23 sites across the United States.

Weinstein (1974) discovered that in comparison with controls, Re-ED children experience more academic gains, increases in self-esteem, behavioral improvement, and higher ratings of child improvements by mothers and referring agency workers. Other supportive evaluation studies have been done; more are in process. The model has contributed several important innovations to ecological treatment. A panel of nationally known visitors to the program explained it as follows:

> Among the most significant achievements of Project Re-ED is the creation of an entirely new profession within the mental health field, that of teacher-counselor. The new profession has many attractive features: it draws on an abundant pool of talented and caring young adults; it requires less extensive and expensive graduate training than does psychiatry or clinical psychology; it provides a rich experience in socially valuable and personally rewarding work for those who stay in the role, if only for a few years; and it is a stepping-stone to longer-term administrative and instructional positions in reeducation or to further graduate study. Panel members were especially impressed by the competence and high morale of the teacher-counselors in the schools visited. . . .
>
> Among other innovations associated with reeducation (though not necessarily invented in that context) are: the insistence on removing the child from home, school, and community for the shortest possible period consistent with achieving a favorable outcome; the five-day residential week, with children going home every weekend to maintain and nurture family ties; the insistence on small size in programs—not more than forty or fifty residents; the limitation of services to a restricted geographical area, to permit constant engagement with the ecosystem of which the child is the defining member; the emphasis on the achievement of competence, especially in basic educational skills so necessary for effective living; the training of parents to work positively with younger children; the preparation of adolescents for further education or work; the incorporation of wilderness camping for highly antisocial adolescents; the emphasis on adventure for all children. The panel was especially impressed by the fact that reeducation is not a grim process but one that is infused with an affirmative spirit and a deep appreciation of people, of children especially, and of life's simple satisfactions. (Hobbs, 1982, pp. 365, 386)

The psychological and educational principles that govern the day-to-day running of the program have changed little since Hobbs explained them in 1966. However, the interpretation of those policies is continuously unfolding, according to the expertise of the teacher-counselors, their mental health consultants, and the needs of the children. Hobbs states that "the continuing vitality of the Re-ED program springs, in part at least, from an understanding that every person involved in the program is responsible for inventing what Re-ED should become" (1982, p. 30–31). The 12 principles of the Re-ED program are as follows:

1. Life is to be lived now, not in the past, and lived in the future only as a present challenge.
2. Trust between child and adult is essential. It is the foundation on which all other principles rest, the glue that holds teaching and learning together, the beginning point for reeducation.

3. Competence makes a difference; children and adolescents should be helped to be good at something, especially schoolwork.
4. Time is an ally, working on the side of growth in a period of development when life has a tremendous forward thrust.
5. Self-control can be taught, and children and adolescents can be helped to manage their behavior without the development of psychodynamic insight; and symptoms should be controlled by direct address, not necessarily by an uncovering therapy.
6. The cognitive competence of children and adolescents can be considerably enhanced; they can be taught generic skills in the management of their lives as well as strategies for coping with the complex array of demands placed on them by family, school, community, or job. In other words, intelligence can be taught.
7. Feelings should be nurtured, shared spontaneously, controlled when necessary, expressed when too long repressed, and explored with trusted others.
8. The group is very important to young people; it can be a major source of instruction in growing up.
9. Ceremony and ritual give order, stability, and confidence to troubled children and adolescents, whose lives are often in considerable disarray.
10. The body is the armature of the self, the physical self around which the psychological self is constructed.
11. Communities are important for children and youth, but the uses and benefits of community must be experienced to be learned.
12. In growing up, a child should know some joy in each day and look forward to some joyous event for the morrow. (Hobbs, 1982, pp. 22–23)

If we were to add to the list of principles today, we would emphasize the importance of ambient expectancies in ReEd schools as a source of affirmative, purposeful, and even zestful living by students and staff alike. When programs are going poorly, expectations of failure generate failure. But when programs are going well, the schools are so positive, so alive with learning, that students and staff are caught up in a deeply fulfilling adventure every day. Affirmative expectations are contagious; they often spread to families, to regular schools, and to cooperating social agencies (Hobbs, 1982, pp. 22–23).

The Family Empowerment Model

Just as Project ReEd strengthens the ecological system in which the child is the defining member, the Family Matters program (Cochran, 1987) functions to strengthen the ecological system in which parents are the defining members. Research has suggested that an important factor in mediating stress and risk in parents is the availability of a friend, extended family member, or professional who can offer support, interpretation, or redirection of behavior (Wahler, 1980). The Family Matters program was designed to explore the capacity of urban environments to serve as support system to parents and other adults directly involved in the care of children.

The key concept in this model is empowerment, defined as "an interactive process involving mutual respect and critical reflection through which both people and controlling institutions are changed in ways which provide those people with greater influence over individuals and institutions which are in some way impeding their efforts to achieve equal status in society, for themselves and those they care about" (Cochran, 1987, p. 11). The program is based on five assumptions about families:

1. All families have some strengths.
2. The most valid and useful knowledge about the rearing of children is lodged among the people—across generations, in networks, and in the culturally rooted folkways or ethnic and cultural traditions.
3. A variety of family forms are legitimate and can promote the development of healthy children and adults.
4. Fathers as well as mothers can play an active role in activities with the child and household tasks.
5. Cultural differences are both valid and valuable (Cochran, 1987, pp. 14–15).

The study involved 276 families in Syracuse, New York. Each family had a 3-year-old child. The families were evenly distributed among 18 neighborhoods. Families in 10 of the 18 neighborhoods were offered the family support program; families in other neighborhoods served as controls. Families participated in the program for an average of 26 months.

Two approaches were used to involve families in activities related to their children: (1) a home-visiting approach and (2) a cluster-building approach. At the parents' request, eventually both approaches were offered to all families. In the home-visiting approach, trained paraprofessionals visited with parents and children, gave recognition to the parenting role, reinforced and enriched parent-child activities, and shared information about child care and community services. Early meetings were spent seeking out the parents' points of view and learning about current activities that parents thought were germane to their development. These activities were then shared with other parents in a standard format, an approach which emphasized the importance of parents' ideas and established the program as one that gathered information from parents for parents. In the cluster-building approach, workers first got to know parents and then arranged for group meetings (with child care) to introduce families to one another, to get a sense of what joint activities might be useful, and to create a forum for sharing information and resources.

Over the 2 years of the program, changes occurred in parents in predictable, developmental ways: from positive changes in self-perception; to new efforts to reach out to spouse, child, relatives, neighbors, and friends; to social action. White, single mothers were especially responsive to the program as reflected in more positive self-perceptions and involvement with larger numbers of people. Contacts between home and school were less for these families than for controls because contact seemed to be initiated only when children were having difficulty.

Positive outcomes were noted for those children whose families occupied less advantageous positions in the social structure, such as less educated parents, including some two-parent and most one-parent families. There is some anecdotal evidence to suggest that parents became more empowered in their efforts to influence key individuals or institutions (e.g., bosses, city or human services), but no baseline measures were gathered at the outset. Elements of the program that the author feels are particularly important for others to consider include the noncategorical, nondeficit approach to delivery of services, and the opportunities for families to become involved in the program in different ways. If, as we have seen, children's low school achievement and asocial behavior are strongly correlated with parental attitudes, behaviors, roles, and parenting skills, then the potential benefit of this kind of program as a preventive measure and as a support to families is enormous.

ASSESSMENT

For the practitioner, assessment is a major contribution offered by the ecological model. By evaluating troubling behaviors in context, the practitioner (e.g., teacher, psychologist, or counselor) is given extensive opportunities to understand and alter disturbing behavior cycles. Each effective ecological assessment approach contains two elements: (1) a process or sequence of steps to follow and (2) a particular selection of variables for evaluating the interaction of child and setting.

As the simplest level, an assessment sequence includes these elements:

1. **Identify the disturbing interaction.** Exactly what is happening? What happens before and after the disturbance? When does it occur? What times of day are free from the disturbance? Who is involved? What does the behavior accomplish for the child?
2. **Identify who is disturbed by the interaction.** Who is not? What norms or expectations are being violated? Are the norms reasonable? Should the expectations be changed?
3. **Consider what might be causing the problem.**

   - physical setting
   - inappropriate contingencies
   - lack of match between the child's characteristics and the curriculum
   - peer pressures and expectations
   - discrepancy between home and school expectations
   - physical or psychological stress factors

4. **Gather information about past and potential interventions.** Has anything worked before? What strengths and resources can be built upon? What are the reality constraints?
5. **Develop, implement, and evaluate a solution package.** What are your goals? Who is responsible for what? What is the timeline? What will be the evidence for success?

The experience and sophistication of the assessor emerge in the identification of variables that are scanned to determine what is causing the troubling behavior(s). Bulgren and Knackendoffel (1986), for example, have included six elements to scan: physical milieu, classroom patterns, personal interactions, learner styles and academic deficits, expectancy factors, and factors outside school. Each element is further delineated. Physical milieu, for example, includes open versus closed space, classroom seating, and classroom density.

Morse's (1985) wisdom emerges especially in his breakdown of factors that may affect a child's behaviors. He examines **cognitive-academic attributes and behavior** (cognitive ability, achievement, learning disability, study skills, school institution, cognitive mediation ability, reality testing), **affective interpersonal components** (self-concept, self-esteem, identity, identification targets, level of trust, value incorporation, self-responsibility, empathic potential, affective states, view of the world), **social-interpersonal components** (peer role, authority relationships, attention/relationship seeker, likability/winsomeness, out-of-school activities) and **biophysical factors** (physical state/health, neurological integration, appearance and body image, birth conditions and prenatal trauma, medication/drugs, developmental rate, temperament). (See Figure 9.1.)

Muscott (1987) has a particularly elegant approach to assessment that he calls a "conceptual behavior management process." He divides the process into three phases: developing policy, gathering information, and developing the management plan. His approach is particularly sensitive to the influence that personal values, system values, and realities may have on the behaviors identified, the interventions considered, and the choices one must make about rules, policies, and procedures.(See Figure 9.2).

Hobbs (1982) has articulated a very complete implementation aid which he calls an "ecological assessment and enablement plan." A chart for each child specifies the service required, who's responsible, by whom, service completion dates, costs, source of funds, criterion, and follow-up information. Critical to the plan are mechanisms for building linkages with key components of the child's ecosystem.

Several articles provide helpful suggestions for locating assessment instruments that allow the practitioner to gather valid data. (See Cantrell & Cantrell, 1985: Rogers-Warren, 1984.)

For the inexperienced teacher, the abundance of potentially relevant variables in an ecological assessment may seem overwhelming. If one's goal is surviving, the first year of teaching may be devoted to survival or coping with crises rather than a careful analysis of individual and setting match.

In my experience, the adding of levels of analysis come slowly, with new dimensions added through observation, reading, and experience with children. Each new dimension adds color and depth to one's perception of the setting. For me, an understanding of developmental stages and temperament provided the first tools for evaluating child-setting match; an understanding of family and school culture was another focus; understanding how family culture and learning style affect the way individuals learn and teachers teach is a current interest. No single variable, such as temperament, will provide the key to unlock every puzzling situation. However, the quest is fun and the wisdom is cumulative!

As we have seen, the ecological perspective provides an alternative approach to assessment and intervention based on an understanding of child/setting interactions. Our understanding of these interactions continues to grow as

Sequence

Information Areas for Consideration	A	B	C	D	E	F	G
	Nature and source of referral problem	Ecological: Past and present	Past interventions tried/results	Individual self-synthesis assets, limitations, needs	Overall behavioral style	Interventions planned: Short-term Long-term	Reassessment Replanning
Individual Child 1. Cognitive-Academic 2. Affective-interpersonal 3. Social-interpersonal 4. Biophysical							
School							
Family							
Community							

FIGURE 9.1

Assessment Tool for Tracking a Child's Behaviors

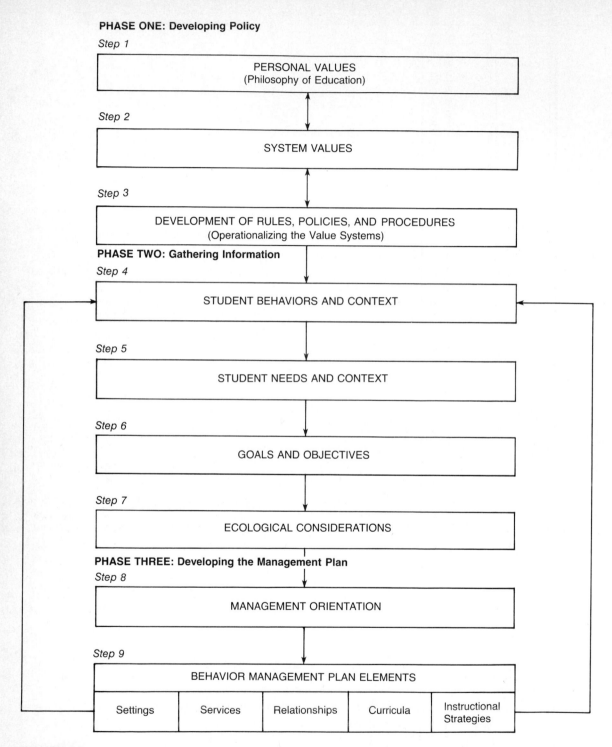

FIGURE 9.2
Conceptual Behavior Management Process

we develop new templates for assessing the characteristics of children and settings. In the future we need to take further advantage of the ecological model to
design interventions that foster productivity and zestful enjoyment in our children and youth.

SUMMARIES

The ecological model views emotional disturbance as a product of discordance
in the reciprocal interactions of the child and components of his social system.
No one is blamed for causing emotional disturbance or for its effects. Rather, the
child and significant participants in the child's environment are viewed as contributing and receiving members of transactions in an interactive system. Responsibility for altering disturbing interactions is shared among the participants.
Assessment must examine the child-environment interactions as the basis for
planning interventions. The goal of interventions is to improve the interactions
and to make the social system work better. Since the early work of Hobbs and
Rhodes in applying the ecological model to educating emotionally disturbed
children, several ecological interventions have been developed focusing on improving the goodness of fit between children and settings. This view has been
useful in expanding the focus of interventions to include families, schools, community networks, and other systems in which the child interacts.

DISCUSSION QUESTIONS

1. Think back over your own experiences in school. What particular situations
   made you feel most productive, confident? Least productive, confident? Why?
   Try to assess the **interactions** between you (i.e., temperament, motivation,
   and needs) and the characteristics of the physical and social setting. Compare
   your discoveries with others. Is there any consensus on what kinds of interactions caused trouble? Do you find important differences in your group?
2. What is the role of parents in contributing to disturbance according to this
   model? What role do parents play in contributing to disturbance according to
   the behavioral and psychodynamic models? What implications do these different views have for how a teacher would work with parents?
3. This model requires that we evaluate our own culturally based expectations
   and values in judging whether our interaction is disturbed. One might even
   suggest that the very models we develop for understanding deviance are
   rooted in a particular culture and historical period. Would you agree? Why or
   why not?
4. What are the strengths and weaknesses of the ecological perspective in assessing and treating disturbance?
5. Most theories of disturbance focus attention on the microsystem level as
   described in Bronfenbrenner's typology. What opportunities and risks to our
   understanding of disturbance do you see in extending the ecological model
   to include mesosystem, exosystem, and macrosystem levels?
6. Consider a child from your reading or experience whose behavior was considered disturbing. Assess all the variables that you think were contributing to
   the disturbing interaction. Discuss what further questions you have and what
   you learned from the activity.

REFERENCES

Apter, S., & Conoley, J. (1984). *Childhood behavior disorders and emotional disturbance.* Englewood Cliffs, NJ: Prentice-Hall.

Banks, J. (1987). *Teaching strategies for ethnic studies* (4th ed.). Boston: Allyn and Bacon.

Barker, R. (1963). *The stream of behavior.* New York: Appleton-Century-Crofts.

Barker, R. (1968). *Ecological psychology.* Stanford: Stanford University Press.

Barker, R. (1987). *Recollections of the midwest psychological field station.* Unpublished manuscript.

Bennett, W. (1986). *First lessons: A report on elementary education in America.* Washington, DC: Superintendent of Documents, U.S. Government Printing Office.

Bristol, M., & Gallagher, J. (1982). A family focus for intervention. In C. Ramey & P. Trohanis (Eds.), *Finding and educating the high-risk and handicapped infant.* Baltimore: University Park Press.

Bronfenbrenner, U. (1979). *The ecology of human development: Experiments by nature and design.* Cambridge, MA: Harvard University Press.

Bulgren, J., & Knackendoffel, A. (1986). Ecological assessment: An overview. *The Pointer, 30,* 23–29.

Cantrell, M., & Cantrell, R. (1985). Assessment of the natural environment. *Education and Treatment of Children, 8,* 275–295.

Carbo, M., & Hodges, H. Learning styles strategies can help children at risk. *Teaching Exceptional Children, 20,* 55–58.

Carnegie Forum. (1986). *A nation prepared: Teachers for the 21st century.* Hyattsville, MD: Carnegie Forum on Education and the Economy.

Chess, S., & Thomas, A. (1984). *Origins and evolution of behavior disorders.* New York: Bruner/Mazel.

Chinn, P., & Hughes, S. (1987). Representation of minority students in special education classes. *Remedial and Special Education, 4,* 41–46.

Clark, R. (1983). *Family life and school achievement. Why poor black children succeed or fail.* Chicago: University of Chicago Press.

Cochran, M. (1987). The parental empowerment process: Building on family strengths. *Equity and Choice, 4,* 9–23.

Daniels, S., Wilkinson, C., & O'Connor, W. (1984). The psychosocial ecology of urban black youth. In W. O'Connor and B. Lubin (Eds.), *Ecological approaches to clinical and community psychology.* New York: Wiley.

Education Commission of the States. (1986). *Transforming the state role in undergraduate education.* Denver, CO: ECS Distribution Center.

Feagans, L. (1972). Ecological theory as a model for constructing a theory of emotional disturbance. In W. Rhodes & M. Tracy (Eds.), *A study of child variance* (Vol. 1). Ann Arbor: ISMRRD, University of Michigan.

Forness, S., Guthrie, D., & MacMillan, D. (1982). Classroom environments as they relate to mentally retarded children's observable behavior. *Journal of Mental Deficiency, 87,* 259–265.

Goodlad, J. (1984). *A place called school: Prospects for the future.* New York: McGraw-Hill.

Gump, P. V. (1975). Ecological psychology and children. In M. Hetherington (Ed.), *Review of child development research* (Vol. 5). Chicago: University of Chicago Press.

Gump, P. V. (1977). Ecological psychologists: Critics or contributors to behavior analysis? In A. Rogers-Warren & W. Warren (Eds.), *Ecological perspectives in behavior analysis.* Baltimore: University Park Press.

Heath, S. (1983). *Ways with words.* Cambridge, England: Cambridge University Press.

Hobbs, N. (1966). Helping disturbed children: Psychological and ecological strategies. *American Psychologist, 21,* 1105–1115.

Hobbs, N. (1982). *The troubled and troubling child.* San Francisco: Jossey-Bass.

The Holmes Group. (1986). *Tomorrow's teachers: A report of the Holmes group.* East Lansing, MI: The Holmes Group.

Kauffman, J. (1984). Saving children in the age of big brother: Moral and ethical issues in the identification of deviance. *Behavior Disorders, 10,* 60–70.

Kounin, J. S. (1970). *Discipline and group management in classrooms.* New York: Holt, Rinehart, & Winston.

Lentz, F., & Shapiro, E. (1986). Functional assessment of the academic environment. *School Psychology Review, 15,* 346–357.

Lichstein, K., & Wahler, R. (1976). The ecological assessment of an autistic child. *Journal of Abnormal Child Psychology, 4,* 31–54.

Lieberman, L. (1985). Special education and regular education: A merger made in heaven? *Exceptional Children, 51,* 513–516.

Montero-Sieburth, M. (1988). Conceptualizing multicultural education: From theoretical approaches to classroom practice. *Equity and Choice, 4,* 3–12.

Moos, R., & Trickett, E. (1974). *Classroom environmental scale manual.* Palo Alto, CA: Consulting Psychologists Press.

Morse, W. (1985). *The education and treatment of socio-emotionally impaired children.* Syracuse: Syracuse University Press.

Muscott, H. (1987). Conceptualizing behavior management strategies for troubled and troubling students. *The Pointer, 31,* 15–22.

Nielsen, H., & Moos, R. (1978). Exploration and adjustment in high school classrooms: A study of person-environment fit. *The Journal of Educational Research, 72* (1), 52–57.

Ramirez, B. (1988). Culturally and linguistically diverse children. *Teaching Exceptional Children, 20,* 45–46.

Ramsey, E., & Walker, H. (1988). Family management correlates of antisocial behavior among middle school boys. *Behavior Disorders, 13,* 187–201.

Reynolds, M., Wang, M., & Wahlberg, H. (1987). The necessary restructuring of special and regular education. *Exceptional Children, 53,* 391–398.

Rhodes, W. (1970). A community participation analysis of emotional disturbance. *Exceptional Children, 36,* 309–314.

Rhodes, W. (1967). The disturbing child: A problem of ecological management. *Exceptional Children, 33,* 449–455.

Rhodes, W., & Paul, J. (1972). *A study of child variance: Conceptual project in emotional disturbance.* Ann Arbor, MI: University of Michigan Press.

Rhodes, W., & Paul, J. (1978). *Emotionally disturbed and deviant children..* Englewood Cliffs, NJ: Prentice-Hall.

Rieth, H., Polsgrove, L., Okolo, C., Bahr, C., & Eckert, R. (1987). An analysis of secondary special education classroom ecology with implications for teacher training. *Teacher Education and Special Education, 10* (3), 113–119.

Rogers-Warren, A. K. (1984). Ecobehavioral analysis. *Education and Treatment of Children, 7* (4), 283–303.

Rubin, R., & Balow, B. (1978). Prevalence of teacher identified behavior problems: A longitudinal study. *Exceptional Children, 45,* 102–111.

Schalock, R., & Jensen, C. (1986). Assessing the goodness-of-fit between persons and their environments. *Journal of the Association for Persons with Severe Handicaps, 11,* 103–109.

Smith, D., Adelman, H., Nelson, P., Taylor, L., & Phares, V. (1987). Students' perception of control at school and problem behavior and attitudes. *Journal of School Psychology, 25,* 167–176.

Swap, S. (1978). The ecological model of emotional disturbance in children: A status report and proposed synthesis. *Behavior Disorders, 3,* 186–196.

Swap, S. (1984). Ecological approaches to working with families of disturbing children. In W. O'Connor & B. Lubin (Eds.), *Ecological approaches to clinical and community psychology.* New York: Wiley.

Swap, S., Prieto, A., & Harth, R. (1982). Ecological perspectives of the emotionally disturbed child. In R. McDowell, G. Adamson, & F. Wood (Eds.), *Teaching emotionally disturbed children.* Boston: Little, Brown.

Thomas, A., Chess, S., & Birch, H. (1968). *Temperament and behavior disorders in children.* New York: New York University Press.

Valero-Figueira, E. (1988). Hispanic children. *Teaching Exceptional Children, 20,* 47–49.

Wahler, R. (1980). The insular mother: Her problems in parent-child treatment. *Journal of Applied Behavioral Analysis, 13,* 27–42.

Weinstein, L. (1974). *Evaluation of a program for reeducating disturbed children.* Washington, DC: Department of Health, Education and Welfare. (ERIC Document No. ED 141–966)

Willems, E. P. (1967). Sense of obligation to high school activities as related to school size and marginality of student. *Child Development, 38,* 1247–1260.

Wood, F. (1988). Learners at risk. *Teaching Exceptional Children, 20,* 4–9.

10
Educators of the New Paradigm*

MAIN POINTS

1. Classic science posits that the learning self and what is learned are two separate things. In other words, the world can and does exist separately from the person who is learning about that world.

2. The new paradigm maintains that what a child sees and what she learns is based on what the child is. Much of what the learner sees and learns is grounded largely on her own projections.

3. What an individual learns changes both her world and what she is. Learning and becoming are one and the same thing.

4. Ideas are actions and actualize all aspects of reality. Ideas that are not actions are not real, but only potentially real. Mental knowing is active, not passive.

5. Breaking material down into bits and pieces leads to fragmented thinking. Objectivity in the classic science framework is the vehicle by which we learn to separate our selves from facts. Conversely, the new paradigm emphasizes holistic thinking and connectedness.

6. The new paradigm sees man or woman as a participator and not simply as an observer of nature and reality.

7. Object, time, space, and causality are orienting concepts relative to who and where an individual is. These concepts are simply modes of thinking about reality. They are not concrete conditions externally placed in the environment.

8. In the new paradigm, knowledge is a creative process rather than a discovery or recovery process. Education, then, is a process of helping the child become a creator of knowledge.

---

*This chapter was written by William C. Rhodes, research professor, and Mary Sue Rennells, post-doctoral fellow; Department of Special Education, University of South Florida.

9. The development of thinking skills is critical to a child's being able to know and experience a richer and more rewarding world.

10. Education teaches children *how* to learn even more than specifically *what* to learn. The child is taught how to develop her mind in ways that help her order and organize her world into more meaningful wholes.

11. Instruction directly patterns the child's mind so that it, in turn, can pattern her world into a more understandable and coherent unity.

The thinker makes a great mistake when he asks after cause and effect. They both together make up the indivisible phenomenon.

Goethe

The twentieth century teems with change. From the scientific revolution of Einstein at the beginning of the century to the political revolutions of Eastern Europe at the end of the century, the world has catapulted from an industrial society to an information society. Classic, Newtonian science has captured many of our hearts and minds as the driving force behind a new global village: men on the moon, organ transplants, instantaneous visual information, and personal computers. Yet the implications and ramifications of Einstein's profound thought experiments and of other physicists are gradually insinuating themselves into our society, radically altering the way we think, see, believe, and act. This new scientific paradigm, intriguing and provocative, holds a promise for resculpting our lives and how we educate our children. This chapter explores this new paradigm in theory and in application.

PIONEERS OF THE SHIFTING PARADIGM

A small group of special education researchers and teachers have embraced the new paradigm of science, and have written eloquently about its implications and applications to special and general education.

Lous Heshusius (1982, 1984, 1986, 1988), for instance, attacks the underpinnings of the mechanistic model that has guided the sciences and special education. Heshusius posits that the cornerstones of the mechanistic model—control, prediction, sequentiality, linearity, and additivity—robs meaning and spontaneity from the teacher/learner relationship. In this view, the student is a reactive and passive organism, easily manipulated and controlled by outside forces. Conversely, the teacher, as the behavior-change agent, dissects both disparate curriculum areas and emotions into discrete, measurable, and observable segments.

Heshusius

According to Heshusius,

> These steps can be arranged sequentially, taught to the child, and measured quantitatively as outcome. This view dictates that the time period necessary for training or teaching can be predicted; that "the best way" (in terms of methods, materials, and teaching strategies) can be determined; and that such planning can cover periods as long as one year. (1982, p. 8)

Heshusius notes that academic and behavioral objectives are often constructed by adults outside the classroom who neither know nor teach children. It must be emphasized that Heshusius is not decrying the use of concrete methods and teaching strategies. Rather, she exposes the educational juxtaposition of means for ends.

She contrasts the mechanistic view with the nonmechanistic model afforded by the new paradigm, which places the teacher and the student as active participants in the learning process. Heshusius explains:

> In effect, they [teachers and students] change reality as they participate in it. Thus the use and place of teaching strategies, learning principles, methods, and materials cannot be exactly predetermined. Ideally, the teacher and student must work with an open-ended planning approach which continuously matches the direction taken with the ever-changing conditions. (1982, p. 11)

She stresses that special education has tried to do the impossible by framing unpredictability within predictability, the unmeasurable within the measurable, and wholeness within fragmentation. Heshusius interprets holistic thought, the linchpin of the nonmechanistic model. In contrast to reductionistic thought, holistic thought struggles to directly apprehend and understand both the integrity of complexity and also the overarching "relationship of the whole to its parts (which derive their very existence from the whole and are not independent from it)" (Heshusius, 1986a, p. 463). Holism can advocate for data-based instructional procedures while opposing mechanistic data and data-gathering procedures.

Heshusius frames conceptions of effectiveness squarely within the paradigm from which they emerged. Paradigms evolve criteria for selecting and subsequently evaluating problems. Heshusius extrapolates:

> Therefore, the relevant questions to ask are **how** holism conceives learning, what **kinds** of data should be gathered, and **how** should they be gathered to support the contention that learning is occurring (1986b, p. 463).

Heshusius (1986b) questions rigorous methodology. Invoking once again the interdependency of observer-observed, fact-value, objectivity-subjectivity, she maintains that the mechanistic method's inviolable independent status is eroding, that the new paradigm is beyond method, beyond objectivity, beyond subjectivity, beyond reductionistic rationality. Instead, contemporary thinkers (Jurgen Habermas, Richard Rorty, and Hans Gadamer) are metamorphosing the reductionistic rationality of technique and method into human rationality (Bernstein, 1983). "This rationality, instead of being grounded in method and technique, is grounded in discourse, dialogue, and morality—for both our theoretical and research endeavors and for the conduct of our practical lives" (Heshusius, 1988, p. 61).

Indeed, Heshusius gathers together various ways of knowing other than reductionistic rationality: poetry, literature, art, values. She attributes Prigogine and Stengers (1984, p. 23) with suggesting the twentieth century symbol for science: "art forms that bridge the confrontation between formal/theoretical and intuitive/tacit understandings of the world" (Heshusius, 1988, p. 61). In short, a fusion exists between inner and outer worlds, inseparable and interdependent. Heshusius urges that we, as teachers of exceptional students, develop within ourselves that self-reflection, that deep understanding of the fundamental needs and complex interdependencies of mankind which lie outside the boundaries of reductionistic rationality. To Heshusius, the tacit knowledge inherent in the arts and humanities is essential to preparing teachers to work within the complexities and moral demands of human exceptionality.

Poplin

Mary Poplin (1988a, 1988b) applies the principles espoused by Heshusius to the field of learning disabilities. We think these principles also apply to emotions and behaviors. While describing the differences between the four prevalent models of learning and emotional-behavior problems (i.e., medical, psychological process, behavioral, and cognitive/learning strategy models), Poplin (1988b) delineates 12 characteristics common to the four models and indicative of reductionistic thinking. She applies these only to learning disabilities. We can see that they also apply to behavioral problems. The 12 characteristics are as follows:

1. Learning and behavioral problems are a discrete phenomenon rather than an explanation of a phenomenon.
2. Each model ultimately places the responsibility for cause and/or the cure for diagnosed problems directly on the student.
3. Each model proposes a diagnosis, the goal of which is to document specific deficits.
4. Each model attempts to segment learning and affect into parts.
5. Teaching techniques proposed under each model assume that instruction is often most effective when it is tightly controlled, leaving the learner predominantly passive.

6. The proposed diagnosis for each model forms the essence of the intervention.
7. Instruction in each model is deficit driven.
8. Teaching and learning are viewed in each model as unidirectional; that is, the teacher knows what is to be learned and the student is to learn it.
9. Each model assumes a right and wrong posture about the teaching and learning process.
10. Each model almost exclusively promotes school goals rather than life goals.
11. Each model supports the segregation of students into different categories.
12. Steps and sequences are valued within the delivery system itself (Poplin, 1988b, pp. 394–398).

Poplin (1988b) stresses that, although specific assumptions about etiology, assessment, diagnosis, and instruction have changed, the fundamental beliefs and values have remained constant. In essence, we believe that (1) special education problems can be reduced to a single identifiable, verifiable construct; (2) the process of teaching and learning is most effective when most reduced; and (3) this reduction of educational services benefits all learning disabled children.

To counterbalance these assumptions, Poplin (1988a) describes a melding of three complementary perspectives, consistent with the new paradigm: structuralist philosophy, constructivist theory, and holistic beliefs. Poplin identifies Piaget (1970) as the activator of both structuralism and constructivism. Philosophical structuralism posits a method for collecting, organizing, perceiving, and interpreting phenomena. Constructivism, on the other hand, describes how learning constructs new knowledge through the processes of both self-regulation and transformation. Piaget, according to Poplin, saw constructivism and structuralism as inseparable and integral. Holism comprises noncognitive variables related to learning, particularly feelings, intuitive thought, and motivation.

To explore the implications of these perspectives to special education, Poplin identifies 12 principles of the structuralist, constructivist, and holistic teaching/learning process:

Structuralist Values

1. The whole of the learned experience is greater than the sum of its parts.
2. The interaction of the learned experience transforms both the individual's spiral (whole) and the single experience (part).
3. The learner's spiral of knowledge is self-regulating and self-preserving.

Constructivist Beliefs

4. All people are learners, always actively searching for and constructing new meanings, always learning.
5. The best predictor of what and how someone will learn is what she already knows.
6. The development of accurate forms follows the emergence of function and meaning.
7. Learning often proceeds from whole to part to whole.
8. Errors are critical to learning.

Holistic Thought

9. Learners learn best from experiences about which they are interested and involved.
10. Learners learn best from people they trust.
11. Experiences connected to the learner's present knowledge and interest are learned best.
12. Integrity is a primary characteristic of the human (learner's) mind (Poplin, 1988a, p. 405).

These principles suggest how we learn. What is lacking is an explanation of *not* learning, of learning problems. Poplin suggests five possible reasons for learning failure in the classroom: "developmental unreadiness, inactive teaching techniques, insufficient previous and current experiences, insufficient interest, and mismatch of previous experiences" (1988a, p. 411).

Poplin concludes that viewing the teaching/learning process from the new paradigm perspective will transform what we see as disabilities and who we see as disabled. Poplin (1988a) posits several tenets of the constructivist/holistic theory to special education:

1. New experiences are integrated into the whole spiral of knowledge so that the new pieces of knowledge, the new meanings, are much larger than the sum of their parts.
2. Two or more learning experiences transform one another and transform the structure of present knowledge. Thus, learning is not merely additive, it is transformative.
3. The learner is always learning, and the process of self-regulation, not reinforcement theory, determines best when, what, and how things are learned.
4. Instruction is best derived from student interest and talent and not from deficits or curriculum materials.
5. The assessment of student development, interests, and involvement is more important to teachers than student performance on reductionistic subskills and subprocesses.
6. Good teaching is interactive rather than unidirectional.
7. Real-life activities form better educational experiences than synthetically contrived ones.
8. Errors are necessary, and should not be penalized.
9. Goals of instruction should be more life related (e.g., literacy and cooperative learning) than school related (e.g., reading basals, worksheets, and textbooks).
10. Reflection, creation of questions, and construction of personal interpretations are more critical than "correct," "accurate," "right" answers to prepared questions.
11. Problems in learning are the result of interactions of personalities, interests, development, expectations, and previous experiences.
12. Learning involves a process of going from whole to part to whole with accurate forms (parts) being secondary to the whole.

13. Form follows purpose (function) and meaning, and premature instruction in accurate forms will inhibit fluency.
14. Passion, trust, and interest are paramount—subjectivity surrounds learning, and cognitive processes are only one part of the picture.

Poplin maintains that viewing the educational experience with these principles in mind will bring a different picture into sharp focus. She offers that relinquishing a reductionistic approach to education will yield richer knowledge of the student and greater knowledge of designing meaningful experiences around who the child is rather than who the child is not.

The concepts of the new paradigm are gradually infiltrating disparate factions of education and special education. Thomas Skrtic (1986) comprehensively examines the intricacies of the new paradigm as it applies to special education knowledge and organizational theory. Sam Crowell (1989) extends the characterization of content and process in education within the context of the new paradigm. He offers succinct, concrete examples of paradigmatic classroom applications: cooperative learning, complex instruction, whole language, and brain-based learning. The new paradigm has been applied to science teaching (e.g., Wagner, 1983) and holistic language arts (e.g., Bender, 1987). Scientific methodology, particularly as it applies to education, has also been investigated and restructured within the framework of the new paradigm (e.g., Stainback & Stainback, 1985).

SHIFTING THEMES AND PRACTICES

Connectedness and Knowledge

The central theme of the new paradigm is "connectedness." That is, the connectedness of everyone and everything to everyone and everything else. The glue of this connectedness is knowledge that is generated rather than acquired. We propose that the child and the teachers together are knowledge generators and that the generic base of education is teaching the child **how** to generate knowledge as a way of life. This may deviate somewhat from classic education, but reflects the shifting view of knowledge which science is beginning to uncover. The new physics has stimulated this new science of knowledge. It is shifting our overarching image of the universe from that of a great machine to that of a great thought.

The first part of this chapter presents some of the elements of this changing view which sees the universe as an information-generating network rather than a clockwork machine. The last part of the chapter addresses the need for an active, generic curriculum to help children become part of this new information-generating society. Too many of our children are falling out of this knowledge-connected network in the world of reality which is emerging from the new scientific paradigm.

The sample of the Life Impact curriculum presented in this chapter which is being tested for our rapidly increasing number of at-risk children is designed to change the child's life rather than to give her a set of school skills. If such a generic curriculum could help transform such marginalized children, it would fit the old homily, "If you give a starving man a fish you have relieved his present hunger; but if you teach him how to fish, you have taught him how to live." If you can teach a child how to generate knowledge, you have taught her how to live in a real world of information explosion.

Table 10.1 contrasts the classic science view with the shift that is taking place in the new scientific paradigm. Table 10.1 also presents the implication of these changes for the educator. It may help you grasp the underlying structural knowledge shift that is occurring in this paradigm. Also, at the end of the chapter is a set of figures (see Figures 10.2, 10.3 and 10.4) that illustrate how "inside" and "outside" might become one and the same thing, and thus represent how thinking, and the things thought about, can coalesce in the new view of knowledge.

TABLE 10.1
The Contrast Between the Classic View and the New Paradigm

The Classic Science View	The Shifting View in Science	Implications for Education
The universe is a great machine.	The universe is a great thought.	Thinking patterns and processes are the basic subject matter of education.
Knowledge is acquired.	Knowledge is generated.	The fundamental task of education is generation of knowledge.
Knowledge is accumulated in bits and pieces which eventually come together to make a total pattern.	Knowledge is holistic and holographic webs of mental responses. New insight changes the web configuration and all of its multifacets.	Curricula should be constructed in web fashion, or in a holistic and holographic fashion.
Inside and outside are two different things.	Inside and outside are the same thing.	Changing the child's web of knowledge changes the child's whole being.
Total objective observation is ideal.	Objectivity, as taught in classic science, cannot occur without including the observer and her own meaning of what is being observed.	Subjective or self-meaning is basic to the educative process.
The world has a single pattern.	The world has multiple, kaleidoscopic (or ever-changing) patterns.	The child must learn to view knowledge as a kaleidoscope of patterns.
Self and world are separate.	Self and world are the same.	The child cannot learn about the world without learning about the self and vice versa.

Paradigm Themes

Science has changed radically in the twentieth century. It has overthrown most of its cherished beliefs and basic ways of knowing about its world. Education was founded on the belief system of science before it began to change in the early 1900s. That belief system is now referred to as "classic science." The changed belief system, based on the revolution in science that began to take shape in the twentieth century, is called **the new scientific paradigm.** It is a radically different way of seeing the world and viewing how we come to know what we know. This makes a difference in how we look at teaching children. For one thing, it brings the learner and what she learns together into one whole. What the child learns is what she is and vice versa. Classic science separates these two realities. The learning self and what was learned were two separate things.

This view firmly holds that the world can and does exist separate from the person who is learning about that world. The classic view tends to make the act of learning a very passive process, because the learner gains knowledge of something "outside," apart from herself and from who she is. In fact, the learner is encouraged to try to keep out of the entire process as much as possible. The reason for this is that the child has to learn to be "objective." Classic scientists and classic educators hold that the personal stuff inside the learner gets in the way of clear-eyed knowledge of stuff outside the child. The new way of looking at acquiring knowledge in science and education (the new paradigm) is tied to the astounding finding in science that what you see and what you learn is based in large measure on what you are and vice versa. In a sense, what you find in the world is shaped by what you are, and what you are looking for, at that particular time. There is no way a learner can keep herself out of what is learned because the person, the world, or the material that that person comes to know are one and the same thing. There is no way for the learner to keep from mixing all the messy stuff inside herself into what she knows or learns. There is no such thing as being really objective in the way we generally think of it, for much of what the person sees and learns is based largely on her own projections of herself. In fact, if we try to separate the learner's self from what we are teaching, we can create serious problems for that learner.

The Learning Self

According to the new educational paradigm, since what one learns changes both one's world and what one is, learning and becoming are one and the same thing. That is, new knowledge, generated largely by the knower, folds back into the knowledge reservoir already existing in the mind of that knower. Then a magical transformation takes place in this occurrence. The holistic pattern is changed; and in the process, this changed pattern is dynamically charged to accept new knowledge. This is shown in Henry Pierce Stapp's (1971) mathematical analysis of the quantum transformation. This transformation process changes both the knower and what he comes to know. What this tells us is that learning and becoming are one and the same thing. Therefore, there is no way to separate self-development from teaching. What a child becomes is largely what she learns. We can say that the teacher is not a "psychologist," a "parent," a "therapist" or a "physician," but this is not wholly true because it assumes that the education is not infusing the child's whole being and making her a totally different person than she was before she learned new things.

The tricky problem in teaching is to get the child to put the whole self into whatever it is that we are trying to teach. When we try to be too objective, the child feels that we are rejecting who she is, and that we do not appreciate and understand what she stands for.

Theory vs. Practice

Some educators will say, "The new paradigm is only theory. It isn't practical." The central point of the new paradigm is that ideas and actions cannot be separated. Ideas that are not actions are not real, but only potentially real. They are ghost material until the person activates them. Then they become live ideas which can "move the earth." It is ideas that shape, form, and transform reality. Ideas are the energy source of every educational or social revolution. In fact, according to the new paradigm, ideas actualize all aspects of reality. Stapp (1971), who is one of the new breed of scientists, shows us mathematically that the only events known to exist are mental events. That is hard to understand until you think about it. The classic perspective says that we can only know about things through our senses. All learning **about** reality has to come through eyes, ears, nose, mouth, and skin. The new paradigm says, "No, we do not simply 'sense' reality. We 'know' reality directly with the mind." Mental knowing is active, not passive. It crystallizes reality. It does not just know **about** reality. It transforms possible reality into actual reality. We do not know how it does this. But experiments in the new physics show us that it does. As you read this chapter, this central point in the new paradigm may be the hardest thing to grasp. However, once you have grasped it, everything else makes sense.

We Create Our Own Reality

The fact that the child constructs her world out of the ideas developed in her mind, and spins her world around herself, is something that Piaget (1986) also believed and demonstrated in his studies of child development. The kind of self-world reality that the child constructs out of her mind depends on how well-developed her mental processes are. Education is the means by which the child's mental processes are developed and elaborated. If the child's mental processes are narrow and blighted, the world she constructs around the self will be narrow and blighted and vice versa. Likewise, if her mental processes are limited, the self, which to a large extent she also constructs, is similarly limited.

Fragmented Thinking

Classic science has taught us to think in fragmented ways. We firmly believe that we and our students learn better if we break knowledge down into bits and pieces. This is how classic science goes about the process of learning.

This classic view of learning teaches us first to draw a clear line between ourselves and our world. The idea is that we can be objective this way and learn more clearly about our world of reality without clouding this knowledge with personal feelings and intentions. This harsh rejection of our humanness has led to tremendous accomplishments in classic science. Since the industrial revolution, it seems to have accomplished miracles. We developed cars and assembly-line pharmaceutical factories, assembly-line appliances, and assembly-line chemicals, synthetics, radios, and so on. Our scientific skies were unlimited.

We are now beginning to notice what that scientific control over things was doing to the environment. We did not notice what it was doing to the delicate balance of nature—destroying the ozone layer, increasing acidity of rain and snow, killing trees and vegetation. We did not notice that we were running out of space to bury those things we developed with classic science when they were no longer useful. We never dreamed we would have to put them on floating barges that would not be able to land and dump them elsewhere. We did not notice that we were polluting our drinking water, our lakes, our oceans. Now we are aware that there are costs in the way we conducted science.

We did not notice what the classic science world view was doing to our objectively excluded selves in our scientific pursuits. Our fragmented way of thinking, with a deliberately objective mind set, left us out of our universal picture altogether.

In the classic style of education, objective teaching may cause alienation. Too many children feel separated from their world and disconnected from other people. They feel alone, unimportant, and incompetent. Fragmenting styles of thinking make them feel their world is chaotic and lacks any logical sense. Classic science has generated many theories and practices to account for the learning and socialization problems we find in our children. Mainly, these theories fall into two or three categories that can be combined in various ways. Emotional disturbance may be viewed as a problem of "physical" heredity. It may be attributed to the environment. It is because of the child's behavioral history. These theories show how our classic sciences separate the self from the world, and then break knowledge and people into various "manageable" categories.

When we teach children, we convince them to think of themselves as a **product** of their heredity, their environment, and their behaviors. They buy into this thinking, and consequently lose any sense of having control over themselves or their world. They learn the lesson well that they "can't help it" because of this lack of control. Therefore, among even our most-favored children, we see alcoholism, drug addiction, and dangerous sexual practices. We see a beautiful, vibrant, but drunk coed being gang-raped by a group of drunken favored sons in a college dormitory. We see two wealthy preppies practicing violent sex games, with the girl ending the game in death. We see alienated, disconnected youth hanging out on mean streets, pushing drugs or robbing homes, stores, and people. We see younger and younger teenage girls caught in unwanted and unmanaged pregnancies. These youngsters do not feel they have any real control over their lives. They do not know about the power of the mind in nature discovered by the new breed of physical scientists. They have not experienced an education that teaches wholeness and connectedness. They do not know the power that thinking has over "things." Their teachers have not known these experiences, either. Our impulse in education is to ignore the self of the learner because classic views tell us that self-development is not education's business. The parent, the doctor, the psychologist, the social worker, or some other specialist is responsible for that isolated and partialized social, physical, or psychological self.

As educators, our objective attitude conveys to our children that who they are is relatively unimportant in the educative process. We seem to think that they can leave their "selves" at the door of the classrooms. Our only interest is in this vast body of knowledge we own "out there" that we have to put "in there." In the primary grades the main classic lesson we have to teach children is objectivity. We do not want them to contaminate knowledge with their feelings, desires, and fantasies. We train them how to "think" independently of feelings or beliefs. Thus, knowledge is objectified and put outside the self.

Above all, we tend to teach children to separate "selves" from "facts." Once we teach this we, then, teach them to break down those facts into smaller units or pieces in order to assimilate them. After children master the task of "objectivity," they are encouraged to turn to the "outside" world and divide it into manageable chunks of knowledge. We teach language arts, science, math, and social studies as though they are independent of each other and separate from the child's self.

This is the classic view of knowledge. However, the new paradigm tells us that even nature cannot be broken down into parts. It is a unity. This view teaches that our mind, freed from fragmented thinking skills, is capable of grasping knowledge in holistic terms. In fact, when we put knowledge of our world outside ourselves, and try to break down phenomena, events, occurrences, facts, and processes into manageable bits and pieces, we lose all sense of meaning. Some of the newer approaches to education such as "whole language," "whole brain learning," and "holistic education" are all based on this precept of the new paradigm. They all say we do not teach meaning. When we lose meaning, we experience a sense of disorientation and disorder; of being disconnected. In fact, some scientists (Bohm, 1984; Wolf, 1984) tell us that when we teach children to break things into bits and pieces, we train the total mind to think in a discordant, disjunctive fashion. A fragmented teaching style is at the heart of our personal alienation from ourselves and our world. Some scientists feel that such fragmented thinking is responsible for separating person from person, country from country, race from race, class from class. Such a way of thinking, they say, divides us rather than unites us. Even the "thinking skills" people have not looked at this danger as we begin to teach children how to think, how to reason, how to be intelligent.

According to the new paradigm scientists, we have to learn to see and experience the whole. We have to cure our thinking of the fragmented style in order to heal ourselves and our world. We must learn to experience connectedness in our lives. Teachers must learn to teach in holistic ways. We must constantly teach connectedness. We must teach the child that she is a whole being, not a cognitive being, as opposed to an affective being; not a body separate from a "soul;" not a self separate from a world. We cannot teach a child to think without teaching her to feel. We cannot teach her to behave without teaching her to socialize. We cannot teach her mind without teaching her total self. We must teach the child that she is a unity connected to the world, and that the world is a unity that connects all things to the thinking self.

Creating Knowledge

Teaching the child in the classic sense convinces her that knowledge comes strictly from outside the self, in a hidden world that reveals itself to her reluctantly, one piece at a time. In contrast, the new paradigm suggests that what we come to know is largely what we project into the world. New knowledge links to old knowledge. In the process, this new knowledge changes old meanings. Knowledge is a creative process, rather than a discovery or recovery process.

If we consider teaching in light of this new paradigm view, then instruction is a process of helping the child become a knowledge creator. It is a growth and development process in which the child builds and expands her own knowledge-creating capacities in the company of other knowledge creators; this process includes all of us. The child continually enlarges and deepens her personal world as she enlarges and deepens the self. He becomes a more and more enriched projector of reality as he reflects upon the self as knower. Thus, for the child, as for all of us, the quality of life expands as the knowing self expands.

If we look at reality this way, the educators discussed in this chapter have captured the essence of the change which was precipitated by the new breed of scientists. These writers are not just interested in changing the way we teach children to relate to knowledge. They are interested in entering the minds of the readers and helping them directly experience this radically changed reality in all of its implications for a new type of education.

A Humanistic Science

Within the new paradigm, science has turned humanistic. The new physics is actually not about physical processes at all. Rather, it is about the human observer or participator who spins those processes into existence. It emphasizes thinking rather than things. Surprisingly, science has become subjective. Classic science viewed man as an accident of nature. Classic nature was totally oblivious to humans, unmoved by their alien passions, cares, concerns, and needs. Men came and went and nature went on without them, knowing nothing of their existence. Classic science was a history of man's longing for connection and communication with nature. In spite of man's entreaties, classic science viewed nature as aloof and utterly unmoved, responding to man's plea for knowledge with endless silence, only indirectly revealing bits of itself. In the new science, nature speaks in a human voice and answers back as man projects himself into it. Man finds the endlessly creative products of his own mind in nature's midst. He recovers from nature what he puts into nature. At long last, with the new scientific paradigm, connectedness finally is established. Man finds himself a part of infinite consciousness that brings everything together. In this process, the new physics, a major revolutionary source of the new paradigm, has become a dynamic, intuitive science in which the "Self and its Brain" (Eccles, J., & Popper, K. 1977) seek greater understanding and knowledge rather than more predic- tion and control of nature. It has become a humanistic physics, a creative phys- ics, with the personal participator at the heart of the scientific revolution.

Classic education, like all of the classic social sciences, imitated the meth- ods of knowing used by classic physics. The classic physics tried as much as possible to eliminate the knower from the knowing process. We have done the same illogical thing in classic education, in spite of the fact that all our experience in teaching children tells us this is impossible. In the model of knowing used by strictly deterministic, logical-empirical physics, there was little space for human- ities or art. For nature itself, the very source of knowledge was neutral, passion- less, nonhuman. In the new physics, Wheeler (1982) says that the whole uni- verse is a self-exciting circuit, which could not have been real until there were human observers. The new paradigm is predicated upon a human reality cre- ator, a **participator** and not simply an **observer**. Suddenly nature is humanized. It is no longer **neutral** and passionless. Nature takes on all the characteristics of the human participator. Any knowledge we generate regarding "nature" is now knowledge also about ourselves in nature. Nature opens up to us, resonates to us, communicates with us.

Learning to Project Reality

It is very important that we make children aware that science, arts, and human- ities are all unified projections of themselves. When they come to know these fields, they come to know themselves. In this sense, their premier field of studies is the arts and humanities, because it is most directly or immediately about themselves (Heshusius, 1986). Science tells them about the way they locate themselves in and relate to a context of object, time, space, and causality. In the new paradigm, these orienting concepts are only relative to who and where they are. They are reality-anchoring concepts or mental constructs of objects, space, time, causality; not absolute, concrete conditions or variables in the universe. They are, as Einstein said of time and space, simply modes of thinking about reality and not concrete conditions in the environment. This means that the humanities rather than the sciences are the basic subject matter. Science helps children use their minds to structure their world coherently, to give order and organization to their own chaotic experiences. It helps them make everything real, but it does not speak directly to their inner spirit, only to their minds as messengers of their inner selves. Humanities and the arts should not be taught separate from the sciences, or else they will remain aloof and meaningless bodies of knowledge unrelated to the reality of children's lives. Science has to be viewed by children as relative to themselves as persons. If it is seen this way, it is quite possible that when children become developers of knowledge, they will not generate outcomes in science which will be detrimental or destructive to themselves and their world in the way that classic science has done.

Questions

Two major questions about this new world view are raised in the minds of educators: Does everybody live in her own separate world? Do we teach our children that their own reality, no matter how different from everybody else's reality, is what they should live by? These are complex questions. One of the major explanations of the new physics phenomena is a strangely disquieting explanation. It is the "many worlds" view in which each of us has multiple selves living in many possible worlds. However, at every moment in time we choose one of these views and "pop" that particular one into reality. In a science fiction sense, we could "pop" into existence a different world from that "popped" by most people. This is still a very controversial explanation, one that is much too difficult to grasp at this point.

Another answer to the question "Is everybody's own world personally different from everyone else's?" is "No, because over a long period of time, our individually generated worlds come into convergence." We have sort of a mainstream world with moderate variations. Only a few people are like van Gogh, who saw color, form, and structure totally different from the way we perceive our world. Even van Gogh's closest artist friends could not see the world the way he did. Even though van Gogh's brother, who ran an art gallery, was able to sell the strange paintings of van Gogh's artist friends who were supposed to be using the view of reality that was allied to van Gogh, he could not sell van Gogh's paintings. These paintings were worthless products of van Gogh's weird projections of himself into reality. So, the loyal brother paid for all of these crazy pictures of reality out of his own pocket, letting van Gogh assume that there were buyers. Years after van Gogh's suicide, people reached the "Ah-Hah!" experience and could say, "Now I see the world the way van Gogh sees it." Many so-called schizophrenics are not so lucky as van Gogh to be able to show to the world the strange reality they see and experience. The mainstream flows on, unperturbed by the schizophrenic vision they have revealed. Yet, our reality can be much richer because of persons like van Gogh.

The second question that comes to mind regarding the new paradigm is, if the world is not separate from our selves, what happened to the basic building blocks of physical reality? What about that concrete physical reality that we see with our own eyes? What about the real physical conditions of object, space, time, and causality? How is it that we all know what these conditions are and how they exist?

There are two answers given to this question. One is that "something" is transmitted to us across the generations which provides our minds with the potential to mentally construct object, time, space, and causality. Second, although there is no physical reality apart from our mental construction, there are ghostly, half-real physical potentials in the universe, which come out of their potential state into reality when we actualize them by intent and attention. In a sense, we are keeping the world going by paying attention to it. We "pop" it into existence. What a strange idea! Yet, it holds up, experiment after experiment, and mathematical treatment after mathematical treatment in the new scientific paradigm.

What does this mean to educators? It means we have to help the child develop her thinking capacities so she can participate in the continued creation of her world. Since we literally "think" things into existence, the development of thinking skills is critical to the child's being able to know and experience a richer and more rewarding world. Not only do we have to teach holistic thinking, we also have to develop all of the child's projective and reality-processing capacities in order for her to feel a sense of active contribution to this world. If she can grasp this meaning of the learning process, we can help her realize that, through learning, she is gaining greater control over her own personal reality.

Experience Your Own Projections

At this point you might want to have a direct experience of how you project your own reality. Figure-ground photos, picture completion photos, and ink blots require your personal projections into them to make them meaningful. Look at Figures 10.1, 10.2, and 10.3. Try projecting your own meanings into them. Then, independently of each other (and of your perception), present them to two or three friends to see if they find something different in them. This will give you an idea of the intimate connection or mutuality of "inside" and "outside." The holistic scientific view of reality denies a separation between observer and observed, subject and object, person and environment.

MIND-IMPACT EDUCATION

A Generic Curriculum

Along with the growth of special education, a new dimension has emerged in education's conception of curricula. For a while, the full scope of this subtle change was obscured by the enthusiasm for specific curricula to modify children's behavior. However, alongside the growth of behavioral curricula other attempts at modification of various aspects of a child's development were underway. Curricula for the education of social-personal and affective capacities

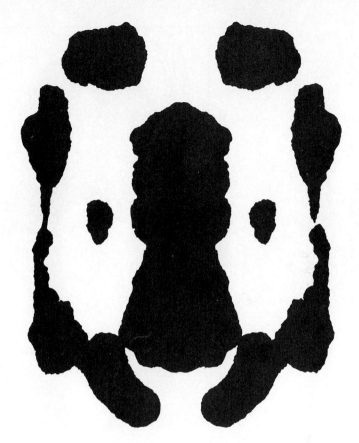

FIGURE 10.1
What Do You See in This Ink Blot?

evolved. There was a flood of cognitive and metacognitive development curricula. We also are beginning to see the welding together of affective-cognitive
curricula, cognitive-behavioral curricula, and so on. Previously, the classic science framework encouraged assessment of and intervention into separate segments of the child's total life. The new paradigm, however, sees everything as
connected. For instance, knowledge and being are unified. Therefore, what a
child comes to know changes her whole being. Thus, not only does the new
paradigm encourage holistic education, it also shows learning and development
to be reciprocal or refluent processes. They are mutually dependent growth
processes.

Whole-Mind Patterning

Mind patterning and the child's construction of reality go together. The more
developed the patterning capacities of the child's mind, the richer the reality
within which the child lives.

FIGURE 10.2
Is She Young or Old?

In the rest of this chapter, we will attempt to develop a generic "mind-patterning" form of instruction. Mind patterning actively involves the child and her inner way of knowing. Instead of devoting all of the child's school time to learning **what** to know, the child is also given in-depth instruction in **how** to know about her world. She is taught to connect herself to her world through the generation of new knowledge.

At the University of South Florida, we are experimenting with a particular generic curriculum that attempts to do this. It is a supplementary curriculum that goes directly to the child's mental-patterning ability with which she constructs her reality. We call it the Life-Impact curriculum. It is being used experimentally with children who have been labeled disordered, deprived, disabled, disruptive, discordant, and so on. Educators generally see these children as disconnected, or poorly connected, to the goals and content of the classic school. Many of these children find our classic style of teaching, which is fragmented, to be confusing or threatening to them. They either withdraw from learning, or they reject and attack it. Sometimes they project the problem outward onto the teacher. Sometimes they project the problem inward and blame themselves for being inade-

FIGURE 10.3
What Is It?

quate and incompetent. Educators do not help much with the labels they attach to these children.

The type of instruction we are developing to help these children reorganize themselves and their learning can be called a Life-Impact curriculum or a holistic thinking curriculum because that is exactly what it tries to do. Rather than concentrating simply upon putting facts into the child's mind, this curriculum teaches the child how to process the content of her life and world so that she can have some control over her reality. Rather than simply focusing upon the assimilation of content, we teach the child how to construct and process reality. This Life-Impact curriculum bears some resemblance to thinking skills curricula, in that it assumes that generic change can be made in mental capacities through education. However, unlike cognitive development curricula, it does not segregate the child's cognition from her total mental configuration which includes her social-personal and affective-behavioral capacities. As a holistic curriculum, it also has the potential of helping the child improve and integrate her self-concept, self-awareness, and self-confidence because she begins to feel in command of her own world.

The three interactive and integrative components of this Life-Impact curriculum are (1) context structuring, (2) constructing self-world relationships or refluences, and (3) constructing meaning.

Context Structuring.   This component teaches the child how to mentally pattern the holistic context of the self in relationship to other persons, objects, time, space, and causality (i.e., those ingredients of her world that provides a structure around the self). Context structuring also underlies all curriculum content in the classic school. This is the context or the basic grounding within which the self operates and knows its world. When the child learns that she can help produce these personal structures with her mind (as Jean Piaget has shown), she immediately feels a sense of control over her own reality.

Constructing Self-World Relationships or Refluences.   A second component of the Life-Impact curriculum is teaching the child to improve her conscious realization of herself, or her self-reflective capacity, as a central figure in the person-object-space-time-causality context which relates to herself (Piaget, 1986). Instead of feeling outside this physical grounding, the child begins to feel directly connected to her own life-world. In a sense, she is then an integral and determining part of her world, and is free to develop and expand her own self into that world. Thus, we deliberately teach self-development in much the same way we teach the modes of thought related to person, object, space, time, and causality.

Constructing Meaning.   The final component of this Life-Impact curriculum teaches the child to give meaning to reality as a holistic process in action which involves her directly. Reality is no longer a buzzing confusion of fragmented things floating around in a world outside the child. We teach her that there can be more than bits and pieces which make up her world, and that she can help determine the actual meaning of her reality just as everyone else can give personal meaning to reality.

These three components, like a hologram, cannot be separated from each other. Each is contained and reflected in the other. Context, self-world relationships, and meaning are alternating special manifestations of the same reality.

Hands-on or Laboratory Teaching

Hands-on activities show the child literally how to construct reality (Piaget, 1986). The tasks or activities are basic learnings that provide the foundation for all of the child's future learnings.

Teachers recognize that "hands-on" exercises that revolve around object, space, time, and causality are ways of teaching the familiar educational patterning of order, organization, relationship, classifications, sequencing, attribute "treeing," correlating, enumerating, and so on. The materials used resemble those used in **thinking skills** curricula, but they also encompass social-personal and affective-behavioral learning.

The child learns the vocabulary associated with constructing the reality context of person, object, space, time, causality. She also learns the mental-patterning processes of sorting, ordering, organizing, classifying, attribute-treeing, segmenting, and correlating. Gradually she learns that she has "tacit" knowledge or "intuitive" knowledge of these construction processes, but has to learn to make these more explicit, more precise, more elaborated, and more usable. We would like to emphasize that this particular component is not a perceptual-deficit correction effort. It is personal-context development aimed at helping the child make explicit her own connection to person, object, space, time, and causality. In the new paradigm a child does not perceive a contextual environment existing outside herself. The child is an active constructor of her personal life, which moves from inside toward the outside as an extension of the self into an information-bound world. As Piaget illustrated, the child **projects** person, object, space, time, and causality, and literally constructs what classic science conceives of as a substantive, existing external reality. In this component of the curriculum, we follow the new physics extension of Einstein's special relativity theory. Person, object, space, time, and causality are a unified network of thought rather than conditions in the environment. We teach the child how to strengthen and deepen her extension of herself into the outward manifestation as an environing context. We teach her to create rather than perceive reality through unified modes of thought about person, object, space, time, and causality. The exercises which follow teach the child to project her mind outward into a shared personal-social and affective reality.

Let us use an exercise in projecting time as an example. We want the child to see that time is always self-referenced. One of the ways of doing this is to turn the child's life into a time-sequenced history.

Objective of This Exercise: To have the child demonstrate to herself that time is always a relative to herself.

Task: Have the child construct her own timeline history.

Material: A wide strip of paper Scotch-taped to the chalkboard and around the room.

Procedure: Tell the child to construct a time system that is made up of critical incidents in her life (e.g., "Sister born, my age 4. Father to Vietnam, my age 10. Cousin died, my age 12").

Discussion Process: When three or four personal time histories have been taped to the walls, the class discusses the varying time systems as personal constructs of a meaningful time series.

A mirror exercise is another example of the differences between the teaching of directions in space as relative to the self-observer. This exercise can be performed after the child has a firm mental concept of right and left and compass directions.

Objective: To teach the personal relativity or mental projection of directions in space.

Materials: A full-length mirror, the child's body, a set of verbal directions.

Procedure: Tell the child to turn left, then left again, then right. Say to the child, "Verbalize the direction your mirror image is facing. Verbalize the direction your own body is facing. Trace the compass sequence of movements your mirror image took and you, yourself, took."

As you can visualize when you read this, the child has to construct and reconstruct the directional movement of both herself and her mirror image and

TABLE 10.2
Hands-On Activities

Object Construction

Loud Thinking	Classification Exercises
Attribute Exercises	Classification Tree Exercises
Bead-Stringing Exercises	Coding Exercises
Mirror Exercises	Hidden Figure Exercises
Block Design Exercises	Object Reconstruction Exercises
Object-Patterning Exercises	

Space Construction

Floor Compass	Identifying Objects in Space
Magnet Bar	Mazes
Directions	Blue Printing
Map Skills	Geo Boards
Star Machine	Mirror Exercises

Time Construction

Clocks	Self-History Timeline
Time Zones	Floor Compass
Speed of Light and Sound	Space-Time Travel
Time Events	Historical Time
Other Planets	Time Words and Order
Time Sequences	Time Schedules
Military Time and Space	Time Travel

translate from one to the other in her head. She learns that she can produce the image inside her head.

The laboratory exercises in the self-construction and self-projection learning component of the reality-processing curriculum moves beyond a personal context of object, space, time, and causality. The child is forced to become aware of the central source of her own constructive powers. She also becomes aware of other people. We teach the child what the new paradigm, generated by the new physics, is teaching us. We are the authors of almost all that we behold. Because of who we are, we cannot look upon the world without changing it in accordance with our intentions. What we come to know in the world is largely a result of what we put into the world. We teach the child to watch herself watching, to be conscious of her inner creative powers at work upon an outside world. We try to teach the child to order and organize her capacities for self-creation and self-projection which occur together. We teach the child about the "self" being made manifest in the world.

We do not attempt to teach this material about the self independent of contextual construction. Rather, we teach about this self in conjunction with object, space, and time. **Environment** is the operational term. In these exercises, the child begins to understand that her environment includes much more than her world. Environment is a composite and ever-flowing stream of reality that includes the child's psychosocial, cultural, interpersonal, and intrapersonal projections. It is a reality configuration which her mind projects outward into a manifest world. The environment contains her feelings, meanings, perceptions, intentions, expectations, and desires. Therefore, the world that the child thinks is outside herself is actually emanating from inside herself. That is, although there is a shared reality "out there," each individual experiences her own unique, personally created reality. No two realities are exactly alike. Therefore, no two "ways of knowing" are exactly alike. The child is taught to claim her ownership in this component of laboratory exercises.

We use some of the same symbol language in these exercises as we do in the context-building exercises, but the child begins to learn much more personal-construct terms which refer to self-awareness, self-projection, self-understanding, self-description, self-regard, self-image, self-concept, and self-determination.

The child keeps a "Me Book," a self-talk journal in which she talks to herself about herself. Thus, she learns about who she is and who she is becoming. In becoming a self-conscious person, the child becomes aware that she is always talking to herself about herself, and that such self-talk is terribly important in what happens to her in life. Thus, she learns about her own self-authorship of her world.

Some specific exercises used in this self-creation, or self-construction, component of the reality-processing curriculum include:

- Sorting, ordering, classifying, and "treeing" (i.e., developing branches of) people according to physical attributes in the same way inanimate objects are sorted in the curriculum component.
- Comparing, contrasting, and ranking oneself with a group of significant other people on these attributes. Group sharing.
- Sorting, ordering, classifying, and "treeing" people according to psychological attributes. Group sharing of these solutions.
- Surfacing one's self-attribute or self-defining language, and learning how one dimensionalizes these self-talk images on a most-liked, least-liked, sliding scale.
- Teaching the child that these self-talk images are not fixed and unchangeable things inside herself, but are evolving processes related to their projected environments in which their own thinking, feeling, and doing are enmeshed in a netlike fashion.
- Teaching the child how to modify these self-defining nets, as an important part of learning to know her own world.
- Empathic projection of oneself into a dramatic human crisis scene which can be interpreted in multiple ways, and developing scenarios about other persons in that scene. Group sharing of these scenarios.
- Interpreting and giving meaning to figure-ground-reversal pictures to teach the extent to which reality is a projection from inside oneself. Group sharing of these projections.
- Projecting personal meaning into a set of ink blots and comparing and contrasting the multiple projections of the group.

From the perspective of classic education, these self-constructive and self-projective laboratory exercises are not a part of the pedagogic process, because learning is believed to come from an external source. In the classic segmented view of the child, not only does reality exist independent of the child, but cognition is separated from the child's feelings, the child's behavior, and her social-personal life. In short, reality exists independent of the child's holistic being. However, even apart from the new paradigm, Jean Piaget's research shows that we cannot separate self from environment; that the child constructs her reality, including the physical constructs of person, object, space, time, and causality. He tells us that the child projects her self-world into existence. Therefore, whatever energy may come from the outside is simultaneously structured and shaped into personal meanings by the whole child.

The new physics has shown us in its experiments and mathematics that all we can know of physical reality is mental responses. In a sense, this is the same psychophysical view of reality that Piaget discovered in his extensive developmental studies. Within the new paradigm, it is impossible to continue in an education that tries to leave out the self from its pedagogical processes.

In the final component of our generic curriculum which teaches the child how to process information, we have developed laboratory exercises that help the child to tie everything together. This is the most critical part of our curriculum. In it not only does the child learn that reality is a holographic process which is constantly unfolding rather than a fixed, substantive thing out there; but she learns that, as in a kaleidoscope, there are endless facets and endless variations of reality. This is particularly important for the kind of children we are working with in our research. The reality they experience seems to be frozen and impervious to their efforts to make sense of it. For them, reality seems to be a rigid wall, separating them from the world. Their own experiences are like the behavior of a rat running in a wire-mesh wheel. They can't stop the circular motion, nor do they foster any hope of escaping this rigid confinement and moving out into the larger environment surrounding them. In these exercises we emphasize that reality is not a "thing" but a flowing process that is shaped in various ways by the individual's participation in it. We teach the child to be aware of how her own version of reality differs from those of other people in her environment. We teach flexible thinking and perception about reality. We have specific exercises in this component that teach the child how to pattern and repattern her reality in conjunction with that part of reality that is consensually validated in the specific world which she inhabits.

Mental patterning extends the idea of Piaget's schema. In mental patterning, we teach children to consciously pattern, map, or make associations within their worlds. Different patterns of the same landscape can reflect different levels of apperception or expectation. This mental patterning provides the context from which the child may thrust her projections. By choosing mental patterns, the child is able to align her patterns and thereby her projections to the situations she faces. Among these patterns are the following:

• Mental patterning and projection of thinking processes such as ordering, organizing, sorting, categorizing, comparing, contrasting, classifying, sequencing, and enumerating.
• Mental patterning and projection of modes of self-consciousness such as self-talk, "loud thinking," self-imaging, and self-reflection.

- Mental patterning and projection of "psychological sets" toward one's world.
- Mental patterning and projection of modes of thought vis-a-vis person, object, space, time, and causality.
- Mental patterning and projection of simultaneous and alternating subject-object, "psychological sets" (like convex and concave surfaces) toward thinking and things, self and others, images and symbols, and the social, cultural, physical, behavioral, and affective contexts in which they operate.
- Mental patterning, projecting, and transposing of multiple symbol forms (i.e., verbal, mathematical, imaginal, musical, etc.).
- Holistic mental patterning that includes differing forms of abstraction; causal definition; logical styles, problem definition, analysis, and solutions; and boundary setting. ("Differing forms" refers to levels of thinking, such as Jean Piaget's concrete and formal operations stages of thinking, Bertalanffy's "systems" thinking, or quantum mechanics' holistic thinking.)
- Mental patterning of meanings and belief systems.

The preceding is only a partial list of the patterning and repatterning of thought processes that take place in generic curricula. **Generic curricula** includes not only this particular specific Life-Impact curriculum, but also other generic, but segmented, curricula designed to teach cognitive development, social-personal skills, affective education, or behavior modification. This list should give you an idea of the vast scope of education's influence on the lives of children.

A Case Study

Let us complete this chapter by giving a brief sketch of a child who had less than 2 years of training in the Life-Impact curriculum which we are researching. Figure 10.4 is a sketch of a "Mobius" which shows how inside and outside are the same. That is, "inside" and "outside" are continuous, or one and the same thing. Therefore, teaching self-understanding and development influences the environment in which the child lives. This is the case of J. We make no claims that the changes in J's whole being were a result of the curriculum, because he was in a residential treatment center when he participated in the curriculum. We only claim that the curriculum was apparently compatible with his total needs.

Case Review

J was a teenaged male who was thought to be borderline schizophrenic. However, because he was such a confusing child to the professional staff, a specific diagnosis was not pinned on him. Nevertheless, he was quite different from most children seen in this particular center. He seemed blissfully content with himself and made no trouble for the staff, even though he did not really participate with them. He was totally unconnected or ungrounded in time and place. His own self-concept was unrelated to any external picture of him in achievement, per-

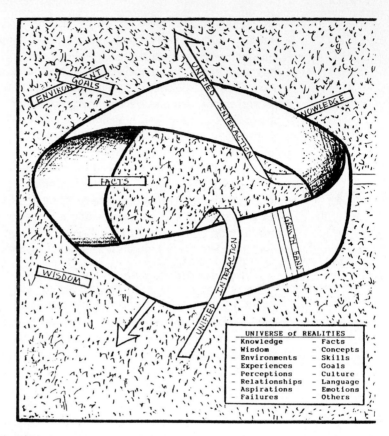

FIGURE 10.4
Topological/Mobius Model of Interactive Growth and Learning Within the New Paradigm

sonality tests, external observations, or actual relationship abilities. He saw himself as perfect in every way. He verbalized this self-satisfaction at the drop of a hat. He could not read, could not fit in with other children, and could not show up at the times and in the places scheduled for him. But, he blissfully ignored all these strange characteristics that were obvious to everyone else. If the children cornered him about not being able to read, he rejected reading as having any importance. When they responded that he could not even get a driver's license, he claimed he could go anywhere he wanted to go on his own two feet. The Tennessee Self-Concept Scale supported his own apparent self-confidence. Although he repeatedly showed up in the wrong classroom at the wrong time, he declared that he had no trouble with time or place. As far as he was concerned, causality did not exist. Whatever happened in his life, he felt he always made it happen. As far as he was concerned, he was a perfect person in a perfect world. At the end of the first year of participating in the life-impact curriculum (along with psychotherapy), there were definite and startling changes.

First, his self-confidence on the Tennessee Self-Concept Scale showed a decided drop. He became concerned about his poor reading achievement. He, who had little or no attachments to other children in the school, formed a friendship with a close buddy. Together they began to create behavioral problems for the school. From an innocuous and benign presence in the school, J became a boisterous critic of the school and its policies. It was as though he had suddenly become aware of his context of time and place, and became contentious within it. From simple-minded conformity to, and removal from, his world, he seemed to awaken to being in the world and to having some real control over it.

Descriptive Analysis of J

From a classic perspective which segments a child into a cognitive part, a behavioral part, a social-skills part, and an affective part, none of these segments were working very well when J was admitted. Even in the residential center, his intervention program was separated into these different functional areas. He was in "regular" subject-matter classes. There was a "behavioral specialist" to work with his behaviors. There was a social-skills class to work with his social effectiveness, and he was assigned to a psychotherapist to deal with his affect. Apparently, this was a total residential treatment center that was supposed to be providing a holistic system's intervention program for J. In spite of internal structures for interprofessional communication, each separate department approached the child from its departmental specialty. The child was thus divided among the specialized professions.

He was assigned to the holistic reality-processing curriculum in which he participated in the exercises previously described. The dramatic personal changes described briefly in the case sketch occurred after a year and a half spent within the curriculum.

If these changes were analyzed from the perspective of the classic paradigm, one would probably note deterioration in most segments of this child's functioning. Behaviorally, he had become a problem to the school in the residential center. Affectively, he had become aggressive, mercurial, and an acting-out, or conduct-disordered child. He had developed a disturbing personal relationship with an acting-out buddy. If the center attributed these changes to the experimental curriculum, it was a failure.

On the other hand, from the holistic point of view of the Life-impact curriculum, the child has come to life, suddenly becoming conscious of the world and his anchoring in the time, place, and causality dimensions of that world. He has become concerned about his grades in class, which previously had no meaning to him. His self-confidence had "deteriorated." From a person who was totally uncritical about himself and personally unaware of his being, he had become self-critical and self-aware and was able to see himself as others see him. Having developed self-reflective ability, he was dissatisfied with himself in his world. There was a composite change in his total persona—cognitively, behaviorally, socially, and affectively. Only time (which he now recognizes) will tell whether this is a total regrouping of himself in his world or whether this is deterioration. But there are definite changes in thinking, feeling, and doing which have taken him out of his frozen and meaningless reality state.

SUMMARIES

There are critical differences between the classic segmented paradigm and the new holistic paradigm. In the classic paradigm knowledge is put into the child. In the new paradigm, knowledge about life and the world is constructed by the child.

In the classic paradigm, the environment is separate from and independent of the child. It is extraneous to what the school teaches. In the new paradigm, to a large extent the environment is continuous with the child, and is constructed and projected by the child. Such environmental construction and projection can be taught in the school.

In the classic paradigm, education is responsible only for teaching cognitive content. The teaching of segmented behavioral skills, social skills, or affective skills only become part of the educational mission when these are viewed as problematic to the school or community environment. In the new paradigm, education teaches cognitive content, affect, behavior, and socialization as part of a comprehensive and holistic curriculum. It is not possible to separate and teach the child as if these functions are independent of each other.

In the classic paradigm, school is a specialized agency separate from the community. In the new paradigm, education is a coordinating vehicle for the total community's fostering of child growth and development.

In the classic paradigm, achievement is reflected by grades and objective test scores. In the new paradigm, achievement is age-related transformation in the child's whole being.

In the classic paradigm, the primary emphasis is teaching the child *what* to learn. In the new paradigm, the primary emphasis is teaching the child *how* to learn.

Thus, it can be seen that the world views adopted by the two scientific paradigms—the classic and the new—have a profound effect on educational epistemology and ontology. Epistemology addresses how the child comes to know herself in her world. Ontology deals with the state of the child's being in her world. These critical dimensions of education are now undergoing a profound shift as a result of the discoveries of the new physics.

DISCUSSION QUESTIONS

1. What are some of the implications of the new paradigm for education?
2. How might the role of a new paradigm teacher differ from that of a classic teacher?
3. How do Jean Piaget's concepts of space, time, object, and causality fit with the new paradigm life-impact curriculum described in this chapter?
4. What does Jean Piaget mean when he talks about the child's "construction" of reality?

5. "Time and space are modes of thought and not conditions in the universe." What does this statement mean?
6. When we say that in the new paradigm "learning and becoming are the same thing," what do we mean?
7. Name some of the implications of the new paradigm for education.
8. What are three components of the curriculum described in this chapter?

REFERENCES

Bender, W. (1987). Holistic language arts: Remedial strategies and procedures. *Techniques: A Journal of Remedial Education and Counseling, 3,* 273–280.

Bernstein, R. J. (1983). *Beyond objectivity and relativity, science, hermeneutics, and praxis.* Philadelphia: University of Pennsylvania Press.

Budish, T. (1989). Class presentation.

Bohm, D. (1984). *Wholeness and the implicate order.* London: Routledge and Kegan Paul.

Crowell, S. (1989, September). A new way of thinking: The challenge of the future. *Educational Leadership,* 60–63.

Heshusius, L. (1982). At the heart of the advocacy dilemma: A mechanistic world view. *Exceptional children, 49,* 6–13.

Heshusius, L. (1984). Why would they and I want to do it? A phenomenological-theoretical view of special education. *Learning Disabilities Quarterly, 7,* 363–368.

Heshusius, L. (1986a). Pedagogy, special education, and the lives of young children: A critical and futuristic perspective. *Journal of Education, 168(3),* 25–38.

Heshusius, L. (1986b). The arts, science, and the study of exceptionality. *Exceptional Children, 55(1),* 60–65.

Piaget, J. (1970). *The child's conception of time.* New York: Bantam Books.

Piaget, J. (1986). *The construction of reality in the child.* New York: International Universities Press.

Poplin, M. (1988a). Holistic/constructivist principles of the teaching/learning process: Implications for the field of learning disabilities. *Journal of Learning Disabilities, 7,* 401–415.

Poplin, M. (1988b). The reductionistic fallacy in learning disabilities: Replicating the past by reducing the present. *Journal of Learning Disabilities, 7,* 389–398.

Popper, K. R., & Eccles, J. C. (1985). *The self and its brain.* New York: Springer International.

Prigogine, I., & Stengers, I. (1984). *Order out of chaos.* New York: Bantam Books.

Skrtic, T. (1986). The crisis in special education knowledge: A perspective on perspective. *Focus on Exceptional Children, 18(7),* 1–10.

Stainback, S., & Stainback, W. (1984). Broadening the research perspective in special education. *Exceptional Children, 50,* 400–408.

Stainback. S., & Stainback, W. (1985). Quantitative and qualitative methodologies: Competitive or complementary? A response to Simpson and Eaves. *Exceptional Children, 51,* 330–334.

Stapp, H. P. (1971). S-matrix interpretation of quantum theory. *Physics Review, D3,* 1303.

Wagner, P. (1983). The nature of paradigmatic shifts and the goals of science education. *Science Education, 67*(5), 605–613.

Wheeler. (1982). Bohr, Einstein and the strange lesson of the quantum. In Richard Elvee (Ed.) *Mind in Nature: Nobel Conference* 17. San Francisco: Harper & Row.

Wolf, F. (1984). *Starwave: Mind conscience and quantum physics.* New York: Macmillan.

PART THREE

Behavior rating scales are used frequently in the identification and diagnosis of emotionally disturbed children. They were designed to be objective behavioral ratings, but research suggests that the rater's biases influence ratings.

Applying Theory to Assessment and Instruction

Following the theoretical foundations that have already been established in this text, Part Three presents the specific technologies and methods for assessing and teaching emotionally disturbed children. Chapter 11 examines different approaches to assessment. Emphasis is placed on integrating perspectives and on collaboration among different professional disciplines in understanding the needs of these children.

Chapter 12 presents instructional approaches that have been evaluated and found effective with emotionally disturbed children. Again, the focus is on integrating different perspectives in formulating a theory of instruction and approaches to teaching. Chapter 13 describes specific clinical technologies for behavior management. Both behavioral approaches and cognitive and dynamic approaches are discussed with reference to when and under what circumstances different approaches are appropriate. One of the major needs of emotionally disturbed children, which was recognized in the 1980s with the development of cognitive developmental theory, has to do with their lack of social competence. Chapter 14 deals with the social skills curriculum and methods for teaching social skills.

11
Assessment of Social and Emotional Problems*

MAIN POINTS

1. The assessment of behavioral, emotional, and social problems is a complex process that necessitates sensitivity to the needs of both the client and the consumer.

2. Assessment should begin by examining the instructional setting in which a child is functioning. A child should be referred for more extensive special education evaluation only after modifications in the regular classroom have been tried.

3. Identification procedures should use different methods and tools and should sample the opinions and perceptions of different persons such as peers, parents, different teachers, and the child.

4. A systematic problem-solving approach in which hypotheses are generated and tested should be used when assessing the emotional and social problems of a child.

5. A thorough assessment should focus on more than the child's problems. Strengths the child possesses and strengths within the ecological system should also be examined.

6. Assessment in educational systems differs from assessment in mental health settings. Because diversity of opinion and perspective aids in the understanding of the child and his problems, collaboration and consultation with mental health workers is desirable when feasible.

---

*This chapter was written by Betty Epanchin, University of South Florida.

> The mind of man is keener than it is rational and embraces more than man is able to clearly explain.
>
> *Vauvenargues*

Assessment refers to the process of gathering information about a person for the purpose of planning and evaluating interventions. Assessment activities are shortcuts to getting to know a person. A good assessment conveys what a person is like and what he can and cannot do. It also describes what the person is expected to be able to do. It may describe the person's reactions to various situations and settings and the situations in which he typically functions. While assessment data may be used to determine eligibility for services, they should also contain more complex information about the person and why the problems may be occurring.

When P.L. 94–142 was passed, many public schools did not provide services for emotionally disturbed children. Many of the schools that had programs were just beginning to learn how to deal with these students. At that time, assessment procedures were heavily influenced by either traditional educational models or mental health models. Educational approaches focused on academic and intellectual deficits, but had little to do with emotional problems. Mental health models focused on the inner conflicts of a child, but often they ignored the educational implications of these data. Mandates specified in P.L. 94–142 provided limited direction for assessing social and emotional problems. Specifically, this legislation requires that assessment be nondiscriminatory, that each child be assessed in all areas related to the suspected disability, that the assessment be conducted by a licensed or certified professional, that no single procedure be used as the sole criterion for determining a program, and that the tests be validated for the specific purpose for which they are being used. Currently, the field is debating how these guidelines are best applied.

Most emotionally disturbed children are evaluated by professionals in either public instruction or mental health. While there are common elements in how the two institutions approach the assessment process, there are also significant differences.

ASSESSMENT PRACTICES IN EDUCATIONAL SETTINGS

In educational settings the assessment process is a three-step process that involves screening, identification, and diagnostic procedures. Typically, data gathered during the screening/prereferral processes are used to determine specific issues in need of further study. If a child is believed to have problems, identification and diagnostic procedures are undertaken. This usually involves addressing several standard questions. Academic functioning in comparison to measured ability is considered, and problems associated with specific learning disabilities, mental retardation, sensory handicaps, and language disabilities are ruled out. In addition to the questions having to do with academic ability and functioning, the nature and the extent of the emotional and/or behavioral problems are defined and described through a variety of procedures: behavior check-lists, self-reports, projective testing, classroom observations, clinical interviews, and developmental and social histories. Assessment is a multistage process in which potential hypotheses regarding why the problem is occurring are tested, usually in order of their intrusiveness. The least intrusive procedures are used first and the most intrusive used last.

These steps are not always clear-cut, however, because of the way school districts actualize the process. Since districts vary in the belief systems about how children should be served, the amount of resources available with which to work, and the level of sophistication among available personnel, they also vary in the policies and procedures they institute. Three models (The Iowa Assessment Model, the multiple gating approach, and the preferred assessment strategy) that have been described in the literature illustrate how this process may work.

The Iowa Assessment Model (Wood, Smith, & Grimes, 1985) delineates recommended major steps that should take place in the process of determining eligibility for services. This model emphasizes the importance of maintaining the child in the natural environment as long as is reasonable. This model is outlined in the following steps:

- **Step 1: Classroom or Home Adjustments.** The teacher, parent, or other significant adult who is concerned about a child's behavior makes adjustments in the environment. Outside help is not sought and no further action is necessary if the adjustments result in the desired outcome.
- **Step 2: Prereferral Activities.** Additional resources in the school may be sought, but no labels are affixed and no formal assessments undertaken. The regular education teacher is responsible for the intervention that may involve contracts, tokens, home-school report cards, or direct teaching of social skills. If these interventions are successful, no further resources are needed. If, however, problems persist, actions detailed in the next step occur.
- **Step 3: Referral for Special Education Services—Eligibility.** Parental permission is obtained to formally assess the child and a special education team is called upon to gather data. These data should be purposeful, multifactored, and related to linguistic, physical, and developmental characteristics of the child. Data should enable a team to determine whether the child is benefiting from his present placement.
- **Step 4: Referral for Special Education Services—Placement.** If the child is not considered to be benefiting from his current placement, the team must specify the necessary conditions for the child to benefit. Contrary to what apparently happens in some districts, the Iowa Model specifically states that "when a student is eligible, the district has the responsibility for finding or creating an appropriate alternative placement or service" (p. 49).
- **Step 5: Implementation of the Special Education Plan.** Eligibility and placement decisions result in the creation of an individualized education program (IEP) that must be approved by the parents.
- **Exceptions.** Steps 1 and 2 may be bypassed if a child's problems are so severe and so disruptive that the team feel such action is justified, but Steps 3, 4, and 5 must be followed.

A multiple gating approach has been developed by researchers at the Universities of Oregon and Washington (Walker, Severson, & Haring, 1985). This system reflects a behavioral orientation and involves three separate stages of assessment, each one being more rigorous than the previous stage. The first gate involves the teacher ranking students according to a behavioral profile of internalizing (worrying and anxiety) and externalizing (acting out and blaming others) dimensions. The second gate requires the teacher to rank the 10 top students of both lists in relation to critical problem behaviors. The frequencies and types of problem behaviors are then compared to normative data. If the comparisons exceed the norms, the child proceeds to gate three. Gate three involves observing the child in the classroom. Academic engagement time during classroom seat work and the quality and amount of social interaction on the playground and during recess are observed. If the child is still found to significantly deviate from the norm, he is then referred for special education evaluation.

The systematic approach to screening distinguishes this system. Such an approach should aid in the identification of unhappy, quiet children as well as the aggressive children, and it focuses on variables that are within the teacher's control to alter. Potential problems may arise if systems are unable to provide services for all screened children. Additionally, schools are still struggling with what to do with some of these children; thus, identifying them without also providing appropriate services may create greater problems.

Morgan and Jenson (1988, p. 92) identified 12 steps in their **preferred assessment strategy.** These steps are as follows:

1. Refer.
2. Obtain parental permission for assessment procedures.
3. Interview the teacher, parent, and child using a structured format.
4. Observe the referred and a nonreferred child in both structured and unstructured settings to assess the discrepancy between the referred child's behavior and the behavior of other children in the classroom.
5. Have teachers and parents complete a behavior checklist.
6. Assess the child's academic skills using standardized achievement tests, criterion-referenced tests, curriculum-based assessment approaches, and functional assessments of the learning environment.
7. Administer IQ tests. If retardation or a learning disability is suspected, also administer an adaptive behavior measure.
8. Assess social skills through behavioral observations and checklists completed by the teacher or parent about the child's social skills.
9. Obtain the child's perspective through a youth self-report.
10. Meet with the parents and other involved professionals to discuss recommendations for services and placement.
11. Plan collaboratively with parents and other professionals the child's individual education plan.
12. Select method for ongoing evaluation of the effectiveness of the services or placement.

Many other good systems exist, all of which emphasize the importance of systematic, ongoing decision making that uses data from multiple informants and from multiple instruments. They also require that decisions be made by a multidisciplinary team which includes persons involved with the child at school and the parents or guardians.

ASSESSMENT IN MENTAL HEALTH SETTINGS

Many similarities exist between the assessment process conducted in educational settings and the one conducted in mental health settings. Most, if not all, of the diagnostic tools are the same, and many of the same disciplines are involved. There are, however, some very important differences that teachers need to understand in order to work effectively and collaboratively with mental health professionals.

The traditional mental health assessment procedures start when a child's parent or guardian requests service. An intake worker sees the parent(s) or guardian and determines the nature of the problem. Depending upon the perceived needs of the case, the intake worker assigns the case to psychiatrists, psychologists, social workers, teachers, nurses, or pediatricians. These professionals see the child and the parents/guardian in individual or family interviews. The type of interview that is utilized is determined by the professional biases of the clinicians involved and the needs of the clients. Psychological testing is done—again, the tests that are used vary in relation to the child's needs and the clinician's preferences. This process typically involves two or three interviews with the parents, two or three interviews with the child, and one or two testing sessions.

When the evaluation data are collected, the diagnostic team assembles to discuss their findings and to determine a diagnosis. The prevailing diagnostic system currently in use is the American Psychiatric Association's *Diagnostic and Statistical Manual of Mental Disorders,* Third Edition, Revised, more commonly known as the DSM-III-R. This system utilizes a multiaxial evaluation system to describe the nature and severity of mental disorders. Axes I and II deal with mental disorders; Axis III with physical disorders; and Axes IV and V with severity of psychosocial stressors and global assessment of functioning. The system is described as a biopsychosocial approach to assessment. It is also described as atheoretical, meaning that the intention of the manual is to describe disorders, not to explain etiology. This position was taken in an effort to make the system more acceptable to clinicians from varying theoretical orientations. Each disorder is described systematically on the basis of current knowledge in the following areas: essential features, associated features, age at onset, course, impairment, complications, predisposing factors, prevalence, sex ratio, familial pattern, and differential diagnosis.

Once the mental health team agrees upon a diagnosis, interventions are planned. As mentioned in Chapter 2, psychological interventions are typically directed at the inner life of the person, the psychic conflicts and emotional distortions. Thus, planning for these interventions is based on clinical speculation about how and why the client feels and thinks about his emotional and social world. Confirmation of this clinical speculation is reached in therapy as the client expresses his feelings and the therapist helps the client learn about his inner life. The therapist, after listening to the client's statements and feelings, poses possible explanations with which the client either agrees or disagrees. At the diagnostic conference, assessment data are used to aid the clinician in understanding the emotional issues of a client so that a reasonable and empathetic explanation and set of recommendations may be given to the client.

After the diagnostic team has integrated the assessment information, interpretive interviews are scheduled. During these interviews, the results of the evaluation studies are discussed with, or interpreted to, the parents and the child. This phase is an important stage in the process because it is during this process that the family and the treatment team must acquire the same understanding of the problem. This phase is the basis for the psychological working contract between the family and the mental health workers; that is, the set of expectations that each has of the other.

Much of the data used by clinicians is speculative and very dependent upon the skill of the clinician. When the clinician is not skilled or when there is a poor fit between clinician and client, misunderstandings can easily arise. Inaccurate or insensitive information can alienate the client or, worse, can contribute to the client's problems. Much care must be given to be ethical and cautious in the use of such speculative data.

As can be seen from this brief discussion, the assessment processes in mental health and education both use a systematic problem-solving approach. Many of the same tools are used in both settings as well; and in both settings, confidential information is obtained that must be dealt with professionally and empathetically. Differences in how professionals approach the assessment process have to do with the systems in which they work, the service mandates of these systems, and the professional biases associated with the professionals in different settings.

Education is mandated to serve all children. On the other hand, mental health is a voluntary system, serving persons who seek the service. Funding to education is often tied to specific programs such as the percent of children identified as SED (seriously emotionally disturbed). Funding in mental health is tied to insurance, third-party payments, number of client office visits, and so on. Because of these structural differences as well as programmatic differences, mental health professionals tend to be less concerned with comparisons of children or with equity issues. They seek to serve their clients and their actions and interventions are significantly determined by what their client wants. While many regulations govern their work, they do not have federal legislation such as P.L.94-142 dictating what they must do. Although many of the same tools are used in educational and mental health settings, mental health clinicians are allowed to make professional judgments about what tests to use. In many school districts, regulations determine which instruments may be used for particular purposes (e.g., in some states, some individually administered intelligence scales are not considered acceptable for determining eligibility for services).

The diagnostic systems are also different. Public schools focus on determining eligibility for service. Comparisons with other children in the school system are made, and equity is a major concern of service providers. Beyond these issues, diagnostic attention to the nature of the problem depends upon the professionals involved. Some formulate a shared understanding of the child's problems, but many do not. The mental health diagnostic system is medically oriented to fit its funding sources. Mental health professionals almost always determine a specific diagnosis, but, in contrast to education, they do not always specify in detail what the treatment will be.

It is the view of this text that collaborative approaches that integrate both views are most helpful, especially with difficult, seriously disturbed children and their families. Because educators are with children for significant periods of time and often are the only professionals serving children, an understanding of psychological and emotional problems may aid teachers in promoting development of children's social and emotional skills and maturity.

In the section that follows the types of instruments and procedures used in these evaluations are briefly reviewed.

TECHNIQUES/MEASURES USED TO ASSESS EMOTIONAL AND BEHAVIORAL PROBLEMS

Behavior Checklists

Behavior checklists are lists of behaviors, gathered from record reviews and teacher reports, that have been standardized on groups of children in regular classrooms and on groups of children receiving special services for emotional and behavioral problems. Some checklists include prosocial, positive behaviors along with negative, disruptive behaviors, but many contain only items that deal with problem behavior. Raters check items that describe the child being rated.

Table 11.1 lists and describes a number of the frequently used behavior checklists. As can be seen from this table, behavior checklists vary considerably in format, intended rater, psychometric sophistication, and function. Although behavior checklists have their roots in behavioral psychology, a number of measures now reflect psychodynamic and ecological tenets (Burks, 1977; Miller, 1981; Wirt, Seat, Broen, Lachar, & Kinedst, 1982). These characteristics impact on the usefulness of the measures.

Recommended uses of behavior checklists include comparing the magnitude of one child's behavioral problems with the behavior of children in the normative sample as a means of determining severity of problems, evaluating the effectiveness of an intervention by comparing children's pre- and postscores on checklists, and describing the characteristics of children in a sample for research purposes.

TABLE 11.1
Behavior Checklists (pp. 314–318)

Name	Purpose	Scales	Unique Features
Behavior Dimensions Rating Scale (L. Bullock & M. J. Wilson, 1989)	To screen for behavior problems and to monitor progress. Appropriate for ages 5–19.	43 items that are bipolar descriptors. Scales are: • Aggressive/Acting out • Socially withdrawn ▪ Irresponsible/Inattentive ▪ Fearful/Anxious	Printed on carbonless NCR paper. Responses automatically transferred to scoring summary sheet. Takes 5 to 10 minutes to complete. 1,900 children in nationally standardized norms—validated with juvenile delinquents.
Behavior Evaluation Scale (BES) (S. B. McCarney & J. E. Leigh, 1983)	To aid teachers and school personnel in identifying problem behavior. Appropriate for grades K–12.	52 items contribute to the following 5 scales: • Learning problems ▪ Interpersonal difficulties ▪ Inappropriate behavior ▪ Unhappiness/depression ▪ Physical symptoms/fears	Scales correspond to P.L. 94–142 definition of emotional handicaps, which may facilitate translation of data into goals and objectives on IEP.
Behavioral Rating Profile (L. L. Brown & D. D. Hammill, 1983)	Ecologically based screening instrument. Grades 1–7.	Teacher Scale, 30 items. Parent Scale, 30 items. Child Scale, 60 items. These scales yield 3 subscale scores: School, Peer, Home (20 items per scale). Also a score on sociogram.	Child rates same problem areas as parents and as teachers (e.g., Child = "I argue a lot with my family"; Parent = "Is verbally aggressive to parents").

TABLE 11.1
continued

Name	Purpose	Scales	Unique Features
Burks Behavior Rating Scales (H. F. Burks, 1977)	To identify patterns of pathological behavior. Appropriate for primary and junior high school students.	110 items yield 19 factor-analytically derived scales such as excessive self-blame, poor ego strength, excessive suffering, poor anger control.	Identifies patterns or profiles of children with problem behaviors.
Child Behavior Checklist (T. M. Achenbach, 1981; T. M. Achenbach, 1986; T. M. Achenbach & C. S. Edelbrock, 1980)	To provide standardized parental descriptions of a wide range of problem behaviors	8–9 factor-analytically derived scales (depending upon form) grouped into 2 major factor scales: internalizing and externalizing.	Parallel forms for teachers, parents, and children. Also has a Social Competence Scale and a scale for direct observation of behavior.
Comprehensive Behavior Rating Scale for Children (R. Neeper, B. B. Lahey, & P. J. Frick, 1990)	To provide information for diagnosis and treatment planning for children having problems in school. Ages 6–14.	70 descriptive statements on which teachers rate students using a 5-point scale. Specific scales include Inattention/Disorganization, Reading Problems, Cognitive Deficits, Oppositional/Conduct Disorder, Motor Hyperactivity, Anxiety, Sluggish Tempo, Social Competence, and Daydreaming.	Contains items about learning difficulties as well as emotional and behavioral problems. Corresponds to DSM-III-R categories on representative sample of over 2,200 in 12 states. Takes 10 to 15 minutes.

TABLE 11.1
continued

Name	Purpose	Scales	Unique Features
Conners Parent Rating Form (Conners, C. K., 1982a) and Conners Teacher Rating Form (Conners, C. K., 1982b)	To identify children with hyperkinetic behavior and to evaluate the effects of pharmacological intervention.	Parent form has 48 items that constitute 5 scales: learning problems, conduct disorders, psychosomatic, impulsive-hyperactive, and anxiety. Teacher form has 28 items that form 3 scales: conduct problems, hyperactivity, and inattentive-passive.	Used extensively in drug studies.
Devereux Elementary School Behavior Rating Scale (G. Spivak & M. Swift, 1967)	To help teachers focus on behavioral difficulties that interfere with successful academic performance. A screening instrument that is appropriate for grades K–6.	47 items form 11 behavior factors such as impatience and classroom disturbance. Both proactive and problem behaviors rated on a 7-point scale.	Easy to score. Profile on answer sheet.
Eyberg Child Behavior Inventory (S. M. Eyberg, 1980)	Behavioral-specific instrument for assessing parental perceptions of problem behaviors. Ages 2–16.	36 items yield 2 scores: Intensity Score (cumulative ratings of problem behaviors on a 7-point scale); Problem Score (total number of problem behaviors).	Response format is clever approach to differentiating parental concern about behavior from behavior occurrence.
Hahnemann High School Behavior Rating Scale (G. Spivak & M. Swift, 1977)	Screening tool for teachers of junior and senior high students. Appropriate for ages 12–19, grades 7–12.	45 items yield 13 behavior factors, all related to achievement. Each scale has 3 or 4 items on it.	Includes prosocial and problem behaviors. Easy to score. Profile on answer sheet.
Jesness Inventory (C. F. Jesness, 1972)	For classification of delinquents. Ages 8–19.	155 items form 11 scales such as Value Orientation and Alienation.	Has both a self-report and a behavior checklist. Shorter version available.

TABLE 11.1
continued

Name	Purpose	Scales	Unique Features
Kohn Problem Checklist, Research Edition (KPC) (M. Kohn, 1986a) Kohn Social Competence Research Edition (KSC) (M. Kohn, 1986b)	KPC assesses presence or absence of behavior problems in preschool children. KSC assesses range of social-emotional functioning in preschool children.	KPC is a 49-item rating scale that measures dimensions of angry-defiant and apathetic-withdrawn behaviors. KSC is a 73-item, bipolar rating scale that measures behavior on dimensions of cooperative-compliant vs. angry-defiant and interest-participation vs. apathetic-withdrawn.	Items of the two measures can be combined to yield pooled-instrument scores.
Louisville Behavior Checklist (L. C. Miller, 1981)	To help parents communicate concerns about their child. Different forms for ages 4–7 and 7–13.	164 items yield 3 broad and 8 specific, factor-analytically derived scales. Also has a total disability, a prosocial, and 6 clinical screening scales.	Has a scale for assessing tolerance of rater which helps in understanding rater bias.
Personality Inventory for Children (R. D. Wirt, P. D. Seat, W. Broen, D. Lachar, & J. Kinedst, 1982)	To provide a comprehensive clinical description of a child based upon parental ratings. For ages 3–16.	600 items contribute to 33 scales.	Similar to the Minnesota Multiphasic Personality Inventory (MMPI) except it is for children. Is a thorough, comprehensive tool for assessing personality to be used only by mental health professionals. Scales measure both magnitude of problems and parental tendency to be defensive about themselves and their child.

TABLE 11.1
continued

Name	Purpose	Scales	Unique Features
Revised Behavior Problem Checklist (H. Quay, & D. Peterson, 1984)	To describe children's behavioral functioning in different situations. To develop treatment plans and monitor treatment impact.	89 items contribute to the 6 scales which are: • Conduct disorders • Socialized aggression • Attention problems/immaturity • Anxiety-withdrawal • Psychotic behavior • Motor tension excess	Takes approximately 10 minutes to administer. Spanish translation available. Norm sample of 1,126 children from a variety of settings. Has solid research base.
Social Skills Rating System (SSRS) (F. Gresham, & S. N. Elliott, 1990)	Screening for and assessing social and behavioral problems that become the focus of intervention. Appropriate for preschool through grade 12.	Social Skills Scale • Cooperation • Assertion • Responsibility • Empathy • Self-control Problem Behaviors Scale • Externalizing Problems • Internalizing Problems • Hyperactivity Academic Competence Scale	Items are rated according to their perceived frequency of occurrence and to their importance for successful functioning. 3 forms for teachers, 3 for parents, and 2 for students (by age).
Walker Problem Behavior Identification Checklist (H. Walker, 1983)	Screening tool for problem behaviors.	50 items contribute to total score; 5 subscales: Acting Out, Withdrawal, Distractibility, Disturbed Peer Relations, and Immaturity.	Short, easy to use. Scoring and profile on same sheet.

Initially, behavior checklists were intended to be objective ratings of behavior. The research literature, however, has been fairly consistent in reporting that raters have strong biases which affect the way they perceive children (Cairns & Green, 1979; Epanchin & Rennells, 1989; Kazdin, Esveldt, Unis, & Rancurello, 1983; Simpson & Halpin, 1986). Raters appear to rate the same child consistently over time, but the same child is not consistently rated across different raters.

Not only do raters' biases affect the way in which a child is perceived but children also behave differently in different settings. For example, a child with learning disabilities may clown and misbehave at school as a way of hiding his learning problems, whereas at home where his problems are understood and accepted, he may be quiet and cooperative. Likewise, children from unstructured, disorganized family settings may experience the structure and expectations of school as oppressive and unpleasant; consequently, they may be oppositional and hostile at school. At home, with less demands, they may seem reasonable and cooperative.

The nature of the directions given to the rater also may affect the reliability of the ratings. Many checklists specify that the rater should know the child for a specified period of time. Some checklists specify that the rater should only endorse items that have been observed within a specified recent time period (Achenbach & Edelbrock, 1978). The more specific the directions, the higher the reliability across raters. Some checklists have dichotomous answers or a 3-point scale while others have a 7-point scale. The more options offered, the greater the need for definitions regarding what the ratings mean.

Typically, behavior rating scales and self-ratings are given to the rater who completes the form and gives it to someone who scores it. Little, if any, discussion occurs about the ratings. Miller (1977) has suggested that behavior checklists may be used as a guide for interviewing. If this is done, clinicians use the checklist as a basis for discussing rater perceptions. For example, the clinician might say, "I see that you checked that Karen steals. Can you tell me more about her stealing?" This enables the clinician to understand more about the problem—a process that often greatly enhances the utility of behavior checklists. Stealing to some parents is taking food from the refrigerator without asking, while to others taking small items from a local store is no cause for concern. Discussion of specific items often illuminates individual rater biases and also provides a detailed picture of the type of expectations significant persons have for the child.

When selecting a behavior checklist, teachers and administrators need to consider the intended uses. If the measure is to be used for program evaluation purposes, the behaviors listed on the checklist should match the goals of the intervention. For example, the Parent Symptom Questionnaire (Conners, 1970) has been used extensively in drug research. Behaviors listed on the questionnaire are behaviors which are affected by medication; thus, the measure fits its intended use. If longitudinal information is to be collected about children, the age range of the selected measure needs to fit the intended range in the study.

If schools are using the behavior checklist to write goals and objectives for IEPs, items that focus on school issues are more useful.

The intended consumer also must be considered. Clinical psychologists who are using the checklist for diagnostic purposes may prefer checklists that focus on clinical syndromes. Jargon is not offensive to them. Parents, on the other hand, may be offended by too many negative, judgmental statements and incomprehensible language. Teachers often become impatient with checklists that take too long to complete or that ask questions that are unrelated to school.

Time also must be considered. Some checklists take as little as 10 or 15 minutes to complete, while others take an hour. Some, like the Walker Problem Behavior Identification Checklist (Walker, 1983), are scored quickly and conveniently. No extra forms are needed. Ratings are simply added up for each scale. Other checklists must be hand-scored with templates, or consumers must purchase computer scoring systems.

There are a number of available behavior checklists that may be used for assessing emotionally disturbed children. These checklists vary in relation to the characteristics of the child being rated, the settings in which the rater has observed the child, the way in which the checklist is administered, and the biases and perceptions of the rater rating the child (Carnes & Green, 1979). Given the number of factors which affect behavioral ratings, their greatest value may come not as objective measures of behavior but rather as reflections of how various persons perceive the child being rated. Such information is useful in determining what type of treatment goals to set with whom. Another advantage has to do with ease of use: most behavioral checklists are not time-consuming and most can be administered, scored, and interpreted by teachers. Their most significant disadvantages are related to what they really mean. When using these measures for identification purposes, data should be gathered from several different raters. If the ratings correspond and if all the raters endorse similar problems, it is likely that the child is exhibiting the same type of problems in a variety of settings and that these problems are occurring with such frequency and intensity that intervention is warranted. If, however, the ratings do not correspond, the child may still need help. The ratings may merely be reflections of the differing views held by different raters.

Self-Report/Self-Concept Measures

Self-report measures include a variety of tools that require the child to rate himself on specified dimensions. Self-concept measures are the most frequently used and best known of the self-report measures. Other approaches included in this category include measures of locus of control, depression, anxiety, and hopelessness. Table 11.2 describes some of the more frequently used measures.

Typically, these measures are paper-and-pencil measures that require the child to read and respond to items about himself. If the child is a nonreader, items may be read to him. Older children circle their responses while younger children may mark smiling or frowning faces (smiling faces = yes or true;

TABLE 11.2
Self-Report Instruments

Name	Purpose	Description
Coopersmith Self-Esteem Inventory (Coopersmith, 1967)	To measure feelings of self-worth in children.	58 items constitute 5 subscales. For ages 9 and up (to adulthood). Requires approximately 10 minutes to complete. Normed on 1,850 students in the Northeast.
Friendship Questionnaire (Bierman & McCauley, 1987)	To assess children's perceptions of their relationships with peers through a simple, straightforward questionnaire. Designed as an adjunct to sociometric ratings.	Contains 8 open-ended questions about friends and 32 items on which children rate the frequency of different types of interactions with peers using a 5-point scale.
Hopelessness Scale (How I Think About the Future)(Kazdin, French, Unis, Esveldt-Dawson, & Sherick, 1983)	Developed as a screening tool for hopelessness, depression, and suicidal intent.	17 items are answered true/false. Score indicative of magnitude of negative expectations for the future. Normed on children between 8–13 years old.
Multidimensional Measure of Children's Perceptions of Control (Why Things Happen) (Connell, 1980)	To measure children's multidimensional perceptions of their locus of control.	2 parallel forms with 48 items on each. 4-point response format on items. Measures sources of control: internal, powerful others, and unknown. Also measures perceptions of outcome: success or failure in regard to expectations of cognitive, social, or physical competencies. For children 8–14. Administered orally to children under 11.
Nowicki-Strickland Locus of Control Scale for Children (Nowicki & Strickland, 1973)	To measure generalized locus of control.	40 items yield one general locus of control score. Uses yes-no response format. For children in grades 3–12. Has a 5th grade reading level. 2 short forms and a preschool scale are also available.
Piers-Harris Children's Self-Concept Scale (Piers & Harris, 1969)	To measure relatively stable self-attitudes in children ages 3–12.	80 items yield global measure of self-concept and 6 factor-analytically derived subscale scores: behavior, intellectual and school status, physical appearance and attributes, anxiety, popularity, and happiness and satisfaction.

TABLE 11.2
continued

Name	Purpose	Description
Revised Children's Manifest Anxiety Scale (What I Think and Feel)(Reynolds & Richmond, 1978)	To identify chronic manifest anxiety in children.	28 anxiety items and 9 "lie" items yield a total score for anxiety and a score on the lie scale. Items in a true/false format. For children in grades K–12.
Self-Perception Profile for Children (Harter, 1985)	To tap children's self-perceptions of themselves in various domains of their lives.	36 items yield scores on the following 6 subscales: scholastic competence, social acceptance, athletic competence, physical appearance, behavioral conduct, and global self-worth. There are versions for children in age ranging from preschool (a pictorial measure) to adolescence. Form for children with learning disabilities. Uses a unique response format that minimizes child answering in a socially desirable manner.
Tennessee Self-Concept Scale (Fitts, 1965)	To measure self-concept and specific aspects of self-esteem.	100 items yield a total self-concept score and 8 self-esteem scores in the areas of identity, self-satisfaction, behavior, physical self, moral-ethical self, personal self, family self, and social self. Requires approximately 10–20 minutes to take. For ages 12 and over.

frowning faces = no or false). Scores on these measures have been derived in a variety of ways; some yield factor-analytically derived scores for several scales, while others have one score that is derived from a small normative sample.

Self-report measurement has waxed and waned in popularity over the past 30 years. When ego psychology and phenomenology dominated the field, these techniques were popular, but as behavioral thought became more influential, many clinicians became disenchanted with the "inaccuracy" of children's reports. Critics charged that children could determine the socially desirable responses and engage in "impression management"; that is, children could report what they want others to think rather than what they actually think. Additionally, some critics questioned whether children's immature cognitive and language skills limited their ability to report their feelings. As ecological concepts have gained in popularity, self-reports are once again seen as valuable. "To ignore a person's own perception of reality is to lose a vital data base from which to draw treatment goals" (Finch & Rogers, 1984).

Projective Testing

Projective testing is another method of gaining information about a child's inner life. But unlike the self-report measures, the child is largely unaware what he is revealing about himself in projective tests. This procedure has its roots in the psychodynamic perspective. The method involves presenting the child an ambiguous stimuli and asking him to share his associations. The procedure is based on the assumption that the child will project personal feelings and thoughts onto the stimuli.

There are several different types of projectives that range from very unstructured stimuli to relatively structured stimuli. The primary tools are the Rorschach Inkblot Method (Rorschach, 1942), the Thematic Apperception Test (Murray, 1938), the Children's Apperception Test (Bellak & Bellak, 1949/1974), the Roberts Apperception Test for Children (Roberts, 1982), and the semiprojectives such as the Sentence Completion Test (Hart, 1972; Rotter & Rafferty, 1950), the Draw-A-Person (Koppitz, 1968; Machover, 1949), the Draw a House-Tree-Person (Buck & Hammer, 1969); Draw Your Family (Deren, 1975); Kinetic Family Drawing (Burns, 1982); and Three Wishes.

The Rorschach Inkblot Test was developed by Hermann Rorschach in 1921 as a perception test called the Form Interpretation Test. Rorschach died shortly after the publication of his monograph when the procedure, in his opinion, was still in the experimental stages. Other investigators saw the potential of the measure as a projective technique, and began using and researching it as a personality measure. Since its initial publication, six different approaches to scoring and interpreting the measure have been developed and over 1,000 studies have been conducted using the measure. The scoring procedures enable trained psychologists to evaluate the respondent's characteristic approach to the blots and unconscious wishes and feelings expressed during the testing.

The Thematic Apperception Test (TAT), the Children's Apperception Test (CAT), and the Roberts Apperception Test are examples of more structured projective instruments. These measures consist of ambiguous pictures, photographs or drawings of people or animals, in various situations which are designed to draw out feelings about significant emotional issues in a child's life. For example, one of the cards on the Roberts Apperception Test is intended to elicit stories about sibling rivalry and having dependency needs met when one has to contend with siblings. Children are instructed to tell a story about the picture. Their story is to have a beginning and an ending and should name the major characters. They are to tell what is happening to the person, how the character feels, and what the outcome will be. The stories are analyzed for themes and repetition of conflicts.

Projective testing should be done by a trained psychologist, usually a clinical psychologist. This technique has been the topic of much controversy, particularly when it is used in schools. Peterson and Batsche (1983) have argued that projected tests do not meet the requirements of P.L. 94–142 and Section 504 of the Rehabilitation Act of 1973 because of their "overreliance on high inference techniques" which increase "the likelihood of bias and misidentification" (p. 442). On the other hand, Knoff (1983) pointed out that clinical interviews are considered acceptable procedures; yet, they are also very subjective. Perhaps the validity of this measure rests not with the instrument itself but with the clinician using it. In the hands of a skilled, well-trained clinical psychologist, much valuable information about the nature of the respondent's conflicts can be obtained. On the other hand, when used by unskilled, poorly informed clinicians, this procedure could be used in a destructive, invalid manner.

The semiprojectives are the most structured of these procedures. The Sentence Completion Test consists of stems of sentences which the child is supposed to complete. With the Draw-a-Person, the child is given one of several sets of directions: "Draw a picture of yourself." "Draw a picture of yourself doing something." "Draw a picture of you and your family." "Draw a picture of you and your family doing something." The Three Wishes technique consists of asking the child, "If you had three wishes, what would they be?"

Especially if they are part of an identification battery, semiprojectives must be administered and scored by a licensed or certified psychologist. Again, when used by a skilled clinician, these tools can provide rich and insightful information, but they can also be easily misused. Although a number of systems for objectively scoring these systems have been developed, most have not been reliable. Furthermore, questions of validity have been raised about this approach. Koppitz stated that "drawings are not tests and cannot be treated as such. The value derived from children's drawings depends on the knowledge, experience, and skill of the examiner" (1983, p. 426). She also noted that "drawings should only be used in combination with other diagnostic instruments, observations of the student, and with developmental and background information to diagnose specific emotional problems present in children and adolescents" (p. 426).

Currently, these techniques appear to be more commonly used in mental health settings than in public schools, probably because their greatest value seems to be in their usefulness for generating hypotheses about children's conflicts (see Figure 11.1). Therapists use such information in their therapy with children, but teachers have tended to be more concerned with "here-and-now," everyday interactional patterns. Many teachers are not sure what to do with information about children's more private feelings and thoughts, and many school psychologists are not trained in these procedures so they are unable to help interpret these data. For these reasons, projective tests have not been used as frequently in schools as in mental health settings.

The semiprojectives, however, have been widely used in schools, not for identification purposes, but merely to get to know children better. Teachers,

FIGURE 11.1

Children's art can provide diagnostically rich information to teachers. This picture was drawn by a 9-year-old girl who lives in a residential treatment center for troubled children. Her mother is an exotic dancer and her father has received treatment for paranoid schizophrenia. He currently is in jail for abusing his wife and children. On more than one occasion the child watched her father tie her mother to a chair and burn her with a cigarette. The child, who typically is reluctant to talk about her concerns and feelings, volunteered an explanation of the drawing to her teacher. She said it is a picture of her family. Even though she is the middle child, in the drawing she is the largest child with long hair. She dreams of being a hairdresser when she grows up. The mother, whose head was colored in bright fuchsia, describes herself as being overwhelmed by the children and her need to make a living. She acknowledges that she is short-tempered with them and ineffective as a disciplinarian.

counselors, and school psychologists report that children enjoy these procedures and that the procedures are helpful tools for learning more about children's feelings, wishes, hopes, and perceptions.

Classroom Observations

Classroom observations provide data about the child in his natural environment. They also add validity to data gathered through other procedures. Because observations may be conducted in different ways, they are flexible and easily adapted to the needs of the situation. These data allow one to learn about what is going on between the child and the teacher, the child and his peers, the child in interaction with the physical space, and the child in relation to the expectations of the classroom.

The value of these data is highlighted by the following, frequently observed scenario. A special education teacher entered the teacher's lounge after school on a Thursday and collapsed into a chair, moaning that she had had a terrible week. Indeed, during the hour and a half prior to her observation, she had been dealing with several very upset, angry boys who had disrupted her group. In reality, however, the rest of the week had gone quite smoothly and none of the children had been disruptive. The intensity of the recent crisis clouded her vision and distorted her perception of the entire week. When she began reviewing her records of each child's performance, the observational data that she had recorded all week helped her put the events in perspective.

Observations may be done by the teacher, the child, or by an outside observer. They may be conducted in several ways: anecdotal records, critical incident reports, antecedent-behavior-consequence (A-B-C) observations, direct measures of target behaviors, sampling behavior, and setting analysis. With each iteration, the data vary, but all provide more objective, descriptive data about the classroom.

Anecdotal Records. These are diaries about the day. They contain the teacher's recollection of what transpired. The usefulness of this procedure depends in large part on the nature of the descriptions recorded by the teacher. Accounts that are behavioral and specific are more useful than accounts that are general and judgmental. Statements such as "Joie was so manipulative today!" lose their meaning over time, whereas an account such as the following provides more in-depth data that may be useful at a later time.

> Joie asked me for permission to miss gym today. When I told him no, he went to Mr. Miles and asked for permission. When Mr. Miles said no, he wrote a note and put his mother's name on it. He took the note to the office and claimed that he had not been able to find his homeroom teacher; therefore, he was bringing his note to the office. They gave him permission!

Likewise, reporting that Richard was 17 minutes late to class on Monday, 10 minutes late on Tuesday, 3 minutes late on Wednesday, 1 minute late on Thursday, and entered with the bell on Friday is more useful than reporting that Richard was late all but one day during the week.

When kept on a regular basis, anecdotal records can help teachers see what has transpired over time and how aspects of the classroom are changing. They are, however, highly subjective and limited by the selectivity of the recorder.

Critical Incident Reports. These are descriptions of specific events that occur in the classroom. Teachers may use this approach every time a crisis, or a significant disruption, occurs in the classroom. If the same children are involved in disruptions, the teacher may use these observational data to determine what type of pattern exists. Disruptions may be occurring at the same time each day, suggesting a problem with the schedule, or they may involve the same children, suggesting the need for different groupings.

This format prompts the teacher to record information that may be useful in analyzing precipitating stimuli and reinforcing consequences. Sugai (1986) suggested using this procedure for accountability purposes. For example, he noted that he was subpoenaed to testify in a custody case for one of his students. In court he was asked many specific questions about phone calls with the parents, availability of parents, and so on. Without records, answers to these questions are impossible. Sugai noted that maintaining a critical incident log aids teachers in making informed instructional decisions and in advocating for students.

Antecedent-Behavior-Consequence (A-B-C) Observations.   These are observations that are organized in three columns to highlight the precipitating conditions, the behaviors, and the consequences. This format facilitates analysis of environmental variables that may be maintaining problematic behavior.

Direct Measures of Target Behaviors.   These are actual quantifiable accounts of how often or for how long a target behavior was observed. Depending upon the nature of the target behavior, there are several different ways of counting the frequency or duration of the behavior. Table 11.3 summarizes alternative approaches to quantifying target behaviors or dependent measures (e.g., the behavior you wish to change).

Sampling Behavior.   If observers cannot record every occurrence of a behavior or if they are observing multiple behaviors or multiple children, they should consider methods of sampling behavior. This involves periodic but systematic recording of target behaviors. There are two approaches to sampling observed behaviors: interval recording and time sampling. **Interval recording** is a procedure used when several different behaviors or pupils are being observed simultaneously. It is also used for recording behaviors that occur too frequently for each instance to be counted separately. When using this approach, observers devote full attention to observing and recording data—teachers do not carry out the procedure while they are teaching, although aides and volunteers in the classroom have been successfully trained to collect these data.

In interval recording, intervals for observation are established and the observer records whether the target behavior(s) occurred during an interval. Intervals may range in length of time, but typically are short (no more that 1 minute). Gelfand and Hartmann (1984) recommend that intervals be at least as long as the average duration of a single response. When the observational system is complex, an alternating system may be used in which the observer observes for one interval and records for one interval.

TABLE 11.3

Summary of Alternative Methods for Quantifying Target Behaviors

Method	Issues to Consider
1. Count of frequency of occurrence	1.1 To make comparisons, time or trials must be held constant.
2. Percent of occurrences (Number of occurrences/opportunities for occurrence $\times$ 100)	2.1 Equalizes unequal data. 2.2 Easily understood. 2.3 Efficient when summarizing many responses. 2.4 Generally, only used when there are 20 or more opportunities to respond. 2.5 Does not refer to the time when the behavior was observed.
3. Rate of occurrences (Number of occurrences/minutes or hours—Reported as responses per minute or per hour)	3.1 Converts behavior to a constant scale. 3.2 Reveals proficiency as well as accuracy.
4. Duration of time behavior occurred during observation (reported as percent of time engaged in behavior)	4.1 Does not indicate number of times behavior occurred nor duration of occurrences.
5. Duration per occurrence (amount of time engaged in each episode of behavior)	5.1 Reports information about frequency, average duration per occurrence, and total duration.
6. Latency time (amount of time between the presentation of a stimulus and the occurrence of the desired behavior)	6.1 Appropriately used when noncompliance is a problem. May also provide valuable information with high error rates when there is a short response time period.
7. Trials to criterion (actual number of trials used to reach the desired criterion)	7.1 Provides information about how long it takes to learn.

Source: Adapted from Tawney, J. W., & Gast, D. L. (1984). *Single subject research in special education.* Columbus, OH: Merrill.

Observations based upon interval recording techniques yield percents of intervals during which the behavior was observed, not the number of times the behavior occurred. The following formula yields the percent of intervals:

$$\frac{\text{Number of intervals in which behavior was observed}}{\text{Number of intervals during observation}} \times 100 = \text{percent of occurrence}$$

Time sampling is another procedure used to record complex observational data. Teachers can use this approach while they teach, and it is appropriate for sampling behaviors across settings or extended time periods. Time sampling involves dividing the observation time into equal or variable time units. At the end of the observation, the observer records behavior that is occurring at that moment.

Regardless of which approach is used, repeated measures should be taken. It is important that the observations be gathered over several days so that patterns and trends can be established. (For more detailed discussion of these issues, see Cooper, Heron, & Heward, 1987, and Tawney & Gast, 1984.)

Setting Analysis.   The systematic analysis of the context in which behavior occurs provides important data for understanding the world in which the child is functioning. While this could be done in many settings, the most relevant setting for educational evaluations is the classroom. The importance of studying these variables stems from the seductive influence of space, props, activities, and time (Redl, 1966). These variables affect behavior. As has been mentioned many times, children respond differentially to different settings. Knowing how a child responds to different setting variables is important diagnostic data. It helps teachers know how to adjust their classroom environment to help a child function more appropriately.

In conducting a setting analysis, observers can simply describe the classroom environment, focusing on variables that are most salient to them, or they can use a structured format to guide their observations. Miller (1985) has developed an environmental analysis procedure specifically for studying classroom influences on behavior problems. Miller, Epp, and McGinnis (1985) suggested recording information about the following factors when studying the classroom.

Class size or density. A high student-teacher ratio interferes with the teacher's ability to individualize instruction and may increase teacher stress. It also increases the noise level and potential for distraction.

Utilization of space. The arrangement of desks and other classroom furniture influences teacher-student interactional patterns. (See Chapter 13 for additional discussion of specific seating arrangements that match instructional expectations.) The location of the school facilities such as the bathroom, playground, cafeteria, and drinking fountains also affect teacher-pupil and pupil-school interactions.

Props. The classroom props, such as desks, carpets, bulletin boards, and tables affect pupil behavior. Desks need to be reasonably comfortable and the appropriate size for a child. The type of desk is also important. Desks with lift-up tops or separate desks and chairs can pose problems for some children.

Scheduling teachers' use of time also impacts on student behavior. Activities that are too long for a child's ability to attend contribute to problems. Schedules that involve frequent movement from activity to activity and from setting to setting are likely to be disruptive for some children.

The Classroom Environment Scale-CES (Moos & Trickett, 1974) is a tool that may be used to assess how students perceive their educational environment. This measure is based on the assumption that "personality and other individual difference variables (traits) only partially account for variance in behavior. . . . The social environment has important effects on satisfaction, learning, and personal growth. . . . One can distinguish different types, or dimensions, of social environments. . . . These dimensions can have distinct influences, and . . . such influences may differ from one person to another" (Moos, 1979, p. 2).

The CES contains 90 items that constitute three domains and nine subscales. There are also three forms for the CES: Form R (Regular), Form I (Ideal), and Form E (Expectations). Form R measures students' and teachers' perceptions of the classroom as it exists when they complete the form. Forms I and E measure perceptions of the ideal classroom and expectations for a new classroom. Items on the various forms are the same; thus, the format enables comparison of student and teacher perceptions of actual versus expected and actual versus ideal. Moos and his colleagues have used these tools to investigate differences in perceptions between students and teachers.

The Instructional Environment Scale-TIES (Ysseldyke & Christenson, 1987) is another system for observing and recording information about a classroom and the exceptional child's response to the classroom. The system has appeal for many reasons: It is flexible, yet thorough. Observers record data in 10 dimensions of the classroom, but the observer is given latitude in deciding what to record. Guidelines are furnished for each of the 10 categories, but the observer is instructed to record strengths and weaknesses. After the observation, the observer interviews the teacher and the child using a structured interview. For the teacher, the questions have to do with the teacher's expectations for the child. For the child, the questions have to do with the child's understanding of the lesson. This system enables description of both the classroom and the child's response to the classroom. What is particularly appealing about this system is the focus of the instrument—to describe the setting and the child's response to it. The measure is based on the philosophy of utility—do what works.

Clinical Interviews

Clinical interviews are the most frequently used diagnostic tool, probably because they are flexible and easily adapted to many settings and to differing clinical perspectives (Prout, 1983). Interviews may be conducted with children to learn more about how they perceive themselves and their difficulties. Interviews may be conducted with parents to learn about their perspective on the child's problems. Parent interviews also may be used to obtain developmental and social histories. Also, interviews may be structured or unstructured.

Unstructured Clinical Interviews.   These interviews are conducted in many different ways by some elementary school counselors and school psychologists, and by most clinical psychologists and child psychiatrists. The traditional approach stems from the psychodynamic perspective and involves placing the child in a relatively unstructured playroom and observing his behavior. Typically, crayons, paper, a dollhouse, puppets, Play Doh, toy weapons, and games are available for use. The assumption is made that what the child chooses to do with the materials has preconscious and unconscious significance. The interviewer follows the symbolic meaning of the play while interacting with the child around the literal content of the play.

The interview typically has three phases: introduction, free play, and closing (Workman, 1965). The introductory phase involves the clinician discussing with the child the purpose of the session and what the limits are. Once the child begins to play, the clinician responds to the child's play by observing, participating, and encouraging the child to elaborate and explain his play. Through the clinician-child interaction, fantasy and the expression of affect and attitudes are encouraged.

At the end of the session, the clinician summarizes her perception of what transpired, her view of the child's problems, and her recommendations for future action. After the child leaves, the clinician records her observations and the content of what transpired. These data are used to address the following topics: the child's relationship with the interviewer (trust, intimacy, warmth), the child's expression of affect, the child's ability to express his opinions and attitudes, the child's coping mechanisms and reality testing, and the content of the child's concerns. Clearly, this technique is subjective and dependent upon the skill of the clinician in facilitating the child's participation in the format.

Structured Clinical Interviews.   More structured formats have been developed by Hodges, Kline, Fitch, McKnew, and Cytryn (1982) and Edelbrock, Costello, Dulcan, Conover, & Kalas (1986). These instruments were developed to enable the clinician to obtain more systematic and relevant diagnostic information. They are used primarily to obtain psychiatric diagnoses and for research purposes. Alternatively, clinicians in schools can blend techniques, using self-report measures and behavior checklists as structures for interviews in addition to the unstructured format described previously.

Developmental and Social Histories.   These histories are gathered during a clinical interview that is specifically designed to obtain information about a child's growth and development. These interviews are conducted for two purposes: (1) to obtain information about how the child has mastered developmental milestones and about his medical and social history in order to rule in or out specific problems that might explain the child's problem behavior, and (2) to discern how the child is perceived by his parents or guardians. Skilled clinicians often conduct these interviews in an informal, conversational manner while also exploring the following topics:

- Description of problems child is experiencing
- Current level of functioning at home and at school
- Intensity and chronicity of the problems
- A description of medical problems (illnesses, operations, etc.)
- Family relationships
- Family history (more often in mental health settings)

It is recommended that interviewers use a structured format when gathering these data. Graham and Rutter (1968) compared the information that 268 parents reported during spontaneous open-ended interviews with the information these same parents reported in response to a series of specific questions. They found that the systematic approach yielded more useful and more consistent information than the open-ended interviews. Chess, Thomas, and Birch (1966) compared parents' recollections of events with notes taken about the children's development at the time the developmental milestones were met. The children and parents in their study were part of a study known as the New York Longitudinal Study. The researchers found significant distortions of parental recall in 12 of the 33 cases.

Because of parents' apparent problems in accurately remembering their children's development, interviewers may encourage parents to bring a child's baby book or they may inform parents prior to the interview what they are going to discuss. Parents may be able to obtain more accurate information with better preparation. Some professionals believe that the value of these interviews is found in the data about parents' attitudes toward their children, rather than in actual data about the child's development. Factual information about a child's medical history or mastery of developmental milestones can be obtained from the pediatrician or family physician.

Two measures described in the research literature also may be useful to teachers engaged in assessing children's life situations, especially if the measures are administered during interviews with the child and his parents. The Life Events Record by Coddington (1972) is a life stress measure for children and adolescents. There two versions of the scale, a 36-item scale for children and a 40-item scale for junior high students. The items are listings of events and the respondent indicates whether the event has been experienced within the last year and if so, how often. Parents and children can both respond to the items. Life stress scores are derived by summing values termed life change units that are associated with the various events that have been experienced. The units were determined by 243 raters who were teachers, pediatricians, and mental health workers. Table 11.4 lists the most stressful life stress by age groups, based on ratings gathered during the development of the Life Events Record. Although the rank order of these events may change in relation to social changes, it is likely that most of these events are still very stressful. It is also likely that younger children continue to find the loss of a parent through death, divorce, and so on most stressful while older children's stressors continue to be caused by multiple issues that incorporate family and their social world.

The second measure, COPES (Children's Own Perceptions and Experiences of Stressors), is a 60-item instrument composed of items taken from other stress measures and items constructed on the basis of interviews with children (Colton, 1985). The measure includes both major life events and daily hassles experienced by children, such as having to wait. The measure includes items about family, social, internal, and school-related stressors. There is a 5-point rating scale which asks how upsetting each item is for most children, with 1 being not upsetting at all and 5 being extremely upsetting. After rating each item, children are then asked to indicate whether the event has ever happened to them and, if so, whether it was upsetting to them. Additionally, there are two questions having to do with how stressful school and teachers are in general. Respondents also can add other events that have upset them that were not on the list.

The items constitute seven factor-analytically derived scales: isolation, major life events, family disruptions, cognitive overload, financial concerns, step-families, and school problems. The measure was normed on children between

TABLE 11.4
The Most Stressful Life Events Listed on the Coddington Life Events Record by Age Groups

Preschool

Death of parent
Divorce of parents
Marital separation of parents
Jail sentence of parent for 1 year or more
Marriage of parent to stepparent
Death of brother or sister and hospitalization of self
Acquiring a visible deformity
Hospitalization of parent for serious illness
Birth or adoption of sibling

Elementary

Death of parent
Divorce of parents
Marital separation of parents
Acquiring a visible deformity
Death of sibling
Jail sentence of parent for 1 year or more
Marriage of parent to stepparent
Hospitalization of self
Becoming involved with drugs/alcohol
Having a physical congenital deformity
Failure of a year in school
Hospitalization of parent for a serious illness

Junior High

Unwed pregnancy
Death of parent
Divorce of parents
Acquiring a visible deformity
Marital separation of parents
Jail sentence of parent for 1 year or more *and* fathering an unwed pregnancy
Death of brother or sister
Discovery of being an adopted child *and* having a visible congenital deformity *and* becoming involved with drugs/alcohol
Change in acceptance by peers
Death of a close friend
Marriage of parent to stepparent
Failure of a year in school
Pregnancy of an unwed teenage sister
Hospitalization of self
Beginning to date
Hospitalization of parent with serious illness
Suspension from school

TABLE 11.4
continued

Senior High

Unwed pregnancy
Death of parent
Acquiring a visible deformity
Divorce of parents *and* fathering an unwed pregnancy
Becoming involved with drugs/alcohol
Jail sentence of parent for 1 year or more
Marital separation of parents
Death of sibling
Change in acceptance by peers
Pregnancy of unwed teenage sister *and* discovery of being an adopted child
Death of close friend *and* marriage of parent to stepparent
Having a visible physical deformity
Hospitalization of self
Failure of a year in school *and* change to a different school
Hospitalization of parent *and* not making a desired extracurricular activity (e.g., athletic team, band, etc.)

Source: Adapted from "The Significance of Life Events as Contributing Factors in the Diseases of Children" by J. S. Heisel, S. Ream, R. Raitz, M. Rappaport, and R. D. Coddington, *Journal of Pediatrics,* 1973, *83,* 119–123.

the ages of 8 and 13. Although care has been taken with psychometric development of the measure, its greatest value to educators may not be in the scores obtained, but in the information learned about the child during the administration of the measure.

When selecting and using measures, consumers need to consider the purpose for which the measures are being used. Some of the measures described in this chapter are not appropriate for comparing a child with others. Their psychometric properties are not sound enough for making decisions about eligibility for services. The measures are, however, useful for learning about a child and what he is thinking or how he perceives his world.

PROBLEMATIC ISSUES IN THE ASSESSMENT PROCESS

Assessment issues are among the most problematic issues currently being considered in the professional literature. In a recent white paper published by the executive committee of the Council for Children with Behavior Disorders, the statement was made that "it is clear that our current assessment, referral, and intervention practices do not reflect best practice, and in fact, prevailing practices may be contributing to our misrepresentation problems. These practices (e.g., norm-referenced assessments, nondata-based decision making, pull-out service delivery options, uncooperative interdisciplinary relations, etc.) remove teacher accountability and increase opportunities for bias and subjective decision-making—all of which results in the inequitable treatment of culturally diverse students with or without behavioral disorders'' (p. 272). Some of these problematic issues, and others, are briefly described below.

Evaluation Often Means Placement

Research has shown that the majority of children who are evaluated for special education services are found eligible (Algozzine, Christenson, & Ysseldyke, 1982). Increasingly, the professional bias appears to be against pull-out services because (1) the label **emotionally disturbed** has negative associations for teachers, parents, and other students, and (2) research has reported limited benefits from special placements (Wood, 1985). Thus, Wood contends, ''We should be conservative in advocating the placement of students in segregated special programs. Such placements should be made only after strenuous efforts to manage the problem behavior while maintaining the student in a regular classroom environment'' (p. 226). Wood states:

> Our message to the prospective student client and his/her guardians must be something to this effect: If you are willing to accept the negative label that must be attached to all who receive special education services, we will help you to meet more adequately the expectations of the school so long as you are under our direct supervision. The skills you learn and practice in this setting may or may not enable you to function more successfully in other settings. We can offer only a limited warranty for the outcomes of special education programs for the behaviorally disordered. If the student's major problems are school-related, the services we can provide under this limited warranty agreement may be enough. Once free of the pressures of the school environment, he/she may find a more comfortable niche in society. For the student with more pervasive problems, what is offered may not be sufficient without the availability of noneducational supportive services. (p. 226)

Who Is Eligible for Services?

Another controversy in the assessment process centers around criteria for determining eligibility for services. At present, the legal mandate for who should be served is unclear (Wood, 1985). This lack of clarity stems from at least two sources: (1) the definition presented in P.L. 94–142 suggests that there are children who are socially maladjusted but not emotionally disturbed, but many disagree (Bower, 1982), and (2) the ''intent of Congress'' when the legislation was passed is not clear. To date, there has been only one Supreme Court case dealing with eligibility and appropriate placement; that is, the Board of Education of the Hendrick Hudson Central School District v. Rowley et al. (1982). Rowley is a deaf child, but Wood (1985) maintains that this case addressed certain principles that relate to emotionally disturbed children. In the Rowley case, the attorneys for the school district argued that P.L. 94–142 charged local school districts to provide services so that children are able to make academic progress, but that school districts are not obligated to provide optimal services. The majority of the Court concurred that once a child is making academic progress, the school's responsibility is fulfilled. Wood (1985) maintains that definition in the implementing legislation and Rowley "threaten to limit the ability of special educators to provide full services to behaviorally disordered students." He identified five subtypes of emotionally disturbed/behaviorally disordered children, noting that only the first two groups are unequivocally to be served (see Figure 11.2).

Given the ambiguity of guidelines regarding who should be served, it appears that school district philosophies and individual clinician's personality and disciplinary biases appear to exert a great deal of influence over the decisions that are made about children. Long (1983) conducted telephone interviews to address this issue, and found that the level of available specialized services exerted significant influence in determining eligibility. "ED children re-

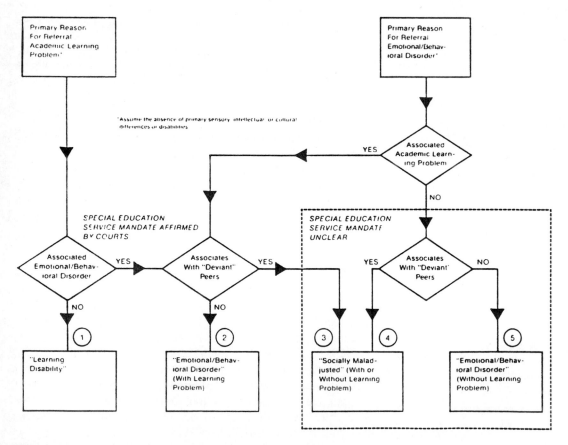

FIGURE 11.2
Subgroups of Emotionally Disturbed Students

siding in school districts with above average per capita income, higher school budget expenditures, and a higher proportion of mental health professionals were found to receive more specialized and expensive services" (p. 52).

Some Assessment Procedures Have Little Value to Practitioners

Most states mandate how children may be identified as eligible for special education services, and most of these procedures are norm-referenced tests. Teachers and clinicians maintain that many of these tests and procedures have little value to them when they are planning interventions for children. Norm-referenced assessment data are typically collected in clinical settings, not in classrooms, where the problematic behavior is occurring. Many of the measures are technically inadequate and lack instructionally relevant information. Morse charged that "procedures are often ritualized and easy answers are sought from the use of a mandated set of tests. Often the child gets lost in the data: If you have ever read a case file and then met the youngster, you may have had the shock of comparison" (p. 55). He also observed that "current diagnostic methods emphasize tests that tell the teacher nothing and psychiatric studies that have no relevance" (1985, p. 55).

Zabel, Peterson, Smith, and White (1982) conducted a study in which they found that teachers of emotionally disturbed children considered descriptions of interventions already attempted, behavior ratings, and behavior observations to be the most useful assessment data. Unfortunately, these were among the least available data in students' records. IQ test scores; achievement test scores; and vision, hearing, and language screening were considered among the least useful; yet they were the data most likely to be available. Rizzo and Zabel (1988) reported that a replication study conducted 5 years later found improvements in availability of data, although many of the same problems persisted.

Assessments Need to Solve the Mystery of the Child

A related problem has to do with making the child understandable. Scores about levels of acting out or reports generated by computers detailing the child's ability do little to help teachers understand more about their puzzling children. Shectman (1979) has suggested that assessment information is valuable to consumers when it helps make the child "understood from the inside, rather than described from the outside" (p. 787). Teachers see these children behaving in mystifying and maddening ways. They know, better than an outside evaluator, what the child is doing. What they often do not know is why the child is behaving as he is. This lack of understanding between teacher and child often leads to alienation and mutual rejection. If an evaluation can make sense of the child's behavior and if it can help the teacher know how to respond to the child, consumers are more likely to use and be satisfied with the data.

Many assessment reports inaccurately or incorrectly convey characteristics about a person because the team conducting the evaluation failed to appreciate the complexity of personality evaluation. Shectman's solution to this problem is to focus on how the individual experiences situations, not on what he does. This focus enables the person being evaluated to be considered in his own environmental context. Because children respond differently to different settings, such a focus is important. These differences help clarify the nature of the problem, the characteristics of the child, and the stressors and the supports in the environment. It is this complex picture, not the static scores generated in several testing situations, that portrays the individual more sensitively.

Parental and Multidisciplinary Team Involvement Is Needed

The specifics detailed in P.L. 94–142 make it clear that the authors of the law intended that the process encourage parental involvement in educational planning, multidisciplinary thinking in developing plans, and individualized programs that are tailored to children's needs. Unfortunately, in many systems it appears that the letter of the law is followed, but the intent is missed. Decisions about educational placement are made on the basis of what is available, rather than what is needed (Rizzo & Zable, 1988). The receiving teacher writes the IEP independently, often pulling goals and objectives from computer banks, and the IEP meeting is a formality, conducted primarily for the purpose of signing the IEP and documenting the occurrence of the meeting. Parents are presented information, but rarely participate in the decision making (Yanok & Derubertis, 1989).

When the assessment process is reduced to such mechanistic practices and bureaucratic restraints, quality suffers. The opportunity is lost for all participants to acquire a shared perception about the child, his needs, and his future. Opportunities for effective and productive collaboration also are lost. Such actions convey the impression that schools do not have enough time for or they are not concerned about the parents, the other professionals who participated in the process, and the child.

Reports Often Pay Little Attention to Their Intended Audience

In an insightful article about why consumers tend to disregard diagnostic information provided to them, Shectman (1979) suggested that persons conducting assessments need to be sensitive to the needs of the persons consuming the diagnostic information. "To put oneself truly in the role of the other is, of course, no small feat. For one to achieve this internally re-created state, one must be able to empty oneself temporarily of one's self; in other words, to sense from the inside what life is like for the other person, whether client or colleague; to look at things from a mutually shared 'inside' while simultaneously keeping a sense of separateness and one's own frame of reference against which the other person's viewpoint and experience are contrasted" (Shectman, 1979, p. 787). Erikson (1958) called this "disciplined subjectivity." The needs of the consumer need to be addressed as the feelings, perceptions, and realities of the person being evaluated are explained.

Clinicians' Need to Have the Right Answers May Interfere With Obtaining a Shared Understanding of the Problems

Another problem diagnosticians often face arises when their formulations of the child's and family's problems do not match others' opinions. It is often difficult to give up well-thought-out formulations when others disagree. It is easy to see the client, the less knowledgeable actor, as wrong or defensive. Shectman (1979) made an important point when he stated that differences among groups or differences between a group and the diagnostician are to be regarded as useful data, not as "wrong" or "resistance." It is the diagnostician's job to unearth these differences, to clarify the nature of the differences, and to work toward greater understanding of these differences among all parties.

Gibb observed the pitfalls of the diagnostician "having the answer" in these observations:

Listeners often perceived manifest expressions of certainty as connoting inward feelings of inferiority. They saw the dogmatic individual as needing to be right, as wanting to win an argument rather than solve a problem, and as seeing his ideas as truths to be defended. This kind of behavior often was associated with acts which others regarded as attempts to exercise control. . . . One reduces the defensiveness of the listener when he communicates that he is willing to experiment with his own behavior, attitudes and ideas. The person who appears to be taking provisional attitudes, to be investigating issues rather than taking sides on them, to be problem-solving rather than debating, and to be willing to experiment and explore tends to communicate that the listener may have some control over the shared quest or the investigation of the ideas. If a person is genuinely searching for information and data, he does not resent help or company along the way. . . . The implications of the above material for the parent, the teacher, the manager, the administrator, or the therapist are fairly obvious. Arousing defensiveness interferes with communication, and thus makes it difficult—and sometimes impossible—for anyone to convey ideas clearly and to move effectively toward the solution of therapeutic, educational, or managerial problems. (1973, pp. 248–249)

Culturally Diverse Children May Be Misrepresented in Current Procedures

Culturally diverse students enter the referral-to-placement process at higher rates than other children, thus they are particularly at-risk for misdiagnosis (Executive Committee of CCBD, 1989). Language and social interaction differences may be perceived by teachers as deficits, which may lower teacher expectations and lead to unfavorable teacher-student and student-student interactions.

RECOMMENDATIONS FOR CONDUCTING QUALITY EVALUATIONS

Professional and Attitudinal Stance During an Assessment

As the team of persons conducting an assessment go about their work, it is important that they focus on learning how others perceive the situation and helping to find answers that others concur with. The team should not seek to be the authority. Evaluations need to conform with federal, state, and local requirements, but these should not be the focus of the process. Many of the problems currently facing educational diagnosticians stem from misplaced and misguided concerns brought on by institutional pressures.

Questions that Need to Be Addressed

Rather than focusing on rules and policies that must be followed, it may be more beneficial clinically to address what knowledge is needed in order to have an adequate picture of the child, his family, and his instructional needs. The information-gathering process should start by examining the environment and alterable variables before focusing on child characteristics.

1. **Who is bothered by what?** It is important to determine who is in pain (Morse, 1985). More in-depth analysis may not legitimize the concern, but that too is diagnositically important. When an intervention is planned, it is important that attention be given to who feels the problem, regardless of what the assessment team thinks, because this person may be a source of motivation or of potential sabotage, if ignored.

2. **What interventions have been used in the past and how has the child responded to them?** If past interventions were implemented properly, the child's response to them will be helpful in determining what is needed in the future. The Council for Children with Behavior Disorders recommends a functional assessment perspective that involves three basic premises:

   a. Assessment data should be directly relevant to instructional decision making. Ysseldyke and Algozzine (1984) maintain that the most relevant variables to collect are the extent to which instruction is presently occurring and the duration and appropriateness of that instruction. How much instructional time is the child receiving and how much of that time is the child engaged?

   b. Assessment should focus on alterable instructional variables (Bloom, 1980), that is, variables that influence student performance and are also under the teacher's control. What is the instruction like? Are the rewards sufficient to maintain motivation?

   c. Assessment should reflect how the student is responding to existing instruction. This involves conducting repeated teaching trials to determine whether the child is making academic progress. How is the child responding to the curricular materials? To what materials does the child respond most positively?

Such an approach enables the child to receive help in the mainstream without being labeled and forces assessment of the learning environment before referral and certification.

3. **Do the stressors in the child's life explain his survival tactics?** It is important that the assessment team realize that the child's home environment is not *the* problem, rather it may have left a residue that is currently hurting the child (Morse, 1985). Some children behave as if their pasts are also their present. For example, an abused child may view all adults as threatening and abusive or a child from a family deserted by the father may view men as not worthy of trust.

4. **How is the child perceived?** This picture needs to be complete; thus, it must be more than a description of the child's problems. To provide a comprehensive view of the child, Morse (1985) identified the following four major subheadings:

    a. **Cognitive-academic attributes and ability.** How does the child perform in school? How capable is the child? How is he performing in relation to his ability? How is he performing academically in relation to his peers (e.g., on norm-referenced tests)? What academic skills does the child currently have? (How are his criterion-referenced test results?) What are his study skills like? How are his cognitive mediation skills? (Is he using inner language or thinking to control actions?) Is his reality testing intact? Does the child have a learning disability?

    b. **Affective-intrapersonal components.** How does the child perceive himself? With whom does the child identify? Is the child capable of trusting, or is he too trusting? What values (morals) does the child hold? How responsible does the child feel for his actions? How empathetic is the child toward others? What are the child's dominant feelings? How does the child view the world? (Is it friendly or threatening, just or unjust?)

    c. **Social-interpersonal factors.** How does the child relate to his peers? What role does he fill in his social group? How does the child relate to adults? (Is he a limit-tester or an attention-seeker?) Is he likeable? What does he do with his out-of-school time?

    d. **Biophysical factors.** Is the child in good physical health? Does he have any physical or neurological problems? What is his physical appearance like? What are his perceptions of his body, his body image? What were his birth conditions like? Were there any postnatal trauma? Is he using medication and if so, what kind and for what purpose? How effectively is it working? How is the child progressing developmentally? What is the child's temperament (or personality style)?

5. **What is the child's overall behavioral style?** Morse (1985) identifies four major affective/behavioral styles that have clear intervention implications:

a. **Reactive** (25% of emotionally disturbed children)—This category refers to children who react to situational stressors in their lives. The treatment for these problems has a dual focus: teach the child to cope with the stressors (e.g., birth of new child, death of loved one, or moving to new area) and try to alleviate the stressors. Prognostically, these children have relatively hopeful futures presuming the stressors can be minimized and there are no other major problems. Typically, these children are placed in mainstream classes.

b. **Neurotic syndrome** (25% of all emotionally disturbed children)—This category includes children who are in acute internal conflict. These youngsters have internalized standards for behaving and are unable to meet their own standards. Their symptoms vary from acting out, aggressive symptoms to depression and psychosomatic concerns, but common to all is the low self-esteem and self-value. Treatment for these children focuses on teaching deficit social skills and fostering relationships that convey acceptance and appreciation of the child. Assuming these issues are addressed appropriately, it is reasonable to assume these children also will have positive adjustments and can remain in mainstream settings.

c. **Significant deficiency in appropriate value internalization** (approaching 30% of all emotionally disturbed children)—This category includes children who have not developed age-appropriate social and interpersonal values. These children often have experienced deprivation of love and care that establishes loving human bonds. These are antisocial children who are at great risk for serious adult problems. Treatment for these children is often not successful, but most believe they need clear, unambivalent limits and structure—milieu interventions. These are often the children nobody seems to want—they are the "throw-away" children. They are unrewarding to work with because they often defeat our interventions, but as Morse asserts, "We cannot excuse ourselves by scapegoating the victims any more than we can go sentimental in the presence of a career of violence" (1985, p. 112). These children typically disrupt classrooms and programs; thus, they tend to be the children referred for pull-out programs. Programs that successfully serve these children tend to have small classes and additional personnel so that limits can be clearly set and consequences controlled.

d. **Psychotic children** (approximately 8% of emotionally disturbed children)—This category includes children who are experiencing severe, pervasive impairment in their cognitive, emotional, and social functioning. Their reality testing is deficient and they differ significantly from their age mates. Psychoeducational interventions and family intervention and family involvement in the child's treatment are the recommended clinical approaches. Most of these children are also served in pull-out programs, although with early and effective interventions, some of these children can be returned to mainstream settings.

Data such as these provide the diagnostic team with information about the child's characteristics and the environment's characteristics, past and present. If assessment data are to be useful, they present such completeness and such sensitivity.

SUMMARIES

The assessment of emotional and behavioral problems is a complex practice that requires skill, knowledge, clinical sensitivity, time, careful fact finding, and attention to a multitude of issues. When done well, this is the first, and a very critical, step in the intervention process. Too often, however, the pressure of service demands have overwhelmed assessment teams and the thorough, individualized, multidisciplinary approach that should be used has been ritualized and reduced to rather useless practices.

A thorough assessment process focuses on both student and environmental characteristics. Information is obtained from teachers, family, peers, the classroom, and the community. Data include information about the individual student's academic ability, current functioning level, physical health, self-perceptions, and attitudes toward the social world. This effort to obtain information from many persons in the child's environment is based upon a belief that there is no "right" way of perceiving the child's problem; rather, the most useful or desirable view of the problem is a complex view that provides a picture of the social world in which the student is functioning.

Furthermore, children's problems are manifested in different settings in different ways; thus, diagnostic approaches need to be flexible and individualized so that needs are addressed. Some emotionally disturbed students function adequately in academic areas, but have significant problems in social situations. Assessment for such children needs to focus on gaining greater understanding of the nature of the child's social knowledge, his perceptions of himself and others, and his worries and inhibitions. Academic data are not so important.

A thorough assessment also utilizes a variety of assessment tools and techniques because of the limitations of existing ones and because of the mandate of P.L. 94–142. The assumption is made that the validity of conclusions is increased by the convergence of data gathered from different measures.

Finally, quality assessments are useful to persons working with the child. They provide answers to the questions that precipitated the assessment. Thus, assessment data should be presented with the consumer in mind. Providing teachers with information about a child's past conflicts with his parents may help the teacher empathize with the child, but the information may not have a great deal of practical, applied value. Pointing out that the child is mistrustful of authority figures and frequently engages in control struggles as a way of dealing with this mistrust may help teachers avoid such struggles. In contrast, specific information about the conflicts between the parents and a child may be very useful to the parent worker (e.g., social worker or counselor) who is trying to help parents understand the link between their actions and the child's problems.

DISCUSSION QUESTIONS

1. Currently a great deal of attention is being given to early identification and intervention. With most problems, authorities generally agree that dealing with problems as they are emerging and developing is more likely to result in a positive outcome. How should this be done with emotionally disturbed children? What instructional setting is appropriate? Weigh this argument against the problems discussed in this chapter about the negative effects of the label **emotional disturbance** and the questionable benefits of pull-out programs. How do you resolve these issues ethically?

2. Discuss the type of data obtained from behavior checklists, self-report measures, projectives, observations, and interviews. Specify the circumstances and types of problems for which each of these is appropriately used.

3. Describe what Morse means by "ritualized" assessment activities. Identify barriers in the schools to more individualized and appropriate assessment procedures. Think of ways in which safeguards could be employed to prevent such behavior.

4. Compare and contrast educational and mental health approaches to assessment and diagnosis. Discuss the advantages and disadvantages of each.

5. What is a functional approach to assessment? Discuss the advantages of this approach for emotionally disturbed children.

REFERENCES

Achenbach, T. M. (1978). The child behavior profile: I. Boys aged 6–11. *Journal of Consulting and Clinical Psychology, 46,* 478–488.

Achenbach, T. M. (1981). *Child Behavior Checklist for Ages 4–16.* Burlington, VT: University Associates in Psychiatry.

Achenbach, T. M. (1986). *Child Behavior Checklist for Ages 2–3.* Burlington, VT: University Associates in Psychiatry.

Achenbach, T. M. & Edelbrock, C. S. (1978). The classification of child psychopathology: A review and analysis of empirical efforts. *Psychological Bulletin, 85,* 1275–1301.

Achenbach, T. M., & Edelbrock, C. (1980). *Teacher's Report Form.* Burlington, VT: University Associates in Psychiatry.

Algozzine, B., Christenson, S., & Ysseldyke, J. E. (1982). Probabilities associated with referral-to-placement process. *Teacher Education and Special Education, 5,* 19–23.

American Psychiatric Association. (1987). *Diagnostic and statistical manual of mental disorders* (3rd edition, revised). Washington, DC: American Psychiatric Association.

Bellak, A., & Bellak, S. S. (1974). The Children's Apperception Test. New York: CPS Company. (Original work published 1949.)

Bierman, K. L., & McCauley, E. (1987). Children's descriptions of their peer interactions: Useful information for clinical child assessment. *Journal of Clinical Child Psychology, 16,* 9–18.

Bloom, B. S. (1980, February). The new direction in educational research: Alterable variables. *Phi Delta Kappan,* 352–356.

Bower, E. M. (1982). Defining emotional disturbance: Public policy and research. *Psychology in the Schools, 19,* 55–60.

Brown, L. L., & Hammill, D. D. (1983). *Behavior Rating Profile.* Austin, TX: PRO-ED.

Buck, J. N. & Hammer, E. F. (Eds.). (1969). *Advances in House-Tree-Person Technique: Variations and applications.* Beverly Hills, CA: Estern Psychological Services.

Bullock, L. & Wilson, M. J. (1989). Behavior Dimensions Rating Scale. Allen, TX: DLM.

Burks, H. F. (1977). *Burks' Behavior Rating Scales (BBRS).* Los Angeles: Western Psychological Services.

Burns, R. C. (1982). *Self-growth in families: Kinetic Family Drawings (K-F-D) research and application.* New York: Bruner/Mazel.

Cairns, R. & Green, J. (1979). How to assess personality and social patterns: Observations or ratings? In R. Cairns (Ed.), *The analysis of social interactions: Methods, issues, and illustrations.* Hillsdale, NJ: Lawrence Erlbaum.

Chess, S., Thomas, A., & Birch, H. G. (1966). Distortions in developmental reporting made by parents of behaviorally disturbed children. *Journal of the American Academy of Child Psychiatry, 5,* 226–234.

Coddington, R. (1972). The significance of life events as etiological factors in the diseases of children: A study of a normal population. *Journal of Psychomatic Research, 16,* 205–213.

Colton, J. A. (1985). Childhood stress: Perceptions of children and professionals. *Journal of Psychopathology and Behavioral Assessment, 7,* 155–173.

Connell, J. P. (1980). *A new measure of children's perceptions of control: Individual differences, situational determinants, and developmental change.* Unpublished manuscript, University of Rochester.

Conners, C. K. (1970). Symptom patterns in hyperkinetic, neurotic, and normal children. *Child Development, 41,* 667–682.

Conners, C. K. (1982a). *Conners Parent Rating Scale (CPRS).* Toronto, Canada: Multihealth Systems.

Conners, C. K. (1982b). *Conners Teacher Rating Scale (CTRS).* Toronto, Canada: Multihealth Systems.

Cooper, J. O., Heron, T. E., & Heward, W. L. (1987). *Applied behavior analysis.* Columbus, OH: Merrill.

Coopersmith, S. (1967). *Coopersmith Self-Esteem Inventory.* San Francisco: W. H. Freeman.

Deren, S. (1975). An empirical evaluation of the validity of the Draw-A-Family Test. *Journal of Clinical Psychology, 31,* 47–52.

Edelbrock, C., Costello, A. J., Dulcan, M. K., Conover, N. C., & Kalas, R. (1986). Parent-child agreement on child psychiatric symptoms as assessed via structured interview. *Child Psychology and Psychiatry, 27,* 181–190.

Epanchin, B. C. & Rennells, M. S. (1989). Parents' and teachers' sensitivity to unhappiness reported by undercontrolled children. *Behavior Disorders, 14,* 166–174.

Erikson, E. H. (1958). The nature of clinical evidence. *Daedalus, 87,* 65–87.

Executive Committee of the Council for Children with Behavioral Disorders. (1989). White paper on best assessment practices for students with behavioral disorders: Accommodation to cultural diversity and individual differences. *Behavioral Disorders, 14,* 263–278.

Eyberg, S. M. (1980). Eyberg Child Behavior Inventory. *Journal of Clinical Child Psychology, 9,* 29.

Finch, A. J., & Rogers, T. R. (1984). Self-report instruments. In T. H. Ollendick and M. Hersen (Eds.), *Child behavioral assessment: Principles and procedures.* New York: Pergamon.

Fitts, W. (1965). *Tennessee Self-Concept Scale.* Los Angeles: Western Psychological Services.

Gelfand, D. M. & Hartmann, D. P. (1984). *Child behavior analysis and therapy* (2nd ed.). New York: Pergamon.

Gibb, J. (1973). Defensive communication. In H. Leavitt & L. Pondy (Eds.), *Readings in managerial psychology* (2nd ed.). Chicago: University of Chicago Press.

Graham, P., & Rutter, M. (1968). The reliability and validity of the psychiatric assessment of the child. II. Interview with the parent. *British Journal of Psychiatry, 114,* 581–592.

Gresham, F. M., & Elliott, S. N. (1990). *Social Skills Rating System (SSRS).* Circle Pines, MN: American Guidance Service.

Hart, D. H. (1972). *The Hart Sentence Completion Test for Children.* Unpublished manuscript, Salt Lake City, UT: Educational Support Systems.

Harter, S. (1985). *Self-Perception Profile for Children.* Available from the author, Psychology Department, University of Denver, Denver, CO.

Hodges, K., Kline, J., Fitch, P., McKnew, D., & Cytryn, L. (1982). The child assessment schedule: A diagnostic interview for research and clinical use. *Catalog of Selected Documents in Psychology, 11,* 56.

Jesness, C. F. (1972). *Jesness Inventory.* Palo Alto, CA: Consulting Psychologists Press.

Kazdin, A. E., Esveldt-Dawson, K., Unis, A. S., & Rancurello, M. D. (1983). Child and parent evaluations of depression and aggression in psychiatric inpatient children. *Journal of Abnormal Child Psychology, 11,* 401–413.

Kazdin, A., French, N., Unis, A., Esveldt-Dawson, K., & Sherick, R. (1983). Hopelessness, depression, and suicidal intent among psychiatrically disturbed inpatient children. *Journal of Consulting and Clinical Psychology, 51,* 504–510.

Knoff, H. M. (1983). Justifying projective/personality assessment in school psychology: A response to Batsche and Peterson. *School Psychology Review, 12,* 446–451.

Kohn, M. (1986a). *Kohn Problem Checklist* (Research Edition). San Antonio, TX: Psychological Corp.

Kohn, M. (1986b). *Kohn Social Competence Scale* (Research Edition). San Antonio, TX: Psychological Corp.

Koppitz, E. M. (1968). *Psychological evaluation of children's human figure drawings.* New York: Grune & Stratton.

Koppitz, E. M. (1983). Projective drawings with children and adolescents. *School Psychology Review, 12,* 421–427.

Long, K. A. (1983). Emotionally disturbed children as an underdetected and underserved public school population: Reasons and recommendations. *Behavioral Disorders, 9,* 46–54.

Machover, K. (1949). *Personality projection in the drawings of a human figure.* Springfield, IL: Charles C. Thomas.

McCarney, S. B., & Leigh, J. E. (1983). *Behavior Evaluation Scale.* Austin, TX: PRO-ED.

Miller, L. C. (1981). Louisville Behavior Checklist. Los Angeles, CA: Western Psychological Services.

Miller, L. E. (1985). Environmental analysis. In F. Wood, C. R. Smith, & J. Grime (Eds.), *The Iowa Assessment Model in Behavioral Disorders: A Training Manual.* Des Moines: State Department of Public Instruction.

Miller, L., Epp, J., & McGinnis, E. (1985). Setting analysis. In F. H. Wood, C. R. Smith, & J. Grimes (Eds.), *The Iowa Assessment Model in behavioral disorders: A Training Manual.* Des Moines, IA: State Department of Public Instruction.

Moos, R. H. (1974). Family Environment Scale. Palo Alto, CA: Consulting Psychologists Press.

Moos, R. H. (1979). *Evaluating educational environments.* San Francisco: Jossey-Bass.

Moos, R. H., & Trickett, E. J. (1974). *Classroom Environment Scale manual.* Palo Alto, CA: Consulting Psychologists Press.

Morgan, D. P., & Jenson, W. R. (1988). *Teaching behaviorally disordered students: Preferred practices.* Columbus, OH: Merrill.

Morse, W. C. (1985). *The education and treatment of socioemotionally impaired children and youth.* Syracuse, NY: Syracuse University Press.

Murray, H. A. (1943). *Thematic apperception test.* Cambridge, MA: Harvard University Press.

Neeper, R., Lahey, B. B., & Frick, P. J. (1990). *Comprehensive Behavior Rating Scale for Children.* San Antonio, TX: Psychological Corp.

Nowicki, S., & Strickland, B. (1973). A locus of control scale for children. *Journal of Consulting and Clinical Psychology, 40,* 148–154.

Peterson, D. W., & Batsche, G. M. (1983). School psychology and projective assessment: A growing incompatibility. *School Psychology Review, 12,* 440–445.

Piers, E. V., & Harris, D. B. (1969). *Children's Self-Concept Scale (The Way I Feel About Myself).* Nashville: Counselor Recordings and Tests.

Prout, H. T. (1983). School psychologists and social emotional assessment techniques: Patterns in training and use. *School Psychology Review, 12,* 377–383.

Quay, H., & Peterson, D. (1984). *Revised Behavior Problem Checklist.* P.O. Box 248074, Coral Gables, FL 33124.

Redl, F. (1966). *When we deal with children: Selected writings.* New York: Free Press.

Reynolds, C. R., & Richmond, B. O. (1978). What I Think and Feel: A revised measure of children's manifest anxiety. *Journal of Abnormal Child Psychology, 6,* 271–280.

Rizzo, J. V., & Zabel, R. H. (1988). *Educating children and adolescents with behavioral disorders: An integrative approach.* Boston: Allyn and Bacon.

Roberts, G. (1982). *Roberts Apperception Test for Children.* Los Angeles: Western Psychological Corp.

Rorschach, H. (1942). *Psychodiagnostics.* New York: Grune & Stratton.

Rotter, J. B., & Rafferty, J. E. (1950). *Manual: The Rotter Incomplete Sentences Blank.* New York: Psychological Corporation.

Rowley. (1982). Board of Education of the Hendrick Hudson Central School District v. Rowley et al. 73 L. Ed 2d 690, 102 S. Ct. 3034.

Shectman, F. (1979). Problems in communicating psychological understanding: "Why won't they listen to me!" *American Psychologist, 34,* 781–790.

Simpson, R. G., & Halpin, G. (1986). Agreement between parents and teachers in using the Revised Behavior Problem Checklist to identify deviant behavior in children. *Behavioral Disorders, 12,* 54–59.

Spivak, G., & Swift, M. (1967). *Devereux Elementary School Behavior Rating Scale (DESB).* Devon, PA: Devereux Foundation.

Spivak, G., & Swift, M. (1977). Hahnemann High School Behavior Rating Scale (HHSB) Rating Scale. *Journal of Abnormal Child Psychology, 5,* 299–307.

Sugai, G. (1986). Recording classroom events: Maintaining a critical incidents log. *Teaching Exceptional Children, 18,* 98–102.

Tawney, J. W., & Gast, D. L. (1984). *Single subject research in special education.* Columbus, OH: Merrill.

Walker, H. M. (1983). Walker Problem Behavior Identification Checklist (WPBIC)—revised. Los Angeles: Western Psychological Services.

Walker, H. M., Severson, H., & Haring, N. (1985). *Standardized screening and identification of behavior disordered pupils in the elementary age range: Rationale, procedures and guidelines.* Eugene: University of Oregon.

Wirt, R. D., Lachar, D., Kinedinst, J. K., & Seat, P. D. (1977). *Personality Inventory for Children.* Los Angeles: Western Psychological Services.

Wirt, P., Seat, P., Broen, W., Lachar, D., & Kinedinst, J. (1982). *Personality Inventory for Children (PIC).* Los Angeles, CA: Western Psychological Services.

Wood, F. H. (1985). Issues in the identification and placement of behaviorally disordered students. *Behavioral Disorders, 10,* 219–228.

Wood, F. H., Smith, C. R., Grimes, J. (1985). *The Iowa Assessment Model in Behavioral Disorders: A training manual.* Des Moines, IA: State Department of Public Instruction.

Workman, S. L. (1965). The psychiatric diagnostic interview with children. *American Journal of Orthopsychiatry,* 1965, *35,* 764–771.

Yanok, J., & Derubertis, D. (1989). Comparative study of parental participation in regular and special education programs. *Exceptional Children, 56,* 195–199.

Ysseldyke, J. E., & Christenson, S. L. (1987). *TIES—The Instructional Environment Scale.* Austin: PRO-ED.

Ysseldyke, J. E., & Thurlow, M. L. (1984). Assessment practices in special education: Adequacy and appropriateness. *Educational Psychologist, 9*(3), 123–136.

Zabel, R. H., Peterson, R. L., Smith, C. R., & White, M. A. (1982). Availability and usefulness of assessment information for emotionally disabled students. *School Psychology Review, 11,* 433–437.

12
Teaching Emotionally Disturbed Children*

MAIN POINTS

1. Poor academic achievement is often associated with children and adolescents who are emotionally disturbed.

2. Improvement of academic skills can have positive social and emotional consequences.

3. Individualization does not mean that students work alone on isolated tasks. Rather, individualization is a process of systematically delivering instruction so that achievement of every student is maximized.

4. Effective teachers start each lesson with a short review of the previous day's learning. Then they explicitly convey the goals and expectations of the lesson about to begin.

5. When presenting new material, effective teachers demonstrate each skill in small steps, provide varied examples, and check for student understanding.

6. During the guided practice phase of instruction, effective teachers ask many questions, prompt students to correct responses, provide feedback and encourage successful repetition.

7. Overlearning is the main goal of the independent phase of instruction that can be conducted in at least three ways: by teacher-led practice, through seat work, or by students helping each other.

8. The transition from elementary to secondary school presents critical challenges to youngsters with emotional or behavior problems. Metacognitive instruction is emerging as a means to address these challenges effectively.

---

*This chapter was written by Ann M. Cranston-Gingras, Department of Special Education, University of South Florida.

Each person searches for positive recognition of
his worth and he comes to view himself as adequate
in those areas where he received assurance of his
competence or success.

Benjamin Bloom, 1981, p. 173

Inspired by a growing body of evidence demonstrating the effectiveness of
skillful teaching in producing optimal levels of both academic competence and
personal growth among students with emotional handicaps, improvement of the
quality of instruction received by these individuals in special and regular education settings has emerged as a priority area. The acquisition of academic
competence is integrally related to social and psychological development (Erikson, 1963, 1968). Just as positive personality characteristics frequently are the
by-products of scholastic success (Coie & Krehbiel, 1984), poor academic
achievement with its concomitant lowering of self-esteem often exacerbates
emotional disturbance. Covington and Beery (1976) contend that individuals
incapable of succeeding view themselves as unworthy of love and approval and
see their value as persons diminished.

Basic skill deficiencies are reported to be the single common characteristic
of children at risk for educational and social failure (Smith & Lincoln, 1988).
Several researchers have demonstrated relationships between academic underachievement in basic skill areas and emotional disturbance. Wright (1974) found
that more than 70% of the conduct-disordered students he studied had reading
difficulties. Cawley and Webster (1981) found insufficient functional literacy to
be an educational characteristic of more than 50% of a group of emotionally
disturbed and socially maladjusted eleventh graders. Furthermore, Coutinho
(1986) reported significant relationships between poor reading achievement at
the elementary level and disorders in behavior at the secondary level.

While reading is perhaps the skill area in which deficiencies have the most
impact on a student's total curriculum, academic underachievement among
students with emotional disturbance is not limited to reading. Motto and Wilkins
(1968), Bower (1981), and Glavin and Annesley (1971) reported deficiencies in
mathematics, as well as in reading, among children receiving educational services for emotional or behavioral disorders.

Encouragingly, when students improve their skills in academic areas, positive social consequences also occur. Coie and Krehbiel (1984) reported that
when the academic skills of a group of children they studied improved, these
students also improved their social standing from that of "extremely rejected
children" to that of "average status children." Although it is generally recognized
that academic proficiency development should be an essential component of
any total intervention program for students with emotional disturbance, no evidence currently exists to suggest that as a group children with emotional and/or
behavior disorders learn differently than other children. However, individual
characteristics, as well as child-specific anticipated outcomes, warrant compre-

hensive instructional planning, delivery, and feedback to insure maximum educational attainment for every student.

An essential component of effective instruction for students with behavior disorders is individualization. Unfortunately, this component has very often come to be viewed as a practice which requires students to work alone on isolated tasks. Contrary to this misconceived notion, individualization involves the organization of instruction in such a way as to maximize learning by every student (Payne, Palloway, Smith, & Payne, 1981). In order for individualization to be effective, according to Stevens and Rosenshine, it must imply "helping each student to succeed, to achieve a high percentage of correct responses and to become confident of his or her competence" (1981, p. 3). The direct instruction and learning strategy practices described in this chapter are effective means of achieving these outcomes.

While no methodological panacea for teaching children with behavior disorders currently exists, several instructional practices, philosophically and methodologically related to direct instruction (Becker, Engleman, Carnine, & Rhine, 1981; Rosenshine, 1976), are being increasingly recognized as effective in promoting student success (Englert, 1984; Rhine, 1981; Rosenshine, 1979). It should be noted that the term **direct instruction** has a range of meanings. Here, it refers to a comprehensive system of teacher-directed activities that have been related to student success.

Rosenshine and Stevens (1986), after analyzing several successful teacher-training and student achievement programs, found that the most effective teachers most often display the following teacher functions:

- Begin lessons with a short review of previous, prerequisite learning.
- Begin lessons with a short statement of goals.
- Present new material in small steps, with student practice after each step.
- Give clear and detailed instructions and explanations.
- Provide a high level of active practice for all students.
- Ask a large number of questions, check for student understanding, and obtain responses from all students.
- Guide students during initial practice.
- Provide systematic feedback and corrections.
- Provide explicit instruction and practice for seat work exercises and, where necessary, monitor students during seat work.

STRUCTURING INFORMATION

In contrast to less effective teachers who launch into new material with vague statements such as, "Let's pick up where we left off yesterday," more effective teachers begin each lesson with a short review of the previous day's concepts and skills. Research with both low-achieving (Englert, 1984) and normally achieving students (Good & Grouws, 1979; Rosenshine, 1983) has demonstrated that by reviewing relevant prior knowledge, teachers provide both a cognitive structure for the student to relate new information and the opportunity for skill reinforcement and reteaching of problem areas. Rosenshine and Stevens (1986) recommend several specific procedures for reviewing prerequisite learning. Among their suggestions are the following:

- Ask questions about concepts or skills taught in the previous lessons.
- Have students meet in small groups (two to four students per group) to review homework.
- Have students prepare questions about previous lessons or homework and ask them to each other, or have the teacher ask them to the class.
- Have students prepare a written summary of the previous lesson.
- Have students ask the teacher about problems on homework. Then the teacher reviews, reteaches, or provides additional practice.

Implicit in any definition of success is the notion of clearly defined purpose. Successful teachers know what goals they expect their students to attain, and they explicitly communicate these expectations to all their students. By immediately focusing attention on what is to be accomplished, teachers awaken their students' sense of mission, affirming the importance of the endeavor about to begin. Rather than viewing goals as static, terminal components of instruction, special educators should perceive them as catalytic components of the instructional process (Fuchs, Fuchs, & Deno, 1985). By linking new learning to previous instruction and emphasizing overall purposes, teachers can avoid the pitfall of teaching isolated skills that may severely restrict the range of instruction. Figure 12.1 shows that by linking explicitly stated lesson goals with relevant

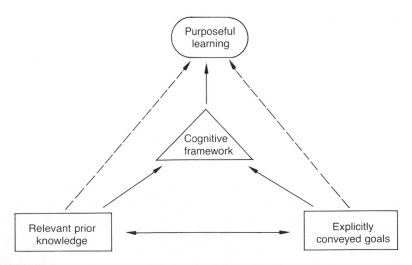

FIGURE 12.1
Linking Explicitly Stated Lesson Goals With Relevant Prerequisite Knowledge and Skills

prerequisite knowledge, teachers can create a cognitive framework through which students organize and process information.

PRESENTATION

During the presentation phase of instruction, effective teachers clearly present new material in small, rapidly paced steps, systematically demonstrating each new skill and explaining in detail all information presented. The teacher provides concrete and varied examples at this stage and checks for student understanding (Rosenshine & Stevens, 1986).

Although the small-step method of instruction has been found to be particularly beneficial for teaching younger students and those with learning difficulties (Engleman & Carnine, 1982; Idel-Maestas, Ritter, & Lloyd, 1983), its usefulness for teaching new material to learners of all ages and abilities has been demonstrated (Berliner, 1982). Small-step instruction is essentially related to the instructional phase of task analysis, a technique commonly used by special educators in sequencing successive approximations toward predetermined objectives. Silbert, Carnine, and Stein (1981) provide three guidelines for sequencing steps in the presentation of new information and strategies:

1. Preskills of a strategy are taught before the strategy.
2. Easy skills are taught before more difficult ones.
3. Strategies and information that are likely to be confused are not introduced consecutively.

Demonstration

Effective teachers spend more time demonstrating new skills and give more examples than do less effective teachers (Englert, 1984; Rosenshine & Stevens, 1986). Students whose teachers develop concepts through lecture and demonstration achieve more than their counterparts who spend most of their time working independently (Brophy & Good, 1986). A major design flaw of many instructional programs for special needs learners is that students are expected to work alone most of the time and have few instruction-related interactions with teachers (Wang & Lindrall, 1984). With practice, teachers can become proficient at providing explicit explanations resulting in greater student awareness of what is being learned, as well as how and when to use it (Duffy, Roehler, Meloth, Varrus, Book, Putnam, & Wesselman, 1986).

Students report better concentration levels when listening to presentations by teachers rather than by fellow students (Mayers, Csikeszentmihalyi, & Larson, 1978). Other activities that may promote low concentration and high off-task behavior among students with emotional disturbance during the presentation phase of instruction include group presentations and role plays. These activities are particularly problematic since they are often characterized by lags in the flow of information, allowing for student distraction and opportunities for inappropriate behavior to occur.

GUIDED PRACTICE

During the guided practice phase of instruction, teachers lead students in practice until all students are responding firmly to teacher prompts. The amount of time devoted to guided practice varies according to age and ability levels of students, as well as difficulty level of the material. More time should be spent in guided practice with younger students and/or difficult material, while more time should be spent presenting new material and less time should be spent on teacher-prompted practice when working with older students and/or less difficult material (Rosenshine & Stevens (1986).

As summarized by Rosenshine and Stevens (1986), during the guided practice phase of instruction, the teacher

- Asks a large number of questions.
- Guides students in practicing the new material, initially using prompts to lead students to the correct response and later reducing them when students are responding correctly.
- Checks for student understanding.
- Provides feedback.
- Corrects errors.
- Reteaches when necessary.
- Provides for a large number of successful repetitions.

Questioning Strategies

Effective questioning involves the successful integration of several variable factors. Essential subprocesses of questioning which require consideration on the part of teachers are as follows: frequency and difficulty level of questions; wait time between questions and expected responses; opportunities for individual students to respond; percentage of correct responses and feedback dimensions.

A high frequency of teacher questions is significantly related to student achievement (Anderson, Evertson & Brophy, 1979; Evertson, Anderson, Anderson & Brophy, 1980; Good & Grouws, 1979; Stallings & Kaskowitz, 1974). Inconsistent results regarding the difficulty level of questions used by effective teachers have been reported. However, according to Brophy and Good (1986), who reviewed several studies relevant to this issue, approximately three quarters of questions asked should elicit immediate correct answers. Generally, difficulty level should vary with content. During basic skill instruction, questions should be fast-paced and answered rapidly and correctly. Complex cognitive content, where students may be called upon to evaluate, apply, or generalize information presented, will require that teachers ask questions that few students can answer immediately (Brophy & Good, 1986). Interestingly, Korinek (1987) reported that during 256 reading instruction sessions observed in elementary level special education classes, teachers "almost never" asked students questions requiring them to elaborate or evaluate.

Response and Feedback

Utilizing data from their review of the relationship between teacher behavior and student achievement, Brophy and Good (1986) reported higher student achievement when teachers pause for about 3 seconds after a question, giving all students time to think of the correct answer before calling on one of them or soliciting a group response. Brophy and Good also recommended that teachers wait for students to offer a substantive response, asking for help or clarification or overtly saying, "I don't know," before probing further.

Anderson, Evertson, and Brophy (1979) and Brophy and Evertson (1976) found higher levels of academic achievement among learners whose teachers called on students in ordered turns, insuring that all students have opportunities to practice and participate. This approach is beneficial to classroom management because it eliminates overt, distracting attempts for attention by students hoping to be called on by the teacher (Brophy & Evertson, 1976). Morse (1985), however, discourages the use of this approach for children with emotional disturbance because it may cause these pupils to "play dumb" to prolong their turn and the teacher's attention. Also, while the ordered turns approach to responding has been found to be useful when teaching small groups of students, it is impractical in most large-group instructional situations with emotionally disturbed students because of the large amounts of time students are expected to wait between opportunities to respond.

In situations where students may be severely withdrawn or fearful of responding, student call-outs may be a desirable way to elicit responses (Brophy & Evertson, 1976). In studies by Anderson, Evertson, and Brophy (1979) and Brophy and Evertson (1976), student call-outs were found to be negatively related to achievement gain among higher-achieving students and positively related to achievement gain among low-achieving students.

An effective way to obtain a high frequency of responses per student as well as to maintain maximum student attention is through group or choral responding. McKenzie (1979) demonstrated that students in classes where group response was used had significantly higher engagement rates than students in classes using individual response. Becker (1977) suggested that teachers use both choral and individual responding, with choral responses being solicited approximately 70% of the time. During individual responding times, teachers can assess the level of understanding of specific children, allowing for additional practice or reteaching if necessary.

Immediate feedback about the quality of responses is an essential component of the learning process (Berliner, 1984; Brophy & Good, 1986; Rieth, Polsgrove, & Semmel, 1981; Rosenshine & Stevens, 1986). Among children with mild handicaps, both student engagement (Rieth & Frick, 1983) and academic achievement (Gersten, Woodward, & Dorch, 1986; Rosenshine & Stevens, 1984) have been positively related to corrective feedback. However, several researchers examining feedback provided to handicapped learners have demonstrated that low frequencies of this behavior have occurred (Morsink, Soar, Soar, & Thomas, 1986; Rieth & Frick, 1983; Thurlow, Ysseldyke, Graden, Greener, & Mecklenburg, 1982). While this lack of feedback may be used as a way to avoid confrontation when teaching children with emotional disturbance, it also has a stagnating effect on pupil achievement, exacerbating the problems of emotionally disturbed children.

In their review of research on effective teaching functions, Rosenshine and Stevens (1986) identified four major types of student responses, as well as strategies for providing corrective feedback for each of these response types. Most importantly, they pointed out, responses should not go unacknowledged. When errors are uncorrected, they can interfere with subsequent learning. Table 12.1 is derived from the suggestions of Rosenshine and Stevens.

In general an 80% rate of correct responding has been recommended for optimal learning of new material (Brophy & Evertson, 1977; Rosenshine, 1983; Stevens & Rosenshine, 1981). A 95% rate of correct responding has been recommended for review of already learned material (Rosenshine & Stevens, 1986). Korinek (1987) found an average of 63.5% of questions answered correctly by varying exceptional elementary students receiving instruction in reading. This low rate of success may have been caused, according to Korinek, by a curriculum lacking small, sequential steps and opportunities for students to practice and master skills before being presented with new material. Korinek recommended that teach-

TABLE 12.1
Student Responses and Corrective Feedback Strategies

Response Type	Strategy for Providing Feedback
	Teachers should:
1. Correct, quick, and firm	Provide short statement of acknowledgement (e.g., "right") and simply ask a new question, maintaining momentum
2. Correct, but hesitant	Provide short, positive statements (e.g., "correct" or "very good"), along with process feedback to reexplain the steps used to arrive at the correct answer
3. Incorrect, but careless	Simply correct student and move on
4. Incorrect, due to lack of knowledge of the facts or the process	Provide the students with prompts or hints to lead them to the correct answer OR Reteach the material to the students who do not understand

ers ask more questions that students can answer correctly, model correct respond-ing, and provide more practice so that students can actively participate in correct responding.

INDEPENDENT PRACTICE

The major purpose of the independent practice phase of instruction is to provide opportunities for overlearning to occur. Without overlearning, it is unlikely that there will be long-term retention of newly learned material (Brophy, 1980). Independent practice can be conducted in at least three ways: teacher leading the practice, students working alone, and students helping each other (Rosen-shine & Stevens, 1986).

Teacher-Led Practice

Especially at the elementary level, independent practice can often be a teacher-led activity with repetition, drills, and question-and-answer sessions frequently used until students demonstrate that overlearning has occurred. Overlearning is evident when students are able to automatically provide quick and firm correct answers without prompts from the teacher (Rosenshine & Stevens, 1986).

Seat Work

When students work alone, the activity is usually termed **seat work.** Seat work is the most commonly used method of independent practice (Evertson, Ander-son, Anderson, & Brophy, 1980; Stallings & Kaskowitz, 1974). Unfortunately, seat work is also an activity characterized by low engagement levels on the part of students (Rieth, Bahr, Polsgrove, Okolo & Eckert, 1987; Rosenshine & Stevens, 1986). As explained by Rosenshine and Stevens (1986), the level of students' engagement is affected by two main factors: (1) the degree to which they are adequately prepared to do the seat work exercises, and (2) the man-agement of seat work activity.

Material presented to students during seat work activities should be directly related to information and skills demonstrated and practiced during the presen-tation and guided practice phases of instruction. It should also be interesting and challenging so that it does not become mere busywork. When teachers fully explain the work presented and run through some practice examples prior to expecting independent work, student success rates and the effectiveness of seat work assignments are enhanced (Brophy & Good, 1986). Clear, explicit, and even redundant instructions should be given so that every student is fully pre-pared to engage in seat work (Rieth & Evertson, 1988). Teachers should also be sure to walk quickly around the room and check for understanding while stu-dents are beginning to settle into their seat work so that no student is left sitting idly, waiting for help.

Continuous monitoring during all stages of seat work has been demonstrated to improve student task engagement (Berliner, 1984; Rieth & Frick, 1983). Rieth and Evertson (1988) described effective monitoring as a process whereby the teacher circulates throughout the classroom, checking student progress and providing encouragement, specific feedback, and assistance. The duration of these contacts should be approximately 30 seconds or less, provided initial preparation has been adequate (Rosenshine & Stevens, 1986). In instances where continuous teacher and/or aide circulation is not possible, such as when simultaneous small-group instruction is taking place, Brophy and Evertson (1976) suggested that the classroom be arranged in such a way that the teacher is facing both the instructional group and the students engaged in seat work. A preestablished seat work routine prescribing exactly how students are to proceed during seatwork also has been found to be effective in instances where simultaneous seat work and small-group instruction is taking place (Brophy, 1983). Such a routine might include instructions on how to get help when needed, how and when to approach the teacher, and what to do when assignments are complete.

Some guidelines for effective Seatwork are as follows. Teachers should

1. Assist students through practice examples (Brophy & Good, 1986)
2. Give clear, explicit, even redundant instructions (Rieth & Evertson, 1988)
3. Continuously monitor student progress (Berliner, 1984; Rieth & Frick, 1983)
4. Circulate through the classroom, providing encouragement, specific feedback, and assistance (Rieth & Evertson, 1988)
5. Generally limit individual contacts to 30 seconds or less (Rosenshine & Stevens, 1986)
6. Arrange classroom so the teacher is facing both small instructional group and students engaged in seat work (Brophy & Evertson, 1976)
7. Use preestablished seat work routine (Brophy, 1986)

Peer-Facilitated Practice

As mentioned previously, the third way that the independent practice function can be carried out is by students working together. Recently, several researchers (Gable & Kerr, 1980; Maheady, Sacca, & Harper, 1988; Maheady, Harper, & Sacca, 1988; Sasso, Mitchell, & Struthers, 1986; Scruggs, Mastropier, & Richter, 1985; Slavin, 1984) have demonstrated both academic and social benefits of peer tutoring involving students with emotional disturbance. Doyle (1986) reported that one type of peer tutoring, utilizing cooperative teams of students, has been found in several studies across grade levels and subject areas to have positive effects on achievement, race relations, and mutual concern among students. As defined by Slavin (1984), cooperative learning involves students working in mixed-ability groups, usually receiving rewards based on group performance or learning. Similarly, Maheady, Harper, and Sacca (1988) described peer-mediated instruction as a teaching arrangement which uses students as instructional agents for their classmates or other children.

Peer tutoring and student teams are effective strategies for improving both academic and social skills.

Three peer-teaching approaches that have recently received attention are: (1) Team Assisted Individualization (TAI) (Slavin, Leavey, & Madden, 1984); Classwide Peer Tutoring (CWPT) (Delquadri, Greenwood, Whorton, Carter, & Hall, 1986); and Classwide Student Tutoring Teams (CSTT) (Maheady, Harper, & Sacca, 1988).

Team Assisted Individualization (TAI) (Slavin, Leavey, & Madden, 1984) involves students working on individualized mathematics units in heterogeneous, cooperative learning groups while the teacher works on the demonstration and guided practice phases of instruction with small groups of homogeneous ability students. In the cooperative learning groups, each student's completed work contributes to her team's score. A reward system, based on the number of work units completed each week, as well as the accuracy of the work completed, is used to recognize teams. While working in cooperative groups, students engaged in Team Assisted Individualization (TAI) comply with specific procedures designed to insure that students are able to obtain help within their teams before asking the teacher for help and also that subject matter is fully mastered.

Classwide Peer Tutoring (CWPT) (Delaquadri et al., 1986), developed at the Juniper Garden Children's Project in Kansas City, Kansas, is designed to improve basic skill performance. Students engaged in CWPT are randomly divided each week into two competing teams. Within each team, students are then assigned to tutoring pairs. Each student in the pair assumes the role of both tutor and tutee for 15-minute time periods with prescribed instructional procedures governing their behavior. The tutor presents questions and the tutee must say and write the answer. Correct answers are awarded two points. If the student answers incorrectly, the tutor tells her how to answer the question and requires the student to write the correct response three times. One point is awarded when the tutee corrects the mistake. While the students are working in tutoring pairs, the teacher circulates through the class and awards points for good tutor and tutee behavior. At the conclusion of the tutoring session, students total all daily points and record them on a laminated scoreboard located at the front of the classroom. These points together with individual test scores are tallied each week to determine both team and individual winners (Maheady, Harper, & Sacca, 1988).

Classwide Student Tutoring Teams (CSTT) (Maheady, Harper, & Sacca, 1988) is an outgrowth of Classwide Peer Tutoring and operates in much the same manner. However, certain differences in the two systems exist. CSTT uses several small, three- to five-member teams, rather than two large teams of tutoring pairs. CSTT students work with all team members at the same time and are assigned systematically, instead of randomly, to teams. This systematic assignment is accomplished by having the teacher confidentially rank all students in the class. Teams are compared of equal numbers of high-, middle- and low-achieving students. Daily point earning, structured instruction procedures, and public performance displays are essentially the same as in the Classwide Peer Tutoring System.

STUDENT-ACTIVATED LEARNING

While the majority of practices and procedures presented in this chapter can be classified as teacher directed, a need exists also, particularly at the secondary level, for students to take a more active role in their learning. Kauffman (1986) identified confusion as the dominant characteristic of an emotionally disturbed student's life. The transition from elementary to secondary school further exacerbates this confusion. Faced not only with adapting to the inherent differences in curriculum, methodology and instructional materials found from one school setting to the next, adolescents with behavior disorders also must adjust psychologically to the shift from elementary school teacher-directed control of learning to secondary school student responsibility for learning. According to Schumaker, Deshler, Alley, and Warner (1983), as students progress from elementary to junior and senior high school, the demands for successful academic performance increase. These increased demands in combination with deficiencies in basic academic skill and nonacademic anxieties in areas such as social interaction, vocational competence, and future plans further add to the student's sense of confusion and helplessness.

Cognitive and Metacognitive Instruction

Acknowledging the many barriers to academic and social success faced by adolescents with learning and behavior problems, several researchers (Alley & Deschler, 1979; Armbruster, Echols & Brown, 1982; Wong, 1985) have investigated the effectiveness of cognitive and metacognitive learning strategies for increasing learning effectiveness and control of learning among these individuals. Without altering academic content, this approach places the instructional emphasis on teaching students how to learn and how to themselves apply what is learned to all subject areas and settings (Masters & Mori, 1986).

Any attempt to differentiate among the terms, **learning strategies, cognitive strategies,** and **metacognition,** risks oversimplification and confusion since many authors use the terms interchangeably or define one with the same explanation another author gives for a different term. However, in this chapter the definition of learning strategies provided by Alley and Deshler (1979) will be utilized. They define learning strategies as "techniques, principles, or rules that will facilitate the acquisition, manipulation, integration, storage, and retrieval of information across situations and settings" (Alley & Deshler, 1979, p. 13). Under this definition, learning strategies incorporate features of both cognitive and metacognitive training (Ellis, Lenz, & Sabornie, 1987). In distinguishing between metacognitive and cognitive strategies, Flavell (1981) suggests that while cognitive strategies involve actual performance and the monitoring of that performance, metacognitive strategies focus more on the monitoring aspect. Palincsar provides an illustration of this point:

> Metacognitive knowledge is indicated when a student notes that it is necessary to prepare differently for essay and true/false tests. When a student plans her approach to studying, for example, by writing the main idea and supporting detail statements for each segment of the text; monitors how effectively this approach is working; and evaluates the outcome of using such a strategy, the student is regulating cognition. (1986, pp. 118–119)

Incorporating cognitive and metacognitive elements, learning strategy instruction is designed to teach students how to learn and how to demonstrate knowledge (Deshler, Schumaker, Lenz, & Ellis, 1984). Three major rationales underlie use of learning strategies with adolescents. According to Deshler and Schumaker (1986), these rationales are as follows:

1. The development and application of learning strategies is significantly related to age with older students found to be consistently more proficient in the use of such behaviors.
2. Adolescents who "learn how to learn" while in secondary school will be able to learn new skills and adapt to future demands.
3. A learning strategies approach requires students to take responsibility for their learning and progress, a commitment required if they are to become independent.

A growing body of research supporting the use of learning strategies to improve academic performance is emerging. Meichenbaum and Asarnow (1979) reviewed research on instruction designed to teach self-regulated learning strategies for various academic tasks. As described by these reviewers, a typical training session, representative of the studies they examined, began with the student modeling the teacher's instructions, progressed to overt rehearsal, and then to covert rehearsal. During this sequence, learners were encouraged to develop and use self-statements to guide and control performance. Examples of self-statements might be

- "Okay, what do I need to do next?"
- "Stop, reread the instructions."
- "Good, I'm doing this right."

This model was used by Bommarito and Meichenbaum (1979) to train secondary school students to monitor their reading comprehension. Students in the experimental group who participated in six 45-minute training sessions performed better on a test of reading comprehension than did students in the control group. In addition, 1 month after the treatment was completed, another test of reading comprehension yielded similar results. These findings relative to the positive relationship between instruction in learning strategies and improved reading comprehension are supported in studies by Malamuth (1979), Richards and August (1975) and Wong and Jones (1982).

Learning Strategies Curriculum

A collection of learning strategy instructional packets comprising the Learning Strategies Curriculum (Schumaker, Deshler, Alley, & Warner, 1983) have been developed at the University of Kansas. Consisting of three strands of several strategies each, the Learning Strategies Curriculum was designed to match the major curriculum demands of the secondary school curriculum. The first strand consists of strategies that help students acquire information from written material. An example of such a strategy is the Multipass Strategy (Schumaker, Deshler, Alley & Denton, 1982) that is used by students to survey, obtain key information, and study critical information in textbook chapters. Strategies, such as the FIRST-Letter Mnemonic Strategy (Nagel, Schumaker, & Deshler, 1986), that enable students to identify and store important information are included in the second strand of the curriculum. Finally, the third strand of the Learning Strategies Curriculum includes strategies aimed at enabling students to cope with the heavy written expression demands of the high school curriculum. For example, the Sentence Writing Strategy (Schumaker & Sheldon, 1985) provides students with a specific routine for writing various types of sentences and the Assignment Completion Strategy (Deshler & Schumaker, 1986) is used by students to organize their time in order to complete assignments.

An integral component of the Learning Strategies Curriculum is the teaching methodology (Deshler, Alley, Warner, & Schumaker, 1981) which enables students to master the strategies. This methodology, consisting of acquisition and generalization phases, is summarized in the following eight steps:

1. Pretest and obtain commitment to learn
2. Describe
3. Model
4. Verbal rehearsal
5. Controlled practice and feedback
6. Grade appropriate practice and feedback
7. Obtain commitment to generalize
8. Generalization

GENERALIZATION TRAINING

While much attention has been given in this chapter to various aspects of knowledge and skill acquisition, the need to directly promote generalization of learned behaviors cannot be overemphasized. In other words, it is essential that students with behavior disorders be deliberately taught to apply the knowledge, skills, and strategies learned in controlled settings to novel situations and conditions. Several researchers (Cranston-Gingras, 1987; Tracy, Briddell, & Wilson, 1974; Vaughn, Bos, & Lund, 1986) have demonstrated that students with learning and behavior problems do not automatically generalize knowledge and skills acquired during structured training sessions to new, although sometimes similar, situations and circumstances. Thus, training for generalization cannot be left to chance (Sulzer-Azaroff & Mayer, 1977).

Even among teachers who recognize the critical importance of teaching specifically for generalization, it is often treated as an afterthought, something with which to deal after students have acquired new skills or information (Ellis, Lenz, & Sabornie, 1987). Rather than being viewed as a terminal stage in the instructional process, however, training for generalization should be a "framework" on which all phases of instruction are "couched" (Deshler, Schumaker, & Lenz, 1984). Ellis, Lenz, and Sabornie (1987) view instruction for generalization as a continuum of activities, beginning with the teacher as primary control agent and evolving into a student-controlled phenomenon. They identify four levels of generalization along this continuum: (1) antecedent, (2) concurrent, (3) subsequent, and (4) independent.

Antecedent Generalization

During antecedent generalization training, which occurs prior to direct instruction, the focus is on techniques and activities aimed at enticing students to learn the skill or strategy and motivating them to use it. As mentioned at the beginning of this chapter, children with emotional disturbance often have very negative feelings about their academic competence. Repeated failure can cause them to develop an attitude of helplessness and inactivity (Torgeson, 1982). Rather than risk increased damage to already weakened self-esteem, many students do not attempt to apply new skills in situations where they perceive the chance for failure (Ellis, 1986). This can be especially true of secondary level students. To counteract this avoidance behavior, researchers (Adelman & Taylor, 1983; Ellis, Lenz, & Sabornie, 1987) recommend making students immediately aware of the range of possible applications of the skills to be learned, as well as of methods and techniques for succeeding at the new skill in its broadest contexts. According to Ellis, Lenz, and Sabornie (1987), teachers can determine if students are sufficiently motivated to learn a new skill and willing to attempt generalization if they can spontaneously do the following:

- Identify the relationship between the pretest and the needed skills.
- Provide rationales for learning the skill.
- Explain why the skill might be difficult to use or remember.
- Identify where the skill that is to be learned can be used immediately (e.g., in another classroom) and when it might be used in the future.
- Identify where the skill can be applied ultimately (e.g., job, community).

Concurrent Generalization

During concurrent generalization which occurs during the acquisition phase of instruction, the emphasis is on having the students acquire the skill well enough for it to become a generalized procedure (Ellis, Lenz, & Sabornie, 1987). At this stage, students should be provided with multiple exemplars; daily reminders about where the skill, knowledge, or strategy can be used; and actual application to class assignments (Deshler & Schumaker, 1986). Meichenbaum (1980) as cited by Ellis, Lenz, and Sabornie (1987) recommends the following procedures for facilitating generalization during the acquisition phase of instruction:

1. Provide feedback on correctness of attempts to use the new strategy.
2. Emphasize principles or aspects of the strategy so that the skill is meaningful to every student.
3. Encourage the student to problem solve and believe the skill is achievable.
4. Determine whether the prerequisite subskills are present in order for the strategy to be learned.
5. Choose tasks that insure a sequential gradation of transfer difficulty.
6. Actively involve the learner during skill acquisition.
7. Gradually fade instructor prompts to insure student involvement.
8. Teach the strategy in multiple settings and involve different agents. Tell students to generalize the skill to specific settings.
9. Reinforce strategy use and encourage self-satisfaction.

Improvement of academic skills often leads to more positive social and emotional development.

Subsequent Generalization

After students have mastered new skills and strategies, but are not automatically applying them in other settings, subsequent generalization training is applied. Subsequent generalization consists of three phases: orientation, activation, and implementation. During orientation, students are required to make decisions about how they will use the new knowledge or skills they have acquired (Ellis, Lenz, & Sabornie, 1987). The activation phase is intended to provide students with opportunities to practice the strategies and skills in a variety of settings and to receive feedback regarding their use (Deshler & Schumaker, 1986). During the implementation phase, the student begins assuming responsibility for maintaining the new skill. Ellis, Lenz, and Sabornie (1987) recommend the following teacher functions at this time:

1. Have the student make a plan to remember the new learning.
2. Have the student provide herself with feedback regarding use of the skill, or ask someone else to provide feedback.
3. Have the student decide what is an acceptable level of performance for applying the skill in different contexts.

4. Have the student set goals and make a long-term plan for applying the strategy. If the student does not have goal-setting skills, then teach these skills at this time.

Independent Generalization

The final level of generalization training, independent generalization, represents a greater shifting of responsibility for applying new skills and knowledge away from the teacher and to the student. At this training level, students are coached in the use of self-control procedures, goal-setting techniques, and self-reinforcement behaviors (Ellis, Lenz, & Sabornie, 1987). At this stage, students strive to truly become self-regulated learners, actively engaged in their own learning processes. According to Zimmerman, self-regulated learners are those who motivationally perceive themselves as "competent, self-efficacious and autonomous" (1986, p. 308).

SUMMARIES

Poor academic achievement is a characteristic common to many students with emotional disturbance. By providing effective instruction, teachers of individuals with emotional disturbance can empower their students to maximize academic achievement, and to improve social and emotional functioning. Direct instruction with its varied components and metacognitive strategy training appear to be promising approaches toward helping students with emotional disturbance gain competence and confidence.

DISCUSSION QUESTIONS

1. Discuss the relationship between academic underachievement and behavior disorders.
2. How do effective teachers structure information for presentation?
3. Which demonstration practices have been found to be most effective? Least effective?
4. What specific factors determine the amount of time spent on the guided practice phase of instruction?
5. How can questioning strategies be modified to accommodate individual student characteristics?
6. What are the essential features of each of the three types of independent practice?
7. What factors contribute to the need for student-activated learning at the secondary level?
8. How do cognitive and metacognitive instructional strategies promote independent learning?
9. What specific practices can teachers implement during each phase of instruction to facilitate generalization?

REFERENCES

Adelman, H., & Taylor, L. (1983). *Learning disabilities in perspective.* Glenview, IL: Scott, Foresman.

Alley, G., & Deshler, D. (1979). *Teaching the learning disabled adolescent: Strategies and methods.* Denver: Love Publishing Co.

Armbruster, B. B., Echols, C. H., & Brown, A. L. (1982). The role of metacognition in reading to learn: A developmental perspective. *Volta Review, 84,* 45–56.

Anderson, L., Evertson, C., & Brophy, J. (1979). An experimental study of effective teaching in the first grade reading groups. *Elementary School Journal, 79,* 193–223.

Becker, W. C. (1977). Teaching reading and language to the disadvantaged: What have we learned from field research? *Harvard Educational Review, 47,* 518–543.

Becker, W. C., Engleman, S., Carnine, D. W., & Rhine R. (1981). The direct instruction model. In R. Rhine (Ed.), *Encouraging change in America's schools: A decade of experimentation.* New York: Academic Press.

Berliner, D. (1982). '82 issue: Should teachers be expected to use direct instruction? *A.S.C.D. Update, 24,* 5.

Berliner, D. (1984). The half full glass: A review of research on teaching. In P. L. Hosford (Ed.), *Using what we know about teaching.* Alexandria, VA: Associates for Supervision and Curriculum Development.

Bloom, B. (1981). *All our children.* New York: McGraw-Hill.

Bommarito, J., & Meichenbaum, D. (1979). Enhancing reading comprehension by means of self-instructional training. In P. Kendall & S. Hollon (Eds.), *Cognitive-behavioral interventions: Theory, research and procedures.* New York: Academic Press.

Bower, E. M. (1981). *Early identification of emotionally handicapped children in the school* (3rd ed.). Springfield, IL: Charles C. Thomas.

Brophy, J. (1980). *Recent research on teaching.* East Lansing, MI: Institute for Research on Teaching, Michigan State University.

Brophy, J. (1983). Classroom organization and management. *Elementary School Journal, 183,* 265–286.

Brophy, J., & Evertson, C. (1976). *Learning from teaching: A developmental perspective.* Boston: Allyn and Bacon.

Brophy, J., & Evertson, C. (1977). Teacher behavior and student learning in second and third grades. In G. D. Borich (Ed.), *The appraisal of teaching: Concepts and process.* Reading, MA: Addison-Wesley.

Brophy, J., & Good, T. L. (1986). Teacher behavior and student achievement. In M C. Wittrock (Ed.), *Handbook of research on teaching* (3rd ed.). New York: Macmillan.

Cawley, J. F., & Webster, R. E. (1981). Reading and behavior disorders. In G. Brown, R. L. McDowell, & J. Smith (Eds.), *Educating adolescents with behavior disorders.* Columbus, OH: Merrill.

Coie, J. D., & Krehbiel, G. (1984). Effects of academic tutoring on the social status of low-achieving, socially rejected children. *Child Development, 55,* 1465–1478.

Coutinho, M. J. (1986). Reading achievement of students identified as behaviorally disordered at the secondary level. *Behavioral Disorders, 10,* 200–207.

Covington, M. C., & Berry, R. (1976). *Self-worth and school learning.* New York: Holt, Rinehart & Winston.

Cranston-Gingras, A. (1987). *The effect of learning strategy instruction on the written expression of migrant adolescents enrolled in a dropout prevention program.* Unpublished doctoral dissertation, University of South Florida, Tampa.

Delquadri, J., Greenwood, C. R., Whorton, D., Carter, J. J., & Hall, R. V. (1986). Classwide peer tutoring. *Exceptional Children, 52,* 535–542.

Deshler, D. D., Alley, G. R., Warner, M. M., & Schumaker, J. B. (1981). Instructional practices for promoting skill acquisition and generalization in severely learning disabled adolescents. *Learning Disability Quarterly, 4,* 415–421.

Deshler, D. D., & Schumaker, J. B. (1986). Learning strategies: An instructional alternative for low-achieving adolescents. *Exceptional Children, 52,* 583–590.

Deshler, D. D., Schumaker, J. B., & Lenz, B. K. (1984). Academic and cognitive interventions for LD adolescents: Part I. *Journal of Learning Disabilities, 17,* 108—117.

Deshler, D. D., Schumaker, J. B., Lenz, B. K., & Ellis (1984). Academic and cognitive interventions for LD adolescents: Part II. *Journal of Learning Disabilities, 17,* 170–187.

Doyle, W. (1986). Classroom organization and management. In M. C. Wittrock (Ed.), *Handbook of research on teaching* (3rd ed.). New York: Macmillan.

Duffy, G.G., Roehler, L., Meloth, M., Varrus, L., Book, C., Putnam, J., & Wesselman, R. (1986). The relationship between explicit verbal explanations during reading skill instruction and student awareness of achievement: A study of reading teacher effects. *Reading Research Quarterly, 21,* 237–252.

Ellis, E. (1986). The role of motivation and pedagogy on the generalization of cognitive training by the mildly handicapped. *Journal of Learning Disabilities, 19,* 66–77.

Ellis, E. S., Lenz, B. K., & Sabornie, E. S. (1987). Generalization and adaptation of learning strategies to natural environments. Part 2: Research into practice. *Remedial and Special Education, 8,* 6–23.

Engleman, S., & Carnine, D. W. (1982). *Theory of Instruction.* New York: Irvington.

Englert, C. S. (1984). Effective direct instruction practices in special education settings. *Remedial and Special Education, 5,* 38–47.

Erikson, E. (1963). *Childhood and society* (2nd ed.). New York: Norton.

Erikson, E. (1968). *Identity: Youth and crisis.* New York: W. W. Norton.

Evertson, C., Anderson, C., Anderson, L., & Brophy, J. (1980). Relationship between classroom behavior and student outcomes in junior high math and English classes. *American Elementary Research Journal, 17,* 43–60.

Flavell, J. H. (1981). Cognitive monitoring. In P. Dickson (Ed.), *Children's oral communication skills.* New York: Academic Press.

Fuchs, L. S., Fuchs, D., & Deno, S. L. (1985). Importance of goal ambitiousness and goal mastery to student achievement. *Exceptional Children, 52,* 63–71.

Gable, R. A., & Kerr, M. M. (1980). Behaviorally disordered adolescents as academic change agents. *Severe Behavior Disorders of Children and Youth, 3,* 117–124.

Gersten, R., Woodward, J., & Dorch, C. (1986). Direct instruction: A research-based approach to curriculum design and teaching. *Exceptional Children, 53,* 17–31.

Glavin, J. P., & Annesley, F. R. (1971). Reading and arithmetic correlates of conduct-problem and withdrawn children. *Journal of Special Education, 5,* 213–219.

Good, T. L., & Grouws, D. A. (1979). The Missouri mathematics effectiveness project. *Journal of Educational Psychology, 71,* 355–362.

Idel-Maestas, L., Ritter, S., & Lloyd, S. (1983). A model for direct, data-based reading instruction. *Journal of Special Education Technology, 6*(3), 61–77.

Kauffman, J. M. (1986). Educating children with behavior disorders. In R. J. Morris & B. Blatt (Eds.), *Special education: Research and trends.* New York: Pergamon Press.

Korinek, L. (1987). Questioning strategies in special education: Links to teacher efficacy research in general education. *Journal of Research and Development in Education, 21,* 16–22.

Maheady, L., Harper, G. F., & Sacca, M. K. (1988). Peer-mediated instruction: A promising approach to meeting the diverse needs of LD adolescents. *Learning Disability Quarterly, 11,* 109–113.

Maheady, L., Sacca, M. K., & Harper, G. F. (1988). Classwide peer tutoring with mildly handicapped high school students. *Exceptional Children, 55,* 52–59.

Malamuth, Z. (1979). Self-management training for children with reading problems: Effects on reading performance and sustained attention. *Cognitive Therapy and Research, 3,* 279–289.

Masters, L. F., & Mori, A. A. (1986). *Teaching secondary students with mild learning and behavior problems.* Rockville, MD: Aspen Systems Corporation.

Mayers, P., Csikeszentmihalyi, M., & Larson, R. (1978). *The daily experience of high school students.* Paper presented at the annual meeting of the American Educational Research Association, Toronto.

McKenzie, G. (1979). Effects of questions and testlike events on achievement and on-task behavior in a classroom concept learning presentation. *Journal of Educational Research, 72,* 348–350.

Meichenbaum, D. (1980). Cognitive behavior modification with exceptional children: A promise yet unfulfilled. *Exceptional Education Quarterly, 1,* 83–88.

Meichenbaum, D., Asarnow, V. (1979). Cognitive-behavior modification and metacognitive development: Implications for the classroom. In P. C. Kendall & S. D. Hollon (Eds.), *Cognitive-behavioral interventions: Theory, research and procedures.* New York: Academic Press.

Morse, W. C. (1985). *The education and treatment of socio-emotionally impaired children and youth.* Syracuse, NY: Syracuse University Press.

Morsink, C. V., Soar, R. S., Soar, R. M., & Thomas, R. (1986). Research on teaching: Opening the door to special education classrooms. *Exceptional Children, 53,* 32–40.

Motto, J. J., & Wilkins, G. S. (1968). Educational achievement of institutionalized emotionally disturbed children. *Journal of Educational Research, 61,* 218–221.

Nagel, D., Schumaker, J. B., & Deshler, D. D. (1986). *The learning strategies curriculum: The FIRST-letter mnemonic strategy.* Lawrence, KS: Excel Enterprises.

Palincsar, A. S. (1986). Metacognitive strategy instruction. *Exceptional Children, 53,* 118–124.

Payne, J. S., Palloway, E. A., Smith, J. E., & Payne, R. A. (1981). *Strategies for reaching the mentally retarded* (2nd ed.). Columbus, OH: Merrill.

Rhine, W. R. (1981). *Making schools more effective: New directions from follow through.* New York: Academic Press.

Richards, J., & August, G. J. (1975). Generative underlying strategies in prose recall. *Journal of Educational Psychology, 67,* 860–865.

Reith, H., Bahr, C., Polsgrove, L., Okolo, C., & Eckert, R. (1987). The effects of microcomputers on the secondary special education classroom ecology. *Journal of Special Education Technology, 8*(4), 36–43.

Rieth, H., & Evertson, C. (1988). Variables related to the effective instruction of difficult to teach children. *Focus on Exceptional Children, 20*(5), 1–8.

Rieth, H., & Frick, T. (1983). *An analysis of the impact of instructional time with different service delivery systems on the achievement of mildly handicapped students.* Bloomington: Indiana University, Center for Innovation in Teaching the Handicapped.

Rieth, H., Polsgrove, L., & Semmel, M. I. (1981). Instructional variables that make a difference: Attention to task and beyond. *Exceptional Education Quarterly, 2,* 61–82.

Rosenshine, B. (1976). Classroom instruction. In N. L. Gage (Ed.), *The psychology of teaching methods.* Chicago: University of Chicago Press.

Rosenshine, B. (1979). Content, time and direct instruction. In P. Peterson & H. Walberg (Eds.), *Research on teaching: Concepts, findings and implications.* Berkeley, CA: McCutchan.

Rosenshine, B. (1983). Teaching functions in instructional programs. *Elementary School Journal, 83,* 335–352.

Rosenshine, B., & Stevens, R. (1984). Classroom instruction in reading. In D. Pearson (Ed.), *Handbook of research on teaching.* New York: Longman.

Rosenshine, B., & Stevens, R. (1986). Teaching functions. In M. C. Wittrock (Ed.), *Handbook of research on teaching* (3rd ed.). New York: Macmillan.

Sasso, G. M., Mitchell, V. M., & Struthers, E. M. (1986). Peer tutoring versus structured interaction activities: Effects on the frequency and topography of peer initiations. *Behavioral Disorders, 11,* 249–259.

Schumaker, J. B., Deshler D. D., Alley, G. R., & Denton, P. H. (1982). Multipass: A learning strategy for improving reading comprehension. *Learning Disability Quarterly, 5,* 295–304.

Schumaker, J. B., Deshler, D. D., Alley, G. R., & Warner, M. M. (1983). Toward the development of an intervention model for learning disabled adolescents. The University of Kansas Institute. *Exceptional Education Quarterly, 4*(1), 45–74.

Schumaker, J. B., & Sheldon, J. (1985). *Learning strategies curriculum: The sentence writing strategy.* Lawrence: University of Kansas.

Scruggs, T. E., Mastropier, M. A., & Richter, L. (1985). Peer tutoring with behaviorally disordered students: Social and academic benefits. *Behavioral Disorders, 10,* 283–294.

Silbert, J., Carnine, D., & Stein, M. (1981). *Direct instruction mathematics.* Columbus, OH: Merrill.

Slavin, R. E. (1984). Team assisted individualization: Cooperative learning and individualized instruction in the mainstreamed classroom. *Remedial and Special Education, 5,* 33–42.

Slavin, R. E., Leavey, M., & Madden, N. A. (1984). Combining cooperative learning and individualized instruction: Effects on student mathematics achievement, attitudes and behaviors. *Elementary School Journal, 84,* 409–422.

Smith, R. C., & Lincoln, C. A. (1988). *America's shame, America's hope: Twelve million youth at risk.* Chapel Hill, NC: MDC.

Stallings, J., & Kaskowitz, D. (1974). *Follow through classroom observation evaluation 1972–1973.* Stanford, CA: Stanford Research Institute.

Stevens, R., & Rosenshine, B. (1981). Advances in research on teaching. *Exceptional Education Quarterly, 2,* 1–9.

Sulzer-Azaroff, B., & Mayer, G. R. (1977). *Applying behavior-analysis procedures with children and youth.* New York: Holt, Rinehart & Winston.

Thurlow, M., Ysseldyke, J., Grader, J., Greener, J., & Mecklenburg, C. (1982). *Academic responding time for LD students receiving different levels of special education services* (Research Report No. 78). Minneapolis: University of Minnesota.

Torgeson, J. K. (1982). The learning disabled child as an inactive learner: Educational implications. *Topics in Learning and Learning Disabilities, 2,* 45–52.

Tracy, D. A., Bridell, D. W., & Wilson, G. T. (1974). Generalization of verbal conditioning to verbal and nonverbal behavior: Group therapy with chronic psychiatric patients. *Journal of Applied Behavior Analysis, 7,* 391–402.

Vaughn, S., Bos, C. S., & Lund, K. A. (1986). But can they do it in my room: Strategies for promoting generalization. *Teaching Exceptional Children, 18,* 176–180.

Wang, M. C., & Lindrall, C. M. (1984). Individual differences and school learning environments. In E. W. Gordon (Ed.), *Review of research in education.* Washington, DC: American Educational Research Association.

Wong, B. Y. (1985). Issues in cognitive-behavioral interventions in academic skill areas. *Journal of Abnormal Child Psychology, 13*(3), 441–455.

Wong, B. Y., & Jones, W. (1982). Increasing metacomprehension in learning disabled and normally achieving students through self-questioning training. *Learning Disability Quarterly, 5,* 228–240.

Woolf, V. (1936). *Three guineas.* New York: Harcourt, Brace & World.

Wright, L.S. (1974). Conduct problem or learning disability? *Journal of Special Education, 8,* 331–336.

Zimmerman, B.J. (1986). Becoming a self-regulated learner: Which are the key subprocesses? *Contemporary Educational Psychology, 11,* 307–313.

13
Discipline and Behavior Management*

MAIN POINTS

1. The best approach to behavior management is prevention or positive programming.
2. Effective behavior management focuses on meeting individual children's needs rather than requiring children to fit into the needs of the program.
3. Successful classroom managers maximally engage children in the learning process. When children are positively involved in the learning process, they do not pose behavioral problems.
4. Effective behavior management is grounded in a clearly articulated philosophy or belief system that guides decision making. The type of philosophy espoused probably is not as important as the consistency with which the philosophy is implemented by all persons involved with the child's program.
5. Careful planning of classroom procedures and practices helps teachers anticipate and avoid many disruptions.
6. Time spent teaching children expectations and orienting them to classroom routines and practices is time well-spent.
7. Expectations must be presented clearly, and consequences for compliance or noncompliance need to be consistently administered. Point and level systems are highly effective tools, particularly in classrooms for behavior-disordered children.
8. An effective behavior management system individualizes the program when the standard procedures are not sufficient for an individual child.
9. Teaching children desirable behaviors or behaviors that are inconsistent with undesirable behaviors is preferable to punishment.

---

*This chapter was written by Betty C. Epanchin, University of South Florida.

10. Time-out, exclusion, seclusion, and physical restraint are to be used when other, less aversive procedures have failed. Frequent use of these procedures is usually an indication of an inappropriate behavioral plan.

I think one must finally take one's life in one's arms.

Arthur Miller, 1980

Historically, behavior management or discipline has been viewed in both American and European schools in a reactive manner; that is, the focus has been on "stopping unwanted behaviors through punishment" (Sabatino, 1987, p. 8). We now realize that punishment is a poor deterrent for unwanted behaviors. Instead of focusing on punishment, we are now seeing a shift to prevention and to proactive teaching. This shift appears to be broad-based, as writers from different conceptual frameworks are supporting actions in this direction. Horner, Dunlap, Koegel, Carr, Sailor, Anderson, Albin, & O'Neill (in press) advocate positive programming, while Morse (1987) and a number of his colleagues discuss preventive discipline. While there are differences in these concepts, both are proactive and positive in focus.

A related issue that has arisen from research in this area is that of generalization. A number of studies have suggested that without careful programming, skills learned in one setting may not be transferred to other settings. Apparently, children need to be taught skills that will enable them greater access to less restrictive settings (Horner et al., in press).

This shift has resulted in response to a growing body of research that casts doubt on the effectiveness and the ethics of suppressing or punishing unwanted behavior. Kounin (1970) reported that effective classroom managers are distinguished from their less effective peers, not by their ability to manage crises and problems but rather by their ability to prevent problems from ever arising. Thus, as Morse notes, "The challenge is to convert the vast, exhausting task of mopping up after incidents to forward-looking strategies that are far more productive for both pupils and teachers" (1987, p. 4).

A related issue that has arisen from research in this area is that of generalization. A number of studies have suggested that without careful programming, skills learned in one setting may not be transferred to other settings. Apparently, children need to be taught skills that will enable them greater access to less restrictive settings (Horner et al., in press).

The position developed in this chapter is consistent with this emphasis on prevention discipline or positive programming. Behavior management, or the disciplinary process, is viewed as multifaceted, involving much more than managing inappropriate behavior. It refers to actions taken by the teacher and the school to establish and maintain a productive learning environment. Discipline, or effective behavior management, enables students to achieve optimally, to participate and benefit maximally, and to learn how to function effectively both as a student and as a group member. Behavior management helps children "incorporate socialized behavior, not just classroom compliance" (Morse, 1987, p. 4).

As teachers set up behavior management systems, they act upon their beliefs and knowledge. There is no single "right" instructional or management decision. Rather, teachers must consider the professional knowledge base, their own personal beliefs, characteristics of their teaching environment, and their students in deciding how to intervene. The "rightness" of an intervention is determined by its effectiveness, and efficacy is judged by multiple factors such as child, family, and teacher satisfaction or change in behavior.

Based on the sparse information in the literature regarding actual practice, it appears that teachers currently are using a variety of techniques from different theoretical orientations in an effort to establish effective systems (Grosenick, George, & George, 1988; Kavale & Hirshoren, 1980). The major difficulty of an eclectic approach is it requires the teacher to organize and synthesize the theoretical assumptions and practices into a pragmatic program that meets the needs of individual students and that fits the context in which the teacher is functioning. This is a very complicated process because it requires an understanding of many aspects of the educational environment. Until an integrated paradigm emerges, teachers must be the integrators, drawing theory and techniques from multiple sources to fit the situations they face.

This chapter and Chapter 14 focus on current practices that are effective when establishing management systems. Content discussed in this chapter deals with environmental interventions that the teacher can use to control behavior. Chapter 14 focuses on affective and cognitive interventions that teachers may use to help children learn how to manage their own feelings and thoughts more effectively. Both are important parts of a behavior management system.

SYSTEM SUPPORT

If teachers are to have effective behavior management systems, they must have support from the system in which they work. Even the best of teachers will have problems in a school that views special education as a "dumping ground" rather than an instructional program. Systems that have strong special education programs typically have administrative support as evidenced by inclusionary administrative action and policy, the presence of clinical supervision and consultation, and clarity of role expectations within the school or district.

Administrative Inclusion

Principals and administrators who value special education programs generally attend to details that make teachers feel included and valued. Teachers are provided access to the decision making, and their ideas are incorporated into the school. When feasible, their students are included in school-wide activities such as student government and sports. Rather than being housed in a "portable" classroom or in the basement of the building, teachers and their classrooms are in the mainstream of the school. Thus, physically and psychologically special education and regular education are both valued and included.

The author has observed two incidents in schools that stand out as illustrations of this type of support. In one school, services for the emotionally handicapped were away from the main building in an old trailer that had a leaking roof. Consistent with the district policy, emotionally handicapped children were assigned to regular homerooms, but spent most of their day in the special classroom. When class pictures were being taken, more than one of the regular education teachers excluded the emotionally handicapped children. After 2 years in this school, the special education teacher, who was very effective with the children, transferred to another school because he was so discouraged. In another school in the same school district, the principal made her philosophy clear from the start of the year. All children enrolled in a homeroom were the responsibility of the homeroom teacher. In this school, class parties, pictures, trips, and so on included all children in the class. Individual arrangements were sometimes necessary, but both the emotionally handicapped children and their teacher felt valued and included in the school. Cherniss (1980) cites helplessness as a major cause of burnout among teachers. Isolation from the decision-making process contributes to a sense of helplessness.

Clinical Supervision/Consultation

Decisions about behavior management are difficult under the best of circumstances, but when teachers work with aggressive, hostile children in isolated settings, the decisions are even more difficult. Research on teacher burnout and staff morale is underscoring what many clinicians have noted for years—that consultation and clinical supervision help teachers feel less stressed by the demands of their jobs.

Gillet (1987) outlines a number of techniques that supervisors can use to provide support to teachers of emotionally handicapped children. These strategies enable teachers to have opportunities to learn from their mistakes, experiment with new approaches, and have control over their teaching situation. In such environments, teachers can be more effective.

Some of these techniques are as follows:

1. Develop clear, decisive guidelines for disciplinary action so that teachers know what the system recommends.

2. Review IEPs and behavior management plans to ensure that teachers have been realistic in their expectations for their students and themselves.
3. Maintain on-site, specific visitation schedules.
4. Follow up on staff requests.
5. Be predictable and available.
6. Permit the teacher to control the class.
7. Provide demonstration teaching.
8. Take decisive action when necessary (e.g., call a multidisciplinary staff conference to plan how to deal with a violent student), and assist teachers in "letting go" of cases that cannot be remediated.
9. Organize a meaningful staff development program.
10. Develop a support system for teachers.

Enabling teachers to talk with other teachers who are dealing with similar problems or with professionals from other disciplines helps teachers think more objectively and learn to deal with situations and individual children and their families more effectively.

Role Clarity

In addition to having colleagues with whom to problem solve, teachers need to know what is expected of them and what they may expect of their system. For example, they need to know who will help if a child becomes violent and how they will access the help. They need to know what resources are available for providing help to individual children and how they can access involvement from mainstream teachers. They also need to know and clearly understand the goals and philosophy of their school and school system. Beliefs about programs and children affect programming in significant ways. For example, in some school systems emotionally handicapped children are considered the responsibility of special education, while in other systems all exceptional children are assigned to regular education. Such differences in philosophy affect individual teacher's approaches to behavior management.

COMPONENTS OF PREVENTION

Most authorities agree that a well-run classroom for emotionally disturbed children is structured, organized, predictable, and orderly. Children spend most of their time working; they follow their teacher's directions; they understand the class rules and expectations; and, at least most of the time, students are cooperative. However, an orderly classroom climate does not happen without a great deal of planning and teaching of expectations.

Effective Academic Activities

When setting up a classroom, teachers make a number of decisions that determine how well their classroom will work and therefore the number of problems

High student involvement in academic activities is related to low rates of student disruption.

that will be prevented. The first and most important decision is what to teach. The presentation of an interesting lesson in which the child can be successful is the most basic approach to managing behavior (DeLuke & Knoblock, 1987; Morse, 1987). When children are actively engaged in their school activities, they do not have time to misbehave (Carnine, 1976; Greenwood, Delquadri, & Hall, 1984; Morgan & Jenson, 1988). Thus, a wise approach to behavior management is one that rewards academic performance, rather than compliant behavior (Blankenship, 1986; Sabatino, 1987).

Room Arrangement and Classroom Props

An important aspect of preventing behavior problems is attention to ecological variables that affect behavior—that is, matching the learning activity with the physical room arrangement (Stainback, Stainback, & Froyen, 1987). When props in the classroom support the instructional goals, problems are prevented (Evans & Lovell, 1979; Nash, 1981). As Paine, Radicchi, Rosellini, Deutchman, and Darch (1983) point out, proper use of space and equipment also impacts upon teachers. It enables them to improve student performance, to be more positive, and to spend more time teaching. The following examples illustrate this point:

1. When teachers are lecturing, demonstrating, or using guided practice to reinforce new skills, students' tables and desks should face the teacher and the teacher should be able to survey the class to monitor student reactions. Space is needed between desks or tables so the teacher can move with ease around the room. These arrangements discourage talk among students and thereby aid students in complying with teacher expectations.

2. Cooperative, small-group work is facilitated by arrangements that focus student attention on other students and enable the sharing of materials or equipment. Small tables or desks in clusters of four or five support this activity.

3. Group discussions, an activity used in many classrooms to start and end the day, work well with chairs arranged in a circle. Such an arrangement can also be flexible, enabling students to move chairs from a study carrel to a circle and back again, but it can also create problems of noise and unwanted contact among children.

4. In classrooms where children spend significant amounts of time engaged in seat work, the most desirable arrangement may be study carrels or the placement of desks in isolated places around the perimeter of the room and behind or between bookcases or file cabinets. When teachers have the luxury of ordering furniture and designing rooms, built-in study carrels are often requested and effectively used.

5. Classrooms that use learning centers need to be divided into work areas, allocating sufficient space to each learning center, so that students at one center do not distract students at another center. This approach is particularly effective with young children who have difficulty attending to any one task for long periods of time and who learn best through applied activities.

Thus, teachers prevent many problems through careful attention to creating a match between their classroom physical arrangement and their instructional approach. Without such a fit, many problems arise that could have easily been prevented.

Materials and Equipment

The potential for problems to develop also increases when the materials and equipment in a classroom do not fit the educational activities or the students' needs. For example, problems often develop when students have to share materials and equipment or when equipment is not ready to use or breaks down while in use. Few research studies have focused on procedures for managing materials and equipment effectively, but many authors attest to the importance of this practice (Cangelosi, 1988; Hewett & Taylor, 1980; Paine et al., 1983; Rinne, 1984). The following are practices that have wide clinical support.

Problems are avoided if children have sufficient quantities of materials and supplies. If materials must be shared, teachers are wise to place books, paper, pencils, and other materials needed for work at or close to the student's work station. In a similar vein, it is also wise to assign cubbies, coat hooks, chairs, desks, and lockers so that arguments over territory and possessions are eliminated. Without such attention to instructional props, a teacher's lessons can easily be disrupted by a fight between two children who want the same magic marker or chair.

In addition to preventive planning, teachers need to teach students how to share and how to manage equipment and materials so that chaos does not occur when unexpected and unplanned problems arise. Presenting and discussing concrete suggestions about working together and following procedures are also preventive practices.

The type of furniture used in classrooms can also help minimize problems. Desks that have tops which may be opened and closed can be problematic because students can disrupt an entire class by banging their desk tops. Likewise, open bookshelves with alluring books and equipment can be problematic to distractible students. Storing equipment out of the children's sight removes potential problems.

Minimizing Downtime

Using equipment such as tape recorders, filmstrip projectors, computers, and record players on a regular basis is an excellent way to attract and keep children's attention and interest, but the equipment needs to be kept in good working order and ready for use (Hewett & Taylor, 1980). Students' attention can be easily lost while the teacher is fumbling with a movie projector. Likewise, children can become distracted and frustrated when equipment they are using does not work.

Overhead projectors with prepared transparencies can eliminate the time students waste waiting for the teacher to finish writing on the board. Systems that require children to wait for their assignments or wait to have their work checked also create fertile opportunities for problems (DeLuke & Knoblock, 1987). Classrooms that enable children to move easily and quickly from one activity to another, without long and frustrating starting and stopping, are classrooms that run more smoothly. Kounin (1970) observed the importance of pacing. His data indicated that good classroom managers were well prepared, kept up a brisk instructional pace, and focused on the lesson, not disruptions. In these classrooms children had little downtime when they were not sure what to do or had nothing to do. Children were engaged in the business of learning. This is especially important in classrooms for behavior-disordered children, who are easily distracted and lured into disruptive, nonproductive activities.

Scheduling

Preventive planning is based upon careful scheduling of all classroom components: the class, each student, the teacher, and the teaching assistant. Detailed scheduling for everyone helps maintain the momentum from one activity to another and helps teachers situate themselves or their aides where they are needed to prevent disruptions from occurring. To accomplish this level of organization, teachers may need to develop three types of schedules: class schedules, individual student schedules, and teacher schedules.

Class Schedules.   Daily and weekly schedules for the class help everyone orient themselves to upcoming activities. They inform students about what will occur when, which helps children with learning and behavior problems anticipate activities and organize themselves. Class schedules also help teachers insure that time is allocated in accord with their goals and objectives. Having the schedule posted in a prominent place and referring to it frequently also helps teachers remember what activities are planned throughout the day. This also helps teachers guide students from one activity to another while also maintaining a brisk pace.

To set up an effective schedule, teachers first need to decide what and how they want to teach. This information needs to be integrated with information about characteristics of the class. With both sets of data, teachers can plan schedules that maximize the instructional time. The following guidelines may help when planning schedules:

1. Identify content that is new and challenging and content that is practice. Intersperse challenging new work with practice work. Also schedule more appealing work after demanding work. This enables the teacher to use subsequent activities as motivators.
2. Identify times of the day when the class is most settled and least settled. Some students typically come to school unsettled and benefit from a quiet, calming activity before they transition into more demanding activities. Other children are freshest and most alert early in the morning; thus, they respond well to having the most challenging material early. Teachers have to match their instructional objectives with their knowledge of their students' characteristics.
3. Whenever new material is presented, time needs to be allocated for the presentation and for practice and feedback.
4. Schedules should also have time for transitions. Teachers need to determine how much time is needed to transition from one activity to another. When students take more time than is scheduled, teachers may need to plan activities to help students move through transitions more efficiently because transitions are potentially one of the most disruptive times during the day for behavior-disordered children (Rhodes, 1985; Strain & Sainato, 1987; Kuergeleis, Deutchman, & Paine, 1980).
5. Plan for the unexpected. If teachers value adherence to the schedule, provisions must be made for adjusting the schedule when the unexpected occurs, such as a fire drill, a child getting sick, or unexpected pleasure and excitement about an activity. By scheduling some flexible time in a schedule, teachers enable themselves to keep to a basic schedule and thereby reinforce the importance of the schedule to the students.
6. Determine the length of schedule intervals by assessing the length of time students can stay on task independently. For young children and for

behavior-disordered children, this may be only 15 minutes. Schedule activities for every period, be the period 15 or 45 minutes long. Verbal reminders that a period is almost over help children anticipate an upcoming transition better. Kitchen timers and large, easily visible clocks also help children move from one activity to another more easily.

7. In self-contained classrooms, opening and closing activities are usually important. Many teachers start the day with planning activities or with a morning meeting, much like "sharing" in early childhood programs. This is intended to help children get oriented to the school day. Likewise, a group discussion time at the end of the day helps to wrap up the day's activities and helps children transition out of school. Often these opening and closing sessions have rituals that help students get through the housekeeping tasks.

8. Post the class schedule in a highly visible place in the classroom and refer to it often. For young children, pictures to match the content help nonreaders use the schedule.

9. Expect that students finish one task before starting another, but try to assign work that can be done in a day. If work is unfinished at the end of the day, it is usually not a wise idea to carry it over to the next day. Students need to be given a fresh start each day.

10. Teachers of resource rooms and of high school students usually have students for periods during the day, not for most of the day. They typically have minischedules for each class. The same principles discussed previously apply to these miniperiods; only the amount of available time is altered.

Individual Student Schedules.   After the class schedule is made, teachers need to develop schedules for individual students. With the overall class format in mind, individual student's needs are considered as teachers plan individual schedules. This enables teachers to individualize. For example, in a class where most children are working on different levels, the teacher may assign each child a different activity. On each child's schedule, specific work will be detailed during each activity. Teachers may set up individual schedules to be used much like a checklist; time periods will be listed and activities detailed. Children and teachers check off progress as work is done. Some teachers also use this as a place to record points earned in the reward system.

Persons working with junior and senior high school students in mainstream settings have different scheduling concerns. To insure that students are placed with teachers who are able to work with emotionally handicapped students, it may be necessary to individually schedule students so that good matches are obtained between the teacher, the class expectations, and student.

Teacher and Teaching Assistant Schedules.   Once the class schedule and the student schedules are planned, teachers may plan their assistant's schedule and their own schedule. As teachers go over the schedules to determine which children will have adult help and when they will have it, they are able to anticipate potential problems and plan ways of deflecting them. For example, knowing that Suzy tends to give up on math easily, the teacher may decide to have the aide monitor Suzy during the first 10 minutes of math. This type of "hurdle help" may help Suzy get started and motivated to finish.

Teachers must provide students and assistants with information about the schedules and what is expected. Students need to be taught how to read and use the schedule. Teaching assistants also need to be taught expectations. Sometimes teachers complain about the quality of their assistant's help without first providing training and guidance in how to help. Assistants need to know where materials and supplies are located, what they are expected to do with the students, where they are to work with the students, and how they should deal with problems if they are to follow the schedule and be helpful.

Establishing Routines

Routines provide order that enables most students to feel comfortable. Knowing what to expect and how to do it provides a sense of security to most students. In planning how the classroom will run, teachers should think about what they want students to do throughout the day. For example, some occasions that teachers must consider are listed below:

- Small-group Behavior
    - Are students allowed to whisper?
    - Do they have to raise their hands when they want to talk?
    - Can they help each other?
    - How should they be seated?
- Starting a Lesson
    - Where do students sit?
    - What should they have ready to use?
- Paperwork
    - How should papers be headed?
    - When and where is paperwork turned in?
    - What type of grades/checking can the student expect?
    - Are notebooks expected? Will they be checked? What type of notebook does the teacher want?
- Movement Through the School
    - Are students expected to go to the lunchroom and gym in a line?
    - How should students line up?
    - Is a pass needed to go to the bathroom independently during class time?
    - What are the consequences for being late?
- Getting Help During Seat Work
    - Should students raise their hands and teachers rotate around the room when students need help?
    - Is it the assistant's responsibility to rotate around the room checking papers and providing help while the teacher works with a small group?
    - Can students get help from their classmates?

- When Work Is Finished
    - What should students do when they finish their work?
    - Are they free to do what they wish, or is there work to do?
- Transitions From One Activity to Another
    - How should students move from one activity to another?
    - What should students do if one child is misbehaving while others are waiting to start an activity?

Teachers need to plan what they will do to encourage students to abide by the established routines. They also need to inform the students what will happen if established routines are not followed. Once the structure is developed, teachers need to teach students their expectations for how the class will operate and what cooperative and noncooperative behavior will yield.

Determining Class Rules

Rules are different from routines. Rules should apply to all children and they should be consistently enforced. Breaking a rule is a serious transgression, whereas not following a routine may result in loss of points or privileges, but it is not so serious. There should be as few rules as possible so that all children know and remember the rules and so that teachers can consistently enforce the rules. To ensure that a rule is necessary, Cangelosi suggests that a rule should serve at least one of the following four purposes:

1. To maximize on-task behaviors and minimize off-task, especially disruptive, behaviors.
2. To secure the safety and comfort of the learning environment.
3. To prevent the activities of the class from disturbing other classes and persons outside of the class.
4. To maintain acceptable standards of decorum among students, school personnel, and visitors to the school campus. (1988, p. 116)

In most classrooms rules that meet these criteria have to do with respecting persons and property (e.g., "don't hit or hurt oneself or others," and "don't destroy property.")

Most authorities recommend that teachers display the class rules in a prominent place and, as with the class schedule, refer to the rules often (Strain & Sainato, 1987). In listing the rules, teachers should try to phrase them in a positive manner; however, if clarity requires negative statements, clarity is more important than positive phrasing. For example, "We respect each other" is a common rule, but some behavior-disordered children, especially young ones, need more explicit instructions such as "We do not hit" and "We do not harm others' property."

Some teachers, especially those of older children, involve their students in developing the rules. By engaging students in the process, teachers maximize students' knowledge of and commitment to the rules. Research indicates that student-imposed rules are at least as effective as teacher-imposed ones (Dickerson & Creedon, 1981; Felixbrod & O'Leary, 1974).

When children do break a rule, the consequences should be immediate and should function as a punisher for the child. A punisher in this context is a consequence that helps reduce the occurrence of the behavior in the future. As Walker (1979) pointed out, rules alone produce minimal or no effect on child behavior, especially when dealing with ''acting out'' aggressive children, unless the rules are backed up by effective consequences.

In his discussion of controlling victimization, Floyd stated:

> Fighting as a way of settling a score in school should be categorically condemned; it is incompatible with the educational mission of schools. The school forbids it, the teacher will not condone it, and the police will be called in the event of fights. School personnel must take this position openly and firmly, and not merely to protect potential victims. They must take this position for the sake of the bully as well. They must clearly enunciate these rules so as to help potential bullies control their aggression. Bullies need to believe that teachers are in control and that adults believe in the rules they make. . . . Many teachers are uncomfortable when asked to convey to students what they consider to be the message of ''law and order.'' This message may seem incompatible with the principles of free inquiry, liberal education, unmolested learning, and especially the least restrictive approach to the learning environment. Nevertheless, it should be stated unequivocally: Children need rules! And children in special education desperately need rules, precepts, and values. Perhaps none is more important than their need to understand that actions have consequences. . . . Special educators are often on the front lines and in the trenches trying to bring the ''rules of civilization'' to the emotionally disturbed. Keep in mind that to be authoritative is not to be authoritarian! More than ever, children need adults to embody the legitimate claims of society and the school for security and stability. (1985, p. 12)

Grouping

For years teachers have used the procedure of placing more disruptive students next to quiet, compliant rule followers, assuming that the disruptive student will model the behavior of the well-behaved models or that peer pressure will help the disruptive student behave. Stainback, Stainback, Etscheidt, and Doud (1986) studied this practice by placing a 10-year-old boy, described by teachers and the principal as the most disruptive boy in the class, with groups of well-behaved students and with other disruptive students. Direct observations indicated that he consistently exhibited fewer disruptive behaviors when placed in work groups with well-behaved students. Based on these data, the authors questioned the wisdom of placing disruptive students in classes with other disruptive students, as often happens in special education settings.

This issue is particularly important in light of current pressures to segregate conduct-disordered children from other seriously emotionally disturbed children. Some teachers and administrators are arguing that conduct-disordered students should not be grouped with socially maladjusted children because both groups suffer (Center, 1989). "For this reason, differentiating these two groups and not exposing the undersocialized, conduct-disordered student to inappropriate socialization are important factors. Although the service needs of both groups involve programming directed at socialization, co-placement of members of the two groups runs a considerable risk of being counter-productive for the conduct-disordered student" (Center, 1989, p. 11). More data are needed regarding the effects of grouping.

MATCHING CONSEQUENCES WITH BEHAVIOR

Prior to the start of school, effective teachers make a number of critical decisions that impact on student behavior. They decide what they expect of students and what they will do to elicit such behavior. They also specify consequences for noncompliance. Predetermined consequences that are matched to cooperative and noncompliant behavior help teachers develop an organizational framework for managing behavior that has a preventive, proactive approach.

Establishing a Continuum of Reinforcers

When organizing the classroom, teachers may consider a continuum of reinforcers that range from concrete, tangible, teacher-imposed, authoritarian ones to naturally occurring, intrinsic ones. In selecting reinforcers, teachers should choose naturally occurring and less tangible consequences, whenever possible. Concrete reinforcers are used primarily for behaviors that are being developed and not easily within the child's control.

The basic approach involves setting up a carefully structured, organized class with predictable consequences that enable children to learn and behave appropriately. For most children with behavioral and learning problems, a well-run classroom in which the child experiences success is sufficient treatment; however, some children need more individualized interventions. Skillful therapeutic teachers interpret chronic misbehavior as an indication for individualized attention and remedial assistance, not punishment. Teachers view chronic misbehavior as a failure of the system and an indication of the need for more help; thus, they reevaluate their management system. For example, when a reinforcer is not effective in helping a child control his behavior, they reevaluate and revise their reward system rather than continue to punish. More frequent, more concrete, and more immediate rewards are often effective modifications that help children gain better control over their problem behavior. Therapeutic teachers also prefer teaching children what to do when a problem arises or teaching behaviors that are incompatible with the problem behavior rather than punishing.

Administering Standard Reinforcers

In a comparison of the reward preferences of students in mainstream and special education settings for grades 6 through 9, Martens, Muir, and Meller (1988) found that good grades and free-time privileges were the preferred rewards for all students. Middle school children also rated academic work with peers or teacher as very desirable. No significantly different ratings were found among regular and special students in their reward preferences. The authors interpreted this finding as having significant implications for students being moved from special to regular classroom settings. Using the same rewards in both settings may be helpful to students as they move from more restrictive to less restrictive settings.

In addition to social praise, reinforcers that are easily used in regular and special education classrooms include special privileges and class jobs such as the ones listed below:

storing audiovisual equipment	stapling papers
setting up projectors	running errands
setting up screens	answering phone
closing shades	patrolling crosswalks
operating lights	leading lines
caring for plants	caring for pets
collecting materials	decorating room
erasing boards	cleaning erasers
choosing a special seat	having free time
leading a discussion	visiting the principal

For a group of children, the following reinforcers may be used:

a class soft drink break	party or popcorn break (fun Friday)
extra time at recess	playing games
watching a movie	a field trip

Token Economies.   When social praise, grades, free time, privileges, and class jobs are **not** effective in helping students gain control over their behavior, a token economy or point system may be used. In these systems, tokens or points are given to students contingent upon desired behavior. The tokens or points have no value of their own; they must be "backed up" by rewards that have value to the students. For example, tokens can serve as currency in a class or school store where toys or other rewards may be purchased.

A token economy has three defining characteristics: (1) behaviors that are to be reinforced, (2) a symbolic medium of exchange called a token, and (3) backup reinforcers that may be purchased with tokens (Cooper, Heron & Heward, 1987). The behaviors to reinforce, the types of tokens used, and the nature of the backup reinforcers vary in relation to teacher preference and student characteristics, including both age and severity of problems. Young, more handicapped children may need frequent, concrete rewards, whereas older students may be able to monitor and reinforce themselves.

A token economy system should be tailored to meet the needs of the class. Variables that teachers must consider include the type of tokens, how often they will be dispensed, when the tokens can be traded for backup reinforcers, what behaviors will be rewarded, and what the backup reinforcers will be.

A variety of tokens can be used: poker chips placed in cups on children's desks, paper clips chained together over a child's study carrel, marks on a point card, stars on a chart, and holes punched in the point card. Ease of use should determine choice of token. A system works best that does not disrupt the flow of the classroom. Quiet, quick dispensing of tokens is desirable. Thus, if members within a group are likely to knock over the cup of chips or if the children are likely to steal the chips, poker chips in cups are not likely to be the best system. Likewise, teachers usually want to use a special colored pen when marking points on a card so that children do not mark their own cards.

Some teachers keep the points on a paper on their clipboard, away from children and their possible efforts to change points. This, however, prevents the children from seeing how they are doing. Concrete, visual reminders of progress are helpful to some children.

Young children often need reinforcers more frequently than older children. Some teachers set the classroom up on the basis of 15-minute activity periods that are followed by reward time, and this type of schedule is used during the school day. As children mature or with older groups, the intervals may be longer. Other teachers set kitchen timers at variable intervals and reward when the time chimes.

The behaviors to be rewarded may dictate the schedule. For example, if a teacher wishes to increase attending behavior, she may use a concealed timer and intermittent reinforcements. When the chime sounds, all children who are attending are rewarded; hence, children must be continuously attentive to earn their rewards. If, however, following class rules is the desired behavior, intervals may be more appropriate. The system would reward all children who followed the rules during the interval.

Likewise, determining when children can trade in their tokens may vary in relation to age and the group. Young children may need daily or even twice daily trade times; older children can go for a week or more.

Since the goal is to help children be more self-sufficient and responsive to naturally occurring rewards, teachers should encourage children to move toward less frequent exchanges. Some teachers accomplish this through a school store that has rewards of varying value. The more expensive items require more tokens than can possibly be acquired during one trade-in period. In such a system, children are allowed to save their tokens until they have enough for the more expensive reward. After children have successfully demonstrated that they can control their behavior for longer periods of time without concrete rewards, the teacher can use their success as a concrete indication of their readiness to move to less contrived reward systems. In instigating such changes, teachers encourage the student's self-pride in successful performance and use social praise and attention as reinforcers.

Teachers select behaviors to be rewarded on the basis of their goals for the children. The goals may be for all children in the class or each child may have his own goal. Teachers frequently blend these two systems. When this is done, they award tokens for following specified class rules such as "respecting others" and "following instructions" and they also award tokens for individual goals. By blending the two systems, teachers can individualize within the class while not being overwhelmed by keeping track of many different goals. This can be very important when a class is composed of diverse children. For example, a class might have a few disruptive, very immature children who are struggling to meet the basic class rules and a few bright, self-controlled children who are depressed, passive, and withdrawn. Quite likely, class rules will be easy for the quiet children to accomplish, but difficult for the disruptive children. To equalize the system so all children have to work about the same for their rewards, the teacher may give the quiet children a goal that requires social interaction and that, while certainly within the child's ability to accomplish, is more challenging than following the class rules.

Again, the objective of a token economy is to teach children how to behave appropriately. As children grow and learn behaviors, the teacher should move from concrete backup rewards to rewards that are more readily available in most classrooms. Older children may prefer to choose their own rewards or privileges. Pencils, stickers, erasers, and little toys are frequently available in school stores. Models, notebooks, or posters are examples of more expensive items that students may save points to earn.

Some teachers have tied privileges or free time to tokens or points. For example, children may work all week to earn a "fun Friday." "Fun Fridays" are times for the children who earned their points to have popcorn, play games, and so on. In such systems, children who do not earn the Friday reward are assigned the work that they did not complete during the week, a natural consequence of not completing assignments during the assigned time.

Some teachers, especially those in day treatment programs, tie their reward system to out-of-school activities. When this is implemented, parents or other responsible adults typically contract with the teacher to monitor the specified behaviors in settings other than school. For example, daily report cards informing families of a student's good behavior are a means of decreasing inappropriate behavior (Ayllon, 1975; Lahey, 1977).

For some young, severely disturbed, low-functioning children, it may be necessary to use direct and basic rewards, such as objects or food, that are contingent upon desired behavior. The reward may or may not have been specified through a contract in which the teacher and student agree upon expectations and consequences. Examples of objects given directly as rewards are candy, peanuts, pretzels, pencils, and stickers.

Regardless of the system used, it should be carefully developed and explained to the students, parents, and all other persons within the school who will interact with the students. When other important persons in the child's life understand the behavior system, they are able to support and enforce the expectations, thereby increasing the effectiveness of the system.

Level Systems. Level systems are structures that establish predetermined contingencies for student behavior. The level system has been described as "an application of the principle of shaping, where the goal is self-management (i.e., developing personal responsibility for social, emotional, and academic performance" (Bauer, Shea, & Keppler, 1986, p. 28). Level systems may be used with a variety of treatment programs from different conceptual bases; however, it is probably most easily used with behavioral approaches.

In a level system, desirable and undesirable behaviors are detailed, along with the consequences for each. Lower levels tend to be teacher-directed, to have external reward systems, and to be associated with more restrictive environments. Higher levels tend to place more responsibility on the student, to allow more autonomy to the student, and to rely upon more intrinsic rewards. As students move from lower to higher levels, they also become more self-directed. In most systems, the top level reflects behaviors and expectations of mainstream settings.

Level systems originated in more restrictive settings; however, in recent years they have been used successfully in public school classes. Braaten (1979) described a level system used in the Madison School Program in Minnesota. In this system students gradually move from one class to another as they progress through levels. Mastropieri, Jenne, and Scruggs (1988) describe two different level systems that were used successfully in high school resource rooms. In these classrooms, students worked on a level for four days of the week. At the end of the day on Thursday, students were allowed to request a level change. Requests for change were submitted to the teacher who reviewed the requests. On Friday students and the teacher discussed and voted on the requests. If a student met an 85% accuracy criterion on assignments and received a majority vote in favor of change, the level for the student was changed the next week. Each time a student made a level change, a new contract was signed with the teacher.

Level systems are easily combined with point systems when establishing a behavior management system. If a level system is used in conjunction with a point system, points are designated for each level. Students must earn the specified points to move from level to level. Typically in such systems students earn points for following behavioral rules and completing academic work. Additionally, teachers usually make provisions to give bonus points to children who do something that is especially pleasing to the teacher. For example, ignoring a child who is misbehaving or accomplishing a task that is especially difficult are behaviors which might be rewarded with bonus points.

The use of a point and level system enables teachers to specify in concrete ways what they expect of their students. These expectations are detailed at the outset so they are not reactive responses. Rather, such an approach helps teachers to administer consequences consistently.

It has always been assumed that the backup rewards are what makes point and level systems effective. However, as Hoefler and Bornstein (1975) pointed out, other variables may be equally or more influential. For example, point and level systems teach appropriate social behavior and they create situations for children to see appropriate models and receive social approval. Phillips and his colleagues at Achievement Place initially described their point system as the "heart of the program," but as they learned more about their system, they concluded that the social aspects were the "heart of the program," not the token economy system per se (Phillips, Phillips, Fixsen, & Wolf, 1973). "While tokens are facilitators of behavior change, the main effects are attributed to social interaction and modeling" (Hoefler & Bornstein, 1975, p. 160).

Teaching Alternative Behaviors

A desirable alternative to punishing undesirable behavior is differential reinforcement of incompatible (DRI), alternative (DRA), or other (DRO) behaviors. For example, to decrease a child's out-of-seat behavior, a teacher might reinforce on-task behavior (DRI). A child cannot be on task and out of his seat simultaneously. If the teacher chooses to use DRA, she might place the student with a group that is assigned to finish a group project. Rewards would be contingent upon productive group work. While the student might be able to be out of his seat and also participate in the group work, it is likely that the out-of-seat behavior will decrease as the student becomes involved in the project. If the teacher uses DRO, she will reinforce any reasonable behavior other than out-of-seat behavior.

These techniques are effective in decreasing unwanted behaviors while also maintaining a positive focus in the classroom. They also are less controversial than punishment procedures. However, behaviors that disrupt the classroom and consistently interfere with a student's educational progress need to be stopped immediately.

Administering Punishment

Although punishment is ethically less desirable than other approaches and may not generalize to other settings, it is an effective and relatively quick way to suppress unacceptable behavior. According to Braaten, Simpson, Rosell, and Reilly (1988), at least five different forms of punishment are commonly seen in the classroom: (1) response cost, (2) time-out, (3) overcorrection, (4) contingent exercise, and (5) aversive conditioning.

Response cost is paying back rewards contingent upon unwanted behavior. It is most often seen in conjunction with point systems.

Time-out is denying a student access to reinforcement contingent upon inappropriate behavior. Time-out can be administered in a number of ways. Inclusionary time-out is administered while the child is in the classroom. For example, allowing the child to stay in his seat but not earn reinforcers is a form of inclusionary time-out. Seclusionary time-out requires the child to leave the classroom.

Overcorrection involves restitution and practicing an appropriate response to a problem situation. Restitution is used when damage to property occurs. Examples are cleaning a wall after scribbling on it, or taping a paper back together after ripping it up.

Contingent exercise involves physical exercise, such as push-ups or running laps, as a consequence of inappropriate behavior.

Aversive conditioning involves the use of painful or noxious consequences (e.g., electric shock or lemon juice squirted into the student's mouth) in response to dangerous or potentially injurious behaviors. This is a very controversial technique used only in extreme behaviors, such as head banging, pulling out one's hair, or scratching oneself.

When selecting a punisher, teachers must be careful to match the transgression with the consequence. Mild misbehaviors warrant small punishers, while serious misbehaviors require more aversive consequences. In addition to matching behaviors with consequences, teachers need to consider the age of their students. Apparently teachers use somewhat different punishers with young children than with older children. For example, Zabel (1986) reported that time-out is used more commonly with younger children than with older students.

Matching misbehaviors with punishers is a complex process that is best done prior to the transgression. Relying on the teacher to make consistent judgments at the moment a child is challenging her authority is likely to produce inconsistent and reactive punishment. Using critical incident reports prepared by teachers in a residential treatment center, Epanchin, Rennells, Rhoades, Simmers, and Wasik (1988) found that teachers underestimated the frequency with which they used time-out, even though they were required to complete a report each time a child was sent to time-out. Because it is so difficult for teachers to make reasoned decisions when a child is misbehaving, some programs have carefully developed guidelines that detail for teachers how to administer punishment. If no guidelines exist for using time-out, teachers are wise to develop their own and share them with the principal, other faculty, the students, and the students' families prior to using the procedure.

Teachers also need to be mindful that punishment can be upsetting to some children; therefore, it can add to a problem, rather than stopping it. When planning consequences, teachers need to consider whether the child's potential for reacting in anger is worth the consequence. Some children respond to limits as though they were criticism and they become angry. In effect, they use their anger to ward off further criticism. A teacher may decide that the more important lesson is teaching the child that his anger does not control others and that the child can be corrected and still be perceived as good. With another child, the teacher may feel that confrontation is undesirable; consequently, another approach may be used.

Finally, as Braaten et al. note, "no use of punishers is appropriate in the absence of a comprehensive plan for teaching and reinforcing desired behaviors" (1988, p. 80). Whenever punishment is used, teachers should carefully plan how to teach desirable substitute behaviors and they should monitor children's response to the punishment. Punishers, such as time-out, can serve as negative reinforcers to teachers. The teacher removes the noxious child from the classroom. Because she feels relief, she may perceive the intervention as helping, even though the child's inappropriate behavior may not be decreasing. In effect, removal of the child is reinforcing the teacher to use time-out whether or not it helps the student. Epanchin et al. (1988) reported this happening with a few students when the teachers were not regularly monitoring students' time-outs. Because of this potential, it is essential that teachers maintain accurate and complete documentation of the use of time-out and that the time-out data be carefully monitored to ensure that time-out is having the desired effect on the child.

Group-Oriented Rewards and Punishments

Teachers often find that focusing on individual students when establishing a reward-punishment system is too complex. Keeping track of several individual students can be cumbersome and, more importantly, not effective, often because peer reinforcement is more influential than teacher-administered consequences. An alternative approach is the use of group-oriented systems. Salend (1987) describes several such approaches:

1. Hero Method—One child earns points for the entire group by meeting his individual behavioral goals. Since the group reward is dependent upon the success of the individual child, group members tend to help the individual child behave appropriately (Patterson, 1965).
2. Group-Response Cost System—The group is given a set number of tokens, and each time a group member misbehaves a token is removed. At the end of the specified period of time, if a predetermined number of tokens remain, the entire group is rewarded (Salend & Kovalich, 1981; Salend & Lamb, 1986).
3. Good Behavior Game—(Barrish, Saunders, & Wolf, 1969) The group is divided into teams and each team works to keep its total number of points under the specified criterion. Rewards are given to all team members on teams that meet criterion. For example if the criterion was no more than 5 points, B team would not receive the reward, but teams A and C would.
4. Group Time-Out Ribbon—A time-out ribbon is placed on a board and as long as the group is behaving in accord with teacher expectations, the group can receive rewards, but if an individual student misbehaves, the ribbon is removed for a predetermined period of time and the group is unable to receive rewards during the time the ribbon is off the board (Salend & Gordon, 1987).
5. Peer Mediated Extinction—Peers are rewarded for not reinforcing another student's inappropriate behavior. When this approach is used, Salend suggests that teachers explain to the peers that the behavior may get worse before it improves (Salend & Meddaugh, 1985).

While each of these techniques has been demonstrated to be effective in helping control inappropriate behaviors, teachers need to monitor them carefully. Occasionally, groups will respond to these techniques by scapegoating one child or by placing excessive and inappropriate pressure on one child, which defeats the purpose of these approaches.

Self-Monitoring

Teaching students to monitor their own behavior is an excellent way to teach students to be more independent and self-reliant. A number of studies have successfully taught students to observe and record their own behavior (James, Trap, & Cooper, 1977, Lovitt, 1973; Stevenson & Fantuzzo, 1984; Sugai & Rowe, 1984). Often having a student collect data on his behavior has a "reactive effect" (Alberto & Troutman, 1986), which means the behavior changes in the desired direction as a function of the self-recording. These changes may dissipate over time unless other self-management procedures are employed, such as self-reinforcement.

When teaching students to self-monitor, the following strategies are recommended:

1. Define the target behavior and teach the student the definition of the target behavior.
2. Select a system for collecting data and teach the student how to collect the data.
3. Both student and teacher (or some other adult) collect and compare data for a few observations.
4. Once the teacher is satisfied that the student understands the system and is collecting data appropriately, the student self-records independently.

Another approach to students' use of self-recording is seen when teachers encourage students to move from teacher-collected data to student-collected data as part of the progression towards greater independence. Students who consistently stay at the top level in a level system are likely candidates for self-monitoring.

MAINTAINING A PREVENTIVE BEHAVIOR MANAGEMENT SYSTEM

To maintain a preventive behavior management system, teachers need to continuously communicate expectations and to use the behavior management systems that they have planned. Without continuous use and refinement, systems are ineffective. Teachers who use their system effectively teach it all year.

At the beginning of the year when children first come into the classroom, effective teachers spend time teaching children what is expected of them. Anderson, Evertson, & Emmer (1980) and Emmer, Evertson, & Anderson (1980) studied how effective teachers started the school year and found that they spent a great deal of classroom time in the early weeks introducing rules and procedures. Room arrangement, materials storage, and other physical aspects that had been prepared in advance were taught. On the first day of school, these teachers attended to student concerns about the teacher and classmates, the daily schedule, where to put personal belongings, and when and where to go to lunch, the bathroom, and to get a drink of water. The information was gradually presented to the students so they could understand it. The tone of the classroom was one of teaching, not controlling. Key procedures and routines were taught to students during more or less formal lessons, and prior to implementing activities students were reminded of what the teacher expected.

From the first of the year, effective teachers maintained control of their classrooms, not by criticizing and/or threatening, but rather by monitoring and following through with expectations about what children should be doing. Reminders such as "You're not earning your points. You need to be finishing this page" are usually more effective than "Stop daydreaming." Such responses teach the children what to do, rather than only what not to do. Responses to failure should be instructive corrections, not criticism.

Brophy and Evertson (1978) suggest that the amount of time teachers must devote to teaching expectations varies in relation to the developmental level of the students. For example, young primary children (K–grade 2 or 3) tend to be compliant and eager to please their teachers, but they need to be socialized into the student role. They require a great deal of formal instruction, not only in rules and expectations, but in classroom procedures and routines. Teachers of children in this stage need to plan a number of repetitious activities that help children learn how to behave like students.

Elementary age students (grades 2–3 through grades 5–6) have learned most of what they need to know about school rules and routines, and most remain oriented toward obeying and pleasing their teachers. Consequently, less time needs to be devoted to classroom management at the beginning of the year, and less cuing, reminding, and instructing are required thereafter.

Early adolescents (grades 5–6 through 9–10) become less oriented toward pleasing teachers and more oriented toward pleasing peers. Many become resentful or at least questioning of authority, and disruptions due to attention seeking, humorous remarks, and adolescent horseplay become common. Classroom management once again becomes more time-consuming, but in contrast to stage one, the task facing teachers is not so much one of instructing willing but ignorant students about what to do as it is motivating or controlling students who know what to do but are not always willing to do it. Also, individual counseling becomes more prominent, as the relative quiet and stability that most students show in the middle grades give way to the adjustment problems of adolescence. Thus, in planning for children in this stage, teachers need behavior management systems that detail expectations and remove the teacher from the power struggles. When a good behavior management system is in place, the teacher's role is to enforce the system. On-the-spot reactions that can appear personal are minimized.

High school students (after grades 9–10) become more personally settled and more oriented toward academic learning again. As in Stage two, classroom management requires less teacher time and trouble, and the classroom takes on a more businesslike, academic focus.

Teaching the system at the beginning of the year is not sufficient, however. Teachers must use it continuously. Reminding a student of the system and of consequences that will occur depending upon student behavior helps to reinforce a system and make it effective. Teaching a system without using it continuously is akin to telling students, "Do what I say, not what I do."

INDIVIDUALIZATION

Individualization is the antithesis of indifference. It means that teachers accommodate, within reason, individual needs when planning programs, rather than forcing the child to fit program structure. It means attending to each child and being sensitive to each child's individual needs. It does not mean implementing an individual program for each child in the classroom. In the context of behavior management, individualization means ensuring that each child in the classroom is enabled to behave appropriately most of the time.

For most emotionally handicapped children, implementing an organized and structured educational program will prevent many classroom problems from occurring, but for some children more is needed. No matter how well a teacher plans to prevent problems and no matter how effectively the rewards system is used, behavioral outbursts and disruptions will occur. With some children the disruptions will be infrequent, and are but manifestations of "down" times that all children have.

For other children, such outbursts should be interpreted as indications of a need—a plea for help and a statement that the current program is not sufficient or appropriate. Children who are not successful in the highly structured, organized special education classroom need additional and even more individualized planning in order to be successful.

As has been pointed out repeatedly in this book, emotionally handicapped children frequently display behaviors which threaten, anger, discourage, and shock teachers. Teachers and administrators sometimes conclude that the child is incorrectly placed or that he is "untreatable." Rather than individualizing for the child's unique needs, the teacher may refer him for more restrictive services. In some instances such a referral may be appropriate, but often it reflects a failure to effectively individualize. If teachers view problematic episodes as opportunities to learn what the child needs, they will probably be successful in planning for the child's individual needs and the child is likely to learn new values and ways of behaving.

Individualized plans are developed on the basis of diagnostic information. The teacher needs to answer the question, Why is the child having difficulty? Two sources of information that can be particularly informative are classroom observations and the child's own statements. A-B-C observations conducted by the teacher in the classroom or critical incident records can be helpful approaches to identifying where and when the problems seem to occur most frequently. For example, if the observation reveals that problems occur most often during transitions from one activity to another, it may be hypothesized that the child needs even more structure to accomplish the daily changes in activities and settings. If, on the other hand, the child reports concerns about a bully picking on him during recess, the teacher may hypothesize that the child needs to learn how to deal with bullies and the bully needs to be watched and dealt with as well. Based on the hypothesis, intervention plans are generated, implemented, and evaluated, using the child's response to treatment as the criterion of success.

Contracting

One procedure that is frequently used for individualizing an educational program is contingency contracting. As the name implies, this is a procedure that involves an agreement, usually written, between two or more parties. The contract may involve the teacher, student, a group of students, a class, parents, or other significant persons. In the contract, expectations are detailed for all parties. The teacher specifies what she will do, the student specifies what he will do, and other parties specify their responsibilities. Additionally, the consequences for completing the contract are detailed. The following guidelines have been recommended for writing classroom contracts (Homme, Csanyi, Gonzales, & Rechs, 1970):

1. Contracts should specify the target behavior or level of achievement/competence.
2. They should be used systematically as an integral part of the classroom.
3. Rewards should be immediate, once the conditions are met.
4. Rewards should provide for frequent reinforcers in small amounts that approximate target behaviors.
5. Contracts should make the rewards consistent with the terms on the contract.
6. The contract should be negotiated and mutually agreed upon by all parties.
7. Contracts should be clear, honest, positive, and fair to both parties.
8. Accomplishments, not compliance, should be the focus of a contract.

Contracts facilitate flexible programming for individual students. There are concrete, specific means of specifying expectations and inviting cooperation and support.

DEALING WITH UNACCEPTABLE BEHAVIOR

There are days when it seems that no matter what a teacher does, emotionally handicapped children have difficulty. Thus, programs must be prepared to handle emotional outbursts and physical aggression. Although such outbursts may be indicative of an inappropriate program, teachers, teaching assistants, and other personnel need a system in place so they can intervene at the moment aggression begins. They need to know what to do when a child becomes physically aggressive or destructive. If the teacher waits until a child behaves unacceptably to decide what the consequences will be, she is in a reactive position and may find she is too punitive or too indecisive. Anger at the child for behaving as he did or guilt about being too punitive may impair the teacher's decision-making skills.

When a student has an outburst that disrupts the class or hurts himself or other children, the teacher needs to intervene quickly and decisively. Other students are often frightened by such outbursts and find comfort when the teacher is clearly in charge. Furthermore, when the teacher is not clearly in charge, the setting is conducive to classroom bullies victimizing vulnerable children. Victims need protection from intimidation by bullies, and bullies need help in controlling their aggression.

Removal from the Classroom

One response to physical aggression is removal from the classroom, often called exclusionary time-out. This provides the misbehaving child with privacy, and it protects the other students. How the child is removed and what happens after the child is removed are critical issues.

If rules are clearly explained and consistently enforced, children know that physical aggression and destruction lead to removal from the classroom. Furthermore, if the classroom is a positive place for students and if students have a positive relationship with the teacher, removal from the classroom is an undesirable consequence. Therefore, the success of removal from the classroom depends upon students wanting to be in the classroom, trusting the teacher to be fair and reasonable, and knowing that their actions were clearly and unequivocally in violation of expectations. When these conditions exist, students typically leave when asked and return more calmly in a relatively short period of time.

Procedures for Using Time-Out.   When time-out rooms are available to a teacher, plans for using time-out should be detailed in the child's individual treatment and educational plan. These plans should be approved by the families and principal before a child is sent to time-out. In the plan, the following parameters should be detailed.

Reason/behavior that requires time-out. Time-out should be used only when the child exhibits specific target behaviors such as hitting another child. The practice of using time-out for an unspecified variety of inappropriate behaviors is likely to dilute the effectiveness of the procedure (Brantner & Doherty, 1983).

Use of warnings. With some children, it is effective to give a warning when they first begin to misbehave. It also protects the child's due process rights by providing a reminder that a punishment will be used if he does not change his behavior (Yell, 1990). Thus, it is ethically and legally preferable to warn a child before sending him to time-out. However, some children may use the warning as an opportunity to argue or may perceive it as nagging attention; thus, data should be taken on the effects of warnings and alternatives selected when the data indicate that warnings are not effective.

Providing explanations. Teachers must decide whether the child needs an explanation for why he is being sent to time-out or whether a simple directive will be issued. For example, when using a directive, a teacher might simply say, "Howard, go to time-out." An explanation might be, "Howard, you hit Jimmy. Hitting is not allowed. You must go to time-out for 2 minutes."

Some children use such an occasion to argue; hence, directives are more appropriate. Other children appear to need an explanation of what they did and why they are being sent to time-out. For these children, brief explanations are appropriate. MacDonough and Forehand (1973) found that brief explanations neither helped nor hindered effectiveness; thus, decisions should be made on the basis of data gathered about an individual child.

Time spent in time-out. Most authorities agree that short periods of time spent in time-out are most effective, unless the child has a history of long time-outs (Harris, 1985). Children are typically placed in time-out for a short period of time (preferably 1–5 minutes). Release from time-out is contingent upon appropriate behavior.

Requirements for release. Requirements for release should be determined prior to putting a child in time-out, and these expectations should be conveyed to the child. A typical requirement for release is a short period (1–5 minutes) of appropriate behavior prior to release (Brantner & Doherty, 1983).

Discussion after release. Some children use the time in time-out to calm down. When they first leave the room, they are more receptive than at other times to discussions about what they did and why they did it. With these children, it is appropriate to schedule time to discuss the incident after the child leaves the time-out room. With other children, such discussion may simply reinforce the misbehavior. The child may want attention so much that it is worth it to go to time-out.

When Children Refuse to Leave the Classroom.

Occasionally children refuse to leave when they are sent to time-out. When this happens, teachers have several options. They may overpower the child and physically remove him, or they may try verbal tactics. Successful management of such situations requires knowledge of the individual child.

Physical removal provides the class and the child with a model of power, which may not be what the teacher wants to convey. Conversely, seeing that the teacher can deal with a disruptive, aggressive child may comfort some children, even the misbehaving child. It will be frightening to all, however, if the teacher struggles with the child but cannot successfully get him out of the room. Thus, this strategy should not be tried unless the teacher is confident she can remove the child without hurting the child or herself.

An alternative to physical removal is verbally reminding the child that he is making a decision not to cooperate. The teacher should also remind the child of the particular consequences of not cooperating (e.g., losing points and privileges). A number of problem-solving strategies are described in Chapter 14. Often such verbal reminders help children move on their own.

Teachers of children who are occasionally assaultive should have systems established that access help when it is needed. If a child refuses to leave a classroom and continues to behave unacceptably (destroying property, threatening others, hurting others, etc.), teachers must have a preestablished method for obtaining help, such as a buzzer to the office. With such a system, if a child refuses to leave and the teacher doubts her ability to get the child out of the room, a call for help is necessary. Figure 13.1 lists tasks to follow when implementing time-out.

Court Rulings. Courts have restricted the use of time-out in public and private institutions. In *Wyatt v. Stickney* (1972), it was mandated that students should not be put in locked rooms. In *Rogers v. Okin* (1986) and *Wyatt v. Stickney* (1972), it was ruled that children in time-out should be constantly supervised. In *Morales v. Turman* (1974), it was determined that time-out should be used for brief periods—those lasting less than 50 minutes.

Schools, however, have been given wide latitude in determining what is acceptable educational practice (Center, 1989; Yell, 1990). In *Cole v. Greenfield-Central Community Schools* (1966), the court ruled that contingent observation was a "relatively innocuous" disciplinary technique and that its use was warranted by the plaintiff's behavioral problems. In *Dickens v. Johnson County Board of Education* (1987), the court ruled that exclusionary time-out

Step	Task	Date Completed	Teacher's Initials
1.	Try less aversive techniques and document results.	_____	_____
2.	Operationally define disruptive behaviors.	_____	_____
3.	Record baseline on target behaviors.	_____	_____
4.	Consider present levels of reinforcement (strengthen if necessary).	_____	_____
5.	Decide on time-out procedure to be used.	_____	_____
6.	Decide on time-out area.	_____	_____
7.	Decide on length of time-out.	_____	_____
8.	Decide on command to be used to place child in time-out.	_____	_____
9.	Set specific criteria that will signal discontinuance of time-out.	_____	_____
10.	Set dates for formal review of the time-out procedure.	_____	_____
11.	Specify back-up procedures for typical time-out problems.	_____	_____
12.	Write up the entire procedure.	_____	_____
13.	Have the procedure reviewed by peers and supervisors.	_____	_____
14.	Secure parental/guardian approval and include the written program in the child's IEP.	_____	_____
15.	Explain procedure to the student and class (if appropriate).	_____	_____
16.	Implement the procedure, take data, and review progress daily.	_____	_____
17.	Formally review procedure as indicated.	_____	_____
18.	Modify the procedure as needed.	_____	_____
19.	Record results for future teachers/programs.	_____	_____

FIGURE 13.1

Time-Out Implementation Checklist (From "The Use and Abuse of Using the Timeout Procedure for Disruptive Pupils" by T. H. Powell and I. Q. Powell, 1982, *The Pointer,* *26*(2), p. 21. Copyright 1982 by *The Pointer.* Reprinted by permission.)

(a large, three-sided refrigerator box that had an open top and a desk placed inside the box) was reasonable in light of the offenses. Furthermore, the court ruled that this procedure was particularly appropriate for handicapped children because they would not be denied an appropriate education. In *Hayes v. Unified School District No. 377* (1987), the court ruled that seclusionary time-out in a time-out room was used to ensure the safety of other students and to teach appropriate behavior to the acting-out student.

A number of states and many local school districts have instituted their own regulations for the use of time-out, and these regulations tend to be more restrictive than those of the courts. Common to most of these policies are the following guidelines for seclusionary timeout (Gast and Nelson, 1977, p. 464):

The time-out room should

- Be at least 6 ft. × 6 ft. in size.
- Be properly lighted (preferably recessed lights with the switch outside the room.
- Be properly ventilated.
- Be free of objects and fixtures with which a child could harm himself.
- Provide a means by which an adult can continuously monitor—visually and aurally—the student's behavior.
- Not be locked—a latch on the door should be used only as needed and only with careful monitoring.

Many states and local school districts also require that time-out rooms be constructed from nonflammable materials in order to meet fire regulations and insurance requirements.

Records should be carefully kept when time-out is used. According to Gast and Nelson, the records should include

- The student's name
- The episode resulting in the student's placement in time-out (behavior, activity, other students involved, staff person, etc.)
- Time of day the student was placed in time-out
- Time of day the student was released from time-out
- The total time in time-out
- The type of time-out (e.g., conditions necessary for release)
- The student's behavior while in time-out (1977, pp. 464–65)

The importance of record keeping cannot be emphasized enough for both ethical and legal reasons. Nelson and Stevens (1983) identified failure to evaluate records as a common abuse in many applied settings. Unless careful records are kept and analyzed, teachers could be placed in tenuous positions. Although the courts have generally ruled in favor of schools, inadequate documentation could jeopardize a teacher's claim that the procedure was appropriate. Yell (1990) cautions that decisions made in courts other than the Supreme Court are not nationally binding; thus, teachers must be informed about local regulations.

Effectiveness of Time-Out.   Numerous studies have demonstrated time-out to be an effective procedure if the classroom or setting from which the child is sent is a rewarding place for the child. If the child is content to be out of the setting, however, it is unlikely that the procedure will be effective.

When time-out rooms are readily available, they can be overused by adults (Garrison, 1984). If programs are not carefully monitored, staff can slip into a practice of sending a child to time-out for a number of transgressions. When time-out becomes the institutionalized response to problematic behavior, it loses its effectiveness for many children. Therefore, it should be used only for specific, predetermined behaviors, and it should be carefully monitored and charted. Furthermore, if a child's behavior is not improving, the program should be reexamined and other interventions planned.

Irwin (1987) questioned the necessity of time-out rooms on psychiatric impatient wards, a setting in which they have been commonly used. He suggested that a structured, predictable, consistent milieu where the ratio of adults to children is high may prevent the necessity of seclusionary rooms. Epanchin et al. (1988) found that when teachers were taught what to do instead of placing children in time-out, teachers' use of time-out decreased.

Manual Restraint

Occasionally, behavior-disordered children lose control and need to be physically restrained. Schloss and Smith (1987) define physical restraint as "the direct restriction of a student's movements by applying force to his or her limbs, head, or body" (p. 207). It typically is not a punishment. Rather, it is a means of preventing the child from hurting himself or others. While there are mechanical restraints (e.g., seat belts or harnesses), such devices are rarely used in classrooms for emotionally disturbed children. However, physical restraint is used when a child loses control, hits or hurts another child, and does not regain control of himself. Teachers should use physical restraint only when they are confident that they will be able to remove the child from the immediate setting and prevent further aggressiveness.

Several systems have been developed that teach staff how to physically restrain a child. Most of these systems emphasize the importance first of assessing a situation, then intervening only if the teacher has backup help or is confident that she can manage the child without hurting herself or the child. Generally, the physical restraint training involves learning ways to deflect hits and kicks, release hair pulls or bites, hold children's arms and legs so that they can no longer hit or kick, and carry a child to another location, if necessary.

Teachers working in self-contained classrooms or in residential treatment centers may wish to obtain training in one of these systems (see Harvey & Schepers, 1977; Samuels & Moriarty, 1975; Upchurch, Ham, Daniels, McGhee, & Burnett, 1980). Residential treatment centers and mental health facilities often provide such training for their staff and allow teachers from the public schools to participate in the training, if the teachers express an interest and need. The training involves practicing the holds until proficiency is reached. It should be emphasized that reading about physical restraints in no way prepares teachers to use the procedures. Teachers who plan to use physical restraint should participate in training sessions.

Whenever a child loses control and requires physical intervention, the teacher should review the situation as soon as she is calm and has a minute for reflection. Cues for what upsets an individual child need to be identified. In the future, the teacher can either avoid such situations or anticipate them and thus be prepared to deal with the resulting problems. If teachers use crises as opportunities to learn more about the child, future problems can be avoided or at least faced with knowledge. Rather than viewing these times as failures, teachers need to be prepared to view and use crises as opportunities for teaching and learning.

Expulsion and Suspension

One response to assaultive, destructive behavior is the use of expulsion or suspension. Yell (1989) summarized a number of court cases involving suspension and expulsion of handicapped students. He proposed a model for making disciplinary decisions about handicapped children in which three basic questions are addressed by a team of specialized persons (see Figure 13.2). He maintained that parents should always be involved and that unilateral decisions by persons such as a principal or school board member should never be allowed.

Cullinan (1986) also developed a set of guidelines based upon a review of court cases. His guidelines are similar to Yell's. Cullinan recommended the following:

1. Immediate but temporary suspension may be used when a student is presenting a substantial disruption or danger in the educational setting.
2. Immediate but temporary suspension also may be used as a consequence to less threatening behaviors when ordinary due process procedures are followed.
3. When a handicapped student is excluded for more than 10 days per year, the placement team should schedule a review of the placement, notify the family of the review, and insure the family's right to an impartial hearing and appeal.
4. When a handicapped student is excluded from school, another educational placement must be provided.
5. Disciplinary school exclusion is not appropriate for handicapped children when the misbehavior is related to the student's handicapping condition.

Restrictions on the practice of suspending or expelling emotionally handicapped students from school have spawned considerable controversy. The debate centers around several fundamental questions about fairness and equitable treatment of handicapped children. Critics charge that we are creating a dual system of discipline because an emotionally handicapped student may not be expelled for an act of misconduct that would automatically result in the expulsion

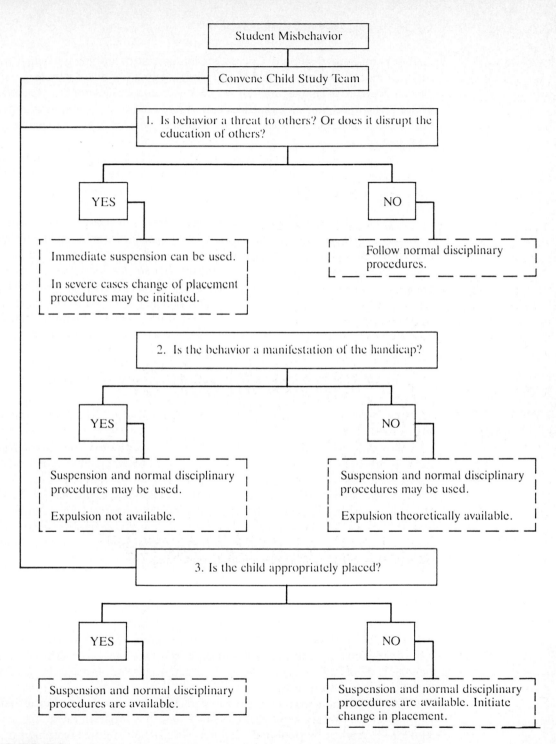

FIGURE 13.2
Policy Models for the Discipline of Handicapped Students (From "Honig v. Doe: The Suspension and Expulsion of Handicapped Students" by M. L. Yell, 1989, *Exceptional Children, 56*(1), p. 68.)

of a nonhandicapped student. Critics also charge that determining whether the student's misconduct was related to the handicapping condition is both a very difficult decision to make and an additional bureaucratic burden. Cullinan (1986) pointed out that such practices may impede the process of normalization by shielding the emotionally handicapped student from ordinary consequences of misbehavior.

The intent of the restrictions was to insure emotionally handicapped students access to treatment designed to correct their handicapping condition. Advocates maintain that these restrictions are needed to protect the rights of the handicapped.

Another alternative to expulsion and suspension is the practice of in-school suspension. This practice removes the offending student from his assigned class and places him in the in-school suspension room for a specified period of time, ranging from a few hours to days or weeks. There are many variations for managing this practice, some of which are tied to level systems. Most involve the student losing privileges and freedom, but still being required to complete assignments. Often a crisis teacher is available to help the student with academics and to discuss with the student his transgression and future possible reactions that might be more socially acceptable.

SUMMARIES

Behavior management is a complex process that involves careful orchestration of the classroom, explicit teaching of expectations, constant monitoring and evaluation of student progress and behavior, and a readiness to deal with crises if and when they arise. Teachers who focus on academic achievement when setting up a behavior management system appear to be more successful than teachers who focus only on behavioral control. Additionally, positive, proactive systems are more effective than reactive, punitive systems. To maintain a proactive stance, teachers need to monitor themselves and guard against their reacting to their students' hostility and oppositionalism. Setting up clearly articulated systems for reinforcing and punishing students early in the year helps teachers be consistent and nonpunitive, if the teacher uses the system regularly.

Teachers also need to consider how to help students learn skills that will transfer to mainstream settings. One of the great challenges facing special education is how to support and promote more movement of special students into mainstream settings. Thus, special education teachers need to carefully assess the skills students will need in mainstream settings and plan strategies for helping students acquire those skills.

Finally, teachers need to be prepared to deal with outbursts and view them as opportunities to help or as indicators of a need for program revision, not as situations that must be punished. Children with behavioral and learning problems will have difficult days, and teachers need to use these as opportunities rather than as failures for the child.

DISCUSSION QUESTIONS

1. Observe students in regular education classrooms. Then observe students in classrooms for the emotionally disturbed. What differences did you notice in the structure of the classrooms and in the teachers' expectations?
2. Think about several recent disruptions that you have observed in a classroom. Can you think of ways that these disruptions could have been prevented?
3. How do highly structured special education classrooms with explicit systems for rewards and punishers prepare students for mainstream settings?
4. Think of incidents when a child has been sent to time-out. What interventions could have been tried earlier to prevent the child from being sent to time-out?
5. Do you believe that isolating a child in a time-out or seclusion room is acceptable? Why or why not?
6. Bobby, a 15-year-old boy who has been in a self-contained classroom for emotionally disturbed students for 4 years, is being gradually mainstreamed into a regular, remedial program. He has voiced concerns to his special education teacher about his ability to meet the expectations of the program he is entering. The teacher repeatedly has assured Bobby that he is ready because he has made significant academic and behavioral gains. Then one day he does poorly on an assignment in the special education class and has a temper tantrum, much like those he had when he first entered the special education program. He shoved his desk to the side, hitting and hurting a student sitting beside him. He also threw his hard-cover book at his teacher, barely missing her head. The standing rule in his school is a 3-day suspension for hurting a student or teacher. Should Bobby be suspended? Why or why not? How should this episode be handled? What issues should be considered?

REFERENCES

Alberto, P. A., & Troutman, A. C. (1986). *Applied behavior analysis* (2nd ed.). Columbus, OH: Merrill.

Anderson, L., Evertson, C., & Emmer, E. (1980). Dimensions in classroom management derived from recent research. *Journal of Curriculum Studies*, 12, 343–356.

Ayllon, T. (1975). The elimination of discipline problems through a combined school-home motivational system. *Behavior Therapy*, 6, 616–626.

Ayllon, T., & Roberts, M. D. (1974). Eliminating discipline problems by strengthening academic performance. *Journal of Applied Behavior Analysis*, 7, 71–76.

Barrish, H. H., Saunders, M., & Wolf, M. M. (1969). Good behavior game: Effects on individual contingencies for group consequences on disruptive behavior in a classroom. *Journal of Applied Behavior Analysis*, 2, 119–124.

Bauer, A. M., & Shea, T. M. (1988). Structuring classrooms through levels systems. *Focus on Exceptional Children*, 21(3), 1–12.

Bauer, A. M., Shea, T. M., & Keppler, R. (1986). Levels systems: A framework for the individualization of behavior management. *Behavioral Disorders*, 12, 28–35.

Blankenship, C. S. (1986). Managing pupil behaviors during instruction. *Teaching Exceptional Children, 19,* 52–53.

Braaten, S. (1979). The Madison School Program: Programming for secondary severely emotionally disturbed youth. *Behavioral Disorders, 4,* 153–162.

Braaten, S., Simpson, R., Rosell, J., Reilly T. (1988). Using punishment with exceptional children: A dilemma for educators. *Teaching Exceptional Children, 20*(2), 79–81.

Brantner, J. P., & Doherty, M. A. (1983). A review of timeout: A conceptual and methodological analysis. In S. Axelrod & J. Apsche (Eds.), *The effects of punishment on human behavior* (pp. 87–132). New York: Academic Press.

Brophy, J., & Evertson, C. (1978). Context variables in teaching. *Educational Psychologist, 12,* 310–316.

Cangelosi, J. S. (1988). *Classroom management strategies: Gaining and maintaining students' cooperation.* New York: Longman.

Carnine, D. (1976). Effects of two teacher presentation rates on off-task behavior, answering correctly, and participation. *Journal of Applied Behavior Analysis, 9,* 199–206.

Center, D. B. (1989). Social maladjustment: Definition, identification, and programming. *Focus on Exceptional Children, 22* (1), 1–12.

Cherniss, C. (1980). *Staff burnout: Job stress in the human services.* Beverly Hills: Sage.

Cole v. Greenfield-Central Community Schools, 657 F. Supp. 56 (S. D. Ind. 1986).

Cooper, J. O., Heron, T. E., & Heward, W. L. (1987). *Applied behavior analysis.* Columbus, OH: Merrill.

Cullinan, D. (1986). Disciplinary exclusion and the behaviorally disordered. *The Pointer, 30,* 11–13.

DeLuke, S. V., & Knoblock, P. (1987). Teacher behavior as preventive discipline. *Teaching Exceptional Children, 19,* 18–24.

Dickens v. Johnson County Board of Education, 661 F. Supp. 155 (E. D. Tenn. 1987).

Dickerson, E. A., & Creedon, C. G. (1981). Self-selection of standards by children: The relative effectiveness of pupil-selected and teacher-selected standards of performance. *Journal of Applied Behavior Analysis, 14,* 425–433.

Emmer, E., Evertson, C., & Anderson, L. (1980). Effective management at the beginning of the school year. *Elementary School Journal, 80,* 219–231.

Epanchin, B. C., Rennells, M. S., Rhodes, W. R., Simmers, D., & Wasik, B. H. (1988). *A case study of the modification of the use of time-out in a residential treatment program.* Unpublished manuscript. Available from the senior author, Department of Special Education, University of South Florida, Tampa, FL.

Evans, G., & Lovell, B. (1979). Design modification in an open school. *Journal of Educational Psychology, 71,* 41–49.

Felixbrod, J., & O'Leary, K. (1974). Self-determination of academic standards by children: Toward freedom from external control. *Journal of Educational Psychology, 66*, 845–850.

Floyd, N. (1985). "Pick on somebody your own size!": Controlling victimization. *Pointer, 29* (2), 9–17.

Garrison, W. (1984). Aggressive behavior, seclusion and physical restraint in an inpatient child population. *Journal of American Academy of Child Psychiatry, 23*, 448–452.

Gast, D. L., & Nelson, C. M. (1977). Legal and ethical considerations for the use of timeout in special education settings. *The Journal of Special Education, 11*, 457–467.

Gillet, P. (1987). Discipline-related teacher stress. *Teaching Exceptional Children, 19*, 62–65.

Greenwood, C. R., Delquadri, J. C., & Hall, R. V. (1984). Opportunity to respond and student academic performance. In W. L. Heward, T. E. Heron, D. S. Hill, & J. Trays-Porter (Eds.), *Focus on behavior analysis in education.* Columbus, OH: Merrill.

Grosenick, J., George, N. L., & George, M. P. (1988). The availability of program descriptions among programs for seriously emotionally disturbed students. *Behavioral Disorders, 13*, 108–115.

Harris, K. R. (1985). Definitional, parametric, and procedural considerations in timeout interventions and research. *Exceptional Children, 51*, 279–288.

Harvey, E., & Schepers, J. (1977). Physical contact techniques and defensive holds for use with aggressive retarded adults. *Mental Retardation, 15*(5), 29–31.

Hayes v. Unified School District No. 377, 669 F. Supp. 1519 (D. Kan. 1987).

Hewett, F. M., & Taylor F. D. (1980). *The emotionally disturbed child in the classroom: The orchestration of success* (2nd ed.). Boston: Allyn & Bacon.

Hoefler, S., & Bornstein, P. (1975). Achievement Place: An evaluative review. *Criminal Justice and Behavior, 2*, 146–168.

Homme, L., Csanyi, A. P., Gonzales, M. A., & Rechs, J. R. (1970). *How to use contingency contracting in the classroom.* Champaign, IL: Research Press.

Horner, R. H., Dunlap, G., Koegel, R. L., Carr, E. G., Sailor, W., Anderson, J., Albin, R. W., & O'Neill, R. E. (in press). *Toward a technology of "nonaversive" behavioral support.*

Irwin, M. (1987). Are seclusion rooms needed on child psychiatric units? *Journal of the American Orthopsychiatric Association, 57*, 125–126.

James, J. C., Trap, J., & Cooper, J. O. (1977). Students' self-recording of manuscript letter strokes. *Journal of Applied Behavior Analysis, 10*, 509–514.

Kavale, K., & Hirshoren, A. (1980). Public school and teacher training programs for behaviorally disordered children: Are they compatible? *Behavioral Disorders, 5*, 151–156.

Kuergeleis, B., Deutchman, L., & Paine, S. (1980). Effects of explicit timings on students' transitions. Eugene, OR: Direct Instruction Follow Through Project, University of Oregon.

Kounin, J. (1970). *Discipline and group management in classrooms.* New York: Holt, Rinehart & Winston.

Lahey, B. (1977). An evaluation of daily report cards with minimal teacher and parent contacts as an efficient method of classroom intervention. *Behavior Modification, 1,* 381–394.

Lovitt, T. C. (1973). Self-management projects with children with behavioral disabilities. *Journal of Learning Disabilities, 6,* 138–150.

MacDonough, T. S., & Forehand, R. (1973). Response-contingent time out: Important parameters in behavior modification with children. *Journal of Behavior Therapy and Experimental Psychiatry, 4,* 231–236.

Martens, B. K., Muir, K. A., & Meller, P. J. (1988). Rewards common to the classroom setting: A comparison of regular and self-contained room student ratings. *Behavioral Disorders, 13,* 169–174.

Mastropieri, M. A., Jenne, T., & Scruggs, T. E. (1988). A level system for managing problem behaviors in a high school resource program. *Behavioral Disorders, 13,* 202–208.

Miller, A. (1980). *After the fall.* New York: Penguin.

Morales v. Turman, 364 F. Supp. 166 (E.D. Texas 1973).

Morgan, D. P., & Jenson, W. R. (1988). *Teaching behaviorally disordered students: Preferred practices.* Columbus, OH: Merrill.

Morse, W. C. (1987). Introduction to special issue on preventive discipline in special education. *Teaching Exceptional Children, 19,* 4–6.

Nash, B. (1981). The effects of classroom spatial organization on four- and five-year-old children's learning. *British Journal of Educational Psychology, 51,* 144–155.

Nelson, C. M., & Stevens, K. B. (1983). Time-out revisited: Guidelines for its use in special education. *Exceptional Education Quarterly, 3,* 56–67.

Paine, S. C., Radicchi, J., Rossellini, L. C., Deutchman, L., & Darch, C. B. (1983). *Structuring your classroom for academic success.* Champaign, IL: Research Press.

Patterson, G. R. (1965). An application of conditioning techniques to the control of a hyperactive child. In L. P. Ulman & L. Krasner (Eds.), *Case studies in behavior modification* (pp. 370–375). New York: Holt, Rinehart & Winston.

Phillips, E. L., Phillips, E. A., Fixen, D. L., & Wolf, M. M. (1973). Achievement Place: Development of the elected manager system. *Journal of Applied Behavior Analysis, 6,* 541–561.

Powell, T. H., & Powell, I. Q. (1982). The use and abuse of using the timeout procedure for disruptive pupils. *The Pointer, 26*(2), 18–22.

Rhodes, W. R. (1985). *The efficacy of instructional routines in reducing the duration of transitions for behaviorally disordered students in a residential treatment center.* Unpublished dissertation, University of North Carolina at Chapel Hill.

Rinne, Carl. (1984). Attention: The fundamentals of classroom control. Columbus, OH: Merrill.

Rogers v. Okin, 638 F. Supp. 934 (D. Mass. 1986).

Sabatino, D. A. (1987). Preventive discipline as a practice in special education. *Teaching Exceptional Children, 19*, 8–11.

Salend, S. (1987). Group-oriented behavior management strategies. *Teaching Exceptional Children, 20*, 53–55.

Salend, S. J., & Gordon, B. (1987). A group-oriented timeout ribbon procedure. *Behavioral Disorders, 12*, 131–137.

Salend, S. J., & Kovalich, B. (1981). A group response-cost system mediated by free tokens: An alternative to token reinforcement in the classroom. *American Journal of Mental Deficiency, 86*, 184–187.

Salend, S. J., & Lamb, E. M. (1986). The effectiveness of a group-managed interdependent contingency system. *Learning Disabilities Quarterly, 9*, 268–274.

Salend, S. J., & Meddaugh, D. (1985). Using a peer-mediated extinction procedure to decrease obscene language. *The Pointer, 30*, 8–11.

Samuels, M., & Moriartry, P. (1975). CRYCON: The concept of crisis classroom control (a training manual). (Available from Martin Samuels, 142 Pennlear Dr., Monroeville, PA 15146 or (412) 622–4619).

Schloss, P. J., & Smith, M. A. (1987). Guidelines for ethical use of manual restraint in public school settings for behaviorally disordered students. *Behavioral Disorders, 12*, 207–213.

Stainback, W., Stainback, S., Etscheidt, S., & Doud, J. (1986). A nonintrusive intervention for acting-out behavior. *Teaching Exceptional Children, 19*, 38–41.

Stainback, W., Stainback, S., & Froyen, L. (1987). Structuring the classroom to prevent disruptive behaviors. *Teaching Exceptional Children, 19*, 12–16.

Stephens, T. M. (1977). *Directive teaching of children with learning and behavioral handicaps.* Columbus, OH: Merrill.

Stevenson, H. C., & Fantuzzo, J. W. (1984). Application of the "generalization map" to a self-control intervention with school-aged children. *Journal of Applied Behavior Analysis, 17*, 203–212.

Stokes, T. F., & Osnes, P. (1989). An operant pursuit of generalization. *Behavioral Therapy, 20*, 337–355.

Stokes, T. F., & Baur, D. M. (1977). An implicit technology of generalization. *Journal of Applied Behavior Analysis, 10*, 349–367.

Strain, P., & Sainato, D. M. (1987). Preventive discipline in early childhood. *Teaching Exceptional Children, 19*, 26–30.

Sugai, G., & Rowe, P. (1984). The effect of self-recording on out-of-seat behavior of an EMR student. *Education and Training of the Mentally Retarded, 19*, 23–28.

Upchurch, T., Ham, L., Daniels, R., McGhee, M., & Burnett, M. (1980). *A better way: An illustrated guide to protective intervention techniques.* Butner, NC: Murdock Center.

Walker, H. M. (1979). *The acting out child: Coping with classroom disruption.* Boston: Allyn & Bacon.

Wyatt v. Stickney, 344 F. Supp. 373 (M. D. Ala. 1972).

Yell, M. L. (1989). Honig v. Doe: The suspension and expulsion of handicapped students. *Exceptional Children, 56,* 60–69.

Yell, M. L. (1990). The use of corporal punishment, suspension, expulsion, and timeout with behaviorally disordered students in public schools: Legal considerations. *Behavioral Disorders, 15,* 100–109.

Zabel, M. K. (1986). Timeout use with behaviorally disordered students. *Behavioral Disorders, 12,* 15–21.

14
Teaching Social Behavior*

1. Teaching social skills lessons and conducting here-and-now problem-solving discussions can help children become more skillful and successful in social situations.

2. When teaching social skills, teachers need to identify the situations in which a child is having problems and the type of problems the child is having. Children have many different types of social problems, and if teachers are to deal successfully with these problems, they need to know what the specific problems are.

3. Social problems can result from the way in which children perceive their social world, the way they think about solutions to social problems, the behavioral skills children possess, or a combination of any of these three areas.

4. Teachers need to individualize their social skills instruction, not through individual lessons, but through knowledge of individual children's strengths and needs.

5. Language facility is an important factor in children's ability to function effectively in social situations. Many emotionally handicapped children do not use language effectively as a social tool.

6. Teachers need to learn to use counseling techniques in the classroom so that "here-and-now" problems can be used as learning experiences.

7. Teachers should focus their training on behaviors that will help the child survive in less restrictive settings.

---

*This chapter was written by Betty C. Epanchin, University of South Florida.

Here is Edward Bear, coming downstairs now, bump, bump, bump,
on the back of his head, behind Christopher
Robin. It is, as far as he knows, the only way of
coming downstairs, but sometimes he feels that there
really is another way, if only he could stop bumping
for a moment and think of it. And then he feels that
perhaps there isn't.

A. A. Milne, Winnie-the-Pooh

Many emotionally disturbed children engage in self-destructive social behaviors.
Like Edward Bear they sometimes think there is a better way, but they are so
enmeshed in a self-defeating cycle that they see neither how to change nor that
solutions are possible. It is the teacher's task to help these students learn about
productive alternatives. It is also the task of the teacher to help students believe
in themselves and their potential for change. This chapter focuses on two basic
approaches frequently used by teachers to facilitate the development of appropriate social behavior in school—(1) proactive, didactic lessons and (2) on-the-
spot, here-and-now counseling.

PROACTIVE TEACHING APPROACH

Basic Assumptions

Many of the treatment approaches discussed earlier in this book emphasize
changing the environment or the child as solutions to a child's social, emotional,
and behavioral problems. Such approaches assume that the child has the ability
to behave appropriately if environmental and/or emotional barriers are removed. While this often may be the case, it is not always so. Some children do
not have the ability to behave in prosocial, self-enhancing ways. For many
children, it is not enough to help them understand their conflicted feelings, to
reward them for their prosocial behavior, or to provide a safe, accepting environment. They also must be taught how to behave and how to understand their
social world.

One of the tenets accepted by traditional psychodynamic therapists has
been that substitute behavior must be available to the client before one confronts
or interprets a client's defensive approach to dealing with difficult or stressful
situations (Paul, 1973). Stated differently, a child must have the skills to deal with
situations in an alternative way before we can realistically remove the child's
coping behavior, even though the coping strategies are problematic. Likewise,
behavioral therapy has advocated teaching appropriate social behaviors that are
incompatible with the problematic behaviors (Horner, Dunlap, Koegel, Carr,
Sailor, Anderson, Albin, & O'Neill, in press). Teaching social skills is a way of
developing desirable behavior so that less desirable behavior can be decreased
or eliminated.

This chapter reviews the approaches and the specific strategies currently being used to help children develop competence in social situations. Although the focus of this discussion is on teaching and developing skills, the assumption is made that a positive, working teacher-student relationship must exist if the teacher is to help students develop these skills. Perhaps in no other area is the student-teacher relationship so important as when the teacher is trying to help the child learn how to be more skillful socially.

Historical Perspective

From the beginning of public education, one of the primary goals has been to train children to become productive, contributing members of society. Citizenship has always been part of the public school curriculum. In the early days of public education, emphasis was placed on teaching students to read the Bible and behave in a moral fashion. Later, as increasing numbers of immigrants were enrolled in the public schools, emphasis was placed on citizenship training. During the 1960s when society was concerned with rectifying many social ills, a number of school systems and teachers incorporated affective education programs in their curriculum. In recent years, the emphasis has been placed on teaching children social skills. While each of these approaches focuses on somewhat different issues, they all represent public education's effort to help children become more productive and useful citizens.

Social Competence

Social competence is a judgment about whether a person performs competently in a social situation. To be socially competent, a person must possess a number of social skills. Combs and Slaby defined social skills as "the ability to interact with others in a given social context in specific ways that are socially acceptable or valued and at the same time personally beneficial, mutually beneficial, or beneficial primarily to others" (1977, p. 162). Implicit in this definition is the recognition that consideration must be given to situation-specific and age-sensitivity issues. Thus, based on this definition, a person who is socially competent may be described as possessing age-appropriate social skills that enable her to determine what is expected in a given social situation, to behave in the expected manner, and to satisfy her own needs and wishes in the situation.

At a minimum, a person needs to possess the following specific social skills:

- To read social rules and expectations
- To interpret social and interpersonal cues
- To communicate effectively in social situations
- To initiate social interactions in an age-appropriate manner
- To establish and maintain friendships
- To solve problems when they arise
- To negotiate tactfully and successfully with others

- To understand and be sensitive to one's feelings and wishes
- To be comfortable with and tolerant of one's self
- To understand and value ethical behavior
- To control oneself when upset or angry
- To present oneself in an attractive, appropriate manner.

After studying socially accepted children, Drabman and Patterson (1982) identified the following characteristics of these children. Socially accepted children conformed to accepted standards of social behavior, were cooperative, adapted well to routines, accepted the situations in which they found themselves, conformed to the requirements of various settings, and exhibited extroverted behavior. Gresham (1982) identified six skills necessary for successful mainstreaming: ability to cooperate, interact positively, share, greet others, ask for and provide information, and converse with others.

APPROACHES FOR HELPING CHILDREN BECOME MORE SOCIALLY COMPETENT

Teaching children how to behave and how to be socially competent is increasingly becoming a basic part of curricula, especially for emotionally handicapped children. The impetus for this approach comes from the belief that children are unsuccessful in social situations because they do not know how to behave. As Goldstein and Glick (1987) noted, helping children to understand and recognize their conflicts is not a sufficient intervention if the children do not have the skills to act upon their feelings and insights.

As was described in Chapter 7, a growing body of research is informing us about how specific social skills develop; however, much of this research has progressed along diverse lines, seldom relating one line of research to others. Consequently, no structured comprehensive body of knowledge has developed. Furthermore, considerably more attention has been given to assessment of social skills than to the training and development of these skills. Much of the research on social skills training has failed to consider the social implications of the training. That is, Is the client better off as a result of the training? Few studies have "demonstrated the integrity of independent variables" (Schloss, Schloss, Wood, & Kiehl, 1986, p. 11). Rarely have the studies operationally defined and monitored the treatment that was implemented and seldom do researchers study the generalization effects of social skill training to other settings, responses, and times. In short, the "technology of social skill development for behaviorally disordered individuals is only beginning to emerge" (Schloss et al., 1986, p. 12).

When deciding which social skills to teach, teachers need a framework for thinking about social skills. Without such direction, it is easy to be overwhelmed by the myriad of socially maladaptive behaviors seen in the classroom for emotionally handicapped children. Two models for conceptualizing how children process social information are presented as examples of structures that facilitate the integration of the diverse research and intervention studies. Both models view social information processing as a complex process of receiving or perceiving social information, thinking about the information or understanding and making sense of it, and acting upon it. These two models utilize a problem-solving approach that involves identifying the social situations in which problems are occurring and then determining which specific cognitive and behavioral skills are lacking.

The first model, developed by Dodge (1986), is a five-step process: encoding, representation, response search, response decision, and enactment (see Figure 14.1).

The **first step,** encoding social cues in the environment, involves receiving sensory cues from the social environment and attending to appropriate social cues. To perform this adequately, a child must be free of debilitating biases and must be able to attend to relevant and important social cues.

The **second step,** representation or interpretation, is often indistinguishable from the first. It involves integrating the social cues with memories of past experiences, the data base.

The **third step,** response search, involves searching for behavioral responses. In so doing, the child applies rule structures as a way of deciding how to behave. For example, the child might think, "I have been victimized, thus I can hit back."

The **fourth step,** response decision, occurs when the child decides what to do. Ideally, the child will learn to weigh the possible outcomes of different behaviors and determine what behavior will result in a favorable outcome.

The **fifth step,** enactment, refers to the action the child takes or the script the child elects to follow.

Dodge's model is based upon several assumptions:

1. The child comes to a social situation with her own "hardware" (biologically determined response capabilities) and her own "data base" (memory storage of past experiences). These predispose a child to process social information in certain ways.
2. Social information processing is assumed to occur in sequential stages, and each is essential to competent behavior.
3. Most processing occurs unconsciously. Only under novel or complex situations does the child think about her thinking.
4. Idiosyncratic processing presumably leads to idiosyncratic, or deviant, behavior.
5. The model is transactional, meaning the process does not stop when the child acts, or at enactment, because the model involves others. When the child receives cues from others, she monitors her own behavior in accordance with the information she receives. Dodge likens the process to a chess match.
6. The steps exist in dynamic relation to each other, meaning that as information is processed, it may change how the information is encoded.
7. Information is processed rapidly.
8. The steps are sequential, building one upon the other. This is important because it means the model has testable hypotheses.
9. While the process occurs rapidly and dynamically, the steps are believed to be separable—that is, they can be measured independently.

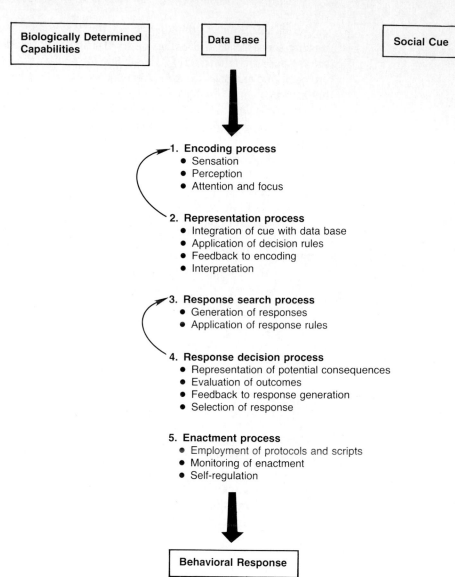

FIGURE 14.1
Dodge's Social Information Processing Model of Competence. (From *Cognitive Perspectives on Children's Social and Behavioral Development: Minnesota Symposium of Child Psychology* (vol. 18, p. 84), ed. M. Perlmuler. Hillsdale, N.J.: Lawrence Erlbaum Associates.)

By Dodge's own admission, his model only provides "a crude framework" for integrating the complex issues related to social information processing. One major area that needs further consideration is the role of affect in the processing of social information. Dolgin (1986) suggested that greater attention be given to developmental differences.

The second social information-processing system, developed by Hughes and Hall (1987), is a three-step model: reading, generating, and applying. The basic questions asked in this model are as follows: Can the child "read" the social situation? Can she "generate" the appropriate problem-solving strategies in a given situation? and Can the child "apply" appropriate problem-solving strategies in a problem social situation? Clearly, this model also emphasizes the importance of systematically assessing skills at each step to determine the type of problems a child is having and to pinpoint needs for an intervention.

In this model, there are three types of social incompetence: behavioral skill deficits, cognitive deficits, and cognitive/behavioral deficits.

- **Behavioral skill deficits** refer to an inability to perform social behaviors. A child with this type of problem knows what should be done but has difficulty performing the behavior. An illustration of this type of problem is seen in the child who knows one should speak and be friendly when trying to make friends, but when meeting another child, she does not look the child in the face and smile. Another illustration might be found in the child who is not able to conduct an age-appropriate conversation with a peer.
- **Cognitive deficits** refer to distortions or delays in thinking about social information. These types of problems include the child who misunderstands how to relate to peers. She acts silly to gain their friendship, but they perceive her as weird. She is too competitive in a friendly game of croquet. In both cases, the child possesses the skills to behave appropriately, but misunderstands the nature of the social environment.
- **Cognitive/behavioral deficits** include problems in both realms. The child has deficits in both understanding her social environment and in performing social behaviors. For example, a child with such deficits is standing in line waiting for a drink of water. Another child accidentally bumps her. The child with the cognitive/behavioral deficit hits the child who bumped her because she perceived the bump as intentional. The child misperceived the social situation and she utilized behavioral responses that are maladaptive.

As can be seen from these descriptions, both models provide frameworks for analyzing social behavior. When faced with a socially incompetent child, without such frameworks, it is difficult to determine what is needed and how to proceed.

Schloss et al. charged that "current research lacks evidence of attention to specific subject characteristics in selecting independent and dependent variables" (1986, p. 11). Current clinical practice also seems to suggest that teachers provide general social skills lessons, but specifically targeted, individualized programs are rarely implemented. Perhaps this lack of individualization has to do with the difficulty teachers face in assessing specific skills.

Both the Dodge and the Hughes/Hall models stress the importance of assessing the specific skill deficit before planning an intervention. Assessment involves determining where and when the child is having social problems as well as what type of social problems the child is having. Approaches for determining where and when the child is having social problems were discussed in Chapter 11. Most of the assessment strategies for determining what type of social problem a child is having are typically process-oriented tools that involve observing the child perform social skills or deal with social problems. Once the child's skills have been assessed, teachers may plan individual teaching programs. Deficit skills may be taught during interactions throughout the day as issues arise, or they may be taught during targeted lessons.

Individualization occurs through the teacher's knowledge of an individual child's skills and needs, not necessarily from individual lessons. Regardless of the teaching plan used, to be effective, the teaching approach needs to be consistent. Teachers will help children understand the relevance of the lesson if it is applied and discussed throughout the day as situations arise. In the section that follows, sample assessment questions are listed, and techniques for assessing the skill and possible interventions are described.

DEALING WITH PROBLEMS OF ENCODING AND INTERPRETING SOCIAL DATA

There are a number of questions that might be asked in an effort to determine whether the socially incompetent child has difficulties because of cognitive distortions of social cues or delays in social cognition development. Children with these problems have difficulty because of the way they think about the social world or because of their lack of knowledge regarding the social world. Some of the more salient questions are discussed in this section.

Does the child understand that people have multiple and differing perspectives? One skill that many believe underlies a number of more complex skills is the ability to perceive various points of view. As was discussed in Chapter 7, egocentrism is an inability to differentiate one's own personal perspective from that of others. Egocentric children do not realize that other people may have perspectives, views, or opinions that are different from their own. An illustration of this behavior is found in the following vignette.

> A four-year-old boy was in an automobile wreck. In telling his grandmother about the wreck, he asked "Did you hear the bang?" He proceeded to discuss the wreck as though she had been there and witnessed the entire event. His grandmother was at her home at the time, many miles away, and the child also knew that. To this child, however, his awareness and experiences were also hers.

Perspective taking is clearly a developmental skill acquired by most children roughly between the ages of 6 to 8. Because children who lack this skill believe that their view is the world view, they cannot understand that another child has an opinion or feelings different from their own. Until this skill is acquired, higher level negotiation and interpersonal problem solving are unrealistic. Egocentric children do not appear to be interested in or respectful of other's opinions. They may lack empathy (Chandler & Greenspan, 1972). They tend to view the world as being clearly one way or the other—shades of gray are not understood. They do not appreciate compromise and the legitimacy of several points of view. Self-reflection and self-evaluation are also difficult.

Several techniques have been developed for assessing egocentric behavior in research studies (Chandler, 1973a; Chandler, 1973b; Flavell, Botkin, Fry, Wright, & Jarvis, 1968; Kurdek & Rodgon, 1975; Mullis & Hanson, 1983; Simeonsson, 1973). Perhaps the best-known technique is Chandler's Bystander Task (1973a). This involves showing the child a series of cartoons depicting a central character who experiences an upsetting event in the first part of the story sequence and then interacts with another person (the bystander) during the latter part of the story sequence. The central character's behavior is understandable and logical **only** if one is privy to the entire sequence, but it is puzzling if one does not know the entire sequence. Children are required to tell two stories in response to each of the cartoons. The first story, called a spontaneous story, establishes that the child understands the thematic sequences. For the second story, the child is to tell the story from the viewpoint of the bystander.

Figure 14.2 illustrates one of these stories. In this sequence the child tells the entire story first. Then she tells the story from the baker's perspective. Responses are scored on a scale of 0 to 4. Egocentrism is defined as not being able to discriminate between privileged and nonprivileged information. In the story, an egocentric response would be any response suggesting that the baker understood why his cookies made the girl sad.

Training children to be less egocentric usually involves helping them develop the ability to take another's perspective. There are perceptual perspective-taking tasks, cognitive perspective-taking tasks, and affective perspective-taking tasks (Kurdek & Rodgon, 1975). One of the more successful studies was reported by Chandler (1973a). He trained delinquent boys in affective perspective-taking by involving them in drama and video filmmaking. The boys wrote several dramas that had parts for everyone in the group of five. The mini-dramas had to be about real-life events that would happen to kids the age of the boys. Each boy had to play each role. All episodes were videotaped, viewed by the group, and discussed; thus, each boy played all five parts in the mini-drama as well as saw and discussed the videotape of himself in each role. It was assumed that such training experiences would help the boys learn how to step outside of their own egocentric viewpoints and assume the role or perspective of persons different from themselves.

A postintervention assessment and an 18-month follow-up were conducted. When compared to both the placebo and nontreatment control groups, the experimental group showed the most significant gains on the perspective-taking tasks and they had half as many known delinquencies during the postintervention period.

Can the child communicate effectively with others? Is her language socially useful and adequate? A skill that appears to be related to egocentrism is that of referential communication, or the ability to use descriptors and referents that enable one to be understood. Children who lack referential communication skills are unable to assess the informational needs of others. Again, this is a developmental skill. Young children use words and phrases that are so vague that others do not understand their meaning. For example, a young child may tell her mother that she wants to wear ''that one'' and point to a closet full of

FIGURE 14.2
Chandler's Bystander Task.

FIGURE 14.2
continued

clothes. We expect ineffective communication in young children, but in older children it can be debilitating. Children without referential communication skills will have difficulty dealing competently with their social environments that increasingly require effective communication to participate in games, conversations, and other social activities of middle childhood and adolescence.

Ineffective language has been associated with behavioral problems (Camp, 1977; Chandler, Greenspan, & Barenboim, 1974,) and with academic problems (Strayhorn & Strain, 1986). Chandler et al. (1974) conducted a study in which they compared the performance of a control group with an experimental group that participated in role taking and filmmaking and an experimental group that received training and feedback in referential communication. As hypothesized, they found that institutionalized emotionally disturbed children performed lower than their better adjusted normal peers in role-taking and referential communication tasks, that remediation in social decentering was partially effective, and that improvements in these skills were associated with behavioral improvements. To their surprise, however, they also found that training in referential communication resulted in significant improvement in performance on both role-taking and referential communication tasks, whereas the training in role taking resulted only in improvments in role-taking skills.

In the research literature, referential communication skills have been measured in the COMTASK (Simeonsson & Grube, 1983). In this task, there are tall rectangular boxes, short square boxes, tall cylinders, and short cylinders of different colors. They may be placed on a top and bottom shelf. Several items such as a nail, key, and a ball are given to the child, one at a time. The child is instructed to hide the items under the boxes and then to tell the examiner where the item is hidden. Children who lack referential communication skills will leave out critical information. They may say "under the round blue one," leaving out the dimension or height.

Training in referential communication is easily done in the classroom through a variety of gamelike activities that force children to communicate with each other. The assumption is made that children placed in such situations will realize they are not communicating adequately and their desire to communicate more adequately will motivate them to learn more effective skills. For example, children may be assigned to work in pairs. They are seated facing each other with a screen between them. One child is instructed to create a design with plastic shapes; then she is to give her partner directions so that he can create the same design. Points are given for successful matches.

Teachers may find a number of activities that are appropriate for teaching these skills in language workbooks under the heading of teaching pragmatics. In selecting activities, teachers should pick ones that are only slightly above the child's ability level. Tasks that are too difficult will be frustrating for the child. Teachers should also pair children who are on approximately the same skill level. Boyce and Larson (1983), Simon (1980), and Wiig (1982) have developed materials for practitioners that are useful for helping students learn to be more effective, less egocentric communicators.

In addressing the question of why language skills are important to social competence, Strayhorn and Strain (1986) suggest two possible explanations.

The first has to do with establishing a success cycle in which competent language leads to academic success which leads to positive feedback from teachers which contributes to student compliance and peer acceptance. The other mechanism that may operate is based on the notion that self-language, or inner language, helps to regulate behavior and contributes to self-control. Children who are verbally facile may also have more inner behavioral controls.

Can the child accurately read others' social cues and intentions? Very young children think all behavior is "on purpose" and directed at them or for their purpose, but as children mature, they develop skills in processing social information. They acquire rules for behaving, and these rules are dependent upon how others react to the child. Friendly children elicit different responses than unfriendly children. Thus, it is critically important that children learn to read others' intentions accurately. Many aggressive children, however, lack this skill. As discussed in Chapter 7, **attributional bias** describes the process of misreading others' social cues. As expected, children who tend to perceive hostile cues are also prone to retaliatory or aggressive counterresponses.

Aggressive children often have a number of other biases in processing information from their social worlds. They often attend to the most recent cues (recency bias), and they tend to conduct shorter than average searches for cues before attributing cause of a behavior. They are quick to decide why things happen—a characteristic of younger children as well. Such "premature cue search skills" are predictive of later problems with social competence (Mischel, 1983).

To assess social information-processing skills such as attributional bias, cue recall, and cue search, researchers have developed several fascinating and effective measures (Dodge, 1980; Dodge, Murphy, & Buchsbaum, 1984; Lochman, 1987), but most are time-consuming to administer and score and some are based on videotaped sequences that are available only for research purposes. Few teachers have the time to seek out the measures and learn the time-consuming scoring procedures that have been used in research studies; however, less formal techniques are effective for classroom use. Teachers may interview children, especially after an altercation with a peer, and discern whether a child is having problems perceiving social information. When interviewing the child for such a purpose, the teacher should do so privately and simply ask her about the recent episode: "What happened?" "Who started it?" "Is this the type of problem you usually have?" "How do you feel about it?" "How does the other child feel about it?" The teacher should probe to find out which factors the child identifies as having caused the problem. A child with an attributional bias is likely to blame the other child for the problem—"He started it because he called my mother a name." "He shot me the bird," etc. Such a child may also distort the situation, failing to remember the start of the problem, and failing to attend to many of the cues in the interaction.

Although a large amount of literature deals with the nature of social information-processing deficits and delays, few data exist about how best to intervene. Teachers may wish to teach several affective lessons that deal with distorted attributions and the consequences of such thought. For example, reading and discussing stories about motives, intentions, and consequences of actions might be worthwhile. It seems unlikely, however, that children with this type of problem will be able to generalize from impersonal lessons to their own personal lives. Attributional biases are typically part of a cycle that involves distortion, aggression based on the distorted view, counteraggression based on the hostility, and an expectation of aggression. Because attributional biases are affectively bound and self-reinforcing, it seems unlikely that an impersonal lesson or series of lessons will be sufficient for dealing with the problem.

Teachers will probably need to de-bias the child's deviant processing through individualized techniques. Dodge suggested that "creative interventions involving repeated direct experience with stimuli that are incompatible with deviant processing may be most appropriate" (1986, p. 119). For example, creating and maintaining a positive, affirming relationship with a child who expects rejection and hostility creates dissonance for the child. Most likely, the child will respond by being more provocative and hostile, certain that retaliation and punishment are on the way. Accordingly, the teacher must be prepared *not* to respond as the child expects—not to fit into the child's expectations of hostility. Once a relationship of trust and positive expectations is established between the teacher and child, the child is psychologically in a position to listen to and seriously think about the teacher's ideas. The relationship may provide the vehicle that enables the teacher to engage in productive problem-solving discussions with the child when the need arises and the situation permits. Life-space interviewing, a technique discussed later in this chapter, may be a worthwhile approach for conducting these discussions.

Does the child possess adequate social knowledge about how to get one's needs met? Does she understand cause and effect or means-ends thinking in social interactions? Can the child anticipate consequences of her actions? Does she consider the moral implications of social interactions? As discussed in Chapter 7, research indicates that many socially incompetent children lack the knowledge of how to deal with problematic social situations. They know that they should say "please" when they want something, but if that does not work, it appears that they know few other socially appropriate approaches for getting their needs met and their wishes honored. As with many of the other social skills discussed in this chapter, problem-solving skills are also developmentally based. As children grow older, they are able to generate more solutions to social problems, their solutions are more varied, and they understand the consequences of various actions. Aggressive and unpopular children often have superficial knowledge about how to deal with social problems and their social reasoning often resembles the thinking of younger children. Thus, when assessing the type of social problem a child might have, we evaluate the child's ability to think about social problems.

A popular technique for assessing these skills involves showing the child a picture of two children and presenting a story that involves one child having something that the other child wants. After the dilemma is presented, the examinee is asked what the child could do to get what he wants. After the examinee responds, he is asked, "If that doesn't work, what else could he do?" Finally, the child is asked, "What would you do?" With this measure it is possible to observe the child's characteristic approach to problem situations, and the child's flexibility in solving problems. If probes regarding consequences and means-ends thinking are added, it is also possible to determine how the child thinks through a problem. For example, the examiner might also ask, "What would happen if . . .?" and "How can she be certain that that will happen?"

Moral reasoning is interwoven with social interpersonal reasoning. Kohlberg (1966) suggested that moral reasoning is developmentally based and that it is related to the ability to organize, integrate, and act upon social information in a consistent manner.

A number of curricula have been developed with the purpose of promoting social and moral reasoning and problem solving. These programs involve teaching the child or the class how to solve problems. A step-by-step problem-solving strategy is taught, and once it is mastered, it is used during subsequent lessons and whenever problems arise. Most programs approach the task by exposing the child to real-life dilemmas and helping the child think through the problem. Once the child is confronted with the realities of the problem, she is motivated to work on the issue.

Think Aloud (Camp & Bash, 1981) is a program that was initially designed for improving self-control in young, aggressive boys, but as the authors worked with the program, they expanded it for use in the regular classroom because they realized it was appropriate for many different children. The program draws heavily on the work of Meichenbaum and Goodman (1971) and Spivack and Shure (1974).

The program starts by teaching children a four-step approach to solving problems. The teacher models problem-solving thinking through self-talk, and the children copy the teacher by playing a game of "copy cat." Figure 14.3 shows the cue cards posted in the classroom and used to help children remember the steps in the problem-solving approach. The group starts with a simple coloring task in which the teacher guides the class through the steps by such statements as, "What is my problem? I need to stay in the lines and make this a neat picture. How can I do that? Well, if I color slowly and carefully, I can do a better job." As the teacher colors, he might say, "Am I using my plan? Am I working slowly? Yes, I am doing that. Am I being careful? Well, most of the time, but I did look up and messed up when I did that." After the picture is completed, the teacher would then ask, "How did I do?" Then he would discuss the self-evaluation.

Bash and Camp (1986) discussed several problems that they observed teachers to have when learning to teach the Think Aloud curriculum. First, teachers had difficulty feeling comfortable with children talking out loud. To illustrate what can happen, they told the following story:

> Second graders were productively verbalizing as they attempted to organize 12 pictures into a logical matrix. Every student was in his seat and a few students were explaining to their neighbors their rationale for categorizing a few of the pictures. There were no obvious disruptive behaviors and the Think Aloud trainer did not hear any off-task conversation. But when the assistant principal walked into the room he admonished the class: "I want everyone of you to be

FIGURE 14.3
The Think Aloud Classroom Program

quiet. There is no reason for all this noise. You know what your work is. Get it done quietly.'' The powerful effect of self-instruction was blotted from the lesson. (Bash & Camp, 1986, p. 202)

A second area in which teachers must adjust their teaching is becoming comfortable in allowing children time to organize their thoughts and to think about an issue. Teachers appeared to want children to answer immediately, so they rephrased questions and essentially gave the children the answer. After considerable experimentation, Bash and Camp developed the following training sequence to help teachers learn to teach the Think Aloud curriculum effectively. They teach teachers to use the problem-solving paradigm by giving them tasks that allow them to learn to problem solve and to observe instructors emphasizing process, not end product, generating and accepting alternatives equally, and predicting potential problems.

Bash and Camp also noticed teachers were having difficulty in learning how to teach emotions. To help teachers learn how to teach children about emotions, they developed the following instructional sequence:

1. Identify need for recognizing a particular emotion.
2. Show facial expression that characterizes emotion.
3. Label emotion for students.
4. Define emotion.
5. Provide personal examples.
6. Restate definition.
7. Show picture. What might have provoked the emotion?
8. Show different picture. What might have evoked the emotion?
9. What's something the person could say or do to lessen or to intensify the emotion?
10. Follow up by using the emotion label during class or by identifying the emotion in literature.

Think Aloud has been evaluated both empirically (Camp, 1980; Camp, Blom, Hebert, & Van Doorninck, 1977; Watson & Hall, 1977) and informally through observation and anecdotal records. Bash and Camp (1986) report a number of positive outcomes—children are able to identify and empathize with others' feelings, monitor their own actions, and work cooperatively. Teachers have learned to involve their students in finding solutions for problems. They are more willing to allow students to assume responsibility.

Problem-solving programs for older children also teach the steps of problem solving. Coie, Lochman, Thompson, and Katz (1986) proposed a problem-solving ladder. In their curriculum, children are taught how to perform each of the component tasks of the problem-solving process. Once the specific skills are mastered, children practice the entire process during repeated exercises throughout the training program.

Curricula that emphasize problem solving and moral reasoning typically present children with social dilemmas to resolve. For example, when teaching such a unit, the teacher presents the children with a story like the following:

What Should Christy Do?[1]

Unlike lots of girls, Christy was crazy about her little brother. Not only was he the cutest little towhead in the second grade, but he was always telling wild tales that made her laugh.

It was fun for sixth-grader, Christy, to meet Charlie in the hall, or watch him on the playground, or peep into the second-grade room where he sat with his little sneakered feet tucked under his chair.

One afternoon at recess, Christy and some other sixth-grade girls were making mats out of dandelion stems. Christy had gone around the side of the building to get more dandelions when the bell rang. Just as she turned the corner, she saw her little brother pick up a big rock, throw it through the cafeteria window, and scurry to the back of the building.

---

[1] From *Today's Education*, May 1966, pp. 41.

Although no one else was in sight outdoors, Christy felt that someone inside the building would certainly have seen Charlie break the window and report to the principal. She went to her room, but was so worried about Charlie that she finally asked her teacher for permission to leave the room. She went to the office prepared to stand by her little brother during what she was sure would be an unpleasant interview.

When she got to the office, sure enough, there was Charlie talking to the principal. He didn't look unhappy, however.

When he saw her, he said cheerfully, "Hi Christy. I'm telling Mr. Clark how I saw Michael Lansing throw a rock through the cafeteria window."

"Michael Lansing!" Christy said.

Charlie nodded. "He just picked up a big stone and—pow—right through the window. Miss King asked if anybody knew about the window, so I told her, and she sent me to tell Mr. Clark."

Christy knew Michael Lansing. He was always getting into trouble. But this was one thing he hadn't done. She had seen Charlie throw the rock, and now, to make matters worse, he had made up a deliberate lie about it.

She hated to think what the principal would say to Charlie if he learned the truth, and she hated to imagine how their parents would punish her brother when they heard the story. Of course, he had done two very bad things and deserved to be punished, but was it up to her to tell on him? It certainly wasn't fair to Michael Lansing to be blamed, but how she hated to be the one to get Charlie into trouble. What should Christy do?

Another curriculum that includes a unit on moral reasoning is Goldstein's Aggression Replacement Training (Goldstein & Glick, 1987). This curriculum, developed for aggressive juveniles, has three components: structured learning (teaching of prosocial skills through behavioral methods), anger control training (dealing with affective issues through counseling and self-control methods), and moral education (utilizing structured discussions to explore and understand moral dilemmas). Goldstein utilized these three components in his curriculum because of the effectiveness of interventions that focus on change strategies in different domains.

Does the child possess adequate self-control skills? Can the child stop and think before acting? Self-control skills are not separate from some of the skills discussed in this chapter, but they are so basic to many of the skills that they merit attention. To problem solve and to play cooperatively with others, children must be able to control their impulsive thoughts and actions. Self-control or self-management procedures have become popular in many classrooms because of the following reasons:

- Students must become involved in the behavior change process.
- Self-control skills can be generalized to other settings.
- These procedures may save the teacher time.

Most self-control training approaches emphasize the importance of several component skills: self-recording, self-evaluation, self-determination of contingencies, and self-instruction (Hughes, Ruhl, & Misra, 1989; O'Leary & Dubey, 1979; Rosenbaum and Drabman, 1979). **Self-recording** involves teaching the child how to observe and record her own behavior. This is an especially important task that often results in positive behavior change. As children learn to observe and monitor themselves, they self-correct problem behaviors. Furthermore, self-recording does not have to be accurate to result in positive behavior change. Studies comparing child-recorded data with observer's data have yielded low correlations, but positive behavioral change in the child did occur. These changes, however, may be short-term. **Self-evaluation** requires the child to compare herself to predetermined criteria and to evaluate her performance. **Self-determination of contingencies** involves allowing the child, instead of the teacher, to choose her rewards. Generally, self-determined rewards are more effective than externally determined rewards. **Self-instruction** involves teaching children to self-talk, to guide themselves through a problem, or to provide themselves with self-instructions. This procedure has been demonstrated to be effective in research studies, although there do appear to be developmental variations in the type of self-instruction to which children of different ages are most responsive.

Kendall and Braswell (1985) developed a treatment program that has six components: a problem-solving approach, self-instructional training, behavioral contingencies, modeling, affective education, and role-play exercises. Their program, developed for impulsive children, focuses on teaching the child self-instruction and self-monitoring skills. Children are taught to use self-statements that are not overly negative and to evaluate their performance and reward themselves regularly.

After a review of the literature, Hughes, Ruhl, and Misra (1989) concluded that studies dealing with self-management procedures generally report positive behavioral change; however, most studies are unclear regarding whether the changes are socially significant. It is also unclear which behaviors lend themselves to self-management procedures. The authors described studies that focus on generalization over time as encouraging, but more needs to be known about the effects of teacher-controlled and naturally occurring reinforcers.

Does the child possess skills for making and keeping friends? Does she have age-appropriate group entry and interactional skills? Friends are people from whom we gain a great deal of support and validation. When we are troubled, an understanding friend can be comforting and affirming. When we are joyous, our joy is made all the more special by sharing it with friends. As children grow and develop, friends exert an increasingly significant influence over behavior. Thus, skills in making and keeping friends are important components of social competence because friends are means of gratifying personal needs.

Unlike some of the other skills previously discussed, friendship making is not a skill that is entirely within the control of the child. Making friends involves other persons. Research indicates that proximity and chance often exert as much influence over who our friends are as do the person's personal qualities. If you ask a child why a certain person is her friend, she will name personal qualities such as niceness, kindness, trustworthiness, honesty, or fun and interesting to be around—all of which may be true. But, another reason children become friends is they see a lot of each other. With time and exposure, children learn to trust and like the persons with whom they associate the most.

For emotionally disturbed children this is an especially important issue because they often do not come into prolonged contact with children whose friendship will provide a positive influence. Rather, they tend to associate with children who are also having difficulties. Many of these children are highly suggestible; thus, associating with children who exert a negative influence can lead them into greater difficulty. Teachers and other adults working with these children need to find techniques for helping children have positive associations with children who can be positive role models and helpful friends.

Not only do teachers need to ensure contact with positive role models, they also need to provide opportunities to learn to behave in socially appropriate ways. Observations of unpopular children have found that many do not know how to start conversations with their peers or join play activities. They tend to draw attention to themselves and disrupt ongoing activities. They also tend to use more aversive verbal comments. In contrast, popular children employ more group-oriented statements and react to the social give-and-take of children's groups with an easygoing ability to accept and return in similar spirit the teasing, insults, and disagreements that typically occur. That is, they are not quick to react in a hostile, negative manner that creates more problems (Dodge, Schlundt, Schocken, & Delugach, 1983).

Some of these skills may be taught, especially if the teaching is individualized. Oden and Asher (1977) conducted a study in which they compared pre- and postsociometric ratings of three different groups of socially isolated children: a group that received social skills coaching in play situations; a group in which children were paired and allowed to play, with no instruction provided; and a control group. Posttesting and follow-up evaluations indicated that the coached group improved immediately after the coaching and continued to improve over time in play situations but not in work situations. Gresham and Nagle (1980), Covill-Servo (1982), and Ladd (1981) have utilized similar approaches and obtained basically the same results. Coie and Krehbiel (1984) combined tutoring and social skills coaching for a group of unpopular, low-achieving children. They found the treatment enhanced both the children's social acceptance and academic achievement.

Social skills that are valued by friends evolve as children develop. Young children consistently describe their friends in concrete terms such as, "We play Transformers together" or "We live next door to each other." Scarlett (1980) suggested that isolated preschoolers are the ones who tend to watch other children and not engage in as much active play as the nonisolated children. Therefore, they are less interesting and attractive as social partners. Because they play less, they lack a vehicle for including peers in an interaction. Scarlett proposed that teachers play with isolated children as a means of facilitating their skill development in play activities.

As children grow older, the qualities they value in friends appear to shift. Fourth graders speak of doing the same thing with friends, whereas eighth graders speak of intimacy, loyalty, and trust. Between fourth and eighth grade there appears to be another stage, one in which conformity and skills are valued: "He doesn't cause trouble." "He plays soccer well." "She's smart." When helping children learn how to make friends, teachers need to keep these developmental differences in mind. Children apparently seek somewhat different qualities in friends as they mature.

Teachers who are interested in setting up programs to teach children social skills that will promote social acceptance may simply structure time for games and discussion. Especially if consultation is available from a professional who can spend time observing the children and helping to identify deficit skills and appropriate interventions, this approach may be successful. If, however, such collaboration is not available, teachers may wish to use one of the many curricula currently available. As teachers become more proficient with a program and as they learn more about their students, they will be able to adapt the curriculum to individual needs. Some of the programs currently available are as follows: Getting Along With Others: Teaching Social Effectiveness to Children (Jackson, Jackson, & Monroe, 1983), Skillstreaming the Elementary Child (McGinnis & Goldstein, 1984), Skillstreaming the Adolescent (Goldstein, Sprafkin, Gershaw, & Klein, 1980), The ACCEPTS Program (Walker, McConnell, Holmes, Todis, Walker, & Golden, 1983), and Social Skills in the Classroom (Stephens, 1978). Table 14.1 provides a brief description of several commercially available social skills programs.

Does the child possess classroom survival skills? Socially competent children survive the demands of school reasonably well. They do not get in trouble with their teachers, nor do they engage in fights and disruptions at school. They understand how one is expected to behave in school, and they conform to these expectations. Even if they are subjected to trying situations such as insensitive teachers or boring lessons, they are able to control themselves and cope in the situation.

Many emotionally disturbed children lack such coping skills. If a lesson is boring or the teacher insensitive, these children are likely to react in a hostile, negative, problematic manner, which often gets them in trouble. Schools do not tend to excuse a child's rudeness because a teacher was boring or insensitive. For this reason, it may be necessary to actively teach children how to survive in a classroom when they do not like the teacher or the learning activities.

Arnold Goldstein and his colleagues (Goldstein, Sprafkin, Gershaw, & Klein, 1980; McGinnis & Goldstein, 1984) have developed the Skillstreaming programs, which are structured learning curricula designed to teach children prosocial skills. Both the elementary and secondary levels contain a number of lessons that are intended to help children learn how to cope more effectively with classroom situations. On the elementary level, McGinnis & Goldstein (1984) present classroom survival skills in the first training module. Listening, asking for help, saying thank-you, bringing materials to class, following instructions, completing assignments, contributing to discussions, offering help to an adult, asking a question, ignoring distractions, making corrections, deciding on something to do, and setting a goal are included in this unit. Although the secondary curriculum does not contain a specific section entitled classroom

TABLE 14.1
Commercial Curricula for Teaching Social Skills

Curriculum	Brief Description
ACCEPTS Social Skills Curriculum (Walker, McConnell, Holmes, Todis, Walker, & Golden, 1983)	Uses a 9-step instructional approach in which the teacher (1) defines skill and explains how it is used, (2) models positive example of the skill (through role play or videotape) and discusses it, (3) models negative example and discusses it, (4) reviews and restates skill definition, (5) models positive example again, (6) provides additional appropriate applications of the skill and initiates student role plays, (7) provides additional modeling of the skill, (8) encourages role play among students and provides feedback and additional instruction, and, if necessary (9) contracts homework assignment with student for completion by next lesson.
Cognitive-Behavioral Therapy for Impulsive Children (Kendall & Braswell, 1985)	Uses a cognitive approach to developing self-control in impulsive children. Teaches self-instructional talk as a means of internalizing control. A 4-step process is taught in which the child learns to (1) recognize that there is a problem and identify its features, (2) initiate a strategy that will help resolve the problem, (3) consider the alternatives, and (4) take action on the chosen plan. Children are also taught to evaluate their performance and to reward themselves.
Getting Along With Others: Teaching Social Effectiveness to Children (Jackson, Jackson, & Monroe, 1983)	Uses a model of telling children what to do, showing them how to do it, and requiring that they practice the skill. Contains activities in 17 skill areas such as following directions, joining a conversation, compromising, problem solving, and handling name-calling and teasing.
Social Skills Assessment and Training With Children: An Empirically Based Handbook (Michelson, Sugai, Wood, & Kazdin, 1983)	Developed for aggressive and withdrawn children. Emphasizes assessing skills and planning interventions based on assessment data. Contains over 16 different assessment and training modules.

survival skills, there are a number of skills included in the curriculum that help secondary students cope more successfully with the demands of the classroom. For example, asking a question is taught as part of the unit entitled "Beginning Social Skills." Following instructions and asking for help are taught as part of the unit on advanced social skills. Deciding on something to do, setting a goal, deciding on your abilities, gathering information, and concentrating on a task are taught as part of the unit on planning skills.

TABLE 14.1
continued

Curriculum	Brief Description
Skillstreaming the Adolescent (Goldstein, Sprafkin, Gershaw, & Klein, 1980)	Uses a structured learning format that involves (1) modeling the skill, (2) practicing the skill through role playing, (3) providing feedback regarding the performance, and (4) using the skill in other settings (transfer of training). Training activities are provided in the following six general areas of social skills: beginning social skills (having a conversation, saying thank you, giving a compliment, etc.), advanced social skills (asking for help, joining in, apologizing, convincing others, etc.), dealing with feelings, alternatives to aggression, dealing with stress, and planning (setting a goal, deciding on your abilities, arranging problems by importance, etc.).
Skillstreaming the Elementary School Child (McGinnis & Goldstein, 1984)	Based on the same general structured learning approach previously described. Differences in programs have to do with developmental differences of intended population. Training activities are provided in five general areas: (1) classroom survival skills, (2) friendship-making skills, (3) skills for dealing with feelings, (4) alternatives to aggression, and (5) skills for dealing with stress.
Think Aloud (Camp & Bash, 1981)	Cognitive approach to developing problem-solving skills as a means of improving impulsive, inadequate responses. Teaches students to use the following paradigm: (1) What is my problem? or What am I supposed to do? (2) How can I do it? or What is my plan for doing it? (3) Am I using my plan? and (4) How did I do?

Is the child attractive? Does she present herself well? In exploring reasons why children were rejected by their peers, Coie, Rabiner, and Lochman (in press) found that physical appearance is one of the factors that contributes to peer rejection. In their sample of school children from an inner-city school district, children who were physically unattractive and who presented themselves as dirty, unkept, and poorly groomed were often rejected by their peers. Thus, when helping children learn how to become more competent socially, the teacher needs to stress physical appearance along with interactional skills.

It is usually best to deal with problems involving poor hygiene and inadequate grooming privately. Teachers may need to refer children with these problems to the school nurse or to a school counselor, or the teacher may need to make arrangements to see the child before or after school.

Many children with these problems come from backgrounds of neglect and poverty; thus, teachers must be very careful about how they present the problem and what solutions they suggest. It is important that children perceive school officials as helpful and concerned about them, not critical of their families and backgrounds. Once the issue of self-presentation is raised and discussed in a sensitive manner, and once the child agrees she wants to improve her appearance, it is relatively straightforward to teach lessons in grooming, care of clothing, hygiene, and so on.

Self-presentation is interwoven with other complex feelings about the self. Many children who are not well groomed and who do not practice good hygiene habits also have poor self-perceptions. The two are interrelated. Improvements in self-appearance sometimes can help a child feel better about herself, and sometimes a child's very negative self-perceptions seem to work against consistent, positive improvements in self-presentation. Thus, when working with a child with such problems, teachers need to plan how to help the child continue to be motivated to maintain a schedule of self-care. Contracts and self-charting have been used for this purpose.

CLASSROOM COUNSELING TECHNIQUES

As was mentioned at the beginning of this chapter, there are several approaches to teaching children social behaviors. Two significant ones are didactic skill development and here-and-now problem solving. The latter utilizes techniques in the classroom that have been developed in clinical, counseling settings but that may also be used in the classroom in response to everyday problems that develop. When implemented competently, both approaches are effective.

Classroom counseling techniques are especially appropriate when sensitizing children to their own problematic reactions and when helping children think through their own web of conflict. Some children have developed such elaborate rationalizations about why they have problems that they are not motivated to change. They blame others for their problems. In situ discussions can help these children become aware of their behavior and link their behavior to its effects. Such discussions can also help children who are struggling with their troubled, conflicted feelings and who are disconnected from themselves, their feelings, and their behaviors. These children may become so enmeshed in their own conflict that they are unable to see how to disengage themselves.

To be effective, classroom counseling must be done with care and skill. All teachers discuss with students reasons for being late, for not completing homework, and for being preoccupied; but if these discussions are not conducted appropriately, little may be accomplished. In fact, children may find them annoying rather than helpful.

To conduct a discussion about a child's problems, the teacher needs to have basic skills and knowledge in counseling as well as a clear understanding of

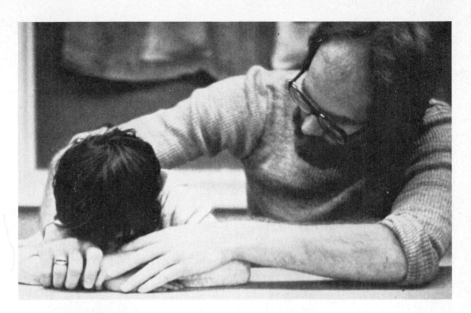

The crisis teacher provides support and assistance to children who are having difficulty coping at school.

the child's problems. Most authorities also think the focus needs to remain on the
here and now, rather than on the past. For example, problems that occur in the
classroom are generally considered appropriate content for classroom counseling, whereas family problems or family crises may not be. Several systems have
been developed to help teachers counsel with children in the classroom.

Life Space Interviewing

In 1959, Fritz Redl introduced the phrase **life space interview,** or LSI, to describe a reality-oriented, here-and-now interview technique that was appropriate
for "clinical exploitation of life events" and "emotional first aid." Clinical exploitation of life events means using the here-and-now routine occurrences as
material for helping children gain insight into their problems and learn new ways
of coping. Examples of exploiting life events include dealing with children's
distortions of a social situation, helping children become aware of their maladaptive attitudes, and teaching children new problem-solving skills. Providing
emotional first aid involves functioning as an alter ego or supplying the child with
needed direction, organization, and control. Giving emotional support to children who are overwhelmed by intense feelings or who are frustrated by daily
annoyances is an example of emotional first aid.

When compared to typical classroom discussions, the life space interview
is different in a number of ways. DeMagistris and Imber (1980) found that in
many classroom discussions, children's behavior was criticized immediately, and

little attention was directed toward understanding the children's perception of a specific incident. The discussions were rarely private and often ended in a teacher-student standoff or with the child being punished for the inappropriate behavior. During life space interviews, an effort is made to determine how the child perceives the problem, discussions are usually private or only with concerned parties, and the focus is on sorting out the issues and preventing future problems rather than on determining punishment.

Morse (1980) has outlined seven steps to follow when conducting a life space interview.

1. The teacher should start by finding out how the child (or the group) perceived the event which precipitated the LSI.
2. The teacher determines whether the child perceives the event as an isolated event or as a typical problem. If the teacher sees the problem as a typical event but the child does not, the teacher must help the child attend to similar episodes so that with time the child realizes the significance of such events.
3. After the child has explained her view of the problem, the teacher explains his view of what happened in a nonevaluative manner. As the event is reconstructed, concomitant feelings and impulses are recognized.
4. Throughout the LSI, but particularly as the child's distortions are challenged, the teacher strives to convey a feeling of acceptance to the child. The teacher's attitude reflects the belief that the child has a right to be heard without condoning the problem. The feelings underlying the child's behavior are addressed, rather than the defensive behavior that precipitated the problem in the first place.
5. To help the child learn better ways of dealing with similar situations, the child is encouraged to think about the implications or logical consequences of her behavior in a nonpunitive, nonjudgmental manner.
6. After the problem is discussed and analyzed, the teacher searches for sources of motivation to change the child.
7. If a plan can be worked out for resolving the problem or for preventing similar problems in the future, steps are taken in that direction. Before agreeing to the plan, the teacher should feel confident that the plan will be successful.

Before employing a life space interview, teachers need to consider a number of factors.

1. **Is there sufficient time to talk about the problem?** To start a serious discussion 5 minutes before the school bus comes ensures that the discussion will be rushed and probably less productive.
2. **Is the child in the right frame of mind?** The child must be psychologically ready to enter into a discussion. When a child is acutely upset, she is not in a condition to calmly consider the situation. Likewise, once a child has settled down and put the problem out of her mind, bringing up the problem again may reactivate her fury.
3. **Is the teacher in the right frame of mind?** When a teacher is still recovering from fury triggered by a child's outburst, it is clearly not a good time to initiate an LSI. The teacher's own feelings would interfere.

4. **Is the setting appropriate?** Airing private issues in public can make the child uncomfortable and can interfere with the interview and the teacher-student relationship. Likewise, conducting an interview in a highly stimulating environment may be too distracting to the youngster.

5. **Is the issue closely related to other issues the child is presently working on?** To bombard children with all their problems at once is likely to overwhelm them and accomplish nothing. Problems should be raised one at a time and in a carefully considered sequence.

6. **Is the issue one that the child is psychologically ready to understand?** To focus on issues about which the child is strongly defensive is to risk either antagonizing the child or being dismissed as not understanding or being incompetent. For the child to be ready to discuss the problem, it must be understood. Underlying this issue is the belief that people understand and remember selectively; hence, issues should be raised when children are ready to understand.

Proponents of the life space interview technique maintain that it combines therapeutic tools with educational tools so that teachers can help children learn about themselves and their feelings and motives (Long, 1990). For troubled children, this can be especially helpful as they often believe they are "bad" but do not understand what causes their "badness." Helping them to understand their feelings and then linking these feelings to actions helps explain their "badness." Further, helping them to think through the situation so that distortions are addressed and gradually diminished, helps them improve their social thinking skills. Life space interviewing lends itself to dealing with attributional biases and to teaching problem-solving and consequential thinking. It also can be used to help "rub numb values" (i.e., to activate a child's sense of right and wrong) (Redl & Wineman, 1957).

Critics charge that sound empirical support does not exist to support the use of the technique, that it takes too much time away from academics, and that it enables students to project blame onto others (Gardner, 1990). Unquestionably, more research is needed that deals with this technique, but essentially, the basic arguments about whether or not to use the technique stem from the fundamental, philosophical beliefs of the critics and the advocates (Wood, 1990).

Teacher Effectiveness Training

Another approach to conducting discussions about problems in the classroom has been suggested by Gordon (1974). This system, known as the No-Lose Method, is a process of working through conflicts from beginning to end. The steps in this method are (1) defining the problem, (2) generating possible solutions, (3) evaluating the solutions, (4) determining how to implement the decision, (5) deciding which solution is best, and (6) assessing how well the solution solved the problem. This approach may be used with groups or with individuals, but in order to use this method, the teacher must have a good relationship with students and possess good communication skills.

Listening is a critical component of constructive talk. Gordon describes two types of listening. **Passive listening** includes silent listening, consisting of verbal or nonverbal acknowledgment responses (e.g., nods, smiles, "Uh-huh") and verbal or nonverbal acknowledgment responses (e.g., "That's interesting," "Do you want to go on?"). **Active listening** is the process of decoding a student's uniquely coded message and then trying to give feedback.

Gordon provides the following as an example of active listening. The student complains, "This school sure isn't as good as my last one. The kids there were friendly." The teacher hypothesizes that the student feels lonely and left out. Therefore, the teacher responds, "You feel pretty left out here?" The student's agreement confirmed that the teacher had correctly heard and decoded the child's message. This process is akin to Morse's recommendation that teachers not counterattack defenses. If the teacher had become defensive and replied, "Why, that is a great school—the kids are known for being friendly," the teacher would have been responding to the literal meaning of defensive behavior, or counterattacking a defense.

Gordon also stresses the importance of determining who "owns" the problem. If the student owns the problem, Gordon believes that the teacher should become a counselor and help the student deal with the problem, primarily through active and passive listening. If the teacher "owns" the problem, Gordon recommends confronting the student with an "I-message."

I-messages consist of three parts: a description of what is causing the problem, a description of the tangible effect of the behavior, and identification of the resulting feelings. An example is: "When art supplies are not put up after they are used in the art center, I have to do it and it takes a lot of time. This upsets me, especially when I'm in a hurry."

The advantage of an I-message, according to Gordon, is that it helps keep the responsibility for the problem where it belongs. By not accusing the child, it helps prevent the child from becoming defensive. This, in turn, helps the child hear the message and discuss the problem rationally. Gordon maintains that by using an I-message, the teacher usually elicits the student's feelings. When this happens, the teacher should listen actively.

Finally, in describing effective communication, Gordon (1974) presents what he calls the "Dirty Dozen," 12 roadblocks to effective communication. He maintains that these 12 kinds of messages inhibit or block two-way communication, and without two-way communication, it is not possible, he believes, to help students with their problems. The "Dirty Dozen" are

1. Ordering, commanding, directing. Example: "You stop complaining and get your work done."
2. Warning, threatening. Example: "You'd better get on the ball if you expect to get a good grade in this class."
3. Moralizing, preaching, giving "shoulds" and "oughts." Example: "You know it's your job to study when you come to school. You should leave your personal problems at home where they belong."
4. Advising, offering solutions or suggestions. Example: "The thing for you to do is to work out a better time schedule. Then you'll be able to get all your work done."

5. Teaching, lecturing, giving logical arguments. Example: "Let's look at the facts. You better remember there are only 34 more days of school to complete that assignment."

6. Judging, criticizing, disagreeing, blaming. Example: "You're just plain lazy or you're a big procrastinator."

7. Name calling, stereotyping, labeling. Example: "You're acting like a fourth grader, not like someone almost ready for high school."

8. Interpreting, analyzing, diagnosing. Example: "You're just trying to get out of doing that assignment."

9. Praising, agreeing, giving positive evaluations. Example: "You're really a very competent young man. I'm sure you'll figure how to get it done somehow."

10. Reassuring, sympathizing, consoling, supporting. Example: "You're not the only one who ever felt that way about tough assignments, too. Besides, it won't seem hard when you get into it."

11. Questioning, probing, interrogating, cross-examining. Examples: "Do you think the assignment was too hard?" "How much time did you spend on it?" "Why did you wait so long to ask for help?" "How many hours have you put in on it?"

12. Withdrawing, distracting, being sarcastic, humoring, diverting. Examples: "Come on, let's talk about something more pleasant." "Now isn't the time." "Let's get back to our lesson." "Seems like someone got up on the wrong side of the bed this morning."[2]

Other writers, notably Ginot (1971), Glasser (1969) and Dreikurs (1968), have also developed techniques for communicating with children in the classroom. Ginot (1971) advocates "congruent communication," which he believes enables teachers to communicate with students about problems without attacking the student. In this approach to verbal processing, teachers convey the message, "I like you but I don't like what you are doing." By using congruent communication, Ginot believes teachers can be helpful, accepting, and constantly aware of their impact upon children.

Glasser (1965) developed a technique for problem solving which he calls "reality therapy." He then applied this technique in school situations. He maintains that people's past experiences influence but do not determine their present functioning, that people have choices about how they behave, and that the teacher's role is to help children make wise choices.

Dreikurs (1968) proposes a model for disciplining children that relies upon the use of logical and natural consequences. He views consequences as actions that naturally and logically follow behavior. Good behavior results in rewards, and unacceptable behavior causes unpleasant consequences. Dreikurs sees children's misbehavior as stemming from mistaken goals (e.g., gaining attention). In his approach teachers are responsible for helping children acquire better, more adaptive goals and ways of behaving.

---

[2] From *Teacher Effectiveness Training* (pp. 48–49) by Thomas Gordon, 1975, New York: David McKay.

It is critical that teachers do not perpetuate the maladaptive patterns of emotionally disturbed children by reacting as people in the past have reacted. Whatever technique is used, it is important that teachers find a way to respond to emotionally disturbed children in a way that conveys both the belief that the child has the ability to behave appropriately and the expectation that the child can acquire better ways of behaving.

Effective classroom counseling is a complex process. It requires the teacher to possess a technical knowledge of interpersonal dynamics, but it also requires personal qualities such as sensitivity to others and the ability to empathize. If a classroom discussion is conducted in a judgmental or intrusive manner, it may create more problems. On the other hand, if it is conducted appropriately, it can cement the student-teacher relationship. The use of appropriate counseling techniques can contribute to emotional growth in children as well as to an effective behavior management system.

SUMMARIES

Teaching children to be appropriate in social situations is a proactive approach to discipline and behavior management. It is, however, a complex process that requires the teacher to possess knowledge of emotional and social development, skills in helping children learn about themselves and their social world, and empathy for children engaging in such an endeavor.

Teaching social behavior requires the teacher to be clear about what he wants the children to learn. Children's levels of social competence vary significantly, and teachers need to have clear notions about what each child needs to learn. Although most of the issues may be dealt with in a group, the understanding of the child must be individualized and focused if it is to be effective.

The teacher-student relationship probably has a great deal to do with the effectiveness of teaching social behavior. Unlike mathematics and reading skills, social lessons are most often and probably best learned through social relationships. While little empirical data exist to detail what the teacher-student relationship should be like, clinical literature suggests that the relationship should be characterized by empathy, respect, a belief in the individual's ability to perform, and trust in the person to deliver what she promises.

Consistency in actions and words is also important. Telling children how to behave, but acting in another manner is not likely to be effective. Teachers need to use their teaching time to explain and amplify issues that they want the children to think about. Then the rest of their teaching day can be used to demonstrate and apply the lessons. On-the-spot counseling and problem solving reinforces and clarifies topics discussed in class, if teachers are able to use crises and problems as content for teaching.

Respect for children's right to participate and right to privacy is also necessary. When social and interpersonal problems become the content of class discussion, some children will feel uncomfortable and uneasy about the lesson. Forcing such children to participate only antagonizes and alienates them. Children (and adults) will deal with their problems when they can and want to do so. Teachers are most helpful when they create safe, supportive environments conducive to risk taking. They are not helpful when they struggle overtly with children.

Finally, when teachers implement a program for teaching social behavior to emotionally disturbed children, they need to consider what they can and cannot accomplish and what their limits are. Teachers also need to be able and willing to ask for help. During the course of teaching lessons in social skills and conducting counseling in the classroom, it is likely that teachers will encounter problems which make them uncomfortable or children who puzzle or annoy them. Discussing these problems with another professional or getting another person's opinion about how to proceed is often necessary if teachers are to maintain a helping, empathetic, proactive stance in the classroom.

DISCUSSION QUESTIONS

1. When faced with an aggressive child who threatens her peers when things don't go as she wants, how might a teacher go about deciding what skills to teach? Of the various approaches discussed in this chapter, which seem most appropriate?
2. When dealing with a shy, withdrawn child who has few friends and makes few social overtures, what skills might the teacher expect this child to lack? How can a teacher assess whether the child has the skills? Which programs might be appropriate for such a child?
3. Do these programs seem appropriate for the child who apparently knows how to behave, but who for a variety of reasons chooses not to do so? Why or why not?
4. Identify the assumptions upon which a didactic approach to skill development is based. Contrast these assumptions with the ones upon which counseling approaches are based.
5. Do you think a teacher should engage in personal problem-solving discussions with children if he has not been trained? Why or why not?

REFERENCES

Bash, M. A. S., & Camp, B. W. (1986). Teacher training in the Think Aloud Program. In G. Cartledge & J. F. Milburn (Eds.), *Teaching social skills to children: Innovative approaches* (2nd ed.). New York: Pergamon Press.

Boyce, N. L., & Larson, V. L. (1983). *Adolescents' communication development and disorders.* Eau Claire, WI: Thinking Ink Publications.

Camp, B. W. (1977). Verbal mediation in young aggressive boys. *Journal of Abnormal Psychology, 86,* 145–153.

Camp, B. W. (1980). Two psychoeducational training programs for aggressive boys. In C. Whalen & B. Henken (Eds.), *Hyperactive children: The social ecology of identification and treatment.* New York: Academic Press.

Camp, B. W., & Bash, M. A. (1981). *Think Aloud.* Champaign, IL: Research Press.

Camp, B. W., Blom, G. E., Hebert, F., & Van Doorninck, W. J. (1977). "Think Aloud": A program for developing self-control in young aggressive boys. *Journal of Abnormal Child Psychology, 5,* 157–169.

Chandler, M. J. (1973a). Egocentrism and antisocial behavior: The assessment and training of social perspective-taking skills. *Developmental Psychology, 9,* 326–332.

Chandler, M. J. (1973b). The Picture Arrangement Subtest of the WAIS index of social egocentrism: A comparative study of normal and emotionally disturbed children. *Journal of Abnormal Child Psychology, 1,* 340–349.

Chandler, M. J., & Greenspan, S. (1972). Ersatz egocentrism: A reply to H. Borke. *Developmental Psychology, 7,* 104–106.

Chandler, M. J., Greenspan, S., & Barenboim, C. (1974). Assessment and training of role-taking and referential communication skills in institutionalized emotionally disturbed children. *Developmental Psychology, 10,* 546–553.

Coie, J. D., & Krehbiel, G. (1984). Academic versus social skills training with low-achieving, socially rejected children. *Child Development, 55,* 1465–1478.

Coie, J. D., Lochman, J. E., Thompson, T., & Katz, J. (1986). *Social relations training manual for preadolescent intervention program.* Durham, NC: Duke University.

Coie, J. D., Rabiner, D. L., & Lochman, J. F. (in press). Promoting peer relations in a school setting. In L. A. Bond, B. E. Compas, & C. Swift (Eds.), *Prevention in the schools.* Newbury Park, CA: Sage.

Combs, M. L., & Slaby, D. A. (1977). Social skills training with children. In B. B. Lahey & A. E. Kazdin (Eds.), *Advances in clinical child psychology* (vol. 1). New York: Plenum Press.

Covill-Servo, J. (1982). *A modification of low peer status from a sociopsychological perspective.* Unpublished doctoral dissertation. University of Rochester, Rochester, NY.

DeMagistris, R. J., and Imber, S. C. (1980). The effects of life space interviewing on academic and social performance of behaviorally disordered children. *Behavior disorders, 6,* 12–25.

Dodge, K. A. (1980). Social cognition and children's aggressive behavior. *Child Development, 51,* 162–170.

Dodge, K. A. (1986). A social information processing model of social competence in children. In M. Perlmutter (Ed.), *Cognitive perspectives on children's social and behavioral development.* Hillsdale, NJ: Lawrence Erlbaum.

Dodge, K. A., Murphy, R. R., & Buchsbaum, K. (1984). The assessment of intention-cue detection skills in children: Implications for developmental psychopathology. *Child Development, 55,* 163–173.

Dodge, K. A., Schlundt, D. G., Schocken, I., & Delugach, J. D. (1983). Social competence and children's sociometric status: The role of peer group entry strategies. *Merrill Palmer Quarterly, 29,* 309–336.

Dolgin, K. G. (1986). Needed steps for social competence: Strengths and present limitations of Dodge's model. In M. Perlmutter (Ed.), *Cognitive perspectives on children's social and behavioral development.* Hillsdale, NJ: Lawrence Erlbaum.

Drabman, R., & Patterson, G. (1982). Disruptive behavior and the social standing of exceptional children. In P. Strain (Ed.), *Social development of exceptional children.* Rockville, MD: Aspen.

Dreikurs, R. (1968). *Psychology in the classroom: A manual for teachers* (2nd ed.). New York: Harper & Row.

Flavell, J. H., Botkin, P. T., Fry, C. L., Wright, J. W., & Jarvis, P. E. (1968). *The development of role taking and communication skills in children.* New York: Wiley.

Ginot, H. (1971). *Teacher and child.* New York: Macmillan.

Glasser, (1965). *Schools without failure.* New York: Harper & Row.

Gardner, R. (1990). Life space interviewing: It can be effective, but don't. . . . *Behavioral Disorders, 15,* 111–119.

Goldstein, A. P., & Glick, B. (1987). *Aggression replacement training.* Champaign, IL: Research Press.

Goldstein, A. P., Sprafkin, R. P., Gershaw, N. J., & Klein, P. (1980). *Skillstreaming the adolescent.* Champaign, IL: Research Press.

Gordon, T. (1974). *Teacher effectiveness training.* New York: David McKay.

Gresham, F. M. (1982). Misguided mainstreaming: The case for social skills training with handicapped children. *Exceptional Children, 48,* 422–433.

Gresham, F. M., & Nagle, R. J. (1980). Social skills training with children: Responsiveness to modeling and coaching as a function of peer orientation. *Journal of Consulting and Clinical Psychology, 48,* 718–729.

Hughes, C. A., Ruhl, K. L., & Misra, A. (1989). Self-management with behaviorally disordered students in school settings: A promise unfulfilled? *Behavioral Disorders, 14,* 250–262.

Hughes, J. N., & Hall, R. J. (1987). A proposed model for the assessment of children's social competence. *Professional School Psychology, 2,* 247–260.

Horner, R. H., Dunlap, G., Koegel, R. L., Carr, E. G., Sailor, W., Anderson, J., Albin, R. W., & O'Neill, R. E. (submitted for publication). *Toward a technology of "nonaversive" behavioral support.*

Jackson, N., Jackson, D., & Monroe, C. (1983). *Getting along with others: Teaching social effectiveness to children.* Champaign, IL: Research Press.

Kendall, P. C., & Braswell, L. (1985). *Cognitive-behavioral therapy for impulsive children.* New York: Guilford.

Kohlberg, L. (1966). Moral education in the schools: A developmental view. *The School Review, 74,* 1–30.

Kurdek, L. A., & Rodgon, M. M. (1975). Perceptual, cognitive, and affective perspective taking in kindergarten through sixth-grade children. *Developmental Psychology, 11,* 643–650.

Ladd, G. W. (1981). Effectiveness of a social learning method for enhancing children's social interaction and peer acceptance. *Child Development, 52,* 171–178.

Lochman, J. E. (1987). Self and peer perceptions and attributional biases of aggressive and nonaggressive boys in dyadic interactions. *Journal of Consulting and Clinical Psychology, 55,* 404–410.

Long, N. J. (1990). Comments on Ralph Gardner's article "Life space interviewing: It can be effective, but don't. . . ." *Behavioral Disorders, 15,* 119–125.

McGinnis, E., & Goldstein, A. (1984). *Skillstreaming the elementary school child.* Champaign, IL: Research Press.

Meichenbaum, D., & Goodman, J. (1971). Training impulsive children to talk to themselves: A means of developing self-control. *Journal of Abnormal Psychology, 77,* 115–126.

Michelson, L., Sugai, D. P., Wood, R. P., & Kazdin, A. (1983). *Social skills assessment and training with children: An empirically based handbook.* New York: Plenum Press.

Morse, W. C. (1980). Worksheet on life space interviewing in N. J. Long, W. C. Morse, and R. G. Newman (Eds.), *Conflict in the Classroom: The education of emotionally disturbed children* (4th ed.). Belmont, CA: Wadsworth.

Mullis, R. L., & Hanson, R. A. (1983). Perspective-taking among offender and nonoffender youth. *Adolescence, 18,* 831–836.

Oden, S. L., & Asher, S. R. (1977). Coaching children in social skills for friendship making. *Child Development, 48,* 495–506.

O'Leary, S. G., & Dubey, D. R. (1979). Applications of self-control procedures by children: A review. *Journal of Applied Behavior Analysis, 12,* 449–465.

Paul, I. H. (1973). *Letters to Simon: On the conduct of psychotherapy.* New York: International Universities Press.

Redl, F. (1959). *Mental hygiene and teaching.* New York: Harcourt Brace Jovanovich.

Redl, F., & Wineman, D. (1957). *The aggressive child.* New York: Free Press.

Rosenbaum, M. S., & Drabman, R. S. (1979). Self-control training in the classroom: A critical review. *Journal of Applied Behavior Analysis, 12,* 467–485.

Scarlett, W. G. (1980). Social isolation from agemates among nursery school children. *Journal of Child Psychology and Psychiatry, 21,* 231–240.

Schloss, P. J., Schloss, C. N., Wood, C. E., & Kiehl, W. S. (1986). A critical review of social skills research with behaviorally disordered students. *Behavioral Disorders, 12,* 1–14.

Simeonsson, R. J. (1973). Egocentric responses of normal and emotionally disturbed children in different treatment settings. *Child Psychiatry and Human Development, 3,* 179–186.

Simeonsson, R. J., & Grube, C. (1983). *COMTASK.* Unpublished manuscript available from authors, Department of Special Education, University of North Carolina, Chapel Hill, NC 27514.

Simon, C. (1980). *Communicative competency: A functional-pragmatic language program.* Tucson, AZ: Communication Skill Builders.

Spivack, G., & Shure, M. B. (1974). *Social adjustment of young children.* San Francisco: Jossey-Bass.

Strayhorn, J. M., & Strain, P. S. (1986). Social and language skills for preventive mental health: What, how, who, and when. In P. S. Strain, M. J. Guralnick, & H. M. Walker (Eds.), *Children's social behavior: Development, assessment and modification.* Orlando: Academic Press.

Stephens, T. (1978). *Social skills in the classroom.* Columbus, OH: Cedars Press.

Walker, H., McConnell, S., Holmes, D., Todis, B., Walker, J., & Golden, N. (1983). *The Walker social skills curriculum: The ACCEPTS program.* Austin, TX: PRO-ED.

Watson, D. L., & Hall, D. L. (1977). *Self-control of hyperactivity.* La Mesa, CA: Pupil Services Division, La Mesa–Spring Valley School District.

Wiig, E. (1982). *Let's talk: Developing prosocial communication skills.* Columbus, OH: Merrill.

Wood, F. (1990). When we talk with children: The life space interview. *Behavioral Disorders, 15,* 110.

Name Index

Subject Index